Book of
PROVERBS

Book of
PROVERBS

Expository and Homiletical
Commentary

by
David Thomas

KREGEL PUBLICATIONS
Grand Rapids, Michigan 49501

Book of Proverbs by David Thomas
Copyright © 1982 by Kregel Publications,
a division of Kregel Inc. All rights reserved.

Library of Congress Cataloging in Publication Data

Thomas, David, 1813-1834.
  Book of Proverbs.

   Reprint. Originally published: The Practical
Philosopher. London : R.D. Dickinson, 1885. (The
Homilistic Library ; v. 5)
   Includes index.
    1. Bible. O.T. Proverbs—Meditations.
2. Devotional calendars. I. Title. II. Series:
Homilistic Library ; v. 5.
BS1465.4.T47   1982   242'.2   82-18682
ISBN 0-8254-3813-6

Printed in the United States of America

Contents

Publisher's Preface		*xv*
Proverbs 1:1	Solomon's Life, Its Spiritual Significance	9
Proverbs 1:1-6	A Great Teacher and a Genuine Student	12
Proverbs 1:7-9	Piety	15
Proverbs 1:10-16	The Young Man	18
Proverbs 1:17-19	Moral Traps	20
Proverbs 1:20-23	The Voice of Wisdom to the World	22
Proverbs 1:24-33	God and the Sinner in Time and Eternity	25
Proverbs 2:1-5	Spiritual Excellence	27
Proverbs 2:6-9	Good Men and Their God	30
Proverbs 2:10-22	Wickedness and Wisdom: the Bane and the Antidote	32
Proverbs 3:1,2	The Philosophy of Health and Happiness	35
Proverbs 3:3,4	Mercy and Truth	37
Proverbs 3:5-7	God-trusting and Self-trusting	40
Proverbs 3:9,10	The Highest Giving, the Condition of the Highest Getting	43
Proverbs 3:11,12	Affliction	44
Proverbs 3:13-18	The Blessedness of Wisdom	46
Proverbs 3:19,20	Wisdom, the Source and Sovereign of Worlds	48
Proverbs 3:21-26	Fidelity to Principle	49
Proverbs 3:27-29	Beneficence	51
Proverbs 3:30,31	Strife and Oppression	53
Proverbs 3:32-35	Moral Contrasts	54
Proverbs 4:1-4	A Religious Home	56
Proverbs 4:5-9	The *Summum Bonum*	58
Proverbs 4:10-17	The Moral Paths of Men	61
Proverbs 4:18	The March of the Good	63
Proverbs 4:19	The Darkness of Sin	65
Proverbs 4:20-23	Self-improvement and Self-control	67
Proverbs 4:24-27	Laws of Life	69
Proverbs 5:1-20	The Strange Woman and the True Wife	71
Proverbs 5:21-23	Man as Known of God and Punished by Sin	73
Proverbs 6:1-5	Social Suretyships	75

Contents

Proverbs 6:6-8	Little Preachers and Great Sermons	78
Proverbs 6:9-15	The Lazy Man and the Wicked Man	81
Proverbs 6:16-19	Seven Abominations	84
Proverbs 6:20-35 } 7:1-17 }	Counsels to Young Men in Relation to Bad Women	88
Proverbs 8:1-14	The Voice of Divine Wisdom	90
Proverbs 8:15-21	The Authority of Divine Wisdom	92
Proverbs 8:23-31	The Autobiography of Wisdom	95
Proverbs 8:32-36	The Claims of Divine Wisdom	97
Proverbs 9:1-6	The Educational Temple: or Christianity, a School	99
Proverbs 9:7-9	Reproof	102
Proverbs 9:10-12	Character	104
Proverbs 9:13-18	The Ministry of Temptation	105
Proverbs 10:1	The Influence of the Child's Character Upon the Parent's Heart	107
Proverbs 10:2,3	Cash and Character	109
Proverbs 10:4,5	Idleness and Industry	111
Proverbs 10:6,7	Opposite Characters and Destinies	113
Proverbs 10:8-10	Man in a Threefold Aspect	114
Proverbs 10:11	Speech	117
Proverbs 10:12	The Great Mischief-maker and the Great Peace-maker	118
Proverbs 10:13-18	Contrasts	120
Proverbs 10:19	The Sin of Loquaciousness	123
Proverbs 10:20, 21, 31, 32 }	The Speech of the Righteous and the Wicked Compared	125
Proverbs 10:22-28	Moral Phases of Life	127
Proverbs 10:29	Might and Misery	131
Proverbs 11:2	The Advent and Evil of Pride	132
Proverbs 11:7	The Terrible in Human History	134
Proberbs 11:8	Trouble in its Relation to the Righteous and the Wicked	135
Proverbs 11:9	Hypocrisy and Knowledge	137
Proverbs 11:10,11	The Public Conscience in Relation to Moral Character	139
Proverbs 11:12,13	Types of Character in Social Life	140
Proverbs 11:14	Wisdom, the Want of States	142
Proverbs 11:17	The Generous and Ungenerous	145
Proverbs 11:18-20	The Evil and the Good	146
Proverbs 11:22	Adornment	148
Proverbs 11:24,25	The Generous and the Avaricious	150
Proverbs 11:27,28	Seeking and Trusting	152
Proverbs 11:29	Family Life	154

Contents

Proverbs 11:30,31	The Life of the Good	156
Proverbs 12:1-3	The Righteous and the Wicked	157
Proverbs 12:4	The Queen of the Household	159
Proverbs 12:5-8	The Righteous and the Wicked	160
Proverbs 12:9	Domestic Modesty and Display	161
Proverbs 12:10	The Treatment of Animals	163
Proverbs 12:11	Manly Industry and Parasitical Indolence	164
Proverbs 12:12,13	The Crafty and the Honest	166
Proverbs 12:14	Retributions of the Lip and Life	167
Proverbs 12:15	The Opinionated and the Docile	169
Proverbs 12:16-23	Speech	170
Proverbs 12:24	Diligence and Dignity. Slothfulness and Servility	173
Proverbs 12:25	The Saddening and the Succoring	174
Proverbs 12:26,28	The True Pathway of Souls	176
Proverbs 12:27	Labor as Enhancing the Relative Value of a Man's Possessions	177
Proverbs 13:1	The Teachable and the Unteachable Son	179
Proverbs 13:2,3	Man Speaking	181
Proverbs 13:4	Soul Craving	182
Proverbs 13:5,6	Moral Truthfulness	183
Proverbs 13:7,8	Poverty and Wealth	184
Proverbs 13:9	The Light of Souls	187
Proverbs 13:10	Pride	188
Proverbs 13:11	Worldly Wealth	190
Proverbs 13:12	Hope Deferred	191
Proverbs 13:13	The Word	193
Proverbs 13:14	The Law of the Good	194
Proverbs 13:15a	A Sound Intellect	195
Proverbs 13:15b	The Way of Transgressors	197
Proverbs 13:16	The Wise and the Foolish	198
Proverbs 13:17	Human Missions and Their Discharge	200
Proverbs 13:18	The Incorrigible and the Docile	201
Proverbs 13:19	Soul Pleasure and Soul Pain	203
Proverbs 13:20	The Grand Fellowship and Assimilation in Life's Path	205
Proverbs 13:21	Nemesis: Destiny Following Character	207
Proverbs 13:22,23	Material Wealth	208
Proverbs 13:24	Parental Discipline	210
Proverbs 13:25	The Satisfaction of the Body Determined by the Condition of the Soul	212
Proverbs 14:1	Housewifery	214

Contents

Proverbs 14:2	Human Conduct	215
Proverbs 14:3	Speech, a Rod	216
Proverbs 14:4	The Clean Crib, or Indolence	218
Proverbs 14:5,6	Veracity and Wisdom	219
Proverbs 14:7-9	The Society to be Shunned	221
Proverbs 14:10	The Heart's Hidden Depth	223
Proverbs 14:11	The Soul's Home	225
Proverbs 14:12	The Seeming Right Often Ruinous	227
Proverbs 14:13	Sinful Mirth	229
Proverbs 14:14	The Misery of the Apostate, and the Happiness of the Good	231
Proverbs 14:15-18	The Credulous and the Cautious	232
Proverbs 14:19	The Majesty of Goodness	234
Proverbs 14:20-22	A Group of Social Principles	236
Proverbs 14:23,24	Labor, Talk, Wealth	238
Proverbs 14:25	The True Witness	240
Proverbs 14:26,27	Godliness, Safety and Life	241
Proverbs 14:28	The Population of an Empire	243
Proverbs 14:29	Temper	244
Proverbs 14:30	Heart and Health	246
Proverbs 14:31	Godliness and Humanity	248
Proverbs 14:32	Death Depending on Character	250
Proverbs 14:33	Reticence and Loquacity	252
Proverbs 14:34,35	The Political and Social Importance of Morality	254
Proverbs 15:1,2	Words	256
Proverbs 15:3	God's Inspection of the World	258
Proverbs 15:4,7	Speech	260
Proverbs 15:5,6	Diverse Families	262
Proverbs 15:8-11	The Man-ward Feeling and the Infinite Intelligence of God	264
Proverbs 15:12	The Scorner	266
Proverbs 15:13-15	Human Hearts	268
Proverbs 15:16,17	The Dinner of Herbs and the Stalled Ox	270
Proverbs 15:18	Social Discord	273
Proverbs 15:19	Indolence and Righteousness	274
Proverbs 15:21,22	Contrasts	276
Proverbs 15:23	Useful Speech	277
Proverbs 15:24	The Way of the Wise	279
Proverbs 15:25,26	The Procedure and Propensity of God	281
Proverbs 15:27	The Evils of Covetousness and the Blessedness of Generosity	282
Proverbs 15:28,29	The Righteous and the Wicked	284
Proverbs 15:30	The Highest Knowledge	286

Contents

Proverbs 15:31,32	Reproof	288
Proverbs 15:33	Godly Fear and Genuine Humility	290
Proverbs 16:1	Man Proposes, God Disposes	292
Proverbs 16:2	The Self-complacency of Sinners and the Omniscience of God	294
Proverbs 16:3	The Establishment of Thoughts	296
Proverbs 16:4	Universal Existence	298
Proverbs 16:5,6	Evil	300
Proverbs 16:7	Pleasing God	302
Proverbs 16:8	The Good Man and His Worldly Circumstances	303
Proverbs 16:9	The Plan of Man, and the Plan of God in Human Life	305
Proverbs 16:10-15	Model Monarchs	308
Proverbs 16:16	Moral and Material Wealth	312
Proverbs 16:17	The Way of the Upright	314
Proverbs 16:18,19	Pride and Humility	316
Proverbs 16:20,21	The Conditions of a Happy Life	318
Proverbs 16:22	The Two Interpreters	320
Proverbs 16:23,24	Ideal Eloquence	322
Proverbs 16:26	Labor	324
Proverbs 16:27-30	Mischievous Men	326
Proverbs 16:31	The Glory of the Aged Piety	328
Proverbs 16:32	The Conqueror of Self, the Greatest Conqueror	331
Proverbs 16:33	Life, a Lottery and a Plan	333
Proverbs 17:1,2	Family Scenes	335
Proverbs 17:3	Divine Discipline	337
Proverbs 17:4	Conversational Likings of Bad Men	339
Proverbs 17:5	The Unfortunate Poor	341
Proverbs 17:6	Posterity and Its Ancestors	343
Proverbs 17:7	Speech Incongruous and False	345
Proverbs 17:8	The Power of Patronage	347
Proverbs 17:9	The Right Concealment and the Wrong Revealment of Offences	349
Proverbs 17:10	Moral and Corporeal Chastisement	351
Proverbs 17:11-13	The Genius and Punishment of Evil	353
Proverbs 17:14	Strife	355
Proverbs 17:15	Perverse Treatment of the Characters of Men	357
Proverbs 17:16	Capacity Without Will	359
Proverbs 17:17; 18:24	Degrees and Duties of True Friendship	361
Proverbs 17:21,25	The Fool: Negatively and Positively	365

Contents

Proverbs 17:22	Bodily Health Dependent on Mental Moods	369
Proverbs 17:23	Bribery	371
Proverbs 17:24	A Double Picture	373
Proverbs 17:26	Persecution and Treason	375
Proverbs 17:27,28	Frugality in Speech	377
Proverbs 18:1,2	A Student's Spirit	379
Proverbs 18:3	Wickedness Contemptible and Contemptuous	382
Proverbs 18:4	The Words of Inspired Wisdom	383
Proverbs 18:5	Three Bad Things	386
Proverbs 18:6-8	The Speech of a Splenetic Fool	388
Proverbs 18:9	Miserable Twinship	390
Proverbs 18:10-12	The Soul's Tower	392
Proverbs 18:13	Impetuous Flippancy	394
Proverbs 18:14	The Unbearable Wound	396
Proverbs 18:15,16	The Attainment of Knowledge and the Power of Kindness	398
Proverbs 18:17-19	Social Disputes	401
Proverbs 18:20,21	The Influence of the Tongue	404
Proverbs 18:22	A Happy Marriage	405
Proverbs 18:23; 19:4,6,7	Poverty, Riches and Social Selfishness	408
Proverbs 19:1	The Better Man	410
Proverbs 19:2,3	The Soul Without Knowledge	412
Proverbs 19:5,9	Falsehood	414
Proverbs 19:11, 12,19	Anger Controlled and Uncontrolled	416
Proverbs 19:13,14	A Cursed Home and a Blessed Home	418
Proverbs 19:8,16	Goodness and Happiness	420
Proverbs 19:17	The Deserving Poor	422
Proverbs 19:18,20	Parental Discipline and Filial Improvement	424
Proverbs 19:21	The Mind of Man and the Mind of God	426
Proverbs 19:22	Kindness	429
Proverbs 19:23	The Fruits of Personal Religion	431
Proverbs 19:24	Laziness	432
Proverbs 19:25	Man Chastising the Wrong	433
Proverbs 19:26-27	Filial Depravity and Parental Warning	436
Proverbs 19:28,29	The Character and Doom of the Wicked	438
Proverbs 20:1	An Intemperate Use of Strong Drink	439
Proverbs 20:2	The Terrific in Human Government	440
Proverbs 20:3	Unlawful Strife	441
Proverbs 20:4	Indolence	443

Contents

Proverbs 20:5	The Getting of Wisdom from the Wise	444
Proverbs 20:6,7	A Prevalent Vice and a Rare Virtue	447
Proverbs 20:8	The Picture of a Noble King	449
Proverbs 20:9	Moral Purity	451
Proverbs 20:10,23	The Market	453
Proverbs 20:12	The Hearing Ear and the Seeing Eye	455
Proverbs 20:13	Early Rising	458
Proverbs 20:14	Chicanery	460
Proverbs 20:15	Material Wealth and Intelligent Speech	462
Proverbs 20:16, 18,21	Business Economics	464
Proverbs 20:19,20	The Idle Talebearer and the Wicked Son	467
Proverbs 20:22	The Duty of Man Under a Sense of Injuries	469
Proverbs 20:24	A Providence Over Man	471
Proverbs 20:25	Selfishness in Religion	474
Proverbs 20:26,28	A Strong Government	478
Proverbs 20:27	Conscience	480
Proverbs 20:29	The Glory of Godliness, Both in Youth and Age	481
Proverbs 20:30	God's Discipline of His Children	483
Proverbs 21:1-3	God and the Human Race	485
Proverbs 21:4	The Prosperity of the Wicked is Sin	488
Proverbs 21:5-7; 22:29	The Right and Wrong Road to Plenty	490
Proverbs 21:8	The Unregenerate and the Regenerate	492
Proverbs 21:9, 19; 25:24	Matrimonial Misery	494
Proverbs 21:10-12	The Wicked	497
Proverbs 21:13	The Cry of the Poor	500
Proverbs 21:14	Social Anger	503
Proverbs 21:15	Moral Contrasts	504
Proverbs 21:16	Hopeless Apostasy	505
Proverbs 21:17	Self-indulgence, a Source of Poverty	507
Proverbs 21:18	The Wicked, a Ransom for the Righteous	509
Proverbs 21:20	Wealth in Relation to Character	511
Proverbs 21:21	The True Pursuit of Mankind	514
Proverbs 21:22	The March of the Good	516
Proverbs 21:23	The Government of the Tongue	518
Proverbs 21:24	The Infamous	520
Proverbs 21:25,26	Sloth	522
Proverbs 21:27	Wickedness	524
Proverbs 21:28,29	Moral Qualities and Their Results	526

Contents

Proverbs 22:1	Reputation and Riches	528
Proverbs 22:2,3	Contrasts in Conditions and Characters	531
Proverbs 22:4,5	Life, Prosperous and Perilous	533
Proverbs 22:6	Child-training	536
Proverbs 22:7	The Social Rule of Wealth	539
Proverbs 22:8	Human Life	541
Proverbs 22:9	Genuine Philanthropy	543
Proverbs 22:10	The Scorner	545
Proverbs 22:11,12	The Good Man	547
Proverbs 22:13	The Excuses of Laziness	549
Proverbs 22:14	The Influence of a Depraved Woman	551
Proverbs 22:15	A Terrible Evil and a Severe Cure	553
Proverbs 22:16	The Evils of Avarice	555
Proverbs 22:17-21	Spiritual Verities	557
Proverbs 22:22,23	The Oppression of the Poor	561
Proverbs 22:24-28	Interdicted Conduct	563
Proverbs 23:1-3	The Epicure; or Gastric Temptation	566
Proverbs 23:4,5	Riches Not to be Labored for as an End	568
Proverbs 23:6-8	A Spurious Hospitality	570
Proverbs 23:9	The Incorrigible Sinner	573
Proverbs 23:10,11	Social Injustice	574
Proverbs 23:12	Spiritual Knowledge	576
Proverbs 23:13,14	Parental Discipline	578
Proverbs 23:15-23	An Appeal of Parental Piety	580
Proverbs 23:26	Man's Heart	582
Proverbs 23:29-35	The Drunkard's Effigy Hung Up as a Beacon	584
Proverbs 24:1,2	The Villany and Absurdity of Sin	589
Proverbs 24:3-7	Enlightened Piety	591
Proverbs 24:8,9	Aspects of Depravity	594
Proverbs 24:10	The Day of Adversity	596
Proverbs 24:11,12	The Neglect of Social Benevolence	597
Proverbs 24:13,14	Spiritual Science	599
Proverbs 24:15,16	The Hostility of the Wicked Towards the Good	602
Proverbs 24:17,18	Revenge	604
Proverbs 24:19,20	An Example of the Folly of Envy	606
Proverbs 24:21,22	Human Government	608
Proverbs 24:23-26	Social Conduct	610
Proverbs 24:27	Human Labor	612
Proverbs 24:28,29	Types of Corrupt Testimony	615
Proverbs 24:30-34	Idleness	617
Proverbs 25:1	Solomon's Three Thousand Proverbs	619
Proverbs 25:2-5	Kinghood	622

Contents

Proverbs 25:6,7	A Corrupt Ambition 625
Proverbs 25:8-10	The Worst and Best Way of Treating Social Dissensions 628
Proverbs 25:11	The Excellency of Fitly-spoken Words . 630
Proverbs 25:12	The Beauty of a Reprovable Disposition 633
Proverbs 25:13	The Value of a Good Messenger to His Employers 635
Proverbs 25:14	Swaggering Generosity 637
Proverbs 25:15, 21,22 }	The Manifestation and Mightiness of Moral Power 638
Proverbs 25:16	The World's Honey 641
Proverbs 25:17-20	Bad Neighbors 643
Proverbs 25:23	Righteous Anger 647
Proverbs 25:25	Good News from a Far Country 651
Proverbs 25:26	Religious Apostasy 653
Proverbs 25:27	Natural Desires Running too Far 655
Proverbs 25:28	The Lack of Self-mastery 657
Proverbs 26:1,8	Honor Paid to Bad Men is Unseemly and Pernicious 658
Proverbs 26:2	Human Anathemas 661
Proverbs 26:3-11	Aspects of a Fool 664
Proverbs 26:12,16	Vanity, One of the Greatest Obstructions to Soul-Improvement . . 668
Proverbs 26:17-22	Mischievous Citizens 670
Proverbs 26:23-28	Clandestine Hatred 672
Proverbs 27:1	Man and Tomorrow, a Fact and a Failing 675
Proverbs 27:2	Self-praise 677
Proverbs 27:3-6	Social Wrath and Social Friendliness . . 679
Proverbs 27:7	An Appetite for Good Things Essential for Their Enjoyment 682
Proverbs 27:8	The Evil of a Roaming Disposition 684
Proverbs 27:9-11	A Genuine Friendship and a Happy Fathership 688
Proverbs 27:12,14	Imprudence and Flattery 691
Proverbs 27:17	The Soul, Its Bluntness and Its Whetstone 693
Proverbs 27:18	Man Honored in Service 696
Proverbs 27:19	The Uniformity and Reciprocity of Souls 698
Proverbs 27:20	The Insatiability of Man's Inquiring Faculty 700
Proverbs 27:21	Popularity, the Most Trying Test of Character 702

Contents

Proverbs 27:22	The Moral Obstinacy of Sin	704
Proverbs 27:23-27	A Picture of Life, Rural and General	707
Proverbs 28:1	Conscience	709
Proverbs 28:2-5	A Threefold Glimpse of Life	711
Proverbs 28:7-9	Life in the Home, the Market and the Sanctuary	715
Proverbs 28:10	Opposite Characters and Opposite Destinies	717
Proverbs 28:11	Vanity in the Rich and Penetration in the Poor	720
Proverbs 28:12, 28; 29:2	Secular Prosperity	722
Proverbs 28:13	Man's Treatment of His Own Sins	725
Proverbs 28:14	Reverence and Recklessness	727
Proverbs 28:15-17	Types of Kings	729
Proverbs 28:20-23	Avarice	731
Proverbs 28:24	Robbery of Parents	734
Proverbs 28:25,26	Self-sufficiency and Godly Confidence	736
Proverbs 29:1	Restorative Discipline	739
Proverbs 29:3, 15,17	Parental Life	741
Proverbs 29:4, 12,14	Human Rulership	745
Proverbs 29:5	Flattery, a Net	748
Proverbs 29:6	The Snare and the Song	750
Proverbs 29:7	The Treatment of the Poor, a Test of Character	752
Proverbs 29:8,9, 10,11,20,22,23	The Genius of Evil	755
Proverbs 29:16	The Fall of Evil	758
Proverbs 29:18	Divine Revelation	761
Proverbs 29:19,21	Types of Servants	763
Proverbs 29:24	Commercial Partnerships	765
Proverbs 29:25-27	Social Life	768
Proverbs 30:1-9	Agur, as a Philosopher, a Bibleist and a Suppliant	771
Proverbs 30:10	The False Accuser	775
Proverbs 30:11-14	Many Races in One	778
Proverbs 30:24-28	Practical Lessons from Insect Life	782
Proverbs 31:1-9	The Counsels of a Noble Mother to Her Son	784
Proverbs 31:10-31	A Noble Woman's Picture of True Womanhood	788
Index		*799*

Publisher's Preface

Gems and jewels are neither dimmed by time nor superceded by fashion. A queen will wear an old one as proudly as a new one. Often the older are more valuable. Such are these Proverbs, words tried and pure, spoken by Solomon in the book of Proverbs.

Their value is enhanced for today's reader by the warm flowing and refreshing illumination by David Thomas in his book, the *Book of Proverbs*. His priceless thoughts sparkle and brighten every page. The warm outflow of Thomas' loving heart blends with the practical, moral and spiritual remedies of Proverbs for the evident needs of men and nations today.

Although Proverbs is preeminently a practical book of the Bible, radiating, in almost every sentence, the ethics of trade and of all secular occupations, Biblical exegetes have regarded it in its theological and ecclesiastical aspects rather than in its broad human relations; they have treated it as a creed rather than a code.

xvi / Publisher's Preface

Dr. David Thomas wrote in his Preface to the early edition of this work, "With this conviction which time deepens in me, I have gone through this book of Proverbs and have sought to develop and enforce its worldwide axioms in their relation to every person's daily life. Axioms that bear down with their divine might against indolence, intemperance, fraud, falsehood, incontinence, extravagance, selfishness and all the themes that work in the domestic, social, mercantile, professional and political life of men. My purpose has been to produce a work that will help, in some humble measure, to raise the standard of personal and public morals."

The publishers trust that the re-issue of this relevant classic will challenge and inspire Bible students, both clergy and lay people, to again make these Biblical truths a part of the moral fiber of society today.

—The Publishers

Homiletical Commentary on Book of Proverbs

Proverbs 1:1

Solomon's Life, Its Spiritual Significance

"The Proverbs of Solomon the son of David, King of Israel."

MAN'S life is a book, by which the Great Father educates the human race. By man He teaches man. As in the smallest dew-drop glistening on the blade we may see the measureless ocean, in man He the Eternal is manifest. Some men give a fairer and fuller revelation of Him than others; they have a higher type of being, and a nobler character. Jesus of Nazareth was "God manifest in the flesh." Solomon, although a depraved man, revealed not a little of the Divine. A really great man he was not, for no man can be really great who is not good—and he was not that. True, he had an intellect of the highest order, an intellect whose thoughts are the seeds of libraries; an experience, too, that measured life in its varied phases. The Eternal teaches the ages through him. What are the lessons his life teaches? In it we read

THE CO-EXISTENCE OF GOOD AND EVIL IN THE SAME HUMAN SOUL.—In early life we are told that Solomon "loved the Lord and walked in all the statutes of David his father." He appreciated wisdom as the chief good;

he reared the magnificent temple at Jerusalem, and consecrated it by his devotions. He spake "three thousand proverbs," containing the germs of universal truth and virtue. All this shews that in his great heart there were the seeds of many virtues and the spirit of noble deeds. But sad to say, vice as well as virtue had a place and a power within him. He displayed revenge; encouraged, at times, idolatry; and revelled in a voluptuousness and a carnality unsurpassed. Good and evil are, in different measures, found in the best of men on earth. In the spirits of heaven there is good, and good only; in hell, evil, and evil alone; in those of earth, they co-exist in different degrees. "The web," says Shakspeare, "of our life is of mingled yarn, good and bad together." The recognition of this fact is important in estimating the characters of our fellow men. A man is not to be pronounced utterly bad because he has fallen into wrong, nor completely good because he has performed some virtuous deed. In his life we read

THE FORCE OF THE DEGENERATIVE PRINCIPLE IN HUMAN NATURE.—There was much in this man's soul to raise him, and keep him high up in the realm of virtue. His father, although not a good man, on his death-bed addressed him thus, "I go the way of all the earth, be thou strong therefore, and show thyself a man, and keep the charge of the Lord, thy God, to walk in His ways and keep His statutes." The sacred impressions he received in childhood, and the noble truths which, his proverbs show, dwelt in his mind,—all indicate that there was a strong force within him, to make and keep him right. Albeit, there was at the same time in his heart a principle stronger than all, stronger than early impressions, and his own clear convictions of right; a principle that often overcame all the good, and dragged him down into the abysses of depravity. "Let him that thinketh he standeth, take heed lest he fall." In his life we read

THE UTTER INSUFFICIENCY OF ALL EARTHLY GOOD TO SATISFY THE MIND.—What has the earth to give that this man possessed not in rich abundance?

Wealth? His riches were enormous: "the kings of Tarshish and the isles, the kings of Sheba" offered to him their gifts. *Power?* He sat on a throne of ivory and gold; he was the idol of his age; princes came from afar to witness his glory and to render him homage. *Beauty?* Whatever was lovely in nature and exquisite in art were at his command. "Vineyards, orchards, gardens, fruitful trees, artistic streams, men singers and women singers, and musical instruments of all sorts." *Knowledge?* "God gave him wisdom and understanding; largeness of heart even as the sand which is on the sea-shore." He was a sage, a poet, and a naturalist. "He spake three thousand proverbs, and his songs were one thousand and five." With all this was he happy? He pronounces all "Vanity and vexation of spirit." "Great riches have sold more men than ever they have bought out," says Lord Bacon. The fact is, the world has nothing wherewith to satisfy that soul within us, which will outlive the stars and yet be young, comprehend the universe and yet be empty without a God. In his life we read

THE SUPERIORITY OF TRUE THOUGHTS TO ALL THE OTHER PRODUCTIONS OF MAN.—Solomon was an active man; few men worked harder than he, few accomplished more material work: but what are all his buildings, his fleets, his ornaments, his gardens, his artistic devices, compared to his *proverbs?* His thoughts have lived, and worked, and spread for three thousand years. They are working now, and will continue to work as generations come and go, and as kingdoms rise and break like bubbles on the stream. What Lord Bacon says of fame is true of all earthly things, "it is like a river that beareth up things light, and drowneth things weighty and solid." True thoughts live and give life. They are the seeds of coming literatures, philosophies, characters, institutions.

Such are the lessons which Solomon's history teaches. The real life of every man is in his *love*. "Show me," says Fichte, "what thou truly lovest, show me what thou seekest and strivest for with thy whole heart, when thou hopest to attain to true enjoyment, and thou hast hereby shown me thy life. What thou lovest is that thou livest. This very love is thy life; the root, the seat, the central point of thy being."

Proverbs 1:1-6

A Great Teacher and a Genuine Student

"The proverbs of Solomon the son of David, king of Israel; To know wisdom and instruction; to perceive the words of understanding; To receive the instruction of wisdom, justice, and judgment and equity; To give subtilty to the simple, to the young man knowledge and discretion. A wise man will hear, and will increase learning; and a man of understanding shall attain unto wise counsels: To understand a proverb, and the interpretation; the words of the wise, and their dark sayings."

THESE six verses give us two subjects for study.

A GREAT TEACHER.—Solomon the son of David, king of Israel, was not only a passive but an active teacher—a voluntary as well as an involuntary one. All men teach by their lives whether they will or not; they are "living epistles known and read of all men." We all become objects of human observations, subjects of human thought and enquiry, though we ourselves may be utterly unconscious of the fact. Solomon taught by his life, but he also taught by conscious determination. These verses bring under our notice the form and design of his lessons. What is the *form?* He spoke in "Proverbs." A proverb is the wisdom of ages crystallized into a sentence: a gold coin in the currency of thought. Earl Russell defines a proverb as "the wisdom of many and the wit of one." The proverbs of Solomon being inspired, are the rays of eternal ideas mirrored in the diamonds of human genius.

"Jewels five words long,
That on the stretch'd forefinger of all time
Sparkle for ever."—*Tennyson*

No style of instruction is more ancient than the proverbial.

The most ancient nations have their aphorisms, and not a few of them sparkle with a "beam divine." We have become so wordy, our books so numerous, and our intellects so speculative, that we have ceased to make proverbs. What should be wrapped in one round sentence we spread out into volumes in these days. Instead of "apples of gold in pictures of silver" we have grains of gold in heavy waggons, and these often painted in gaudy hues. What is the *design?* *Soul*-culture. "To know wisdom and instruction, to perceive the words of understanding." There is much for man to know. Much in outward nature—the essence, laws, uses, of the material system to which he belongs. Much in his own nature, his mental, physical, and moral constitution; much in the relations which he sustains to the universe and his Maker, and much in the obligations springing therefrom. Man instinctively craves for knowledge, and greatly does he need it. He needs intellectual enlightenment and discipline: the soul without knowledge is not good. These proverbs were intended to enlighten the human reason, to conduct the human intellect through phenomena into the universe of reality, and make it acquainted with "the reason of things." But the design of the proverbs is more than mental culture, it is *moral*. It is instruction in "judgment and equity." They contain rules of life, nay, principles of action. They teach duty not only in every department of life and social grade, but in every separate movement of the individual man. "If the world," says a modern writer, "were governed by this single book, it would be a new earth wherein dwelleth righteousness." The suggestive character of these proverbs is admirably adapted to the great work of spiritual culture; it is not systematic but sententious. It agrees with Locke's idea of education. "The business of education," says this great philosopher, "is not to perfect a learner in all or any of the sciences, but to give his mind that freedom, that disposition, and those habits that may enable him to obtain any part of knowledge he shall apply himself to or stand in need of, in the future course of his life." In these verses we have

A GENUINE STUDENT.—Who is the true learner? He is described as a "wise man." A wise man is he who chooses the highest end and the best means to attain it. There are many very intelligent men who are unwise. Some set before them a low and unworthy end, some a good end but employ ill-adapted means. A genuine student, however ignorant, is a man who aims at wisdom, and gives his mind to those things that make for it. He is a man who pursues resolutely, and in a right way, the highest end of his being. He is described as an *attentive* man. "A wise man will hear." The mental ears of some are so heavy that they hear not the voice of wisdom, and the ears of others are so full of the rush and din of worldly concerns, that even truth in thunder rolls over their heads unheard. A genuine student "opens his ear," bows his head, and listens attentively and earnestly, anxious to catch every word. He is described also as an *improving* man. It is said of him that he "will increase learning" and "attain unto wise counsels." By listening he gains; the words he catches he forms into sentences, and the sentences extend into chapters. The more the genuine student knows the more he feels his ignorance, and the more he craves for light. Our knowledge is "but to know how little can be known." He is described as an *interpreting* man. He "understands a proverb and the interpretation: the words of the wise and their dark sayings." "Dark sayings," says Wardlaw, "mean properly enigmas or riddles. These were used of old as one of the methods of conveying instruction. It was conceived that by giving exercise to the understanding in finding out the solution of the enigma, it was calculated to deepen on the mind the impression of the lesson which was wrapt up in it. This was not done for mere amusement, but for imparting serious instruction; although to the young there might, in some instances, be the blending of an intellectual entertainment, with the conveyance of useful information of salutary counsel." These enigmatical maxims of wisdom were sometimes rendered the more attractive by being thrown into the form of verse, and even being set to music. A poetic taste and a musical ear were thus made subservient to the communication and impression of truth. The great thoughts of great men are luminous in themselves, but dark to the thoughtless because their eyes are closed. Let us remember the words of John Milton, that "the end of learning is to know God, and out of that knowledge to love Him, and to imitate Him, as we may the nearest, by possessing our souls of true virtue."

Proverbs 1:7-9

Piety

"The fear of the LORD is the beginning of knowledge: but fools despise wisdom and instruction. My son, hear the instruction of thy father, and forsake not the law of thy mother: For they shall be an ornament of grace unto thy head, and chains about thy neck."

FROM this short passage the following great truths may be learned.

Piety IS REVERENCE FOR GOD.—"The fear of the Lord." What fear? Not slavish fear, or foreboding apprehension. There is no virtue in this;—it means a loving reverence, which implies a recognition of the divinely good and great. For who can reverence the mean, the unkind, or the unvirtuous? An impression of greatness and goodness lies at the foundation of holy veneration, and into it there enter the sentiments of gratitude, love, and worship. Piety is love, venerating the majestic and adoring the good. It has nothing in it of the fear that hath torment. On the contrary, it is full of that love that "casteth out fear" and fills the soul with the ecstasies of hope.

Piety IS THE GERM OF INTELLIGENCE. It is the "beginning of knowledge." What knowledge? Not merely intellectual. Many an impious man knows the circle of the sciences. The devil is intelligent. But though he grasp the universe with his intellect, penetrate its essence, and interpret its laws, he is ignorant. Spiritual knowledge —the knowledge of self, the universe, Christ, and God,—is the true knowledge. This grows out of piety — grows out of reverent love. "The secret of the Lord is with them that fear Him." He knows nothing rightly who knows not God experimentally. "In the rules of earthly wisdom," says Lord Bacon, "it is not possible for nature to attain any mediocrity of perfection, before she be humbled by knowing herself and her own ignorance." God is love, and he that loveth not, knoweth not God. Knowledge of Him is the root of that great tree of science, under whose branches all holy spirits live, and on whose immortal fruit they feast and flourish.

Piety IS DESPISED BY FOLLY.—"Fools despise wisdom and instruction." Who are the fools in Solomon's sense? Not the brainless madmen or the illiterate dolts. But the morally perverse, the men whose sympathies are all earthly, carnal, devilish, the men who practically ignore the greatest facts in the universe, trifle with the serious, and barter away the joys of eternity for the puerilities of time. All unregenerate men are such fools, and they despise wisdom and instruction. They look on the pious not only with the eye of indifference, but with the eye of scorn. They do this because they are fools, and they are fools for doing it. To despise piety is to despise that moral salt which prevents society from sinking into putrefaction, those sunbeams that lighten their path, warm their atmosphere, and fill their world with life and beauty. "It is," says Archer Butler, "among the most potent of the energies of sin, that it leads astray by blinding, and blinds by leading astray; that the soul of man, like the strong champion of Israel, must have its 'eyes put out,' when it would be bound with fetters of brass, 'and condemned to grind in the prison house.'" *

Piety INVOLVES FILIAL OBEDIENCE.—" My son,

* Judges xvi. 21.

hear the instruction of thy father, and forsake not the law of thy mother." Family life is a divine institution; obedience to its laws is a part of piety. "Filial love," says Dr. Arnot, "stands near and leans on godliness. It is next to reverence for God. That first and highest commandment is like the earth's allegiance to the sun by general law; and filial obedience is like day and night, summer and winter, budding spring and ripening harvest, on the earth's surface. There could be none of these sweet changes and beneficent operations of nature on our globe if it were broken away from the sun. So when a people burst the first and greatest bond—when a people cast off the fear of God, the family relations, with all their beauty and benefit, disappear. We may read this lesson in the fortune of France. When the nation threw off the first commandment, the second went after it. When they repudiated the fear of God, they could not retain conjugal fidelity and filial love. Hence the wreck and ruin of all the relations between man and man. As well might they try to make a new world as to manage this one wanting the first and second, the primary and subordinate moral laws of its nature."

This filial obedience is a moral adornment. "They shall be an ornament of grace unto thy head and chains about thy neck." "You may read at times," says one, "on festive days, in the high places of the earth, of the elegance and splendour of royal and courtly attire, and your imagination may be dazzled by the profusion of diamonds, and pearls, and brilliants, and tasteful decorations and gaudy finery; indicating the anxiety felt and the pains expended to adorn this 'painted piece of living clay.'" What is the worth of all this decoration? Virtue is the only true ornament of a moral intelligence,—a jewel this, which set in the centre of the immortal spirit, will flash on through every turn of life,

> "When gems, and ornaments, and crowns,
> Shall moulder into dust."

Proverbs 1:10-16

The Young Man

"My son, if sinners entice thee, consent thou not. If they say, Come with us, let us lay wait for blood, let us lurk privily for the innocent without cause: Let us swallow them up alive as the grave; and whole, as those that go down into the pit: We shall find all precious substance, we shall fill our houses with spoil: Cast in thy lot among us; let us all have one purse: My son, walk not thou in the way with them; refrain thy foot from their path: For their feet run to evil, and make haste to shed blood."

THE LIFE OF THE YOUNG MAN IS AMONGST SINNERS.—This is implied in the passage, and this is a fact. Sinners encompass us, as servants, masters, clients, customers, and sometimes as parents, brothers, sisters. We must go out of the world to go from them. The text teaches us the following things concerning sin:—It is *cruel*. They "lay wait for blood." They say let us "swallow them up alive as the grave." Sin extinguishes social love and kindles malignity instead. It carries with it the venom of the devil. It teaches that sin is *cunning*. They are said to "lay wait," to "lurk privily." Sinners are essentially hypocrites. They dare not show their true characters to their fellow men. Were they to do so, instead of enjoying social fellowship and patronage, they would be shunned as monsters. Hence they always work under mask and love the dark. They put on the robes of virtue. They kiss and stab at the same time. It teaches that sin is *greedy*. "We shall find all precious substance, we shall fill our houses with spoil." Avarice is the spring that sets and keeps them in motion. "Precious substance" is what they are after. For this they have an insatiable craving.

"O cursed hunger of pernicious gold!
What bands of faith can impious lucre hold!"

This is the world into which the young are born, brought up and educated. What a morally perilous position! How great the caution required!

THE DANGER OF THE YOUNG MAN IS ENTICEMENT.—
"My son, if sinners entice thee." This they are sure to do. Sin always begets an instinct to propagate itself. No sooner did angels fall, than they became tempters. Eve sins, and entices her husband. Sin is a whirlpool, sucking all into itself. Sinners draw the young into evil, not by violence or hard words, but by simulated love and quiet persuasion. They say, "Come with us." Come with us; we have your interest at heart. We wish you happiness. Come, share our pleasures, our transports, and our gains. Cast in thy lot among us, let us all have one purse." This is the danger. It is fabled of the Syrens, that from the watch tower of their lovely island, they charmed the passing ships to their shore by their music. But the sailors when they landed on their sunny beach, transported by a melody adapted to each heart, were destroyed by their enchanters, and their bones left unburied in the sand. Thus sinners act upon the young. It is by the music of fascinating manners, kind words, and fair promises, that they charm the young away from the straight voyage of life to their shores, in order to effect their ruin.

THE ATTITUDE OF THE YOUNG SHOULD BE RESISTANCE.—"Consent thou not." Learn to say "No"—*No*, with the emphasis of thy whole soul. Thou canst resist. Heaven has endowed thee with power to resist all outward appeals. Thou oughtest to resist. To consent is to insult thy Maker and contract guilt. Thou must resist. Thy well-being, now and evermore, depends upon resisting. "Refrain thy foot from their path." Do not parly with them. Do not take the first downward step, for the hill is steep, and every step adds a strong momentum. One sin leads to another, and thus on. Why resist? "Their feet run to evil, and make haste to shed blood." The path may be smooth and flowery, but it is evil and ruinous.

"The devil," says an old writer, "doth not know the hearts of men, but he may feel their pulse, know their temper, and so accordingly can apply himself. As the husbandman knows what seed is proper to sow in such soil, so Satan finding out the temper, knows what temptation is proper to sow in such a heart. That way the tide of a man's constitution runs, that way the wind of temptation blows. Satan tempts the ambitious man with a crown, the sanguine man with beauty, the covetous man with a wedge of gold. He provides savoury meat, such as the sinner loves."

Proverbs 1:17-19

Moral Traps

"Surely in vain the net is spread in the sight of any bird. And they lay wait for their *own* blood; they lurk privily for their *own* lives. So *are* the ways of every one that is greedy of gain; *which* taketh away the life of the owners thereof."

SIN LAYS TRAPS FOR SOULS.—"The net is spread." Sin has woven a net and laid it along the path of life. This net is wrought of diverse materials, such as sensuality, avarice, ambition. How cleverly the skilful fowler constructs and lays his net. It is placed where the innocent bird is likely to come in the garden or the granary, for the grain or the grub, and where when it comes it will be enthralled even in its first step. It is thus with the moral fowler,—the great tempter of souls and all whom he employs. Enticements are traps. There is the trap of self-indulgence, and carnal gratification. There is the trap of worldly amusements laid in theatres, taverns, and the orgies of revelry and debauch. There is the trap of avarice laid in scenes of unrighteous traffic and reckless speculation. There is the trap of ambition spread out and concealed in all the paths to social influence and political power. Traps abound. They are adjusted for men of every mental type, of every period in life, in every social grade. They are laid for children in the play-ground, for merchants in the exchange, for statesmen in the senate, for all classes—from the pauper to the prince. All ages—from the child to the octogenarian.

THESE TRAPS MUST BE EXPOSED.—" In vain the net is spread in the sight of any bird." The fowler conceals his net. If he laid it in the sight of the bird, instinct would strike the warning and his object would be missed. Sin works insidiously. It takes advantage of men's circumstances, ignorance, and inexperience. It steals into the soul through a word in song, or a note in music, through a glance of the eye, or a touch of the hand. It does not enter the soul by violently destroying its fortress, but by crawling over the walls, and creeping into its recesses. The work of the true philanthropist is to expose the traps and to thunder warning in the ears of the birds as they come swooping down. Young men, remember that sin is insidious, and lays its traps stealthily, in scenes where beauty smiles and syrens chant.

> " Our dangers and delights are near allies ;
> From the same stem the rose and prickle rise."

THESE TRAPS BRING RUIN TO THEIR AUTHORS.—"They lay wait for their own blood, they lurk privily for their own lives." "They lay wait." Who? Not the bird, but the fowler, not the intended victim but the foul deceiver. Whilst the tempters "lurked" privily "for the blood" of others, they "lay wait" for their own blood. Retribution overtakes them. If they escape violence themselves, the Nemesis pursues them. Thus it was with Ahab and his guilty partner, they plotted the destruction of others, but they worked out their own ruin; thus it was with Haman, who sought to murder Mordecai, but hung himself, and thus with Judas too. Sinners the world over, in all their plans and purposes, are " digging a pit for themselves." " So with the ways of every one who is greedy of gain "—it is the inexorable law of retribution. Their schemes may seem to

22 / Book of Proverbs

prosper here, but justice tracks their steps and their ruin is inevitable.

> "There is no strange handwriting on the wall,
> Thro' all the midnight hum no threatening call,
> Nor on the marble floor the stealthy fall
> Of fatal footsteps. All is safe. Thou fool,
> The avenging deities are shod with wool!"
>
> W. ALLEN BUTLER

Proverbs 1:20-23

The Voice of Wisdom to the World

"Wisdom crieth without; she uttereth her voice in the streets; She crieth in the chief place of concourse, in the openings of the gates: in the city she uttereth her words, *saying*, How long, ye simple ones, will ye love simplicity? and the scorners delight in their scorning, and fools hate knowledge? Turn you at my reproof: behold, I will pour out my spirit unto you, I will make known my words unto you."

DIVINE wisdom was an abstraction in the days of Solomon. It is an incarnation in our times. In his days it was personified in language. In ours it is personified in flesh. It is the same thing however clad; the infinite intelligence of love and truth. It is the "mind of God." This wisdom is here represented as speaking to the world.

The voice of wisdom to the world is EARNEST.—"Wisdom crieth." The communications of heaven to humanity are not the utterances of mere intellect. They are the expressions of the heart. The Bible is an earnest book, Christ is an earnest messenger. The eternal Father is in earnest with His human children. "As I live saith the Lord God I have no pleasure in the death of the wicked." "In the last day, that great day of the feast, Jesus stood and *cried*, saying, If any man thirst, let him come unto me and drink." God's communications to men show the earnestness of His heart. Look at their nature. How fervid forceful, vehement. Mark their variety. They come in poetry, prose, prophecy, precept, promise, threat, expostulation, admonition. Note their continuance. They do not cease, they keep on from age to age. Wisdom is ever crying through nature, through the Bible, through the history of past ages, through conscience, and through reason. Earnestness is all heartedness. God's heart is in His communications to men.

The voice of wisdom to the world is PUBLIC.—" She uttereth her voice in the streets; she crieth in the chief places of concourse, in the openings of the gates." "The accumulation," says Kitto, "of phrases implying publicity—the streets, the chief place of concourse, the openings of the gates, the city—probably refer to the custom in the East, particularly among the Arabians, for people to hold discussions and conversations on religion and morals in the open air, and especially in the more public parts of the town, to which the inhabitants resort for the sake of society. It is not unusual indeed for a man respected for his eloquence, learning, or reputed sanctity, to collect in such places a congregation which listens with attention and interest to the address he delivers. Thus such wisdom as they possess may be said to "cry in the streets;" and as the people read very little, if at all, a very large part of the information and mental cultivation which they possess is derived from the discussions, conversations, recitations, and lectures on various subjects, which they hear in the streets and public places." Where is the voice of heavenly wisdom not heard? The whole earth is vocal with it. It echoes in every man's soul. "There is no speech nor language where her voice is not heard." There are three classes here specified to whom it addresses itself. The "*simple.*" "Ye simple ones"—those most unsophisticated and free from the taint of sin, the millions of the rising race as well as those in more advanced life who have retained in some measure the innocency of childhood. "*Scorners*"—men who are so hardened in sin that they resist impressions and sneer at sacred persons and things. To impious scoffers and profane jesters, who are numerous in all ages and are morally the most degraded of men, this Wisdom speaks. "*Fools*"—men who hate knowledge. The simple are weak, the scorner disdainful, the fool malignant—he hates knowledge. How great the mercy of God in condescending to speak to such.

But the earnest and public address of wisdom to these classes is pre-eminently practical. It is in the language of *expostulation*. "How long ye simple ones?" How long? Do you know how brief your life is and how urgent the work of spiritual reformation? How long ye simple ones will ye love simplicity? And the scorners delight in their scorning, and fools hate knowledge?" It is the language of *invitation*. "Turn you at my reproof." Turn away from worldliness and wickedness and come to holiness and truth. Turn, you *can* do it, you *must* do it, you are *bound* to do it. "Let the wicked forsake his ways and the unrighteous man his thoughts, and let him return unto the Lord, and He will have mercy upon him, and to our God, for he will abundantly pardon." It is the language of *encouragement*. "I will pour out my Spirit upon you." "I will make known my words unto you." "I offer," says Bishop Hall, "to you both my word outwardly to your ears, and a plentiful measure of my Spirit to make that word effectual to you."

Such is the voice of Wisdom. "He that hath ears to hear let him hear." Hear that your souls may live—hear at once. Delay is sinful and perilous. Remember the words of John Foster—"How dangerous to defer those momentous reformations which conscience is solemnly preaching to the heart! If they are neglected, the difficulty and indisposition are increasing every month. The mind is receding degree after degree, from the warm and the hopeful zone; till at last it will enter the *Arctic* circle, and become fixed in relentless and eternal ice."

Proverbs 1:24-33

God and the Sinner in Time and Eternity

"Because I have called, and ye refused; I have stretched out my hand, and no man regarded; But ye have set at nought all my counsel, and would none of my reproof: I also will laugh at your calamity; I will mock when your fear cometh; when your fear cometh as desolation, and your destruction cometh as a whirlwind; when distress and anguish cometh upon you. Then shall they call upon me, but I will not answer; they shall seek me early, but they shall not find me: For that they hated knowledge, and did not choose the fear of the LORD: They would none of my counsel: they despised all my reproof. Therefore shall they eat of the fruit of their own way, and be filled with the fruit of their own devices. For the turning away of the simple shall slay them, and the prosperity of fools shall destroy them. But whoso hearkeneth unto me shall dwell safely, and shall be quiet from fear of evil."

GOD AND THE SINNER IN TIME.—Two things are observable here. First, *God's conduct to sinners in time.* What does he do? He "*calls*" them—calls them by teachings of nature, the admonitions of reason and the appeals of His word—calls them away from sin to holiness, from misery to joy, from Satan to Himself. He *stretches* out His hand. "I have stretched out my hand." What for? To rescue from danger, to bestow benedictions, to command attention, to welcome a return. He *counsels* them. "Ye have set at nought my counsels." Counsels that would shed light upon duty and destiny, solve moral problems, and make the path of human life straight and sunny for ever. He *reproves* them. "And would none of my reproof." His reproofs, whilst they are honest, are also loving and tender. This is the attitude of the Eternal towards every human sinner here. He is calling, outstretching His hand, addressing counsels, and administering reproofs. But, mark on the other hand, Secondly, *the conduct of sinners towards God in time.* How do sinners treat the Almighty here? They *refuse* His call. "I have called and ye refused." They *disregard* His attitude. "I have stretched out my hand and no man regarded." They condemn His counsel and reproof. "Ye have set at nought all my counsel, and would none of my reproof." What a spectacle to angels is this! God's treatment of the sinner and the sinner's treatment of Him. Wonder, oh heaven! and be astonished, oh earth!

GOD AND THE SINNER IN ETERNITY.—Here observe, First, *His conduct towards the sinner in eternity*. When sinners pass impenitently into the realms of retribution, how does the Eternal treat them there? He *laughs* at them. "I will laugh at your calamity." Strong metaphor conveying a most terrific idea! What a laugh is this! It is the laugh of mockery and contempt. "I will mock when your fear cometh." A father laughing at his child in trial and anguish! For the suffering child to see his parent looking on without a tear of compassion or a sigh of sympathy, with a heartless indifference, would give poignancy to his pains, but to see him smile and to hear him laugh in his writhing agonies, how unspeakably distressing! To be laughed at by God! Can you have a more terrible picture of misery? A thousand times sooner let the Eternal flash His lightnings, hurl His thunders, and rain His fires on me, than laugh at my calamities. He *disregards* their prayers. Fear is on them as a desolation! *Destruction* has come down upon them as a whirlwind. Distress and anguish has seized them, and they pray, and God says, "I will not answer." He looks on and laughs. What a contrast between His conduct in time, and His conduct in eternity! Observe, Secondly, *the impenitent sinner's conduct towards God in eternity*. He whom sinners ignored and disregarded in *time*, is earnestly prayed to now. "They shall seek me early but shall not find me." They would not listen to my warnings and invitations, and I will not listen to their prayers. They seek God but cannot find Him. Why has all this misery come upon them? Here is the explanation:—"They hated knowledge and did not choose the fear of the Lord. They would none of my counsel; they despised all my reproof. Therefore shall they eat of the fruit of their own way and be filled with their own devices." They said to the Almighty when here, "Depart from us." He says to them there, "Depart from me." Here is retribution. All their misery is but the eating of the fruit of their own ways. They reap what they had sown. As fruit answers to seed, as echoes to sound, their calamities in eternity answer to their conduct in time. " Be not deceived, God is not mocked. Whatsoever a man soweth that shall he also reap."

Notwithstanding all this, mercy still speaks in the close of the passage. " Whoso hearkeneth unto me shall dwell safely, and shall be quiet from fear of evil." Practical attention to God's word will secure safety now and for ever. " The name of the Lord is a strong tower, the righteous flee thereto and are safe." " Seek the Lord while he may be found, and call upon him while he is near."

Proverbs 2:1-5

Spiritual Excellence

"My son, if thou wilt receive my words, and hide my commandments with thee; So that thou incline thine ear unto wisdom, *and* apply thine heart to understanding; Yea, if thou criest after knowledge, *and* liftest up thy voice for understanding; If thou seekest her as silver, and searchest for her as *for* hid treasures; Then shalt thou understand the fear of the LORD, and find the knowledge of God."

WE have here
Spiritual excellence DESCRIBED.—It is described as "*the fear of the Lord,*" and as "*the knowledge of God.*" The twofold description conveys the idea that godliness has to do both with the *intellect* and the *heart*. It is knowledge and fear. It is such a knowledge of God as generates the true emotion towards Him. In true spiritual excellence there is a blending of reverent love and theologic light. Such a blending that both become one, the love is light and the light is love. In this, our perfection and well being consist. This is not the means to

heaven, it is heaven—heaven in all times, circumstances, and worlds. Its influence is beautifully and truthfully described by Sir Humphrey Davy. "Religion, whether natural or revealed, has always the same beneficial influence on the mind. In youth, in health, and prosperity it awakens feelings of gratitude, and sublime love, and purifies at the same time that which it exalts; but it is in misfortune, in sickness, in age, that its effects are more truly and beneficially felt: when submission in faith and humble trust in the Divine Will, when duties become pleasures, undecaying sources of consolation; then it creates powers which were believed to be extinct, and gives a freshness to the mind which was supposed to have passed away for ever, but which is now renovated as an immortal hope. Its influence outlives all earthly enjoyments, and becomes stronger as the organs decay, and the frame dissolves; it appears as that evening star of light in the horizon of life, which we are sure is to become, in another season, a morning star, and it throws its radiance through the gloom and shadow of death."

Here we have

Spiritual excellence ATTAINED.—How is this invaluable state of being to be reached? The text indicates the method. By the *reception* of Divine truth. "If thou wilt receive my words." The receptive faculty must be employed. God's truth must be taken into the soul. It is the glory of our nature that we can take into us ideas from the Eternal Intellect, and this we must do if we would reach the grand ideal of being. His thoughts alone can break the darkness of our spirits and warm them into heavenly life. By the *retention* of Divine truth. "Hide my commandments." What we receive from the Divine Mind we must hold fast. We must keep the seed in the soil, nurse and watch it, that it may germinate and grow. There is a danger of losing it. The winds of temptation and the fowls of evil will tear away the grains unless we watch. By the *search after* Divine truth. "Apply thine heart to understanding." "Incline thine ear unto wisdom." The ear must be turned away from the sounds of earthly pleasure, the din of worldliness, and the voices of human speculation, and must listen attentively to communications from the spiritual and eternal. The search must be *earnest.* "If thou cravest after knowledge, and liftest up thy voice after understanding." Truth never comes where it is not wanted, where its necessity is not felt. It only gives its bread to the hungry, and its waters to those who feel the burning thirst. As hungry children cry out for food, souls must cry to the Eternal Father for light. The search must be *persevering.* "If thou seekest her as silver, and searchest for her as for hid treasures." How indefatigable are men in their search for silver and gold. They excavate the mountains, they plough the seas, they go from market to market and from shore to shore, in earnest quest for gold. But spiritual excellence is infinitely more precious than all worldly treasures. "It cannot be valued with the gold of Ophir, with the precious onyx or the sapphire. The gold and the crystal cannot equal it, and the exchange of it shall not be for jewels of fine gold. No mention shall be made of corals, or of pearls : for the price of wisdom is above rubies. The topaz of Ethiopia shall not equal it, neither shall it be valued with pure gold." By so much as spiritual excellence is more valuable than all worldly treasures, should be our ardent, unwearied diligence in quest of it. " The following relic," says Mr. Bridges, "of our renowned Elizabeth will be read both with interest and profit. It was written on a blank leaf of a black letter edition of St. Paul's Epistles, which she used during her lonely imprisonment at Woodstock. The volume itself, curiously embroidered by her own hand, is preserved in the Bodleian :—'August. I walk many times into the pleasant fields of the Holy Scriptures, where I pluck up the goodlisome herbs of sentences by pruning, eat them by reading, chew them by musing, and lay them up at length in the high seat of memorie, that in gathering them together, and so having tasted their sweetness, I may the less perceive the bitterness of this miserable life.'"

Proverbs 2:6-9

Good Men and Their God

"For the LORD giveth wisdom; out of his mouth *cometh* knowledge and understanding. He layeth up sound wisdom for the righteous: *he is* a buckler to them that walk uprightly. He keepeth the paths of judgment, and preserveth the way of his saints. Then shalt thou understand righteousness, and judgment, and equity; *yea*, every good path."

THESE words bring under our attention the greatest beings on *earth*, good men; and the greatest being in the *universe*, the Great God. Notice:—

THE CHARACTER OF GOOD MEN.—The description given of them here is full, varied, and very significant. They are spoken of as the *"righteous."* The whole duty of man may be included in this word, or in its equivalent, a shorter word still—just. The moral code of the universe may be reduced to two words, "Be just." Be just to yourself, respect your own nature, train your own faculties, guard your own rights, realize your own ideals. This is virtue! Be just to others: "Whatsoever ye would that men should do unto you do ye even so to them." This is morality. Be just to God: The Best Being love the most, the Truest Being trust the most, the Greatest Being reverence, adore and serve the most. This is religion! Virtue, morality, and religion constitute a righteous man. They are spoken of as "*walking uprightly.*" Goodness in all moral creatures is not stationary, but progressive. It is an everlasting walk into new fields of beauty, new scenes of enjoyment, new spheres of service. "The path of the just is a shining light which shineth more and more unto the perfect day." They are spoken of as "*saints.*" They are consecrated to God's service, set apart to His use, they are the living and imperishable temples of the Holy Ghost. Such is the sketch given here of good men, and stand they not in sublime contrast with the canting hypocrites, worldly grubs, fawning sycophants, wretched snobs, which abound in modern society and from which all honest hearts recoil? "The greatest man," says Seneca, "is he who chooses right with the most invincible resolution, who resists the sorest temptation from within and without, who bears the heaviest burdens cheerfully, who is calmest in storms, and most fearless under menaces and frowns, whose reliance on truth, on virtue, and on God is most unfaltering." Kind Heaven, multiply the number of these good men!

Observe

THE GOD OF GOOD MEN.—He is here set forth in *His relation to creation generally.* " For the Lord giveth wisdom, out of His mouth cometh knowledge and understanding." He is the great original, central, exhautless Fountain of intelligence. He is "the Father of lights;" the light of instinct, the light of reason, the light of genius, the light of conscience, all stream from Him as from the sun. Wherever there is a ray of truth, a beam of intelligence, a gleam of virtue, there is God, and in them He should be recognized and worshipped.

"God," says old Quarles, "is a light that is never darkened, an unwearied life that cannot die, a fountain always flowing, a garden of life, a seminary of wisdom, a radical beginning of all goodness."

" Give me unveil'd the source of good to see!
Give me Thy light, and fix mine eyes on Thee!"—BOETHIUS.

He is here set forth in *His relation to the good in particular.* He makes special provisions for them. He provides for their instruction. "He layeth up sound Wisdom." We need not ask the question, Where are "the treasures of sound wisdom" laid up for us? The Son of Man, the Redeemer of the world is the "Wisdom of God." He protects them from their enemies. "He is a buckler to them that walk uprightly." Our path is fraught with danger and beset with temptations, foes lurk about us on all hands, and we need a defence. He is our "buckler." Significant expression this; it does not say that he holds the buckler, or has a buckler for us, but He *is* the buckler.

32 / Book of Proverbs

He Himself is the shield, and our enemies must strike *through* Him to injure us. He superintends their career. "He keepeth the paths of judgment, and preserveth the way of His saints." He vouchsafes their ultimate perfection. "Then shalt thou understand righteousness, and judgment, and equity, yea every good path."

Such is the God of the good! May this God be our God! May He be our guide even unto death!

> " Thou Uncreate, Unseen, and Undefined
> Source of all life, and Fountain of the mind,
> Pervading Spirit! whom no eye can trace:
> Felt through all time, and working in all space,
> Imagination cannot paint that spot,
> Around, above, beneath, where Thou art not!"
>
> R. MONTGOMERY

Proverbs 2:10-22

Wickedness and Wisdom; the Bane and the Antidote

"When wisdom entereth into thine heart, and knowledge is pleasant unto thy soul; Discretion shall preserve thee, understanding shall keep thee: To deliver thee from the way of the evil *man*, from the man that speaketh froward things; Who leave the paths of uprightness, to walk in the ways of darkness, Who rejoice to do evil, *and* delight in the frowardness of the wicked; Whose ways *are* crooked, and *they* froward in their paths: To deliver thee from the strange woman, *even* from the stranger *which* flattereth with her words: Which forsaketh the guide of her youth, and forgetteth the covenant of her God. For her house inclineth unto death, and her paths unto the dead. None that go unto her return again, neither take they hold of the paths of life. That thou mayest walk in the way of good *men*, and keep the paths of the righteous. For the upright shall dwell in the land, and the perfect shall remain in it. But the wicked thall be cut off from the earth, and the transgressors shall be rooted out of it."

Two things of a very opposite character are brought before us in these verses—wickedness and wisdom, and these two things are at work in all literatures, institutions, enterprises, souls, the world over.

WICKEDNESS.—We have here a terrible description of wicked persons. Observe their *character*. Their *speech* is corrupt. "The man that speaketh froward things." Justin said, "By examining the tongue of a patient, physicians find out the diseases of the body and philosophers those of the mind." The wicked use their tongues to express the erroneous, the blasphemous, and perverse. They set their "mouth against the Heavens," and sometimes we hear them say to all moral constraints, "Let us break their bands asunder and cast away their cords from us." Their *habit* is corrupt. "They leave the paths of righteousness to walk in the ways of darkness." Wicked men "love darkness rather than light, because their deeds are evil." Their path is not only dark but crooked. "Whose ways are crooked." The way of goodness is straight, even, and uniform; but that of sin is labyrinthian and rough, as well as dark. Their *heart* is corrupt. They "rejoice to do evil and delight in the frowardness of the wicked." They not only speak the wrong thing, do the wrong thing, pursue the wrong course, but they rejoice in the wrong. Their pleasure is in sin, in debauchery, intemperance, carousings. They revel in wickedness. Their *influence* is corrupt. This is illustrated in the description of the "strange woman" here introduced, who "flattereth with her lips, forsaketh the guide of her youth, and forgetteth the covenant of her God." A description this of the prostitute, not only most touching and humiliating, but true to modern fact. A more horrid sight this side of Hell cannot be seen than a fallen woman, a woman giving her nature up to carnality and wrong. She is ruined and she ruins. Solomon lifts up his warning against such a character, and well he might, for he was led away from God and truth by her seductive wiles. Observe their *peril*. "Her house inclineth unto death, and her paths unto the dead. None that go unto her return again, neither take they hold of the paths of life." The spell of lust palsies the grasp of her victims. Ah! how many a poor, infatuated, deluded youth has been led on step by step the downward road to the chambers of death; led by soft and silken bonds, amidst syren music to adamantine chains and penal fire! Everything dies under the influence of wickedness,—self-respect, spiritual sensibility, mental freedom, the freshness, the vigour, and the beauty of life. Observe their *doom*. "The wicked shall be cut off from the earth and the transgressors shall be rooted out of it." They are rooted out from the esteem of the good, from the sphere of improvement, from the realm of mercy, and the domain of hope.

Eschew sin, my friend! The soul with sin in it is within the central attractions of Hell, and all its motions accelerate its movements thither. If it is in thee, crush it at once; it is easier to crush a spark than a conflagration, to break the egg of the cockatrice than to kill the serpent.

WISDOM.—This is represented here both as the preventative and the antidote to wickedness. Wickedness is terribly powerful, but wisdom is mightier. Its mightiness, however, in man depends upon its right reception. "When wisdom entereth into the heart." Wisdom outside of us is a grand thing for thought and speculation, but it must come into us to be of any real and permanent service. It will not do to flow from the tongue or float in the brain, or to come to us as a strange visitant, to be tolerated or entertained for a short time; but as a friend, of all friends the dearest to the heart. It must come in as a "thing that is pleasant to thy soul." Then it does three things in relation to wickedness. It *guards the innocent.* "Discretion shall *preserve* thee, understanding shall *keep* thee." The way to keep out evil is to fill the soul with goodness. If Divine wisdom takes full possession of thy heart, when evil comes, it will "find nothing" in thee. It *delivers the fallen.* "Deliver thee from the way of evil men," from the "strange woman." If thou hast fallen into evil, if thou art within its sphere of magic infatuation, let wisdom enter thy heart and thou shalt be delivered. It shall break the spell of the enchanter, it shall unlock the door of thy caged soul, and let thee out into the air of sunny truth. Heavenly wisdom in the soul is the only soul-redemptive force. It *guides the redeemed.* "That thou mayest walk in the ways of good men and keep the paths of the righteous." It guides our feet in the way of peace. It is a lamp to our path. Like the star to the mariner, if this wisdom shine within us it will guide us safely over the voyage of life. How shall we get into the heart this wisdom, that guards the innocent, delivers the fallen, and guides the redeemed? "If any man lack wisdom let him ask of God, who giveth to all men liberally and upbraideth not."

> " Who are the wise ?
> They who have govern'd with a self-control,
> Each wild and baneful passion of the soul—
> Curb'd the strong impulse of all fierce desires,
> But kept alive affection's purer fires.
> They who have pass'd the labyrinth of life,
> Without one hour of weakness or of strife :
> Prepared each change of fortune to endure,
> Humble though rich, and dignified though poor.
> Skill'd in the latent movements of the heart—
> Learn'd in the lore which nature can impart ;
> Teaching that sweet philosophy aloud,
> Which sees the 'silver lining' of the cloud ;
> Looking for good in all beneath the skies :
> These are the truly wise."—PRINCE.

Proverbs 3:1-2

The Philosophy of Health and Happiness

" My son, forget not my law, but let thine heart keep my commandments For length of days, and long life, and peace, shall they add to thee."

DIVINE revelation is a law. It is not a mere creed, but a code. It is not given for mere study, speculation, and belief, but for obedience. It has all the attributes of a law, —publicity, authority, practicability. The text teaches two great truths.

OBEDIENCE TO MORAL LAW IS A CONDITION OF PHYSICAL HEALTH.—Mark at the outset what the obedience is. It is the obedience of the heart. "Let thine *heart* keep my commandments." The Bible legislates for mind, for thoughts, affections, impulses, and aims. Its commandment is so broad that it takes the whole soul in, penetrates to its deepest and most hidden springs of action. Obedience is not a thing of tongue, or hand, or foot, it is a thing of the heart. Perfect external conformity to the mere letter of the law, were it possible, would be rebellion if the heart was not in it. We are taught here that this spiritual obedience is a condition of physical health. It secures "length of days and long life." The connection between obedience and physical health is clear from the three following facts:—(1) That physical health requires obedience to the divine laws of our being. (2) That obedience to these divine laws involves a study of them. (3) That the heartiest sympathy with the Divine author is essential to their successful study. These propositions are so evident that they require neither illustrations nor proof. Add to this the fact that sobriety, temperance, chastity, industry, contentment, regularity, amiability, control of the temper, and the passions, which are involved in true obedience, are all conducive to corporeal health and vigour. Some people seem to regard ill-health as a mark of gentility. They are afraid to acknowledge themselves as vigorous and robust, lest they should be considered vulgar. They consider it more respectable to acknowledge feebleness than strength. Others seem to regard ill-health as a virtue—something to be pleased with and commended for. But in truth ill-health often means coarseness and crime. It grows out of the infraction of divine laws. Health of the body depends upon health of soul, and health of soul depends upon obedience to the moral laws of God. Bodily vigour depends upon moral virtue. "Godliness is profitable unto all things, having the promise of the life that now is and of that which is to come." There is a care for health which destroys it. "People," says Sterne, "who are always taking care of their health are like misers who are hoarding a treasure which they have never spirit enough to enjoy." But there is a care that promotes it—it is a care for moral purity and a divine elevation of soul in thought and aim.

OBEDIENCE TO MORAL LAW IS A CONDITION OF SPIRITUAL HAPPINESS.—"And peace shall be added to thee." Peace requires two things. (1) The inward harmony of our powers. The soul is often like a battle-field, on which there is a violent conflict of forces. The suggestions of reason and the dictates of conscience battle against the armies of carnal lusts and selfish impulses. It is like a sea, into whose depths there rush contending currents, heaving it to its centre. (2) The sense of divine favour. The feeling that the Lord is against us gives the throbs of perpetual restlessness to our souls. Now spiritual obedience puts an end to this state of things, crushes inward enemies, hushes inward storms, and gives a blessed consciousness of divine approval.

> ".Peace is the end of all things—tearless peace;
> Who by the immovable basis of God's throne
> Takes her perpetual stand ; and, of herself
> Prophetic, lengthens age by age her sceptre:
> The world shall yet be subjugate to love,
> The final form religion must assume,
> Led like a lion, rid with wreathed reins,
> In some enchanted island, by a child."—FESTUS

Proverbs 3:3-4

Mercy and Truth

"Let not mercy and truth forsake thee: bind them about thy neck; write them upon the tables of thine heart: So shalt thou find favour and good understanding in the sight of God and man."

Two of the greatest moral realities of the universe are mentioned in these verses. They are the greatest themes in all true books, the chief elements in all great lives, the noblest attributes of the Godhead, the primal substances of the Gospel. "Grace and truth came by Jesus Christ." These two direct man's nature as a being possessing intellect and heart, each of which has its respective cravings and claims. We must have "*truth*" in us;—all our faculties must truthfully move in harmony with eternal realities. We must have "*mercy*" in us. All our powers must move by it as their impulse and sovereign. Man's duty in relation to "mercy and truth" is here set forth by two strong metaphors, the metaphors of binding and writing.

Man has to BIND "mercy" and "truth" to him.—"Bind them continually upon thy heart and tie them upon thy neck." The allusion here is probably to the phylacteries with which the Jews were commanded by Moses to bind the law around their foreheads. But here the command is to bind mercy and truth, not upon the hand or the head, but upon the *heart;* and they were to be kept there, not for a time, but "continually;" to be taken off neither day or night. They are to be carried with us as mementoes of our obligations to heaven, and as safeguards to protect us from the wrong and the ruinous. They are so vital to us that we must not part with them. Take mercy and truth from the soul and you take the verdure from the fields, and leave them in barrenness; you take the light from the heavens and leave them in sackcloth. Part with everything; property, friends, reputation, life itself, sooner than part with them. Without them the soul is lost—lost to virtue, nobility, usefulness and heaven.

Man has to WRITE "mercy and truth" within him.— There are two Bibles—one consists of truth written on paper, the other of truth written on the soul. Whilst both are valuable, the latter is for many reasons the most precious. (1) Because it is the most *real*. In the paper Bible we have only "mercy and truth" in *symbol,* but in the loving heart they themselves are there. The figures on your bank book, representing the amount which stands to your credit at the bank, are not real money but the sign; your property is not in your book, but in the bank; so "mercy and truth" are not in the letter-press, but they are in the heart. (2) Because it is the most *legible*. The paper Bible contains many things hard to be understood. The most enlightened interpreter fails to reach its meaning, but what is written on the heart, is written in the language that universal man can read, the savage as well as the sage, the child as well as the octogenarian. (3) Because it is the most *capacious*. The heart is a volume whose pages defy finite arithmetic, whose folios none but God can number. How voluminous the contents of every heart now! But what through the ages! Every impression we receive is a fresh sentence. (4) Because it is the most *endurable*. Paper, parchment, marble, or even brass, on which men have written, time has destroyed; but the heart is immortal, and the sentences written on it eternity cannot obliterate.

Man has to ENJOY " mercy and truth " within him.—If mercy and truth are in the soul, not as mere ideas or as temporary impulses, but as living, regnant, and abiding forces, God's favour will be enjoyed, success will attend our ways, and we shall advance in holy freedom and force. Christ (who brought "grace and truth " into the world), as he grew increased in favour both with God and man, and it will be the same with all those who embody those transcendent elements in their lives.

Conclusion.—The whole implies that "mercy and truth" are outside of men in their unregenerate state. They are in the heart of God, they are in the universe, they are in the Bible as symbols, but they are not inherent in human nature. Men must have them. Embrace them, brother; bind them indissolubly upon thy moral being, and write them indelibly on thy heart!

Proverbs 3:5-7

God-trusting and Self-trusting

"Trust in the LORD with all thine heart; and lean not unto thine own understanding. In all thy ways acknowledge him, and he shall direct thy paths. Be not wise in thine own eyes: fear the LORD, and depart from evil."

GOD-TRUSTING.—"Trust in the Lord." Man is a trusting creature: he is always leaning on some object. So deep is his consciousness of dependence, that he dares not stand alone. This trusting instinct, like all the other instincts of his nature, has been sadly perverted by a wrong direction. Everywhere man is leaning on the unworthy, the unreliable, and the unenduring; hence his constant disappointments and confusion. Observe here the *object* of true trustfulness. "The Lord,"—the All-merciful, the All-wise, and All-powerful;—the Unchanging amidst all changes, the All-loving amidst all malignities, the All-enduring amidst all dissolutions, the One and only One; not *it* nor *them*, but HIM. Observe the *manner* of true trustfulness. It must be *entire;* "With all thy heart." It must be an unquestioned, undivided confidence. He is to be trusted lovingly: not as a matter of expedience or dry duty, but as a matter of supreme affection. It must be *always*. "In all thy ways acknowledge Him." Man's ways are many. All men have different ways. These are determined by organization, idiosyncracies, and other constitutional adventitious circumstances. There is the way of the sensualist, the sceptic, the savage, the sage, the worldling, the saint. Each man has often different ways: he does not continue through life in the same path, he changes it through the force of age, conviction, and experience. But in whatever way he walks, at any time he should trustfully acknowledge Him; acknowledge not merely his existence, personality, power, but His absolute authority over him; His claim to be his grand subject of thought, object of affection, supreme aim of life. Observe the *advantage* of true trustfulness. What is it? Guidance in the right—"He will direct thy paths." He guides those who will trust in Him. His guidance secures safety amidst all perils, and happiness amidst all sorrows. He will make the path clear and secure, as we walk on and upward, for ever. Another advantage is departure from evil. "Fear the Lord and depart from evil." Fear is included in God-trusting, and where this is there is a departure from evil. The soul in which there is this blessed trust breaks away from all evil, and struggles its way into holiness and love. There is yet another advantage specified,—strength in all. "It shall be health to thy navel and marrow to thy bones." True trustfulness excludes all those anxious cares, and crushes all those appetites and passions of the soul, which are ever the seeds of physical discomfort and disease. It gives that evenness of temper, that regularity to the impulses, that tranquil cheerfulness to the heart, which are pre-eminently conducive to corporeal health and force. It is a libel on religion to represent it as in any way inimical to true physical vigour and animal enjoyment. Trust in God is as cheering as the light of heaven, and as healthful as the mountain breeze.

> " Thy God hath said 'tis good for thee
>   To walk by faith and not by sight.
>   Take it on trust a little while,
>   Soon shalt thou read the mystery right,
>   In the bright sunshine of His smile."—KEBLE

SELF-TRUSTING.—"Lean not on thine own understanding." There is a right self-reliance. In relation to our fellow men we are bound to trust our own energies, convictions, and conscience. We have no right to trust to other men's powers and efforts to help us either physically or mentally. Heaven has endowed us all with faculties by which to help ourselves, if they are rightly worked. The man who is not self-reliant in this sense sinks his manhood in the parasite. But that self-trusting, to which Solomon refers, implies an exaggerated conceit of our own powers. Hence he says, "be not wise in your own eyes." Don't put too high an estimate on your own understanding. Thank God for your intellect. Respect it, train it, feed it with the choicest fruits on the tree of science, but don't lean on it as an infallible guide. At its best here, its eyes are very dim, its ears heavy, and its limbs feeble. The sages of all times, who have trusted to it, have gone down in darkness, bequeathing to us such literary productions as show how far they wandered from the light. The light of our own reason is far too feeble to guide us safely through the moral labyrinths of life. "Be not wise, therefore, in thine own eyes." Self-conceit is at once offensive and pernicious; it involves *self-ignorance*. No man, who knows himself, can be vain. The hierarchs of heaven veil their faces. What is the knowledge of the most enlightened compared with what *is* to be known? What is a spark to the central fires of the universe? What compared with what he *ought* to have known? How much more the wisest on the earth might have known if they had properly employed their powers? A man "wise in his own eyes," is self-benighted. He is like a pauper maniac, who fancies himself a king. "Many," says Seneca, "might have attained wisdom, had they not thought they had really attained it." Self-conceit not only involves self-ignorance, but obstructs *mental improvement*. "Seest thou a man wise in his own conceit, there is more hope of a fool than of him." True knowledge requires effort. It neither springs up involuntarily, nor comes to us independently of our own endeavours, or even by efforts, feeble, irresolute, and desultory. It requires an invincibility of purpose, a concentration of faculties. Who will put forth such efforts to gain it, but those who have the profoundest sense of its necessity? There must be a craving, amounting almost to an agony, in order to overcome the inertia and grapple with the difficulty. A man who is "wise in his own eyes," feels no such necessity as this: he is self-sufficient, and imagines that he knows everything. Self-conceit destroys *social influence*. A vain man disgusts rather than pleases, repels rather than draws, he is generally despised, seldom respected. Intelligence, generosity, truthfulness, humility, these are the elements that win social esteem, and gain social command. But these are seeds that can never grow in a self-trusting, self-conceited man.

> " They whose wit
> Values itself so highly, that to that
> All matters else seem weak, can hardly love,
> Or take a shape or feeling of affection,
> Being so self-endear'd."—SHAKESPEARE

Proverbs 3:9-10

The Highest Giving, the Condition of the Highest Getting

"Honour the LORD with thy substance, and with the firstfruits of all thine increase : So shall thy barns be filled with plenty, and thy presses shall burst out with new wine."

THE HIGHEST GIVING.

"HONOUR the Lord with thy substance." The two great functions of men are to gather and to give, to appropriate and to distribute. These two functions bring all his powers into play and fully develope his nature. But man is to gather in order to give, to get in order to impart. "It is more blessed to give than to receive." What is the highest giving? (1) Giving to the *Best Being*. Who is He? "The Lord." The distinguishing glory of a moral intelligence is the *power* of giving to God, and his highest honour is to have his gift *accepted* of Him. (2) Giving the *best things* to the Best Being. "Thy substance." "The firstfruits of all thine increase." "God will not have the dregs that are squeezed out by pressure poured into His treasury. He depends, not like earthly rulers, on the magnitude of His tributes. He loveth a cheerful giver. He can do without our wealth, but He does not bless without our willing service." Giving to God does not merely mean giving contributions to His cause, but the giving of our all, ourselves. The surrender of self is essential to give virtue and acceptance to all other contributions. Until we give ourselves, all other oblations however costly, are impious pretences and solemn mockeries. Self-sacrifice alone can give worth and acceptability to all other presentations.

THE HIGHEST GETTING

By giving thus you get back,—What? The choicest and fullest divine blessings. "So shall thy barns be filled with plenty." This is a figurative expression for the highest good in the highest degree; and good of all kinds— temporal, intellectual, social, spiritual. Surrendering to God is godliness, and godliness is the condition of all true gain. He who yields his all to the Eternal, *attends to the condition of all true prosperity*—industry, temperance, economy, foresight. "Seek ye first the kingdom of God, and His righteousness, and all other things shall be added unto you." He who yields his all to God, *insures the special favour of Heaven*. The Divine blessing rests upon the labour of the truly good. "God is not unrighteous to forget your work and labour of love which ye have showed towards His name." Seneca has well said, "He that does good to another man, does also good to himself; not only in the consequence but in the very act of doing it; for the conscience of well doing is an ample reward." "Good," says Milton, "the more communicated, more abundant grows."

Proverbs 3:11-12

Affliction

"My son, despise not the chastening of the LORD; neither be weary of his correction: For whom the LORD loveth, he correcteth; even as a father the son *in whom* he delighteth."

"AFFLICTIONS" are to be accepted as MEANS OF SPIRITUAL DISCIPLINE.—" The chastening of the Lord."—" His correction." Human sufferings in this world must be regarded, not as *casualties*, or events that come on us by capricious chance or iron necessity. They are from "the Lord." The Lord is in all. "The Lord gave," not chance nor necessity, the Lord "hath taken away." Nor as mere *penalties*. It may be true that sin is the source of all suffering. But suffering here, in the cases of individuals, is not according to the measure, or kind of sin. It is *reformative*, not destructive. " The chastening of the Lord." Affliction does the good man service in many ways. It detaches him from the race and makes him feel his own solemn loneliness. It impresses him with the worthlessness of materialism, and with the awful solemnity of the spiritual world. It brings the idea of death, retribution, eternity, powerfully near to the heart.

Afflictions are to be accepted as TOKENS OF PARENTAL LOVE.—"Whom the Lord loveth he correcteth." The anguish is not caused by the lash of a tyrant, or the infliction of an inexorable judge, but by the love of a father. (1) *The character of God as a benevolent Being attests this*. It is a monstrous profanity to believe that He, the infinitely loving One, can have any pleasure in our suffering. He is Love. (2) *The experience of the good attests this*. What said David? "Before I was afflicted I went astray."* Paul: "I take pleasure in infirmities." And this is the testimony of the good in all ages. (3) *The word of God attests this*. " Happy is the man whom God correcteth." "As many as I love I rebuke." " And He shall sit as a refiner." Affliction is like the winter frost, it kills the pernicious insects which the sun of health has engendered. It acts like the stormy wind upon the tree, it strengthens the fibres and deepens the roots of our virtue. It is like the thunderstorm in nature, it purifies the unhealthy atmosphere that has gathered around the heart. It is the bitter potion which the skilful physician administers to his patient. "As threshing separates the corn from the chaff," says Burton, "so does affliction purify virtue." "Virtue," says Lord Bacon, "is like precious

---

* Psalm cxix. 67.   II. Cor. xii. 8 to 10.   Job. v. 17.
  Rev. iii. 19.   Mal. iii. 3.

odours, most fragrant when they are incensed and crushed; for prosperity doth best discover vice, but adversity doth best discover virtue."

Proverbs 3:13-18

The Blessedness of Wisdom

"Happy *is* the man *that* findeth wisdom, and the man *that* getteth understanding. For the merchandise of it *is* better than the merchandise of silver, and the gain thereof than fine gold. She *is* more precious than rubies : and all the things thou canst desire are not to be compared unto her. Length of days *is* in her right hand; *and* in her left hand riches and honour. Her ways *are* ways of pleasantness, and all her paths *are* peace. She *is* a tree of life to them that lay hold upon her : and happy *is every one* that retaineth her."

THESE words catalogue the blessings that accrue to a godly life. This godliness or wisdom

ENDOWS WITH THE BEST WEALTH.—It is here represented as better than "silver," "fine gold," "precious rubies," and all things that can be desired. What are the greatest temporal possessions in comparison with moral goodness! Can the former be really enjoyed without the latter? Can a corrupt soul be happy with the world? The former have a very transitory existence compared with the latter. The material is transitory in itself, and is ever rapidly passing from the grasp of its possessor. But "he that doeth the word of God abideth for ever." The former are not essential to blessedness; the latter is. A godly soul can be happy in a pauper's home. The Lord is its portion. "What things were gain to me," says Paul, "those I counted loss." The former are really a curse without the latter. The more a man has of the world, if he has not virtue in his heart, the more he has to blacken his future and damn his soul. This Wisdom

ENSURES PERMANENT GOOD.—" Length of days is in her right hand." By length of days here Solomon does not mean mere longevity on earth, although wisdom conduces to this, but evidently permanent *distinctions*. The moral riches and honour connected with wisdom are unlike the earthly, they are enduring, and also permanent *enjoyments*. "Her ways are ways of pleasantness, and all her paths are peace." Her ways are the ways of chastity, justice, truthfulness, holy affections, benevolent activities, and communings with the Great God, and from these, pleasures must inevitably spring. Religion is happiness. It has a "rest for the soul." It has a "fulness of joy." It has sublime delights even in temporal affliction. This Wisdom

RESTORES TO ALL FORFEITED PRIVILEGES.—"She is a tree of life, to them that lay hold upon her, and happy is every one that retaineth her." Adam by sin forfeited the privileges of the "Tree of Life." Would he ever have suffered or died had he continued in connection with its living virtues? Nay, would he not have grown in power and honour for ever? True godliness is a tree of life, a tree of life *in* the soul. Like the Apocalyptic tree, it is in the midst of the street of the New Jerusalem, on either side of the river, yielding twelve manner of fruits, and the leaves of it are for healing the nations. This tree of life was *Central*. "In the midst." Godliness is in the centre of man's nature. This Tree of life was *Well-rooted*. "It was either side of the river." A religious soul is a soul rooted by the stream of Divine love and truth. This tree of life was *Fruitful*. "Twelve manner of fruits." It affords every variety of pleasure, meets every taste and want. This tree of life was *Restorative*. "Leaves of the tree for the healing of the nations." Godliness restores waning faculties, renews decaying powers. Here then is the true riches, the true honour, and the true peace of men.

> " O rich in gold! Beggars in heart and soul!
> Poor as the empty void! Why, I, even I,
> Sitting in this bare chamber with my thoughts,
> Are richer than ye are, despite your bales,
> Your streets of warehouses, your mighty mills,
> Each looming like a world, faint heard in space,
> Your ships unwilling fires, that day and night
> Writhe in your service seven years, then die
> Without one taste of peace."—ALEXANDER SMITH

Proverbs 3:19-20

Wisdom, the Source and Sovereign of Worlds

"The LORD by wisdom hath founded the earth; by understanding hath he established the heavens. By his knowledge the depths are broken up, and the clouds drop down the dew."

THESE words give us two ideas concerning the universe.

THAT IT IS ORGANIZED BY WISDOM.—"The Lord by wisdom hath founded the earth." This stands opposed to two absurd cosmological theories. It stands opposed *to the eternity of the universe.* The universe is not eternal either in its *elements* or its *combinations.* There was a period, far back in the abysses of eternity, when there was nothing, when the absolute One lived alone. It stands opposed *to the contingent origin of the universe.* It sprang from no fortuitous concourse of atoms. "By Wisdom hath He founded the earth; by understanding hath he established the heavens." He has hollowed out the oceans, and arranged the systems of clouds. The scientific student of nature sees design and exquisite adaptations in every part of nature. "By His knowledge the depths are broken up, and the clouds drop down the dew." "We are raised by science," says Lord Brougham, "to an understanding of the infinite wisdom and goodness, which the Creator has displayed in all His works. Not a step can we take in any direction without perceiving the most extraordinary traces of design, and the skill everywhere conspicuous is calculated in so vast a proportion of instances to promote the happiness of living creatures, and especially of ourselves, that we feel no hesitation in concluding, that if we knew the whole scheme of Providence, every part would appear in harmony with a plan of absolute benevolence. Independently, however, of this most consoling inference, the delight is inexpressible, of being able to follow the marvellous works of the Great Author of nature, and to trace the unbounded power and exquisite skill, which are exhibited by the most minute as well as the mightiest parts of His system."

THAT IT IS ORGANIZED BY THE WISDOM OF ONE BEING. "The Lord." It is not arranged on a plan which is the outcome of many intelligences. One intellect drafted the whole. Every part of the stupendous engine, even to the smallest pin, was sketched by Him Who has no counsellor, and Whom none can instruct. *The unity of the universe* shows this. There is the unity of *style, operation* and *purpose*. *The Word of God* declares this. "In the beginning God created." "Thou, Lord, in the beginning hast laid the foundation of the earth, and the heavens are the works of Thine hands." The Bible cosmogony alone agrees with the deductions of true science, the intuitions of the soul, and the claims of religion. He is the

> "Mighty cause
> Of causes mighty! Cause uncaused!
> Sole root of nature!"—DR. YOUNG.

Proverbs 3:21-26

Fidelity to Priniciple

"My son, let not them depart from thine eyes; keep sound wisdom and discretion: So shall they be life unto thy soul, and grace to thy neck. Then shalt thou walk in thy way safely, and thy foot shall not stumble. When thou liest down, thou shalt not be afraid: yea, thou shalt lie down, and thy sleep shall be sweet. Be not afraid of sudden fear, neither of the desolation of the wicked, when it cometh. For the LORD shall be thy confidence, and shall keep thy foot from being taken."

FIDELITY to principle is the idea involved in these words. "My son, let not them depart from thine eyes." What?—The principles of truth. The advantages connected with fidelity to principle are here sketched, and they are—

LIFE.—"Life unto thy soul." The principles of

heavenly wisdom *originate* spiritual life. They are soul-quickening. The words of wisdom are "spirit and life." They are to the soul what the sunbeam and the dew are to the fields. Where they are not, there is darkness and dearth. They *nurture* spiritual life. They are the bread and water of life. The soul apart from them is dead, dead to all high interests, spiritual services, and enjoyments. Another advantage connected with fidelity to principle is—

ORNAMENT.—" Grace to thy neck." These principles clothe the life with the beauty of holiness. They give a refinement, and a gracefulness to character. This " Grace " or ornament is valuable for many reasons. *It is becoming to all.* Some ornaments are only becoming to certain classes or certain positions. It is *within the reach of every man.* There are ornaments that can only be obtained by a few : jewels and diamonds are beyond the reach of the poor. It is *admired by the highest intelligences,* by great men, angels, God Himself. There are ornaments that are prized by some but despised by others. It is *imperishable in its nature.* All other beauties decay, all other brilliancies grow dim, wisdom "is a crown that fadeth not away." There is also connected with fidelity to principle—

SAFETY.—"Shalt walk in thy way safely, thy foot shall not stumble." The twenty-sixth verse assigns the reason for the safety. God is the guide and the guardian of the faithful. Elsewhere we are told that "The steps of a good man are ordered by the Lord." " He that dwelleth in the secret place of the most High, shall abide under the shadow of the Almighty." "The Eternal God is thy refuge." What a blessing to be safe on a path of tremendous precipices, and beset with foes, on a sea rolling tumultuously over quicksands and rocks ! There is yet another blessing associated with fidelity to principle—

COURAGE.—"Thou shalt not be afraid." It is one thing to be safe and another thing to *feel* secure. A feeling of safety may well make us courageous. A man whose soul is in vital alliance with the principles of everlasting truth need not " be afraid of sudden fear, nor of the desolation of the wicked when it cometh." " None of these things move me," said Paul. Hold fast then the principles of sound wisdom, let them not depart from thee, let them be thy pillar to guide thee in the desert, thy pole-star on the sea. It is, to use the language of Carlyle, "an everlasting lode-star, that beams the brighter in the heavens, the darker here on earth grows the night around."

Proverbs 3:27-29

Beneficence

"Withhold not good from them to whom it is due, when it is in the power of thine hand to do *it*. Say not unto thy neighbour, Go, and come again, and to-morrow I will give; when thou hast it by thee. Devise not evil against thy neighbour, seeing he dwelleth securely by thee."

THESE verses teach:

THAT HUMAN BENEFICENCE HAS IT CLAIMANTS.—"Them to whom it is due." To whom do we owe kindness? To all who need it. We are commanded "to do good unto all men." *What you have is given in trust.* It is not yours, you are but the trustees. The Benevolent God gave it to you to use benevolently. It sprang from love, and should be used by love. *It is given for distribution.* God gives light to the sun that it may throw light on all the depending planets, water to the clouds that they may pour it on the barren hills, and property to man that he may use it for the good of his race. "Men," said Cicero, "resemble the gods in nothing so much as in doing good to their fellow creatures." These verses teach:

THAT HUMAN BENEFICENCE IS ONLY LIMITED BY INCAPACITY.—"When it is in the power of thy hand to do it." Our power is the measure of our obligation. No man has a right to keep back that which he can spare when his neighbour needs it. This, in the estimation of heaven, is dishonesty. Property is given, not to hoard, but to circulate for the common good. The withholder is a moral felon. Again, the verses teach :

THAT HUMAN BENEFICENCE SHOULD EVER BE PROMPT IN ITS SERVICES.—" Say not to thy neighbour, go and come again, and to-morrow I will give." The apostle James enjoins the same duty. " If a brother or sister be naked and destitute of daily food, and one of you say unto them, depart in peace, be ye warmed and filled : notwithstanding ye give them not those things which are needful to the body : what doth it profit?" Why be prompt? *Because the postponement of any duty is a sin in itself.* It is a tacit rebellion against heaven. *Because the neglect of a benevolent impulse is injurious to self.* A genuine impulse of generosity is the stirring of what is Divine within us :—the uplifting force of the soul. Our well-being depends upon strengthening it by exercise. Woe to the soul that crushes it! It is a germ of Paradise. *Because the claimant may seriously suffer by a delay of your help.* The delay may facilitate the evil, and hasten his ruin. Furthermore, these verses teach :

THAT HUMAN BENEFICENCE EXCLUDES ALL UNKINDNESS OF HEART.—" Devise not evil against thy neighbour." True "charity thinketh no evil." A selfish heart is an evil deviser. This is seen in the tricks of trade, as well as the stratagems of war. " Benevolence," says Kant, the great German philosopher, " is a duty. He who frequently practises it, and sees his benevolent intentions realized, at length comes really to love him to whom he has done good. When, therefore, it is said, ' Thou shalt love thy neighbour as thyself,' it is not meant thou shalt love him first, and do good to him in consequence of that love, but thou shalt do good to thy neighbour, and thus, thy beneficence will engender in thee that love of mankind which is the fulness and consummation of the inclination to do good."

Proverbs 3:30-31

Strife and Oppression

"Strive not with a man without cause, if he have done thee no harm. Envy thou not the oppressor, and choose none of his ways."

THIS proverb directs our attention to two great evils:
STRIFE.—Look at strife in two aspects.
As a principle inherent in the soul. There is a battling instinct in every human mind. Man is made to antagonize. This principle is in itself neither a virtue nor a vice. But it is a great blessing, since we have so much to oppose us here. It is intended to put us into antagonism not to existence, but to the evils of life, such as disease, poverty, injustice; not to God, but to His enemies, and the enemies of the order and happiness of the universe.

Look at strife again,—*As a principle liable to perversion.* The prohibition of the proverb implies that men are prone to strive against those who have done them "no harm." The striving with men without a cause is that terrible perversion of this principle, and this is the root of all domestic broils, social convulsions, ecclesiastical contentions, and national wars. How contrary this strife is to all the teachings of Holy Writ. "How all the minor cruelties of man are summed in war, conclusive of all crimes."—*Festus.* The other evil which the Proverb directs our attention to is:

OPPRESSION.—"The oppressor" is one who imposes unjust burdens; who crushes others to raise himself. He is always unjust, generally heartless, often cruel. He is, alas! no rarity. He is a *common* character; he belongs to all spheres of life, secular and sacred. There is the *political* oppressor, who crushes nations by unjust imposts. There is the *social* oppressor in the master and the mistress who crush their servants by overwork. There is the *ecclesiastical* oppressor, who seeks a lordship over consciences. The proverb virtually says two things about the oppressor. *His character is not to be envied.* "Envy not the oppressor." Why? *Because envy in itself is an evil.* Emulation is one thing, envy another. The former is not necessarily selfish, malign, or soul-torturing; the latter is, and therefore essentially bad. It is greedy, heartless, and heart-distressing. Because *there is nothing in the oppressor to be desired.* There are some objects of envy that have in them something good. Not so the oppressor; he is bad from branch to root. *His conduct is not to be followed.* "Choose none of his ways." His ways are all bad. He has many ways, private and public, domestic, political, and religious, but they are all crooked by injustice, all noxious with the sin of selfishness, and tending to damnation. Stand aloof! "Fret not thyself because of evil-doers; neither be thou envious against the workers of iniquity." A modern poet has struck off the hideous character of oppressors in a few words—

> "The good old rule
> Sufficeth them, the simple plan,
> That they should take who have the power,
> And they should keep who can."—WORDSWORTH

Proverbs 3:32-35

Moral Contrasts

"For the froward *is* abomination to the LORD: but his secret *is* with the righteous. The curse of the LORD *is* in the house of the wicked: but he blesseth the habitation of the just. Surely he scorneth the scorners: but he giveth grace unto the lowly. The wise shall inherit glory; but shame shall be the promotion of fools."

THESE verses give us a twofold contrast:-

A CONTRAST IN MORAL CHARACTER.—The "froward" and the "righteous,"—the "wicked" and the "just,"—the "scorner" and the "lowly,"—the "wise" and the "foolish." The "froward" is the perverse, refractory, rebellious; the "righteous" is the upright, obedient, and loyal. The differences between the good and bad are at least threefold. *A difference in the grand purpose of being.* The purpose of a wicked man is personal pleasure, worldly gain; that of the good is usefulness and Divine approval. *A difference in the grand impulse of being.* The governing motive of the wicked man is selfishness; self is the centre and circumference of all his activities. That of the righteous is love. He lives not to himself. "The love of Christ constraineth him." A Christ-like benevolence is the spring and sovereign of all his activities. Here is also:

A CONTRAST IN RELATION TO GOD.—The contrast is here set forth very saliently and strongly. *The one is repugnant to the Eternal, the other is in His confidence.* The "froward" is an "abomination,"—an object of loathsomeness. To the Infinitely Holy One sin is an "abominable thing;" it is repugnant to His whole nature. But on the other hand the righteous is in His confidence. "His secret is with the righteous." This is ever so. They "dwell in the secret place of the Most High." "Shall I hide from Abram the thing that I do?" "The secret of the Lord is with them that fear Him; and He will shew them His covenant." "All things that I have heard of my Father I have made known unto you." *The one is under the curse of the Lord, the other under His blessing.* "The curse of the Lord is on the house of the wicked, but He blesseth the habitation of the just." The house of Belshazzar is an illustration of the one, Daniel v. 6; that of Obededom of the other. (2 Sam. vi. 11; 1 Kings, xxi.) *The one is repulsed with scorn, the other is visited with grace.* "Surely he scorneth the scorners: but he giveth grace unto the lowly." He disdains the one with abhorrence, He looks on the other with the smiles of grace. *The one is raised to glory, the other is degraded to shame.* "The wise shall inherit glory, but shame shall be the promotion of fools." "Glory," a word embracing the eternal heaven, which the righteous shall not only enter into, but inherit; but "shame," and everlasting contempt, is the doom of the wicked.

"Shame their promotion"! What an expression! Their fame will be infamous, their grandeur a disgrace, their pageantry a contempt. "Many that sleep in the dust shall awake, some to everlasting life, and some to everlasting contempt." The great question of questions for every man is, What is his moral character? The contrast between the true and the false, the right and the wrong, is so striking, that there is not any difficulty in determining to which we belong. As is our character so are we before God and His universe, and so will our destiny be in the great hereafter; Paradise grows out of it, and from it hell flames and thunders.

Proverbs 4:1-4

A Religious Home

"Hear, ye children, the instruction of a father, and attend to know understanding. For I give you good doctrine, forsake ye not my law. For I was my father's son, tender and only *beloved* in the sight of my mother. He taught me also, and said unto me, Let thine heart retain my words: keep my commandments, and live."

THE words present three things concerning a religious home:

THE LOVE OF A RELIGIOUS HOME.—"I was my father's son, tender and only beloved in the sight of my mother." In a religious home there are two kinds of love for the offspring. *The natural love.* There is an instinctive affection which mankind, like all animals, have for their young—a mere gregarious affection. Though there is no virtue in this, it is a great boon. It is a stream from the heart of the Great Father of the universe, mirroring Himself, and making glad His progeny. *The spiritual love.* An affection this, which has respect to the spiritual being, relations and interests of the children. The former kind of love is in most homes : this is confined to the religious, and the religious only. Spiritually we can only love the morally good. A mutual recognition of excellence is the sacred bond of an imperishable friendship.

THE TRAINING OF A RELIGIOUS HOME.—" He taught me also, and said unto me, let thine heart retain my words." David taught his son Solomon. " And thou, Solomon, my son, know thou the God of thy father and serve him with a perfect heart." The words imply: *That the parent's teaching was worth retaining.* " Let thine heart *retain* my words." It is a great thing to give words worth retaining. There are words, alas! that enter the minds of children that should be expelled the moment of their entrance. They are germs of moral hemlock. *That the parent's teaching was practical.* " Keep my commandments." The highest authority on earth is the authority of a godly parent. His words are laws, and these laws are to be obeyed. It is only as moral teaching is reduced to practice that it promotes the high interest of true manhood. It is only as ideas are embodied in acts that they enrich the moral blood and strengthen the fibre and the limb. *That the parent's teaching was quickening.* " And live." True religious teaching is quickening to all the powers of the soul—intellectual and moral. There is a teaching that is deadening; there are "Finishing Schools," schools that quench the natural thirst for knowledge, emasculate the faculties, and inflate the soul with the noxious gas of vanity. True teaching quickens. " My words" they are " spirit, and they are life."

THE INFLUENCE OF A RELIGIOUS HOME.—The man who gives this counsel as a father, was the child of a religious home, thus described : " Hear, ye children, the instruction of a father, and attend to know understanding. For I give you good doctrine, forsake ye not my law. For I was my father's son, tender and only beloved in the sight of my mother." Here is a religious home reproduced. The child becomes a father, the subject becomes a sovereign, and the influence is thus repeated and transmitted. " Train up a child in the way he should go" when he is young, "and when he is old he will not depart from it." The home is the most potent institution in the world. Parental roofs are more influential institutions than cathedrals. "The old arm-chair," where parents sat, is mightier to me than any pulpits ever have been or ever will be. There are two reasons for this. *The susceptibility of childhood.* Ideas fall on us in the first stages of moral consciousness, with an inspiration, a glow, and a charm, which are wanting in all after periods. *The force of parental affection.* The power of a parent over the character of his child in the first stages is almost absolute, approaching that of the potter over the clay. Parents are instrumental authors, not only of the physical organization of their children, but also of their spiritual character.

> " The fond attachment to the well-known place,
> Whence first we started into life's long race,
> Retains its hold with such unfailing sway,
> We feel it e'en in age, and at our latest day."—COWPER.

Religious homes are the great want of the race. What boots the multiplication of churches and chapels, unless you multiply these?

Proverbs 4:5-9

The *Summum Bonum*

> " Get wisdom, get understanding: forget *it* not; neither decline from the words of my mouth. Forsake her not, and she shall preserve thee: love her, and she shall keep thee. Wisdom *is* the principal thing; *therefore* get wisdom; and with all thy getting get understanding. Exalt her, and she shall promote thee; she shall bring thee to honour, when thou dost embrace her. She shall give to thine head an ornament of grace: a crown of glory shall she deliver to thee."

WE agree with a modern author in regarding the " chief good" as that which unites the following qualities:—" It **must be intellectual, or** adapted to the higher and nobler part of our nature; attainable by all, of whatever sex, age, or mental conformation; unimpaired by distribution; independent of the circumstances of time or place; incapable of participation to excess; composed essentially of the same elements as the good to be enjoyed in a future state." All these qualities are found in that which is called "wisdom" in this passage.

HERE IS THE SUMMUM BONUM DESCRIBED

It is called "Wisdom." This wisdom is the "*principal* thing." In what does it consist? *In the possession of the highest knowledge.* What is the highest knowledge? The knowledge of the highest natures, the highest relationship, the highest duties, the highest interests, the highest Being—GOD. Much of what is called science is but the knowledge of small things—dust and grain. *In the application of the highest knowledge.* The highest knowledge may be possessed—fallen angels, perhaps, have it—and yet have no wisdom. They are fools. Wisdom consists in turning the whole to a right practical account. A life-conformity to spiritual truths, to eternal realities; not temporary phenomena, is true wisdom. He who makes the word of eternal truth flesh, is the wise man and he has reached the chief good.

HERE IS THE SUMMUM BONUM SOUGHT

Man is here exhorted to search after it. How is it to be sought? It does not grow up in us instinctively; nor does it come by miracle. It must be sought. But how? *Attentively.* "Neither decline from the words of my mouth." No prejudice must seal the soul. The ear must be ever open to the voices of wisdom, whencesoever they come. *Constantly.* "Forsake her not." Never turn aside from her, or thou wilt lose her charm. Peter's momentary distance from incarnate Wisdom led to his fall. Forsake her not; let there be no fickleness, but constancy. *Lovingly.* "Love her." Thou wilt never take a step after her if thou hast no love: thou wilt shun her if thou hast hate. Love is the essential inspiration in every successful search. *Supremely.* "Exalt her." She must be felt to be the *chief good*, the " one thing needful." He who seeks her as a subordinate good will never find her. She is the queen in the realms of pursuits, and will be found by none who do not recognise her royalty and seek her out as such.

HERE IS THE SUMMUM BONUM ENJOYED

When possessed, she will be three things to thee. *A guardian*. "She shall keep thee." Keep thee from the carnal, the selfish, and the depraved. Wisdom is the soul's true Palladium. *A patron*. "She shall promote thee." She will raise thee in the estimation of thine own conscience—in the judgment of the universe, and in the eye of God. *A rewarder*. "She shall give to thy head an ornament of grace; a crown of glory shall she deliver to thee." The crown she gives is made not of fading laurels, or of any mouldering gem or metal—a tawdry adornment for a head of clay. But a crown coruscating with the moral perfections of God Himself. "When the chief Shepherd shall appear ye shall receive a crown of glory, that fadeth not away."

Brothers, here is the *summum bonum*—look at it, until it spreads out such a thing of glory in your horizon, as to throw everything else into insignificance and shade. "It is a view of delight," said Lucretius, as quoted by Lord Bacon, "to stand or walk upon the shoreside and to see the ships tossed with tempest upon the sea; or, to be in a fortified tower, and to see two battles join upon a plain; but it is pleasure incomparable for the mind of the man to be settled, landed, and fortified in the certainty of truth, and from thence to descry and behold the errors, perturbations, labours, and wanderings up and down of other men."

Proverbs 4:10-17

The Moral Paths of Men

"Hear, O my son, and receive my sayings; and the years of thy life shall be many. I have taught thee in the way of wisdom; I have led thee in right paths. When thou goest, thy steps shall not be straitened; and when thou runnest thou shalt not stumble. Take fast hold of instruction; let *her* not go: keep her, for she is thy life. Enter not into the path of the wicked. and go not into the way of evil *men*. Avoid it, pass not by it, turn from it, and pass away. For they sleep not, except they have done mischief; and their sleep is taken away, unless they cause *some* to fall. For they eat the bread of wickedness, and drink the wine of violence."

MORALLY, then, there are two paths of life—paths which the Heavenly Teacher represents as the broad and the narrow way. These two are indicated in the text.

THE PATH OF WISDOM.—It is here taught that this *path of wisdom is known only by teaching.* The teaching is by precept. "I have taught thee." Men do not get spiritual wisdom either by the intuitions or deductions of their own nature. It comes to them in its first lessons by teaching. By example. "I have led thee in right paths." This implies that he was in the path himself. He who tries to teach religion by precept, without example, is like the man who would walk on one leg without crutches. However strong the limb may be, he could not make much progress. Precept and example are the two legs of a true teacher. The majority of teachers, alas! are moral cripples.

This path of wisdom is fraught with true blessings. There is *longevity.* "The years of thy life shall be many." Godliness conduces to physical health, and thus to long life. But true longevity does not consist in the number of years, but in the number of great thoughts, lofty purposes, and noble deeds. Many men of twenty have lived a longer life than those of seventy. There is *freedom.* "Thy steps shall not be straitened." On the great highway of life the only free traveller is he who is spiritually wise. Others are so burdened and fettered that there is no spring of liberty in their steps. There is *safety*. "When thou runnest thou shalt not stumble." Speed is often attended with danger, but the celerity of a good man is free from peril. "He will give His angels charge concerning thee. They shall bear thee in their hand, lest thou dash thy foot against a stone." "The lion and the young lion shalt thou trample under foot."

This path of wisdom requires the most vigorous steadfastness. "Take fast hold of instruction, let her not go, keep her, for she is thy life." Hold the lessons of wisdom with a firm and unrelexable tenacity; grasp them as the drowning man the rope that is thrown out for his rescue. There is a danger of losing this path, many have done so. "He exhorted them all that, with purpose of heart, they would cleave unto the Lord." "Firmness," says Burns, "both in sufferance and exertion, is a character which I would wish to possess. I have always despised the whining yelp of complaint, and the cowardly, feeble resolve."

THE PATH OF WICKEDNESS.—"Enter not into the path of the wicked, and go not in the way of evil men." Wickedness has a path. It is a very broad and crooked path. Solomon saw it in his day, and here raises an earnest warning against it. He urges its avoidance. He intimates that—

The avoidance of this path is a matter of great urgency. It is crowded with "evil men" bent on mischief. They live *for* mischief. "Their sleep is taken away unless they cause some to fall." They have an infernal pleasure in doing wrong. They live *by* mischief. "They eat the bread of wickedness, and drink the wine of violence." What they have got to support them, they have got by dishonesty and violence. Wicked men live by falsehood, fraud, and oppression. He intimates that—

The avoidance of the path requires strenuous effort. "Avoid it; pass not by it; turn from it and pass away." It is a very *contiguous* path. It is so near that every man is on the margin of it, and may step into it unawares. It intersects every walk of life. It crosses all our lines of activity. It is a very *attractive* path. The crowds are there, and there is great attraction in a crowd. The stream of sensual enjoyment rolls by it, and the flowers of worldly beauty bloom on either side. It is overhung with clusters of earthly gratifications. The Syrens chant their enticing strains at every opening. It is a very *perilous* path. Good reason, therefore, had Solomon for the strong language of our text—" Avoid it, pass not by it." The prowling beasts of Hell lurk along the line and a fathomless abyss of ruin is at its end. Avoid this path. " Blessed is the man that walketh not in the counsel of the ungodly, nor standeth in the way of sinners, nor sitteth in the seat of the scornful." The moral of the whole is expressed in the words of Christ—" Strive to enter in at the strait gate, for broad is the path that leadeth to destruction and many there be that go in thereat." There is a tremendous whirlpool in the path of sin ; he that comes within the circle of its eddying waters is likely to be sucked down into the central gulf of irremediable ruin.

Proverbs 4:18

The March of the Good

"The path of the just is as the shining light that shineth more and more unto the perfect day."

The march of the good is A BRIGHT march.

It is "as the shining light." Light is the emblem of *intelligence, purity, and blessedness*. The march of the good is like the march of the sun—*glorious*. How glorious is the sun as it rises in the morning, tinging the distant hills with beauty, at noon flooding the earth with splendour, in evening fringing the clouds with rich purple, crimson, and gold. *Commanding.*—The sun is the ruler of the day; at his appearance the world awakes from its slumbers, the winds and waves obey him, as he moves all nature moves. *Useful.*—The sun enlightens the system and maintains harmony throughout every part. He renews the earth, quickens the seeds into life, covers the landscape with beauty, ripens the harvest for man and beast. *Independent.*—Troops of black clouds may roll over the earth, but they touch not the sun, furious storms may shake the globe, but the sun is beyond their reach. He is always behind the darkest clouds, and looks calmly down upon the ocean in fury and the earth in a tempest. *Certain.*—The sun is never out of time, he is ever in his place at the right hour. In all this he is the emblem of the good man—glorious, commanding, useful, independent, and certain.

The march of the good is A PROGRESSIVE march

"Shineth more and more." It has a dawn and a meridian. Godliness is progressive. We are "to follow on to know the Lord." We are "to go from strength to strength." We are to see "greater things than these." We are to be "changed into the same image from glory to glory." We are "to press toward the mark, for the prize of the high calling of God in Jesus Christ." The capacity of the soul for indefinite development, its eternal craving for something better, the increase both of its desire and power for further advancement as it progresses, as well as the assurances of God's Word, demonstrate that we are made for progress. "More and more." This is the soul's watchword—Excelsior! is its cry.

The march of the good is A GLORIOUS march

"Unto the perfect day." Perfect day. What a day is that! They shall shine as the sun in the Kingdom of God. Perfect day—not one cloud of error in the sky; not one ungenial blast in the atmosphere. Perfect—knowledge free from error; love free from impurity; purpose free from selfishness; experience free from pain. The good man's progress excels even the glory of the sun. The sun does not increase in size or splendour; he is not greater in bulk or brighter in lustre now than when he shone on Adam; but growth, everlasting growth, is our destiny. Onward through circling ages without end, is the career which kind Heaven has decreed for sainted souls. They feel

> Their orbit immensity,
> Their work, to make it radiant,
> With the reflected beams of God.

Proverbs 4:19

The Darkness of Sin

"*The way of the wicked is as darkness: they know not at what they stumble.*"

SIN is a dark path.

THE PROOF.—*It yields no true happiness.* There is a dark, chilling shadow resting upon the heart of the traveller. If there be any light in the sky, it is the light of a meteor flashing for a moment, and leaving the darkness more intense. Ignorance, pollution, and sorrow mantle it in gloom. *It leads to an end the reverse of expectation.* "They know not at what they stumble." Difficulties meet them they never anticipated. They always expect something brighter further on, instead of which the scene grows darker and darker, until "outer darkness" is reached. Many bright orbs has the Great Father of spirits set in the firmament of the human soul—such as innocence, faith, trust, hope, love. These in young life shine with more or less brightness for a time; but as men sin they become dimmer and darker. One by one they are quenched, until, when all are lost, the soul's firmament becomes as black as sackcloth.

THE CAUSE.—Why is this road so dark? Darkness arises from one of three causes. Either the want of light;

or the want of the organ of sight ; or the want of the right employment of the organ. In either of these cases, a man is in the dark. But which is the cause of the darkness of the sinner's path ? Not the want of light. There is the light of nature, of reason, and the Bible. Not the want of the organ of vision. There is intellect and conscience. But the want of the *right use* of the faculty. He shuts his eyes. Like the man in noontide splendour, with strong eyes, who wraps himself in gloom, by closing his eyelids : so the sinner makes dark his own path. He loves darkness.

THE CONSEQUENCE.—" They know not at what they stumble." They do stumble. This is a fact implied. " They grope for the wall like the blind." "If a man walk in the night, he stumbleth." *Heaven has put obstructions in the sinner's path.* Conscience, the examples of holy men, Christ, and the Spirit. These are put to obstruct his progress, to prevent him hurrying on to ruin. He stumbles over them and goes down. *These obstructions become great inconveniences.* The greatest blessings are stumbling blocks to them. The very things which should make their path delightful, prove their constant inconvenience, and ultimate ruin. Even Christ is a " stumbling block " and a " rock of offence " to them. They crush themselves into ruin, by stumbling against Him Who came to make their path the path of life. "All sin and wickedness in man's spirit," says an old author, " hath the central force and energy of hell in it, and is perpetually pressing down towards it as towards its own place. Christ's burden, which is nothing else but true godliness, is a winged thing and travels, bears itself upwards upon its own wings, soaring aloft towards God ; so the devilish nature is always within the central attractions of hell, and its own weight instigates and accelerates its motion thither "

Proverbs 4:20-23

Self-improvement and Self-control

"My son, attend to my words; incline thine ear unto my sayings. Let them not depart from thine eyes; keep them in the midst of thine heart. For they *are* life unto those that find them, and health to all their flesh."

SELF-IMPROVEMENT.—"The words of wisdom" are the vehicles of those Divine principles, the reception and embodiment of which by man are essential to his well-being. Notice two things—

The method of gaining them. There must be the attentive ear. "Incline thine ear unto my sayings." What worth are the voices of Divine wisdom if we are inattentive; if the ear is given to other sounds? On a deaf man, or the man whose ear is taken up with something else, the grandest oratorio makes no impression and has no charm. There must be the *steadfast look.* "Let them not depart from thine eyes." Let the eye of the soul be fixed steadfastly upon them. The principles of wisdom must always loom as the grand realities on the horizon of the soul. There must be the *enshrining heart.* "Keep them in the midst of thine heart." It is not enough to have them as sounds in the memory, or as propositions floating in the intellect, or even as passing impressions on the surface of the heart: they must be taken down into the depths of our moral nature. They are germs that will only grow in the deepest soil. Put them there and they will break out into a Paradise. Observe:

The blessedness of having them. "They are *life* to those that find them." They are the soul-quickening elements. "The incorruptible seed which liveth and abideth for ever." They are "*health* to all their flesh." Life without health is scarcely worth having. These principles not only give life to the soul, but supply the nutriment, and stimulate the activities that *ensure health*—health of all kinds: intellectual, moral, and physical. Indeed, the health of each part is essential to the health of the whole man. Disease in the body reaches the mind, and the diseases of the mind affect the body.

SELF-CONTROL.—"Keep thy heart with all diligence, for out of it are the issues of life." Man somehow or other has lost self-control. He is the creature, the instrument, the victim of capricious thoughts, lawless impulses, and passing events. He has no royalty, though millions call him king, who is not the monarch of himself. The text directs us to this, and we notice (1) *The nature* of true self-control. "Keep thy heart." In the corporeal economy the heart is the fountain of life, it pours the blood through all the parts of the body, the most distant and the most minute. What the physical heart is to the body, the moral heart, that is the supreme affection, is to the whole spiritual nature. It is the source of its life, the root, fountain, spring of its being. What is it to keep the heart? To hold it to the right *object* of supreme love. Unless the *chief* love be centred in the chief good there is no regal settledness of soul. To hold it to the right *purposes* of life. What are the grand aims of life? In one word, a devout appropriation of the blessings of being, and a right distribution of the same. Man is made to get and to give, and to get *in order* to give; and to do both evermore in the spirit of true worship.

(2) The *method* of true self-control. "With all diligence." Or, as it might be expressed, "Keep it with all keepings." "Keep it from getting evil, as a garden is kept; keep it from doing evil, as the sea is kept from reclaimed Netherlands." There must be the greatest assiduity. Because there is a great *danger* of its being turned away. There are so many attractive forces, so many seductive influences. Because the turning it away would be a *sad catastrophe*. If the heart as a fountain is not kept pure, all the streams of life will be poisoned; if the heart as a garden is not kept cultivated, the whole sphere of life will be overrun with thorns, weeds, and vermin.

(3) The *argument* for true self-control. " Out of it are the

issues of life." Everything depends upon the state of his heart. " As a man thinketh in his heart so is he." We are, in the scale of being, and in the eye of God, according to the state of the heart. " Out of the heart," said Christ, " proceed evil thoughts, murders, and adulteries." How needful for us to pray, " Create within us clean hearts, O God, and renew within us a right spirit." " He," says Milton, "who reigns within himself, and rules passions, desires, and fears, is more than a king."

Proverbs 4:24-27

Laws of Life

> " Put away from thee a froward mouth, and perverse lips put far from thee. Let thine eyes look right on, and let thine eyelids look straight before thee. Ponder the path of thy feet, and let all thy ways be established. Turn not to the right hand nor to the left : remove thy foot from evil."

HERE are laws for the government of self. Here is a law for the tongue, a law for the eye, a law for the mind, a law for the life.

Here is a demand for PURE LANGUAGE.—" Put away from thee a froward mouth, and perverse lips put far from thee." Speech is one of the grand peculiarities that distinguish man. It is a priceless gift. It is the vehicle through which one man can pour his soul into the heart of not only one but many. The organ by which he can influence the ages. How sadly perverted it has become! Language too often is the channel of damnable errors, blasphemous impieties, and moral filth. " Our speech should be seasoned with salt that it might administer grace unto the hearers." A pure heart is essential to pure speech. Speech is but one of the streams that well out from the fountains of the soul. Would that this stream were always clear, reflecting evermore the rays of love, holiness, and truth!

Here is a demand for a STRAIGHTFORWARD PURPOSE. —" Let thine eyes look right on, and let thine eyelids look straight before thee." Have no *side* glances, no *by*-ends; but have a grand purpose on which the eye of the soul shall be always fixed. Straightforwardness stands opposed to all sly cunning, all vacillation, all ambiguity: all double meanings and aims. Have a purpose in life, clear, well-defined and righteous, and keep it ever before you as the " mark of the prize." Do not look back or turn aside: let the eyes of your soul be ever on it. When the eye is single the whole body is full of light. Straightforwardness is one of the brightest jewels in the crown of virtue, whilst slyness and duplicity are the brands of infamy. He who pursues a good object openly, faithfully, and constantly, will every day command increasing respect from his fellow-men, and find the divine forces within him beating stronger and more harmonious.

Here is a demand for HABITUAL THOUGHTFULNESS. —"Ponder the path of thy feet, and let all thy ways be established." Man was made not only to think but to be *thoughtful*. Thoughtfulness should be the habitude of his nature. He should walk the path of life thoughtfully, not by *impulse*. His steps should have nothing of the caprice of mere instinct. Man is a vessel on a wondrous voyage. Whilst emotion is his propelling force, thought is the helmsman that must hold the rudder. He should walk life's path thoughtfully, not by *prejudice*. He should not be guided by traditional dogmas or unholy preconceptions. Thought must be his pillar in the wilderness. He should go on thoughtfully, not by *custom*. He should not move mechanically, but as a free intelligence; move not from the forces without but within, not from others but from himself.

Here is a demand for UNSWERVING RECTITUDE.— " Turn not to the right hand nor to the left. Remove thy foot from evil." Duty is a straight path. The way of sin is serpentine in its shape as well as in its spirit. Virtue is a straight line running right up to God. Any turn therefore would be wrong, and riskful. Take care; there are by-paths tempting in every direction. " Turn not to the right hand nor to the left." Take no step without thought, and let your thought be on the will of the Great " Taskmaster."

How comprehensive the legislation of heaven! It seeks to control the tongue, the eye, the thought, the foot, the entire man. Its laws reach the motions of every organ, every faculty, and every impulse. He who obeys those laws of life, lives and he only lives. Socrates has well said that " the end of life is to be like unto God: and the soul following God will be like unto him: he being the beginning, middle, and end of all things."

Proverbs 5:1-20

The Strange Woman and the True Wife

" My son, attend unto my wisdom, *and* bow thine ear to my understanding: That thou mayest regard discretion, and *that* thy lips may keep knowledge. For the lips of a strange woman drop *as* an honeycomb, and her mouth *is* smoother than oil: But her end is bitter as wormwood, sharp as a two-edged sword. Her feet go down to death; her steps take hold on hell. Lest thou shouldest ponder the path of life, her ways are moveable, *that* thou canst not know *them*. Hear me now therefore, O ye children, and depart not from the words of my mouth. Remove thy way far from her, and come not nigh the door of her house: Lest thou give thine honour unto others, and thy years unto the cruel: Lest strangers be filled with thy wealth; and thy labours *be* in the house of a stranger; And thou mourn at the last, when thy flesh and thy body are consumed, And say, How have I hated instruction, and my heart despised reproof; and have not obeyed the voice of my teachers, nor inclined mine ear to them that instructed me! I was almost in all evil in the midst of the congregation and assembly. Drink waters out of thine own cistern, and running waters out of thine own well. Let thy fountains be dispersed abroad, *and* rivers of waters in the streets. Let them be only thine own, and not strangers with thee. Let thy fountain be blessed: and rejoice with the wife of thy youth. *Let her be as* the loving hind and pleasant roe; let her breasts satisfy thee at all times; and be thou ravished always with her love. And why wilt thou, my son, be ravished with a strange woman, and embrace the bosom of a stranger."

HERE is a graphic description of an unchaste woman. A description given by a man of genius, culture, and who, to his disgrace, knew the subject from a sad experience. " King Solomon loved many strange women." And he has left us these words : " I find more bitter than death the woman whose heart is snares and nets." The unchaste woman he calls " strange," and truly strange it is that one whom heaven has endowed with such refined sensibilities and lofty powers should prostitute her noble nature to the reign of sensualism.

A WARNING IN RELATION TO A WOMAN.—A "strange woman" is a woman whom in these times we should call a *prostitute*. The warning is given by a description *of her conduct*. Her speech is fascinating—"her lips drop as an honeycomb, and her mouth is smoother than oil." Honied words have a charm for inexperienced souls. Her manners are accommodating, "her ways are moveable." Proteus-like, she puts on many shapes. She adapts herself to the occasion. The warning is given by a description *of her end*. It is "bitter as wormwood, sharp as a two-edged sword," " Her feet go down to death; her steps take hold on hell." Strong figures of misery are these; but not too strong. The horrid memories, the self-remorse, the ruined health and reputation, the blasted hopes—what misery are these! The warning is given by a description *of her victims*. They "mourn at the last, when thy flesh and thy body are consumed." Those whom she enthrals are robbed of their honour, their wealth, and become the victims of terrible remorse.

A RECOMMENDATION IN RELATION TO A WOMAN.— " Drink water out of thine own cistern, and running waters out of thine own well." The reference in these verses is evidently to marriage, which is "honourable in all." Choose one chaste pure-minded woman as thy companion through life : be true to her, find thy happiness in her society, and in hers alone. " Drink waters out of thine own cistern." "Rejoice with the wife of thy youth." Cherish her with gentleness and purity, as "the loving hind and pleasant roe." "Whatsoever interrupts the strictest harmony in this delicate relationship, opens the door to imminent temptation. Tender, well-regulated domestic affection is the best defence against the vagrant desires of unlawful passions." "Marriage," says Jeremy Taylor, "has in it less of beauty, but more of safety than the single life: it hath not more ease, but less danger: it is more merry and more sad: it is fuller of sorrows and fuller of joys: it lies under more burdens, but is supported by all the strengths of love and charity: and those burdens are delightful. Marriage is the mother of the world, and preserves kingdoms, and fills cities and churches, and heaven itself. Celibacy, like the fly in the heart of an apple, dwells in perpetual sweetness, but sits alone and is confined and dies in singularity: but marriage, like the useful bee, builds a house, and gathers sweetness from every flower, and labours and unites into societies and republics, and sends out colonies, and feeds the world with delicacies, and obeys their kings and keeps order, and exercises many virtues, and promotes the interest of mankind, and is that state of good to which God hath designed the present constitution of the world."

Proverbs 5:21-23

Man as Known of God and Punished by Sin

"For the ways of man *are* before the eyes of the LORD, and he pondereth all his goings. His own iniquities shall take the wicked himself, and he shall be holden with the cords of his sins. He shall die without instruction; and in the greatness of his folly he shall go astray."

MAN AS KNOWN OF GOD.—God knows man thoroughly; —knows what he has been, what he is, and what he will be in the great hereafter. This fact, for an incontrovertible fact it is, should be practically realised; and, if practically realised, it will have a fourfold effect upon the soul. *It will stimulate to great spiritual activity.* When the eye of an intelligence falls right on us, the glance stirs the soul. What soul could sleep, if it felt the eye of God ever resting on it? *It will restrain from the commission of sin.* Did we feel His eye ever on us, should we ever yield to temptation? "Thou God seest me," is a powerful preventive. *It will excite the desire for pardon.* God has seen all the errors and sins of the past, and they are great in number and enormity. Since He sees them, they must either be punished or absolved. *It will brace the soul in the performance of duty.* Moses endured as "seeing Him who is invisible." He knows our trials and our difficulties. Therefore let us be magnanimous under trial and brave in danger.

" What can 'scape the eye
Of God, all-seeing, or deceive His heart,
Omniscient ? "

MAN AS PUNISHED BY SIN.—" His own iniquities shall take the wicked himself, and he shall be holden with the cords of his sin."

As virtue is its own reward, sin is its own punishment. The words suggest that sin does three things in punishing the sinner. *It will seize him as its victim:* " Iniquities will take the wicked himself." How ? *It will arrest him in his career.* In the midst of his revelries, as in the case of Belshazzar and Herod, it will bring him to a stop. *It will detach him from his comrades.* It will bring him home to himself, and overwhelm him with the sense of his own responsibilities and guilt. Sin must seize the sinner sooner or later, grasp him with the hand of iron. *It will bind him as its prisoner.* " He shall be holden with the cords of his sins." What are the cords ? There are *the " cords " of causation.* Man's experience to-day grows out of the experience of yesterday, and becomes the source of his experience to-morrow; and thus for ever he is linked indissolubly to the past. Thus, Job said, " Thou makest me to possess the sins of my youth." Out of past sins spring a weakened intellect, a shattered constitution, an accusing conscience. There are *the " cords " of habit.* Every sin contributes to the weaving of the cord that shall one day bind the soul as fast as hell. " Can the Ethiopian change his skin, or the leopard his spots?" What are the chains of darkness that enthral damned spirits, but habits of sin ? There are *the " cords " of despair.* When despair, black and portentous, settles around the heart, all power of free action is gone, and the man is a slave. *It will exclude him from knowledge.* " He shall die without instruction." Sin closes the eyes and seals the ears of souls, and thus shuts out the light and the voice of truth. Men under the influence of sin love darkness rather than light. *It banishes him as an exile.* "In the greatness of his folly he shall go astray." He shall wander away like a prodigal, and never find his home again. Sin banishes the soul from virtue, heaven, God; and reduces it to a homeless, friendless orphan in the universe. "The seeds of our own punishment," says Hesiod, "are sown at the same time we commit sin." Sins tend to hell. "Little sins," says Hopkins, "are the natural stream of a man's life, that do of themselves tend hellwards, and are of themselves enough to carry the soul down silently and calmly to destruction; but when greater and grosser sins join with them, they make a violent tide that hurries the soul away with a more swift and rampant motion down to hell, than little sins would or could do of themselves."

Proverbs 6:1-5

Social Suretyships

"My son, if thou be surety for thy friend, *if* thou hast stricken thy hand with a stranger, thou art snared with the words of thy mouth, thou art taken with the words of thy mouth. Do this now, my son, and deliver thyself, when thou art come into the hand of thy friend; go, humble thyself, and make sure thy friend. Give not sleep to thine eyes, nor slumber to thine eyelids. Deliver thyself as a roe from the hand *of the hunter*, and as a bird from the hand of the fowler."

THE instructions of the Bible are profitable for the life that now is, as well as for the life that is to come. Its principles of domestic, social, and political economy, are far more wise, as well as righteous, than can be found in human book or college. The "Book of Proverbs" is a far better guide for a young man in business than Adam Smith or the *Times* newspaper. Solomon here speaks of suretiships as an evil.

AS AN EVIL TO BE DEPLORED.—"My son, *if* thou be surety." As if he said, it is a sad thing if thou hast. Although suretiship is not always an evil, there are always two things necessary to render it justifiable. *The case should be deserving.* The person whose responsibility you take upon yourself should be one in every way deserving your confidence and help. *You should be fully competent to discharge the obligation.* You should feel that the claims of your family and others upon you would fully justify you to give up the amount to which you are pledged, if required. Where these two things are not, all suretiships are wrong. The most deserving men will seldom ask for suretiships, and the most competent men will seldom undertake the responsibility. Therefore it is often an evil. It constantly presses the surety with anxiety, if he is an honest man, and often brings ruin on himself and on his family, when the person for whom he stands fails in his duty. Solomon represents suretiship

AS AN EVIL VERY EASILY CONTRACTED.—Merely "striking the hand" and uttering "the words." One word, the word "yes," will do it, written or uttered in the presence of a witness. This little word has ensnared and ruined many an honest man. Plausibility will soon extract it from a pliant and generous nature. How easy it is for a man to ruin himself in every way, secularly as well as spiritually; one wrong step often takes into a path that is downward and dark, and gives an impetus never to be overcome. Solomon represents suretiship

AS AN EVIL TO BE STRENUOUSLY REMOVED.—"Do this now, my son, and deliver thyself, when thou art come into the hand of thy friend." Do it *promptly.* The bond may take force to-morrow. Try by every honest means to get the bond back at once. "Give not sleep to thine eyes, nor slumber to thine eyelids" till it be done. Do it *beseechingly.* "Humble thyself." It is no use to carry a high hand; thou art in his power. Bow before him and entreat him to give it up. Do it *effectively.* "Deliver thyself as a roe from the hand of the hunter, and as a bird from the hand of the fowler." Thou art encaged in iron law, break loose honourably somehow and be free. An evil in social transactions kindred to this, is what is known in the business world as *accommodation*. I mean speculation without capital, extensive risks on a baseless credit. This system is false, treacherous, hollow, ruinous. The remarks of Helps on men of business are worthy of note here :—" Rare almost as great poets—rarer, perhaps, than veritable saints and martyrs, are consummate men of business. A man to be excellent in this way must not only be variously gifted, but his gifts should be nicely proportioned to one another. He must have in a high degree that virtue which men have always found the least pleasant of virtues — prudence. His prudence, however, will not be merely of a cautious and quiescent order, but that which being ever actively engaged, is more fitly called discretion than prudence. Such a man must have an almost ignominious love of details, blended with a high power of imagination, enabling him to look along extended lines of possible action and put these details in their right places. He requires a great knowledge of character, with that exquisite tact which feels unerringly the right moment when to act. A discreet rapidity must pervade all the movements of his thought and action. He must be singularly free from vanity, and is generally found to be an enthusiast who has the art to conceal his enthusiasm."

Proverbs 6:6-8

Little Preachers and Great Sermons

"Go to the ant, thou sluggard; consider her ways, and be wise: which having no guide, overseer, or ruler, provideth her meat in the summer, *and* gathereth her food in the harvest."

THE Eternal Father has favoured His human offspring with a two-fold revelation of Himself—the Bible and Nature. Looking at men in their relation to this two-fold revelation, they divide themselves into three distinct classes:—*Those who study neither ; those who study one and disparage the other ; and those who reverentially study the teachings of both.* The allusion in the text, and which is only one of many, plainly shows us that the Bible encourages the study of nature.

The Bible refers us to nature in order *to attest its first principles.* That God is all wise, all-powerful, all-good; that man has a soul and is under moral obligation, are things which the Bible assumes, takes for granted, does not attempt to prove. The man who wants proof it refers to nature's volume.

The Bible refers us to nature *for illustrations of its great truths.* The sower, the harvest field, trees, rivers, vineyards and vales, meads and mountains, skies and seas, it employs as emblems.

The Bible refers us to nature in order to *reprove the sins it denounces.* To reprove us for our ingratitude, it refers us to the ox and the ass. "The ox knoweth its owner and the ass its master's crib." To reprove us for our want of confidence in the paternal providence of God, it points us to the lilies of the field and the fowls of the air; and to reprove us for our *spiritual indolence*, it directs us to the ants. "Go to the ant, thou sluggard."

Now, the sluggard to whom I am going to address myself is the *spiritual* sluggard. Not the man who is neglecting his worldly business—the secularly indolent man—but the man who is neglecting the culture of his own spiritual nature and the salvation of his own soul. These little ants will teach you four great truths. They teach you:

That the feebleness of your power is no just reason for your indolence.—These little creatures are small, they are feeble—you could crush a thousand beneath your foot; yet see how they work. Naturalists have shown their ingenuity as architects, their industry as miners and builders; they have divided them into mason-ants, and carpenter-ants, and mining-ants, and carving-ants, and have shown that whilst their ingenuity in these departments of action is remarkable, their industry would put the most indefatigable of human labourers to the blush. If this tiny insect can do so much, do not you, with your bony limbs, strong sinews, robust frame, the engine of a deathless intellect, memory, imagination, conscience, soul, plead your feebleness as an excuse for your indolence. Remember three things—*that all power, however feeble, is given for work; that you are not required to do more than you have power to accomplish*, and that *all power increases by use.* The man who attempts to do something gets power by the attempt. There was once a man with an arm withered—a mere dried stick: but Christ commanded him to stretch it forth; he might have said, "I cannot;" but he resolved to do it, and with the resolution came the power. This is a symbol of the universal truth, that you can get power by effort. The man who has one talent can make five by it, and the man of five can make ten. Power increases by use. The naturally strong men, who say they cannot work, live and die pigmies. The naturally weak men, who say *try*, often attain Herculean force. They teach you:

That the activity of others is no just excuse for your indolence.—Go to the ant-world, penetrate its little mines, its chambers, store-houses, garrets, workshops

—for it has all these—and you will see millions of inhabitants, but not *one idler:* all are in action. One does not depend upon the other, and expect another to do his work. The teeming population is busy. This is a lesson to the indolent soul. The Christian world is busy, and there are thousands working : some preaching, some praying, some teaching, some writing ; but not one can do *thy* work. Can any one *believe* for *thee? repent* for thee? *think* for thee? *love* for thee ? *worship* for thee ? Can any one *die* for thee or be *damned* for thee ? Like the ant-hill, the Christian world is a scene of action, but not one of the million actors can do *thy* work. They teach you-

That the WANT OF A HELPER IS NO JUST EXCUSE FOR YOUR INDOLENCE.—" Go to the ant"-hill, see them work : each is thrown upon his own resources and powers. "They have no guide, overseer, or ruler." Each works according to his own little nature. Self-reliantly each labours on, not waiting for the instruction or guidance of another. Do you say, I have no minister, no books, no Christian friend, and therefore cannot work ? You cannot say this ; but if you could, that would be no excuse ; you have an intellect that can think, you have a heart that can love, you have a conscience that can guide. You have suggestive nature, you have this wonderful Bible, you have God! You are without excuse. Do not wait and ask for overseers or guides, or rulers, or priests, or bishops ; if they come, and can help you, be thankful. Trust your own instincts, like the ant ; act out your own powers, use the light you have, and look to God for help. While you are looking for greater advantages, your time is passing. Your season for making provision for the future is shortening. Cold, black, bleak winter is approaching. They teach you—

That the PROVIDENCE OF GOD IS NO JUST REASON FOR YOUR INDOLENCE.—Go to the ant-hill and see these tiny creatures laying up for the future. The ant " provideth for meat in the summer, and gathereth her food in the harvest." There is a Divine providence over these little insects. There is no creature, however small, that comes not within the pale of God's providing agency. But

He provides for His creatures by the use of their own powers. *He does not do for any creature what He has given that creature power to do for himself.* He carries provisions to plants, and flowers, and trees, because they cannot go in search of their food. But the creatures to whom He has given locomotive power, must *seek* their food. Let me here remind you, that like these little creatures, *you have a future;* that like these little creatures *you have to prepare for the future,* and then, that like these little creatures you have a *specific time to make preparation.* Do not talk of Providence, as an excuse for your indolence. Say not, God is good, and He will provide. He has provided for you richly, but He only grants the provision on condition of the right employment of your powers. There is an inheritance for the good, but only on the condition of their working. There is a heaven of knowledge, but only for the student; there is a harvest of blessedness, but only to the diligent husbandman; there are scenes of triumph, but only to the victorious warrior. In conclusion, let me remind you that your harvest-time of your life will soon be over. The sun is fading now; the ripened ungathered fruits are falling to the ground; autumn is gradually tinging the scene; nature looks more sterile and sombre every day; the air is getting chilly; the winter is coming,—freezing, furious, black winter is coming. "How long wilt thou sleep, O sluggard?"

Proverbs 6:9-15

The Lazy Man and the Wicked Man

"How long wilt thou sleep, O sluggard? when wilt thou arise out of thy sleep? *Yet* a little sleep, a little slumber, a little folding of the hands to sleep: so shall thy poverty come as one that travelleth, and thy want as an armed man. A naughty person, a wicked man, walketh with a froward mouth. He winketh with his eyes, he speaketh with his feet, he teacheth with his fingers: frowardness *is* in his heart, he deviseth mischief continually; he soweth discord. Therefore shall his calamity come suddenly; suddenly shall he be broken without remedy."

THE LAZY MAN.—In the three preceding verses, Solomon directs attention to the ant. Job, as well as Solomon, directs men to the beast of the field for wisdom "Ask now the beasts and they shall teach thee." So does Christ—"Be wise as serpents and harmless as doves." Lazy people abound. There is scarcely a greater evil in society than laziness. What is laziness? Not inactivity; for a man may be incapable of action. But it is inactivity arising from an indisposition to work. Plenty of power, but lacking desire. A lazy man is a drag upon the wheel of social progress. He consumes the products of other men's labours, and produces nothing himself. His life is one great theft. The text presents two things concerning this laziness. It is *procrastinating*. "Yet a little sleep, a little slumber, a little folding of the hands to sleep." Man, from the constitution of his nature, has not the power to *abandon* altogether the idea of labour. Conscience presses him to labour, and work at every turn urges its claims. The lazy man is too cowardly to say I will never work, I will sleep for ever, and he procrastinates He promises to labour. By this, he does two things, he *quiets his conscience;* and *cheats society*. Thus, the song of his life is—" To-morrow, and to-morrow, and to-morrow."

> "Shun delays, they breed remorse,
>   Take thy time while time is lent thee;
> Creeping snails have weakest force,
>   Fly their fault lest thou repent thee;
> Good is best when sooner wrought,
> Ling'ring labours come to nought."—SOUTHWELL

The text shows that indolence is also *ruinous*. "So shall thy poverty come as one that travelleth, and thy want as an armed man." Laziness brings ruin. Intellectual laziness brings intellectual ruin; commercial, brings commercial ruin; spiritual, spiritual ruin. This is a law. Solomon suggests that the ruin comes—first, *gradually*, "as one that travelleth." It does not gallop; it does not rush on you at once. Like all other natural laws, it proceeds gradually. Secondly, *Irresistibly*, "As an armed man." Ruin comes travelling slowly on. The lazy man does not see his grim visage for days, perhaps years. At last, however, he shows himself, and stands by his side gaunt, ghastly, and fully armed. He clutches him, and all is over. "Idleness," says Hunter, "travels very slowly, and poverty soon overtakes her." "If you ask me which is the real hereditary sin of human nature, do you imagine I shall answer pride or luxury, or ambition, or egotism? No; I shall say indolence. Who conquers indolence will conquer all the rest. Indeed, all good principles must stagnate without mental activity."

THE WICKED MAN.—"A naughty person, a wicked man, walketh with a froward mouth." Idleness is generally connected with wickedness as parent and child. One author says that a state of idleness is a state of damnable sin. Another, that it is the most "corrupting fly that can blow on the human mind." Men learn to do ill by doing that which is next to it—nothing. Here is the *portrait* of the wicked man. He is *perverse in speech*. "Walketh with a froward mouth." In his speech he has no regard for truth or propriety. False, irreverent, impure, and audacious. He is *artful in conduct*. "Winketh with his eyes, speaketh with his feet, teacheth with his fingers." He expresses his base spirit in crafty, clandestine, and cunning methods. He is anything but straightforward and transparent. He is *mischievous in purpose*. "He deviseth mischief continually; he soweth discord." Malevolence is his inspiration. He rejoiceth in evil. Here is the *doom* of the wicked man. "Therefore shall his calamity come suddenly." His doom is *certain*—"shall." The moral laws of the universe and the word of God guarantee his punishment. His doom is *sudden*. "Suddenly shall he be broken." The suddenness does not arise from the want of warning, but the neglect of it. "Because sentence against an evil work is not executed speedily, therefore the heart of the sons of men is fully set in them to do evil." Come it must, and when it comes, it will astound the victim with surprise. His doom is *irremediable*. "Without remedy." When it is fixed, there is no revocation, no alteration. "As the tree falleth, so it must lie."

Beware of indolence; it is a sin in itself; for we are made for action: without it our nature can neither be unfolded nor satisfied, and God and His universe require our service. It is a sin the most prolific: it hatches every form of wickedness. Society swarms with its damning progeny. Bishop Hall has well said that "idleness is the devil's cushion, on which he taketh free ease, and is fitly disposed for all evil motions. The standing water stinketh: the current keeps clear and cleanly."

Proverbs 6:16-19

Seven Abominations

"These six *things* doth the Lord hate; yea, seven *are* an abomination unto him: A proud look, a lying tongue, and hands that shed innocent blood, An heart that deviseth wicked imaginations, feet that be swift in running to mischief, A false witness *that* speaketh lies, and he that soweth discord among brethren."

HERE is a catalogue of evils specially odious to the Holy One, as well as injurious to His creation. Here is—

HAUGHTY BEARING.—"A proud look." Pride is frequently represented in the Bible as an offence to the Holy God. "He resisteth the proud." "Him that hath a high look and a proud heart will not I suffer." "Thou wilt bring down the high looks." Haughtiness is an abomination, because it implies self-ignorance, unkindness, and irreverence. How true is the language of old Quarles concerning pride. "As thou desirest the love of God and man, beware of pride. It is a tumour in the mind that breaks and poisons all thy actions: it is a worm in thy treasure, which eats and ruins thy estate; it loves no man —is beloved of no man; it disparages virtue in another by detraction; it disrewards goodness in itself by vain-glory: the friend of the flatterer, the mother of envy, the nurse of fury, the sin of devils, and the devil of mankind: it hates superiors, it scorns inferiors, it owns no equals;—in short, till thou hate it, God hates thee." Here is—

VERBAL FALSEHOOD.—"A lying tongue." This is a sore evil; David prays against it. "Deliver my soul, O Lord, from lying lips." *Falsehood always implies a corrupt heart.* A pure one supplies no motive for it. Vanity, avarice, ambition, cowardice, are the parents and patrons of all lies. *Falsehood always has a bad social tendency.* It disappoints expectations, shakes confidence, loosens the very foundations of social order. "Whatsoever," says Steele, "convenience may be thought to be in falsehood and dissimulation, it is soon over; but the inconvenience of it is perpetual, because it brings a man under an everlasting jealousy and suspicion, so that he is not believed when he speaks truth, nor trusted when perhaps he means honestly. When a man hath once forfeited the reputation of his integrity he is set fast, and nothing will then serve his turn, neither truth nor falsehood." Here is—

HEARTLESS CRUELTY.—"Hands that shed innocent blood." Cruelty implies an utter lack of sympathy with God's *creatures.* This makes way for the malign that revels in torture. And it implies also an utter lack of sympathy with God's mind. "God is love." He desires the happiness of His creatures. He made them for enjoyment. He who inflicts pain is out of sympathy both with the universe and with his Maker. Cruelty even to dumb animals, which abounds, is an atrocious sin, and must be ineffably offensive to the All-loving Creator. "Wherever it is found, it is a certain mark of ignorance and meanness: an intrinsic mark, which all the external advantages of wealth, splendour, and nobility cannot obliterate. It will consist neither with true learning nor true civility, and religion disclaims and detests it, as an insult upon the majesty and goodness of

God, Who having made the instincts of brute beasts to the improvement of the mind, as well as to the convenience of the body, hath furnished with a motive to mercy and compassion toward them very strong and powerful, but too refined to have any influence on the illiterate or irreligious." Here is-

VICIOUS SCHEMING. "A heart that deviseth wicked imaginations."—The Divine eye penetrates the heart. He sees all that passes there, not only the deep plots of evil, the elaborate schemes of thought, and the deliberate purposes, but ideas and emotions in the most incipient and fugitive forms. He judges the man as He sees him there. Adulteries, robberies, idolatries, murders, He sees perpetrated in the deep and silent districts of the soul. There are some hearts so bad that they are ever inventing evil things. It was said of the antediluvian man that every imagination and thought of his heart was only evil continually. How sad that the heart, which should ever be the nursery of the genial, the generous, and the gracious, should be devising "wicked imaginations!" What a revelation there will be on the last day, when the hidden things of the heart shall be exposed. Here is—

MISCHIEVOUS EAGERNESS.—"Feet that be swift in running to mischief." They not only do mischief, but they do it *eagerly*, with ready vigilance; they have a greed for it. They seize every opportunity. Their pleasure is in mischief. Evil is earnest; its great leader is never at rest, he moves to and fro on the earth; like a roaring lion, he goes about "seeking whom he may devour;" and just in proportion to the power that evil has over a man is his eagerness. What is more swift than revenge, jealousy, or any of the malign passions? These don't walk, they run, they fly on the wings of lightning. "Their feet are swift to shed blood." Here is-

SOCIAL SLANDER.—"A false witness that speaketh lies." The slanderer is amongst the greatest of social curses. He robs his fellow-creature of his highest treasure —his own *reputation* and the *loving confidence* of his friends. "The slanderer does harm to three persons at once: to him of whom he says the ill, to him to whom he says it, and most of all to himself in saying it." It is an accursed thing this slander. It works oftentimes by other means than words: by a look or a shrug of the shoulders it levels its poisoned arrows; it has broken many a virtuous heart and stained many a virtuous reputation. It has nodded away many a good name, and winked into existence a host of suspicions, that have gathered round and crushed the most chaste and virtuous of our kind. It often works in the dark, and generally under the mask of truthfulness and love.

> "He that shall rail against his absent friends,
> Or hears them scandalized, and not defends,
> Sports with their fame, and speaks whate'er he can,
> And only to be thought a witty man,
> Tells tales, and brings his friends in disesteem:
> That man's a knave—be sure beware of him."—HORACE

Here is—

DISTURBING STRIFE.—"And he that soweth discord among brethren." He who by tale-bearing, ill-natured stories, and wicked inventions, produces the disruptions of friendship, is abhorrent to God, Who desires His creatures to live in love and unity. "Ye lovers of strife," says Bishop Jewel, " by whose name shall I call you? I would I might call you brethren: but alas, this heart of yours is not brotherly. I would I might call you Christians: but alas, you are no Christians. I know not by what name I shall call you: for if you were brethren, you would love as brethren; if you were Christians, you would agree as Christians." This subject serves to show three things. (1) *The moral hideousness of the world.* These "seven" evils everywhere abound. They are rife and rampant the world over. (2) *The immaculate purity of God.* He *hates* those things; they are all abominations to Him; eternally repugnant to His Holy nature. (3) *The true mission of the godly.* What is that? To endeavour to rid the world of the evils offensive to Heaven.

Proverbs 6:20-7:17

Counsels to Young Men
in Relation to Bad Women

"My son, keep thy father's commandment, and forsake not the law of thy mother: Bind them continually upon thine heart, *and* tie them about thy neck. When thou goest, it shall lead thee; when thou sleepest, it shall keep thee; and *when* thou awakest, it shall talk with thee. For the commandment *is* a lamp; and the law *is* light; and reproofs of instruction *are* the way of life; To keep thee from the evil woman, from the flattery of the tongue of a strange woman."

"My son, keep my words, and lay up my commandments with thee. Keep my commandments, and live; and my law as the apple of thine eye. Bind them upon thy fingers, write them upon the table of thine heart. Say unto wisdom, Thou *art* my sister; and call understanding *thy* kinswoman: That they may keep thee from the strange woman, from the stranger *which* flattereth with her words."

THESE are some of the counsels which Solomon addresses to the young man, to guide him in his conduct towards the bad woman whom he so graphically describes in the last part of the 6th and the whole of the 7th chapter. He seems to have had no name strong enough to express his disgust of her, no names bad enough by which to designate her. He calls her a "strange woman," an "evil woman," a "harlot," &c., &c. Avoiding all the particular references, we come to the safe-guards of young men. We put these two passages together, because, in spirit, and almost in language, they are identical. They lead us to consider the proper treatment and blessed use of sacred counsels.

The proper TREATMENT of these protective counsels.—They are to be applied. The application of the sacred counsels should be *close*. "Bind them continually upon thine heart, and tie them about thy neck." "Bind them upon thy fingers; write them upon the table of thine heart." This strong figurative language means that they should be brought home to the inner being and experience. They are not merely to be in the brain, or on the lip, but bound up with the very vitalities of existence. They should become strong and ever operative instincts in our moral life. The application should be *constant*. "Bind them *continually*." They are not for mere occasional use. They are not to be used merely for certain things, but for all, and for ever. It will not do to lay them aside at any moment; for wherever thou goest, at every corner of the street, seductive influences will meet thee. The application should be *loving*. They must be regarded " as the apple of the eye," as the tenderest relation. " Thou art my sister and kinswoman." What we do not love soon forsakes us. Love is the retaining faculty of the soul. Prize these as you prize the pupil of your eye, as you prize the dear sister whom love has entwined round your heart. Young man, this is how these counsels must be treated, if they are to be your safeguards. Treat them thus, and you will become invulnerable.

The BLESSED USE of these protective counsels.— *They guide*. " When thou goest, they shall lead thee." They are a lamp to the feet, throwing its radiance before thy steps. This lamp will always burn in advance of thee *They guard*. " When thou sleepest, they will keep thee." They will keep thee from all temptations, shield thee from the honeyed shafts of " the strange woman." Sacred counsels are the only effective police in the empire of evil. *They commune*. "They will talk to thee." They are full of meaning; they are echoes of the Divine mind. They will talk with thee about spiritual relations, about duty and destiny. Blessed companions these! Their converse enlightens, cheers, and ennobles. *They animate*. " Keep my commandments, and live." They are the life-giving power to the soul. The description of the young man's temptress and her beguiling and fascinating methods is so life-like and minute that it needs neither explanation nor comment. We shall pass the verses by, and leave them to speak for themselves, as they do most truthfully, sadly, and warningly. To the " youths " and the " young men void of understanding " we earnestly commend the right treatment of these Divine counsels. Listen not to the voice of the temptress: turn a deaf ear to her, and pass on. "Many strong men have been slain by her: her house is the way to hell, going down to the chambers of death."

Proverbs 8:1-14

The Voice of Divine Wisdom

"Doth not wisdom cry? and understanding put forth her voice? She standeth in the top of high places, by the way in the places of the paths. She crieth at the gates, at the entry of the city, at the coming in at the doors. Unto you, O men, I call; and my voice *is* to the sons of man. O ye simple, understand wisdom: and ye fools, be ye of an understanding heart. Hear; for I will speak of excellent things; and the opening of my lips *shall be* right things. For my mouth shall speak truth; and wickedness *is* an abomination to my lips. All the words of my mouth *are* in righteousness; *there is* nothing froward or perverse in them. They *are* all plain to him that understandeth, and right to them that find knowledge. Receive my instruction, and not silver; and knowledge rather than choice gold. For wisdom *is* better than rubies; and all the things that may be desired are not to be compared to it. I wisdom dwell with prudence, and find out knowledge of witty inventions. The fear of the LORD *is* to hate evil: pride, and arrogancy, and the evil way, and the froward mouth, do I hate. Counsel *is* mine, and sound wisdom: I *am* understanding; I have strength."

DIVINE wisdom here personifies herself, and she has a *right* to do so for two reasons. *She is the highest attribute of person.* Wisdom is not the property of things, but of persons, and the highest property of persons—the property of the spiritual nature. Wisdom is not mere intelligence; it is a compound of intelligence and goodness; it is the "genius of goodness." Wisdom rightly personifies herself, also, because *she has received highest expression in the Highest Person.* She is seen everywhere in the material universe, but her sublimest revelation is in the Person of the Son of God. He is the Logos.

These verses bring under our notice the voice of Divine wisdom.

IT IS A VOICE STRIVING FOR THE EAR OF ALL.—"Doth not Wisdom *cry?*" She is earnest. There is a vehemence in her tone. Christ gave it a wondrous emphasis. "In the last day, that great day of the feast, Jesus stood and cried, saying, If any man thirst, let him come unto me and drink." Observe: She cries in the *most commanding scenes of life*. "In the top of high places." Her voice was heard on Sinai; on the Mount of Beatitudes, and on the brow of Calvary. Observe: she cries in the *ordinary thoroughfares of life*. "In the way of the places of the paths." In the days of Christ the voice rung by the wayside, on the seashore, in the street. So now. It may be heard at every turn in life. Again: She cries in *the most crowded districts of life*. "She crieth at the gates, at the coming in at the doors." In the great cities where men meet together to transact their business. There she is, at the gates and at the doors. As they go in and out of their banks and exchanges, there she is. The voice of Divine wisdom is everywhere. In every event of Providence, in every object of nature, in every dictate of conscience, in every lesson of experience— above all, in every word of Christ.

IT IS A VOICE WORTHY OF THE EAR OF ALL.—Wisdom here utters a commendation of herself; she spreads out her own merits as a reason why her voice should be heard. Why listen ? Because her communications *are perfect*. "I speak of excellent things." They are perfect in an intellectual and a moral sense. The communications are true to the eternal laws of reason and right. Her communications *are intelligible;* "they are all plain to him that understandeth." They are in their nature so congruous with the human soul, and conveyed in such simple language, "that a wayfaring man, though a fool, need not err therein." They are axiomatic to the unsophisticated heart. Her communications *are precious*. "Receive my instruction and not silver, and knowledge rather than choice gold." He who experimentally possesses a Divine truth is infinitely richer than he who is the owner of kingdoms. Her communications *are exhaustless*. "I wisdom dwell with Prudence, and find out knowledge." The idea is, I have vast resources. In Christ, Who is The Wisdom of God, " are hid all the treasures of wisdom and knowledge."

Her communications are *rectifying*. "The fear of the Lord is to hate evil." It religionizes and spiritualizes the soul. Wherever the words of wisdom are really received, a revolution is effected within. Her communications are *original*. "Counsel is mine, and sound wisdom; I am understanding." What Divine wisdom gives is undeniably unborrowed. "Who hath directed the Spirit of the Lord, or being His counsellor hath taught Him." This wisdom is ever in the world. Her voice is everywhere; it rings through the ages. It is high above all the tumults of the nations. The voices of generations are hushed in graveyards and in seas, but this voice sounds on; it cannot be silenced.

> "The works of men inherit, as is just,
> Their Author's frailty, and return to dust;
> But Truth Divine for ever stands secure,
> Its head is guarded as its base is sure.
> Fix'd in the rolling flood of endless years,
> The pillar of th' eternal plain appears,
> The railing storm and dashing wave defies,
> Built by that Architect who built the skies."—COWPER

Proverbs 8:15-21

The Authority of Divine Wisdom

"By me kings reign, and princes decree justice. By me princes rule, and nobles, *even* all the judges of the earth. I love them that love me; and those that seek me early shall find me. Riches and honour *are* with me; *yea*, durable riches and righteousness. My fruit *is* better than gold, yea, than fine gold; and my revenue than choice silver. I lead in the way of righteousness, in the midst of the paths of judgment: That I may cause those that love me to inherit substance; and I will fill their treasures."

WISDOM here speaks of herself as the Queen of the world, possessing the tenderest interest in the good of mankind, and having the choicest gifts to bestow. The words indicate three things concerning Wisdom in the exercise of her authority.

Wisdom, in the exercise of her authority, DETERMINES THE DESTINY OF RULERS.—"By me kings reign." It *inspires all the good actions of kings.* Every measure of their government, every righteous enactment, and every truly loyal act, derives the inspiration from the Wisdom that presides over the universe. All good in earthly rulers proceedeth from it, as sunbeams proceed from the sun. Whatever is wholesome in their laws, Wisdom suggested and inspired. It *controls all the bad actions of kings.* Whilst it originates the good, it guides and directs the evil. It changes the times and seasons, removeth and setteth up kings. It turns the tyrannies and follies of wicked monarchs to its own account, so directs them as to work out its own grand purposes.

> "There is a divinity that shapes our ends,
> Rough hew them as we may."

Wisdom is at the head of the universe, "the hearts of kings are in her hands."

Wisdom, in the exercise of her authority, HAS A SPECIAL REGARD FOR THE GOOD.—"I love them that love me, and those that seek me early shall find me." Divine Wisdom has heart as well as intellect; it glows with sympathies, as well as radiates with counsels. It has love in it: love is its genius, its root, its essence. The highest Wisdom is love. Love is the profoundest seer, the greatest contriver, the most beautiful artist. The universe is the offspring of love. We are taught here, that this Wisdom *loves its lovers.* "I love them that love me." Whoever loves Divine Wisdom, loves it especially as seen in Christ: these are loved of it. "He that hath My commandments and keepeth them, he it is that loveth Me." This Wisdom, built, furnished, and sustains the universe for her friends. We are here taught that this Wisdom is *accessible to its early seekers.* "Those that seek Me early shall find Me." Early life is the time to seek wisdom. Our moral metal is fluid in youth, and we can be run into any mould; in age it becomes hard as the granite or the steel. It must be sought to be obtained, and the sooner in life the better.

Wisdom, in the exercise of her authority, HAS THE DISTRIBUTION OF THE CHOICEST GIFTS.—"Riches and honour are with Me. Yea, durable riches and righteousness. My fruit is better than gold." There is a comparison here between spiritual and material wealth, and the former is declared the better, and so it is: the one enriches the man himself, the other does not. It is all external to him. Worldly riches are all outside our manhood. The one is substantial, the other is not. It is called here, "substance." Material wealth is a mere fugitive form. The one is permanent, the other is not. Material wealth passes away. Poetry depicts fortunes with wings. Those wings are always ready to expand and take flight. Let us seek this true and enduring wealth. "Wherefore do ye spend money for that which is not bread, and your labour for that which satisfieth not? Hearken diligently unto me, and eat ye that which is good." "Lay not up for yourself treasures on earth, where moth and rust doth corrupt, and where thieves break through and steal; but lay up for yourselves treasures in heaven." "I counsel thee to buy of me gold tried in the fire, that thou mayest be rich, ; and white raiment, that thou mayest be clothed." Moral goodness is the true wealth, vital, satisfying, enduring; that which so identifies itself with the soul that it will be as imperishable as its own immortality. "When King Demetrius had sacked and razed the city of Megæra to the very foundation, he demanded of Stilpo, the philosopher, what losses he had sustained. 'None at all,' said Stilpo, 'for war can make no spoil of virtue.' And 'tis said of Bias, that his motto was *omnia mea mecum porto*, I carry all my goods with me, viz., his goodness."

Proverbs 8:23-31

The Autobiography of Wisdom

"I was set up from everlasting, from the beginning, or ever the world was. When *there were* no depths, I was brought forth; when *there were* no fountains abounding with water. Before the mountains were settled, before the hills was I brought forth: While as yet he had not made the earth, nor the fields, nor the highest part of the dust of the world. When he prepared the heavens, I *was* there: when he set a compass upon the face of the depth: When he established the clouds above: when he strengthened the fountains of the deep: When he gave to the sea his decree, that the waters should not pass his commandment: when he appointed the foundations of the earth: Then I was by him, *as* one brought up *with him:* and I was daily *his* delight, rejoicing always before him; Rejoicing in the habitable part of his earth; and my delights *were* with the sons of men."

HERE we must speak of Wisdom as a person, and that person is none other than He who is called the "Wisdom of God." These verses may be well regarded as His autobiographic sketch. He alone can write His own history, for His existence and experience date back to periods anterior to the creation. He speaks of Himself here in four aspects:

AS HAVING EXISTED BEFORE ALL TIME.—"The Lord possessed me in the beginning of His way, before His works of old. I was set up from everlasting, from the beginning, or ever the earth was." How old is the universe? No arithmetic can compute its ages. When was the beginning? When did the first creature start into life? The question baffles all our endeavours for solution. However distant that period might be, Christ was before it: "Before His works of old." "When there were no depths I was brought forth. When there were no fountains abounding with water." When there was no being but God, Christ was. "In the beginning was the Word, and the Word was God." "He is the Alpha and the Omega, the first and the last." The builder is older than his building, the artist than his productions, the author than his books. Christ is older than the universe. He speaks of Himself here:

AS HAVING BEEN PRESENT AT THE CREATION.—
"When he prepared the heavens I was there. When he set a compass upon the face of the deep," &c., &c. The universe had an *origin*. It is not eternal. There was a point in the far distant past, when it was nowhere but in the mind of God as an idea. There was a beginning. It originated with *one* Being. It neither rose by chance, nor by the agency of a plurality of creators. He "prepared the heavens." He "set a compass upon the face of the deep." "He established the clouds above. He strengthened the fountains of the deep. He gave to the sea His decree." He, no one else, no one with Him. Christ *witnessed the process*. "I was there," I was the only spectator. I saw the birth of chaos. And out of it I saw this beautiful world with its circling heavens, floating clouds, and rolling oceans, mountains and valleys, with all the countless tribes of life, arise. He who witnessed the origin of the universe can alone give its genesis, and He does it here. He speaks of Himself here:

AS HAVING BEEN IN ETERNAL ASSOCIATION WITH THE CREATOR.—"Then I was by Him, as one brought up with Him. I was daily His delight, rejoicing always before Him." "The same was in the beginning with God." In that mysterious fellowship He was at once the object and subject of Infinite love. *The Father loved Him.* "I was daily His delight." The Infinite heart rested in complacency on Him. "He was in the bosom of the Father." *He loved the Father*, "rejoicing always before Him." The Infinite attachment was mutual. We cannot explain that affection, for we understand not the relationship. We accept the statement with wonder and with worship. He speaks of Himself here:

AS HAVING FELT BEFORE ALL WORLDS A DEEP INTEREST IN MAN.—"Rejoicing in the habitable parts of his earth. My delights *were* with the sons of men." To Him the universe was as real before it took an actual form as ever. He saw the human race on this globe with all its generations, crimes, sorrows, sufferings, before it was created. Men were as real to Him before the first man was created, as they were when He mingled with them in the streets of Jerusalem, or on the shores of Galilee. Redemption is no after-thought in the Divine procedure. The world was built as its theatre, and Christ was foreordained before its foundation. Its redemption was contemplated by Him in eternity, and was then a source of joy. "My delights were with the sons of men." He came as no reluctant messenger. "The Word," the Infinite Reason, the Eternal Mind of the universe, "was made flesh, and dwelt among us."

Proverbs 8:32-36

The Claims of Divine Wisdom

> "Now therefore hearken unto me, O ye children: for blessed *are they that* keep my ways. Hear instruction, and be wise, and refuse it not. Blessed *is* the man that heareth me, watching daily at my gates, waiting at the posts of my doors. For whoso findeth me findeth life, and shall obtain favour of the LORD. But he that sinneth against me wrongeth his own soul: all they that hate me love death."

THE claims of Wisdom as here presented are—

VERY SIMPLE.—What are they? *Diligently study* its counsels. "Hearken unto me." "Hear instruction." It is expressed further as "watching daily at my gates; waiting at the posts of my doors." The idea is, render a diligent attention to my counsels. Men are made for contemplation, and this is necessary to bring out their faculties into full play, and to give them health and vigour. The words of Wisdom are the greatest subjects for human contemplation: they explain the rationale of existence, reveal the Infinite, and point out the path to a happy and ever progressive destiny. The study of these words, therefore, is not only proper, but urgent and necessary. *Constantly obey* its precepts. "Blessed are they that keep thy ways." The teachings of Divine Wisdom are not merely speculative, but regulative. They are maxims to rule the life. Too often have they been made subjects for mere theory and debate, but they are in reality laws: they are not so much for creeds as for codes. They come with authority from the Great King, and they have a binding force. The claims of wisdom as here presented are—

VERY IMPORTANT.—*Obedience* to them is *happiness.* "Blessed is the man that heareth me; watching daily at my gates, waiting at the posts of my doors." Human happiness consists in a loyal obedience to the Divine counsels. Happiness is not in thought but in deeds. It is action that alone can ring the chimes of Heaven in the heart. "Blessed are they that hear the word of God and keep it." To *neglect* them is *ruin.* "He that sinneth against me wrongeth his own soul." "All that hate me love death." Sin is a self-injury. This is a fact, and this fact shows, First: That God's laws are essentially connected with the constitution of man. It is the characteristic of all His laws that they are written on the constitution of the subject. The atom, the flower, the beast, the man, the angel, all have their laws deep in their own nature. All sin is unnatural, and an evasion of its penalties is impossible. The sinner must flee from himself before he can flee from the misery which his sin entails. Secondly: That God's counsels are the expressions of benevolence. We wrong our souls by not keeping them. The voice of His prohibitions is, "do thyself no harm," and the voice of all His injunctions is, "rejoice evermore." All His laws are but His love speaking to man in the imperative mood. Thirdly: That God's counsels should be studiously obeyed. The sinner "wrongeth his own soul." Sin is folly, and the greatest sinner, whatever his talents and attainments may be, is the greatest fool. In every sin he quaffs that cup of poison, which shall produce anguish but never kill. In sinning,

> " We rave, we wrestle with Great Nature's plan,
> We thwart the Deity: and 'tis decreed,
> Who thwart His will shall contradict their own."

Proverbs 9:1-6
The Educational Temple:
or Christianity, a School

"Wisdom hath builded her house, she hath hewn out her seven pillars: She hath killed her beasts; she hath mingled her wine; she hath also furnished her table. She hath sent forth her maidens: she crieth upon the highest places of the city, Whoso *is* simple, let him turn in hither: *as for* him that wanteth understanding, she saith to him, Come, eat of my bread, and drink of the wine *which* I have mingled. Forsake the foolish, and live; and go in the way of understanding."

THE highest end the Great Father of spirit can have in His dealings with his intelligent and moral offspring is their education, the full and perfect development of all their powers in harmony with themselves and His everlasting will. For this purpose He has provided man with two schools—*Nature and Christianity*. The former is a magnificent one. All the true sciences of the world are but a few of its lessons which intelligent pupils have learnt in the school of nature. The latter—Christianity—is reared to meet man's spiritual condition as a fallen creature. In nature God is revealed as the Creator, in Christianity as the Redeemer. Christianity does not supersede nature; on the contrary, it trains man properly to study and appreciate it. We regard the passage as a highly poetic representation of the school which Wisdom has reared for man in Christianity, and it leads us to notice—

THE FIRMNESS OF ITS STRUCTURE.—"She hath hewn out seven pillars." A "pillar" is the emblem of strength, and "seven" of perfection. In what does the firmness of the Christian school consist? In its *truth*. Its lessons are true to human instincts, to human experience, to human reason: true, also, to a man's deep-felt moral wants as a sinner. The firmness of a school consists in the truthfulness of its doctrines. Time, which will mar the beauty of the architecture of a school, and crumble its structure to dust, though built of marble or granite, can never touch its truth with the breath of decay. The famed schools of Egypt and Greece are no more. They were ornaments and attractions in their day. Upon them Socrates and Plato, Aristotle and Pythagoras shed the lustre of their genius. Kings and heroes were their pupils. But they are gone. They did not deal in lessons true to man. Their metaphysical dreams and pompous hypotheses passed away as the intellect of the world advanced. But the school which Wisdom "hath builded" by the hand of the Galilean some eighteen centuries ago is as firm as ever.

THE ADAPTATION OF ITS PROVISIONS.—"She hath killed her beasts, she hath mingled her wine, she hath also furnished her table." The adaptation of the provision is seen in their *nature*. The things specified here were the staple commodities of life among the Easterns. The idea suggested is, that Christian truths sustain a relation to the soul analogous to the relations that the necessaries of physical life do to the body. As the body could not live without the right appropriation of food, no more can the soul without the right appropriation of Christian truth. Christ taught this frequently. He is the Bread of Life, that came down from Heaven. The adaptation of the provisions is seen in their *variety*. There is a variety in the provisions mentioned here; "beasts," "wine," "bread." Physiologists say that man's body not only requires food, but a variety of food—animal and vegetable. Why else such a rich variety of these productions in nature? and why else such an appetite for variety? Be this as it may, the Christian school presents this diversity. There is truth here suited to every faculty and sentiment of our nature—intellectual truth, religious truth, moral truth, redemptive truth—truth for the past, truth for the future. The soul can no more be fed upon one doctrine than the body upon one element. Some regard a few dogmas only as food for the soul, but when once pardoned by God's grace, and renewed by His Spirit, it wants universal truth to feed on. His smallest flower that grows in your garden cannot feed upon any one element. Does it not require sun and air, soil and shower, and all the various gases of the world to lend their aid. And can the soul feed upon a few dogmas? No; nor need it: Christianity has provided a boundless variety.

THE INVITATION OF ITS MESSENGERS.—" She hath sent forth her maidens; she crieth upon the highest places of the city, Whoso is simple, let him turn in hither." The invitation is *earnest :* " She crieth." It is not a cold, half-hearted, formal invitation. The great Teacher, on the great day of the feast, stood and cried. His messengers are commanded to go into the highways and hedges, and "compel." "The Spirit and the bride say, Come." The invitation is *universal.* "Whoso." There is no restriction—the banquet is spread for all. There are places and provision at the banquet for the sage as well as the rustic—for the old and the young. Provisions are suited to every class of mind. Truths here are sublime enough for the greatest philosopher, and simple enough for the untutored child. Plato had inscribed on the door of his school, " Let none but geometricians enter here;" but on the portals of the Christian school is written, "Whoso is simple let him turn in hither."

THE BLESSEDNESS OF ITS AIM.—What is the great design of this school? It is to give life. "Forsake the foolish and live." There are some schools that kill—kill the love of enquiry—kill the moral sensibility. But this is a life-giving school. Its *lessons* are most quickening. What so adapted to revive the downcast energies of the soul as the doctrines of Christianity? Its *teachers* are most quickening. A dull teacher, without genius and inspiration, will make his pupil dull, even though he deal in the most inspiring truths. But prophets and apostles are full of genius and life: They are full of the Great Spirit that quickeneth all things.

Let us learn from this the relation which we should sustain to this Divine Temple of Education. We should all be *teachers.* Few in the Temple are so ignorant as not to be able to impart something of which others are ignorant. We should all be *inviters*—go into the street as messengers of Wisdom, crying upon the highest place in the city, "Whoso is simple let him come in *hither*."

Proverbs 9:7-9

Reproof

"He that reproveth a scorner getteth to himself shame: and he that rebuketh a wicked *man getteth* himself a blot. Reprove not a scorner, lest he hate thee: rebuke a wise man, and he will love thee. Give *instruction* to a wise *man*, and he will be yet wiser: teach a just *man*, and he will increase in learning."

"HERE," says Lord Bacon, "caution is given how we tender reprehension to arrogant and scornful natures, whose manner is to esteem it for contumely, and accordingly to return it." All men, even the wisest and the best, at times may require reproof, but the administration of it is generally very difficult. "The most difficult province in friendship is letting a man see his faults and errors, which should, if possible, be so contrived that he may perceive our advice is given him, not so much to please ourselves as for his own advantage. The reproaches, therefore, of a friend should always be strictly just, and not too frequent."

The verses lead us to consider reproof in two aspects.

As INJURIOUSLY ADMINISTERED.—He that reproveth a scorner getteth to himself shame, and he that rebuketh a wicked man getteth himself a blot." The "scorner" is a man distinguished by self-ignorance, audacity, callousness, vanity, and irreverence. His grand aim is by little sallies of wit and ridicule, to raise the laugh against his superiors. He belongs to the lowest type of moral character, he occupies the lowest grade of depravity, he lives next door to hell. The "wicked man" is of the same class. Probably

Solomon intends by both expressions to point to those who are in the lowest grade of sin, hardened and incorrigible. To reprove these is injurious. It does them no service, whilst it brings pain to yourself. It will give you " shame and a blot." The man who resents reproof is like the fabled lady who, because the looking-glass reflected the wrinkles of her face, dashed it to the ground. The Heavenly Teacher has taught us the same lesson. " Give not that which is holy unto dogs. There are men beyond the reach of elevating influences, and it is worse than waste of labour to endeavour improving them. It is said of Pericles, that as he was sitting in a meeting before others one day, a foul-mouthed fellow railed upon him all the day long; at night, when it was dark and the meeting broke up the fellow followed him and railed at him, even to his doors, and he took no notice of him; but when he came home he said to him, "It is dark, I pray let my man light you home." These wicked scorners are incorrigible, the ministry of discipline has done with them and retribution has laid its hand on their heart. Their day of grace is over, their day of judgment has commenced. The verses lead us to consider reproof—

AS USEFULLY ADMINISTERED.—"Rebuke a wise man and he will love thee." By rebuking a wise man you enlist his affection. "He will love thee." Every true man will feel more grateful for honest reproofs than for unmerited commendation. The false man loves flattery, the true welcomes honest rebukes. "Let the righteous smite me; it shall be a kindness." By instructing a wise man you render him a benefit. " Give instruction to a wise man, and he will yet be wiser." He will take the suggestion, he will correct the error pointed out. Wise men are not so perfect as not at times to require correction, and we must not connive at their faults because of their reputation for wisdom. They are not beyond improvement. "None," says Matthew Henry, "must think themselves too wise to learn, nor so good that they need not be better, and therefore need not be taught. We must still press forward and follow on to know till we come to the perfect man. 'Give to a wise man,' give him advice, give him comfort, give him reproof, and he will yet be wiser; give him occasion to show his wisdom and he will show it, and the acts of wisdom will strengthen the habit." Some one has said that " reproof is like fuller's earth, it not only removes spots from our character, but rubs off when it is dry."

Proverbs 9:10-12

Character

"The fear of the LORD *is* the beginning of wisdom: and the knowledge of the holy *is* understanding. For by me thy days shall be multiplied, and the years of thy life shall be increased. If thou be wise, thou shalt be wise for thyself: but *if* thou scornest, thou alone shalt bear *it*."

NOTHING is so important to man as character. It is the only thing that he can call his own: the only property that will go with him into the other world, and the only thing that will determine his condition through all ages of the future. Here we have-

THE FOUNDATION AND BLESSEDNESS OF A GOOD CHARACTER.—The *foundation*. What is it? "The fear of the Lord." Not slavish dread, but loving reverence. "The knowledge of the holy is understanding." Solomon links the knowledge of the holy things, or, as some suppose, holy ones, with the "fear of the Lord;" and, in truth, they may be considered as identical, for an experimental knowledge of "the holy" is essentially related to the "fear of the Lord," which is the beginning of wisdom and the germ of all spiritual goodness. All true sagacity takes its rise here. The two things may be expressed by intelligent piety, and this is the foundation of a true character. The character that is organised on this principle is good; all others are corrupt. The *blessedness*. "For by me thy days shall be multiplied and the years of thy life shall be increased." Piety, as we have stated more than once elsewhere, is conducive to long life. What is it to live? Not merely to exist. A man may exist here seventy years and not really live a day. Life means a full and happy discharge of all the functions of our being, a full development of all our powers. To live is to realise the grand ideal of character as embodied in the life of Jesus. "For me to *live*," says Paul, "is Christ." Here we have—

II. THE SOLEMN PERSONALITY OF CHARACTER, WHETHER GOOD OR BAD.—"If thou be wise, thou shalt be wise for thyself; but if thou scornest thou alone shalt bear it." Character is a *personal* thing. It concerns the man himself and him only. It is true that a good character by influence may be of service to others, but it is of no benefit whatever to the Almighty. "Can a man be profitable unto God as he that is wise may be profitable unto himself?" It is also true that a bad character may by influence be injurious to others. "Thy wickedness may hurt a man." But it concerns the man himself infinitely more than any one else. The good man is blessed in his own deed, and the evil man is cursed in all his work. "Be not deceived; God is not mocked: whatsoever a man soweth, that shall he also reap." "Every man," says Sir J. Stevens, "has in himself a continent of undiscovered character. Happy is he who acts the Columbus to his own soul."

Proverbs 9:13-18

The Ministry of Temptation

"A foolish woman *is* clamorous : *she is* simple and knoweth nothing. For she sitteth at the door of her house, on a seat in the high places of the city, To call passengers who go right on their ways : Whoso *is* simple, let him turn in hither : and *as for* him that wanteth understanding, she saith to him, Stolen waters are sweet, and bread *eaten* in secret is pleasant. But he knoweth not that the dead *are* there : *and that* her guests *are* in the depths of hell."

THE "foolish woman" here stands opposed to wisdom in the first verses of the chapter. The former is an emblem of the power of wickedness in the world, prosecuting its work of temptation.

The other represents the power of goodness inviting the world to holiness and peace. Every man moves between these rival invitations in every step of life. The text presents to us the ministry of temptation in three aspects :

AS CONDUCTED BY DEPRAVED WOMAN.—"A foolish woman" is here the emblem of wickedness in the world. It is a sad thing to find woman a tempter, but from the first great mother of us all down to the present day, she has often been found sustaining this character. The devil has made her one of his most efficient organs. The tempting woman is here described :—She is *ignorant*. "She is simple and knoweth nothing." She is blind to spiritual realities and claims. She may be clever, acquainted with the ways of the world, and crafty; still the great spiritual world is concealed from her. She is in the kingdom of darkness :—She is *clamorous*, full of noise and exciting talk, bearing down all objections to her entreaties :—She is *audacious*. "She sitteth at the door of her house on a seat in the high places of the city." Modesty, which is the glory of her sex, has left her. She is bold and brazen :—She is *persuasive*. "Whosoever is simple let him turn in hither." "Stolen waters are sweet." This is her argument. She admits that her pleasures are wrong, and on that account the more delectable. She is a portrait of all whom the devil employs as his emissaries of evil. Mark her features, and take warning. The ministry of temptation is here presented.

AS DIRECTED TO THE INEXPERIENCED.—To whom does she especially direct her enticements? Not to the mature saint, stalwart in virtue. She calls "passengers" who go right on their ways. "Whoso is simple let him turn in hither." All men are "*passengers*." All are going "right on their ways." Step by step each moves on. Moves on constantly by day and night, asleep or awake; moves on irresistibly; no one can pause a moment on his journey to eternity. *Temptation* is busy in the path of each.

Appeals are made on all hands to the ruling passions of our nature, avarice, ambition, and lusts. Beware! The ministry of Temptation is here presented.

AS TENDING TO A MISERABLE END.—"He knoweth not that the dead are there, and that her guests are in the depths of hell." This ministry of temptation is very successful, as conducted by depraved woman. This woman obtained "*guests.*" More, alas! accept the invitation of folly than wisdom, wickedness than virtue. "Broad is the road that leadeth to destruction, and many there be that go in thereat." Her guests were *ruined.* "They were *dead*, and they were in the depths of hell." Lust bringeth forth sin; "sin, when it is finished, bringeth forth death." "To be carnally minded is death." "The stolen waters," however sweet, are poisonous. Her guests were ruined, *contrary to their intention.* "He knoweth not." Every man who accepted her invitation entered her chamber for pleasure; this was his purpose. But he met with ruin.

Brother, the devil has a ministry here as well as Christ. Which ministry exerts the most influence on thee? Remember that-

> "It is one thing to be tempted,
> Another thing to fall."—SHAKESPEARE

Proverbs 10:1

The Influence of the Child's Character Upon the Parent's Heart

"A wise son maketh a glad father: but a foolish son *is* the heaviness of his mother."

WHAT does Solomon mean by "a wise son?" A son of precocious intellect, who grows at once into a great scholar, or one who proves himself to have such business aptitudes as to rise to fortune and power at a bound? Many would call such a son wise. He evidently means a godly son, for in a previous verse he states, "the fear of the Lord is the beginning of wisdom." Observe:

The HOLY character of a child GLADDENS the heart of the parent.—"A wise son maketh a glad father." The father, however, must himself be a godly man before a godly son could gladden his heart. A worldly father is generally disposed to regard a religious son with mortification and disappointment, and deem him weak-minded and fanatic. But what on earth can be more delightful to the heart of a pious father, than the conduct of an intelligent, pure-minded, generous, brave, godly son? It is the brightest earthly sunbeam that can fall upon his soul. It delights him for at least two reasons. Because he sees in such conduct the best results of his training. He has the happy assurance that his arduous efforts and self-sacrifices have not been fruitless, that he has not laboured in vain. He looks at his son's life as a rich reward. Because he sees in such conduct the best guarantee for his son's happiness. He feels the goodness he discovers in him, has the promise of the life that now is and of that which is to come. Thus he is glad. Is not this a worthy end for every son to aim at? He whose life gladdens not the heart of a pious father is an offence to God, and will prove a curse to himself and to society. Observe:

The UNHOLY character of a child SADDENS the heart of the parent.—"A foolish son is the heaviness of his mother." "Here is distinguished," says Lord Bacon, "that fathers have most comfort of the good proof of their sons : but the mothers have most discomfort of their ill proof; because women have little discerning of virtue but of fortune." It wounds her, because she discovers that all her toils, labours, anxieties, have been fruitless, and that one who is dear to her heart is moving towards infamy and ruin ; his conduct is a "heaviness" to her heart. It rests as a leaden cloud upon her spirit. What a wretched life is this! The life that bruises the bosom that nursed and nurtured it, that tortures the heart whose love has made a thousand sacrifices on its account ; it is a life that must be execrated by universal conscience, and by Heaven. Of all men, no man is in a more hopeless condition than he who has lost his love for his mother, and clouds her life with sadness. All great men have always been distinguished by love for their mother. How touching was Cowper's address to his mother:

> " My mother, when I heard that thou wast dead,
> Say, wast thou conscious of the tears I shed ?
> Hover'd thy spirit o'er thy sorrowing son—
> Wretch even then, life's journey just begun ?
> Perhaps thou gav'st me, though unseen, a kiss ;
> Perhaps a tear, if souls can weep in bliss.
> I heard the bell toll'd on thy burial day,
> I saw the hearse that bore thee slow away,
> And turning from my nursery window drew
> A long, long sigh, and wept a last adieu."

Proverbs 10:2-3

Cash and Character

"Treasures of wickedness profit nothing ; but righteousness delivereth from death. The LORD will not suffer the soul of the righteous to famish : but he casteth away the substance of the wicked."

HEAVEN'S estimate of human possessions differs widely from those of conventional society. In the judgment of the world money is of all things most to be prized, and moral character a thing of inferior importance. The text expresses an opposite estimate. Note:

The WORTHLESSNESS of a wicked man's WEALTH.— It will "profit nothing." The wicked man gets treasures here, and often, indeed, the more wicked he is the more he succeeds. His avarice is stronger, and his conscience is less scrupulous. The "fool" in the Gospel became rich. But of what real profit is wealth to the wicked ? True, it feeds and clothes him well as an animal, and gives him gorgeous surroundings. But what "profit" is all this to a man whose character is bad ? It "profits" him "nothing" in the way of making him happy. It cannot harmonize those elements of his nature which sin has brought into conflict; it cannot remove the sense of fault from his conscience; it cannot fill him with a bright hope for the future. It "profits" him "nothing" in the way of obtaining the true love of his contemporaries. Men bow in servility to the wealthy, but there is no genuine reverence and love, where there is not the recognition of goodness. It "profits" him "nothing" in the dying hour or in the future world. It cannot prepare him for death, or be of any service in the dread future. He leaves it all behind. "Naked came ye into the world and naked must ye return." Riches "profit nothing" in the day of wrath. "Thou fool, this night thy soul shall be required of thee." In truth, instead of profit it is a loss, a curse. Was it not so with Judas? When his conscience was touched with a sense of guilt, "he brought again the thirty pieces of silver to the chief priests and elders, saying, I have sinned in that I have betrayed innocent blood." The fires of his guilt made the coins so red hot that he could not hold them any longer in his hands. He himself "casteth away his substance:" it is thrown away as rubbish. Note:

The VALUE of a RIGHTEOUS man's CHARACTER.— "But righteousness delivereth from death. The Lord will not suffer the soul of the righteous to famish." They shall be delivered from death. Not from physical dissolution, for we must all die, there is no discharge in that warfare. But from that which is the very essence in the evil of physical death, the sting of sin. And also from spiritual death, which is separation from God, the root of life. "The soul of the righteous shall never famish." On the contrary, it shall increase in vigour for ever. There is no want to them that fear him. "The young lions do lack and suffer hunger, but they that seek the Lord shall not want any good thing." "I have been young and now am old, yet have not I seen the righteous forsaken nor his seed begging bread." And Paul says, "I have all, and abound; I am full." Let us accept Heaven's estimate of human possessions, take rectitude of character as infinitely more valuable than all the wealth of wicked men. The latter enables a man to enjoy, and inherit the whole world; whether he has any legal hold upon it or not. In a pauper's hut he can say, all things are mine, whether Paul or Cephas, life or death, things present or things to come. I am Christ's and Christ is mine.

> " Seas roll to waft me,
> Suns to light me rise ;
> My footstool earth, my canopy the skies."

Proverbs 10:4-5

Idleness and Industry

"He becometh poor that dealeth *with* a slack hand: but the hand of the diligent maketh rich. He that gathereth in summer *is* a wise son; *but* he that sleepeth in harvest *is* a son that causeth shame."

HERE we have industry contrasted with slothfulness and sin. What is industry? "It does not consist," says one, "merely in action, for that is incessant in all persons. Our mind being like a ship in the sea, if not steered to some good purpose by reason, gets tossed by the waves of fancy, or driven by the winds of temptation some whither: but the direction of our mind to some good end without roving, or thinking in a straight and steady course, and drawing after it our active powers in execution thereof, doth constitute industry." There are three points of contrast—

The hand of the one is DILIGENT the other is SLACK.— The hand of the industrious is active, prompt, skilful, and persevering; and often very brown and bony through labour. The hand of idleness is "slack," loose, unskilled, and inapt. It hangs by the side as if it were made for nothing but to be carried about. Activity braces the muscles, and strings up the limbs for work. Indolence slackens the limbs, aye, and slackens the whole frame. Physical debility and half the disease of the body spring from indolence.

The soul of the one SEIZES OPPORTUNITIES, the other NEGLECTS them.—The one "gathereth in summer," the other "sleepeth in harvest." The industrious man not only watches for opportunities, but makes them. He does the work of the season; leaves not for to-morrow what should be done to-day. But he does "more." By skilful diligence, he makes the tide of circumstances flow favourably for him, and the winds breathe propitiously. He is the creator rather than the creature of circumstances, their master rather than their serf. The other, on the contrary, lets the opportunities pass; he "sleepeth in harvest." When he should be busy reaping the ripened fields, binding up the sheaves, and garnering the crops as provision for coming months, he "sleepeth," and allows the precious grain to fall into the earth and rot amongst the weeds. Instead of seizing opportunities, still less creating them, he leaves them to pass away unimproved. The tide which flowed up strong enough to bear him to prosperity, he has allowed to ebb away, and leave him a starving pauper on the shore.

The destiny of the one is PROSPERITY; that of the other RUIN.—Two things are said of the diligent. That his hand "maketh rich." In another place it says, "maketh fat," and in another place, "The hand of the diligent shall bear rule," shall conduct authority. The man in the gospel, who employed his talents, got the "well-done" of his Master, and the rulership over many things. But on the other hand, the destiny of the idle is poverty and shame. "He becometh poor that dealeth with a slack hand," and he also "causeth shame." Laziness, as we have elsewhere said, brings ruin. "Drowsiness," as Solomon has it, " clothes a man in rags."

Proverbs 10:6-7

Opposite Characters and Destinies

"Blessings *are* upon the head of the just: but violence covereth the mouth of the wicked. The memory of the just *is* blessed: but the name of the wicked shall rot."

HERE we have two opposite characters—the wicked, and the just. These terms we have frequently explained, and they represent the two great moral classes of mankind— the good and evil. From these opposite characters there spring opposite destinies.

The good are blessed in their EXISTENCE, the wicked are not.—"Blessings are upon the head of the just." He is blest by true men, his character is admired, and his usefulness appreciated. Heaven smiles on him, what he has he enjoys with a thankful heart, he is filled with the "peace of God, which passeth all understanding." He is blessed in himself, and he blesses all others. But what of the wicked? "Violence covereth the mouth of the wicked." Of this clause a different rendering has by some been proposed. That of our received version, however, seems preferable, and we accept it. It yields a natural contrast to the first. Some conceive that there is an allusion to the practice of covering the face of the condemned. According to this view, the import will be that the violence of the wicked will bring him to condemnation. More probably, however, "covering the mouth" means making ashamed, putting to silence. His detected and exposed iniquity, rapacity, and selfishness, shall be like a muzzle upon his mouth, shutting it in silent confusion. He is struck speechless. He has nothing to say in the way of defending or extenuating his crimes.

The good are blessed in their MEMORY, the wicked are not.—"The memory of the just is blessed, but the name of the wicked shall rot." Most men desire posthumous fame. The text implies this, otherwise why appeal to it? No man wishes to be forgotten. All would have their name survive their death. Nor do any desire to be remembered with unkindness. All would have their names mentioned with pleasure and gratitude. In one's more thoughtful mood there is something overwhelmingly crushing in the idea of being forgotten in the world in which we have lived and toiled. The just alone can secure posthumous fame. "The memory of the just is blessed, but the name of the wicked shall rot." The human mind is so constituted that it can only willingly remember the pleasant. It turns away from the disagreeable. The crimes and character of the wicked are themes for thought distasteful to the soul, hence their very names are allowed "to rot." They are putrid and noxious, and men would bury them in the grave of forgetfulness. The memory of the "just" shall be blessed with *long continuance*. Their contemporaries will continue while they live to speak of them with gratitude and esteem, raise monuments to perpetuate their memory, and thus hand down their names to the men of coming times. The memory of the "just" shall be blessed with *holy influence*. The remembrance of their virtues will be an ever multiplying seed. Though dead, like Abel, they will continue to speak.

Proverbs 10:8-10

Man in a Threefold Aspect

"The wise in neart will receive commandments: but a prating fool shall fall. He that walketh uprightly walketh surely: but he that perverteth his ways shall be known. He that winketh with the eye causeth sorrow: but a prating fool shall fall."

Here is man in SAFETY.—The man who is secure is described as doing two things—receiving law and practising it. "The wise in heart will receive commandments."

He adopts them intelligently, being convinced of their Divine authority, and implicitly believing them to be holy, just, and good. There are men ever ready to *give* commandments, to *modify* commandments, to *repeal* commandments; but the true man receives them loyally and lovingly as the expressions of the Divine Will. He receives with "meekness the engrafted word" of law. The secure man not only receives law but practises it. He "walketh uprightly." What he has received rules and regulates his life, he reduces the Divine precepts to practice. Such a man is *safe*. "He that walketh uprightly walketh safely."

The path of duty is the path of safety. Why? Because *omnipotence guards the traveller.* He who moves on the path of duty, though surrounded by enemies, has the Almighty as his Companion and Guard. "The Lord God is a sun and shield." The good have always this assurance, and undauntedly have they pursued their course, even unto death. He is safe, however perilous the path may sometimes appear. Moses, at the Red Sea, felt it perilous, but onwards he went and was secure. Joshua, at the Jordan, felt it perilous; he proceeded, and the waters made him a safe passage. David confronted Goliath and was delivered out of his hand. Daniel in the lion's den came forth unharmed. The just are safe. "Their defence shall be in the munitions of rocks." "Mark the perfect man and behold the upright, for the end of that man is peace."

Here is a man in PERIL.—"A prating fool shall fall." Literally a "lip fool." The self-conceited are generally superficial, and the more superficial as a rule the more talkative: the smaller and lighter the thoughts the bigger and more plentiful the words. Light matter floats to the surface and appears to all, the solid and precious lies at the bottom; the foam is on the face of the waters, the pearl is below. Sir Walter Raleigh has well said:—"Talking much is a sign of vanity; for he that is lavish in words is a niggard in deed." Such a man is in danger; his words are so reckless and rash that he exposes himself to individual resentment. They create stumbling blocks to his feet, and he falls. He falls into contempt, confusion, and suffering, through his vapouring, reckless, and blasphemous talk. The "prating fool" is one of the most popular characters in this age. He gains the platform in every public agitation. Societies hire him to "stump" the country. He lives to prate and prates to live. In the course of time he falls. The public begin to read him, find him a sham, and he falls. "A prating fool shall fall." As a rule the more true in heart and affluent in thought a man is, the more reticent and retired. Plato has well said, "As empty vessels make the loudest sound, so they that have the least wit are the greatest babblers."

Here is a man in MISCHIEF. — "He that winketh with the eye causeth sorrow." Deceivers are winkers, professing kindness to their neighbours, by a wink of the eye they give a hint to their accomplices to cheat or rob. Sly and artful men are referred to. A man who does his work by looks or words, hints and inuendoes, rather than by words like the "prating fool," such a man "causeth sorrow." He destroys social confidence, he slackens and snaps the bond of friendship, he sows the seeds of jealousies, and evokes the querulous tones of dissensions. The artful character is the most mischievous in society. He works his diabolic designs by a "wink." Blackens reputations, creates quarrels, breaks hearts by a "wink." "In dealing with cunning persons," says Lord Bacon, "we must ever consider their ends to interpret their speeches; and it is good to say little to them, and that which they least look for. In all negotiations of difficulty, a man may not look to sow and reap at once, but must prepare business, and so ripen it by degrees."

Proverbs 10:11

Speech

"The mouth of a righteous *man is* a well of life; but violence covereth the mouth of the wicked."

SPEECH is one of the most distinguishing faculties of man—a faculty this that gives immense influence either for good or evil. "The chief purpose for which it is given," says Bishop Butler, "is plainly that we might communicate our thoughts to each other in order to carry on the affairs of the world for business, and for our improvement in knowledge and learning." Solomon and the Bible say much about this faculty. Here we have,

The speech of the GOOD.—"The mouth of a righteous man is a well of life." The speech of a righteous man is here compared to a "well of life." It is like a "well" in many respects. *It is natural.* A well springs from the heart of nature. It is sin that gives to speech its affectations and artificialities. A thoroughly good man speaks out with a free and natural flow like the well, the thoughts that are in his breast. Natural speech is always eloquent. *It is clean.* The well, unlike the pool, is ever pure. It is clear as crystal. You can see the pebbles at the bottom. There is nothing impure in the speech of a truly "righteous man." No corrupt communication proceedeth out of his mouth. His speech is clean. Of all the dirty things in this world, the most loathsome is dirty speech. A clean soul is essential to clean speech. *It is refreshing.* What is more refreshing to the thirsty traveller than a sip from the well? What is more refreshing to a soul than good, pure, vigorous, godly talk? *It is life-giving.* The well gives life. It skirts all around it with verdure, and the streams it sends forth touch into life the banks along their course. The words of truth and holiness are the means by which God gives life to the souls of men. Such is the speech of the good; nothing so valuable on earth as this. "The tongue of the just is as choice silver; and the lips of the righteous feed many." Here is,

The speech of the WICKED. — "Violence covereth the mouth of the wicked." "From the mouth of the righteous," says Wardlaw, "there proceed the words of comfort, truth, and joy; under the tongue of the wicked there lie concealed cursing and bitterness, wrath and clamour, and evil speaking. There is something more fearful in the idea of the mouth covering violence than in that of uttering it. If the mouth is kept close, it is only covering, till a convenient season, the violence that is within—intimating that the wicked is well aware when it is best for his nefarious purposes to keep silence as well as when to speak out. Even when he compresses his lips, and says nothing, there is no good there." His mouth is not a well, it is a stagnant pool, covered up with noxious weeds, thorns, and thistles, and filled with moral filth. What goes from it is poison.

Tupper's description of speech is worth quoting here:

" Speech is the golden harvest that followeth the flowering of thought,
Yet oftentimes runneth it to the husk and the gains be withered and scanty.
Speech is reason's brother, and a kingly prerogative of man
That likeneth him to his maker, who spake and it was done.
Spirit may mingle with spirit, but sense requireth a symbol,
And speech is the body of a thought, without which it were not seen."

Proverbs 10:12

The Great Mischief-maker and the Great Peace-maker

"Hatred stirreth up strifes: but love covereth all sins."

A BETTER division for this proverb it is impossible to get than the one put forth by an old expositor:—"The great mischief-maker, and the great peace-maker."

Here we have the GREAT MISCHIEF-MAKER—"Hatred."

"Hatred stirreth up literally as one lifteth up a spear that had been at rest." Hatred disturbs the existing quiet by railings: it stirs up dormant quarrels, oftentimes by mere suspicions and trifles. "Strifes" of all kinds, domestic, social, religious, and political, are great evils in themselves, and in their influence. The history of them is the history of crime, lamentation and woe. All the strifes have one great promoter—that is, "hatred" and malice. This fiend is ever busy in this work. It is the great disturber of the moral universe; it sets man against himself, against his Maker, against society, and the universe.

Plutarch's remarks on hatred are worthy the Christian's study and regard. "A man," says he, "should not allow himself to hate even his enemies: because, if you indulge this passion, on some occasion it will rise of itself on others: if you hate your enemies, you will contract such a vicious habit of mind, as by degrees will break out upon those who are your friends, or those who are indifferent to you."

Here we have the GREAT PEACE-MAKER. — "Love covereth all sins." "As hatred by quarrels exposes the faults of others, so love 'covers' them: except in so far as brotherly correction requires their exposure. The reference is not to the covering of our sins before God, but the covering of our fellow men's sins in respect of others. Love condones, yea, takes no notice of a friend's errors. The disagreements which 'hatred stirreth up,' love allays; and the offences which are usually the causes of quarrel it sees as though it saw them not, and excuses them. It gives to men the forgiveness which it daily craves from God. It condones past offences, covers present, and guards against future ones. To abuse this precept into a warrant for silencing all faithful reproofs of sin in others would be to ascribe to charity the office of a procuress." Love is at once a specific element and a specific agent. As an *element*, its home is the heart of God—the God of peace. As an *agent*, it is Christ—the Prince of peace. Love restores order. It is in the moral system like the sap in the tree. It strives to heal the broken branches. Love pardons offences.

Instead of parading and magnifying the fault that disturbs, it seeks to blot it out. "It covereth a multitude of sins."

> "Love is the happy privilege of mind;
> Love is the reason of all living things.
> A Trinity there seems of principles,
> Which represent and rule created life,
> The love of self, our fellows, and our God."—FESTUS

Proverbs 10:13-18

Contrasts

"In the lips of him that hath understanding wisdom is found : but a rod *is* for the back of him that is void of understanding. Wise *men* lay up knowledge : but the mouth of the foolish *is* near destruction. The rich man's wealth *is* his strong city : the destruction of the poor *is* their poverty. The labour of the righteous *tendeth* to life : the fruit of the wicked to sin. He *is in* the way of life that keepeth instruction : but he that refuseth reproof erreth. He that hideth hatred *with* lying lips, and he that uttereth a slander, *is* a fool."

THERE is a three-fold contrast here in the character and condition of men : an intellectual, social, and moral contrast. Here is :

AN INTELLECTUAL contrast. Here is a man that "hath understanding," and a man that is "void of understanding." The difference existing between men in relation to the amount of knowledge is of vast variety. Between the most enlightened mind and the most ignorant, there is almost as great a gulf as between the most sagacious animal and the most uncultured savage. The disparity arises from a difference in mental constitution. Some have a far higher mental order of faculties than others. And also from a difference in educational opportunities. Whilst some have had the advantages of the great universities of Europe, and others of humbler schools down to the lowest "dame establishment," the great majority of the human race have been left to the unaided light of nature. Hence it is no wonder that, if there are those who have understanding, there are those who are "void" of it. Solomon states two things here concerning the intelligent man. First: He *communicates* wisdom. "In the lips of him that hath understanding wisdom is found." When he speaks men are enlightened, their minds are set to think, and their spirits are refreshed. Secondly: He *accumulates* wisdom. "Wise men lay up knowledge." It is a characteristic of knowledge in the mind, that with its increase there is an increase both in the mind's desire for larger intelligence, and in its capacity for it. The more a man knows the more he craves for intelligence, and the more ample his capacities for an augmented stock become. It is anything but this with the ignorant man—the man "void of understanding." Solomon says two things of him, that there is a "rod for his back," and that his "mouth is near destruction." He is the subject of coercion; he has not intelligence enough to be swayed by argument. His language is so mischievous, he babbles and blabs so recklessly, meddles so much with other men's concerns, that he brings ruin on himself; his mouth is always "near destruction." Here is:

A SOCIAL contrast.—"The rich man's wealth is his strong city; the destruction of the poor is their poverty." The social differences amongst men are as great as their mental. We have princes and paupers, millionaires and mendicants. Solomon here indicates that the rich man's confidence of protection is in his "strong city:" its bulwarks of massive granite and gates of ponderous iron; vigilant police and invincible soldiers, he imagines will keep him safe. He is mistaken! for if he be safely guarded from human invaders, there are other enemies that he cannot shut out: Disease, bereavements, death, cares, anxieties, sorrows; these can scale the highest fortresses and assail him. Alas! the tendency of wealth is to dispose its possessor to trust to safety where no safety is. On the other hand, "the destruction of the poor is their poverty;"

what awakens their foreboding and alarm is their destitution. Poverty often drives men to desperation, suicide, and murder. Here is:

A MORAL contrast.—"The labour of the righteous tendeth to life, the fruit of the wicked to sin." It is said of the righteous that his labour "tends to life." According to the constitution of things, righteous labour tends to life, bodily, mental, and spiritual; the life of self and the life of others. It is said that he "keepeth instruction." He keepeth it to increase it, to use it to guide and strengthen him in the path of duty. Because he does this he is in the "way of life." In contrast with this, look at the description of the wicked. "The fruit of the wicked is sin." Sin is here put in contrast with life, and it is the true antithesis. Sin is death, the death of the true, the divine, and the happy. The "fruit of the wicked" is his conduct, his conduct is sin, and sin is death. It is also said of him, that he "refuseth reproof," and that in this he "erreth." The man who refuses righteous reproofs is like the bewildered traveller who, rejecting all directions, pursues his course until he tumbles over the precipice and is dashed to pieces. He is further represented as one that "hideth hatred with lying lips," and uttereth slander. Wickedness hides hatred by lies, and slays reputations by slanders. It is often honey on the lips and venom in the heart. It is always associated more or less with a villany that hides itself under flattering words, and works out its ends by treachery and lies. "Of all the vices," says an able author, "to which human nature is subject, treachery is the most infamous and detestable, being compounded of fraud, cowardice, and revenge. The greatest wrong will not justify it, as it destroys those principles of mutual confidence and security by which only society can subsist. The Romans, a brave, generous people, disdained to practise it towards their declared enemies: Christianity teaches us to forgive injuries: but to resent them under the disguise of friendship and benevolence, argues a degeneracy at which common humanity and justice may blush.

Proverbs 10:19

The Sin of Loquaciousness

"In the multitude of words there wanteth not sin : but he that refraineth his lips is wise."

"THERE is very great necessity indeed of getting a little more silent than we are. It seems to me that the finest nations in the world—England and America—are going away into wind and tongue ; but it will appear sufficiently tragically by-and-by, long after I am away of it (the world). Silence is the eternal duty of a man. 'Watch the tongue,' is a very old precept, and a most true one." So said Carlyle, in his characteristic and remarkably enlightened and vigorous address at Edinburgh, in the beginning of April, 1870. The most thinking men of all ages have felt a similar conviction of the enormous evil of garrulousness. Solomon evidently did so. The sage of Chelsea is in this, as he is in many other things, one with the old royal sage of Jerusalem, "In the multitude of words there wanteth not sin."

LOQUACIOUSNESS IS A SIN AGAINST THE SPEAKER HIMSELF.—"A man whose tongue is always wagging," as Carlyle has it, is doing a serious injury to his own intellectual and spiritual nature. Great volubility *is a substitute for thought.* The man who has the love and faculty of great speaking is naturally prone to mistake words for thoughts. Hence it turns out as a rule that the most fluent utterers are the most shallow thinkers. Who has not heard long sermons and speeches, delivered oftentimes in graceful diction and impressive tones and attitudes, all but destitute of any idea worth carrying away ? Great volubility is a *quietus to thought.* The man who has the power of talking without thinking, will soon cease to think. The mechanism of thought will not work amid the rattling of the jaw. Thus the man who is always speaking injures himself. "The prating fool shall fall," says Solomon. True : he does fall.

His mental faculties fall into disuse under the constant pressure of verbosities.

LOQUACIOUSNESS IS A SIN AGAINST THE HEARER.—The men in the senate who in long debate spin out their yards of talk, as well as the garrulous on platforms and in pulpits, injure society in many ways. They *waste the precious time of the hearer.* The hours the listener is bound to give to those wordy discourses might be employed in other ways, to high mental and spiritual advantage. The men who occupy the time of assemblies with speech without thought are the perpetrators of enormous theft. They steal away men's precious time. They *foster self-deception.* The people who listen to them often fancy that they have derived good from their addresses, whereas, in most cases, they have not derived one single idea of any practical worth in life. They have been feeding, not on the bread of thought, but on the gilded confectionery of words ; aye, and often on nothing but wind. Hence, as a fact patent to every thoughtful observer in the religious world, the most ignorant as well as often the largest congregations, are those who attend the ministry of the garrulous preacher. They *propagate crude opinions instead of divine principles.* As a rule, the things their words convey are not truths which the speaker has reached, as living convictions, by an earnest and independent search of divine revelation. They are opinions that have come into him by education, and which he has never digested, or the untested notions which start from his brain in the excitement of the hour. Thus tares are sown instead of wheat.

Beware, then, of garrulousness in yourself; and, for your soul's sake, do not put yourself under its influence. "We have two ears and but one tongue," says an old writer, "that we may hear much and talk little." "Set a watch, O God, before my mouth : keep the door of my lips."

Proverbs 10:20-21; 31-32

The Speech of the Righteous and the Wicked Compared

"The tongue of the just *is as* choice silver: the heart of the wicked *is* little worth. The lips of the righteous feed many: but fools die for want of wisdom."

"The mouth of the just bringeth forth wisdom: but the froward tongue shall be cut out. The lips of the righteous know what is acceptable: but the mouth of the wicked *speaketh* frowardness."

HERE again Solomon is on the question of speech. He attaches great importance to the power of the tongue to work good or ill. As a philosopher, he knew that the character of a man's language depended upon the character of his heart, that the speech of a corrupt man would always be vile and pernicious, and that of the upright pure and sanitive. There is in these verses a comparison between the speech of the two characters.

The speech of the good man is VALUABLE; that of the other is WORTHLESS.—"The tongue of the just is as choice silver." Just before Solomon had said, that the mouth of the righteous is "as a well of life," indicating that his language was natural, clean, and life-giving. Here it is spoken of as "choice silver." It is intrinsically valuable, it contains truths of priceless worth, truths that reflect the Creator, and bless His creation. But the speech of the evil man is worthless. "The heart of the wicked is little worth." Why does Solomon bring the heart and the tongue into comparison, rather than the tongue of each? Probably to express the idea that speech is always the outcome and exponent of the heart. Truly the speech of a corrupt man is "little worth." He may be a man of distinguished genius, of high mental culture, a brilliant author, and a commanding orator. Still all his sentences are of "little worth." They stream from a corrupt heart, and have in them more or less of the vile and pernicious.

The speech of the good man is NOURISHING, that of the other is KILLING.—"The lips of the righteous feed many, but fools die for want of wisdom." How one soul can nourish and invigorate another by the language of truth and love! Thus Christ strengthened His disciples, and the Apostles the churches they planted. A few suitable words falling from the lips of a noble man have often braced the heart of the hearer with a martyr's heroism. But what of the words of the wicked man? Are they nourishing? Here is the contrast—"fools die for want of wisdom." Their words, beautiful as they may sound, are not grain, but chaff; however delicious to the palate, they are not aliment, but poison. The spiritual destroyer of humanity makes corrupt words his wings to bear him through the world; his poisoned javelins to strike death into the heart of his victims.

The speech of the good man is WISE, that of the other is FOOLISH.—"The mouth of the just bringeth forth wisdom; but the froward tongue shall be cut out." The words of him whose intellect is under the teaching of God, and whose heart is in vital sympathy with Him, are wise words: they tend to explain the facts of life, throw true light on the path of duty, and supply stimulants to pursue it without deviation or pause. The policies propounded by the wicked may seem wise at first, but time always exposes their folly, and brings its disciples to confusion and shame. "The froward tongue shall be cut out." "Cut out," as a corrupt tree which brings forth evil fruit is hewn down and cast into the fire. Take the books written by corrupt men for sceptical and sensational objects. Many of them are philosophic in structure, elaborate in argument, mighty in rhetoric, decked with learning, and sparkling with genius. What are they? They are the "froward tongue," the perverse uttering of perverse men, and they shall be "cut out." The *cutting* process, thank God, is going on.

The speech of the good man is ACCEPTABLE, that of the other is PERVERSE.—"The lips of the righteous know what is acceptable; but the mouth of the wicked speaketh frowardness." The words of truth are always acceptable to God. "We are unto God a sweet smelling savour," said the Apostle. And acceptable are they also to all thoughtful and candid men. Though they clash with prejudice, and strike against strong inclinations, still, inasmuch as they are true they "commend themselves to every man's conscience." Not so the utterances of the wicked. There is a "frowardness" that is distasteful to all consciences, and repugnant to the heart of God and the good.

Jesus taught that the reformation of language must proceed from the reformation of the heart. "How can ye being evil speak good things?" What are the elements of good moral speech? *Sincerity* and *Purity*. By sincerity, I mean the strict correspondence of the language with the sentiments of the heart; and by purity I mean, the strict correspondence of those sentiments with the principles of everlasting right. Sincerity without purity, were it possible, would be of no moral worth. But sincerity of expression without purity of sentiment seems to me all but socially impossible. A corrupt man is both ashamed and afraid to expose the real state of his heart to his fellow men. But let the sentiments be pure, let the passion be chaste, let the thoughts be generous, let the intentions be honourable, let the principles be righteous, and then, instead of there being any motive to insincerity of language, there will be all the incentives to the utmost faithfulness of expression.

Proverbs 10:22-28

Moral Phases of Life

"The blessing of the LORD, it maketh rich, and he addeth no sorrow with it. *It is* as sport to a fool to do mischief: but a man of understanding hath wisdom. The fear of the wicked it shall come upon him: but the desire of the righteous shall be granted. As the whirlwind passeth, so *is* the wicked man no *more:* but the righteous *is* an everlasting foundation. As vinegar to the teeth, and as smoke to the eyes, so *is* the sluggard to them that send him. The fear of the LORD prolongeth days: but the years of the wicked shall be shortened. The hope of the righteous *shall be* gladness: but the expectation of the wicked shall perish."

HUMAN life has its spiritual and moral as well as its material and intellectual side. Actions are performed by a man and events occur in his history which reveal his moral nature and relations. There are five things in these verses of great moral significance.

WEALTH MAKING HAPPY. — "The blessing of the Lord it maketh rich, and he addeth no sorrow with it." Great temporal blessings are often, perhaps generally, the occasion of mental suffering. They awaken in the mind harassing cares, painful anxieties, and distressing suspicions. What distress wealth brought upon Lot! and Ahab, though he wore a crown, was "sick on his bed." Through discontent the young man in the gospel was rich but not happy. But here we are reminded that it need not be, that it never is so, if the blessing of the Lord is connected with it. Wealth, when it is reached in harmony with the will of God, and employed in the service of benevolence and truth, has no sorrow, but tends to happiness in many ways. It is held with a loose hand, and if it departs there is no great regret; it is regarded as a trust, to be used in the service of another rather than for ourselves. A man who has got his wealth rightly, holds and uses it rightly, will find that, instead of adding sorrow, it conduces not a little to his happiness.

MISCHIEF DONE IN SPORT.—"It is as sport to a fool to do mischief, but a man of understanding hath wisdom." There is an innocent sport. Many natures, especially the young, have in them much of the frolicsome and the humorous. The sport of innocent childhood and youth, and that of rich and generous-natured manhood, is not a thing for censure. But the "sport" to which Solomon here refers is "To do mischief." A "sport" which does injury to the reputation, the property, the peace, the comforts of others. It is a sport that turns the serious into ridicule, that makes merry in deeds of nefarious wickedness. How much mischief is done in sport. There is a malign as well as a generous sport! There is the hilariousness of innocence and the hilariousness of crime. It is only a fool that doth mischief by sport. A "man of understanding hath wisdom,"—that is, he would not do it. Mischief to him is too serious for sport. The exuberance of his spirits and humour could never tempt him to wound the feelings or damage the interests of his fellow men. It is the fool that makes a mock of sin, to the wise man sin is too grave a matter to laugh at. Here is:

JUSTICE DONE TO ALL.—"The fear of the wicked it shall come upon him; but the desire of the righteous shall be granted." The anticipation of the righteous and the forebodings of the wicked shall both one day be realised. There is at times in every guilty conscience a fearful looking for of judgment; that judgment will surely come, it will be a terrible fact in his history. There is on the other hand in every godly soul a desire for a higher spiritual good, for sublimer attainments in excellence; that desire shall meet with its realization. "The desire of the righteous shall be granted." What are forebodings in the wicked and what are hopes to the good, shall before long become great conscious facts. It shall come to the wicked very *suddenly*. "As the whirlwind passeth so is the wicked no more." Mighty, rushing, resistless, it comes and bears them away. But it establishes the righteous. "The righteous is ('is' is not in the original) an everlasting foundation." Perhaps there may be a reference to the violence of the wicked being directed against him, and his remaining under the protection of the Divine power, unmoved, unharmed. The whirlwind assails the mountain; sweeps and eddies along with tempestuous and tearing fury; leaves here and there traces of its raging course; but the mountain stands unshaken on its deeplaid and unmovable basis. Such shall be the amount of the wicked man's power, such the harmlessness of its results, against those who are under the protection of Jehovah. It shall spend itself, and pass away: and the righteous shall not be moved. If God be for them, who can be against them? Here is:

INDOLENCE CAUSING VEXATION.—"As vinegar to the teeth and smoke to the eyes, so is the sluggard to them that sent him." Vinegar sets the teeth on edge, and smoke gives pain to the eyes. Both irritate and annoy, so an indolent messenger provokes his master. Who has not felt this? You entrust a man on an important errand, you despatch him, and you bid him hasten his steps and return with speed, but he is an indolent man; after he has left your sight he lags and crawls slowly on, sometimes sitting down and sometimes lounging at the side of the hedge: you get anxious, you wonder what has become of him, you have misgivings as to his safety, you fear that the mission with which you entrusted him has failed; every minute increases your anxiety and heightens your irritation. Truly the lazy, yawning loiterer is to you as "vinegar to the teeth," and as "smoke to the eyes." Laziness is not only bad for the man himself, but is most vexatious to those who are unfortunate enough to employ him in their service. Here is:

CHARACTER REVEALED IN ITS ISSUES.—The character of the good is here represented, as in many other places in this book, as prolonging life and yielding joy. "The fear of the Lord prolongeth days. The hope of the righteous shall be gladness." Here is the character of the good lengthening the life and filling it with gladness. On the contrary, the character of the wicked is represented as abbreviating life and ending in ruin. "The years of the wicked shall be shortened. The expectations of the wicked shall perish."

How full is the Bible of human life, its follies and its wisdoms, its vices and its virtues, its friendships and bereavements, its prosperities and adversities, its sorrows and its joys. God has filled the Bible with humanity, in order that it might interest men and improve them. The crimes of ancient men are here used as beacons flashing their red light, from the dangerous rocks and quicksands, and their virtues as bright stars to guide us safely on our voyage.

Proverbs 10:29

Might and Misery

"The way of the LORD *is* strength to the upright : but destruction *shall be* to the workers of iniquity."

NOTICE :

The way to STRENGTH.—The Lord has "*a way*" for man to walk in. He has a way for *Himself*. He does not move without foresight and plan. His course is mapped out. He knew the end from the beginning. His way, though righteous and benevolent, is nevertheless inscrutable to us. His way is in the sea and his paths are in deep waters. What seraph can trace His goings?

> We cannot find thee out, Lord, for infinite thou art,
> Thy wond'rous works and word reveal thee but in part ;
> The drops that swell the ocean, the sands that girt the shore,
> To measure Thy duration, their numbers have no power.

He has a way for his *creatures*. He has mapped out a path for all, according to their constitutions. He has given an orbit to all the globes of matter, a sphere to all irrational life ; has described a course for angelic hierarchies, and planned out a specific path for fallen men to tread in. What is the way He has marked out for us ? It is the way of *social justice* and *Divine worship*. In other words, the way that Christ pursued. Our course is to follow Him ; the great law binding on us is to be animated by His spirit, controlled by His principles, and engrossed in His purposes. *The man who walks in this way gets strength.* "The way of the Lord is strength to the upright." It is the "upright' who walks in this way. The man who has been made erect in Christian principles and virtues shall get intellectual strength :—in every step along this path he finds truths to challenge and nurture thought, and mental fruit clusters on all sides. Moral strength :—strength to resist temptation, to bear trial, to discharge duty, to serve man, to glorify God. "They that wait upon the Lord shall renew their strength." The righteous shall hold on his way, and he that hath clean hands shall be stronger and stronger." Notice again:

The way to RUIN.—"But destruction shall be to the workers of iniquity." Destruction of what? Conscience, memory, moral obligations, existence? I trow not. But the destruction of hopes, loves, friendships, and all that make existence worth having. The way to this terrible condition is iniquity. The word is negative—the want of equity. Men will be damned not merely for doing wrong, but for not doing the right. The want of air, bread, water, will destroy the body; the want of righteousness will ruin the soul. " He that believeth *not* shall be damned."*

Proverbs 11:2

The Advent and Evil of Pride

" *When* pride cometh, then cometh shame: but with the lowly *is* wisdom."

NOTICE:

THE ADVENT OF PRIDE.—"When pride cometh." What is pride? It is inordinate self-appreciation. It is the putting of too high an estimate on self. This feeling *comes* to a soul. It is not born in it. How does it come? By associating only with inferiors. Constant intercourse with those whose talents, beauty, accomplishments, wealth, or position, are manifestly inferior to our own, is favourable to its advent. By practically ignoring the true standards of character. When we lose sight of the eternal law of rectitude, and judge ourselves only by the imperfect standards around us, pride is likely to come.

> " Pride (of all others the most dangerous fault)
> Proceeds from want of sense, or want of thought.
> The men who labour and digest things most,
> Will be much apter to despond than boast."

By a practical disregard to the majesty of God. He who

* Verses 30 to 32 have been noticed in a previous reading.

shuts Him out from his sphere of habitual thought and experience will be accessible to pride. The conscious presence of God humbles. "When I consider the heavens, the work of Thy hands, the moon and stars that Thou hast made. What is man that Thou art mindful of him?" Notice:

THE EVIL OF PRIDE.—What is the evil? First: It brings shame. "Then cometh shame." The man who has formed such a false and exaggerated estimate of self must be disappointed one day, and the disappointment will fill him with "shame." The pride of Herod reduced him to the worms. Man like water must find his level; he must come to realities. How frequently and earnestly the Heavenly Teacher inculcates humility. "When thou art bidden, go and sit down in the lowest room." "Whosoever exalteth himself shall be abased." It brings the shame of folly. The soul blushes with a sense of its own foolish estimate. And also the shame of guilt. Pride is a wrong state of mind, and hence follows a blushing sense of guilt. It was so in the case of our first parents; shame covered them when they discovered the folly and guilt of their pride. "Pride goeth before destruction, and a haughty spirit before a fall."

> "Of all the causes which conspire to blind
> Man's erring judgment, and misguide the mind,
> What the weakest head with strongest bias rules,
> Is pride, the never-failing vice of fools!
> Whatever nature has in worth denied,
> She gives in large recruits of needful pride;
> For as in bodies, so in souls, we find
> What wants in blood and spirits filled with wind:
> Pride, where wit fails, steps in to our defence,
> And fills up all the mighty void of sense.
> If once right reason drives that cloud away,
> Truth breaks upon us with resistless day.
> Trust not yourself; but your defects to know,
> Make use of every friend and every foe."—POPE

Secondly: It excludes wisdom. Wisdom cannot dwell with pride; indeed, pride will not allow it to enter. The proud man is so self-sufficient, has such a high estimate of his own knowledge, that he feels no need of further light.

He is so satisfied with the rushlights that his pride has kindled within him, that he draws the curtains and shuts out the sunbeams. But if wisdom could enter, it could not live there, the atmosphere of pride would smother it. Truly pride is a bad thing. "Pride," said old Thomas Adams, "thrust proud Nebuchadnezzar out of men's society, proud Saul out of his kingdom, proud Adam out of paradise, proud Haman out of the court, proud Lucifer out of Heaven."

Proverbs 11:7

The Terrible in Human History

"When a wicked man dieth, *his* expectation shall perish: and the hope of unjust *men* perisheth."

THERE are two terrible events here—

DEATH MEETING THE WICKED MAN.—"A wicked man dieth." Death everywhere is a sad event—in the flower, in the bird, in the beast, it is a saddening sight. Death in the babe; death, even in a righteous man, is sad. But death in connection with the wicked is of all sights the saddest under these heavens. The wicked man dieth. Then death does not wait for reformation in character. Procrastination may adjourn duties, but not death. Death will not wait an hour or a minute: when the appointed hour has struck he is there. He has an appointed work to do and a time for doing it, and nothing can delay his course. "A wicked man dieth." Then the greatest enemies of God and His universe are overcome. Wicked men rebel against God, battle with everlasting right, but death is stronger. Death comes and puts an end to all. His cold touch freezes the heart, stills and silences them for ever.

* The subjects contained in verses 3 to 6 have been discussed in previous Readings.

It is well for the world that death does come to the wicked. Were they to remain for ever, or for any very lengthened period, our planet would become a Pandemonium. Terrible as death may be to them, their death is a blessing to humanity. The other terrible event here is:

Hope leaving the human soul. — "His expectation shall perish: and the hope of unjust men perisheth." What is dearer to the soul than hope? It is dearer than life itself, for life is a curse without it. The soul lives in its hope and by its hope. "The miserable hath no medicine but only hope," says Shakespeare. But when the wicked man dieth, he loseth this hope. Hope says adieu to him, plumes her pinions, and departs for ever. The hope of *liberty, improvement, honour, happiness*, gone, for ever gone. Every "star of hope" quenched, and the sky of the soul black as midnight. "He dieth, and carrieth nothing away; his glory shall not descend after him." "He shall go to the generations of his fathers, and shall never see light." How strong the language of despair, as expressed by Milton:

> "So farewell hope, and with hope farewell fear,
> Farewell remorse—all good to me is lost;
> Evil be thou my good."

Proverbs 11:8

Trouble in Its Relation to the Righteous and the Wicked

"*The righteous is delivered out of trouble, and the wicked cometh in his stead.*"

All men have their troubles. "Man is born to trouble, as the sparks fly upwards." But while the good and the bad have both trouble, their relation to it is strikingly different, as indicated in this proverb.

The righteous are going out of "trouble."—"The

righteous is delivered out of trouble." The righteous have their troubles—troubles arising from physical infirmities, mental difficulties, secular anxieties, moral imperfections, social dishonesties, falsehoods, and bereavements. But the glorious fact in their history is, they are being "delivered out" of these troubles. They are emerging out of darkness into light, out of discord into harmony. *Partially* : They are being delivered out of trouble *now*. There are many striking instances of deliverance on record. Abraham, Noah, Moses, Mordecai, Daniel. Every righteous man can refer to troubles from which he has been delivered, enemies that he has overcome, difficulties that he has surmounted, storms that he has left behind. *Completely.* They will be delivered out of all trouble at death. With the last breath all their sorrows depart as a vision of the night. The whole of the mighty load is left on this side of the Jordan. John, in vision, saw the righteous who had " come out of great tribulation," clothed in white robes, and exulting in bliss.

Take heart, ye righteous ones ; yet a little while, and all your storms will be hushed—all your clouds will melt into azure.

The wicked are GOING INTO TROUBLE.—" And the wicked cometh in his stead." They are in trouble now, but they are going deeper into it every step they take. Their heavens are growing darker, and the clouds more heavy : they are forging thunder-bolts and nursing storms. The trouble they are going into is unmitigated. They are not mixed with blessings, which lighten their pressure or relieve their gloom. The trouble they are going into is unending. " The worm dieth not, and the fire is not quenched."

Brother, mark the difference between the righteous and the wicked. See the former moving on, with his troubles receding like a cloud behind him, with sunshine breaking on his horizon : see the wicked advance under a sky growing more and more dark and thunderous.

Proverbs 11:9

Hypocrisy and Knowledge

"An hypocrite with *his* mouth destroyeth his neighbour : but through knowledge shall the just be delivered."

THE hypocrite is one who feigns to be what he is not—one whose life is a lie. Selfish, he wears the costume of benevolence: false, he speaks the language of sincerity and truth. "A hypocrite," says Bowes, "is like the painting at one time exhibited in London, of a friar habited in his canonicals. View the painting at a distance, and you would think the friar to be in a praying attitude. His hands are clasped together and held horizontally to his breast, his eyes meekly demised like those of the publican in the gospel; and the good man seems to be quite absorbed in humble adoration and devout recollection. But take a nearer survey, and the deception vanishes. The book which seemed to be before him is discovered to be a punch-bowl, into which the wretch is all the while, in reality, only squeezing a lemon." How lively a representation of a hypocrite! Observe:

Hypocrisy is DESTRUCTIVE. — "A hypocrite with his mouth destroyeth his neighbours." By his deception he has often destroyed the *reputation*, the *peace*, and the *soul* of his neighbour. Hypocrites are ravenous wolves in sheep's clothing. Under the pretence of loyalty, Haman would have destroyed a whole nation. Hypocrisy *implies* the pernicious. A consciousness of wrongness within is the cause of all hypocrisy. The corrupt heart dares not show itself as it is. Hence it puts on the garb of goodness. It is theatrical: it appears to be what it really is not. It is a difficult character to keep up. It is a battle against nature and reality. "If the devil ever laughs," says Colton, "it must be at hypocrites. They are the greatest dupes he has. They serve him better than any others, and receive no wages; nay, what is still more extraordinary, they submit to greater mortifications to go to hell than the sincerest Christian to go to heaven. Hypocrisy *employs* the pernicious. Misrepresentations and errors, the curse of the world, are its instruments. A false man is a "moral murderer; his mouth the lethal weapon, and his neighbour the victim." He is an assassin, striking down reputations. Observe:

Knowledge is RESTORATIVE.—" But through knowledge shall the just be delivered." Knowledge is here put in antithesis with hypocrisy, and they are essentially opposites. Real knowledge enables its possessor to defeat the crafty and malicious designs of the deceiver. A spiritually enlightened man can penetrate the mask of the hypocrite and defeat his pretensions. Divine knowledge is the restorative power of the world. "This is life eternal, to know Thee the only true God, and Jesus Christ whom Thou hast sent." It scatters the clouds of ignorance and error, and raises the soul to light, freedom, purity, and blessedness. The knowledge, however, to deliver and redeem must be practical.

> " Only add
> Deeds to thy knowledge answerable : add faith,
> Add virtue, patience, temperance : add love,
> By name to some call'd charity, the soul
> Of all the rest. Then wilt thou not be loath
> To leave this Paradise, but shalt possess
> A paradise within thee happier far."—MILTON

Proverbs 11:10-11

The Public Conscience in Relation to Moral Character

"When it goeth well with the righteous, the city rejoiceth: and when the wicked perish, *there is* shouting. By the blessing of the upright the city is exalted but it is overthrown by the mouth of the wicked."

DOWN deep beneath the errors, follies, vanities of the community, there is a *conscience*. A something that concerns itself not with the truth or falsehood of propositions, or the expediency or inexpediency of actions, but with immutable right; it points evermore to the just, as the needle to the pole.

The words lead us to notice—

The public conscience in relation to the RIGHTEOUS.— "When it goeth well with the righteous the city rejoiceth." Public conscience is *gratified by the prosperity* of the righteous. The moral heart of the city exults when it sees a truly good man prosper, even though his doctrines may clash with its prejudices, and his conduct with its selfish interests and gratifications. So did the people of old in relation to Mordecai and Hezekiah. Public conscience *acknowledges the usefulness* of the righteous. "By the blessings of the upright the city is exalted." All history shows the truth of this. "Righteousness exalteth a nation." All that is great and good in our England to-day must be ascribed to righteous principles. These principles, scattered broad-cast by our ancestors, have taken root, grown, and worked off the superstition, the barbarism, and the tyranny of former times. Who is the true patriot and real benefactor? Not the man of brilliant genius, oratoric power, or skilful finance, but the righteous man.

Righteous men are the salt of society, preventing it from putrefaction: the pillars of the State, preventing kingdoms crumbling into confusion. Notice also:

Public conscience in relation to the WICKED.—
"When the wicked perish there is shouting." *It rejoices in their ruin.* There is shouting when they fall. When the oppressor and tyrant fall, the public shout. "So let all Thine enemies perish, O Lord, but let them that love Thee be as the sun when he goeth forth in his might." When the Pharaohs, the Nebuchadnezzars, the Herods, the Alexanders, the Neros fall, the people may well rejoice. *It proclaims their mischief.* "The city is overthrown by the mouth of the wicked." The "mouth of the wicked," the channel of impieties, falsehoods, impurities, and innumerable pernicious errors—has caused in all ages, and is still causing, the overthrow of States.

Pope has well described the kind of statesman that blesses nations:

> "Stateman, yet friend to truth! of soul sincere,
> In action faithful and in honour clear!
> Who broke no promise, served no faithless end,
> Who gain'd no title, and who lost no friend;
> Ennobled by himself, by all approved,
> Praised, wept, and honour'd by the race he loved."

Proverbs 11:12-13

Types of Character in Social Life

"He that is void of wisdom despiseth his neighbour: but a man of understanding holdeth his peace. A talebearer revealeth secrets: but he that is of a faithful spirit concealeth the matter."

IN these verses there are four distinct types of character, which Solomon observed in the social life of his age, and they are to be found now in every social grade in every country under heaven.

THE INSOLENT.—"He that is void of wisdom *despiseth* his neighbour." There are men destitute of all true respect for their fellows. Always uncivil and rude. They are insolent in their speech and their bearing, ever saucy, and abusive. Such were those in the multitude that surrounded the cross, who "wagged" their heads at Infinite dignity. The remarks of Fielding on this class are to the point. "As it is the nature of a kite to devour little birds, so it is the nature of some minds to insult and tyrannise over little people. This being the means which they use to recompense themselves for their extreme servility and condescension to their superiors; for nothing can be more reasonable than that slaves and flatterers should exact the same taxes on all below them, which they themselves pay to all above them." "Such a man," says Solomon, "is void of understanding." He does not know himself, he does not know the respect due from him even to the humblest of his fellow creatures. Here is

The RESPECTFUL.—"A man of understanding holdeth his peace." He is neither precipitant in the judgment he forms of men, nor hasty in his language. He listens, reflects, weighs, and then speaks with deference; he is the true gentleman of society, cautious, prudent, polite. He does not blab out secrets entrusted to his confidence, nor break forth into language of indignation, even under strong provocation. He is master of his own temper, and rules his own tongue. He acts ever under the impression of what is due from man to man. He is uncringing to his superiors, and courteous to those below him. "As the sword of the best tempered metal is most flexible, so the truly generous are most pliant and courteous in their behaviour to their inferiors." Here is

The TATTLER.—"The talebearer revealeth secrets." A talebearer is one who will take in your secrets, and hastens to his neighbour to pour them into his greedy ears. He has an itching to know your concerns, and no sooner do you impart them, than he itches for their communication. There is, perhaps, a strong propensity in all to reveal secrets, and this in proportion to the strength of the man's vanity. When a man breaks a secret he gratifies his vanity in two ways. By revealing knowledge which the hearer has not, and by showing at the same time how much he is trusted. A more odious and mischievous character is scarcely to be found than a talebearer. Sheridan spoke in his day of a set of " malicious, prating, prudent gossips, both male and female, who murder characters to kill time; and will rob a young fellow of his good name before he has years to know the value of it." He is not always malicious in spirit, but he is always dangerous. He is always disturbing friendships, starting suspicions, and creating animosities. Here is

The TRUSTWORTHY.—"But he that is of a faithful spirit concealeth the matter." This man is the antithesis to the talebearer. He is a dependable friend; he will listen to your secrets as things too sacred for speech. You can trust him with your life, he will never betray you.

Of course such a man will not receive a secret in confidence which endangers the interests, rights, and lives of others; the man who would offer such a secret to him he would repel with indignation or hand over to the police. But secrets that involve no injustice or injury to others, he will hold as sacred as his life.

> " His words are bonds, his oaths are oracles;
> His love sincere, his thoughts immaculate:
> His tears pure messengers sent from his heart:
> His heart as far from fraud as heaven from earth."
> SHAKESPEARE

Proverbs 11:14

Wisdom, the Want of States

"Where no counsel *is*, the people fall: but in the multitude of counsellors *there is* safety."

"IT is obvious enough," says an able expositor, "that there is something here to be understood. The 'counsel' that keeps the people from ruin must be wise and good: and when given, it must be taken and followed. There may be no lack of counsel, but it may be counsel that 'causeth to err from the way of understanding,' and both ruler and people would have been better without it. But the case supposed, appears to be that of a self-willed, self-sufficient, head-strong ruler, who glories in his power; who determines to wield the rod of that power in his own way, and who plays the hasty, jealous, resolute, sensitive, and vindictive tyrant; who disdains to call in counsel, or who does it only for the pleasure of showing his superiority to it, by setting it at nought. I conceive the phrase, 'where no counsel is' to be intended to convey not a little of the character of him, by whom it is declined or disregarded. He is a character under whose rule 'the people fall.' We have an example of such a character—foolish, high-minded, insolent—in Solomon's own successor Rehoboam."

This verse implies three facts—

THE PEOPLE REQUIRE A GOVERNMENT. — Human governments are not arbitrary institutions. They spring from the instincts and necessities of society. A few men in every age are made to rule. They are, as compared with the multitude, royal in capacity, intelligence, aspiration, power. The millions are made to obey. They are uninventive, unaspiring, cringing, and servile. From such a state of things government must flow. The tree of human government is a Divine seed, which Heaven has implanted in the social heart. The tree, it is true, is often hideous in aspect and pernicious in fruit. This is the fault of the air and the soil, not of the seed, its origin is Divine.

The verses, moreover, imply that:

The GOVERNMENT REQUIRED IS THAT OF INTELLIGENCE. — Not force, not passion, not caprice, not despotism, but "counsel." The common will must be swayed by reason. Men are not to be governed as brutes, by force or violence, but by enlightened legislation. Rulers should be men not only of incorruptible justice, but of the most enlarged information and practical philosophy. It is a sad thing to send men to the senate house as England now sends them. In our ignorance we are making legislators of joint-stock jobbers, reckless speculators, uncultured manufacturers, broken down journalists and brainless Lords. Bancroft has well described the true statesman. "He is inviolably constant to his principle of virtue and religious prudence. His ends are noble, and the means he uses innocent. He hath a single eye on the public good : and if the ship of the state miscarry, he had rather perish in the wreck than preserve himself upon the plank of an inglorious subterfuge. His worth hath led him to the helm. The rudder he uses is an honest and vigorous wisdom, the star he looks to for direction is in Heaven, and the port he aims at is the joint welfare of prince and people."

Again the verses imply that :

The NECESSARY INTELLIGENCE MUST BE REACHED BY CONSULTATION.—" In the multitude of counsellors there is safety." The wisest men must meet, compare opinions, weigh suggestions, and thus, by the honest process of inquiry, travel to a wise conclusion, in which they all agree. If in the multitude of counsels, the safety of a state consists, our country ought to be secure. What with our free discussions in club, in senate, in hall, and in journalism, we truly have a multitude of counsellors. What we want is more intelligence, independency, and virtue in the people, so that they may be able to understand what a statesman should be, and may send no one to Parliament as their representative, who has not the noblest attributes of man.

> "A pillar of state : deep on his front engraven,
> Deliberation sat and public care,
> And princely counsel in his face shone
> Majestic."   MILTON

⁎ The subjects of the 14th and 15th verses have already been discussed, and will be in future Readings.

Proverbs 11:17
The Generous and Ungenerous

"The merciful man doeth good to his own soul: but *he that is* cruel troubleth his own flesh."

WE learn—

That a GENEROUS disposition is a BLESSING to its possessor.—"A merciful man doeth good to his own soul." A merciful man doeth good to his *intellectual faculties*. It is a psychological fact that the intellect can only see clearly, move freely, and progress vigorously, as it is surrounded by the atmosphere of disinterested affection. Selfishness blinds, cripples, enervates the understanding. It is only as the eye is single with disinterested love, that the whole intellectual body can get full light. In truth the mental faculties can only grow to strength and perfection in the soil and sunshine of the benevolent affections. A merciful man doeth good to his *moral sentiments*. Conscience approves only of the actions that spring from love. And our faith in the spiritual, the eternal, the Divine, can only live and thrive under the influence of the generous. "The good Samaritan," says Arnot, "who bathed the wounds and provided for the wants of a plundered Jew, obtained a greater profit on the transaction than the sufferer who was saved by his benevolence."

"The quality of mercy is not strain'd,
It droppeth as the gentle rain from heaven
Upon the place beneath; it is twice bless'd:
It blesses him that gives and him that takes.
'Tis mightiest in the mightiest: it becomes
The throned monarch better than his crown.
His sceptre shows the force of temporal power,
The attribute to awe and majesty.
Wherein doth sit the dread and fear of kings:
But mercy is above this sceptred sway,
It is enthroned in the hearts of kings,
It is an attribute of God Himself:
And earthly power doth them show likest God's,
When mercy season's justice. Therefore,
Though justice be thy plea, consider this,—

> That in the course of justice none of us
> Should see salvation: we do pray for mercy;
> And that same prayer doth teach us all to render
> The deeds of mercy."
>
> SHAKESPEARE

We learn from this proverb also:

That an UNGENEROUS disposition is A CURSE to its possessor.—"He that is cruel troubleth his own flesh." Unmercifulness of temper breeds envy, jealousy, malice, remorse, fear, suspicion, pride, and all the fiends that torment the soul. The selfish man is his own curse, he creates his own devil, and hell. God has so constituted the world that the man who injures another injures himself the more. The malign blow he deals out has a rebound more heavy and crushing to himself.

Proverbs 11:18-20

The Evil and the Good

> " The wicked worketh a deceitful work: but to him that soweth righteousness *shall be* a sure reward. They that are of a froward heart *are* abomination to the LORD: but *such as are* upright in *their* way *are* his delight."

SOLOMON'S classification of men was generally *moral*. He looked at them through the glass of eternal law, and they separated before his eye into two great divisions, the good and the evil. These he characterises by very varied epithets. To the former he applies such terms as "wise," "upright," "righteous," "just;" and to the latter, "fools," "wicked," "hypocrites," "froward," "unjust." To him all men were either good or bad in a moral sense.

His words before us exhibit these two classes in four aspects.

As they appear in WORK.—They both work, and they both reap the results of their work. "The wicked worketh a deceitful work." The good "serveth righteousness." The evil worketh " deceitfully." Evil deludes the individual *himself*. It makes his very life a fiction. He walks in "a vain show:" he is filled with illusory hopes. "Thou sayest that thou art rich and increased in goods, needing nothing." Paul, speaking of evil, says, "it deceived me, and by it slew me." The whole mental fabric in which the soul of the evil man lives, however large in dimensions, magnificent in architecture, and splendid in its furniture, is founded on the sand of fiction. It deceives *others*. Evil makes man a deceiver. It fabricates and propagates falsehood, it is like the great father of lies, who by a deceit, tempted the mother of our race. The serpent said unto the woman, "Ye shall not surely die." On the other hand, the good works righteously. "Soweth righteousness." Charged with righteous principles, he sows them as seed in the social circle to which he belongs. He sows them not merely by his lips, but by his life : by his spirit as well as his speech.

The words before us present good and evil,

As they appear in RETRIBUTION.—All works, the bad as well as the good, bring results to the worker. These results are the retribution ; they are God's return for labour. The righteous reap life. "To him that soweth righteousness shall be a sure reward." Righteousness tendeth to life. Life of the highest kind—*spiritual*, and of the highest degree—*immortal blessedness*.

The wicked reap *death*. "He that pursueth evil pursueth it to his death." What is this death ? The death of all usefulness, nobility, and enjoyment. "Be not deceived; whatsoever a man soweth, that shall he also reap. He that soweth to the flesh, shall of the flesh reap corruption. He that soweth to the Spirit shall of the Spirit reap everlasting life." Again the words before us present good and evil :—

As they appear before GOD.—"They that are of a froward heart are abomination to the Lord; but such as are upright in their way are his delight." God *observes* moral distinctions. This is implied. "His eyes run to and fro, beholding the evil and the good." God *is affected* by moral distinctions. What he sees he *feels*. He looks at the evil with disgust, and at the good with delight. "The righteous Lord loveth righteousness."

The words before us moreover present good and evil,

As they appear in COMBINATION.—Men, like sheep, are gregarious. They live in flocks. In the text their combination is supposed. "Though hand join in hand." This combination is *natural*. The wicked in these verses are supposed to be in danger, and nothing is more natural than for men to crowd together in common peril. Fear as well as love brings men together: the one drives, the other draws. A divided family comes together under a common calamity; a divided church under a common danger, and a divided nation runs into compactness at the sight of a foreign invader. But such combination is *useless*. "Though hand join in hand, the wicked shall not go unpunished." No combination of men, however great in number, vast in wisdom, mighty in strength, affluent in resources, can prevent punishment from befalling the wicked. It must come. The moral constitution of the soul, the justice of the universe, and the almightiness of God, render all human efforts to avoid it futile. "Be sure your sin will find you out."

Proverbs 11:22

Adornment

"*As* a jewel of gold in a swine's snout, *so is* a fair woman which is without discretion."

BY a fair woman, Solomon probably means a woman of personal attractions, either natural or artificial; and by "discretion" he means virtue, or moral worth. His idea therefore is, that the external attractions of a woman devoid of mind-excellencies, are "as a jewel of gold in a swine's snout."

Here is a very INCONGRUOUS conjunction in one

person.—Here are external charms and moral deformity united. Personal beauty, the beauty of form and face, is not a thing to be despised, but to be admired. It is an expression of the divine tastefulness and love. God created beauty; it radiates in the heavens, it adorns the earth, it sparkles in the seas, it overflows the universe.

Nor should we despise artistic ornament. But when personal attractions, either natural or artificial, especially the latter, are united to a corrupt character, the *conjunction* is as incongruous as "jewels of gold in a swine's snout." It is true this hideous incongruity is not generally seen, for the lack of true spiritual insight. But there it is, and if we saw things as they really are, as we shall one day see them, as angels and God see them now, the incongruity would be most manifest and distressing. Again:

Here is a very REVOLTING conjunction in one person. —Incongruity is not always disgusting. It is sometimes *ridiculous*, and is one of the chief forces in exciting and gratifying the risibilities of our nature. But this incongruity is disgusting when it is seen in the light of healthy moral sentiments. As the jewel in the swine's snout makes the swine appear more thoroughly the swine, so personal ornaments associated with moral corruption make, by way of contrast, the character appear more truly revolting. The reason why this incongruity is not more abhorrent to us is, that we do not see, as we ought to see, the putrescent character. Our eye rests upon the personal attraction, and peers not into the moral heart. We are taken up more with the "jewel" on the body than with the "swine" in the soul. Furthermore,

Here is a very COMMON conjunction in one person.—This is a sadly common spectacle; one of the elements united —namely, corrupt character—is all but universal; and the other element, personal attraction, though in its natural form limited, yet in its artificial form is extensive and rapidly extending. The desire for personal decoration has become a raging passion, and creates half the trade of the world. Wickedness is *promoted* by personal ornament. Those whom heaven has blessed with natural charms are exposed to far greater temptations than those who have but little of the comely. Wickedness is *fond of* personal attractions. It is perhaps the inspiring genius in all the costumal fashions of the world. Vulgarity always likes finery—sin is always fond of making a grand appearance. Moral swine like jewels.

Reader, do not, in forming your fellowships, be carried away with one side of life. Do not follow the "swine" for the sake of the "jewel." If God has blessed you with the grace of personal beauty, try to get the higher grace of spiritual goodness. In proportion, I trow, to the beauty of a person's mind and character, will be the disregard for ornamental costumes, or spangling jewels. Old Fuller's words are so true and quaint that they are worth quotation here:

"He that is proud of the rustling of his silks, like a madman, laughs at the rattling of his fetters. For, indeed, clothes ought to be our remembrancers of our lost innocence; besides, why should any brag of what is but borrowed? Should the ostrich snatch off the gallant's feather, the beaver his hat, the goat his gloves, the sheep his suit, the silkworm his stockings, and neat his shoes (to strip him no farther than modesty will give leave), he would be left in a cold condition."

"Dress," says Cowper, "drains our cellars dry, and keeps our larder lean."

Proverbs 11:24-25

The Generous and the Avaricious

"There is that scattereth, and yet increaseth; and *there is* that withholdeth more than is meet, but *it tendeth* to poverty. The liberal soul shall be made fat: and he that watereth shall be watered also himself."

THIS proverb is paradoxical in expression, but unquestionably true in principle. The philosophy of the human mind, and the experience of ages, attest its truth. There is a distribution that enricheth the soul of the distributor, and there is an acquisition that impoverishes. The words bring under our notice the respective operations, the reactive influence, and the social estimate of the generous and avaricious in human nature.

THE RESPECTIVE OPERATION of both those principles.—The one "*scattereth.*" It is like the hand of the sower scattering the seeds of kindness in all directions. Whatever is suited to ameliorate the woes and to bless the lives of men, whether it be ideas, wealth, influence, or effort, it willingly gives. Like the sun, it lives and shines by distributing influences to bless. The other "*withholdeth.*" The avaricious disposition is a withholding power, keeping back that which society claims and wants. What is the hoarding of wealth but the keeping back of that which the poverty and sufferings of humanity require. The withholding of the avaricious in England, explains much of that pauperism and distress which, unless speedily checked and overcome, will ruin our country. Avarice is an anomaly in the universe; all else gives out what it receives, but as a monster this clutches and retains. "Had covetous men, as the fable goes of Briareus, each of them one hundred hands, they would all of them be employed in grasping and gathering, and hardly one of them in giving and laying out, but all in receiving, and none of them in restoring. A thing in itself so monstrous, that nothing in nature besides is like it, except it be death and the grave, the only things we know of which are always carrying off the spoils of the world, and never making restitution. For otherwise all the parts of the universe, as they borrow of one another, so they still pay what they borrow, and that by so just and well balanced an equality that their payments always keep pace with their receipts." Again, in relation to the avaricious and generous, the verses lead us to notice:

THE REACTIVE INFLUENCE of both.—Every effort has a reaction. Action and reaction are the law of the universe, material and spiritual. The scattering "*increaseth.*" The liberal soul "gets fat." Not unfrequently does liberality bring *temporal* wealth. There are many signal instances of this in the history of generous men; it is invariably so in *spiritual* life. It always brings wealth of soul. Every generous act enricheth our spiritual being. " Give, and it shall be given unto you, good measure, pressed down, running over, and shaken together." The withholding "*tendeth to poverty.*" Avarice not unfrequently leads to temporal pauperism, always to moral. The man who receives all and gives nothing, sinks lower and lower into the depths of spiritual destitution. The soul of the miser always runs into a miserable grub. Strongly does Paul show the truth of this—" He which soweth sparingly shall reap also sparingly ; and he which soweth bountifully shall reap also bountifully." Moreover, in relation to the avaricious and the generous the verses teach :

THE SOCIAL ESTIMATE of both.—" He that withholdeth corn, the people shall curse him ; but blessing shall be upon the head of him that selleth it." *The people shall curse the avaricious.* Who knows the imprecations that fall every day on the head of grasping greed ? " The cries of them which have reaped are entered into the ears of the Lord of Sabaoth." *The people shall bless the generous.* Hear Job's experience, " The blessing of him that was ready to perish came upon me : and I caused the widow's heart to sing for joy. Unto me men gave ear and waited, and kept silence at my counsel. After my words they spoke not again, and my speech dropped upon them."

> " The truly generous is the truly wise ;
> And he who loves not others lives unblest."

Proverbs 11:27-28

Seeking and Trusting

" He that diligently seeketh good procureth favour : but he that seeketh mischief, it shall come unto him. He that trusteth in his riches shall fall : but the righteous shall flourish as a branch."

HERE we have man in two attitudes, pursuing and resting. He is in quest of something, " for man never is, but always to be blest:" and then he is trusting in something that he has attained. Here we have :

MAN SEEKING.—All men pursue one of two opposite moral objects—good or evil. The text speaks of both. Some are in pursuit of *good*. "He that diligently seeketh good." There are those who are industrious in the search and service of goodness, and that both for themselves and society. But some are in pursuit of *evil*. "He that seeketh mischief." There are those who are as industrious in doing evil, as others in doing good; they are always in mischief.

The destiny of these, the text suggests, is widely different. *The one procureth favour* :—favour with conscience, society, and God, and *The other disfavour*. "It shall come unto him." That is, mischief shall come unto him. He shall have what he deserves. The disapprobation of his own conscience —the denunciation of society—the frown of Heaven. "Behold, he travaileth with iniquity, and hath conceived mischief, and brought forth falsehood. He made a pit, and digged it, and is fallen into the ditch which he made. His mischief shall return upon his own head, and his violent dealing shall come down upon his own pate." Here we have

MAN TRUSTING.—"He that trusteth in his riches shall fall." This is a common tendency. Men are everywhere trusting in their wealth for happiness and honour. Like the fool in the Gospel, they say, "Soul, thou hast much goods laid up for many years." Wealth as an object of trust is not only spiritually unsatisfactory but *necessarily evanescent*. Man's wealth cannot stay long with him, his connection with it is very brief, and very uncertain, too; they may part at any moment. He, therefore, who trusteth to his wealth shall "fall." *Whence?* From all his hopes and mundane pleasures. *Whither?* To disappointment and despair. *When?* Whenever moral conviction seizes the soul, whether before or after death. *Why?* Because wealth was never a fit foundation for the soul to trust on. "Lo, this is the man that made not God his strength; but trusted in the abundance of his riches, and strengthened himself in his wickedness." "The first of all English games," says Ruskin, "is making money. That is an all-absorbing game: and we knock each other down oftener in playing at that than at football, or any other roughest sport; and it is absolutely without purpose. No one who engages heartily in the game ever knows why. Ask a great money-maker what he wants to do with his money—he never knows. He doesn't make it to do anything with it. He gets it only that he may get it. 'What will you make of what you have got?' you ask. 'Well, I'll get more,' he says. Just as at cricket you get more runs. There is no use in the runs, but to get more of them than other people is the game. So all that great foul city of London there, rattling, growling, smoking, stinking—a ghastly heap of fermented brickwork, pouring out poison at every pore. You fancy it is a city of work. Not a street of it. It is a great city at play, very nasty play, and very hard play, but still play. It is only Lord's Cricket Ground without the turf: a huge billiard table without the cloth, and with pockets as deep as the bottomless pit; but mainly a billiard table after all."

Proverbs 11:29

Family Life

"He that troubleth his own house shall inherit the wind: and the fool *shall be* servant to the wise."

"HOME," says F. W. Robertson, "is the one place in all this world where hearts are sure of each other. It is the place of confidence. It is the place where we tear off that mask of guarded and suspicious coldness, which the world forces us to wear in self-defence, and where we pour out the unreserved communications of full and confiding hearts. It is the spot where expressions of tenderness gush out without any sensation of awkwardness, and without any fear of ridicule." It is a Divine institution, the best of human kingdoms, the type of heaven. The proverb implies three things concerning family life:

That PEACE should be the grand aim of all its members.—It is here implied that to trouble the house is an evil. And so it is. Each member should studiously endeavour to maintain an unbroken harmony in the family sphere. Every look, expression, thought, word, calculated to disturb should be carefully eschewed. Whatever storms rage without, there should be serenity within the household door.

It is implied—

That there are some members WHO BREAK the peace of their domestic circle.—There are some who "trouble" their own house. Who are they? The illnatured, impulsive, false, selfish. These are domestic troublers. He who breeds feuds in families creates wars in man's earthly heaven. The homes of England are the glory of our country, the dearer, sweeter spots than all the rest.

"The stately homes of England,
How beautiful they stand,
Amidst their tall ancestral trees,
O'er all the pleasant land;
The free fair homes of England,
Long, long in hut and hall,
May hearts of native proof be rear'd
To guard each hallow'd wall!"
MRS. HEMANS.

But, alas! how often the peace of English homes is broken. An intemperate husband, an irascible wife, a reckless son, make scenes that should be the abode of harmony and love those of discord and anger.

It is implied—

That those who break the peace of their domestic circle are FOOLS.—"He that troubleth his own house shall inherit the wind: and the fool shall be servant to the wise of heart." Two things show their folly. *They get no good by it.* "They inherit the wind." What if they gratify for a moment their vanity, their selfishness, their

156 / Book of Proverbs

pride, their passion by it? Their gratification is but wind. There is nothing substantial or lasting in it. The "wind" they "inherit," too, is a blasting typhoon. *They get degradation by it.* "The fool shall be servant to the wise of heart." The habitual disturber of the family circle soon, by his folly, sinks into a base servitude. The loving and the peaceful, by the wisdom of their conduct, rule him with a dignified despotism, and this fills him with the mortification of vassalage.

Proverbs 11:30-31

The Life of the Good

> "The fruit of the righteous *is* a tree of life; and he that winneth souls *is* wise. Behold, the righteous shall be recompensed in the earth: much more the wicked and the sinner."

THESE verses suggest three things in relation to the life of the good on earth:

THE INVOLUNTARY INFLUENCE of a good man's life. —"The fruit of the righteous is a good man's life." The "*fruit*" of a life is the involuntary and regular expression of what the man is in heart and soul. All *actions* are not the *fruit* of life, inasmuch as man in the exercise of his freedom, and indeed even by accident, performs actions that, instead of fully expressing, misrepresent his life. Hence says Christ, "By their fruit," not by their action, "ye shall know them." The regular flow of a man's general activity is the *fruit*, and this, in the case of a good man, is a "tree of life." It is so for three reasons. It expresses real life; communicates real life; nourishes real life. Again the verses suggest:

THE HIGHEST PURPOSE of a good man's life —"He that winneth souls is wise." This implies that souls are lost, and so they are lost to truth, love, usefulness, and God. It implies that souls may be saved, and so they may.

Christ came to save them. Millions have been restored. The Gospel dispensation continues for the purpose. It implies, moreover, that souls may be saved by man. This is a glorious fact. Men have saved, and are still saving, their fellow men. And then it is asserted that the man who succeeds in saving souls is "wise." And so he is in the sublimest sense. Once more the verses suggest:

THE INEVITABLE RETRIBUTION of a good man's life.—"Behold the righteous shall be recompensed in the earth." The recompense here is supposed to refer rather to the *suffering* he experiences, in consequence of his remaining imperfections, than to the *blessings* he enjoys as a reward for the good that is in him. The sins of good men are punished on this earth, and Solomon uses the fact as an argument for the certainty of the greater sufferings that must be endured by the wicked. "Much more the wicked and the sinner." The argument is *à fortiori*: if God visits the sins of His people here with chastisement, much more will He visit the sins of the wicked. "For the time is come that judgment must begin at the house of God: and if it first begin at us, what shall be the end of them that obey not the gospel of God? And if the righteous scarcely be saved, where shall the ungodly and the sinner appear?"

Proverbs 12:1-3

The Righteous and the Wicked

"Whoso loveth instruction loveth knowledge; but he that hateth reproof *is* brutish. A good *man* obtaineth favour of the LORD: but a man of wicked devices will he condemn. A man shall not be established by wickedness: but the root of the righteous shall not be moved."

THE righteous and the wicked are here presented in three aspects.

In relation to INTELLIGENCE.—*The good loves intelligence.* "Whoso loveth instruction, loveth knowledge." A truly good man is a truth seeker. The constant cry of his soul is for more light. "Where shall wisdom be found, and where is the place of understanding?" *The evil hates intelligence.* "He that hateth reproof is brutish." Reproof is a form of knowledge. It shows to a sinner, in the light of great principles, either the imprudence or immorality, or both, of his conduct. He hates this, and is thus "brutish." He who does not desire to have his faults exposed to him in the light of law and love is irrational. "I have surely heard Ephraim bemoaning himself thus: Thou hast chastised me, and I was chastised, as a bullock unaccustomed to the yoke."

The righteous and the wicked are here presented:

In relation to DIVINE TREATMENT.—*The good secures the favour of God.* "A good man obtaineth favour of the Lord." Heaven smiles upon the righteous. "Thou, Lord, wilt bless the righteous; with favour wilt thou compass him as with a shield." To obtain the favour of God is the highest object of life. "Wherefore we labour, that, whether present or absent, we may be *accepted* of Him." *The evil incurs his condemnation.* "A man of wicked devices will he condemn." The frown of eternal justice shadows the path of the wicked. "He that believeth not is condemned already."

The righteous and the wicked are here presented:

In relation to THEIR STANDING.—*The evil have no stability.* "A man shall not be established by wickedness." How insecure are the wicked! They are in "slippery places." They live in a house whose foundation is sand. *The good are firmly established.* "The root of the righteous shall not be moved." "God is our refuge and strength, a very present help in time of trouble." The righteous are like the monarch of the forest, whose roots strike wide and deep into the heart of the earth, and stands secure amidst storms that wreck the fleets of nations and level cities in the dust.

Proverbs 12:4

The Queen of the Household

"A virtuous woman *is* a crown to her husband."

FEW men understood more of woman than Solomon. He knew her frailties and her virtues. His writings abound with many sage remarks upon the female character. Here he speaks of a "virtuous woman," and a virtuous woman is a *true* woman, chaste, prudent, modest, loving, faithful, patient in suffering, and brave in duty, keeping within the orbit of her sex, and lighting it with all the graces of womanhood. Such a woman, Solomon says, is "a crown to her husband." This language implies two things.

That she exercises A CONTROL over him.—A "crown" is the insignia of *rule*. A virtuous woman rules, not by intention, or arrangement, or legislative command, but by the power of her love, and the graces of her life. Woman has more force in her looks than man has in his laws, more force in her tears than man has in his arguments. A virtuous woman is really queen of the world. Beauty, tenderness, love, purity, are the imperial forces of life, and these woman wields.

> "She who ne'er answers till a husband cools,
> Or, if she rules him, never shows she rules;
> Charms by accepting, by submitting sways,
> Yet has her humour most when she obeys."—BEN JONSON

The proverb moreover implies:

That she confers A DIGNITY upon him.—A "crown" is a sign of *dignity*. She dignifies her husband, as well as rules him. Her *excellence* justifies his choice. In her character and deportment all see his wisdom, taste, and judgment in making her his bride. Her *management* enriches his exchequer. By her industry and economy the produce of his labour is carefully guarded, and often increased. Her *influence* exalts his character. Her gentle spirit and manners smooth the roughness of his character, refine his tastes, elevate his aims, and round the angles of his daily life.

Proverbs 12:5-8

The Righteous and the Wicked

"The thoughts of the righteous *are* right: *but* the counsels of the wicked *are* deceit. The words of the wicked *are* to lie in wait for blood: but the mouth of the upright shall deliver them. The wicked are overthrown, and *are* not: but the house of the righteous shall stand. A man shall be commended according to his wisdom: but he that is of a perverse heart shall be despised."

IN these verses Solomon gives us a further description of the righteous and the wicked, and they are here presented in their thoughts, speech, standing and reputation. They are represented

In their THOUGHTS.—Thoughts are the most wonderful things in connection with human life. They are the factors of character, and the primal forces of history. By thought man builds up his own world, and it is ever to him the realest world. Now the thoughts of the righteous and wicked are here brought into contrast. "The thoughts of the righteous are *right*." The righteous man is a man right in heart, and consequently right in all. The heart is the spring of the intellect—the helmsman of the brain. "As a man thinketh in his heart so is he." The thoughts of the wicked are *false*. "The counsels of the wicked are deceit." All the thoughts of a wicked man referring to happiness, greatness, duty, life, God, are false. He lives in a world of illusions. He walketh in a vain show. He is a creature of fiction. Again the two characters are represented

In their SPEECH.—Speech is the instrument by which thought does its work in society. Words are its incarnations, vehicles, and weapons. The words of the wicked are *mischievous*. "They lie in wait for blood." Malice is the inspiration of the wicked man, and he uses words as swords to wound the heart and destroy the reputation of others. "The wicked plotteth against the just." The words of the righteous are *beneficent*. "The mouth of the upright shall deliver them." The good desires good, and the words are not to injure but to bless, not to destroy but to save. To save reputations from calumny, understandings from error, hearts from pollution, souls from perdition. These characters are here given—

In their STANDING.—" The wicked are overthrown and are not, but the house of the righteous shall stand." The wicked are *insecure*. They are to be overthrown. Their hopes, purposes, possessions, pleasures, are all doomed. "I have seen the wicked in great power, spreading himself like a green bay tree. Yet he passed away, and lo, he was not."*These men build their houses on the sand, they totter and must fall. The righteous are *safe*. "The house of the righteous shall stand." They are established on the Rock of Ages. "Him that overcometh will I make a pillar in the temple of my God, and he shall go no more out."† Moreover, these characters are here presented—

In their REPUTATION. — " A man shall be commended according to his wisdom : but he that is of a perverse heart shall be despised." The good commands the *respect* of society. The consciences of the worst men are bound to reverence the right. Pharaoh honoured Joseph, Nebuchadnezzar Daniel. But the wicked man awakes the *contempt* of society. "He that is of a perverse heart shall be despised." Servility and hypocrisy may bow the knee and uncover the head before him when in affluence and power, albeit deep is the contempt for him in the social heart.

Proverbs 12:9

Domestic Modesty and Display

" *He that is* despised, and hath a servant, is better than he that honoureth himself, and lacketh bread."

VANITY, or love of display, is one of the most contemptible and pernicious passions that can take possession of the human mind. Its roots are in self-ignorance—its fruits are

* Psalm xxxvii. 35, 36.   † Rev. iii. 12.

affectation and falsehood. Vanity is a kind of mental intoxication, in which the pauper fancies himself a prince, and exhibits himself in aspects disgusting to all observers. The proverb refers to this in families, and when it takes possession of households it often destroys domestic comforts.

The words lead us to three remarks :
THAT THERE ARE DOMESTIC COMFORTS WITHOUT DISPLAY.—" He that is despised and hath a servant." It follows, then, that he who is "*despised*"—that makes himself of no reputation—maintains a humble deportment—may have a "*servant.*" What cares he for appearances? His neighbours may "*despise*" him, because of his humble bearing, still he has comforts in his family. Instead of wasting the produce of his labour upon gilt and garniture, he economically lays it out to promote the comforts of his home. In many an unpretending cottage there is more real domestic enjoyment than can be found in the most imposing mansions.

The second remark suggested is this :
THERE IS DOMESTIC DISPLAY WITHOUT COMFORTS.— " He that honoureth himself, and lacketh bread." There are in this age of empty show increasing multitudes of parents who sacrifice the right culture of their children, and the substantial comforts of a home, for appearances. They all but starve their domestics to feed their vanity. They must be *grand*, though they lack bread. Their half-starved frames must have gorgeous mantles. This love of appearance, this desire for show, is, I trow, making sad havoc with the homes of old England.

And the other remark is this :
THE CONDITION OF THE FORMER IS PREFERABLE TO THAT OF THE LATTER.—It is "*better,*" says the text, to have comforts without show, than show without comforts. "*Better.*" It is more rational. How absurd to sacrifice the comforts of life to outward show! Who cares for your display? None who care for you; but only those who would despise you were you stripped of your costume. "Better." Why? It is more *moral.* It is immoral to make outward grandeur the grand aim. Immoral, because

vanity, the inspiring motive, is a devilish passion. It is a crime to study the wardrobe more than yourself. "Better." Why? It is more *satisfying*. It is the nature of vanity that it cannot be satisfied. No amount of jewellery or tailoring can satisfy it.

> "What so foolish as the chase of fame,
> How vain the prize! how impotent our aim!
> For what are men who grasp at praise sublime,
> But bubbles on the rapid stream of time,
> That rise and fall, that swell and are no more,
> Born and forgot, ten thousand in an hour."
>
> Young

Proverbs 12:10

The Treatment of Animals

"A righteous *man* regardeth the life of his beast: but the tender mercies o the wicked *are* cruel."

THE world of irrational animals is a wonderful world. Its history, which is only begun to be written, is amongst the marvels of modern literature. The Bible not only commands us to study this world, and sends us to the beasts of the field for instruction, but it also legislates for our conduct in relation to it. The proverb suggests two remarks concerning man's conduct towards the beasts of the field.

THAT KINDNESS TOWARDS THE LOWER ANIMALS IS RIGHTEOUS.—"A righteous man regardeth the life of his beast." Three facts will show why we should be kind to them. *They are the creatures of God.* His breath kindled their life, and His hand fashioned both the great and small. Dare we abuse what He thought worth creating? *They are given for our use.* He put all under the dominion of man: some to serve him in one way, and some in another: some to charm his eye with their beauty, others to delight his ear with their music: some to supply him with food, and others with clothing: some to save his own muscular strength in doing his work, and others to bear him about. *They are endowed with sensibility and intelligence.* They all

have feeling, and some a good degree of sagacity, amounting almost to reason itself. They not only feel our treatment, but, peradventure, form judgments of the same. The other remark suggested by the proverb is:
THAT CRUELTY TOWARDS THE LOWER ANIMALS IS WICKED.—"The tender mercies of the wicked are cruel." Cruelty is wickedness. Man sins against God as truly in his conduct towards animals as in his conduct towards members of his own race. There is a divine law—*"Thou shalt not muzzle the ox when he treadeth out the corn." "Send . . . now, and gather thy cattle, and all that thou hast in the field; for upon every man and beast which shall be found in the field, and shall not be brought home, the hail shall come down upon them, and they shall die."† Great is the difference between the heart of a righteous and that of a wicked man in relation to animal life; the one is kind even to his beast, whereas the kindest treatment of the other is cruelty itself.

> "I would not enter on my list of friends
> (Though graced with polish'd manner and fine sense,
> Yet wanting sensibility) the man
> Who needlessly sets foot upon a worm.
> An inadvertent step may crush the snail
> That crawls at evening in the public path;
> But he that has humanity, forewarn'd,
> Will tread aside and let the reptile live."—COWPER

Proverbs 12:11

Manly Industry and Parasitical Indolence

"He that tilleth his land shall be satisfied with bread: but he that followeth vain *persons is* void of understanding."

IT is implied that all men want "*bread*"—the means of physical sustentation—and that this bread is to come through human industry. The earth spontaneously yields what irrational creatures require, because they are not

* Deut. xxv. 4.   † Ex. ix. 19.

endowed with aptitudes for cultivation. Man is thus endowed, and his Maker will not do for him that which He has given him power to do for himself. Labour is not the curse of the fall; it is a blessed condition of life. Man in innocence had to cultivate Eden. The verse presents two subjects of thought:

MANLY INDUSTRY.—Here is manly industry *indicated*. An agricultural specimen of work is given. "He that tilleth his land." Agriculture is the oldest, the divinest, the healthiest, and the most necessary branch of human industry. Here is manly industry *rewarded*. "Bread" comes as the result. He is "satisfied with bread." All experience shows that, as a rule, proper cultivation of the soil is all that man requires to satisfy his wants. God sends round the seasons, and when man does his work, those seasons carry their respective blessings to the race. Skilled industry is seldom in want.

> "Thrift is a blessing
> If men steal it not."
> SHAKESPEARE

The other subject which the verse presents is:

PARASITICAL INDOLENCE.—This Solomon seems to put as an antithesis to the former. "He that followeth vain persons is void of understanding." The word "vain" may perhaps be taken to represent persons in a little higher grade of life, and who are, more or less, independent of labour. First: *There are those who hang on such persons for their support*. Instead of working with manly independence, they are looking to the patronage of others. They fawn, flatter, and wheedle for bread, instead of labouring. These base-natured people are found in every social grade, and they disgrace their race, and clog the wheels of progress. Secondly: *The persons who thus hang on others for their support are fools*. "They are void of understanding." Why? Because they neglect the fundamental condition of manly development. Industry is essential to strength of body, force of intellect, and growth of soul. "It is bad policy," says our great dramatist, "when more is got by begging than working." "Man should not eat of honey like a drone from others' labour." Why? Because they sacrifice self-respect. The man who loses self-respect, loses the very gold of his manhood, and such a loss must come to him who lives the life of a parasite. Why? Because he exposes himself to degrading annoyances. The parasite's feeling will depend upon the looks, the words, and the whims of his patron. He will be subject to exactions, insults, and disappointments.

> " But harden'd by affronts and still the same,
> Lost to all sense of honour and of fame,
> Thou yet cans't love to haunt the great man's board,
> And think no supper good but with a Lord."—JUVENAL

Proverbs 12:12

The Crafty and the Honest

"The wicked desireth the net of evil *men :* but the root of the righteous yieldeth *fruit.* The wicked is snared by the transgression of *his* lips : but the just shall come out of trouble."

THESE words lead us to notice two opposite principles in human character: craftiness and honesty.

CRAFTINESS.—" The wicked desireth the net of evil men." The idea is that the wicked desire to be as apt in all the stratagems by which advantage is obtained of others, as the most cunning of evil men. Two remarks are suggested here: *Craft is an instinct of wickedness.* "The wicked desireth the net of evil men." Men of the world charge Christians with hypocrisy. But no Christly man is a hypocrite. The better a man is, the less temptation he has to disguise himself, and the more inducements to unveil his heart to all. Honesty needs no covering: like the sun behind the clouds, it struggles to break forth on the eyes of men. On the contrary, a wicked man must be hypocritical, and that just in proportion to his wickedness. Were his polluted heart and dishonest purposes fully to appear, society would recoil from him as a demon. To maintain a home, therefore, in social life, and to get on in his trade or profession, he must be as artful as the old serpent himself. Craftiness is essential to sin. Sin came into the world through craft. The devil deceived our progenitors. Sin is ever cunning: wisdom is alone true. Cunning is the low mimicry of wisdom;— it is the fox, not the Socrates of the soul. Secondly: *Craftiness is no security against ruin.* "The wicked is ensnared by the transgression of his lips." Lies are the language of craftiness. The crafty uses them as concealment and defence, but the eternal law of providence makes them snares. One lie leads to another, and so on, until they become so numerous, that the author involves himself in contradictions, and he falls and founders like a wild beast in a snare. The other principle which the words bring under notice is:

HONESTY. —"The root of the righteous yieldeth fruit." First: *Honesty is strong in its own strength.* It has a root. It does not live by cunning and stratagems, but by its own natural force and growth. Honesty has roots that will stand all storms. Secondly: *Honesty will extricate from difficulties.* "The just shall come out of trouble." The just man may get into troubles, and often does, but by his upright principles, under God, he shall come out of them. "Honesty is the best policy." It may have difficulties, it may involve temporary trouble, but it will ultimately work out its deliverance.

> "An honest soul is like a ship at sea,
> That sleeps at anchor on the ocean's calm;
> But when it rages, and the wind blows high,
> She cuts her way with skill and majesty."

Proverbs 12:14

Retributions of the Lip and Life

"A man shall be satisfied with good by the fruit of *his* mouth: and the recompence of a man's hands shall be rendered unto him."

HERE are—

THE RETRIBUTIONS OF THE LIP.—"A man shall be satisfied with good by the fruit of his mouth." The person here must of course be supposed to be a good man, for he speaks " good." What must speech be to be good? *Sincere*. It must accord exactly with what is in the mind; all other speech is hollow and hypocritical. It must be *truthful*. It must agree exactly with the facts or realities to which it refers. Speech may be sincere, and yet not truthful. It may correspond with what is in the mind, but what is in the mind may not correspond with facts. It must be *benevolent*. It must be used for the purpose of usefulness, not to injure, delude, or pain. Now the speech of such a man will satisfy him with " good." "If any man offend not in word, the same is a perfect man, and able also to bridle the whole body."* How will such speech satisfy a man? First: *In its action upon his own mind*. There is a pleasure in the act of speaking a *true* thing, and there is a higher pleasure in the reflection of having done so.

> " Speech is the light, the morning of the mind;
> It spreads the beauteous images abroad
> Which else lie furled and shrouded in the soul."—DRYDEN

Secondly: *In the effect he sees produced upon others*. He will see in the circle in which he moves, intelligence, goodness, spring up around as he speaks. His speech gives brightness and music to the atmosphere of his listening audience.

Thirdly: *In the conscious approbation of God*. "They that feared the Lord spake often one to another: and the Lord hearkened, and heard it; and a book of remembrance was written for them."† Here are also:

THE RETRIBUTIONS OF THE LIFE.—"And the recompense of the man's hand shall be rendered unto him." The "hand" here stands for the whole conduct of life. It means that man should receive the rewards of his works. And this is inevitable. First: *From the law of causation*. We are to-day the result of our conduct yesterday, and the cause of our conduct to-morrow; and thus ever must we reap the work of our own hands. Secondly: *From the law of conscience*. The past works of our hands are not lost. Me-

---

* James iii. 13. † Malachi iii. 16, 17.

mory gathers up the fragments of our life; and conscience stings or smiles, according to their character. Thirdly: *From the law of righteousness.* There is justice in the universe; and justice will ever punish the wicked and reward the good. "Be not deceived: God is not mocked: whatsoever a man soweth, that shall he reap."

> "Heaven is most just, and of our pleasant vices
> Makes instruments to scourge us."

Proverbs 12:15

The Opinionated and the Docile

"The way of a fool *is* right in his own eyes: but he that hearkeneth unto counsel *is* wise."

HERE are two distinct characters—

THE OPINIATED.—He is a "fool," and his way is always "right in his own eyes." He has such a high estimate of himself that he ignores the opinions of others, and adopts his own notions as the infallible criterion and rule. Such a man, Solomon says, is a "fool." Why? First: *Because he deprives himself of the advantages of other men's intelligence.* It is the law of Providence that men should learn by the knowledge which others have reached by observation, study, and experience. The past should be regarded as the schoolmaster of the present. But the conceited man shuts out all this light. He is too clever to learn. He is so inflated with his own opinions, that he cannot admit the ideas of other men. Secondly: *Because he exposes himself to the scorn of society.* Self-conceit is the most contemptible of attributes: all men despise it in others. A vain man is a social offence. The other character here is—

THE DOCILE.—"He that hearkeneth unto counsel is wise." Why? *Because he enriches his mental resources.* His ear is ever open to the voice of intelligence, which drops priceless sentences of truth every hour. He consults books, men, and nature, and "he increaseth knowledge." "Wise," why? *Because he increases his power of influence.* Knowledge is power. The more intelligence a man has, the wider and higher his dominion over others; and "the man that hearkeneth unto the counsel of the wise" is constantly adding to his stock of wisdom. "Wise," why? *Because he increases his securities of safety.* "In the multitude of counsellors there is safety." Young men, avoid, as you would avoid a fiend, the spirit and manners of self-conceited men.

> "There are a sort of men whose visages
> Do cream and mantle, like a standing pond;
> And do a wilful stillness entertain,
> With purpose to be dressed in an opinion
> Of wisdom, gravity, profound conceit;
> As who should say, *I am Sir Oracle,*
> *And, when I ope my lips, let no dog bark!*
> .... I do know of these,
> That therefore only are reputed wise
> For saying nothing."—SHAKESPEARE

Proverbs 12:16-23

Speech

"A fool's wrath is presently known: but a prudent *man* covereth shame. He *that* speaketh truth sheweth forth righteousness: but a false witness deceit. There that speaketh like the piercings of a sword: but the tongue of the wise *is* health. The lip of truth shall be established for ever: but a lying tongue *is* but for a moment. Deceit *is* in the heart of them that imagine evil: but to the counsellors of peace *is* joy. There shall no evil happen to the just: but the wicked shall be filled with mischief. Lying lips *are* abomination to the LORD; but they that deal truly *are* his delight. A prudent man concealeth knowledge: but the heart of fools proclaimeth foolishness."

SPEECH is again the subject of these verses. Thomas Carlyle has said many strong and striking things about speech and silence. But his finest utterance on the subject will scarcely bear comparison in pith, point, and profundity with those of Solomon. In these verses he draws a contrast between different kinds of speech. Here we have—

THE RASH AND THE PRUDENT.—"The fool's wrath is presently known." Anger fires the fool's soul; thoughts are forged in flame, and he speaks them out at once. His wrath is "presently known." "A fool uttereth all his mind." Such rash speech as this is very foolish. Why? Because anger is seldom worthy of speech, and *rash* speech may do immense mischief. In contrast with this is the prudent man, "who covereth shame." An angry passion may blaze up in his nature, but he covereth it; he does not speak it out; but rather quenches it by suppression.

Here we have—

THE TRUE AND THE FALSE.—"He that speaketh truth, showeth forth righteousness." What is it to speak "truth"? Not merely to speak our conceptions of it, for our conceptions may be false. But to speak those conceptions of truth that agree with the nature of things. Speaking such conceptions is a manifestation of righteousness. The words are radiations of right. "But a false witness deceit." The man who speaks falsehood, instead of showing forth righteousness, shows forth "deceit." He cheats with his tongue.

Here we have—

THE WOUNDING AND THE HEALING.—"There is that speaketh like the piercing of the sword." There is a spiteful, malignant speech, that acts as a javelin, it "pierces" —it is designed to wound—and it does wound. There are those in society, whose "teeth are spears and arrows, and whose tongues are sharp swords." David was frequently wounded by such speech. "As with a sword in my bones mine enemies reproach me." How many there are who cannot speak a kind word: "the poison of asps is under their lips." In contrast with this is the *healing* tongue. "The tongue of the wise is health." There is a speech that is calming, succouring, strengthening—a tonic to the heart.

Here we have—

THE PERMANENT AND THE TRANSIENT.—"The lip of truth shall be established for ever." Truth is an imperishable thing. He that speaks it drops that into the world which will outlive all human institutions, survive kingdoms and grow through the ages. It is the incorruptible seed, "that liveth and abideth for ever." In contrast with this is the transient: a lying tongue "is but for a moment." Falsehood cannot live long. The laws of the universe are against it. It is a bubble that floats on the stream, but breaks with one puff of air, and is lost in the whelming current of destiny.

Here we have—

THE MISCHIEVOUS AND THE PACIFIC.—" Deceit is in the heart of them that imagine evil, but to the counsellors of peace is joy. There shall no evil happen to the just, but the wicked shall be filled with mischief." There is a speech that is mischievous : it comes from the heart of him who is unrighteous, and who imagines evil. It disturbs social order, generates strife ; it creates wars. In contrast with this is the pacific : "to the counsellors of peace is joy." "Blessed are the peacemakers, for they shall be called the children of God."

Here we have—

THE CONDEMNED AND THE APPROVED.—The false are condemned. "Lying lips are an abomination unto the Lord." God is a God of truth, and falsehood is an abomination unto Him. On the other hand, they that deal truly are "his delight." A man of truth is a man of God. Honesty is truth in conduct, and truth is honesty in words. "We should make conscience of truth," says an old author, "not only in our words, but in all our actions ; because those that deal truly and sincerely in all their dealings are his delight, and he is well pleased with them. We delight to converse with and make use of those that are honest, and that we may put a confidence in: such, therefore, let us be, that we may recommend ourselves to the favour both of God and man."

Here we have—

THE RECKLESS AND THE THOUGHTFUL.—"A prudent man concealeth knowledge ; but the heart of fools proclaimeth foolishness." The language does not mean that a prudent man never speaks out his knowledge, but that he is not hasty in speech. He reflects and deliberates; whereas the fool speaks out everything at once that comes into his mind; all the absurd and filthy things of his heart. "The tongue of the wise useth knowledge aright, but the mouth of fools poureth out foolishness."* We are told that the prudent man should keep silence. "Let us be silent," says Emerson, "that we may hear *the whisper of the gods*."

Proverbs 12:24

Diligence and Dignity
Slothfulness and Servility

"The hand of the diligent shall bear rule: but the slothful shall be under tribute."

EXPRESSIONS parallel to the text have already frequently occurred, and will occur again as we proceed; our notice, therefore, shall be brief. Here is—

DILIGENCE AND DIGNITY.—"The hand of the diligent shall bear rule." All men desire rule, and some kind of rule every man may obtain. Social, civil, and, what is higher still, mental and spiritual. Rule over men's thoughts and hearts. Any of these dominions diligence can achieve. Diligence in study may get a knowledge that may sway an age. Diligence in business may obtain wealth that shall govern commerce. Diligence in goodness may achieve an excellence before which the soul of nations shall kneel. The remarks of Confucius on this point are good. "The expectations of life depend upon diligence; and the mechanic that would perfect his work must first sharpen his tools." Here is—

SLOTHFULNESS AND SERVILITY.—"But the slothful shall be under tribute." An indolent man will never become royal in anything. He will be the mere tool of society, the mere servile attendant upon others. Men will

* Prov. xv. 2.

use him, make him a rung in the ladder of their ascent. The slothful man gets neither knowledge, wealth, nor goodness. He never reaches an imperial altitude. He shall be under tribute evermore. That which he hath is ultimately taken from him; and into the outer darkness of obscurity he falls. The words of an able writer are worthy of quotation: "I would have every one lay to heart that a state of idleness is a state of damnable sin. Idleness is directly repugnant to the great ends of God, both in our creation and redemption. As to our creation: can we imagine that God, who created not anything but for some excellent end, should create man for none, or for a silly one? The spirit within us is an active and vivacious principle. Our rational faculties capacitate and qualify us for doing good: this is the proper work of reason, the truest and most natural pleasure of a rational soul. Who can think, now, that our wise Creator lighted this candle within us that we might oppress and stifle it by negligence and idleness? that He contrived and destined such a mind to squander and fool away its talents in vanity and impertinence?"

Proverbs 12:25

The Saddening and the Succoring

"Heaviness in the heart of man maketh it stoop: but a good word maketh it glad."

HERE we have—

THE SADDENING IN LIFE.—"Heaviness in the heart of man maketh it stoop." There is a soul-crushing sadness here. Millions of hearts are "stooping" under the weight of sorrow. There is *personal affliction*, that maketh the "heart stoop." Sufferings of the body, mind, conscience, estate. There is *social affliction*, that maketh "the heart stoop. The unfaithfulness of friends, the malice of enemies, the bereavements of death—what a load of sorrow rests on human souls! Here we have—

THE SUCCOURING IN LIFE.—"A good word maketh it glad." First: *What are "good words"?* "Good words" must be true words. False words may be pleasant for a time, but ultimately they will increase the suffering by terminating in disappointment. Good words must be true, true to reason, conscience, character, God. "Good words" must be kind words—words originating in a loving heart, and instinct with a loving spirit. "Good words" must be suitable words, suitable to the particular state of the sufferer—must be fitted exactly to his condition. Secondly: *Where are good words?* Where is the good word to be found that will make the stooping heart glad? The gospel is that word. "The Spirit of the Lord God is upon me, because the Lord hath appointed me to preach good tidings to the meek; he hath sent me to *bind up the broken-hearted*, to proclaim liberty to the captives, and the opening of the prison to them that are bound, to proclaim the acceptable year of the Lord, to comfort all that mourn." Here is a word about *Providence*, to make the man whose heart stoops under the weight of worldly cares "glad." Here is a word about *pardon*, to make the man whose heart stoops under the sense of guilt "glad." Here is a word about the *resurrection*, to make the man whose heart stoops under the weight of bereavement "glad." Oh! here is a word to comfort us in all our tribulations, "that we may be able to comfort them that are in any trouble, by the comfort wherewith we ourselves are comforted of God."*

---

* II. Cor. i. 4.

Proverbs 12:26, 28

The True Pathway of Souls

"The righteous *is* more excellent than his neighbour: but the way of the wicked seduceth them."

"In the way of righteousness *is* life; and *in* the pathway *thereof there is* no death."

THE life of souls is a journey beginning at the first voluntary thought, and running on from stage to stage, through interminable ages. Wonderful pilgrimage is the pilgrimage of souls. What is its true pathway? This is the grand question.

It is a SUPERIOR pathway.—The word "excellent" here stands for *abundance*. The righteous is more abundant than his neighbour. He is richer, seldom in material wealth, but always in spiritual and moral. He has richer themes for thought, nobler principles of action, sublimer objects of hope, and diviner motives of conduct. He is richer. He has an "inheritance incorruptible, and undefiled, that fadeth not away." He has God Himself for his portion.

It is a SAFE pathway.—"The way of the wicked seduceth him." This stands in contrast with the implied way of the righteous. The way of the wicked is illusory; he fancies it a beautiful, pleasant, safe way, whereas it leads to ruin, it cheats him. "He feedeth on ashes; a deceived heart hath turned him aside, that he cannot deliver his soul, nor say, Is there not a lie in my right hand?" But the way of the righteous, however hard and rough, is safe; its end is everlasting life. The pilgrim is well guarded in every step.

It is a RIGHTEOUS pathway.—"The way of righteousness." What is the righteous way? The way that the righteous God has marked out. Nothing can be more axiomatic than this, that the path which the great Proprietor and Creator of souls has marked out is the right one, and the only right one. Why? Because it is the *path in which His character is the supreme attraction of souls.* In it all the affections of the traveller run after Him, as rivers to the ocean. God is always the grand object before the eye, filling the horizon, and brightening all the scenes through which he passes. Why? Because *His will is the supreme rule.* Wherever His will directs is the path of righteousness. His will is revealed in different forms of expression. For example: "This is the will of God, that ye believe on His Son." Again: "This is the will of God, even your sanctification." The true pathway of souls is—

A BLESSED pathway.—"In the way of righteousness is life; and in the pathway thereof is no death." In this pathway is life. The highest mental, social, and religious life. In this pathway is life *only.* There is no death. No death of any kind, no decay of faculties, no waning of hopes, no wreck of purposes, no loss of friendships. Each traveller steps on in the buoyant energy of immortal youth, through lovely Edens of unfading life.

Proverbs 12:27 *

Labor as Enhancing the Relative Value of a Man's Possessions

"The slothful *man* roasteth not that which he took in hunting: but the substance of a diligent man *is* precious."

THE original word, here translated, "slothful," is in several other places rendered "deceitful." Slothfulness is almost necessarily connected with deceit. The idle man is a dreamer, he lives in false hopes. He makes promises that prove fallacious, because he has not the industry to work them out. Slothfulness stands almost always nearly akin to falsehood. The text means one of three things. Either

* Verse 28 has already been discussed.

that the slothful man is too lazy to "roast" and to prepare for food what he happened to strike down without much effort in the field, or, that what he "roasts" and prepares for food he had no hand in procuring, and that he lives on the production of other men's labours. He has "roast" meat, but that which he roasts is not what he himself took in hunting; or, what he caught in the field was so *easily* caught, caught with such little effort, that he did not value it enough to prepare it for food. He did not take it up, carry it home, and prepare it for the table. The last, I think, was the idea that Solomon had in his mind when he wrote this proverb, " But the substance of a diligent man is precious ;" as if he had said, the slothful man does not value sufficiently what he has, without labour, caught in the field to prepare it for food; but what the industrious man has, as the result of his work, is precious to him. The general principle, therefore, contained in these words is this :—*That labour enhances the relative value of a man's possessions.* This principle is capable of extensive illustration; it applies to many things.

It applies to MATERIAL WEALTH.—Two men may possess property of exactly the same amount, of precisely the same intrinsic and marketable value, but whilst the one has gained it by long years of industry, it has come to the other by accident or fortune, or in some way entirely irrespective of his labour. Is the property equally appreciated by these two men? Is there not an immense difference in the value attached to it by its different proprietors? Yes; the very same amount is a vastly different thing to the two owners.

It applies to SOCIAL POSITION.—One man is born to social influence; he becomes the centre of an influential circle, and gets a position of extensive power, with no effort but that which is involved in a small amount of mental culture. He is a country squire; he is a member of parliament; he is a peer of the realm; and all rather by what is called fortune than by anxious and persevering toil. The other man gets to such positions by long years of arduous and indefatigable labour. Are these two positions of the same value? To the eyes of the world they are of the same worth, but to these men they are vastly different things.

It applies to CIVIL LIBERTY.—Civil liberty is an invaluable possession. It is the grandest theme of political philosophy; it is the ideal of patriotic poetry: it is the goal in the race of nations. But what a different thing it is to the men who have just won it by struggle, bloodshed, and sacrifice, from what it is to those who, like us, the modern men of England, have come into it as an inheritance won by the struggles of our forefathers.

It applies to RELIGIOUS PRIVILEGES.—To have the right to form our own religious convictions, and to express them freely and fully, to worship our own God in our own way, what a priceless boon is this! Yet do we value it as those who gained it after long years of persecution and battle? Thus it is that labour enhances the value of our possessions:

> "Weave, brothers, weave! Toil is ours;
> But toil is the lot of man:
> One gathers the fruits, one gathers the flowers,
> One soweth the seed again.
> There is not a creature, from England's king
> To the peasant that delves the soil,
> That knows half the pleasures the seasons bring,
> If he have not his share of toil."—BARRY CORNWALL

Proverbs 13:1

The Teachable and the Unteachable Son

"A wise son *heareth* his father's instruction: but a scorner heareth not rebuke."

THE TEACHABLE SON.—"A wise son *heareth* his father's instruction." Solomon, of course, supposes that the father is what a father *ought* to be. There are men sustaining the paternal relationship who can scarcely be called *fathers*.

They have not the fatherly instincts, the fatherly love, the fatherly wisdom, the fatherly royalty. A son would scarcely be wise in listening to a father of this class. When we are commanded to honour our father, and to honour the king, it is always supposed that the father and the king are honour-worthy, and realize, to some extent, the ideal of the relationship. He who attends to the instruction of a father, Solomon says, is wise. He is wise, because he attends to the Divine condition of human improvement. The Creator has ordained that the rising generation should get its wisdom from the teachings of its parents. It is by generations learning of their predecessors, that the race advances. Because he gratifies the heart of his best earthly friend. The counsels of a *true* father are always sincere, dictated by the truest love, and intended to serve the interests of his children, and nothing is more gratifying to his paternal nature than to see them rightly attended to.

THE UNTEACHABLE SON.—"A scorner heareth not rebuke." Scorn is derision, contempt, and may be directed either to a person or a thing. It is not necessarily a wrong state of mind; its moral character, good or otherwise, depends upon the person or thing to which it is directed. Some *persons* justly merit derision; some *things* merit contempt. A son who scorns either the person or the counsels of his father, is not in a state of mind to hear rebuke—he is unteachable. The son who has got to scorn the character and counsels of a worthy father, has reached the last degree of depravity, and passed beyond the pale of parental instruction :

> " The sport of ridicule and of detraction
> Turns every virtue to its bordering fault,
> And never gives to Truth and Merit that
> Which simpleness and true desert should purchase."
> SHAKESPEARE

Proverbs 13:2-3

Man Speaking

"A man shall eat good by the fruit of *his* mouth: but the soul of the transgressors *shall eat* violence. He that keepeth his mouth keepeth his life: *but* he that openeth wide his lips shall have destruction."

HERE we have several kinds of speech:

THE SELF-PROFITING AND SELF-RUINOUS IN SPEECH.—
We have here, First: *The self-profiting in speech.* "A man shall eat good by the fruit of his mouth." The speech of a good man which is enlightened, truthful, pure, generous, is of service to *himself* in many ways. By it he promotes the development of his own spiritual being, he gratifies his own moral nature, and produces in hearers results which are delightful to his own observation; thus "he eats good by the fruit of his mouth." Here we have, Secondly: *The self-ruinous in speech.* "The soul of the transgressors shall eat violence." The corrupt speech of the ungodly is a violence to reason, conscience, social propriety. The sinful tongue of the transgressor, of all violent weapons, inflicts the most violent injuries on his own nature. We have here also:—

THE SELF-CONTROLLED AND THE SELF-RECKLESS IN SPEECH.—First: Controlled speech may *be useful.* "He that keepeth his mouth, keepeth his life." The tongue is a member that requires controlling. Passion and impulse are constantly stimulating it to action. Hence the importance of its being properly "bridled;" held firmly by the reins of reason. Secondly: Reckless speech may *be dangerous.* "He that openeth wide his lips shall have destruction." Who can tell the evils that a lawless tongue has done the world? One spark from it has often kindled conflagrations in families, churches, and nations. "If any man among you seemeth to be religious, and bridleth not his tongue, but deceiveth his own heart, this man's religion is vain."* "Give not thy tongue," says Quarles, "too

* James iii. 8, 9.

great a liberty, lest it take thee prisoner. A word unspoken is, like the sword in the scabbard, thine; if vented, thy sword is in another's hand. If thou desire to be held wise, be so wise as to hold thy tongue." " Set a watch, O Lord, before my mouth; keep the door of my lips !"

Proverbs 13:4

Soul Craving

"The soul of the sluggard desireth, and *hath* nothing: but the soul of the diligent shall be made fat.".

These words suggest—

THAT SOUL CRAVING IS COMMON TO ALL.—Both the soul of the sluggard and the diligent "desire." Souls have a hunger as well as bodies, and the hunger of the soul is a much more serious thing. You may see physical hunger depicted in the wretched looks of those who crowd the alleys of St. Giles', and you may see the hunger of souls depicted on the faces of those that roll in their chariots of opulence through Rotten-row. What is the *ennui* that makes miserable the rich, but the unsatisfied hunger of the soul? First: *The hunger of the soul as well as the hunger of the body implies the existence of food somewhere.* It is natural to infer from the benevolence of the Creator that wherever hunger exists in any creature there is a provision for its gratification. Observation and science show that it is so. The God of infinite bountyhood has, in his spiritual kingdom, provided for all the cravings of the human heart. Secondly: *The unsatisfied hunger of the soul as well as the body is painful and ruinous.* Nothing is more distressing and destroying than unappeased animal hunger; it tortures the system and breaks it up. It is more so in the case of souls. " My heart and my flesh crieth out for the living God." The unsatisfying of that cry is hell.

SOUL CRAVING CAN BE ALLAYED ONLY BY LABOUR.—"The soul of the sluggard desireth, and hath nothing, but the soul of the diligent shall be made fat." Charity, accident, or fortune may allay the physical hunger of the man, may make *fat* even the sluggard's body; but *personal* labour, diligent effort, is essential to allay the hunger of the soul. Men must labour before they can get the soul's true bread. There must be the sowing, the culturing, the reaping, and the threshing by the *individual* man, in order to get hold of that bread which can make "*fat*" the soul. Spiritually, I cannot live on the produce of other men, and the law holds absolute that he "who does not work shall not eat."

Proverbs 13:5-6

Moral Truthfulness

" A righteous *man* hateth lying : but a wicked *man* is loathsome, and cometh to shame. Righteousness keepeth *him that is* upright in the way : but wickedness overthroweth the sinner."

MORAL TRUTHFULNESS IS AN INSTINCT TO THE RIGHTEOUS.—"A righteous man *hateth* lying." A soul that has been made right in relation to the laws of its own spiritual being, to the universe, and to God, has an instinctive repugnance to falsehood. A right-hearted man cannot be false in speech or life. " He *hates* lying." All tricks in business, all shams in society, all pretences in religion, are to him revolting. He stands for reality, will die rather than desert or disguise fact.

" There is no terror, Cassius, in your threats ;
For I am armed so strong in honesty
That they pass by me as the idle wind
Which I respect not."—SHAKESPEARE

The prayer of his soul is, "Remove from me the way of lying: and grant me thy law graciously."*

MORAL TRUTHFULNESS IS A SAFEGUARD AGAINST EVIL.—The evils specified in these two verses in connection with the wicked must be regarded as kept off from the righteous by his moral truthfulness. This, indeed, seems implied. What are the evils here implied as connected with falsehood? First: *Loathsomeness*. A wicked man is loathsome." A liar is an unlovely and an unloveable object; he is detestable; he attracts none; he repels all. Secondly: *Shame*. He "cometh to shame." A liar either in lip, or life, or both, must come to shame. A rigorous destiny will strip off his mask, and leave him exposed, a hideous hypocrite, to the scorn of men and angels. Thirdly: *Destruction*. "Wickedness overthroweth the sinner." Inevitable destruction is the doom of the false. They have built their houses on the sand of fiction, and the storms of reality will lay them in ruins.

From all these evils, moral truthfulness guards the righteous. His truthfulness guards him against the loathsome, the disgraceful, and the ruinous:

"An honest man's the noblest work of God."—POPE

Proverbs 13:7-8

Poverty and Wealth

"There is that maketh himself rich, yet *hath* nothing: *there is* that maketh himself poor, yet *hath* great riches. The ransom of a man's life *are* his riches: but the poor heareth not rebuke."

THE seventh verse bears a resemblance to the twenty-fourth of the eleventh chapter.—"There is that scattereth and yet increaseth, and there is that withholdeth more than is meet, but it tendeth to poverty." But the meaning is not

* Psalm cxix. 29.

identical. If we are to attach to the words rich and poor a spiritual rather than a literal meaning, the seventh verse would express an important fact, viz., that there is a principle of action which aims at results the opposite of what it attains. Selfishness aims at personal wealth and greatness, but instead of making a man rich, it leaves him with nothing: he works out his ruin by the principle which urges him to work for his happiness. Whereas the principle of benevolence works in the opposite way—whilst it sinks a man's own personal interest so that he becomes poor, he reaches the true riches. And this illustrates Christ's words: "He that seeketh his life shall lose it."

But I take the verses as presenting two subjects of thought:

The MISREPRESENTATION of poverty and riches.—"There is that maketh himself rich, and yet hath nothing; there is that maketh himself poor, yet hath great riches." These characters abound in modern society. There are poor men who profess to be very wealthy, and they often do so not merely from vanity but from greed also. In business they hire large warehouses, embark in extensive speculations, occupy mansions as their homes, and live in a magnificent style in order to create a false credit. Paupers put on the costume of princes, in order to swindle on a gigantic scale; sometimes they succeed, and by a pretence of large capital obtain the real one, and build up the real one—always at the expense of others. But often, on the other hand, the sparkling bubble bursts, the dazzling meteor sweeps into midnight. These characters abound in modern England, they crowd our scenes of merchandise, they create panics, they are a curse to the country. Then, also, we have amongst us a different class, men who appear to be very poor, but who are, nevertheless, very rich. These are, if not so injurious, yet as contemptible as the others; they are the wretched misers; men who are pinching themselves and families, and clutching from others, in order to gratify their wretched greed of pelf.

The POWER of poverty and riches.—"The ransom of a

man's life are his riches; but the poor man heareth not rebuke." There is a kind of protection in both. "The verse," says an able expositor, "has been understood in different ways. The import of it has been given thus :— 'a rich man, when he fears any evil from his enemies, can divert it by a sum of money; but the poor man, when he is threatened, dares not stay, but runs away.' He does not stand to defend or buy himself off, but the moment he hears rebuke or threatening, aware that he has no resources, he stops not to hear it out, but immediately makes good his escape—takes himself off. I prefer another interpretation, according to which the verse sets forth the comparative benefits of poverty and riches. The rich are objects of envy, exposed to false accusation, robbery, theft, and to the risk of life. It is true that in their circumstances they may, in seasons of public calamity, redeem their lives by a ransom from their abundant store. But the poor are still better off. They are not exposed to danger; they are not envied; they are not looked at askance, with 'jealous leer malign,' with the evil eye of covetousness; nor are they molested with the harassing disquietudes arising from such causes. Who thinks of envying, or persecuting, or defrauding, or taking the life of the man who has nothing? Who ever thinks of robbing or murdering a beggar? He is everywhere safe and free from molestation from whom there is nothing to be had. Poverty, then, is not without its advantages. They are, to be sure, of a negative kind, and not likely to make men give the preference to poverty; nor do I mention them because it should, or that it may. All that is meant is, that such considerations should contribute to reconcile the poor to their providential lot."

Mundane wealth and mundane poverty are alike transient; neither can deliver from death, neither can survive it. The wealth essential to us all, is that of moral goodness; the poverty we should aspire to, is that of a lowly heart. "Blessed are the poor in spirit."

Proverbs 13:9

The Light of Souls

"The light of the righteous rejoiceth: but the lamp of the wicked shall be put out."

"Light," if not essential to life, is essential to its well-being. Life without light, could it be, would be cold, chaotic, wretched. There are different kinds of light even in the material world—some feeble, flickering, transient; others as the lights of heaven, strong, steady, permanent. There are different moral lights—the lights of soul. The text leads us to consider two:

The joyous light of soul.—"The light of the righteous rejoiceth." In what does the light of the soul consist? There are at least three elements—faith, hope, love. The first fills the soul with the light of ideas; the second with the light of a bright future; the third, with the light of happy affections. In all souls on earth these three exist. There is a faith in all, a hope in all, a love in all. Extinguish these in any soul, and there is the blackness of darkness for ever. The righteous have these as *divine* impartations, as beams from "the Father of lights," and in their radiance they live, walk, and rejoice. They rejoice in their *faith*. Their faith connects them with the Everlasting Sun. They rejoice in their hope. Their hope bears them into the regions of the blest. They rejoice in their love. Their love fixes their enrapturing gaze on Him in Whose presence there is fulness of joy.

The transient light of soul.—"The lamp of the wicked shall be put out." It is implied that the light of the righteous is *permanent*. And so it is. It is inextinguishable. "It shines brighter and brighter, e'en unto the perfect day." Not so the light of the wicked. Their light, too, is in their faith, their hope, their love. But their faith is in the false, and it must give way. The temple of their hope is built on sand, and the storm of destiny will destroy it. Their love is on corrupt things, and all that is corrupt must be burnt by the all-consuming fire of eternal justice. Thus the lamp of the wicked must be put out. The light of the righteous is an inextinguishable sun—that of the wicked a mere flickering "lamp;" the breath of destiny will put it out. "How oft is the candle of the wicked put out." To live in a world without a sun, were it possible, would be wretched existence—such a world as Byron describes:

> " The bright sun was extinguished, and the stars
> Did wander darkening in the eternal space,
> Rayless and pathless; and the icy earth
> Swung blind and blackening in the moonless air."

But to live without faith, hope, charity, is infinitely more calamitous.

Proverbs 13:10

Pride

" Only by pride cometh contention: but with the well advised *is* wisdom."

PRIDE is an exaggerated estimate of our own superiority, leading often to an insolent exultation. "There is no such thing," says Fuller, "as proper pride, a reasonable and judicious estimate of one's character has nothing to do with it." From the text we learn—

THAT PRIDE GENERATES DISCORDS.—" Only by pride cometh contention." "Pride," says Collier, "is so unsociable a vice, and does all things with so ill a grace, that there is no closing with it. A proud man will be sure to challenge more than belongs to him. You must expect him stiff in conversation, fulsome in commending himself, and bitter in his reproofs." And Colton says, "Pride either finds a desert or makes one; submission cannot tame its ferocity, nor satisfy or fill its voracity, and it requires very costly food—its keeper's happiness." Being in society essentially *exacting, insolent, heartless, detracting*, it is ever generating "contention." "No wise man," says Taylor, "ever lost anything by cession; but he receives the hostility of violent persons into his embraces like a stone into a lap of wool: it rests and sets down softly and innocently. But a stone falling upon a stone makes a collision, and extracts fire, and finds no rest; and just so are two proud persons despised by each other; contemned by all; living in perpetual dissonances; always fighting against affronts, jealous of every person, disturbed by every accident—a perpetual storm within, and daily hissings from without."

THAT PRIDE REJECTS COUNSELS.—This is implied in the last clause rather than expressed. "But with the well advised is wisdom." The proud man is too great to take the counsel of any. "Pride," says Gurnell, "takes for its motto great *I*, and little *you*." Who can teach him? Truly humility becomes us all. "A humble saint," says Secker, "looks most like a citizen of heaven. 'Whosoever will be chief among you, let him be your servant.' He is the most *lovely* professor who is the most *lowly* professor. As incense smells the sweetest when it is beaten the smallest, so saints look fairest when they lie lowest. Arrogance in the soul resembles the spleen in the body, which grows most while other parts are decaying. God will not suffer such a weed to grow in His garden without taking some course to root it up. A believer is like a vessel cast into the sea: the more it fills the more it sinks."

> " Pride (of all others, the most dangerous fault)
> Proceeds from want of sense, or want of thought.
> The men who labour and digest things most,
> Will be much apter to despond than boast;
> For if your author be profoundly good,
> 'Twill cost you dear before he's understood."—POPE

Proverbs 13:11

Worldly Wealth

"Wealth *gotten* by vanity shall be diminished: but he that gathereth by labour shall increase."

THIS verse implies three things—

That worldly wealth IS A GOOD THING.—The universal feeling of man shows this—all men strive after it. The services it can render show this. Man's physical comforts, intellectual opportunities, social resources, and the progress of his religious institutions greatly depend upon this. The Word of God shows this. "Money," says Solomon, "answers all things." The Bible does not despise wealth. It legislates for its employment and denounces its abuse. We infer—

That worldly wealth may be obtained IN DIFFERENT WAYS.—There are two ways referred to in the text. *The way of vanity.* "Wealth gotten by vanity." The word "vanity" may represent all those tricks of trade, reckless speculations, and idle gambling, by which large fortunes are often *easily* gained. Within our own circle of acquaintance, there are not a few who have become millionaires by guilty hits.

Secondly: *The way of labour.* "He that gathereth by labour." Honest, industrious, frugal labour, is the legitimate way to wealth. Honest industry is God's road to fortune. We infer—

That the decrease or increase of worldly wealth IS DETERMINED BY THE METHOD IN WHICH IT HAS BEEN OBTAINED.—" The wealth gotten by vanity shall be diminished: but he that gathereth by labour shall increase." Two facts in human nature will illustrate this principle. First: *What man does not highly value he is likely to squander.*

That which we hold cheaply we are not cautious in guarding or tenacious in holding. Secondly: *What comes to him without labour he is not likely highly to appreciate.* We generally value a thing in proportion to the difficulty in getting it. The man who has toiled hard for what he has got, will take care of it; whereas he who has got it easily by a hit or by a trick, treats it with less caution, and is more likely to squander it away. Thus the text announces a law in human experience: "Wealth gotten by vanity shall be diminished: but he that gathereth by labour shall increase."

Brothers, whilst we would not have you to disparage worldly wealth, we would not have you put it in its wrong place. Use it as the instrument of action, not as the representative of greatness or the source of happiness.

> " To purchase heaven, has gold the power?
> Can gold remove the mortal hour?
> In life, can love be bought with gold?
> Are Friendship's pleasures to be sold?
> No; all that's worth a wish, a thought,
> Fair Virtue gives, unbribed, unbought.
> Cease, then, on trash thy hopes to bind;
> Let nobler views engage thy mind."—JOHNSON

Proverbs 13:12

Hope Deferred

"Hope deferred maketh the heart sick: but *when* the desire cometh, *it is a* tree of life."

HOPE is a complex state of mind—desire and expectation are its constituents. We define it as an expectant desire. It implies the existence of a future good, and a belief in the possibility of obtaining it. The text leads us to make three remarks concerning it.

THAT MAN'S OBJECT OF HOPE IS OFTEN LONG DELAYED. —"Hope deferred." The future good which men hope for they seldom get at once. Long years of struggle often intervene. It looms a far distant thing before their vision. There is kindness in this arrangement, although we may sometimes fail to see it. First: *It serves to stimulate effort.* It is the goal before the eye of the racer, keeping every muscle on the stretch. Secondly: *It serves to culture patience.* We have need of patience. If what we hope for came at once, was not "deferred," not a tithe of our manhood would be brought out.

THAT THE DELAY IS GENERALLY VERY TRYING.—"It maketh the heart sick." It is trying to the *strength*, to the *temper*, and to the *religion* of man. Still, those "sick" men will not give up the hope. "Hope," says Diogenes, "is the last thing that dies in man." Pandora's fabled box contained all the miseries of mankind, and when her husband took off its lid, all rushed away, but hope remained at the bottom. Ay, hope sticks to the last. However sick at heart, we hold it still.

> " The wretch condemned with life to part,
>   Still, still on hope relies;
> And every pang that rends the heart
>   Bids expectation rise.
> Hope, like the glimmering taper's light,
>   Adorns and cheers the way,
> And still, the darker grows the night,
>   Emits a brighter ray."

THAT THE TRIAL OF THE DELAY IS FULLY COMPENSATED IN ITS REALIZATION.—"When the desire cometh, it is a tree of life." The longer and more anxiously you wait and toil for a good, the higher the enjoyment when it is grasped. Hence the delight of Simeon, who waited for the consolation of Israel, when he clasped the infant Jesus in his arms, and said, "Now lettest thou thy servant depart in peace." A realized divine hope is, indeed, "a tree of life," and especially so when realized in the pure heavens of God. Hope in fruition is the Eden of the soul.

> "Oh! how blest,
> To look from this dark prison to that shrine,
> To inhale one breath of Paradise divine;
> And enter into that eternal rest
> Which waits the sons of God."—BOWRING

Proverbs 13:13

The Word

"Whoso despiseth the word shall be destroyed: but he that feareth the commandment shall be rewarded."

THE world abounds with words. Oral ones load the air, and written ones crowd our libraries. Some human words are unspeakably more valuable than others. The word that expresses the noblest heart, the strongest intellect, the loftiest genius, the highest intelligence, is the best human word on earth. A human word is at once the mind's mirror, and the mind's weapon. In it the soul of the speaker is seen, and by it the soul of the speaker wins its bloodless victories over others. But there is one word on earth incomparably and infinitely above all others. It is emphatically *the* "Word"—the Word of God. The text teaches us two things concerning this Word.

This word despised IS RUIN.—"Whoso despiseth the word shall be destroyed." Who is the despiser of this word? *The scorner, the rejector, the unbeliever, the neglector, the trifler.* Why is ruin involved in despising it? First: Because he who despises, *rejects the only instrument of soul-salvation.* The Gospel is the Word of salvation. "Unto you is the word of this salvation sent." It is the only word that can save, the only balm for the diseased, the only quickening power for the dead. Second: Because he who despises it *brings on his nature the condemnation of Heaven.* Most tremendous guilt is contracted in despising this word. "See that ye refuse not him that speaketh, for if they escaped not," &c.*

This word reverenced IS BLESSEDNESS. — "He that feareth the commandment shall be rewarded." The word is a "commandment," it is an authoritative utterance, and to fear it, in a Scriptural sense, is to have a proper practical regard for it. First: Such a man is "rewarded" *in its*

* Heb. xii. 25.

blessed influences upon his own soul. It enlightens, purifies, cheers, ennobles. Second : Such a man is "rewarded" *with the approbation of Heaven.* "Unto that man will I look, who is of a broken heart, and contrite spirit, and trembleth at my word." What a wonderful thing is *the* Word ! Man's character and destiny are determined by his conduct towards it. How few in this age treat this Word as it ought to be treated ! In proportion to its aboundings men seem to despise it. There was a time, in Edward I.'s reign, when one volume cost £37, to gain which, a labouring man would have to work fifteen long years.

Proverbs 13:14

The Law of the Good

" The law of the wise *is* a fountain of life, to depart from the snares of death."

THIS proverb teaches two things :—That—

THE GOOD ARE RULED BY "LAW."—" The law of the wise." What is law ? There are many definitions ; many most unphilosophic, some most conflicting. The clearest and most general idea I have of it is—*rule of motion.* In this sense all things are under law, for all things are in motion. The material universe is in motion, and there is the law that regulates it. The spiritual universe is in motion, and law presides over it. "Of law," says Hooker, "there can be no less acknowledged, than that her seat is the bosom of God, her voice the harmony of the world. All things do her homage, the very least as feeling her care, and the greatest as not exempted from her power ; both angels and men, and creatures of what condition soever, though each in different sort and manner, yet all with uniform consent, admiring her as the mother of their peace and joy." But what is the law of the good —that which rules them in all their activities ? *Supreme love to the supremely good.* It is not a written commandment, but an all-pervading, inspiring spirit, called in Scripture, "the royal law," the "law of liberty," the "law of the Spirit."

This proverb teaches also that—

The "law" that rules the good is BENEFICENT.— "The law of the wise is a fountain of life, to depart from the snares of death." First: *This law delivers from death.* The word "death" here *must not* be regarded as the separation of body from soul, but as the separation of the soul from God. This is the awfullest death, and supreme love to God is a guarantee against this. Secondly: *This law secures an abundance of life.* "The law of the wise is a fountain of life;" a fountain gives an idea of *activity, plenitude, perennialness.* The law of the good is happiness. The happiness of the true soul is not something then and yonder, but it is something in the law that controls him. In the midst of his privations and dangers, John Howard, England's illustrious philanthropist, wrote from Riga these words, "I hope I have sources of enjoyment that depend not on the particular spot I inhabit. A rightly cultivated mind, under the power of religion, and the exercise of beneficent dispositions, affords a ground of satisfaction little affected by *heres* and *theres.*"

> "If solid happiness we prize,
> Within our breast this jewel lies;
> The world has nothing to bestow,—
> From our own selves our joy must flow."

Proverbs 13:15a

A Sound Intellect

"Good understanding giveth favour."

OBSERVE here two things:

THE NATURE OF A SOUND INTELLECT.—What is a "good understanding?" A good understanding must include four things. First: *Enlightenment.* The soul "without knowledge is not good." Some understandings are as dark as midnight; others are illumined by false lights; others are partially lighted by the true. A good understanding is that which is well informed, not merely in general knowledge, but in the science of duty and of God. Secondly: *Impartiality.* A good intellect forms its conclusions and pronounces its decisions according to the merits of the question, regardless of the interest of self, or the frowns or the favours of others. It holds the balance of thought with a steady hand. Thirdly: *Religiousness.* By this I mean that it must be inspired with a deep sense of its allegiance to heaven. No intellect can be healthy and vigorous that does not live and labour in the atmosphere of devotion. Fourthly: *Practicalness.* It is strong and bold enough to carry all its decisions into actual life. " A good understanding have all they that *do* his commandments."* If these elements make up a sound intellect, it follows that a good understanding is tantamount to practical godliness. Observe here, also,—

THE USEFULNESS OF A SOUND INTELLECT.—" Good understanding giveth favour." The greatest benefactor is the man of a " good understanding ; " a man whose mind is well enlightened; impartial, religious, and practical. The thoughts of such are the seeds of the world's best institutions, and most useful arts and inventions. Such a man is the most useful in the family, in the neighbourhood, in the market, in the press, in the senate, in the pulpit, and everywhere. Such a man "giveth favour." His ideas break the clouds of human ignorance, and quicken the faculties of dormant souls. First: *No favours so valuable as a mental "favour."* He who really helps the mind to think with accuracy, freedom, and force, to love with purity, and to hope with reason, helps the man in the entirety of his being, and for ever. Secondly: *No one can confer a mental "favour" who has not a good understanding.* An ignorant man has no favour to bestow on souls.

" Ignorance is the curse of God;
Knowledge the wing with which we fly to heaven."—SHAKESPEARE

Let us, therefore, cultivate a sound intellect, enlightened,

* Psalm cxi. 10.

impartial, religious, and practical, that we may give to our race the highest favours. "I make not my head a grave," says Sir T. Browne, in his quaint way, "but a treasury of knowledge; I intend no monopoly, but a community in learning; I study not for my own sake only, but for theirs that study not for themselves; I envy no man that knows more than myself, but pity them that know less. I instruct no man as an exercise of my knowledge, or with an intent rather to nourish and keep it alive in mine own head, than beget and propagate it in his; and, in the midst of all my endeavours, there is but one thought that dejects me—that my acquired parts must perish with myself, nor can be legacied among my honoured friends."

Proverbs 13:15b

The Way of Transgressors

"But the way of transgressors *is* hard."

NOTICE the two facts here implied:

The transgressor has A "WAY."—How shall the way of a transgressor be described? There are three general features that characterize it. First: *Practical atheism.* From the beginning to the end of the way the traveller does not practically recognise the Supreme; He is not a power in the thoughts of any of the pilgrims. None of them like to retain Him in their thoughts. Secondly: *Practical materialism.* The things that are seen and temporal, are the great dominant and influential powers. None of the travellers have ears to hear or eyes to see the wonders of the spiritual universe. Thirdly: *Practical selfishness.* To every walker on the "way" self is everything; the centre and circumference of life. The interests of others, the claims of God Himself, are all subordinate to self-gratification and aggrandisement. Such is "the way of transgressors." Truly a broad way it is, for the vast majority of the world are marching on it.

The other fact here is that—

The way of the transgressor is "HARD." Though a popular way, a way which millions go, it is anything but easy. First: *It is a "hard" way in the sense of difficulty.* Every step is a "kicking against the pricks." All expect flowers on the path as they proceed, but the thorns thicken and the cutting ruggedness increases. Voltaire said, "I begin to fancy myself in the most deplorable condition, environed by deepest darkness on every side. I wish I had never been born." Colonel Gardiner, before his conversion, envied the existence of a dog. The transgressor's own *conscience*, the *moral sense* of society, the *institutions* of nature, the *whole current* of the Divine government, are against him. He has to struggle hard to make way. Men reach hell with bleeding feet and exhausted natures. Secondly: *It is "hard" in the sense of results.* The happiness aimed at is never got. There is ever miserable dissatisfaction, and moral agony. "The way of peace they know not." They are like the troubled sea, its waters cast out mire and dirt. "There is no peace, saith my God, for the wicked." The "wages of sin is death."

> " In the corrupted currents of this world
> Offence's gilded hand may shove by justice;
> And in worst times the wretched prize itself
> Buys out the law. But 'tis not so above:
> There is no shuffling: there the action lies
> In its true nature; and we ourselves compelled,
> E'en to the teeth and forehead of our faults,
> To give in evidence."—SHAKESPEARE

Proverbs 13:16

The Wise and the Foolish

"Every prudent *man* dealeth with knowledge: but the fool layeth open *his* folly."

OBSERVE the two opposite characters:

THE WISE MAN.—"He dealeth with knowledge." This implies—First: *That he has knowledge.* Knowledge is essential to a wise man. All true knowledge has its foundation in God. It is a tree with many and varied branches, as high and as broad as the universe, but God is the root and the sap, the strength and the beauty of the whole. There is no knowledge that includes Him not. It implies, secondly: *That a wise man treats his knowledge wisely.* " He dealeth with knowledge." Whilst knowledge is essential to wisdom, it is not wisdom. A man may have a great deal of knowledge and no wisdom. Wisdom consists in its right application. The wise man so deals with his knowledge as to culture his own nature and promote the real progress of his race. " Perfect freedom," says Plato, " hath four parts—viz., wisdom, the principle of doing things aright; justice, the principle of doing things equally in public and private; fortitude, the principle of not flying danger, but meeting it; and temperance, the principle of subduing desires and living moderately." " Knowledge," says Dwight, " is never of very serious use to man until it has become part of his customary course of thinking. The knowledge which barely passes through the mind resembles that which is gained of a country by a traveller, who is whirled through it in a stage; or by a bird flitting over it, in his passage to another." Here is also—

THE FOOLISH MAN.—"A fool layeth open his folly." Foolish men show their folly in at least two ways. First: *by talking about things of which they know little or nothing.* There are two notable facts in human nature. The more ignorant a man is, the more garrulous. Empty-minded persons are generally talkative. The law seems to be, the less thought the more talk. The less one knows of a subject, the more copiously he can speak about it. The very fluent preachers are those who have never thought sufficiently on theological subjects to reach their difficulties. The thinker, discerning difficulties in every turn, moves cautiously, reverently, and even with hesitation. "The fool layeth open his folly." Secondly, *by attempting things which they are incapable of achieving.* The foolish man knows not his aptitudes and inaptitudes. Hence he is seen everywhere, striving to be what he never can; to do that which he never can accomplish. He attempts to build a tower without counting the cost. "Thus he layeth open his folly."

Proverbs 13:17

Human Missions and Their Discharge

> "A wicked messenger falleth into mischief: but a faithful ambassador *is* health."

EVERY man has a *message* in life; all have their mission. There are messages from *men*. Few in civilized society could be found who are not entrusted with some message, some commission from their fellow-men. Some as servants, teachers, merchants, rulers. There are messages from *God*. Every man is sent into the world with certain duties to fulfil. These duties constitute his mission in life. The proverb teaches—

THAT THERE IS A RIGHT AND A WRONG DISCHARGE OF THIS MESSAGE.—There is a "wicked messenger" and a "faithful ambassador." The wrong and the right way will be indicated by the question, what is the right discharge of our mission? He only discharges the various messages of life rightly who does it—First: *Conscientiously*. He who acts without a conscience acts beneath his nature. He who acts against his conscience acts against his nature. He alone acts worthy of his nature who acts according to the dictates of his conscience. A man should throw conscience into every act. Every human deed should flash with the supernal light of conscience. Secondly: *Intelligently*. A man should understand the nature of the grounds of his message. Without this, though he acts conscientiously, he acts not rightly. Some of the greatest crimes ever wrought on our earth have been perpetrated conscientiously. Paul was conscientious in his ruthless persecutions. So perhaps were some of the Jews in putting to death the Son of God.

Thirdly: *Religiously.* All must be done with a supreme regard to that God whose we are, and whom we are bound to serve. No message, even that of the humblest servant, is discharged rightly, if not discharged with a due regard to the claims of the Great Master. "Whatsoever you do, in deed or word, do all to the glory of God." The proverb teaches—

THAT EVIL OR GOOD INEVITABLY RESULTS FROM THE MANNER IN WHICH THE MESSAGES ARE TREATED.—"A wicked messenger falleth into mischief, but a faithful ambassador is health." The message of a wicked messenger, perhaps, may be a wrong message, a message of falsehood and injustice; or it may be right, and he may deliver it unfaithfully. In either case *mischief* comes. Mischief to the man himself—mischief to society. He who speaks a wrong thing, and he who speaks a right thing wrongly, is equally a wicked messenger. The world abounds with such, and they produce incalculable mischief. Mischief springs from a wrong act as death from poison. On the other hand, the "faithful ambassador is health"—health to himself, his own conscience approves of it; and health to those whom he represents, their wishes are gratified their interests are served; and he is "health" to those to whom he is sent. At last he will hear the Divine words of approbation addressed to him, "Well done, good and faithful servant, enter into the joy of thy Lord."

Proverbs 13:18

The Incorrigible and the Docile

"Poverty and shame *shall be* to him that refuseth instruction: but he that regardeth reproof shall be honoured."

Two subjects are here to be noted:

THE DOOM OF THE INCORRIGIBLE.—The incorrigible is one who habitually "refuseth instruction." There are men, who, either from stolidity of nature, or the force of prejudice, or the power of habit, are uninstructable. Their natures are closed against new light, they move in a rut from which no force can move them. To such, the text tells us, "poverty and shame" shall come. These two things are not necessarily associated. Poverty that springs from necessity is a misfortune, not a crime, and therefore no cause for shame. Poverty that springs from sacrifice in the cause of duty and philanthropy, is a virtue rather than a vice, and therefore has no connection with shame. A poverty, however, brought on by incorrigibility of character, is associated evermore with shame. It is a disgraceful poverty. That such shameful poverty springs from such conduct, is manifest in the ordinary life of men. We see it—First: In *secular* matters. The farmer, the tradesman, the professional man who doggedly adhere to their own notions, and will not receive the instruction which modern science affords, are often so unable to compete with those who are open to every new and improved theory and method of action, that they come to a dead failure in their undertakings, and meet with poverty and shame. We see it—Secondly: In *intellectual* matters. Those who neglect the culture of their minds from youth up, and will not receive instruction, have such an impoverished mind that it is associated with shame. How often are their cheeks mantled with abashment, when they find themselves utterly incapable to enter into the enlightened conversation of the intelligent circles into which they are sometimes introduced. We see it—Thirdly: In *moral* matters. He who neglects the spiritual culture of his nature has a poverty of soul distressing to contemplate. He is poor and wretched. He feeds on husks. What worse doom can there be than shameful destitution in secular, mental, and moral things? Shame is the worst of the furies:

> " Shame urges on behind; unpitying shame,
> The worst of furies, whose fell aspect frights
> Each tender feeling from the human breast."—THOMSON

The other subject to be noted is—

THE DESTINY OF THE TEACHABLE.—" He that regardeth

reproof shall be honoured." Honour is a popular word, but has many and often diverse meanings :

> " Ask the proud peer what's honour ? he displays
> A purchased patent or the herald's blaze !
> Or if the royal smile his hopes have blest,
> Points to the glittering glory on his breast.
> Yet if beneath no real virtue reign,
> On the gay coat the star is but a stain;
> For I could whisper in his lordship's ear,
> Worth only beams true radiance on the star."—WHITEHEAD

The truly docile man, whose faculties are ever in search of truth, and who makes Christ his great Rabbi, will assuredly be honoured. *His own soul* will honour him. He will have the approbation of his own conscience. *Society* will honour him. So long as mind is mind, society must ever honour those who are the recipients of the true and the divine. *God* will honour him. He smiles on the genuine inquirer, the real truth-seeker. He takes such under His guardianship, and leads them on into higher and still higher fields of thought. There is no honour but in goodness :

> " Howe'er it be, it seems to me
> 'Tis only noble to be good ;
> Kind hearts are more than coronets,
> And simple faith than Norman blood."—TENNYSON

Proverbs 13:19

Soul Pleasure and Soul Pain

"The desire accomplished is sweet to the soul : but *it is* abomination to fools to depart from evil."

THESE words lead us to the contemplation of two subjects :

SOUL PLEASURE.—What is it ? A "*desire accomplished.*" Desire is the spring power of our activities. Locke defines it " as the uneasiness which a man feels within him on the absence of anything whose present enjoyment carries the delight with it." The desires of the soul, which are very varied, are very significant of our destiny. " Our desires," says Goethe, " are the presentiments of the faculties which lie within us, the precursors of those things which we are capable of performing. That which we would be and that which we desire present themselves to our imagination, about us and in the future. We prove our aspiration after an object which we already secretly possess. It is thus that an intense anticipation transforms a real possibility into an imaginary reality. When such a tendency is decided in us, at each stage of our development a portion of our primitive desire accomplishes itself under favourable circumstances by direct means, and in unfavourable circumstances by some more circuitous route, from which, however, we never fail to reach the straight road again." Indeed, pleasure consists in the gratification of desires. The *quality* and *permanency* of the pleasure must ever depend on the object of the desire. If the thing desired is immoral, its attainment may be "sweet to the soul" for a little while, but afterwards it will become bitter as wormwood and gall. The triumph of truth, the progress of virtue, the diffusion of happiness, the honour of God, these are objects of desire that will give a holy and everlasting "sweetness" to the soul. God Himself should be the grand object of desire. "As for me, I will behold Thy face in righteousness. I shall be satisfied when I awake with Thy likeness." "Desire," says John Howe, "is love exercised upon a good which we behold at a distance and are reaching at. Delight is love solacing itself in a present good. They are as wings and arms of love; those for pursuits, those for embraces. Or the former is love in motion, the latter love in rest; and, as in bodily motion and rest, that is in order to this and is perfected in it." The other subject to be noted is—

SOUL PAIN.—"It is an abomination to fools to depart from evil." Fools are always in connection with evil, men are fools because they are in such an alliance. He who allies himself to evil goes against his own reason and his own immortal interests. There is soul pain *in being connected with evil*. Man was never made to be in such an association; he has yoked himself to that which is eternally antagonistic to his moral intuitions. Conscience is always tormenting the sinner; his nature can never be reconciled to an alliance with it. Notwithstanding this, strange to say, there is soul pain in the *dissolution of that connection.* There is a fierce conflict, a tremendous battle in the effort. "It is abomination to fools to depart." Although the connection is agony, he loathes the separation; so infatuated is he that he hugs his enemy; and when he is driven by moral conviction from it he craves at first a reunion. Like the Jews in the wilderness who yearned for the flesh-pots of Egypt, all exhortations addressed to him to leave evil, cause him to wince and fret and spurn his faithful monitors.

Proverbs 13:20
The Grand Fellowship and Assimilation in Life's Path

"He that walketh with wise *men* shall be wise."

OBSERVE two things:

THE GRAND FELLOWSHIP in life's path.—Though fools crowd the path of life there are many "wise men" here and there. Who are the wise men? Those who aim at the highest end of existence. What is the highest end? Not wealth, pleasure, or fame. These are mere bubbles viewed in the light of the greatness of man's nature, and the vastness of his relationships. The highest end of man, the only worthy end, is eternal perfection of character, spiritual assimilation to God's perfection. Who are the wise men? Those who employ the best means to reach that end. What are the best means to secure this eternal perfection of being? Not external moralities, conventional religions, ritualistic observances. These have been tried over and over again and have failed. The Gospel is *the* power. "Beholding as in a glass the glory of the Lord we are changed." Who are the wise men? Those who devote the best time in the employment of those means. What is the best time? Not to-morrow: it is unwise to trust to-morrow; it may never come. *Now* is that time. Who will say that this is not wisdom? Who will say that he has any claim to be regarded as a wise man whose life includes not these three things? Whatever genius, erudition, skill he may have, if he neglect these things he is a fool. The other thing to be observed is—

THE GLORIOUS ASSIMILATION in life's path.—"Shall be wise." First: There is a transforming power in the *ideas* of the truly wise. The ideas of wise and godly men are the greatest spiritual forces of the world. The ideas of other men, even in their highest aspect, are cold, dim, and dead as the beams of the moon. The ideas of wise men are like the rays of the sun, warm, bright, touching all into life. In the Bible you have these ideas in their mightiest forms. Patriarchs, prophets, apostles, and the Great Son of Man Himself, were their organs. Thank God there are "wise men" who speak with their tongues and their pens, even now, and with these you may walk. Secondly: there is a transforming power in the *sympathies* of the truly wise. Sympathy is a mighty power. Even a touch of it in the dropping tear, the faltering voice, the quivering lip, will often move a soul to its centre. The sympathies of the wise man are deep, spiritual, genuine, Christ-like. They are morally electric. Thirdly: there is a transforming power in the *example* of the truly wise. All moral character is formed on the principle of imitation, hence the moral likeness of the child to the parent, the citizen to his nation. But we imitate only what we love and admire; and the character of the wise man has in it what alone can command the highest love and admiration of the soul. It has moral beauty—the beauty of the Lord.

From this subject we learn that the *choice of companions is the most important step in life.* We are social; we must have companions; these must be either fools or wise, sinners or saints. If we choose fools, we shall be fools; wise, we shall be wise; and they that shall be wise shall shine as the stars. We learn from this subject *that godly literature has an inestimable value.* By godly literature I am far enough from meaning all the books that are called *religious*. Many of the so-called religious books, on account of the feebleness of their conceptions, the sickliness of their sentiments, the exclusiveness of their spirit, the flippancy, the coarseness, the irreverence with which they treat the most momentous subjects, are of all books the most to be contemned and avoided. By godly books, I mean books that treat of the great questions of duty and destiny, not only with the highest ability, but with a spirit of Divine reverence and devotion. We learn from this subject,—that *the Church institution is a most beneficial appointment*. The true Church is an assemblage of "*wise*" men. This is the ideal. Hence it is ordained as the organ of heaven's transforming power: thither the world is to resort to become wise and good. Would that the Institution called the Church were indeed a true Church. But in many cases it is an assemblage of what?—not wise men, but fools.

Proverbs 13:21

Nemesis: Destiny Following Character

"Evil pursueth sinners: but to the righteous good shall be repaid."

THAT retributory justice tracks our footsteps, is a doctrine as old as the race. It grows out of the conscience, and is confirmed by the experience of mankind. The Nemesis of the heathen, which was a mysterious pursuer of character, was only a personification of the doctrine. The subject of the text is, Destiny follows character. Misery grows out of sin, and happiness out of goodness.

THE LAW OF MORAL CAUSATION SHOWS THIS.—Man's character is not the creation of a day or an hour, it is the result of past actions. When no change has taken place, like that of regeneration, the man's character to-day is the result of the whole of his past life, and will be, without such a renovation, the cause of the whole of his future. So that if the character is corrupt, misery must come, and the reverse. "Whatsoever a man soweth, that shall he also reap. He that soweth to the flesh shall reap corruption. He that soweth to the spirit shall reap everlasting life." Character draws destiny after it by an almighty magnetism. It is a fruitful tree, it never ceases bearing, every branch is clustered, but the fruit is either misery or happiness, according to its own vital sap.

THE CONSTITUTION OF MORAL MIND SHOWS THIS.—Moral mind has at least two faculties: One to *recall* the past. Memory gathers up the fragments of our bygone years, so that nothing is lost. Every event that has impressed us, and every conscious act must be reproduced. The law of memory compels us to re-live our past lives. The other to *feel* the past. The past does not flit before us as shadows on the wall, as images on the glass, making no impression; it falls on conscience, it stirs it into feeling. The soul is compelled to shudder at a wicked past, whilst a virtuous past fills it with a quiet and ineffable delight.

THE TEACHING OF HOLY WRIT SHOWS THIS.—The Bible is full of the doctrine. It assures us that God will render to each man according to his deeds.* Sinner, take care, the avenger of blood is at your heels. You may not hear the footfall, for the "avenging deities are shod with wool." But they never pause, they never tire, they never mistake their victim.

Proverbs 13:22-23

Material Wealth

"A good *man* leaveth an inheritance to his children's children: and the wealth of the sinner *is* laid up for the just. Much food *is in* the tillage of the poor: but there is *that is* destroyed for want of judgment."

MATERIAL wealth is a good thing. Those who have it not desire it, and struggle earnestly after it. Those who have

* Joshua vii. 20—26; Matt. xxxv.; Rom. ii. 6 – 10.

it clutch it as a precious treasure. No wise man will underrate it. Although, like everything else, it is capable of abuse, it has the power of rendering immense service to the cause of truth and humanity. Sanctimonious hypocrites who have it not denounce it, but wise men value it as a sacred trust. The verses before us lead us to consider it in two aspects:

As entailed by the good and alienated by the evil.—Here we have it: *Entailed by the good.* "A good man leaveth an inheritance to his children's children." It is a characteristic of man that he feels an interest in posterity. The good and evil alike feel concern for unborn generations. This is an indication of the vastness of our sympathies, and the greatness of our nature. It is here intimated by Solomon that the good have some *special security* by which their property shall descend to their "children's children." A security better than that of legal "bequests." And truly they have, and what is it? The *probable goodness* of their "children's children." Goodness may, and ought ever, to descend from sire to son. The strongest purpose and the most earnest prayer of a good man is that it should do so. His endeavour is to train up his children in the way that they should go, to leave in their possession a godly character—a sublimer inheritance this than kingdoms. Now, if his children's children inherit goodness, they are sure to hand down their inheritance to posterity intact; it will not be wasted by intemperance, reckless speculation, or idle gambling. Goodness is the safest law of entail. Here we have property: *Alienated by the evil.* "And the wealth of the sinner is laid up for the just." Wickedness, from its very nature, cannot hold property through many generations; the fortunes it inherits must crumble away. My confidence in the righteous government of God and in the ultimate triumphs of Christianity is such, that I regard all the property that wickedness has accumulated, is accumulating, and will accumulate, as "laid up for the just." One day the property of the world will come into the possession of the good. "Though the wicked heap up silver as the dust, and prepare raiment as the clay, he may prepare it, but the just shall put it on, and the innocent shall divide the silver."

The verses before us lead us to consider material wealth—
As GAINED BY INDUSTRY, AND SQUANDERED BY IMPRUDENCE.—*As gained by industry.* "Much food is in the tillage of the poor." Every acre of land is full of potential wealth. Skilled industry can make more of one rood of earth, than some men can make of acres. God has put man's food not merely in the ground, but in the "*tillage.*" This is a beneficent arrangement. It is a spur to industry. It is a help to the development of manly faculties. If the man who gets not his food by "*tillage*" were allowed to starve, it would be a blessing to the world. Here we have wealth: *As squandered by imprudence.* "But there is that is destroyed for want of judgment." It requires more sense, perhaps, to retain and rightly use property, than to get it. I have known pushing and unscrupulous dolts make fortunes and lose them:

> "Riches, like insects, while concealed they lie,
> Wait but for wings, and in their season fly.
> To whom can riches give repute and trust,
> Content or pleasure, but the good and just?
> Judges and Senates have been bought for gold;
> Esteem and love were never to be sold."—POPE

Proverbs 13:24

Parental Discipline

"He that spareth the rod hateth his son: but he that loveth him chasteneth him betimes."

THREE things are implied in this text—

A TENDENCY IN CHILDREN TO GO WRONG.—This tendency is obvious to all. No sooner does the child begin to act as a moral being than he, by his fretfulness, vanity, greed, falseness, indicates the existence of the wrong in him. Whether this tendency is propagated by generation or imparted by social influence, whether it is inbred or imbreathed, is one of the vexed questions of polemic theology. I am disposed to think that the social atmosphere in which the infant is born, in which it receives its first impressions and begins to unfold its faculties, is abundantly sufficient to account for it. In the present domestic atmosphere of the race there float the germs of evil, and who shall say how soon they drop through the eye and ear into the infant soul?

THE DUTY OF PARENTS TO DESTROY THIS TENDENCY.— This is implied by the injunction, to chasten "*betimes.*" First: The wrong tendency is a great evil. It is the springhead of a pestilential river. It is the germ of an upas. It is an incipient fiend. Secondly: The sooner it is destroyed the better. The better for the child, the parent, society, the universe. The longer it continues the deeper it strikes its roots, and the more difficult the eradication. It must be done "*betimes.*" Thirdly: Its destruction is the work of a parent. This is the grand moral mission of a parent, for which God holds him responsible. He cannot delegate it to nurse, teacher, or priest. It is *his* work.

THE NECESSITY OF CHASTISEMENT FOR THIS PURPOSE. —" He that spareth the rod hateth his son." The rod does not necessarily mean the twig, the cane, or the whip; it is used as the representative of that which inflicts *pain*. First: *The necessary chastisement involves the infliction of pain.* It may be *corporeal* pain. There are cases in which the child may be so destitute of the sense of propriety and reason that it could receive no other pain than physical. It may be *mental* pain. The child may be punished by the restriction of his liberty, the denial of his wishes, or the frown of his parents; by the word of reproof, oftentimes in a way far more painful than any corporeal infliction. What is wanted in chastisement is *pain*. There must be pain. A rod of some kind, either material or mental. And the parent who does not inflict pain has not the true love for his child. He " hateth his son." Secondly: *The infliction of pain by love.* The infliction of pain from caprice or angry passions is no chastisement. Evil cannot be expelled by evil. The devil cannot exorcise the devil. The child must see that the pain inflicted gives more pain to the parent than to him. The infliction of pain must be felt as the "strange work" of the parent—a work foreign to his nature. Children have been called rough diamonds. Parents are to polish them, and they must be neither struck unskilfully nor left uncut.

> " The voice of parents is the voice of gods,
> For to their children they are heaven's lieutenants;
> Made fathers, not for common uses merely
> Of procreation (beasts and birds would be
> As noble then as we are), but to steer
> The wanton freight of youth through storms and dangers,
> Which with full sails they bear upon, and straighten
> The mortal line of life they bend so often.
> For these are we made fathers, and for these
> May challenge duty on our children's part.
> Obedience is the sacrifice of angels,
> Whose form you carry."—SHAKESPEARE

Proverbs 13:25

The Satisfaction of the Body Determined by the Condition of the Soul

" The righteous eateth to the satisfying of his soul: but the belly of the wicked shall want."

BODILY satisfaction is an essential element in our happiness so long as we are in this world. The text implies that the satisfaction of the body depends upon the condition of the soul, and this is a great truth, greatly neglected. Its obviousness would come out by considering what bodily satisfaction requires. We observe—

BODILY HEALTH.—No food can *satisfy* a diseased body, a body whose organs and functions are out of order. But the condition of the soul has much to do with physical health. "A sound heart is the light of the flesh."* The anxieties, ill-tempers, recriminations, impure passions of a wicked heart, will soon reduce the body to disease, feebleness, and ruin. On the other hand, a true, virtuous, and happy soul tends to physical health. "A merry heart doeth good like medicine, maketh a cheerful countenance; but a broken spirit drieth the bones." One thought can disorganize a healthy body and do much to restore a diseased one.

BODILY SUPPLIES.—The supplies necessary to satisfy the body should be—First: *Of a right kind.* A body restless with hunger would scarcely be satisfied with confectionery. Now, the condition of the soul has much to do with the *kind* of food. The soul not only modifies our natural appetites but creates artificial ones, and hence supplies provisions for the body which are unnatural and unhealthy. The soul, by its workings on the body's appetites, has brought to the body's table compounds unsatisfying and deleterious too. Secondly: *A right amount.* An insufficient amount, even of right provisions, would leave the body unsatisfied. But the question of sufficiency also depends greatly on the soul. Indolence, extravagance, intemperance, bad management, often so reduce men's material resources that they are left utterly destitute of the necessary food. These thoughts, we think, give an important meaning to the text, "The righteous eateth to the satisfying of his soul: but the belly of the wicked shall want." "Truly then godliness is profitable unto all things." A corrupt soul will evermore have a dissatisfied body.

* See HOMILIST, vol. iv., second series, p. 647.

Proverbs 14:1

Housewifery

"Every wise woman buildeth her house: but the foolish plucketh it down with her hands."

WOMAN, in these days of novel-scribbling and rhyming sentimentalities, is so often paraded in literature that we are loth to write the sacred word. Our own great dramatist has said,—

" 'Tis beauty that doth oft make women proud;
'Tis virtue that doth make them most admired;
'Tis modesty that makes them seem divine!"

The text leads us to consider housewifery; its great power and necessary qualifications.

ITS GREAT POWER.—First: *It can build up.* "Every wise woman buildeth her house." A good wife builds her house *materially*. By her economy, industry, and wise management, she increases its material resources. Wordsworth describes such a housewife:

"She was a woman of stirring life,
Whose heart was in her house. Two wheels she had
Of antique form: this large, for spinning wool:
That small, for flax; and if one wheel had rest,
It was because the other was at work."

A good wife builds up her house *spiritually*. A good wife by her example, her spirit, her admonitions, her reproofs, her prayers, builds up in her children a noble character; she thus rears in her house a very temple of industry, intelligence, and worship. Thus she becomes the queen of a little empire, where beauty, love, virtue, and reason reign. Housewifery, secondly, *can pull down.* "The foolish plucketh it down with her hands." There are women who bring their houses to ruin. By their miserable tempers and degrading habits, they ruin their husbands, their children, they make the home the haunt of fiends.

ITS NECESSARY QUALIFICATION.—What is the necessary qualification for a good housewife?—"*Wisdom.*" "Every wise woman buildeth her house." Wisdom implies two things. First: *Using the right means.* The means she employs to build up her house are not inconsistent with the chaste in love, the true in statement, the honest in effort. Secondly: *Using the right means for a right end.* The end not to pamper appetites, to feed vanity and pride, but to elevate the household, bless society, and honour God. The hope of England and of the world rests on such housewifery. Kind Heaven promote it! In the East humanity makes, through centuries, scarcely one inch of true progress. In the West it moves onward with the strides of a giant. Why this? In the former there is no housewifery, in the latter there is.

Proverbs 14:2

Human Conduct

"He that walketh in his uprightness feareth the Lord: but *he that is* perverse in his ways despiseth him."

MEN DIFFER WIDELY IN THEIR DAILY CONDUCT.—First: Some men walk *uprightly.* Walking uprightly implies moral strength. The man is not bent and crooked by the infirmities of sin or the weight of depravity. He has the thorough step of a man. Conscious rectitude. He does not bow down his head, as if ashamed to look his neighbour in the face. He is as open as the day and as fearless as the sun. Secondly: Some walk *perversely.* "They are perverse in their ways." They are crooked in their purposes, policies, and performances. There is nothing true, honest, noble, in their course, or in their bearing.

MEN REVEAL THEIR HEART TOWARDS GOD IN THEIR DAILY WALK.—" He that walketh in his uprightness *feareth* the Lord; but he that is perverse in his ways *despiseth Him.*" First: *Right conduct springs from a right feeling towards God.* The man that walketh uprightly "feareth the Lord." There is no true morality without religion. Piety is the first principle of all rectitude. Atheism can have nothing binding in its code of laws—nothing virtuous in its conduct. All good living must have respect to the Supreme. Secondly: *Wrong conduct springs from wrong feeling towards God.* "He that is perverse in his ways despiseth Him." The wrong doer has no feeling of respect for God. He ignores him as much as he can. Thus it is that in the daily conduct of men you can see their state towards the Great One. You may know how men feel inwardly toward Him by observing how they deal outwardly with each other.

The generating in human hearts supreme love to God, is the only effective way to promote true morality in men —morality in the family, in the market, in the nation, in the world.

Proverbs 14:3

Speech, a Rod

"In the mouth of the foolish *is* a rod of pride: but the lips of the wise shall preserve them."

SPEECH is one of the distinguishing faculties of man. It is here spoken of as a "rod," it is an instrument of the soul. It is a *communicating* rod. "Its chief object," says Bishop Butler, "is plainly that we may communicate our thoughts to each other, in order to carry on the affairs of the world, for business, and for learning." Through this rod of speech souls flow and reflow into each other. It is a *conquering* rod. By speech a man often achieves his highest conquests,—conquests over the thoughts, passions, purposes of mankiud. The mystic Rod of Moses smote the rock of Horeb, and caused it to send forth refreshing streams; the rod of speech can smite the rock of souls, and make it stream with influences to refresh the mental desert. What wonders the rod of speech has done!

The text contains two things concerning it.

It may be SELF-INJURIOUS OR SELF-ADVANTAGEOUS.— It is said, "the lips of the wise shall preserve them," and the implied antithesis is, that those of the fool will injure them. First: *There is a speech that is self-injurious.* The hasty speech of evil passion, the unchaste speech of sensuality, the lying speech of untruthfulness: all such speech inflicts an injury upon the speaker. It blunts his moral sensibility; it lowers his relf-respect; it degrades his social credit. The rod of speech is often an instrument of spiritual suicide. Secondly: *There is a speech that is self-advantageous.* "The lips of wise men shall preserve them." A chaste, truthful, benevolent, judicious speech is a guardian rod of souls. It preserves the character and the reputation of the speaker.

Its RESULTS upon the speaker, whether self-injurious or otherwise, DEPEND UPON HIS OWN CHARACTER.—First: *The speech of the foolish must be self-injurious.* His speech is a "rod of pride." It is a rod that grows out of pride. By some, the word "rod" here is understood as a shoot, or branch, as in the expression, "There shall come a rod out of the stem of Jesse, and a branch shall grow out of his roots." Pride and foolishness are nearly related. A proud man is a fool. He does not know himself, the universe, or his God. Proud speech is the rod that grows out of a foolish heart; but the rod which the foolish heart grows, it also uses as its instrument, and its use must tend to self-destruction. Pride works ruin. "Pride goeth before destruction, and a haughty spirit before a fall." Secondly: *The speech of the wise must be self-advantageous.* The wise man is a good man, and a good man's speech will tend to his own spiritual development, and the promotion of his spiritual powers. "Out of the abundance of the heart the

218 / Book of Proverbs

mouth speaketh." "Keep the heart with diligence, for out of it are the issues of life."

"The Lord shall cut off all flattering lips, and the tongue that speaketh proud things; who have said, with our tongue will we prevail; our lips are our own; who is lord over us."*

Proverbs 14:4

The Clean Crib, or Indolence

"Where no oxen *are*, the crib *is* clean: but much increase *is* by the strength of the ox."

OBSERVE two things here:

THE NEGATIVE gain of indolence.—The indolent man will not go to the trouble of keeping oxen, and therefore he has no crib to clean; work brings work. Industry creates business. If a man will go to the trouble of keeping oxen, he must look after them, "keep their cribs clean." *Indolence saves labour.* First: This is true in *secular* matters. A man who will not cultivate his land will save all the toil of harvest. A man who is too lazy to embark in business will be freed from much anxious toil and a thousand cares connected with mercantile life. Secondly: This is true in *intellectual* matters. A man who is too lazy to commence work of self-culture, to strive after science, or to struggle after scholarship, will of course avoid all that study which is a "weariness to the flesh." Thirdly: This is true of *spiritual* matters. A man who will not take the trouble to ascertain the condition of his soul by looking into the glass of the Divine Word, will remain in that state of moral indifference by which he will escape all that battling against inward corruptions, striving after spiritual holiness, which the true feel to be a strenuous and unremitting conflict.

Thus a lazy man saves much work by not keeping oxen; he has no crib to clean.

* Psalm xii. 3, 4.

OBSERVE again—
The POSITIVE loss of indolence.—" But much increase is by the strength of the ox." The man who keeps the ox, cleans out his crib, takes care of him and industriously employs him in his fields, gets from him results that will more than compensate all his toil. Industry is potential wealth. In all true labour there is a profit. Observe—First : What an indolent man loses in *secular* matters. He loses the pleasure of *gaining* wealth. There is often more gratification in the pursuit of riches than in their possession. He loses the pleasure of rightly using wealth. The generous heart alone can tell the exquisite delight connected with the distribution of wealth for the relief of the distressed, the promotion of knowledge, and the advancement of human happiness. Observe—Secondly : What an indolent man loses in *intellectual* matters. What glorious mental results grow out of laborious study, well disciplined faculties, varied treasures of knowledge, great social influence! Mental riches, unlike material, are inalienable; they cannot take to themselves wings and flee away. Observe—Thirdly : What an indolent man loses in *spiritual* matters. How great the joy of a spiritually-disciplined soul! It is " a joy unspeakable, and full of glory." Here, then, is a choice for men. Indolence or industry. Indolence will save work, but lose its splendid results. Industry will have hard work, but out of it comes "*much increase*," increase of the highest good.

Proverbs 14:5-6

Veracity and Wisdom

"A faithful witness will not lie : but a false witness will utter lies. A scorner seeketh wisdom, and *findeth it* not : but knowledge *is* easy unto him that understandeth."

HERE we have the subject of VERACITY.—" A faithful witness will not lie." This is so much like a truism, that it scarcely calls for a remark. It means that a true man will be true in his expressions: an untrue man will be false. Two things, however, may be implied in it. First: That veracity in witness-bearing *is very important.* Lies are bad everywhere—in the family, in the market, in general society; bad in themselves, and bad in their consequences. But they are worse in the "*court of law*" than anywhere else. *Perjury* is the worst form of lying. It frustrates justice, and when the oath is added, it involves the blasphemy of taking God's name in vain. Secondly: That veracity, in witness-bearing, *can only be secured by a truthful character.* The true man will be true everywhere; the false man false everywhere. The only way, therefore, to put down lying in courts of justice, and everywhere else, is the making of men true and right in heart. This Christianity does, and nothing else does it. It dries up the springs of falsehood in the human heart, such as vanity, greed, fear, and inspires it with an invincible attachment to reality and God: it is its glory that it can and does make men *true.* False men often assume this, but they have no vital connection with it; their lives are libels on its character. Christianity is essentially and eternally antagonistic to shams of all kinds; its mission is to bear witness to the truth.

Here we have the subject of WISDOM.—"A scorner seeketh wisdom and *findeth it not,* but knowledge *is* easy unto him that understandeth." Two things are implied in this—First: That the attainment of wisdom *is a very desirable thing.* Wisdom includes

Acquisition of the highest knowledge.—The knowledge of man, his nature, condition, relations, responsibilities; of God, His being, character, laws, works. It includes also the right application of this knowledge. Knowledge is only really useful to us as we practically apply it. What are all the arts that bless and adorn the civilized world, but the practical application of scientific knowledge. And what is the sublime life of godliness, but true theology practically applied? This is wisdom. Secondly: The attainment of wisdom *depends upon the spirit of the seeker.* "A scorner seeketh wisdom and findeth it not." No character is more despicable than the scorner. His spirit includes *pride*—he sneers at truth, thus indicating intellectual pride. It includes *irreverence.*—He scoffs at the Infinite. It includes *heartlessness.*—He is regardless of the feelings of others. Can a man with such a spirit ever get wisdom? No. He has not the eye to see the truth, even though it stands before him incarnated in a glorious personality. Pilate, with this scoffing spirit, saw it in this sublime form, and yet asked, " What is truth?" The scoffer, even in seeking wisdom, attains confounding fictions.

> " Hear the just doom, the judgment of the skies :
> He that hates truth shall be the dupe of lies;
> And he who *will* be cheated to the last,
> Delusions, strong as hell, shall bind him fast."

"But knowledge is easy unto him that understandeth." That is, the man whose spirit is in contrast to that of the scorner, is docile, attentive, humble. He sits at the Great Teacher's feet and listens to His words. He feels, with Cowper, that—

> " Truths, on which depends our main concern,
> That 'tis our shame and misery not to learn,
> Shine by the side of every path we tread
> With such a lustre, he that runs may read."

Proverbs 14:7-9

The Society to be Shunned

"Go from the presence of a foolish man, when thou perceivest not *in him* the lips of knowledge. The wisdom of the prudent *is* to understand his way : but the folly of fools *is* deceit. Fools make a mock at sin : but among the righteous *there is* favour."

MAN is a social being; his natural affinities and relations show that he is made to a great extent for others, and that others are made for him. So far from reaching perfection in isolation, his very existence would be intolerable in absolute solitude. The text holds up the society which we should avoid—the society of the foolish. A "foolish" man here stands for a "bad" man. The text suggests that the society of such should be avoided for three reasons—

It is UNPROFITABLE.—" Go from the presence of a foolish man, when thou perceivest not in him the lips of knowledge." What you want in society is knowledge—true knowledge, knowledge that shall rightly guide, truly comfort, and religiously inspire the soul. But can such knowledge be got from a foolish man? No. Therefore, time spent in his society is waste time, and you have no time to lose. "Be ye the companions," says the Psalmist, "of them that fear Him." From such choose your associates. Let their society be the society you love. They say, "Come with us and we will do you good." Comply with the invitation, if you would imbibe their spirit, learn their wisdom, and participate in their happiness.

It is MISLEADING.—" The folly of fools is deceit." They cheat *themselves*. They fancy they have the true ideas and the true pleasures, but it is a miserable delusion. They live in a world of fiction. Dreamers they are all. "A depraved heart is deceitful above all things and desperately wicked." They cheat *others*. They mislead and entangle by the falsehood of their speech and the craftiness of their policy. "New stratagems," says Lord Bacon, "must be devised, the old failing and growing useless, and as soon as ever a man hath got the name of a cunning, crafty companion, he hath deprived himself utterly of the principles instrumental for the management of his affairs which is trust."

It is WICKED.—"Fools make a mock at sin." Sin, the greatest insult to God, and the greatest curse to humanity, they mock at. The spirit of mocking at sin is the most impious, cruel, infatuating, and from those who possess it we should flee as from the savage beasts of prey. There breathes not on earth a more inhuman and iron-hearted monster than he who makes a mock at sin. He sports with the great curse of the universe, makes fun of hell itself. "Go," then, "from the presence of a foolish man ;"

seek the companionship of the wise, their society is *profitable*, they "have the lips of knowledge," their words are *truthful*. "The wisdom of the prudent is to understand his way." And where can he get understanding? Only in the society of the *good*. "Among the righteous there is favour." With them there is genuine love, faithful attachment, and holy principle; they cleave to each other from a mutual recognition of goodness, and with mutual love as strong as death.

Avoid evil companions.—St. Augustine has well said, "Bad company is like a nail driven into a post which, after the first and second blow, may be drawn out with little difficulty; but being once driven up to the head the pincers cannot take hold to draw it out, but which can only be done by the destruction of the wood." "One rotten apple," says Feltham, "will infect the store, the putrid grape corrupts the whole sound cluster. If I have found any good companions, I will cherish them as the choicest of men, or as angels which are sent as guardians to me. If I have any bad ones I will study to lose them, lest by keeping them I lose myself in the end."

Proverbs 14:10

The Heart's Hidden Depth

"The heart knoweth his own bitterness: and a stranger doth not intermeddle with his joy."

THOUGH men live in towns and cities, and in social gatherings, each man is a world to himself. He is as distinct, even from him who is in closest material or mental contact with him, as one orb of heaven is from another. Though governed by the common laws of his race, he has an orbit of his own, an atmosphere of his own, and abysses of life into which no eye but the eye of God can pierce.

The heart has hidden depths of SORROW.—"The heart knoweth his own bitterness." There is bitterness in most hearts. There is the bitterness of *disappointed love*—the soul recoiling with agony at the discovery that its affections have been misplaced. There is the bitterness of *social bereavement* — Rachels weeping for their children, and Davids for their Absaloms. There is the bitterness of *moral remorse* going forth in the cry, "O wretched man that I am; who shall deliver me from this body of sin and death?" All this is hidden where it is the most deep. The profoundest sorrow in the human heart is hidden from others, from three causes. First: The *insulating tendency* of deep grief. Deep sorrow draws from society, and seeks some Gethsemane of solitude, to pour out its anguish in loneliness. A greater outrage we can scarcely commit than to intrude on the notice of our fellow men in grief. Secondly: *The concealing instinct* of deep grief. Men parade little sorrows, but conceal great ones. "The man of sorrows and acquainted with grief," mentioned His distress to no one but the Infinite Father. Great sorrows roll as the deep river underground. Thirdly: *The incapacity of one soul to sound the depths of another's grief.* There is such a peculiarity in the constitution and circumstances of each soul, that one can never fully understand another. The deepest things in man are unknown even to himself, and his fellow men have no eye to penetrate into that abyss. Souls are strangers to each other; the acquaintance, even of the most intimate, is superficial. Every man has in him what he cannot speak out. The greater the soul the deeper its sense of loneliness, and the more incapable of communicating itself to others.

Observe here also that—

The heart has hidden depths of JOY.—"A stranger doth not intermeddle with his joy." Though joy is less self-concealing than sorrow, yet it has depths unknown to any but its possessor and its God. The joy that rushed into Abraham's heart when Isaac descended with him from the altar of Moriah; the joy of the father when he pressed his prodigal son to his bosom; the joy of the widow of Nain when her only son raised himself from the bier, and returned to gladden her lonely home; the joy of the heartbroken woman when she heard Christ say, "Thy sins are all forgiven thee"—such joys have depths that no outward eye could penetrate or fathom. The joy of the true Christian is indeed a joy "unspeakable, and full of glory." This subject furnishes an argument. First : *for candour amongst men.* We do not fully know each other, therefore we ought to be generous and candid in our treatment. "What man knoweth the things of a man, save the spirit of a man which is in him." Secondly: *For piety towards God.* Though men know us not, He does. He knows what is in man, and more, He has the deepest interest in our sorrows. " In all their affliction He was afflicted, and the angel of His presence saved them. In His love, and in His pity He redeemed them, and He bare them, and carried them all the days of old."*

Proverbs 14:11

The Soul's Home

"The house of the wicked shall be overthrown : but the tabernacle of the upright shall flourish."

THE "house" and the "tabernacle" in the passage here, must be taken in the most generic sense, as meaning more than the mere tenement, whether of bricks, or stone, or canvas, in which the man physically resides. The words may mean all that *externalism* of a man's life in which he feels the most interest, from which he derives the most pleasure, and that is usually his home. The pleasing surroundings of life constitute the real house or tabernacle in which the man lives. The Proverb teaches that—

In the case of the WICKED this home is doomed to ruin.— —"The house of the wicked shall be overthrown." Is *business* the home of his soul? Does he, the thinking,

* Isaiah lxiii. 9.

conscious man, dwell more in it than anywhere else? His business will depart from him—his warehouses, stock-in-trade, clerks, will all be overthrown. Is *wealth* the house of his soul? Some men live in their gold; it is the sphere in which all their faculties operate, the centre of all their sympathies. This house "shall be overthrown." "We brought nothing into this world, and it is certain we can carry nothing out." Is *society* the home of his soul? There are many who live in company, they are never at home on their own hearths—the *fellowship* of others is their home; this is always the case of the wicked, and this house is doomed to be "overthrown." There are no friendships for the ungodly in the future.

It is here further taught that :

In the case of the RIGHTEOUS this house is destined to prosper.—"The tabernacle of the upright shall flourish." Where is the home of the righteous? Where his heart is. And where is that? First : *In the cause of Divine benevolence.* In the advance of truth, in the extension of goodness, the progress of humanity, he feels the strongest interest. His cause shall flourish. It must go on; heaven and earth shall pass away sooner than it shall fail. Secondly : *In the society of the holy and the true.* The fellowship of the true disciple of Christ is the heaven of his nature; and that shall flourish, it shall increase in numbers, purity, goodness, and influence. "We then having received a kingdom that cannot be moved, let us have grace to worship in reverence and godly fear." The upright shall flourish for ever,—what a prospect! "For evermore!"—words easily uttered "but in comprehension," says Archer Butler, "vaster than human thought can grasp; entering upon eternity, men shall rise with faculties fitted for the scene. For evermore! for an existence to which the age of the earth, of the starry heavens, of the whole vast universe is less than a morning's dream; for a life, which, after the reiteration of millions of centuries, shall begin the endless state with the freshness of infancy, and all the eagerness that welcomes enjoyments ever new."

Proverbs 14:12

The Seeming Right Often Ruinous

"There is a way which seemeth right unto a man, but the end thereof *are* the ways of death."

MANY of the ways which men pursue cannot even "*seem right.*" The way of the habitual blasphemer, sabbath-breaker, debauchee, and such characters, can scarcely appear right to any man. They are manifestly wrong. What are the ways that often "seem right" to men and that are ruinous? We may mention three.

The "way" of the CONVENTIONALLY MORAL "seems right," but is nevertheless ruinous.—Civilised society has its recognised rules of conduct. But these rules regard only the external life of man. They take no cognisance of thought, feeling, desire, and the unexpressed things of the soul. Industry, sobriety, veracity, honesty, these are the extent of its demands, and if these are conformed to, society approves and applauds. Thousands consider these conventional rules to be the standards of character, and pride themselves in their conformity thereto. Because they are diligent in their business, deceive no one, pay every man his due, they consider their way right. Without disparaging in the least this social morality, we are bound to say, that what is *conventionally* moral may be *essentially* wrong. It may spring from wrong motives, and be governed by wrong reasons. The Scribes and Pharisees of old were conventionally rignt. Albeit they were rotten to the core. He who read their natures through and through, denounced them as "whited sepulchres." The end of such a way is "death." Death to all the elements of well-being.

The "way" of the FORMALISTICALLY RELIGIOUS "seems right," but is nevertheless ruinous. Religion has its forms, its places, and times of worship, its order of service, its benevolent institutions. A correct and constant attention to such forms is considered by thousands as religion itself. Regularity in church, conformity to all the recognised rites of worship, contributions according to the general standard of the congregation, all this passes for religion, but it is not religion. It is mechanism, nothing more. The motions of machinery, not the actions of the heart. There is no life in it, and it cannot lead to life, but to "death." "The letter killeth." "God is a Spirit, and they that worship him must worship him in spirit and in truth."

"As the strength of sin," says Charnock, "lies in the inward frame of the heart, so the strength of worship in the inward complexion and temper of the soul. Shadows are not to be offered instead of substances. God asks for the heart in worship, and commands outward ceremonies as subservient to inward worship, and goads and spears into it. What is the oblation of our bodies without a priestly act of the spirit in the presentation of it? To offer a body with a sapless spirit, is a sacrilege of the same nature with that of the Israelites, when they offered dead beasts. One sound sacrifice is better than a thousand rotten one."

The "way" of the SELFISHLY EVANGELICAL seems right, but is nevertheless ruinous.—Evangelical religion, in the sense of a participation of the *spirit* of Christ, is the *true* religion of man. But the thing that is now called evangelical, is, to a fearful extent, intensely selfish. Conventional evangelicalism is the devil of selfishness in the costume of piety and benevolence. Its appeals are all to the hopes and fears of men. Its preaching makes men feel, but their feelings are all concerned for their own interest; makes men pray, but their prayer is a selfish entreaty for deliverance from misery, and for the attainment of happiness. Fire and brimstone, not love to God, bring men together into congregations and churches. We fear that much that is called the evangelical religion of this age stands in direct opposition to the teachings of Him who said, "He that seeketh his life shall lose it," and also to the teaching of Paul, who said, "Without charity I am nothing." A *selfish* evangelicalism is the "way of death."

Men go to hell through churches. What, then, is the way that is *really* right? Here it is: "I am the way." Following Christ alone leads to life. "If any man have not the Spirit of Christ he is none of His."

Right and wrong are independent of men's *opinions*, what seems right to men is often wrong, and the reverse. Nevertheless men are held responsible for their beliefs. A wrong belief, however sincere, will lead to ruin.

Proverbs 14:13

Sinful Mirth

"Even in laughter the heart is sorrowful, and the end of that mirth *is* heaviness."

THERE is an *innocent* mirth, a sunny, sparkling, cheerfulness, arising from a happy natural temperament. There is a *virtuous* mirth. A mirth that has moral worth in it, springing from holy states of heart. This mirth, all should have. We are commanded "to rejoice evermore." There is a *sinful* mirth, and of this the text speaks. Three things are suggested concerning this.

IT IS BOISTEROUS IN EXPRESSION.—The "laughter" to which Solomon here refers is of a certain kind. Laughter in itself is not wrong. "It is," says Steele, "that which strikes upon the mind, and being too volatile and strong, breaks out in the tremor of the voice." And this author speaks of different kinds of laughers—the "dimplers," the "smilers," the "grinners," and the "horse laughers." A man's laugh is often the best index to his character. "How much," says Carlyle, "lies in laughter—the cipher-key wherewith we decipher the whole man! Some men wear an everlasting barren simper; in the smile of others lies the cold glitter, as of ice; the fewest are able to laugh what can be called laughing, but only sniff, and titter, and sniggle from the throat outwards, or, at least, produce some whiffling, husky cachinnation, as if they were laughing through wool. Of none such come good. The man who cannot laugh is not only fit for treasons, stratagems, and spoils: but his own life is already a treason and a stratagem." The laughter of which Solomon speaks, however, is not a natural laughter. It is a hypocritical laughter; it is the laughter of a man who has little or no joy in him—a man ill at ease. It is what Solomon calls elsewhere "the laughter of the fool," and he said of it, " it is mad!" The laughter of a corrupt heart. It is the roar of the maniac; the laugh of the drunkard, who is about stepping over a fearful precipice, is not more mad than the laughter of him who goes through life with a heart in hostility to God.

IT IS SAD IN SPIRIT.—" Even in laughter the heart is sorrowful." The jovial merriment of the social board, the joke, and the laugh, as the glass goes round, are but a veil drawn to conceal a world of misery within. Beneath all, the heart is sorrowful, with dark moral memories of the past, with gloomy forebodings as to the future. Sinful laughter is but misery mimicking happiness. Judge not men by appearance. The most miserable may often show the most merriment. A sorrowful heart lies under all that's gay, and jovial, and sparkling in the circles of wickedness. " Mirth at a funeral," says Dr. Young, " is scarce more indecent or unnatural than a perpetual flight of gaiety and burst of exultation in a world like this, a world which ever seems a paradise to fools, but is a hospital to the wise."

IT IS WRETCHED IN END.—" The end of that mirth is heaviness." Sinful mirth will have an end. Its jestings and carousings will not go on for ever. Disease, age, decay, death, hush all laughter, and quench in deepest gloom all the flashes of ungodly merriment. " The end is heaviness." There is a terrible reaction. The glitter gives way to gloom, the shout to shrieks. Is there any laughter in the agonies of death? will there be any laughter in hell?

Proverbs 14:14

The Misery of the Apostate, and the Happiness of the Good

" The backslider in heart shall be filled with his own ways : and a good man shall be satisfied from himself."

THERE are two important subjects here to be observed :

THE MISERY OF THE APOSTATE.—" The backslider in heart shall be filled with his own ways." First : the *description* of the apostate. "He is a backslider in heart." There is a sense in which all men are backsliders. Sin is an apostacy. It is the turning away of the soul from virtue and from God. The backslider here, however, refers to one who, by God's grace, had been restored to moral goodness, but who had fallen away, "left his first love." Such apostacy, or backsliding, is too general in the world ; Judas, Demas, Peter, David, are examples. The real backslider is he that backslides in *heart*. There are many who seem not to backslide in their conduct ; their external life in relation to the true thing continues the same as ever, but their heart has changed. The backslider in the eye of God is the man who apostatizes in heart. Secondly : The *doom* of the apostate. "Filled with his own ways." Misery inevitably follows his conduct. If he is *restored* he will suffer, he will be "filled with his own ways." How deeply did David feel this, and Peter too—how bitterly he wept. But should he not be restored here, how much greater will be his misery. He will be "filled with his own ways." This is the punishment. The upas germ of sin ripened into a harvest. Combustible sin breaking into conflagration.

THE HAPPINESS OF THE GOOD.—" A good man shall be *satisfied* from himself." Who is the good man ? *The man who loves the supreme good supremely.* Such a man "shall be satisfied from himself." As the backslider's misery springs out of himself, so the happiness of the good man wells up in his own nature. The happiness of ungodly men, such as it is, is not *in* themselves, it is something outside of them, their children, their business, their friendships, their position, their property. Not so the happiness of the good man, it is in himself, it is independent of circumstances. He carries it wherever he goes. It is a well of water springing up into everlasting life. It is—

> " What nothing earthly gives or can destroy,
> The soul's calm sunshine and the heartfelt joy."—POPE

Proverbs 14:15-18

The Credulous and the Cautious

> "The simple believeth every word: but the prudent *man* looketh well to his going. A wise *man* feareth, and departeth from evil: but the fool rageth, and is confident. *He that is* soon angry dealeth foolishly: and a man of wicked devices is hated. The simple inherit folly: but the prudent are crowned with knowledge."

"SIMPLE" and "foolish" in these verses must be regarded as convertible, and represent the same character. So also the words "wise" and "prudent." We have, therefore, two characters, the hastily credulous and the cautiously believing.

THE HASTILY CREDULOUS.—"The simple believeth every word." First: *One of the strongest tendencies in man's mental nature is his propensity to believe.* It is one of the most voracious appetites of the soul. The child opens its mental mouth, hungering for tales from the nurse's lips, and will eagerly swallow everything that is said. "As the young birds," says a modern author, "instinctively open their mouths for food, and their mothers not even once since the creation of the world have thrown in chaff to mock their hunger, so the trustfulness of children is the opening of their mouth for truth. If we fling falsehood in, and laugh at their disappointment, the Lord will require it." Alas, this is done, and the child grows up to manhood disappointed, sceptical, and suspicious. (1) This propensity to believe implies a state of society that does not exist. Were men born into heaven, were society free from all error and deception, it would be not only a right, but a beneficial thing to believe every word, to credit every utterance, and to confide in every character. This is the state of society for which man was created, but he has lost it. He comes into a world of sham and falsehood. (2) This propensity to believe explains the reign of priesthood. Priestcraft feeds and fattens on the natural credulousness of the soul. All the errors, superstitions, and absurdities which have ever prevailed in connection with religion, may be accounted for by the soul's hunger for things to believe. Credulity ever has been and still is one of the curses of the world. (3) This propensity to believe shows the easiness of the condition on which God has made the salvation of man to depend. " He that believeth shall be saved." The act of faith is not only the easiest act for a man to perform, but he has a strong tendency to its performance. Hence there is no merit in the act, and Paul says, in speaking of this condition, "that it is of faith that it may be of grace."

Secondly: *The thoughtless yielding to this tendency is an immense loss.* " The fool rageth and is confident." He sees no danger, dreads no harm. He rushes recklessly forward into mischief. He is passionate. He " rageth." Counsels and warnings only irritate him. Advice, cautions, and reproofs, fall on his soul as sparks on combustible matter. They throw his whole nature into a raging flame of passion. He is stubborn. He is " confident." What does he care about your warnings? Nothing. He despises you, he laughs at them. He is foolish. " He that is soon angry dealeth foolishly," and he " inherits folly." In his impetuous irritability he gives rash utterance to things that bring back on him the utmost chagrin and confusion. He is despised. "A man of wicked devices is hated." The man who has given way to his credulity becomes all this. He is passionate, ignorant of the grounds of his belief, he cannot brook contradiction, his opinions being prejudices, he is stubborn in holding them, and in all this he is " foolish " and " hated."

THE CAUTIOUSLY BELIEVING. — "The prudent man looketh well to his going." True prudence is indicated by two things—First: A dread of evil. "A wise *man* feareth." True dread of evil is consistent with true courage Few, if any, displayed more heroism than Noah, yet, being " moved by fear, he prepared an ark." Evil, both physical and moral, is a bad thing in the universe, and it is right to dread it as we dread poisonous serpents and ravenous beasts. True prudence is indicated by, Secondly: A *departure from* evil. "He departeth from evil." Moral evil is the heart of all evil, and this he forsakes. He shuns it as an enemy to God and the universe. The prudence is indicated by, Thirdly: *Mental greatness.* He is " crowned with knowledge." Caution in believing is necessary for three reasons. The strength of man's tendency to believe, the prevalence of error in society, and the damning influence of falsehood on the soul.

Proverbs 14:19

The Majesty of Goodness

" The evil bow before the good: and the wicked at the gates of the righteous."

THREE remarks are suggested by the social state indicated in these words; the state in which the wicked are prostrate in reverence and entreaty before the good.

It is a social state which SELDOM APPEARS TO BE.—The wicked generally sit supreme in society, they have done so through all past ages and are doing so now, and that to a great extent even in what is called " Christian society." The influence, the wealth, the rule of the world, appear to be with the wicked. Evil seems still the " prince of the power" of the social atmosphere. The good are for the most part the destitute, despised, and oppressed. This has always been to reflecting saints one of the greatest difficulties connected with the government of God. "Wherefore doth the wicked prosper?"* "Wherefore are all they happy that deal very treacherously?" "But as for me, my feet were almost gone; my steps had well nigh slipped. For I was envious of the foolish, when I saw the prosperity of the wicked."†

It is a social state which ALWAYS OUGHT TO BE.—It ought to be—First, As a matter of *right*. The good alone are the truly dignified, the truly royal. Their lineage, their inheritance, their characters, their friendships, their engagements, are all regal. "They are kings and priests unto God." There is more royalty in the hut of a godly pauper than in all the palaces of unregenerate monarchs. Secondly: As a matter of *expediency*. What is right is always expedient. The wicked could not even live on the earth without the good. Unmixed wickedness would soon reduce our world to a Sodom and Gomorrah. The good are "the salt of the earth." Governments never stand long that are not fashioned by the principles of the true. Evil, therefore, ought to "bow before the good."

It is a social state which INEVITABLY MUST BE.—First: *conscience* necessitates it. Even the worst men now and here are compelled by the laws of their moral nature to render homage to the good. Chastity, truth, honesty, disinterestedness, moral heroism, where is there a conscience that bows not to these? Secondly: *retribution* necessitates it. When trials, and sufferings and dangers overtake the wicked, do they not always go for refuge to the good? They will cringe at their "gate," they will fawn at their feet. "Give us of your oil, for our lamps are gone out." How did the 260 souls bow before Paul, the prisoner, amidst the dangers of the storm on the Adriatic Sea! He became the moral commander of all on board as the perils thickened around them.

* Jer. xii. 1—3. † Psalm lxxiii. 2, 3.

Proverbs 14:20-22

A Group of Social Priniciples

"The poor is hated even of his own neighbour: but the rich *hath* many friends. He that despiseth his neighbour sinneth: but he that hath mercy on the poor, happy *is* he. Do they not err that devise evil? but mercy and truth *shall be* to them that devise good."

THESE verses indicate certain principles which seem everywhere at work in the social system of our world. Here is—

INHUMANITY.—The poor is here spoken of as "hated," "despised," and injured by those that "devise evil." There have always been men in society, and still are, who hate and oppress the poor. There are many who have professed great friendship to those in wealth, whom they have despised when they have sunk into poverty. These are what an old expositor calls "swallow friends, that leave in winter." Why are the poor thus despised? First, Because of *selfishness*. There is nothing to be got from them—no money, no patronage, no fame. Their good word goes not for much in the world. Their opinions are neither quoted nor respected. Secondly: Because of *pride*. Pride is a form of selfishness. It is not thought respectable to notice the poor. A poor relation must be ignored. All this is *inhuman*, and, therefore, sinful. "He that despiseth his neighbour, *sinneth.*" In such conduct there is sin against the best feelings of our nature, against the arrangements of God's providence, against Heaven's method for developing benevolence amongst men. Here is—

SERVILITY.—"The rich hath many friends." There is a keen satire in these words. There are base-natured people in all Society, and their name is "legion," who court the rich. Even in the "Christian world," as it is called, there are men who will fawn on the man of purse, and flatter him with adulations. Men, though swindlers in heart, are made chairmen of their public meetings and presidents of their societies. It is humiliating to see men, calling themselves the ministers of Christ, cringing before the chair of the wealthy, and cheering every utterance. All sect churches teem with parasites. A more miserable spirit than this know I not; unchristian, unmanly, most pernicious. Never will Christianity be truly represented, until its disciples shall practically regard intellectual and moral worth united, as the only title to honour and position. "The rich hath many friends." Professed friends, for if a man has not the morally excellent and lovable in him, whatever may be the amount of his wealth, the friends he gets will only be the false and the fawning.

GENEROSITY.—"He that hath mercy upon the poor, happy is he." There is mercy for the poor in Society. It is seen in the numerous and varied benevolent institutions that crowd Christendom. Those who have this mercy are happy. First: *In the approbation of their own consciences.* Mercy is an element of happiness. "It is twice blessed; it blesses him that gives and him that takes," &c. They are happy. Secondly: *In the commendation of their God.* " Blessed *is* he that considereth the poor; the Lord will deliver him in time of trouble."* "He hath dispersed, he hath given to the poor, his righteousness endureth for ever; his horn shall be exalted with honour."† Epicurus well said " a beneficent person is like a fountain watering the earth, and spreading fertility: it is therefore more delightful and more honourable to give than to receive."

RETRIBUTION.—" Do not they err that devise evil, but mercy and truth *shall be* to them that devise good ?" Yes, those that have devised evil against the poor will find, sooner or later, that they have greatly erred. They will find that the "measure that they meted out unto others is meted back to them." On the contrary, "mercy and truth *shall be* to them that devise good." The liberal deviseth liberal things, and by liberal things shall he stand. Read the fifteenth chapter of the Gospel of St. Matthew, in order to see the retribution that the unmerciful will meet with at last. Society is like the echoing hills. It gives back to the speaker his words; groan for groan,

* Psalm xli. 1.   † Psalm cxii. 9.

song for song. Wouldest thou have thy social scenes to resound with music? Then speak ever in the melodious strains of truth and love. "With what measure ye mete, it shall be measured to you again."

Proverbs 14:23-24

Labor, Talk, Wealth

"In all Labour there is profit; but the talk of the lips *tendeth* only to penury. The crown of the wise *is* their riches: *but* the foolishness of fools *is* folly."—

HERE we have—

PROFITABLE LABOUR.—"In all labour there is profit." The word "all" here of course must be taken with limitation, for ill-directed labour is not profitable. Labour is profitable to *our physical health*. Exercise is one of the fundamental conditions of corporeal health and strength. Labour is profitable to *our character*. It conduces to force of thought, energy of will, power of endurance, capacity of application. Labour is profitable to *our social comforts*. By honest, well-directed labour, man gets not only the necessities, but the comforts, the luxuries, the elegances, and the elevated positions of life. In all labour, then— —well directed labour—"there is profit." Every honest effort has its reward. There is no true labour that is vain. "It is only by labour," says Ruskin, "that thought can be made healthy; and the two cannot be separated with impunity."

IMPOVERISHING TALK.—"The talk of the lips *tendeth* only to penury." All talk does not tend to penury. There is a talk that is profitable. The talk of the preacher, the lecturer, the statesman, the barrister, more often tend to affluence than to penury. The talk here is the talk of useless gossip. The desire for talk in some people is a ruling passion. Their tongues are in perpetual motion;

they are ever in search of listeners. Their highest pleasure is in prosy, frothy, useless tattle. As a rule, in proportion to the strength of this desire to talk, is the disinclination to work, and hence penury comes. Sir Walter Raleigh says, "He that is lavish in words is a niggard in deeds. The shuttle, the needle, the spade, the brush, the chisel, all are still but the tongue."

DIGNIFYING WEALTH.—"The crown of the wise is their riches." The idea is that a wise man would so use his wealth that it would become a crown to him. By using it to promote his own mental and spiritual cultivation, and to ameliorate the woes and augment the happiness of the world, his wealth gives to him a diadem more lustrous far than all the diamond crowns of kings. "But the foolishness of fools is folly." This looked at antithetically means that the wealth of a fool adds no dignity to his character.

Gotthold saw a bee flutter for a while around a pot of honey and at last light upon it, intending to feast to its heart's content. It, however, fell in, and, being besmeared in every limb, miserably perished. On this he mused and said, "It is the same with temporal prosperity and that abundance of wealth, honour, and pleasure which are sought for by the world as greedily as honey is by the bee. A bee is a happy creature so long as it is assiduously occupied in gathering honey from the flowers, and by slow degrees accumulating a store of it. When, however, it meets with a hoard like this it knows not what to do, and is betrayed into ruin." Man! be thou like the bee abroad in the meadows, drinking the nectar of flowers, sporting in the sunshine and pouring some little music into the air, rather than the bee with its wing crippled and its body submerged even in honey!

Proverbs 14:25

The True Witness

"A true witness delivereth souls: but a deceitful *witness* speaketh lies."

WE make three remarks on this sentence:

In judiciary matters the thing here asserted is NOT ALWAYS TRUE.—The testimony of a true witness in a court of justice, where the facts are *criminatory* must go not to the deliverance but to the condemnation and ruin of the criminal. Though he may be such a merciful man as to desire intensely to save the prisoner, still because he is "true," he must state the facts regardless of the results. It is only when the facts are *vindicatory* the "true" witness can deliver.

In the disposition of the mind the thing here asserted is GENERALLY TRUE.—"It is probable," says an able expositor, "that the intended antithesis relates, not so much to the *actual fact* of truth saving and falsehood condemning, as to the *dispositions and intentions* of the faithful witness on the one hand, and the lying witness on the other. The faithful witness delights in giving testimony that will save life, that will be salutary, beneficial to his fellow-creatures. The lying witness will, in general, be found actuated by a malevolent and wicked purpose, having pleasure in giving testimony that will go to condemn the object of his malice. The sentiment will thus be, *that truth is most generally found in union with kindness of heart, and falsehood with malevolence.* And this is natural; the former being both good, the latter both evil; falsehood is more naturally akin to malice and truth to love."

In the evangelical ministry the thing here asserted is

INVARIABLY TRUE.—" A true witness " to Gospel facts "delivereth souls." The true work of a Gospel minister is that of a witness. "Ye shall receive power after that the Holy Ghost is come upon you, and ye shall be witnesses unto me, both in Jerusalem, and in all Judea, and in Samaria, and unto the uttermost parts of the earth."* A true witness in the evangelical sense must be distinguished by three things. He must be *thoroughly conversant with the facts*. He must *honestly propound the facts*. He must live *in accordance with the facts*. Such a witness "delivereth souls." "Take heed unto thyself and unto the doctrine; continue in them; for in doing this thou shalt save thyself and them that hear thee."† Gospel facts are the great redemptive forces in human history. Silently and constantly as the laws of vegetation do they operate in the moral soul of the world. Ever are they unloosening the prison doors, breaking the fetters, and working out the emancipation of human souls.

Proverbs 14:26-27

Godliness, Safety and Life

" In the fear of the Lord *is* strong confidence : and his children shall have a place of refuge. The fear of the Lord *is* a fountain of life, to depart from the snares of death."

WE learn from these words—

That godliness is SAFETY.—"The fear of the Lord is strong confidence." By " the fear of the Lord" is meant, as we have frequently seen, no slavish emotion, nothing associated with terror, suspicion, and forebodement. It is loyal love and unbounded confidence, it exorcises all that is servile and cowardly. It is the root of true liberty, it is the sun of joy, it is the heart of heroism. The godly are " his children" and they have " a place of refuge." " God is their refuge and strength." They " will not fear though the earth be removed." We make three remarks about

* Acts. i. 8.   † 1 Tim. iv. 16.

this "place of refuge." *It is a provision against immense dangers.* The sinner is exposed to enormous evils, to countless formidable foes. All the "principalities and powers" of the dark worlds of rebellion are marshalled against him. *It admits of the greatest freedom of action.* A prison is a "place of refuge" as well as a fortress. The inmate is well guarded by massive bars and granite walls from all without, but he has no liberty. But here all have ample scope for action. The sphere is as boundless as infinitude. *It is accessible at all times and for all persons.* Its gates are open day and night. It extends to men on every zone of the globe. Yet foolish men will not enter. They stand shivering without, while the overwhelming storm is gathering. Ancient saints, confessors, and martyrs, were in this "place of refuge," and they sang triumphantly while the tempest raged at the height of its fury. Hear the language of one of its inmates, "I am persuaded that neither death nor life, nor angels, nor principalities, nor powers, nor things present, nor things to come, nor height, nor depth, or any other creature, shall be able to separate us from the love of God which is in Christ Jesus our Lord."*

That godliness is LIFE.—"The fear of the Lord is a fountain of life to depart from the snares of death." What is said here of the fear of the Lord is said elsewhere.† Not only life but a fountain of life,—*abundant* and *perennial.* There is nothing circumscribed in the resources of a genuinely religious soul. Its subjects of thought are as vast as immensity, its objects of love are as boundless as the perfections of Jehovah, its sphere of service and its prospects of futurity are wider than the universe, immeasurable as eternity. "The water that I shall give you shall be as a well within you springing up to everlasting life." In the life of the noble and the true—

> "There's no night following on their daylight hours,
> No fading time for amaranthine flowers :
> No change, no death, no harp that lies unstrung,
> No vacant place those hallow'd hills among."
>   R. MONTGOMERY

* Rom. viii. 38, 39. † Prov. xiii. 14.

Proverbs 14:28

The Population of an Empire

"In the multitude of the people *is* the king's honour: but in the want of people *is* the destruction of the prince."

THE text teaches two things concerning the increase of the population of an empire—

IT REFLECTS HONOUR ON THE GOVERNMENT.—Where the population of a country thrives, three good things are implied. First: *Peace*. Murders, insurrections, wars, and violence in all its forms go to thin the population. Hence, wherever it is found to multiply rapidly, the government is more or less a reign of peace. Another good thing implied when the population increases is,—Secondly: *Sufficiency*. Scarcity of provisions, destitution, tend to starvation, and often drive the people to emigrate to distant shores. A country where there is sufficiency of food for the people reflects honour on the government. It shows scope for enterprise and freedom in labour and trade. Another good thing implied when the population increases is,—Thirdly: *Salutariness*. Pestilence thins a population. Diseases spring from a neglect and transgression of sanatorial laws. Where a population grows, therefore, it shows that sanitary ordinances are more or less respected and obeyed. Thus the increase of a population in any country reflects honour on the Ruler. " In the multitude of the people is the king's honour." Another thing taught concerning the increase of the population of an empire is,—

IT PRESERVES THE EXISTENCE OF THE GOVERNMENT.—" In the want of people is the destruction of the prince." First : *The more people the more defence.* The king whose subjects are few and decreasing has but little protection. He is exposed to invasions. Small states are powerless before mighty empires. Secondly: *The more people the more revenue.* Money, which is the sinew of war, is also the architect of noble institutions and the caterer to royal needs, and tastes, and pageantries. Thus it is true, that "in the multitude of people is the king's honour; but in the want of people is the destruction of the prince." In the language of another, "the prince who reigns over a numerous, thriving, and contented people may be likened to the proprietor of a vineyard, where all is rich, flourishing, fruitful, productive, thus fully rewarding his expense, time, and care, bringing him at once credit and profit. Whereas the prince who sways his sceptre over a drained, exhausted, and dispirited people, is like the proprietor whose vineyard, for want of cultivation and judicious management, becomes in its vines stunted and sapless, and in its soil weedy, poor, and sterile—at once his disgrace and its ruin."

Proverbs 14:29

Temper

"*He that is* slow to wrath *is* of great understanding: but *he that is* hasty of spirit exalteth folly."

EVERY man has what is called *Temper*—a kind of inner atmosphere in which he lives, breathes, and works. This atmosphere has great varieties of temperature from zero to blood heat, and great changes of weather too, severe and stormy, cloudy and sunny. This temper, however, unlike the outward atmosphere, is controllable by man. He can regulate his temperatures and weathers. He can change from the arctic to the torrid, from the tempestuous to the serene and the reverse. The passage leads us to look at temper in two aspects—

AS CONTROLLED.—" He that is slow to wrath is of great understanding." First: It *requires* the efforts of a great understanding rightly to control temper. There are some whose tempers are naturally choleric and stormy. They are so combustible that the tiniest spark of offence will set them in flames. Can such tempers be controlled? Some are constantly pleading their natural dispositions as a palliation of their imperfections and their crimes. It is vain to do this. Our Creator has given us an understanding to control our passions. As a rule, the force of intellect in a man is always equal to his impulses. Where there are mighty passions there is generally an understanding that will match and master them. A sublimer sight one can scarcely have than that of a man with powerful passions majestically calm in irritating circumstances. Such a man shows a "great understanding," an understanding that bids the heaving billows within be calm, and they are at peace. Secondly? *It repays* the efforts of a great understanding rightly to control temper. The highest victories are the victories over temper. To raise our nature above those vexatious feelings which the annoyances and contrarieties of life are calculated to excite, is the most remunerative of labours. It gives a royalty to a man's being before which meaner spirits bow. Moses at the Red Sea is an example of disciplined temper, and Christ in the presence of His enemies was a sublime illustration of moral self-command.* The passage leads us to look at temper—

As uncontrolled.—"He that is hasty of spirit exalteth folly." He exalts folly by giving passion the throne and the sceptre, and placing the soul under her capricious and violent dominion. What crimes are committed, what woes created every day, by giving the reins to passion. Cowper has very graphically described an ungoverned, fretful temper,—

> " Some fretful tempers wince at every touch :
> You always do too little, or too much.
> You speak with life, in hopes to entertain ;
> Your elevated voice goes through the brain.
> You fall at once into a lower key :
> That's worse !—the drone-pipe of an humble bee.
> The southern sash admits too strong a light ;
> You rise and drop the curtain : now 'tis night.

* 1 Peter ii. 21—23.

He shakes with cold : you stir the fire, and strive
To make a blaze ;—that's roasting him alive.
Serve him with venison, and he chooses fish ;
With sole—that's just the sort he would not wish.
He takes what he at first professed to loathe,
And in due time feeds heartily on both ;
Yet, still o'erclouded with a constant frown,
He does not swallow, but he gulps it down.
Your hope to please him vain on every plan,
Himself should work that wonder, if he can !
Alas ! his efforts double his distress :
He likes you little, and his own still less.
Thus, always teasing others, always teased,
His only pleasure is—to be displeased."

Proverbs 14:30

Heart and Health

" A sound heart *is* the life of the flesh : but envy the rottenness of the bones."

"A SOUND heart" is a heart *that gives its supreme affection to the Supremely Good.* All other hearts are, more or less, rotten. Such a heart, the text informs us, is the condition of physical health ; it is the very " life of the flesh." True *science* can demonstrate this fact in many ways. The following line of argument would conduct to the conclusion. Physical health requires attention to certain laws ; these laws to be attended to must be understood ;—the understanding of these laws requires study ;—the proper study of them is only insured by a supreme sympathy of heart with the law-giver.

Every man's *experience*, as well as science, attests this fact. The influence of the emotions of the heart upon the state of the body, even the dullest recognises. The passion of grief, disappointment, anger, jealousy, and revenge, in proportion to their strength derange the bodily system. On the other hand pleasurable emotions give buoyancy and vigour to the body. "A merry heart doeth good like a medicine, but a broken-hearted spirit drieth the bones."

Quackery takes advantage of this fact, and often effects its cures by an endeavour to raise pleasurable emotions in the heart. It is, of course, easy to show, that these pleasurable emotions cannot exist in any elevated, true, and lasting form, where the supreme affection is not centred in God. From this undeniable fact the following conclusions may be drawn:

THAT A MAN'S BODILY HEALTH, WHERE THE ORGANIZATION IS NORMALLY GOOD, IS VERY MUCH IN HIS OWN HANDS.—There are not a few in this artificial age, who, in answer to enquiry after the state of their health, seem to think that it is scarcely virtuous or respectable to say that they are well. Robust health is not genteel or pious with many in these days. Many of the complaints of these people deserve more censure than pity. They spring from certain unworthy and unvirtuous states of the heart. Man is responsible for the condition of his heart, and in Christianity gracious heaven has given us at once the means and the motives to cultivate happy conditions of the heart. "Keep thy heart with all diligence." We infer from this fact again:

THAT CHRISTIANITY IS AN INDISPENSABLE AGENT IN REMOVING MAN'S PHYSICAL DISEASES.—If a "sound heart" be the "life of the flesh," and a "sound heart" means a heart centering its affections upon God, then Christianity is indispensable to this health. First: Christianity is the only system that *has* generated in depraved hearts this supreme affection. And, Secondly: Christianity is the only system that ever *can* do so. We infer from this fact further:

THAT MEDICAL SCIENCE WILL ALWAYS BE INEFFECTIVE UNTIL IT PRACTICALLY CONCERNS ITSELF WITH THE MORAL DISEASES AND CURES OF THE MIND.—With all the parade of scientific progress in the medical realm, mortality, it seems, is not lessened. The medical practitioner should know (1) That it is unscientific to ignore the fact that moral evil is the source of all physical evil, and (2) That it is unscientific to ignore the fact that there is no agent to remove moral evil but Christianity. Furthermore we infer from this fact:

THAT AS THE TRUE MORALITY OF THE WORLD ADVANCES, THE PHYSICAL HEALTH OF THE WORLD WILL IMPROVE.—This seems an inevitable conclusion. Let all the morally unwholesome passions of the world's heart be exorcised, and let all its thoughts and emotions be such only, as are the outgrowths of supreme sympathy with the Supremely Good, and then physical health and hilarity will everywhere prevail. Truly in those days the centenarian will be considered a child in years. Whilst we rejoice in sanatory science in its physical department, we feel assured that its advance in its moral department is the most essential. A drainage to carry away all the foul passions of the heart is the desideratum. The man who is the most successful in his efforts, through Christianity, to promote a moral renovation of hearts, is the greatest philanthropist and sucessful physician.

Proverbs 14:31

Godliness and Humanity

"He that oppresseth the poor reproacheth his Maker: but he that honoureth him hath mercy on the poor."

GODLINESS and humanity, in other words piety and philanthropy, are essentially one. Wherever there is genuine piety, there is philanthropy. Philanthropy is at once the offspring, and the ritualism, of all true religion. "Pure religion and undefiled before God and the Father is this, to visit the fatherless and widows in their affliction." *

The text teaches—

THAT INHUMANITY IS UNGODLINESS.—"He that oppresseth the poor reproacheth his Maker." There is a great deal of inhumanity in the world, the poor have to endure

* James i. 27.

not a little "oppression." Superior force is exerted to exact their labours for the most inadequate remuneration, and thus to "grind their faces." He who does it "reproacheth his Maker." First: By disregarding *that identity of nature with which our Maker has endowed all classes.* There is no distinction of nature in rich and poor. "God hath made of one flesh and blood all nations." The same blood flows through all, the same attributes belong to all; the same relations are sustained by all; the same destiny awaits all. Secondly: By disregarding *those laws which our Maker has enjoined concerning the poor.* Everywhere we are exhorted to remember the poor, to compassionate the poor, to help the poor. "And if thy brother be waxen poor, and fallen into decay with thee, then shalt thou relieve him; yea, though he be a stranger, or a sojourner, that he may live with thee. Take thou no usury of him, or increase, but fear thy God; that thy brother may live with thee."* "The poor shall never cease out of the land; therefore I command thee, saying, Thou shalt open thine hand wide unto thy brother, to thy poor, and to thy needy, in thy land."† Inhumanity, then, is ungodliness. "He that saith he is in the light, and hateth his brother, is in darkness, even until now." ‡

TRUE HUMANITY IS GODLINESS.—"But he that honoureth him, hath mercy on the poor." Honoureth Him, How? By loving Him supremely and serving Him loyally. "If we love one another, God dwelleth in us." The way to glorify God, to show our love for Him, is to serve our race. There is, it is true, a fickle, sentimental, mercifulness for the poor, which has no connection with godliness, but this is not true humanity. True philanthropy is that which sympathises with man, as the offspring of God, the victim of moral evil, the child of immortality, and which consecrates itself in the Spirit of Christ to ameliorate his woes, and redeem his soul, and this is godliness in its practical development. "Is not this the fast that I have chosen? to loose the bands of wickedness, to undo the heavy burdens, and to let the oppressed go free, and that ye break every

* Lev. xxv, 35, 36.   † Deut. xv. 11.   ‡ 1 John ii. 9.

yoke? Is it not to deal thy bread to the hungry, and that thou bring the poor that are cast out to thy house? when thou seest the naked, that thou cover him; and that thou hide not thyself from thine own flesh." *

A poet has thus described the spirit of true humanity:

> " A sense of an earnest will
> To help the lowly living,
> And a terrible heart-thrill,
> If you had no power of giving;
> An arm of aid to the weak,
> A friendly hand to the friendless:
> Kind words, so short to speak,
> But whose echo is endless:
> The world is wide, these things are small;
> They may be nothing, but they are all."

Proverbs 14:32

Death Depending on Character

" The wicked is driven away in his wickedness: but the righteous hath hope in his death."

THE word death has different meanings to different men; it is, in fact, a different event to different men. It is evermore to a man according to his character. The words point us to death in relation to two opposite characters—the wicked and the righteous. Observe—

Death in relation to the WICKED.—" The wicked is driven away in his wickedness." Three things are implied in these words concerning death. First: A very solemn change. He is " driven away." *Whence?* From all existing enjoyment, the beauties of nature, the circles of friendship, the pleasures of life. From all secular engagements, those of the farmer, lawyer, and statesman. From all means of moral improvement: from churches, Bibles, teachers. *Whither?* To the grave as to his body, to eternal

* Isaiah lviii. 6, 7.

retribution as to his soul. The death of the wicked implies—Secondly: A great personal reluctance. He does not go away; he is not drawn away: he is "*driven* away." All the sympathies of his nature are centred in this life. They are all twined round earthly objects as the ivy round the old castle. They are all more deeply rooted in the earth than the oak of centuries. He is in the world, and the world is everything to him. The future world is terribly repulsive to him. Not a ray of hope breaks through its tremendous gloom: it is one dense mass of starless thunder-cloud. This being the case, with what tenacity he clings to life! He will not go, he cannot go; he must be "driven." His death is not like the gentle fall of the ripened fruit from its old branch in autumn, but like the oak, uprooted, and dashed into the air by a mighty whirlwind. It is not like a vessel gliding to its chosen haven, but like a barque driven by a furious wind to a shore it shrinks from with horror. "Driven away!" The death of the wicked implies—Thirdly: A terrible retention of character. Is "driven away in his wickedness." He carries his wickedness with him. This is the worst part of the whole. He carries his vile thoughts, corrupt passions, sinful purposes, depraved habits, and accumulated guilt with him. He will leave everything else behind him but this—this adheres to him. He can no more flee from it than from himself. This wickedness will be the millstone to press downward into deeper, darker depths for ever; the poison that will rankle in the veins for ever, the fuel that will feed the flames for ever. O sinner, lay down this wickedness at the foot of the atoning and soul-renovating Cross! Observe—

Death in relation to the RIGHTEOUS.—"The righteous hath hope in his death." A man is not badly off under any circumstances if he has hope in him. Hope in the heart is a great magician; it changes all things to a man by the wave of its wand. Outward clouds break into sunshine, outer thunder-storms sink into zephyrs, hope turns prisons into palaces, darkness into light, and poverty into wealth. Death is nothing to a man who has strong hope in Him. The strength of hope, however, depends always on two things, (1) On the *grandeur* of its object—the smaller the things hoped for, the weaker the hope, and the reverse. Its power depends (2) On the *strength* of its foundation. Hope for the grandest objects with weak reasons, will not be a strong hope. The righteous man has these two conditions of a strong hope. He has the grandest objects, the highest liberty, the most enchanting beauties, the noblest services, the sublimest friendships, the vision of God, the fellowship of His blessed Son, and communion with the illustrious of all mankind. For all this he has the strongest ground—the unalterable promises of God, and the assurances of his own heart. Give me this hope, and I shall transform the " King of terrors " into an angel of mercy; the dark, deep grave into a sunny pathway to a soul-transporting elysium.

Hast thou this hope, my brother ? "The world," says Archbishop Leighton, " dares say no more of its devices than *dum spiro spero* (whilst I breathe I hope), but the children of God can add by virtue of this living hope, *dum expiro spero* (whilst I expire I hope)."

> " The good man's hope is laid far, far beyond
> The sway of tempests, or the furious sweep
> Of mortal desolation."—H. K. WHITE

Proverbs 14:33

Reticence and Loquacity

"Wisdom resteth in the heart of him that hath understanding: but *that which is* in the midst of fools is made known."

THE words suggest two things—

THAT RETICENCE IS OFTEN A MARK OF WISDOM.—We say *often*, not always. It is sometimes a sign of *stupidity*. There are those whose tongues are sluggish, because their souls are dormant and benighted. It is sometimes a sign of *sulkiness.* There is a morose, unsocial nature, that tends to silence. There is " a dumb devil." But reticence is a sign of wisdom when "wisdom resteth"—or, as some read, quietly "abideth in the heart." It is there biding its opportunity; there for use, not for display. As a rule, wise men are slow and cautious in speech. Two things account for this. First: *Humility.* Great intelligence tends to great humility, and humility is ever diffident. It shrinks from parade. It courts the shady and the silent. Pride, on the other hand, is garrulous. Its instinct is display. Another thing that accounts for reticence in a wise man is—Secondly: *Conscientiousness.* A truly wise man is a conscientious man. Feeling the responsibility of language, he weighs his words. He knows for every idle word there is a judgment. The words suggest again—

THAT LOQUACITY IS EVER AN INDICATION OF FOLLY.— "But that which is in the midst of fools is made known." The emptier the mind, the more active the tongue. This is exemplified in the prattle of children and the fluency of unthoughtful preachers. Volubility is the offspring of vacuity. It has been said that the editor of one of our greatest daily journals will never trust a writer to write a "Leader" on a subject which he has thoroughly compassed. The reason is obvious. The article would lack that flippancy, wordiness, and positivity which are attractive to the common reader. Fools are vain and reckless; hence they are loquacious.

Homer, in his *Iliad,* hath appointed unto dreams two doors, the one a door of horn, which was the door of truth, the other a door of ivory, which was the door of deceit, for horn, as they say, may be looked through, but ivory, being thick and dark, is not transparent. "These doors," it has been said, "may very well be applied to the mouths of men, which are as the indices and tables of the heart; for to some it is a door of glass, which is soon broke open, and easily giveth pass to a multitude of words, wherein the folly of their hearts and minds is discerned; to others it is a door of brass, firm and solid in keeping in their

254 / Book of Proverbs

words with more care and circumspection, and showing the firm solidity of their hearts and minds."

Proverbs 14:34-35

The Political and Social Importance of Morality

"Righteousness exalteth a nation : but sin *is* a reproach to any people. The king's favour *is* towards a wise servant : but his wrath is *against* him that causeth shame."

THE text teaches—

The POLITICAL importance of morality.—"Righteousness"—rectitude of character—"exalteth a nation:" but "sin"—immorality—is "a reproach to any people." It is here said, First : Rectitude "*exalts*" *a nation*. It exalts it in many ways. In *material wealth*. Truth, honesty, integrity, in a people are the best guarantees of commercial advancement. Credit is the best capital in the business of a nation as well as in the business of an individual, and credit is built on righteous principles. The more credit a nation has, the more business it can do ; and the more business, if rightly conducted, the more will be the accumulation of wealth. It exalts it in *social enjoyments*. According as the principles of veracity, uprightness, and honour reign in society, will be the freeness, the heartiness, and the enjoyment of social intercourse. It exalts it in *moral power*. The true majesty of a kingdom lies in its moral virtues. The state whose heart beats loyally to the eternal principles of rectitude gains an influence upon the earth mightier than the mightiest armies or battalions can impart. Secondly : *Unrighteousness degrades a nation*. "Sin is a reproach to any people." The prevalence of immorality amongst a people tends, in the very nature of the case, to ignominy and ruin. Neither commerce, nor arms, nor science, nor art, can long sustain a morally corrupt people. Immutable Heaven has decreed their destruction. "At what instant I shall speak concerning a nation, and concerning a kingdom, to pluck up, and to pull down, and to destroy it; if that nation, against whom I have pronounced, turn from their evil, I will repent of the evil that I thought to do unto them. And at what instant I shall speak concerning a nation, and concerning a kingdom, to build, and to plant it; if it do evil in my sight, that it obey not my voice, then I will repent of the good wherewith I said I would benefit them."*

The text teaches—

The SOCIAL importance of morality.—"The king's favour is towards a wise servant, but his wrath is against him that causeth shame." The idea is, that the king, the man worthy of the name, will treat his servants according to their character. The king's servants either mean his ministers of state, those who serve him in his regal capacity, or those who attend upon him in his more private and domestic relations. Rectitude in his service will be pleasing to him, and honourable to him in either case. All employers throughout society are the best served by those whose characters are distinguished by unswerving truth and incorruptible honesty. Few kings, however fallen in character, have so far gone as to feel any real respect for fawning sycophants and unprincipled time-servers. He serves best and is honoured most, whether he is engaged in the interest of a state, a business, or a family, whose conduct in all things is controlled by righteousness. This subject teaches, First: *That men who are ruled by righteousness are the men most to be valued in a country.* It is not the warrior, the merchant, or even the man of science and art, that are the most valuable to a state. It is the man of goodness. Goodness is to a country what the breeze is to the atmosphere, preventing stagnation and quickening the blood of the world. Secondly: *That the promotion of true morality is the best way to promote the interests of a state.* A healthy press, useful

* Jer. xviii. 7—10.

schools, enlightened pulpits, to promote these is to give peace, dignity, and stability to kingdoms.

> "What constitutes a state?
> Not high-raised battlement, or laboured mound,
>   Thick wall, or moated gate;
> Not cities proud, with spires and turrets crown'd,
>   Nor bays and broad-armed ports,
> Where, laughing at the storm, rich navies ride:
>   Nor starred and spangled courts,
> Where low-browed baseness wafts perfume to pride.
>   No! *Men*—high-minded *men.*"—SIR WILLIAM JONES

Proverbs 15:1-2

Words

"A soft answer turneth away wrath : but grievous words stir up anger. The tongue of the wise useth knowledge aright : but the mouth of fools poureth out foolishness."

FEW writers, ancient or modern, say so much about words as Solomon, and no man of extensive observation and deep thought can fail to be impressed with the importance of *words*. "Words," says Richter, "are often everywhere as the minute hands of the soul, more important than even the hour hands of action." "Men suppose," says the father of the inductive philosophy, "that their reason has command over their words; still it happens that words in return exercise authority and reason." The text leads us to consider two things—

THE PACIFYING AND IRRITATING POWER OF WORDS.—First: *The pacifying power of words.* "A soft answer turneth away wrath." Several things are implied in this short utterance. (1) The existence of anger against you. You have an enemy. There is a man whose soul is fired with indignation, speaking to you either by pen or tongue. Whether that anger has been justly excited by you, it matters not: there it is, in thunder and flame. (2) The importance of turning away this anger. It is a very undesirable thing to have indignation burning in an immortal breast toward you; it is not well to be hated and damned by any one, not even by a child. (3) There is an effective method of turning away wrath. What is that? A "*soft answer.*" A response free from excitement and resentment, uttered in the low tone of magnanimous forbearance. At first, in some cases, the display of such calmness towards an enraged enemy may only intensify the passion. But when reflection comes, as come it must, the "soft answer" works as oil on the troubled waves. A "soft answer," like a conducting-rod, can carry the lightning of an enemy into the ground, and bury it in silence. Among many examples of the pacifying power of soft words, the reply of Gideon to the exasperated men of Ephraim may be given, and also the conduct of Abigail to David.* Secondly: The *irritating* power of words. "Grievous words stir up anger." There is a great tendency in the insulting and denunciatory language of your enemy to induce you to use "grievous words," but the use of such words will, instead of mending the matter, increase the evil, and "stir up anger." They only add fuel to the flame. There are men whose natures are so unsocial and splenetic, that their words are always of that "grievous" sort that "stir up anger." Wherever they go, they scratch and irritate. The curs bark, and even the calm mastiffs get excited.

THE RIGHT AND WRONG USE OF WORDS.—First: *The right use of words.* "The tongue of the wise useth knowledge aright." A similar but not identical sentiment has more than once come under our notice in our path through this book.† Knowledge is good; it is well to have the mind richly furnished with useful information, but this good thing may be, and often is, wrongly used by words. There is a right use of knowledge in speech. What is that? It is to communicate it at right times, to proper persons, in suitable places, and in a becoming spirit. Secondly: *The wrong use of words.* "The mouth of fools poureth out foolishness." "Out of the abundance of the

* 1 Sam. xxv. 32, 33.   † See chaps. xii. 23; xiii. 16; xiv. 33.

258 / Book of Proverbs

heart the mouth speaketh." The fool's heart is full of folly, and folly flows from his lips. Foolish words are either words without meaning, empty jargon, or words of bad meaning, the vehicles of filth, insubordination, and blasphemy. Bishop Horne well remarks that, "Among the sources of those innumerable calamities which from age to age have overwhelmed mankind, may be reckoned as one of the principal, the abuse of words."

Proverbs 15:3

God's Inspection of the World

"The eyes of the LORD *are* in every place, beholding the evil and the good."

THE language of the Bible is often very anthropomorphic. It represents the Infinite Spirit as having the *bodily* parts of men—hands, feet, head, back, heart, eyes, ears, and tongue. It also sometimes represents Him as having the mental passions of men—revenge, jealousy, indignation, hope, disappointment, and regret. All this, of course, is an accommodation to our limited faculties and modes of thought. The text is an instance of this feature of Divine revelation; it speaks of the "eyes of the Lord." The language expresses that which undoubtedly belongs to God, an infinite *capacity of discernment*. He knows at *every moment everything, in every place*. The Bible is full of this doctrine.* The text suggests a few thoughts concerning God's inspection of men.

The inspection is PERSONAL.—He does not inspect men through the eyes of others, but through his own. We often get our knowledge of men from the observation of others. Earthly kings get their knowledge of their subjects thus; but God gets His knowledge from Himself. When He

* Psalm cxxxix.; Proverbs v. 21.; Jer. xvi. 17; 2 Chron. xvi. 9.

comes to judge the world, He will not, like earthly judges, depend for information upon the testimony of witnesses. No one will be able to give Him any fresh information; no eloquence will change the judgment that He has formed. He knows all "of Himself."

His inspection is UNIVERSAL.—"The eyes of the Lord are in every place." There is no place where they are not: on ocean, on land, in society, and in solitude, in the bustle of business, and in scenes of recreation; wherever we are, His eyes are. We cannot go from those eyes, we cannot escape their glance an instant. If we ascend to heaven, they are there; if we plunge into hell, they are there. They penetrate the lowest abysses; they peer into the profoundest darkness.

> " What can 'scape the eye
> Of God, all-seeing, or deceive His heart
> Omniscient ? "—MILTON

The inspection is THOROUGH.—"Beholding the evil and the good." There is nothing in the history of man that is not either good or evil. There is no third, no neutral quality. He knows all the good and all the evil in the most incipient, as well as in the most developed stages. "There is not a word on our tongue, but, O Lord, thou knowest it altogether." This subject urges, First; *Courage for the good.* Ye men of truth and virtue, who struggle here against mighty odds, take courage under your trials and afflictions. The great Master sees you. His eyes are on you—take heart. The subject urges, Secondly: *A warning for the wicked.* "Because sentence against an evil work is not executed speedily, therefore the hearts of the sons of men are fully set to do evil." Because of the delay, conclude not, O sinner, that thy conduct has escaped the notice of the just God. Judgment is coming. The subject urges, Thirdly: *Circumspection for all.* Since God's eyes are always on us, let us " walk circumspectly, not as fools, but as wise, redeeming the time, because the days are evil."

"How dreadful," says Dr. J. Todd, "is the eye of God on him who wants to sin! Do you know about Lafayette, that great man who was the friend of Washington? He tells us that he was once shut up in a little room in a gloomy prison for a great while. In the door of his little cell was a very small hole cut. At this hole a soldier was placed day and night to watch him. All he could see was the soldier's eye, but that eye was always there. Day and night, every moment when he looked up, he always saw that eye. Oh, he says, it was dreadful! There was no escape, no hiding; when he laid down, and when he rose up, that eye was watching him. How dreadful will the eye of God be on the sinner as it watches him in the eternal world for ever!"

Proverbs 15:4, 7

Speech

" A wholesome tongue *is* a tree of life: but perverseness therein *is* a breach in the spirit. . . The lips of the wise disperse knowledge: but the heart of the foolish *doeth* not so."

It would seem that Solomon could not say enough about speech; it occurs to him again and again. As he thinks of it, some new point strikes him, and he notes it down. Let us notice what he here says about the speech of the wise and the foolish:

The speech of the WISE.—First: It is a *healing* speech. The "wholesome tongue," or, literally, as in the margin, a "healing tongue," "is a tree of life." There are wounded souls in society; souls wounded by insults, slanders, bereavements, disappointments, losses, moral convictions. There is a speech that is healing to those wounds, and that speech is used by "the wise." There are societies, too, that are wounded by divisions, animosities; the social body bleeds. There is a speech which heals social divisions, and "the wise" employ it. Secondly: It is a *living* speech. It is "a tree of life." It is at once the *product* and *producer* of life. The speech of the wise is not the vehicle of sapless platitudes, it is the offspring of living conviction. It is a germ falling from the ever-growing tree of living thought: it lives and *produces* life. "Cast forth," says Carlyle, "thy act, thy word, into the everlasting, ever-growing universe: it is a seed-grain that cannot die, unnoticed to-day; it will be found flourishing as a banyan grove—perhaps, alas! as a hemlock forest, after a thousand years." But the word of the wise is not as a hemlock seed; it is a seed that falls from that "tree of life," which is to be the healing of the nations. Thirdly: It is an *enlightening* speech. "The lips of the wise disperse knowledge." The words of the wise are beams reflected from the great Sun of Truth, and they break upon the darkness with which error has clouded the world. Solomon was himself an exemplification of this enlightening speech. "He taught the people knowledge; yea, he gave good heed, and sought out, and set in order many proverbs. The preacher sought to find out acceptable words; and that which was written was upright, even words of truth."*

The speech of the FOOLISH.—First: The speech of the foolish is a *wounding* speech. "Perverseness therein is a breach in the spirit." The unkind slanders, irritating words, of wicked men, have often made a "breach in the spirit" of *individuals, societies,* and *commonwealths.* Many a female servant in our England will show you by her haggard and desponding looks what breaches have been produced in her spirit by the querulous and ill-tempered words of her mistress even in one short month. There are annoying, nagging words used by masters, parents, husbands, wives, that slowly kill people, and their authors should be denounced as murderers. The poison of asps is on their lips, and their words instil the venom into the constitutions of their listeners. Secondly: The speech of the foolish is an *empty* speech. "The heart of the foolish doeth not so." "The heart" is here the antithesis to the "lips." The meaning unquestionably is, that the foolish

* Eccles. xii. 9, 10.

man does not disperse knowledge, but that the wise does. The fool has no knowledge to disperse. He has never sought after knowledge, therefore is ignorant; and, being ignorant, his speech cannot enlighten.

Proverbs 15:5-6

Diverse Families

" A fool despiseth his father's instruction: but he that regardeth reproof is prudent. In the house of the righteous *is* much treasure : but in the revenues of the wicked is trouble."

THESE two verses are a domestic sketch. Two families appear before us. In the one there is filial folly; in the other, filial wisdom : in the one, enjoyable riches; in the other, troublesome wealth.

THERE ARE FILIAL FOLLY AND FILIAL WISDOM.—Notice —First : Filial *folly*. "A fool despiseth his father's instruction." Why is he a fool for doing it? A father's instruction is the best kind of tuition. (1) It is authoritative. A father has a right to instruct his child. The Eternal Himself commands him to " train up a child in the way he should go, and when he is old he will not depart from it." (2) It is experimental. He seeks to give to his child what he has learnt not merely from books or from other men, but from his own long-tried and struggling life. (3) It is *loving*. Who feels a deeper interest in his son than he ? His counsels are dictated by the deepest and divinest affections of the human heart. What egregious folly it is, therefore, for a son to despise such instruction ! Despise— not merely neglect, or reject, but to regard it with contempt. A state of mind lost to everything that is true and noble in sentiment. Notice, Secondly : Filial *wisdom*. " He that regardeth reproof is prudent"—wise. It is wise because it is one of the best means to avoid the evils of life. A father's instruction points out the slippery places in the path of life, the rocks ahead on the trackless voyage. It is the best means to attain the possible good. A "father's instruction" will point to the direction where the good things lie. That son is wise therefore who attends to a father's admonitions.

THERE ARE ENJOYABLE RICHES AND TROUBLESOME WEALTH.—First: There are *enjoyable riches*. " In the house of the righteous is much treasure." Whatever is possessed in the house of the righteous, whether children, friends, books, money, is a treasure. "A little that a righteous man hath is better than the riches of many wicked." The righteous man enjoys what he has. His treasures have been righteously won, are righteously held, and righteously used, and in all he has righteous enjoyment. Secondly: There is *troublesome wealth*. " In the revenues of the wicked is trouble." The wealth of the wicked, instead of yielding real happiness engenders anxieties, jealousies, apprehensions, and greatly trouble the spirit. The wicked man often in getting his riches has trouble. He has to go against the dictates of his conscience, and to war with the nobler instincts of his being. In keeping them, too, he has trouble. He holds them with a nervous grasp, fearing lest they should be snatched from his clutch. In leaving them he has trouble. His wealth gives terror to his dying-bed. "There is a sore evil which I have seen under the sun, namely, riches kept for the owners thereof, to their hurt."

> "Gold will make black white:
> Wrong right : base noble : old young : coward valiant :
> Plucks stout men's pillows from below their heads.
> This yellow slave
> Will knit and break religions ; bless the accurst :
> Make the hoar leprosy ador'd : place thieves,
> And give them title, knee, and approbation
> With senators on the bench."—SHAKESPEARE

Proverbs 15:8-11

The Man-ward Feeling and the Infinite Intelligence of God

"The sacrifice of the wicked *is* an abomination to the LORD: but the prayer of the upright *is* his delight. The way of the wicked is an abomination unto the LORD: but He loveth him that followeth after righteousness. Correction *is* grievous unto him that forsaketh the way: *and* he that hateth reproof shall die. Hell and destruction *are* before the LORD: how much more, then, the hearts of the children of men?" *

THE MAN-WARD FEELING of God.—The text speaks of "abomination" and "delight" in God. He is not a being of sheer intellect, One that sees all and *feels* nothing; indifferent alike to the good and the bad, to the happy and the miserable. He has a heart. Within Him there is an infinite ocean of the tenderest sensibilities. The text teaches us that he has *man-ward* feelings—feelings that have relation to sinful men on this little planet. This is wonderful, wonderful that man should affect the heart of the Infinite! Three things are here suggested concerning this man-ward feeling. First: *It is mingled.* There is "abomination" and "delight." His feelings in relation to man partake of the agreeable and the disagreeable, How the Infinite can feel anything like sadness we know not, the idea transcends our loftiest thoughts; but the Bible speaks of Him as being "grieved," "troubled," and as "repenting." There is an undertone, an awful wail of sadness in some of the utterances of the Bible. It is taught that His man-ward feeling, Secondly: *Has respect to character.* His abomination is toward the "wicked," and his "delight" is toward the "upright." "The sacrifice of the wicked is an abomination to the Lord." The wicked make sacrifices sometimes from custom, sometimes from fear, but their sacrifices, however costly in their nature, and Scriptural in their mode and form of presentation, are

* The seventh verse has been discussed in a previous Reading.

evermore an "abomination." Their sacrifice is an acted lie, and is an offence against the Omniscient. On the contrary, the "prayer of the upright *is* His delight, and He loveth him that followeth after righteousness." To Daniel the angel said, "At the beginning of thy supplication the commandment came forth, and I am come to show thee that thou art greatly beloved."* Of Cornelius it was said, "Thy prayer and thy alms are come as a memorial before the Lord."† So pleasing is the prayer of the good to the Great Father, that "He seeketh such to worship him." That the Infinite cannot look at the good and the bad with the same feeling is clear from the testimony of universal conscience, from the history of providential judgments, and from the declarations of holy Scripture. It is taught that God's man-ward feeling *expresses itself in human experience.* "Correction is grievous unto him that forsaketh the way; and he that hateth reproof shall die." There are wrapt in these words three great principles—wrong must meet with suffering,—the man that forsaketh the way must have correction. Suffering must develop character, to the wicked it is "grievous," and he hateth reproof. He murmurs, rebels, and is full of resentment to God. On the contrary it is implied that the righteous accept it in the proper spirit of resignation and acquiescence. The third principle here implied is that character must determine destiny, "he that hateth reproof shall *die.*" But the point to be here observed is that all this experience in man in relation to the right and the wrong, expresses God's feeling. There must be punishment for sin. Punishment is God's abomination working in violated law.

THE INFINITE INTELLIGENCE OF GOD.—"Hell and destruction are before the Lord; how much more then the hearts of the children of men?" Three things are implied in this wonderful passage. First: *That the human heart has secret abysses within it.* "The heart is deceitful above all things, and desperately wicked: who can know it."‡ So profound are some of the secret things of the soul that man does not know his own heart. Circumstances often

* Daniel v. 22. † Acts x. ‡ Jer. xvii. 9.

bring up to life and power things of which he was utterly unconscious before. "Who can understand his errors?" Secondly: *That the secret abysses of the human heart are not so great as hell and destruction.* Hell is the *Sheol* in Hebrew, and the *Hades* in Greek; and it signifies the unseen world, the great universe of spirits. And perhaps special reference is here had to that section which is under the ban of inexorable justice, populated by fallen angels and ruined men. What secret abysses there are in lost souls! We read of the depths of Satan. What depths are those? Thirdly: *God thoroughly knows the abysses of hell and destruction, and therefore He must be thoroughly conversant with the human heart.* "How much more, then, the hearts of the children of men!" "Hell is naked before him, and destruction hath no covering before him," saith Job. His eye peers into the deepest depths of hell. How thoroughly, then, does he understand man! "I the Lord search the heart, I try the reins, even to give every man according to his ways, and according to the fruit of his doings."*

> " Search me, O God, and prove my heart,
>   E'en to its inmost ground:
> Try me, and read my thoughts, if aught
>   Of evil there be found.
> Yea, Lord, instruct my willing feet
>   The paths of ill to flee,
> And lead me on the eternal way—
>   The way to heaven and Thee."

Proverbs 15:12

The Scorner

"A scorner loveth not one that reproveth him: neither will he go unto the wise."

THE general definition of scorn is that disdainful feeling or treatment which springs from a person's opinion of the meanness of an object, and a consciousness or belief of his

---
* Jer. xvii. 10.

own superiority or worth. It is not necessarily bad. Scorn for the mean and immoral is a state of mind both virtuous and praiseworthy, but scorn for the true and the right, the noble and the divine, is a state of mind akin to that of the worst spirit in hell itself. It is to such the text refers. The scorner here is one who scoffs at religion and God. As this character has frequently come under our attention in passing through this book,* we shall very briefly state three things that are here implied concerning him.

He REQUIRES reproof.—Truly if the scorner requires not reproof, who does? He should be reproved, First: for his *self-ignorance*. He who arrogates to himself a superiority to divine teaching, is utterly unacquainted with his own limited faculties, moral relations, and spiritual needs. Of all ignorance, self-ignorance is the most inexcusable, criminal, and ruinous. He should be reproved, Secondly: For his *impious presumption*. The scorner sets his mouth against the heavens. He dares not only to adjudicate on the doings of God, but to ridicule the utterances of infinite wisdom. Surely such a man requires reproof.

He SHUNS reproof.—"He will not go unto the wise." Why? Because the wise would reprove him. The very instinct of a truly wise man leads to the moral castigation of such characters as scorners. The wise man cannot tolerate such iniquity. The scoffer knows it, and he shuns the society of the good. He will not read books that will deal seriously and honestly with his character. He will not attend a ministry that will expose his character in the broad light of eternal law; nor will he join the society that will deal truthfully with its members. The scorner "will not go unto the wise." Not he. He shrinks from the light. He has a horror of having his own proud conceit and haughty imaginations denounced and brought to contempt.

He HATES reproof.—"The scorner loveth not one that reproveth him." He deems the man his enemy who tells him the truth; hence, he hates the honest Christian. Albeit,

* See Reading on chap. xiv, 5, 6.

O scorner! the man who will "ring thee such a piece of chiding," as will make thee feel the moral turpitude of thy character, is thy friend. The man to whom thou canst say, "Thou turn'st mine eyes into my very soul, and there I see such black and grained spots, as will not leave their tint," thou shalt feel one day to be the truest friend thou hast ever met.

Proverbs 15:13-15

Human Hearts

" A merry heart maketh a cheerful countenance: but by sorrow of the heart the spirit is broken. The heart of him that hath understanding seeketh knowledge: but the mouth of fools feedeth on foolishness. All the days of the afflicted *are* evil: but he that is of a merry heart *hath* a continual feast."

THE Bible speaks much *about* human hearts and much *to* human hearts. It is a book pre-eminently for the heart. Why? Because the heart is the spring of man's activities, and the fountain of his history. In the text there is a reference to different kinds of hearts. Here is the "merry" and the mournful heart, the understanding and the foolish heart.

Here is THE MERRY AND THE MOURNFUL HEART.—Notice. First: *The merry heart.* By the merry heart we shall understand the Christly cheerful heart; not the light, frivolous heart of the thoughtless and the gay. Christliness evermore fills the whole soul with cheerfulness. Two things are said in the text of this "merry heart." (1) It is a radiance to the face. It maketh "a cheerful countenance." A man's countenance is a mirror in which you can see his soul. Emotions chisel their features on the brow. Man has an instinct to recognise this fact. We are physiognomists from childhood, judging character always from the face. This fact is a great advantage in our social life. Did men show no soul in their faces their presence would be as uninteresting as statues. Human society, if it could exist, would be oppressively monotonous. This fact suggests also the true method of beautifying the face. Beauty of countenance consisteth not in features, or complexion, so much as in expression. A genial, frank, sunny look is that which fascinates and pleases the beholder. History and observation show that in proportion to the moral depravity of countries is the physical ugliness of the population. Hence, make hearts cheerful by promoting Christianity, and you will make the presence of men and women mutually more attractive and pleasing. Stephen's Christianity made his face beam like that of an angel. Another thing said of this "merry heart" is, (2) It is a feast to the soul. "A merry heart hath a continual feast." The gratitude, the reliance, the hope, the love of Christian cheerfulness, constitute the soul's best banquet. The banquet continues amidst material pauperism. "Although the fig-tree shall not blossom, neither shall fruit be in the vines, the labour of the olive shall fail, and the fields shall yield no meat, the flock shall be cut off from the fold, and there shall be no herd in the stalls, yet I will rejoice in the Lord, I will joy in the God of my salvation."* It is a "continual feast." Notice. Secondly: *The mournful heart.* Two things are here said of the mournful heart." It breaks the spirit. "By sorrow of heart the spirit is broken." There are hearts over which there hangs a leaden cloud of gloom. All is discontent and foreboding sadness. This breaks the spirit. It steals away all vigour and elasticity from the soul. The faculty —rallying force—is gone; and the machine falls to pieces. The mournful heart also curses the whole life. "All the days of the afflicted are evil." The "afflicted" here are those whose sorrow of heart has broken their spirit. Truly this gloom turns the whole of a man's life into a night with scarcely a star to relieve the encircling darkness.

Here is THE UNDERSTANDING AND THE FOOLISH HEART.

* Hab. iii. 17.

First: *The one "seeketh knowledge."* "The heart of him that hath understanding, seeketh knowledge." The man who hath a true understanding, an unsophisticated, unbiassed heart, seeketh knowledge, the highest knowledge, the knowledge of God, which is the centre and soul of all science. Such was the heart of Nicodemus, who came at night to Jesus in quest of truth. Such was the heart of Mary, who sat at the feet of the Great Teacher; such also that of the Bereans, who searched the Scriptures for themselves. Secondly: *The other "feedeth on foolishness."* Souls, like bodies, have different tastes. Some souls have a taste—not a natural, but an acquired one—for "foolishness." They have a relish for things which in the sight of reason and God are foolish, they seize them with voracity, and with a zest ruminate on them afterwards.

Which of these hearts throbs in thee, my brother? Men have different moral hearts. Hast thou the cheerful or the mourning heart, the understanding or foolish? Remember that as thy heart, so art thou—so art thou in thy character, in the universe, and before God.

Proverbs 15:16-17

The Dinner of Herbs and the Stalled Ox

"Better *is* little with the fear of the LORD than great treasure and trouble therewith. Better *is* a dinner of herbs where love is, than a stalled ox and hatred therewith."

THESE words present to us three subjects of thought. The secularly little with the spiritually good, the secularly much with the spiritually bad, and the better conjunction for man of the two.

THE SECULARLY "LITTLE" WITH THE SPIRITUALLY GOOD.—Solomon gives a specimen here of the *secularly little*—"A dinner of herbs." A meaner repast one could scarcely have—the mere food that nature gives the unreasoning cattle that feed in the meadow. The *spiritually good* he describes as "the fear of the Lord"—a loving reverence for the Great One. This is religion, this is moral goodness. The picture he brings before us, therefore, is that of a good man in great poverty. This has ever been, and still is, a common sight. Some of the truest and the holiest men that ever trod this earth have had to feed on such humble fare as "a dinner of herbs." Lazarus, who found his home in Abraham's bosom, was a beggar. The Son of God had "nowhere to lay his head." This shows two things, First: *That poverty is not always a disgrace.* It is *sometimes* so. When it can be traced to indolence, extravagance, and intemperance, it is a disgrace. But where you find it in connection with the "fear of the Lord," it has nothing disreputable about it. The very rags of the good are far more honourable than the purple of the wicked. This shows, Secondly: *That there are higher rewards for virtue than material wealth.* If riches were the Divine rewards for goodness, men would always be wealthy in proportion to their spiritual excellence. But it is not so. There are higher rewards for virtue than money. Spiritual freedom, a commending conscience, uplifting hopes, inspiring purposes, fellowship with the Divine, these are the rewards of goodness. Another subject here presented is—

THE SECULARLY "MUCH" WITH THE SPIRITUALLY BAD.—Here is a specimen of the *secularly much.* "A stalled ox," not a single joint. This brings up to us the picture of a man with his family and friends sitting around the table enjoying a splendid banquet, a well-fed, well-cooked, well-served ox, with all his attendant luxuries before him, but he has no spiritual goodness, he does not "fear the Lord." He has no love in him; spiritually he is "in the gall of bitterness, and in the bonds of iniquity." This is a social scene as prevalent as the former. Wickedness and wealth we see everywhere associated; and this has been felt in all ages, by the thoughtful, as one of the most painful and perplexing enigmas in the government of God. "I was envious," said Asaph, "at the foolish when I saw the prosperity of the wicked."

The other subject here presented is—

THE BETTER CONJUNCTION FOR MAN OF THE TWO.—
"*Better* is little with the fear of the Lord than great treasure and trouble therewith." Mark, he does not say a "dinner of herbs" is better than a feast off the "stalled ox," this would be absurd, contrary to the common sense and experience of mankind. Poverty is not better than riches, but the reverse. Poverty is a serious disadvantage, and wealth in itself is a great blessing. But what he says is this: it is better to be poor with religion, than to be rich without it. Take two men, one shall be an averagely rich ungodly man, the other an averagely poor and pious one. Solomon would say that the condition of the latter is better than that of the former, and truly so for two reasons. First: *His condition would be a more enjoyable one.*[*] He would have a higher happiness. His happiness would spring from within, that of the other from without. The happiness of the one, therefore, would be sensational, the other spiritual; the one selfish, the other generous; the one decreasing, the other heightening. The ungodly rich have their "*portion in this life,*" and in this life only. Secondly: *His condition would be a more honourable one.* The one is honoured for what he *has*, the other for what he *is*. The one is honoured less and less as people get morally enlightened, the other more and more. The one is honoured only *here* by the depraved, the other is honoured *yonder* by angels and by God.

My poor pious brother, let not thy poverty oppress thee: riches and poverty are more in the hand than in the heart; "a man's life consisteth not in the abundance of things which he possesseth." The contented are ever wealthy, the avaricious ever poor. By thy dinner of herbs may rest the foot of that Jacob's ladder, by which thou canst hold company with the skies, and exchange visits with the celestial.

[*] See HOMILIST, second series, vol. ii. p. 591.

Proverbs 15:18

Social Discord

"A wrathful man stirreth up strife: but *he that is* slow to anger appeaseth strife."

THE text leads us to consider three things:

The EVIL of social discord.—It is implied that *strife* is an evil, and so it is. First: In its *essence*. Ill feeling is a bad thing. It is opposed to the great moral law of the creation—the law of universal love.

> "Be not angry with each other;
> Man is made to love his brother."

So said the poet postman of Devonshire; and the utterance is divinely true. Souls are made for love. Conscience and the Bible show this. Ill feeling is everywhere prohibited, and love everywhere inculcated in the New Testament. "He that loveth not, knoweth not God, for God is love." It is evil—Secondly: In its *influence*. Strife in a family, in a church, or in a nation, is most baneful in its influence. It obstructs progress, it entails miseries, it dishonours truth. Strife is one of the worst of social fiends. It is the spawn of hell.

The PROMOTION of social discord.—How is it promoted? By the *malicious*. "A wrathful man stirreth up strife." Men can only give to society what is in them. They sow their own passions, and like begets like; the wrathful man produces strife. There are men and women in society who are, somehow or other, terribly charged with the malign. "The poison of asps is under their lips." They are social incendiaries. By their temper, their inuendoes, their slanders, they kindle, feed, and fan the flame of social strife. Discord is the music of their souls. "Hatred stirreth up strife."*

The APPEASERS of social discord.—" He that is slow to

---

* See Reading on chap. x. 12.

anger appeaseth strife." "A soft answer turneth away wrath."* "It is an easy matter," says Plutarch, "to stop the fire that is kindled only in hair, wool, candlewick, or a little chaff: but if it once have taken hold of matter that hath solidity and thickness, it soon inflames and consumes — advances the highest timber of the roof, as Æschylus saith; so he that observes anger, while it is in its beginning, and sees it by degrees smoking and taking fire from some speech or chaff-like scurrility, he need take no great pains to extinguish it; but oftentimes puts an end to it only by silence or neglect. For as he that adds no fuel to fire hath already as good as put it out, so he that doth not feel anger at the first, nor blow the fire in himself, hath prevented and destroyed it."

As certain as water quencheth fire, love will extinguish strife.

" Peace hath her victories
No less renown'd than war."—MILTON

Proverbs 15:19

Indolence and Righteousness

" The way of the slothful *man is* as an hedge of thorns: but the way of the righteous *is* made plain."

THERE is a very important principle involved in this antithesis. It is this: that indolence is unrighteousness. A principle this, which, though generally overlooked, is obviously true, and of great practical importance. A lazy man, though legally he may pay every man his due, is notwithstanding dishonest. He lives on the labours of other men: his life is a life of larceny. The divine law is, that if a man does not work, neither should he eat. The slothful servant Christ calls "wicked." The text indicates the tendency of the indolent and the righteous.

THE TENDENCY OF THE INDOLENT IS TO CREATE DIF-

* See Reading on chap. xv. 1.

FICULTIES.—" The way of the slothful man is an hedge of thorns." Deep in the moral nature of man is the feeling that he *ought* to work; and the slothful man endeavours to appease this feeling by making excuses. Whatever way is pointed out for him to walk in, intellectual, agricultural, mercantile, mechanical, professional, is full of difficulties. He sees thorns lie thickly everywhere before him. First: In the *commencement* he sees "thorns." Though his lazy limbs are reluctant, his imagination is active in creating difficulties. It plants hedges of thorns, and they lie formidable in his prospect. Secondly: In the *pursuit* he sees "thorns." He has commenced, but he cannot go on. New thorn-bushes appear, and he is afraid of being scratched. "The sluggard will not plough by reason of the cold." A terrible evil is this indolence, and a very prevalent one, too. " Indolence, says Baxter, "is a constant sin, and but the devil's home for temptations and for unprofitable distracting musings." Ask me to characterize indolence, and I would say it is the drag-chain on the wheel of progress; it is the highway to pauperism. It is the incubator of nameless iniquities, it is the devil's couch.

THE TENDENCY OF THE RIGHTEOUS IS TO OVERCOME DIFFICULTIES.—" But the way of the righteous is made plain." Honest industry plucks up the real " thorns " from the road; it levels and paves as it proceeds. What has it not accomplished? It has literally said to mountains. "depart," and they have departed. And in removing these difficulties strength is gotten; the difficulties of labour are, in truth, the blessings of labour. "Difficulty," says Burke, "is a severe instructor, set over us by the supreme ordinance of a parental Guardian and Legislator, Who knows us better than we know ourselves, and He loves us better too. He that wrestles with us strengthens our nerves, and sharpens our skill. Our antagonist is our helper. This amicable conflict with difficulty obliges us to an intimate acquaintance with our object, and compels us to consider it in all its relations. It will not do for us to be superficial."

Proverbs 15:21-22

Contrasts

"Folly *is* joy to *him that is* destitute of wisdom: but a man of understanding walketh uprightly. Without counsel purposes are disappointed: but in the multitude of counsellors they are established." *

THERE seems to be a threefold contrast in these words.

FRIVOLITY AND PROGRESS.—(1) *Frivolity.* "Folly is joy to him that is destitute of wisdom." He does not merely practise his absurdities, but he rejoices in them. He finds his paradise, such as it is, in the nonsense, the fooleries, the empty gaieties, the painted bubbles of life. These are as the "sweet morsel under his tongue." In *realities*, especially those of a moral kind, he has no pleasure, no interest. (2) *Progress.* "A man of understanding walketh uprightly." It is implied that the frivolous man, who is destitute of understanding, makes no progress in righteousness. The man of true wisdom moves in the path of life with a soul erect in virtuous sentiments and godly aims. He turns his eyes away from beholding vanity. He has no delight in foolery. He pursues his course, abhorring that which is evil and cleaving to that which is good.

THOUGHTLESSNESS AND DELIBERATION.—(1) *Thoughtlessness.* "Without counsel." There are those who, either from indolence, stupidity, or pride, act without advice. They will not consult either their own reason by reflection, or the judgment of others, who know life better than themselves. They are "without counsel," therefore, without any true light within them, without any true guide in the intricate journeys of life. (2) *Deliberation.* There are those who do not only take counsel, but who seek as much counsel as they can get. They have a "multitude of counsellors." They act not from impulse, nor do they depend entirely upon their own judgment. They submit their

* Verse 20 has been discussed in a preceding reading.

plans to the opinions of others, they invite counsel. They move on through life with calm and religious thoughtfulness.

DISAPPOINTMENT AND REALIZATION.—(1) *Disappointment.* The man "without counsel" finds that his "purposes are disappointed." His crude projects of rash and hasty formation were wrecked as soon as they were launched on the sea of practical life. The thoughtless and foolish man is doomed to have all his purposes in relation to pleasure, true success, and lasting dignity, broken. Few things are more distressing to men than a broken purpose. The wreck of purpose is a terrible catastrophe to a soul. The shores of wicked men's lives are thickly strewn with the wrecks of broken purposes and disappointed hopes. (2) *Realization.* "In the multitude of counsellors they are established." It is implied, of course, that the counsellors are wise men, and that their counsels have been well weighed and carried out. In this way men's purposes get established. They find their realization. He who makes God his Great Counsellor, in passing through life, will have his purposes fully established. All the moral architecture which his devout thoughts have sketched within him, and which charm his imagination, he will have one day fully embodied in the New Jerusalem, with pearly gates and streets of gold.

Proverbs 15:23

Useful Speech

"A man hath joy by the answer of his mouth: and a word *spoken* in due season, how good *is it!*"

SOLOMON turns our attention again to speech, and his words here suggest two remarks concerning useful speech:

IT IS A JOY-GIVING SPEECH.—"A man hath joy by the answer of his mouth." Useful speech—speech which enlightens, comforts, strengthens souls—affords no small amount of real pleasure to the speaker himself. Three things guarantee him "joy" in such speaking. *The testimony of his own conscience.* Having spoken what he believed to be the true, the generous, and the fitting, his conscience cheers him with its smiles. The sounds of his truthful words wake heavenly melodies within. *The manifestation of the benefit.* When he sees that the men to whom he speaks are evidently being improved in knowledge, in energy, and in true nobility, he has an unspeakable joy. He sees his words ripening into fruit, and he "hath joy." *The gratitude of his hearers.* The appreciation of his hearers is no small joy. Ask the honest minister of the Gospel if the acknowledgments which from time to time he receives from his audience of the useful effects of his ministry upon their hearts hath not joy in it? "What is our hope, our crown of rejoicing? Are not even ye in the presence of our Lord Jesus Christ at his coming?"*

Another remark concerning useful speech is—

IT IS A SEASONABLY UTTERED SPEECH.—"A word spoken in due season how good is it." The value of a word, however good in itself, depends in a great measure upon its seasonable utterance. There is a time for everything. It should be in season as far as the *speaker's* own soul is concerned. Our souls have their seasons, and words that would be suitable in one of their moods would not be so in another. Words of consolation addressed to us are worthless if our souls are not in sadness; words of reproof are offensive if our souls are not deeply impressed with the sense of the wrong to be reproached. Words in season are words suited to soul moods. Secondly: It should be in season as far as the *hearer's* soul is concerned. Different men have different moral tempers, and words that are suitable to one would not be adapted for another; and the same man has different moods or tempers at different times, the words, therefore, that would suit him at one period would be ill adapted at another. The argumentative, the persuasive, the

* 1 Thess. ii. 19.

guiding, the reproving word, must have its appropriate season to be good. The words of Manoah's wife of Abigail to David, the words of Naaman's servant to his master, the words of Paul to the Philippian gaoler, are all examples of words spoken in due season.* May we all have the tongue of the learned, that we may speak as words to him that is weary. "Let thy conversation," says Quarles, "with men be sober and sincere: let thy devotion to God be dutiful and decent: let the one be hearty and not haughty: let the other be humble and not homely: so live with men as if God saw thee: so pray to God as if men heard thee."

Proverbs 15:24

The Way of the Wise

" The way of life *is* above to the wise, that he may depart from hell beneath."

THE way of the wise is AN ELEVATING way.—"The way of life is above to the wise." It is above. The word "above" is to be taken, not in its local sense, for that would indicate a mere relative position. What is above to one creature locally is beneath to another. Nor is it to be taken in a secular sense. Wise men may reach elevated secular positions, but very often their wisdom has led them down to pauperism and prisons. It is to be taken in a spiritual sense. When Paul commands us to "set our affections on things above," he means not on suns, or stars, or thrones, but on the things of spiritual worth and grandeur. The things above mean the Divine principles, the spiritual services, the vital alliances, the immortal honours, of the great and holy kingdom of God. The wise man's way is "above" to these. He presses towards the

---

* Judges xviii. 23.   1 Sam. xxv. 32, 33.
2 Kings, v. 13, 14.   Acts xvi. 28—31.   Isaiah xlv. 40.

mark of true greatness. "Excelsior" is his motto in a spiritual sense. He knows no pause. His destiny is a moral hill. The zone reached to-day is his starting-point for to-morrow. On its high lands that bound his horizon to-day, he will stand with wider and sunnier prospects to-morrow. His way is "above." "It doth not appear what we shall be, but we know that when He doth appear, we shall be like Him, for we shall see Him as He is."

The way of the wise is A SOUL-SECURING WAY.—"Depart from hell beneath." There is a hell. Whether Solomon here points to the scene of retributive misery, or to *Sheol*, the grave, such a scene undoubtedly exists. Hell is "beneath." It is beneath in a moral sense. Its ideas, habits, fellowships, are all degrading. Every sin is a step downward into intellectual darkness and moral debasement. On the other hand, every step of the wise is a departure from this hell. With it he leaves it further in the rear. What myriads of moral leagues lie between the saints in heaven and this hell "beneath"! And these leagues are ever increasing. It is said that Christ shall separate the good from the bad on the Last Day, as the shepherd separateth his sheep; the one "shall go into everlasting punishment, but the other to life eternal." This separation is going on *now*. The good and the bad are here parting company, going farther and farther from each other continually; the good are rising higher and higher on the right hand in the kingdom prepared for them: while the evil are now on the left hand, and going deeper and deeper "into everlasting punishment with the devil and his angels."

Proverbs 15:25-26

The Procedure and Propensity of God

"The LORD will destroy the house of the proud: but he will establish the border of the widow. The thoughts of the wicked *are* an abomination to the LORD: but *the words* of the pure *are* pleasant words."

"From the style of the antithesis between the "proud" and the "widow," we are naturally led to conceive a special allusion to the haughty oppressor of the desolate and unprotected—to the overbearing worldling, who insolently abuses his power in lording it over his poor dependents."

THE PROCEDURE OF GOD.—The Eternal is ever at work. He is never at rest. "He fainteth not, neither is weary." He acts, not from caprice, but from a plan which His own infinite intellect has mapped out for Him, stretching on from eternity to eternity. He sees the end from the beginning. His course is essentially benevolent, absolutely wise, and therefore unalterable. How does that course affect men? The text suggests—First: That it is *ruinous to the proud*. "The Lord will destroy the house of the proud." It is a decree unalterable and resistless, that those who exalt themselves shall be abased. The soul that towers in its own pride must inevitably come down sooner or later. The text suggests,—Secondly: That it is *salvation to the humble*. "He will establish the border of the widow." The word "widow" here suggests that the proud, spoken of in the first part of the verse, has special reference to the ruthless oppressor. Jehovah has special regard for the widow and the fatherless. He will exalt the widow. "He hath showed strength with his arm, he hath scattered the proud in the imagination of their hearts. He hath taken down the mighty from their seats, and exalted them of low degree."* Thus, as sure as God moves on through the world, the proud will be brought down and the humble exalted.

* Luke i. 51, 52.

THE PROPENSITY OF GOD.—The Eternal has a heart. He has sensibilities, and as we have elsewhere seen, He has feelings in relation to man. First: *He has a loathing towards the thoughts of the wicked.* " The thoughts of the wicked are an abomination unto the Lord." Wicked men have thoughts, and what thoughts are theirs? They are hells in embryo. God knows their thoughts. He peers into their deepest recesses. He understands them all " afar off," and they are repugnant to His nature. " They are an abomination." His holy nature recoils from them with an ineffable disgust. Secondly: *He has a pleasure in the words of the good.* " The words of the pure are pleasant words." Or, as the margin has it—" words of pleasantness." Whether they are words of counsel, words of reproof, words of prayer, they are all pleasant to the Divine ear.

"They that feared the Lord spake often one to another; and the Lord hearkened, and heard it, and a book of remembrance was written before him, for them that feared the Lord, and that thought upon his name." " And they shall be mine, saith the Lord of Hosts, in that day when I make up my jewels: and I will spare them, as a man spareth his own son that serveth him."*

Proverbs 15:27

The Evils of Covetousness and the Blessedness of Generosity

" He that is greedy of gain troubleth his own house ; but he that hateth gifts shall live."

THE EVILS OF COVETOUSNESS.—" He that is greedy of gain troubleth his own house." How does the covetous man trouble " his own house "? In many ways. First:

* Mal. iii. 16, 17.

Sometimes by *niggardly provision for the wants of his house*. He frets at every outlay; he grudges every comfort. His hand is ever open to grasp, never to give. Secondly: Sometimes by *his miserable temper* he disturbs the peace of the house. The temper and bearing of a covetous man produce disgust in all with whom he associates. Then, too, his irritability, anxiousness, and niggardly ways, falsehoods, over-reachings, which are ever associated with covetousness, pain all hearts within his circle. Thirdly: Sometimes by his *reckless speculations* he brings ruin on his house. His greed of gain urges him often into hazardous enterprizes. These sometimes break down, and in their crash ruin his family. Lot, Achan, Saul, Ahab, Gehazi, are examples of men who have troubled their house by their covetousness. "Woe to him that coveteth an evil covetousness to his house, that he may set his nest on high, that he may be delivered from the power of evil."* "As the partridge sitteth *on eggs* and hatcheth *them* not, so he that getteth riches and not by right, shall leave them in the midst of his days, and at his end shall be a fool."† "Refrain from covetousness," says Plato, "and thy estate shall prosper."

The BLESSEDNESS OF GENEROSITY.—"He that hateth gifts shall live." It is implied that the man "greedy of gain," in the first clause, is a man anxious for gifts of any sort, even *bribes*. By the man who "hateth gifts," here we are not to understand one regardless of his own interest, but one who would reject any amount of wealth that came not to him in an honest and honourable way, a man who has a stronger disposition to give than to receive. Such a generous man, we are told, "shall live." He "shall live" in the approbation of his own conscience. Conscience smiles upon the benevolent heart. He "shall live" in the love and esteem of his neighbours. Men are made to admire and applaud the generous. He "shall live" in the approval of his God. The man who rejects all earthly good, offered to him in an unrighteous way, and with a self-denying benevolence, follows duty, shall "receive an

---

* Hab. ii. 9. † Jer. xvii. 11.

hundredfold recompense in this world, and in the world to come everlasting life." "He is good," says a French author, "that does good to others. If he suffers for the good he does he has better still; and if he suffers from them to whom he did good, he is arrived at that height of goodness that nothing but an increase of his suffering can add to it, if it proves his death his virtue is at its summit—it is heroism complete."

Proverbs 15:28-29

The Righteous and the Wicked

" The heart of the righteous studieth to answer: but the mouth of the wicked poureth out evil things. The lord *is* far from the wicked: but He heareth the prayer of the righteous."

THESE verses present to us the righteous and the wicked in relation to their speech and in relation to their God.

In relation to their SPEECH.—The speech of the *righteous is properly studied*. "The heart of the righteous studieth to answer." All speech should be studied. The old proverb is "think twice before you speak once." But all studied speech is not good; some study their speech in order to misrepresent their own hearts, to lead others into temptation, to indoctrinate with wrong sentiments, such is not the studied speech to which Solomon refers. "The heart of the righteous" man "studieth to answer," in order that his speech may agree with his own thoughts and feelings, and in order that it may be of real service to his auditors. He feels so impressed with the awful responsibility connected with the power of words and the momentous influence springing from it, that he duly ponders his utterances. He is "swift to hear, but slow to speak." In contrast with this it is taught that the speech of *the wicked is reckless utterance*. "The mouth of the wicked poureth out evil things." There is no conscience in it, it comes forth unfiltered by moral reflection. Hence his mouth is the vehicle of evil. "An evil man, out of the evil treasure of his heart bringeth forth that which is evil, for out of the abundance of the heart the mouth speaketh."* The unchaste, ill-natured, profane, frivolous, immoral, all that is foul and false in the heart, roll out in torrents from the mouth of the wicked. "How can ye, being evil, speak good things?" Unless the fountain be purified the stream will ever be tainted; unless the tree be made good, the pernicious sap at the root will give a tinge to the foliage and a taste to the fruit. Would that men duly pondered the tremendous influence of their words. Science affirms that every movement in the material creation propagates an influence to the remotest planet in the universe. Be this as it may, it seems morally certain that every word spoken on the ear will have an influence lasting as eternity. The words we address to men are written not on parchment, marble, or brass, which time can efface, but on the indestructible pages of the soul. Everything written on this imperishable soul is imperishable. All the words that have ever been addressed to you by men long since departed, are written on the book of your memory, and will be unsealed at the day of judgment, and spread out in the full beams of eternal knowledge. The righteous and the wicked are presented here—

In relation to their GOD.—It is here taught that *God is morally distant from the wicked.* "The Lord is far from the wicked." What meaneth this? Essentially He is alike near to all; all live and move in Him; and from Him none can flee any more than from themselves. But morally he stands aloof from the ungodly, and they from Him. The very existence of moral beings runs with their sympathies, and the sympathies of God and the sinner flow in opposite directions. Hence they are at the antipodes. There is a mutual recoil. The Holy Creator says to the unholy creature, "Depart ye cursed," and the unholy creature says to Him, "Depart from me, I desire not a knowledge of thy ways." So immeasurable is the chasm between them

* Luke vi. 45.

that it can only be bridged by the mediation of the Great Redeeming Man.

It is here taught that *God is morally near to the righteous.* "He heareth the prayer of the righteous." He "is near to them that call upon him in truth." "He is nigh to them that be of a broken heart, and saveth them that be of a contrite spirit." "Prayer," says Dr. McCosh, "is like a man in a small boat laying hold of a large ship; and who, if he does not move the large vessel, at least moves the small vessel towards the large one; so, though prayer could not directly move God towards the suppliant, it will move the suppliant towards God, and bring the two parties nearer to each other."

Proverbs 15:30

The Highest Knowledge

" The light of the eyes rejoiceth the heart ; *and* a good report maketh the bones fat."

KNOWLEDGE is that information which the mind receives, either by its own studies and experience, or by the testimony of others. It is of different degrees of value, according to the order of subjects which it reveals to the mind, and the strength of the testimony by which they are commended. God is the highest subject of knowledge, and evidences of His being amount to the strongest of all demonstrations. Hence, the knowledge of Him is the highest knowledge. All other knowledges to the soul are but stars in its firmament; this is the Sun, all-revealing, all-quickening, flooding the soul with life and beauty. The text suggests two facts in relation to this knowledge.

It is CHEERING.—"The light of the eyes rejoiceth the heart, and a good report maketh the bones fat." We take the expression "*good report*" as expressing not merely a good reputation or good tidings, but as expressing good knowledge; the best knowledge is the knowledge of God. Such knowledge has the same cheering influence upon the soul, as light upon the natural heart. When light breaks in upon the world after a season of thick clouds and darkness, it sets all nature to music. "Truly, light is sweet; and a pleasant thing it is for the eyes to behold the sun."* It is so when the soul sees God. Is not the knowledge of parental Providence, of Divine forgiveness, of a blessed future beyond the grave, cheering as light? Truly, such knowledge "rejoiceth the heart."

Another fact suggested in relation to this knowledge is—

It is STRENGTHENING.—It "maketh the bones fat." "The *bones* may be called the foundations of the corporeal structure, on which its strength and stability depend. The cavities and cellular parts of the bones are filled with the marrow; of which the fine oil, by one of the beautiful processes of the animal physiology, pervades their substance, and, incorporating with the earthly and siliceous material, gives them their cohesive tenacity—a provision without which they would be brittle and easily fractured. "Making the bones fat" means, supplying them with plenty of marrow, and thus strengthening the entire system. Hence "*marrow to the bones*" is a Bible figure for anything eminently gratifying and beneficial. The idea is strongly brought out in the words : "And when ye see *this*, your heart shall rejoice, and your bones shall flourish like an herb : and the hand of the Lord shall be known toward his servants, and *his* indignation toward his enemies."†

What is the strength of the soul? First: *Trust in God is strength.* The soul possessing firm trust in Him, is mighty both in endurance and in action; and true knowledge gives this trust. Secondly: *Love for the eternal is strength.* Love is soul power. Supreme affection for the supremely good is unconquerable energy, and knowledge gives this love. Thirdly: *Hope for the future is strength.* The soul, full of hope, is invincible. And true knowledge

* Eccles. xi. 7.   † Isaiah lxvi. 14.

gives this hope. Thus a good report, good knowledge concerning God, is to the soul as "marrow to the bones."

Proverbs 15:31-32

Reproof

"The ear that heareth the reproof of life abideth among the wise. He that refuseth instruction despiseth his own soul."

"REPROOF" always implies *blame* either real or imaginary. It is a charge of misconduct, accompanied with censure from one person to another. By the "reproof of life" in the text, we shall understand God's reproof to sinners. His reproofs are characterised by at least three things First: *truthfulness*. Men often address reproofs to others that are undeserved, implying a fault which has no existence. Ill-tempered people are proverbially fond of the work of reproaching. They look at others through their own feelings, and all are bad. Divine reproofs, however, are always truthful. The blame which God charges on man is a fact attested by man's own consciousness. Secondly: *necessity*. Men often address their reproofs when they are not needed. The fault is so trivial, that evil rather than good comes to the individual by rebuke. Many persons do incalculable injury to the character of their children, by noticing and rebuking trivial irregularities, which are almost natural to young life. God reproves men because it is necessary that they should be convicted of sin. The world can only be morally restored by convincing it of sin, of righteousness, and of judgment. Thirdly: *kindness*. Men's reproofs are often inspired by unkindness. Unkind reproofs, even when true, are injurious. It is kindness that gives us power for good.

"Ye have heard
The fiction of the north wind and the sun,

> Both working on a traveller, and contending
> Which had most power to take his cloak from him,
> Which, when the wind attempted, he roared out
> Outrageous blasts at him, to force it off,
> Then wrapt it closer on: when the calm sun
> (The wind once leaving) charged him with still beams.
> Quick and fervent, and therein was content,
> Which made him cast off both his cloak and coat:
> Like whom should men do?"

The text leads us to consider two things:

The ACCEPTANCE of God's reproof.—"The ear that heareth the reproof of life abideth among the wise." How is the reproof to be received? It must be accepted in a right spirit, in the spirit expressed by David, when he said, "Let the righteous smite me and it shall be a kindness, let him reprove me, it shall be an excellent oil; it shall not break my head." Two advantages are indicated in the text for the proper acceptance of Divine reproof. First: *permanent social elevation.* "He abideth among the wise." The "wise" are not only the enlightened, but the holy and the good. The man who rightly attends to the approving voice of God, gets a *permanent* place in his circle. He is born into a kingdom of great spirits. He "*abideth* with the wise" in his social intercourse, in his book studies, and in his spiritual fellowships. Another advantage of the proper acceptance of Divine reproof is, Secondly: *acquisition of true wisdom.* "He getteth understanding." He learns to repel the evil, and to pursue the good. He gets that wisdom which not only throws a light upon his path, but vivifies, strengthens, and beatifies his spirit.

But in the words we have also:

The REJECTION of God's reproof.—"He that refuseth instruction, (or, as the margin has it, *correction*) despiseth his own soul." The rejection of Divine reproof is, First: *sadly common.* God is constantly reproving sinners by His providence, His gospel, and their own consciences. Yet they silence His voice, they will not lay His words to heart. The rejection of Divine reproof is Secondly: *Self-ruinous.* "He despiseth his own soul." The rejection betrays the utmost disregard to the highest interests of being. What a description Solomon gives elsewhere of the ruin that will befall such. "And thou mourn at the last, when thy flesh and thy body are consumed, and say, how I hated instruction, and my heart despised reproof; and have not obeyed the voice of my teachers, nor inclined mine ear to them that instructed me." Again, "When I called, ye refused; I stretched out my hand, and no man regarded. But ye have set at naught all my counsel, and would none of my reproof; I also will laugh at your calamity, I will mock when your fear cometh." Brothers, attend to the reproofs from heaven. They are looking-glasses, in which you can see the face of your spirit true to life. Because they reveal the hideous blots of moral disease, you recoil from them. But this is unwise, as they will point you at the same time to means by which your youth may be renewed like the eagle.

Proverbs 15:33

Godly Fear and Genuine Humility

"The fear of the LORD *is* the instruction of wisdom; and before honour *is* humility."

HERE we have—

GODLY FEAR.—"The fear of the Lord, is the instruction of wisdom." There is, as we have had occasion frequently to remark, a slavish fear and a loving fear of the Lord. The former is foreign to all virtue, and is an element of moral misery; the latter is the reverse of this. A loving fear may sound a contradiction, but it is not so. "Perfect love," it is true, "casteth out" slavish fear, but it generates at the same time a virtuous one. I have read of a little boy who was tempted to pluck some cherries from a tree which his father had forbidden him to touch. "You need not be afraid," said his evil companion, "for if your father should find out that you had taken them, he is too kind to hurt you." "Ah," said the brave little fellow, "that is the very reason why I would not touch them; for, though my father would not hurt me, yet I should hurt him by my disobedience." This is godly fear, a fear of wounding the dearest object of the heart. Concerning this fear, it is here said, that it "is the instruction of wisdom." First: It is the great *subject* of Wisdom's instruction. Everywhere in nature, in the events of life, and in the Holy Book of God, does heavenly Wisdom inculcate this godly fear. Secondly: It is the great *end* of wisdom's instruction. Heavenly wisdom, in all its communications, deals with our souls, not merely to enlighten the intellect and refine the tastes, but to fill us with loving reverence for the Great Father. The conclusion of its whole mission is, "fear God and keep his commandments." This is the burden of its divine teaching.

Here we have—

GENUINE HUMILITY.—"Before honour is humility." This is a maxim of very wide application. First: It is sometimes applicable to *secular* exaltation. As a rule, the man who rises to affluence and power in the world has had to humble himself. He has stooped to conquer. He has condescended to drudgeries and concessions most wounding to his pride. Secondly: This always applies to *intellectual* exaltation. A most humbling sense of one's ignorance, is the first step to intellectual eminence, and almost the last. He who feels he knows nothing, is in the surest field where intellectual laurels are won. Thirdly: This invariably applies to *moral* exaltation. The very first sentence the Saviour uttered when describing the members of His kingdom was—"Blessed are the poor in spirit, for theirs is the kingdom of heaven." "He that humbleth himself shall be exalted." The cross is the ladder to the crown.

> "The bird that soars on highest wing
> Builds on the ground her lowly nest;
> And she that doth most sweetly sing
> Sings in the shade when all things rest.
> In lark and nightingale we see
> What honour hath humility."—J. MONTGOMERY

The truly humble spirit is, in society, to the proud and haughty, what the valley is to the mountain: if less observed, more sheltered and more blessed, valleys see the stars more brightly than the mountains that often veil their proud heads with clouds. The mountains filter the waters on which the valleys live, and send down in soft music to their ears the stormy thunders that beat with violence on their lofty brow. The great Sun stoops to the valleys and touches them with a warmth which it denies to the high hills; and kind nature, which leaves the towering heights amidst the cold desolations of death, endows the humble vales with richest life, and robes them in the enchanting costume of sweetest flowers. "Blessed are the poor in Spirit."

Proverbs 16:1

Man Proposes, God Disposes

" The preparations of the heart in man, and the answer of the tongue, *is* from the LORD."

TAKING these words as they stand before us, they give the idea that all goodness in man is from God. First: Goodness in the *heart* is from Him. "The preparations of the heart in man." The margin reads "disposings." All the right disposings of the heart towards the real, the holy, and the Divine, are "from the Lord." How does He dispose the heart to goodness? Not arbitrarily, not miraculously, not in any way that interferes with the free agency of man, or that supersedes in any case the necessity of man's own actions. Still it is a mystery transcending our present intelligence. He has avenues to the human heart of which we know nothing. He can instil thoughts and impressions by methods of which we are entirely ignorant. " The wind bloweth where it listeth, and thou hearest the sound thereof, but canst not tell whence it cometh and whither it goeth ; so is every one that is born of the Spirit." It is enough for us to know, *That He is the Author of all goodness in* the *soul,* and *that we are bound to labour after* it as if its attainment depended on our own efforts. The words of the text teach—Secondly : That goodness in *language* is from God. "And the answer of the tongue." This follows from the other. The language is but the expression of the heart. If the heart is right, the language is right also. All good in man is from God, "every good and perfect gift cometh down from above."

But whilst these words as they stand teach this truth, they themselves are not true to the original. A literal translation would be this : "To man the orderings of the heart, but from Jehovah the answer of the tongue," and the idea undoubtedly is, "man proposes, God disposes."

This is an UNDOUBTED fact.—A fact sustained by the character of God. All the schemes, and plans formed in the human heart must necessarily be under the control of Him Who is all wise and all powerful. They cannot exist without His knowledge, nor can they advance without His permission. A fact sustained by the history of men. Take for examples the purposes of Joseph's brethren, of Pharaoh in relation to Moses; of the Jews in relation to Christ. A fact sustained by our own experience. Who has not found the schemes and plans of his own heart taking a direction which he never contemplated ? Truly, "man proposes, God disposes." "There's a divinity that shapes our ends rough hew them how we will."

> " There is a Power
> Unseen, that rules th' illimitable world,—
> That guides its motions, from the brightest star
> To the least dust of this sin-tainted world ;
> While man, who madly deems himself the lord
> Of all, is nought but weakness and dependence.
> This sacred truth, by sure experience taught,
> Thou must have learnt, when wandering all alone :
> Each bird, each insect, flitting through the sky,
> Was more sufficient for itself than thou."—THOMSON

This is a MOMENTOUS fact.—It is very solemn in its pearing on the *enemies* of God. Their most cherished schemes, of whatever kind, sensual, avaricious, infidel, are under the control of Him against whom they rebel. He will work them for their confusion, and His own glory. It is momentous. The fact is also important in its bearings on the *friends* of God. To them it is all encouraging. Whilst the schemes of the wicked can have no permanent reign, theirs must prosper and continue. " Surely the wrath of man shall praise Thee, the remainder of wrath shalt thou restrain."* The Great Master of the universe has all the worst fiends in creation in harness, links them to His providential chariot, and makes them bear Him on triumphantly in the accomplishment of His Eternal plans.

Proverbs 16:2

The Self-complacency of Sinners and the Omniscience of God

" All the ways of a man *are* clean in his own eyes; but the LORD weigheth the spirits."

Here we have two things :
THE SELF-COMPLACENCY OF THE SINNER.—" All the ways of a man *are* clean in his own eyes." Saul, of Tarsus, is a striking example of this. He once rejoiced in virtues which he never had. The Pharisee in the Temple, too, did the same : he thanked God for excellencies of which he was utterly destitute. Indeed the worst of men are prone to think well of themselves. Why is this ? (1) They view themselves in the light of society. They judge themselves by the character of others, and the best are imperfect. (2) They are ignorant of the spirituality of God's law. The fact that the Divine law penetrates into the profoundest recesses of the soul, takes cognizance of its most hidden workings, they utterly disregard; and (3) their consciences too are in a state of dormancy. Their eyes not open to see the enormity

* Psalm lxxvi. 10.

of sin. Thus, like the Laodiceans, they say they are rich and increased in goods, and need nothing, whereas they "are wretched and miserable, and poor, and blind, and naked."* "All the ways of man are clean in his own eyes." His eyes are so dim and jaundiced, that he mistakes the filth of his ways for cleanliness and beauty.

Here we have—

THE SEARCHING OMNISCIENCE OF GOD.—"The Lord weigheth the spirits." "Ye are they," said Christ, "which justify yourselves before men, but God knoweth your hearts."† He sees the iniquity in those who regard themselves as blameless. "The Lord seeth not as man seeth, for man looketh on the outward appearance, but the Lord looketh on the heart." "He weigheth the spirit." This implies, First: *The essence of the character is in the spirit.* The sin of an action is not in the outward performance, but in the motive. The fox and the man may perform the same act: both may carry off the property of another, but we attach the idea of crime in the case of the latter and not of the former. Why? Because man acts from motive, not from blind instinct. He is a moral agent. The essence of the act is in the motive. God sees all the crimes of the world, and judges them as they appear in the hidden arena of the heart. This urges, Secondly: *The duty of self-examination.* "If Thou, Lord, shouldest mark iniquities, O Lord, who shall stand?" "Search me, O God, and know my heart: try me and know my thoughts, and see if there be any wicked way in me, and lead me in the way everlasting."‡

> " By all means use sometimes to be alone.
> Salute thyself: see what thy soul doth wear:
> Dare to look in thy chest, for 'tis thine own,
> And tumble up and down what thou find'st there."
> WORDSWORTH

* Rev. iii. 17.   † Luke xvi. 15.   ‡ Psalm cxxxix. 23, 24.

Proverbs 16:3

The Establishment of Thoughts

" Commit thy works unto the LORD, and thy thoughts shall be established."

WHAT are the "*thoughts*" referred to in the text? The thoughts of the soul are a large generation made up of various families and innumerable individuals. Some are worthless and some valuable. Some *cannot* be "established," they are airy speculations, day dreams, phantasmagoria passing before us, yielding us amusement for the minute. There are thoughts which *ought* not to be " established." Such are selfish, malicious, impious thoughts. The permanent establishment of such thoughts would ruin the universe. There are thoughts that *should* be " established." These are virtuous thoughts, involving the grand purposes of life, pious and benevolent thoughts, into which we throw our hearts and which govern our activities. The verse implies two things concerning such thoughts.

That their establishment is A MATTER OF VITAL MOMENT TO MAN.—This is implied: it is the grand motive held forth to induce us to commit our " works unto the Lord." The non-establishment of a man's practical thoughts or purposes involves at least two great evils. First: *Disappointment*. What a man purposes he desires, he struggles after, it is the great hope of his soul. The failure of his purpose is always felt to be one of the sorest of his calamities. The disappointment in some cases breaks the heart. The man who has all the purposes of his life broken is of all men the most miserable. It involves, Secondly: *Loss*. A man's purposes occupy his attention, his sympathies, his activities, his time, and when they are frustrated all these are lost. And are they not the most precious things? It may be said of the ungodly man when he dies, in that " very day his thoughts perish." All his purposes are left as wrecks on the black and boisterous billows of retribution. It is therefore of vast importance to man to have his thoughts *established*. So established as to have all desires gratified, all hopes realized, all activities rewarded. It is also taught concerning such thoughts,—

That GODLY WORKS ARE ESSENTIAL to their establishment.—"Commit thy works unto the Lord." Men always work to carry out their purposes, but none of their works can truly succeed that are not of a godly sort. What is meant by " committing thy works unto the Lord ?" It may include two things. First: *Submit them to his approval when they are in embryo.* A thought is work in germ, the protoplasm of all history. We should lay our works before the Lord when they exist in this thought state, and invoke Him if they are wrong to destroy them in their embryo, if they are right to develop them to perfection. We should seek His counsel before the first step is taken. It may include, Secondly: *The invocation of His blessing upon them when they are accomplished.* "Commit thy works unto the Lord." " The Hebrew idiom gives peculiar emphasis to the precept—roll it over on Jehovah." "Whatsoever we do in word or deed, we should do to the glory of God." It is only as we attend to this precept, that we can get our thoughts established, and thus actualize those purposes and aspirations of the soul, in which we really live. Truly all is vain in human labour unless God is in it. " Except the Lord build the house, they labour in vain that build it; except the Lord keep the city, the watchman waketh *but* in vain."* Man's spiritual constitution is such that he cannot be happy in any labour that springs not from the true inspiration of God. Thus labour without God is vain: Farmers, unless the Lord cultivate the field: merchants, unless the Lord effect the transactions; authors, unless the Lord write the book; statesmen, unless the Lord enact the measure: preachers, unless the Lord make the sermons; that is, unless He is the inspiration of all your efforts, your labour is in vain. It will neither meet His approval nor yield you true satisfaction.

* Psalm cxxvii. 1.

Proverbs 16:4

Universal Existence

"The LORD hath made all *things* for himself: yea, even the wicked for the day of evil."

THE verse teaches two things—
That all existence has ONE AUTHOR.—"The Lord hath made all *things* for himself." This statement stands opposed to three cosmological absurdities. (1) To the *eternity* of the universe. Contingency is a law running through all parts of creation : one thing is ever found depending upon another. This contingency implies the incontingent and absolute. (2) To the *chance production* of nature. That the universe rose from a fortuitous concourse of atoms is infinitely more absurd than the supposition that "Paradise Lost" rose out of a promiscuous throwing of the twenty-six letters of our alphabet together. (3) To the *plurality* of creators. There is *one* Being, who has made all. "The Lord." That all existence has One Author is a fact which agrees with all sound philosophy. All scientific induction takes the mind up to one primal origin. It is a fact that is taught in every part of the Holy Scriptures too. The Bible is full of it. "In the beginning the Lord created the heavens and the earth." "Of him, and through him, and to him are all things." "The foootprint," says Hugh Miller, "of the savage traced in the sand is sufficient to attest the presence of man to the atheist who will not recognise God, whose hand is impressed upon the entire universe."

"The heavens are a point from the pen of His perfection;
The world is a rosebud from the bower of His beauty;
The sun is a spark from the light of His wisdom,
And the sky a bubble on the sea of His power.

His beauty is free from stain of sin,
Hidden in a veil of thick darkness.
He formed mirrors of the atoms of the world,
And He cast a reflection from His own face on every atom!
To thy clear-seeing eye whatsoever is fair,
When thou regardest it aright, is a reflection from His face."

SIR WILLIAM JONES

The verse teaches—

That all existence has ONE MASTER.—"The Lord hath made all things *for Himself.*" He is not only the author, but the end of the universe. All stream from Him, all run to Him. This is *right*, for there is no higher end; this is *joyous*, for he is *Love*. He made the universe to gratify His benevolence—His desire to impart His blessedness to others. But the verse says that " even the wicked for the day of evil," He has made for Himself. What does this import? It does not mean, (1) That God ever made a wicked creature. The supposition clashes with all our ideas of Him as gathered from nature, and as welling from the intuitions of our own spirits. Nor, (2) That He ever made a holy creature wicked. This is equally repugnant to our beliefs, and derogatory to His character. Nor, (3) That He ever made a creature to be miserable. All such suppositions are repugnant to the teachings of nature, the doctrines of inspiration, and the intuitions of the human soul. All it means is, that He makes the wicked subserve His own glory. Is not this evident? Were there no wickedness in the world, there are certain attributes of God which would never have come out to view, such as patience, compassion and forgiving love: The black sky of moral evil. God makes the background on which to exhibit in overwhelming majesty, certain perfections of His nature. "I will get me honour on Pharaoh," said He of old. And this He might say of every wicked spirit. " He maketh the wrath of man to praise him, and restraineth the remainder of wrath." How great is God! He is the Cause, the Means, and the End of all things in the universe, but sin, and even sin He subordinates to His own high ends. Let us endeavour to reach after worthy ideas of God. " It were better," says Lord Bacon, "to have no opinion of God at all, than such an opinion as is unworthy of Him, for the one is unbelief, and the other is contumely, and certainly superstition is the reproach of the Deity."

Proverbs 16:5-6

Evil

" Every one *that is* proud in heart *is* an abomination to the LORD: *though* hand *join* in hand, he shall not be unpunished. By mercy and truth iniquity is purged: and by the fear of the LORD *men* depart from evil."

"PRIDE," says an old writer, "had her beginning among the angels that fell, her continuance on earth, her end in hell." The Bible says much against pride, and authors have dealt largely with the hideous theme. It not unfrequently stands in the Bible to represent sin in general, and in some of its forms it is in truth the quintessence of evil. Notice two things in these verses concerning evil in general.

ITS ESSENTIAL ODIOUSNESS, AND NECESSARY PUNISHABILITY.—Note its *essential odiousness*. "Every one that is proud is an *abomination* to the Lord." "God resisteth the proud." Pride in all its forms—pride of self-righteousness—pride of wisdom, station, as well as the pride of rebellion, is abhorrent to Him. "God," says old Henry Smith, "was wroth with the angels, and drove them out of heaven. God was wroth with Adam, and thrust him out of Paradise. God was wroth with Nebuchadnezzar, and turned him out of his palace. God was wroth with Cain, and though he were the first man born of a woman, yet God made him a vagabond upon his own land. God was wroth with Saul, and though he was the first king that ever was anointed, yet God made his own hand his executioner." Note again its *necessary punishability*. "Though hand join in hand, he shall not be unpunished." Evil must be punished; the moral constitution of the soul, the justice of the universe, the Almightiness of God, render all human efforts to avoid it futile. "Woe unto him that striveth with his Maker; let the potsherd strive with the potsherd of the earth."* Though the heathen rage, he that sitteth in the heavens shall laugh and have them in derision, and ultimately vex them with His sore displeasure. "There is no wisdom, no understanding, no counsel against the Lord."* Notice

ITS DIVINE CORRECTIVES, AND THEIR MORAL OPERATION.—Note: Its *divine correctives*. What are they? "Mercy and truth." By them "iniquity is *purged*." These are the two great Divine elements to destroy sin. They came into the world in their perfect form by Christ. "Grace and truth came by Jesus Christ." They constitute the Gospel. They are the fountain opened on this earth for the washing away of sin and uncleanness. They are the fire which Christ kindled in order to burn up the moral corruptions of this planet. Note its *moral operation*. How do they operate in the soul so as to remove sin? "By the fear of the Lord men depart from evil." These two elements, mercy and truth, generate in the human heart that supreme, loving reverence for God, which leads men to "depart from evil." Wherever there is a true godly love in the soul, there is a departure from wrong. Step by step the man walks out of it, until at length he leaves it entirely behind as Lot left Sodom. No man is safe until he gets rid of every sin. Even one sin is the "dead fly in the ointment." One leak in a vessel may cause it to sink, one spark in a house may burn up a city, one sin may damn the soul.

* Isaiah xlv. 9.   † Chap. xxi. 30.

Proverbs 16:7

Pleasing God

" When a man's ways please the LORD, He maketh even His enemies to be at peace with him."

THIS verse directs us to the greatest of all subjects, the subject of pleasing Him who is the Author of the universe, and Whose will decides the destiny of all. This subject is here presented in two aspects.

AS A GLORIOUS POSSIBILITY FOR MAN.—" When a man's ways please the Lord." Then there are ways in which a man can please Him. How? Not by mere *external* services. Some imagine that they can please God by good psalmody, by fine prayers, by flattering addresses, by monetary contributions, by gorgeous ritualism. But all this is an abomination to Him, if the heart is not in love with His character, and in sympathy with His will. " To what purpose is the multitude of your sacrifices unto me? saith the Lord: I am full of the burnt-offerings of rams, and the fat of fed beasts; and I delight not in the blood of bullocks, or of lambs, or of he-goats. When ye come to appear before me, who hath required this at your hand, to tread my courts? Bring no more vain oblations; incense is an abomination unto me; the new moons, and Sabbaths, and calling of assemblies, I cannot away with; it is iniquity, even the solemn meeting. Your new moons and your appointed feasts, my soul hateth; they are a trouble unto me: I am weary to bear *them*. And when you spread forth your hands, I will hide mine eyes from you: yea, when ye make many prayers, I will not hear: your hands are full of blood."* The way to please Him is by a *loving obedience to His will*. The outward service must be the effect and expression of supreme love. He who has this love, and all may and should have it, can please his Maker. As a child may please a man who is the master of empires,

* Isaiah i. 11—15.

so humble man may please the Infinite. To please Him is the *summum bonum* of existence. By so doing we alone can *please ourselves*. Man can never be pleased with himself till he feels that he has pleased his Maker. His moral constitution renders it impossible. Nor can we please the spiritual universe without pleasing Him. What spirit in the creation can be pleased with us if our conduct pleaseth not the Eternal Father? Paul felt this to be the grand end of his existence. "Wherefore we labour, that whether present or absent, we may be accepted of him."* This subject is here presented—

AS WINNING THE GOODWILL OF ENEMIES.—"When a man's ways please the Lord, he maketh even his enemies to be at peace with him." It is here implied that a *good man has enemies*. "The world hated me," said Christ, "before it hated you." The enmity between the seed of the woman and the seed of the serpent is of long standing, inveterate, and ever operative. It is also implied that the overcoming of their enmity is a desirable thing. It is not well to have enmity in any heart towards us, and it is here taught that pleasing the Lord is the surest way to overcome it. Our reconciliation to God is the way to get our enemies reconciled to us. If we please Him, they will not be allowed to harm us, they will respect us with their consciences and may be transformed by our spirit and example. Brothers, let our grand object be to please God. Let us speak and act, not as pleasing men, but God, which trieth our hearts.

Proverbs 16:8

The Good Man and His Worldly Circumstances

"Better *is* a little with righteousness than great revenues without right."

THE verse suggests three facts:
GOOD MEN MAY HAVE BUT LITTLE OF THE WORLD.—

* 2 Cor. iv. 9.

"Better is a little." The great majority of good men in all ages have been poor. This fact, which has been through all time a perplexity to all saints, can be accounted for in various ways. First: The acquisition of wealth is not the grand purpose of a godly man's life. The men who give their energies, their very being to the accumulation of property, are those who of course become the largest inheritors of earthly good. The godly man does not go in for this; he has other and far higher aims, namely, the culture of his soul, the extension of truth, the raising of humanity. Secondly: The principles of a godly man's life preclude him from obeying the conditions by which wealth is generally obtained. Reckless speculation, dishonourable tricks, avaricious over-reachings, greed riding over conscience, are often the most successful means of gaining large possessions. As the world stands, virtue in a man's soul is a hindrance to fortune-making.

The verse suggests—

BAD MEN HAVE MUCH OF THE WORLD. — "Great revenues." Asaph, in his day, observed this, and said, "I was envious at the foolish when I saw the prosperity of the wicked. For there are no bands in their death, but their strength is firm. They are not in trouble as other men: neither are they plagued like other men. Therefore pride compasseth them about as a chain; violence covereth them as a garment. Their eyes stand out with fatness, they have more than their heart could wish."* The fool, the wicked man, referred to by Christ, was so prosperous that he knew not where to store his goods. Who now are your millionaires? What in this age is the character of the men who hold the great prizes of the world in their grasp? Not such as a rule, I trow, that will bear the test of God's holy law. They are not men who "do justice, love mercy, and walk humbly with God."

The verse suggests—

GOOD MEN WITH THEIR LITTLE ARE BETTER OFF THAN BAD MEN WITH THEIR MUCH.—"Better is a little with righteousness, than great revenues without right." First:

* Psalm lxxiii. 3—7.

The condition of such a man is *more enjoyable*. His happiness is spiritual, that of the other is sensational; his is generous, that of the other is selfish; his is imperishable, that of the other is transient. Secondly: The condition of such a man is *more honourable*. He is honoured for what he is not for what he has. He is honoured in proportion to people's intelligence, the other is honoured in proportion to people's ignorance. He is honoured yonder by angels and by God, the other is honoured only here by the depraved.*
The good man then may well be contented with his lot. "The nature of true content," says an old writer, "is to fill all the chinks of our desires, as the wax does the seal. Content is the poor man's riches, and desire is the rich man's poverty. Riches and poverty are more in the heart than in the hand; he is wealthy that is contented, he is poor that wants it. O poor Ahab, that carest not for thine own large possessions, because thou mayest not have another's. O rich Naboth, that carest not for all the dominions of Ahab, so thou mayest enjoy thine own."

Proverbs 16:9

The Plan of Man, and the Plan of God in Human Life

"A man's heart deviseth his way: but the LORD directeth his steps."

THERE are many passages parallel in meaning with this, such as, "O Lord, I know that the way of man is not in himself; it is not in man that walketh to direct his steps."† "The steps of a good man are ordered by the Lord: and he delighteth in his way."‡ "Man's goings are of the Lord: how can a man then understand his own way?"§ Every man's life is ruled by two plans, the one formulated by his own mind, the other by the mind of God. These two plans are referred to in the verse—

* See Reading on chap. xv. 16, 17.
† Jer. x. 23. ‡ Psalm xxxvii. 23. § Prov. xx. 24.

Man's own plan.—"A man's heart deviseth his way." Every man forms a programme of his daily life. He "deviseth his way." He sets before him an object, he adapts the means, and he arranges the time and effort for attaining his purpose. When he moves rationally, he does not move by blind impulse, nor does he even feel himself the creature of grim fate. That man's history is self-originated and self-arranged is manifested by three things. First: *Society holds every man responsible for his actions.* All the laws of society recognise his freedom of action, recognise the fact that he is the sole author of his conduct. Society does not treat him either as a brute or as a machine, but as a free agent, as one whose "heart deviseth his way." Secondly: *The Bible appeals to every man as having a personal sovereignty.* The Holy Word everywhere recognises him as having a power to abandon or modify his old course of conduct and adopt another. All its precepts, menaces, promises, encouragements imply this. It everywhere appeals to his will. Thirdly: *Every man's consciousness attests his freedom of action.* If the sinner felt himself the mere creature of forces he could not control, could he experience any remorse? If the saint felt that the good deed he wrought was forced from him, could he enjoy any self-commendation? Man *feels* that his life is fashioned by his own plan, that he is the undisputed monarch of his own inner world. "It is a contradiction," says F. W. Robertson, "to let man be free, and force him to do right. God has performed this marvel of creating a being with free will, independent so to speak of Himself—a real cause in His universe. To say that He has created such a one is to say that he has given him the power to fail. Without free will there could be no human goodness. It is wise, therefore, and good in God to give birth to free will. But once acknowledged free will in man, and the origin of evil does not lie in God."

God's own plan.—" The Lord directeth his steps." God has a plan concerning every man's life. A plan which, though it compasses and controls every activity, leaves the man in undisturbed freedom. This is the great problem of the world's history, man's freedom and God's control. "Experience," says an able expositor, "gives a demonstrable stamp of evidence even in all the minutiæ of circumstances which form the parts and pieces of the Divine plan. A matter of common business, the indulgence of curiosity, the supply of necessary want, a journey from home, all are connected with infinitely important results. And often when our purpose seemed as clearly fixed, and as sure of accomplishment as a journey to London, this way of *our own devising* has been blocked up by unexpected difficulties, and unexpected facilities have opened an opposite way, with the ultimate acknowledgment, ' He led me forth in the right way.' The Divine control of the apostles' movements, apparently thwarting their present usefulness, turned out rather to the furtherance of the Gospel. Phillip was transferred from an important sphere in Samaria, from preaching to thousands, into a desert. But the Ethiopian eunuch was his noble convert, and through him the Gospel was doubtless widely circulated.* Paul was turned aside from a wide field of labour to a more contracted ministry. A few women and a family were his only church. Yet how did these small beginnings issue in the planting of flourishing churches? After all, however, we need much discipline to wean us from our devices, that we may seek the Lord's direction *in the first place*. The fruit of this discipline will be a dread of being left to our own devices, as before we were eager to follow them. So truly do we find our happiness and security in yielding up our will to our Heavenly Guide! He knows the whole way, every step of the way : ' The end from the beginning.' And never shall we miss either the way or the end, if we only resign ourselves with unreserved confidence to his keeping and *direction of our steps.*"

> " Thou cam'st not to thy place by accident ;
> It is the very place God meant for thee.
> And should'st thou there small scope for action see ;
> Do not for this give room for discontent,
> Nor let the time thou owest to God be spent
> In idle dreaming how thou mightest be,

---

* Acts viii. 37—39.

> In what concerns thy spiritual life, more free
> From outward hindrance or impediment;
> For presently this hindrance thou shalt find
> That without which all goodness were a task
> So slight, that virtue never could grow strong.
> And would'st thou do one duty to His mind—
> The Imposer's overburdened, thou shalt ask
> And own thy need of grace to help ere long."—FRENCH

Proverbs 16:10-15
Model Monarchs

"A divine sentence *is* in the lips of the king: his mouth transgresseth not in judgment. A just weight and balance *are* the LORD'S: all the weights of the bag *are* His work. *It is* an abomination to kings to commit wickedness: for the throne is established by righteousness. Righteous lips *are* the delight of kings; and they love him that speaketh right. The wrath of a king *is as* messengers of death: but a wise man will pacify it. In the light of the king's countenance *is* life; and his favour *is* as a cloud of the latter rain."

THE Bible often speaks of kings as of parents and other relations, not as they are actually found in human life, but as they *ought* to be—the *ideals* are sketched. Thus we are commanded to honour our parents, which command implies that our parents are honour-worthy. It would be an offence to human nature, an offence to God and the universe, to honour some parents. Thus when we are commanded to honour kings, it implies that the kings have in their character and procedure that which is adapted to call forth the reverence of souls. All that is divine within and without us calls upon us to loathe and contemn some of the kings that figure on the page of human history. The sketch which Paul gives of rulers in Rom. xiii. is not that of actual rulers, but of ideal ones. It is the "higher powers," that are "ordained of God," and that are a "terror not to the good works, but to the evil." It is the ruler who is a "minister of God for good," that he "commands every soul to be subject to."* Solomon in

* See HOMILIST, vol. i., second series, p. 141.

this passage sketches such a King. Four particulars he gives concerning him.

He SPEAKS the right.—"A divine sentence is in the lips of the king; his mouth transgresseth not in judgment." Every man is morally bound to be veracious in expressions. But the high office of a king increases the obligation. "A divine sentence" includes two things. First: *Truth in expression*. The sentence must express the real meaning of the *speaker*, no more and no less. No sentence can alone be regarded as "divine" that is not the true exponent of the speaker's soul. It includes also, Secondly: *Truth in meaning*. The meaning of the speaker, his thought, feeling, purpose, must be in accordance with the eternal reality of things. A man may be veracious and yet false, although his words may be true to his own soul, his soul may be untrue to eternal facts. No sentence can be considered a "divine sentence" that does not include these two things. A true king, therefore, is a Divine man; emphatically the "minister of God." His sympathies must be in keeping with the eternal purpose; his judgments ruled by the eternal law, and his pronouncements in keeping with both, and thus his mouth "transgresseth not in judgment."

"He JUDGES the right."—"A just weight and balance are the Lord's; all the weights of the bag are his work." This sentence is evidently intended to characterise the true king. The passage means, First: *That God demands social rectitude*. All impositions, double-dealings, over-reachings, hard bargains struck with over-grasping shrewdness, are enormities in the sight of Heaven, and condemned in the Scriptures. Secondly: *That a true king is a minister of social rectitude*. He sees that equity is done between man and man. He enforces it, not merely by his laws, but by his example too. His prerogative is to be so employed that the golden rule is acted out in every department of his kingdom. "Whatsoever ye would that men should do unto you, do ye even so unto them."

He FEELS the right.—"It is an abomination to kings to commit wickedness: for the throne is established by righteousness." "Wickedness" in all its forms of falsehood, fraud, oppression, greed, cruelty, is an abomination to the heart of the true king, the God-made king. " The God of Israel said, He that ruleth over men must be just, ruling in the fear of God. And he shall be as the light of the morning when the sun riseth, even a morning without clouds, as the tender grass springing out of the earth by clear shining of rain." Shakespeare's idea of a true king was somewhat of this fashion—" The king-becoming graces," said he, " are just, verity, temperance, stableness, bounty, perseverance, mercy, lowliness, devotion, patience, courage, fortitude." The verse suggests two things. First: That the loathing of wickedness in a king is the pursuit of righteousness. Loathing the wrong ever springs from loving the right. And secondly: That the pursuit of righteousness in a king is the stability of his throne. No throne can stand long where righteousness is disregarded, where wickedness is practised or countenanced. No bayonets, swords, armies, navies, bulwarks, can long sustain a throne where virtue is ignored. The nation from whose heart rectitude is gone, in whose soul vice runs riot, has its throne built on moral gunpowder.

He VINDICATES the right.—How ? First : *By approving the right in his subjects.* " Righteous lips are the delights of kings ; and they love him that speaketh right." This accords not with the actual character of kings, either as they appear in the history of the past, or in their present conduct throughout Europe and the world. Actual kings have generally approved of the flatteries and falsehoods of courtiers, and sycophants, and parasites. The tones of adulation are music to their ears ; not so the true king. He " loves him that speaketh right."

> " He's a king,
> A true, right king, that dare do aught save **wrong** ;
> Fears nothing mortal but to be unjust ;
> Who is not blown up with flattering puffs
> Of spongy sycophants ; who stands unmoved
> Despite the jostling of opinion."

Until the world gets kings that will hate flatterers, let it learn to honour and encourage those ministers of kings who have the manly courage to tell their royal masters the truth. "Clarendon, perhaps, was the finest example in modern times of unbending rectitude, boldly reproving his flagitious master, and beseeching him 'not to believe that he had a prerogative to declare vice to be virtue.' Well had it been for Charles had these righteous lips been his delight." Honest lieges are the best lions to guard the throne. Secondly: *By avenging the wrong on his subjects.* "The wrath of a king is as messengers of death; but a wise man will pacify it." "The true king beareth not the sword in vain, for he is the minister of God and a revenger to execute wrath upon him that doeth evil:"—"Upon him that doeth evil." Mark! evil, not as judged by the public sentiment of a corrupt age, nor the edicts of despots, nor the laws of unrighteous governments, but as judged by the moral law of God. Such evil must be punished, and God employs kings to punish it. "But a wise man will pacify it." That is, a wise man will give such proofs of repentance for the wrong, and will make such amends for it as will pacify the wrath. The wrath of a true king is never unappeasable. Thirdly: *By encouraging the true in his subjects.* The light of the king's countenance is life; and his favour is as a cloud of the latter rain." *Life* here means happiness. As the vernal sun to the earth, so is the influence of a true king to his people. The subject teaches that honesty is the best policy in a nation. Honesty is the best policy for a king to pursue to his people, and honesty is the best policy for them to pursue to him. "Constantius, the father of Constantine, tested the character of his Christian servants, by the imperative commands to offer sacrifices to his gods. Some sink under the trial. Those who had *really* 'bought the truth' would sell it for no price. They were inflexible. He banished the base compliants from his service. The true confessors he entrusted with the care of his own person. 'These men,' said he, 'I can trust. I value them more than all my treasures.' This was sound judgment. For who are so likely to be faithful to their king as those that have proved themselves faithful to their God."

Proverbs 16:16

Moral and Material Wealth

"How much better *is it* to get wisdom than gold! and to get understanding rather to be chosen than silver."

THERE are two things implied in this verse. First: *That material wealth is a good thing.* "Gold and silver" are not to be despised. They are good as the creatures of God. All the silver and gold found locked up in the chests of mountains He made. He created nothing in vain. They are good as the means of usefulness. How much good can be accomplished by material wealth. Good of all kinds:—Intellectual, social, moral, religious good. It is implied, Secondly: *That the pursuit of material wealth is a legitimate thing.* The statement of Solomon "that it is better to get wisdom than gold," indicates that it is not wrong to get gold. It is undoubtedly right for men so to develop the resources of nature as to improve their secular condition. Honest industry in the pursuit of wealth is a great blessing to a community. There is no need, however, to urge men to this pursuit. The world gallops after gold. But what the text asserts is this, that moral wealth—the wealth of soul—is better both in its possession and in its pursuit than material.

It is "better" in its POSSESSION.—First: It is better because it enriches the man himself. The wealth of Crœsus cannot add a fraction of value to the man. "The gold is but the guinea stamp." Millionaires are often moral paupers. But moral wealth—the wealth of holy loves, great thoughts, divine aims, and immortal hopes—enrich the man himself. Secondly: It is better, because it creates higher enjoyments. Money has no necessary power to make men happy. It may conduce to human pleasure, but it often produces nothing but heart agony and confusion. Not so with moral wealth. It is in itself a fountain of joy springing up into everlasting life. "I glory in tribulation," says Paul. Thirdly: It is better, because it invests with higher dignities. Material wealth can create the pageantries which the thoughtless populace, the puny-headed mob, and the hollow-hearted parasite mayworship. But moral wealth alone can command the reverence of true men. The true dignity of man is the dignity of moral goodness. A noble heart is the soul of all true royalty. Fourthly: It is better, because it is destined to a longer endurance. All the pleasures and honours of material wealth are of only short duration. "Naked came we into the world, and naked shall we return. We brought nothing into this world, and it is certain we can carry nothing out." But moral wealth produces pleasures and honours everlasting. "Its inheritance is incorruptible and its crown is eternal."

It is "better" in its PURSUIT.—It is better in the *getting*. First: The pursuit is more *ennobling*. The mere pursuit of material wealth, whilst it develops certain faculties, cramps others, and deadens the moral sensibilities. Often in the pursuit of riches we see souls that might have expanded into seraphs running into grubs. Not so with the pursuit of true spiritual wisdom. All the faculties are brought into play, and the whole soul rises in might and majesty. Secondly: The pursuit is more *heavenly*. Amongst the millions in the hierarchies of heaven not one soul can be found pursuing material good as an end. But each presses on to higher intellectual and spiritual attainments. Their "excelsior" is for a nearer approach and a higher assimilation to the Infinite. Thirdly: The pursuit is more *successful*. Thousands try for material wealth and fail. The ditches along the road of human enterprise are crowded with those who ran with all their might in the race for wealth, but who fell into the slough of pauperism and destitution. But you will not find one who ever earnestly sought spiritual wealth who failed. Every true effort involves positive attainment. In every way, therefore, moral wealth is better than material.*

* See HOMILIST, vol. iv., third series, p. 226.

Proverbs 16:17

The Way of the Upright

"The highway of the upright *is* to depart from evil: he that keepeth his way preserveth his soul."

As in every civilized country there are private roads, and high roads, ways that are occasionally used, and roads on which the common traffic runs, so in every man's life there are occasional and incidental lines of action, as well as one regular, common every-day path—the "highway." The man's occasional actions are his by-paths. His general conduct, his average life, his "highway." Every man has his own "highway," the road on which he is to be found during the greater portion of his active life. The "highways" of some are crooked, boggy, perilous. The verse directs us to the "highway" of the upright. The man whose heart is right in sympathy and in aim—the man who has been justified (rectified) by faith—made right by faith in Christ. Two things are here said of this man's "highway."

It is a SIN-DESERTING way.—"The highway of the upright is to *depart* from evil." He departs from evil. Observe, First: *That there is evil in the world.* It is here in a thousand forms—theoretical, emotional, practical, institutional. It is a moral Babylon in which humanity lives. Secondly: *There is a way in which men can escape it.* Without figure, and in Scriptural language, this way is "repentance towards God, and faith in our Lord Jesus Christ." The traveller has been in the evil that lies behind him, like the old "cities of the plain," seething in corruption and black with those combustible elements that will soon take fire. But every step in this "highway" takes him further and further from it, and as he moves on the fire becomes dim in the distance. And though his old world should be wrapt in conflagration, no spark shall fly far enough to reach him. He departs from evil.

It is a SOUL-PRESERVING way.—" He that keepeth his way preserveth his soul." Taking the word " soul" here in its generally accepted sense, two remarks are implied. First : *That man has a soul*. Most men theoretically acknowledge, but at the same time practically deny this. Thousands who are spiritualists in creed are materialists in conduct. Men live after the flesh. Matter rules mind everywhere. The world is busy in obeying the Satanic behest, commanding " stones to be made bread." Out of the earth it is endeavouring to get the staff of its being. Still man has a soul; philosophy, universal consciousness, the word of God demonstrate that we have an existence distinct from matter, that will survive all earthly dissolutions. Philosophy, universal consciousness, and the Word of God prove this. It is implied. Secondly : *That the preservation of his soul depends upon his conduct.* A corrupted and a popular evangelicalism preaches that a certain and sentimental belief is enough to save the soul. But reason and the Bible alike show that upon conduct its growth and destiny depend. It is true that a right conduct must have the right beliefs, and that the right beliefs must be directed to Christ. But the genuineness and worth of those beliefs are alone demonstrated by holiness of life. " Show me your faith by your works." " He that keepeth his way preserveth his soul." Coleridge well says, " Good works may exist without saving principles, and therefore cannot contain in themselves principles of salvation; but saving principles never did, never can exist without good works."

Brothers, enter this " highway," the " highway of the upright," go on no other road. " The miners," says Dr. Arnott, " in the gold fields of Australia, when they have gathered a large quantity of the dust, make for the city with the treasure. The mine is far in the interior; the country is wild; the bush is infested by robbers. The miners keep the road and the daylight. They march in company, and close by the guard sent to protect them. They do not stray from the path among the woods, for they bear with them a treasure which they value, and they are determined to run no risks." Do likewise, brother, for your treasure is of greater value, your enemies of greater power. Keep the way, lest you lose your soul.

Proverbs 16:18-19

Pride and Humility

" Pride goeth before destruction, and an haughty spirit before a fall. Better it is to be of an humble spirit with the lowly, than to divide the spoil with the proud."

AT different times in pursuing our way through this remarkable book, we have had the subject of pride urged on our attention, and so many different remarks have we noted down concerning it, that we must now dismiss the subject with a few words. The verse presents two opposite subjects:

PRIDE AS THE PRECURSOR OF RUIN.—"Pride goeth before destruction, and a haughty spirit before a fall." Pride and haughtiness are equivalents. What is here predicted of pride, First: Agrees with its *nature*. It is according to the instinct of pride to put its subject in an unnatural and therefore in an unsafe position. A proud man is where he ought not to be, and where he does not understand himself to be. His foot is on quicksand instead of on granite rock. He has been borne to his present elevation by the inflation of his faculties, not by the Divine pinions of his nature. Like a paper balloon he must collapse, come down, and descend into the mud. What is here predicted of pride, Secondly: Agrees with its *history*. All history shows that destruction always follows in its march. It entered Heaven, according to Milton. And what a destruction and fall followed. "From Heaven the sinning angels fell." It entered Eden, and inspired our first parents with the wish to become as gods, and what a fall and destruction followed. Examples abound in Sacred History:—Pharaoh, Amaziah, Haman, Nebuchadnezzar, Herod, David, Uzziah, Hezekiah, Peter, are signal and imperishable examples.

The records of their fall flame like red beacons on the rocks of history. This verse presents to us—

HUMILITY AS THE PLEDGE OF GOOD.—"Better it is to be of an humble spirit with the lowly, than to divide the spoil with the proud." What are all the spoils of earth's haughty conquerors to be compared with the blessedness of a genuinely humble soul? "An humble spirit" is better than all worldly good—*better*—more happy, more honourable, more acceptable to God and man. In every respect, both for this world and the next, humility is a blessing. "Humility," said Sir Benjamin Brodie, "leads to the highest distinction, because it leads to self-improvement. Study your own character; endeavour to learn and to supply your own deficiencies; never assume to yourselves qualities which you do not possess; combine all this with energy and activity, and you cannot predicate of yourselves, nor can others predicate of you, at what point you may arrive at last." "Think not," says Sir Thomas Browne, "thy own shadow longer than that of others, nor delight to take the altitude of thyself."

True humility is essentially a Christian virtue. The old Romans knew nothing of it, they had no word in their language to represent it. What they meant by "*humilitas*" was baseness and meanness of spirit; not that calm, moral nobility of soul which we express by the word humility. Gospel humility is moral greatness. As in the ripened cornfields the heaviest ear bends the lowest to the breeze, so amongst men the greatest souls are the most lowly, "The lark," says a modern author, "which mounts so high in singing her hymn of praise, descends afterward to the lowest point, and settles on the ground. So a mind that rises the most in aspirations towards God and heaven, sinks proportionally in its own esteem, and rests on the plains of humiliation and self-abasement. It is as though the element of light to which it soars produced an obscuration of inferior things by the very intensity of its brightness."

> "True dignity abides with him alone
> Who, in the silent hour of inward thought
> Can still suspect and still revere himself
> In lowliness of heart."—WORDSWORTH

Proverbs 16:20-21

The Conditions of a Happy Life

" He that handleth a matter wisely shall find good : and whoso trusteth in the LORD, happy *is* he. The wise in heart shall be called prudent: and the sweetness of the lips increaseth learning."

THESE words lead us to consider two conditions of a happy life. What are they?

SKILFUL MANAGEMENT.—" He that handleth a matter wisely shall find good." Skilful management in every department of life is of the utmost importance. First: It is so in *intellectual matters*. The man who desires to get a well-informed and well-disciplined mind, must arrange both the subjects and the seasons of study with skill. The man of greatest intellect who leaves all his studies to the chances of the hour, will never become distinguished in intellectuals. Method is of primary moment in the business of study. Great intellects become bankrupts for the want of this. Secondly : It is so in *mercantile engagements*. Men of large capital and with industry too often find their way to Basinghall Street for the want of skilful management. Whereas men whose stock-in-trade amounted only to a few shillings, with the faculty for "handling a matter" wisely, have risen to opulence and power. Thirdly : It is so in *spiritual culture*. A wise selection of the best readings, the most instructive pulpits, and the most favourable seasons for devotion cannot be dispensed with if great spiritual good is to be got. Practical philosophy is required we say in every department of action in order to get good out of it. Dr. Tulloch has well said, " Every profession implies system. There can be no efficiency and no advance without it. The meanest trade demands it, and would run to waste without something of it. The perfection of the most complicated business is the perfection of the system with which it is conducted. It is this that brings its complications together and gives a unity to all its energies. It is like a hidden sense pervading it, responsive at every point and fully meeting every demand. The marvellous achievements of modern commerce, stretching its relations over distant seas and many lands, and gathering the materials of every civilization within its ample bosom, are, more than anything, the result of an expanding and victorious system, which shrinks at no obstacles and adapts itself to every emergency." The words lead to consider—

A WELL-STAYED HEART.—" Whoso trusteth in the Lord happy is he." God is the stay of the heart. In Him, and in Him only, can the heart centre its supreme sympathies, and rest its unsuspicious confidence. He is to all the faculties and affections of the soul what the sun is to the planets, keeps them in order, inspires them with life, floods them with brightness, and bathes them with beauty. " Whoso trusteth in Him happy is he." First: He is happy in *himself*. " Happy is he." He feels that his love is approved by his conscience, reciprocated in boundless measure, and employs all his faculties and powers. Secondly: He is happy in his *policy*. " The wise in heart shall be called *prudent*." The right love is the best security for safe policy. Love is inventive genius, and is the best lamp in life's journey. In no light can the intellect see things so clearly and so truthfully as in the sunbeam of love. Thirdly: He is happy in his *speech*. " And the sweetness of the lips increaseth learning." Where the heart is staid on God, not only will there be a wise judgment, but a speech whose mellifluous eloquence will improve society in all true learning. Truly then, "Blessed is the man that trusteth in the Lord, and whose hope the Lord is. For he shall be as a tree planted by the waters, and *that* spreadeth out her roots by the river, and shall not die when heat cometh, but her leaf shall be green; and shall not be careful in the year of drought, neither shall cease from yielding fruit."

Proverbs 16:22

The Two Interpreters

"Understanding *is* a wellspring of life unto him that hath it: but the instruction of fools *is* folly."

LIFE is a school: Nature, human history, and the Bible furnish its lessons. These lessons have two great interpreters—wisdom and folly. These interpreters get opposite meanings out of the same fact, and these meanings exert a directly opposite influence upon the experience, character, and destiny of human souls.

The BENEFICENT interpretation of life.—"Understanding is a wellspring of life." Understanding here undoubtedly means true knowledge, and especially true knowledge concerning the highest truths. What are the highest truths? Truths relating to God as manifested in Jesus Christ. These truths touch all that is vital in man's history, all that is grand in the universe, and glorious in God. "This is life eternal, to know Thee, the only true God, and Jesus Christ whom Thou hast sent." So speaks the only absolutely perfect Teacher the world has ever had or ever will have. This knowledge is a wellspring of life. "Two things" says an eloquent writer, "are necessary to the opening and the flow of wellsprings—deep rendings beneath the earth's surface, and risings above it. There must be deep veins and high mountains. The mountains draw the drops from heaven, the rents receive, retain, and give forth the supply. There must be corresponding heights and depths in the life of a man. Either he is charged as a well spring with wisdom from above, upwards to God and downward to himself, the exercise of his soul must alternately penetrate." This comes of spiritual understanding, which is indeed a "well spring." Ever flowing and refreshing are the powers of the soul. "Whosoever drinketh of the water that I give him shall never thirst," said Christ." "It shall be to him as a well of water springing up to everlasting life." The happiness of a worldly man, such as it is, is from without: it streams in through his senses, yielding in its flow pleasurable but transient sensations. That of a spiritually enlightened man is from within: it is a fountain, not a pool, nor a summer's stream. As the humblest spring of water in the obscure vale has a connection with the boundless ocean that lies behind the hills, perhaps a thousand leagues away, so the joys of a good man flow into him from the Infinite, and as water ever presses upwards to its level, so the happiness of a lowly soul ever presses upward to a participation in the unbounded blessedness of God.

The PERNICIOUS interpretation of life.—"The instruction of fools is folly." In all ages fools have set themselves up as interpreters. In a spiritual sense many of the most illustrious sages of the olden time were fools, and not a few of the *savants*, literati, and priests of our age and land are fools also. They misinterpret the great fact of life, they explain away the divine import and give it a false application. Alas! folly has its philosophies, its sciences, and its religions. Their instruction is ever "folly." "There is nothing," says sensible and sententious Matthew Henry, "that is good to be gotten by a fool. Even his instruction, his acts, his solemn discourses, are but folly, like himself, and tending to make others like him. When he does his best it is but folly in comparison even with the common talk of a wise man, who speaks better at table than a fool in Moses's seat." Folly is pernicious: it brings ruin into every department in which it plays a prominent part—business, politics, or religion. "If the blind lead the blind both shall fall into the ditch."

Proverbs 16:23-24

Ideal Eloquence

" The heart of the wise teacheth his mouth, and addeth learning to his lips. Pleasant words *are as* an honeycomb, sweet to the soul, and health to the bones."

ELOQUENCE is a subject of importance. Much has been written upon it, various definitions have been given of it. Most public speakers aspire after it. It is one of the choicest gifts of genius, and the most potent organ of social influence. Some mistake it for elegance of language, and labour after verbal embellishments, rhetoric periods, and climaxes. Others, for fluency of speech, as if it consisted in a nimble use of the tongue. Elsewhere we have indicated our faith that it is rather a mystic feeling than magnificent words, a natural gift than a human attainment, a magnetic force than articulate sound. Eloquence is often mighty on a blundering tongue, and in lips that quiver too much to speak. These two verses lead us to infer several things concerning true eloquence.

IT IS THE UTTERANCE OF THE TRUE HEART.—" The heart of the wise teacheth his mouth." The moral heart of man is the best teacher. It is the table on which are engraven the laws of God, the eternal principles of virtue : —man's book of life on which experience has written its lessons. It is the mirror that reflects the infinite. The highest wisdom is to be found, not in the *reasoning*, but in the *feeling* regions of our soul. It is when the genuinely patriotic heart " teaches the mouth " of the statesman, that his speeches are really eloquent, and his voice bends the senate to his will. It is when the genuinely justice-loving heart " teaches the mouth " of the counsel, that his address is really eloquent, and he carries the jury with him, and makes the cause of his client triumphant ; and it is when the genuinely Christ-loving heart " teaches the mouth " of the preacher, that his sermons become mighty through God. Another fact here taught concerning true eloquence is that:

IT IS THE MEANS OF USEFUL INSTRUCTION.—It " addeth learning to his lips." True eloquence does more than awaken mere emotion in the hearer. It instructs. Its spirit is in such vital alliance with eternal reality that its very sounds echo such truths as start the highest trains of thought. Out of the heart are the issues of life, mental as well as spiritual life. Who is the best religious teacher? Not the *mere* theologian, however vast his learning, scriptural his theory, or perfect his language, but the *Christ-loving* man, however untutored his intellect and ungrammatical his speech. He dispenses the best " learning;" learning which teaches men rightly to live and triumphantly to die. Aye, the instincts of a true heart furnish the lips with the best lessons of life. Concerning true eloquence the verses further teach that:

IT IS A SOURCE OF SOUL REFRESHMENT.—" Pleasant words are as an honeycomb, sweet to the soul, and health to the bones." Honey was prized by those of old times, not only as a luxury to the palate, but on account of its medicinal and salutary properties. To this there is an allusion here. The words express the twofold idea, *pleasantness* and *benefit*. Many things have the one quality which have not the other. Many a poison is like honey, sweet to the taste, but instead of being " health to the bones," is charged with death. Words of true eloquence, fall ever as drops of honey on the soul, not only delicious to the taste but a tonic to the heart.

Brothers in the ministry, would you have the tongue of the "learned"? Then you must have the heart of the saint, the heart glowing with love to Christ and man. Herein is the soul of eloquence. Who could stand before us if our hearts were rightly and fully affected by Christ and his cross? The force of Whitfield's sermons lay in his heart. Dr. Franklin bears the following testimony to the remarkable power of his eloquence. " I happened to attend one of the sermons of Mr. Whitfield, in the course of which I perceived he intended to finish with a collection, and I silently resolved he should get nothing from me. I had in my pocket a handful of copper money, three or four silver dollars, and five pistoles in gold. As he proceeded I began to soften, and concluded to give the copper. Another stroke of his oratory made me ashamed of that, and determined me to give the silver; and he finished so admirably, that I emptied my pocket wholly into the collector's dish—gold and all. At this sermon there was also one of our club, who being of my sentiments respecting the building of Georgia, and suspecting a collection might be intended, had, by precaution, emptied his pockets before he came from home. Towards the conclusion of the discourse, however, he felt a strong inclination to give, and applied to a neighbour who stood near him, to lend him some money for the purpose. The request was made to, perhaps, the only man in the company who had the coldness not to be affected by the preacher. His answer was, " At any other time, friend Hodgkinson, I would lend to thee freely, but not now, for thou seemest to be out of thy right senses."

Proverbs 16:26

Labor

" He that laboureth laboureth for himself; for his mouth craveth it of him."*

STRANGE that human labour is so generally regarded as an evil to be avoided, as the curse of sin and as a badge of degradation. Though English society allows a man to sign himself a " gentleman " who is free from labour, the arrangements of nature regard him as a felon in the universe. As this subject has frequently come under our attention, in previous chapters of this book, we shall confine ourselves just to the two points referring to it in the verse.

* The preceding verse is an utterance identical to that we have noticed on Prov.. xiv. 12

The PERSONALITY of labour.—"He that laboureth, laboureth for himself." First: There is a sense in which this *must be*. A man's labour must have ever an influence on himself either for good or evil. Every act has a reflex bearing. All the actions of men go to form their habits, their character, and their character is in reality the world they live in, and must live in for ever. "What a man soweth that he also reaps." Whatever a man does for others he really does for himself; simply because all his efforts are seeds that he drops into his own soul—seeds that must germinate and grow; and their fruits become to him either a blessing or a curse. Thus men create their own worlds, and people them either with angels or devils. Secondly: There is a sense in which this *should not* be. Men ought not to labour for themselves, as an end. Men should not seek their own, they should not live to themselves, but to him who "died for them and rose again." The man who makes self the end of his labour degrades his nature and damns his soul. " He that seeketh his life shall lose it." Dr. Cheever gives a striking incident of genuine disinterestedness. "Terantius, Captain to the Emperor Adrian, presented a petition that the Christians might have a temple to themselves in which to worship God apart from the Arians. The emperor tore his petition and threw it away, bidding him ask something for himself and it should be granted. Terantius modestly gathered up the fragments of his petition, and said, with true nobility of mind, 'If I cannot be heard in God's cause, I will never ask anything for myself.'" Again the verse points to :—

The SPRING OF labour.—"For his mouth craveth it of him." Hunger is the spring of human activity. "All the labour of man is for his mouth, and yet the appetite is not filled."* First: Hunger is the spring of *bodily* labour. The toiler in the field, the mariner on the sea, the mechanic in his shop, the merchant in the market, in fact, all men are moved by the same impulse. It is the mainspring in the great machine of human activity, keeping every wheel in motion. Appetite is not an evil to be

* Eccles vi. 7.

mortified, it is a blessing to be valued. Secondly: Hunger is the spring of *intellectual* labour. There is a hunger in the soul for knowledge. " Where shall wisdom be found? and where is the place of understanding?" This thirst for knowledge has given us our philosophies, our sciences, and all the arts that bless and adorn the civilized world. Mental hunger is a blessing; it is the philosophic spirit. Thirdly: Hunger is the spring of *spiritual* labour. Deep in the soul there is a hunger for a better moral state :— Peace of conscience and friendship with God. This hunger stimulates men often, alas, to work with wrong methods. Still it is a good. " Blessed are they that hunger and thirst after righteousness." All hunger indicates health, and implies a provision of suitable supplies. He that hungers for the right proves his moral healthfulness, and may, through Christ, obtain an abundant supply.

Proverbs 16:27-30

Mischievous Men

" An ungodly man diggeth up evil: and in his lips *there is* as a burning fire. A froward man soweth strife: and a whisperer separateth chief friends. A violent man enticeth his neighbour, and leadeth him into the way *that is* not good. He shutteth his eyes to devise froward things: moving his lips, he bringeth evil to pass."

THESE verses represent a mischievous man, a man who makes it the business of his life to injure society. He is designated here by three terms, " ungodly " — in the original, as in the margin, a man of Belial; " froward," —perverse and refractory; " violent,"—fierce, cruel, and bloody. Such is a mischievous man. No uncommon character, alas, this. Throughout all the social circles of the world he is found. His delight is to snap the links of friendship, to sow the seeds of strife in the fields of affection. Quarrels are music to his soul. The verses teach us three things concerning him.

He SEARCHES AFTER evil.—" An ungodly man diggeth up evil." The old quarrel, suspicion, grievance, which had been buried for years, he *digs* for, as a miner for his ore. He belongs to the class described by the Psalmist, "They search out iniquities, they accomplish a diligent search, both the inward thought of every one of them, and the heart is deep." *Time buries the grievances of men.* Years entomb old quarrels. Ages as they roll over this earth like billows bury the memory of its fiercest wars. This is a merciful arrangement. *The mischievous man is an explorer of those tombs.* He opens the graves of old disputes, he brings their ghastly skeletons up, and endeavours to put new life into them. He is a fiend that lives and prowls among the tombs of old disputes. Another fact here taught concerning the mischievous man is this:

He IS INSPIRED BY evil.—"In his lips *there is* as a burning fire." The fires of jealousy, envy, and all other malign emotions that glow in his heart, throw their burning sparks into his words, and kindle flames of discord. "The tongue," says James, "is a fire, a world of iniquity, it defileth the whole body, and it is set on fire of hell." The tongue of the mischief maker burns what? Not falsehoods, suspicions, jealousies, and other dissocializing elements, but all that mutual confidence, trustfulness, and esteem that form the basis of true friendship. On these his syllabic sparks fall as on tinder, and they set on fire the whole course of society. Still further, another fact here taught concerning the *mischievous* man is that:

He PROPAGATES evil.—He soweth strife, he "separateth chief friends," he "enticeth his neighbour," he "bringeth evil to pass." First: *He produceth social strife by insinuations.* "A whisperer separateth chief friends." He whispereth. The whisper is his mode of speech, and for his purpose it is mightier than the loudest thunders of passion. It gives the hearer to understand that there is something so terrible behind, that words cannot, or ought not, to communicate. Ah me! what bright reputations have been stained, what lovely friendships have been destroyed, what pure hearts have been broken, by the whispering inuendo, and the silent shrug of the shoulder. Secondly: *He leads astray by enticements.* "A violent man enticeth his neighbour, and leadeth him into the way that is not good." He uses the winning and seductive in speech to carry out his mischievous designs. Thus he turneth his neighbour into the wrong course. Plausibility is the characteristic and instrument of a mischievous man. Thirdly: *He pursues his designs by deliberation.* "He shutteth his eyes to devise froward things." A man shuts his eyes when he wishes to think closely and undistractedly. The ungodly man does it for the purpose of planning and maturing mischievous devices. When he shuts his eyes, even in bed, while others sleep, it is to meditate on schemes of evil, and then, having digested his schemes inwardly, he employs his "lips" in their artful accomplishment. Thus *mind* and *mouth* are in concert for evil—the latter the agent and servant of the former.

> " He that shall rail against his absent friends,
> Or hears them scandalized, and not defends,
> Sports with their fame, and speaks whate'er he can,
> And only to be thought a witty man,
> Tells tales, and brings his friends in disesteem,
> That man's a knave—be sure beware of him."—HORACE

Proverbs 16:31

The Glory of the Aged Piety

> " The hoary head *is* a crown of glory, *if* it be found in the way of righteousness."

SOME have dispensed with the little word "*if*," and read the text thus, "The hoary head is a crown of glory, it shall be found in the way of righteousness; but this takes away the truth of the passage, for the "hoary head," apart from righteousness, is not a "crown of glory." It is a degradation. The silver-locked sinner deserves shame and everlasting contempt. Age cannot be honoured for its own sake, the older the sinner the more contemptible the character. "The sinner being an hundred years old shall be accursed."* But when age is found in the way of righteousness, then it radiates with the moral diadem, before which our inmost spirits bow in homage. Two things are noteworthy in passing. Although they are not implied in the verse, they are suggested by it. First: *That righteousness is conducive to old age.* This is a fact sustained both by philosophy and history. Physical health depends upon obedience to the laws of our organization. Genuine righteousness insures and includes this obedience. Secondly: *That piety is conducive to honour.* Righteousness is the only true respectability. Goodness alone is true greatness. A crown on the head of ungodliness would be as "a jewel in a swine's snout." We make three remarks concerning the glory of aged piety.

It is the glory of spiritual RIPENESS.—There is something glorious in maturation. The seed ripened into an autumnal crop, the youth ripened into mature manhood, the student ripened into the accomplished scholar, are all objects of admiration. In an old saint there is a truly glorious ripeness. There you have all the seeds of truth and holiness, as sown by holy teachers, cultured by experience, fostered by the sunbeam and the showers of God, tried and strengthened in their roots by the storms of adversity, hanging in rich clusters on the boughs ready to be gathered in. "Thou shalt come to thy grave in a full age, like as a shock of corn cometh in in his season." †

Another remark concerning the glory of aged piety is that:

It is the glory of spiritual COMMAND.—Even Egypt's proud despot bowed before it. "And Joseph brought in Jacob his father and set him before Pharaoh, and Jacob blessed Pharaoh. And Pharaoh said unto Jacob, How old art thou? And Jacob said unto Pharaoh, the days of the years of my pilgrimage are a hundred and thirty years; few and evil have the days of the years of my life been, and have not attained unto the days of the years of the life of my fathers in the days of their pilgrimage. And Jacob blessed Pharaoh, and went out from before Pharaoh."‡ Samuel was an old saint when he died. "And Samuel died, and all the Israelites were gathered

* Isaiah lxv.20.   † Job v. 26.   ‡ Gen. xlvii. 7—10.

together and lamented him, and buried him in his house at Ramah."* "Jehoiada waxed old and was full of days when he died, a hundred and thirty years old was he when he died. And they buried him in the city of David, among the kings, because he had done good in Israel, both towards God and towards his house."† No object on this earth is more truly royal to me, than that man whose noble brow time has whitened with snowy locks, whose intellect, unwarped by prejudice, is still in quest of truth, whose heart beats in sympathy with all that is true, philanthropic, and divine; whose past is sunnied by the memory of useful deeds, whose future is bright with the promises of grace, and who sits in calm majesty, in "the old armchair," on the margin of both worlds, waiting his appointed time. Where on this earth is there a king like him?

Concerning the glory of aged piety we have yet to remark that:

It is the glory of spiritual PROSPECTS.—Simeon, who took the infant Jesus in his arms, and said—"Now lettest thou thy servant depart in peace, for mine eyes have seen thy salvation," is a glorious example of this. Though his foot was on earth, heaven was in his eye, and flooding his heart with joy. The outward man is decaying, but the inner man is strong. The body of an aged saint is to him what the chrysalis is to the insect, whose wings are perfect enough to enable it to break forth into life, sip the nectar of the flowers, sweep the fields of beauty, and bask in the sunshine of day. We conclude with the utterance of a modern author: "As ripe fruit is sweeter than green fruit, so is age sweeter than youth, provided the youth were grafted into Christ. As harvest-time is a brighter time than seed-time, so is age brighter than youth; that is if youth were a seed-time for good. As the completion of a work is more glorious than the beginning, so is age more glorious than youth; that is, if the foundation of the work of God were laid in youth. As sailing into port is happier than the voyage, so is age happier than youth; that is when the voyage from youth is made with Christ at the helm."

* 1 Sam. xxv. 1.   † Chron. xxiv. 15, 16.

Proverbs 16:32

The Conqueror of Self, the Greatest Conqueror

"*He that is* slow to anger *is* better than the mighty; and he that ruleth his spirit than he that taketh a city."

THESE words imply—First: That man has a spirit. By the spirit is to be understood his moral heart, with all its impulses, affections, powers. Secondly: This spirit should be ruled. There should be self-command, self-control. An uncontrolled spirit is a curse to itself, and the universe. Thirdly: That the ruling of this spirit is the greatest of works. It is greater than taking a city.

It is the most NECESSARY of conquests.—It is necessary to the *freedom* of man. A man with an uncontrolled temper is the worst of slaves. He is the victim of a lawless despot. It is necessary to the *peace* of man. An uncontrolled spirit is in eternal conflict with itself. He committeth self-mutilation. Indeed he is like the man in the Gospel, who "fell ofttimes into the fire and oft into the water." It is necessary to the *progress* of man. A man cannot really advance in intelligence and worth, unless he is able to command his own intellect and powers. Men can do without taking "a city," but they cannot without ruling their own spirits.

This is the most RIGHTEOUS of conquests.—Taking cities, physical wars of all descriptions, defensive as well as aggressive, are, to say the least, undertakings of questionable morality. I believe they are wrong, essentially and eternally wrong. But to conquer self is a *righteous* campaign. Man has a right to dethrone evil passions, to crucify old lusts, to pull down corrupt prejudices. His spirit is his own domain. It is the Canaan God has given him to conquer and possess. He must drive out the Canaanites before he can truly enjoy the land; and on this battle he enters with a "Thus saith the Lord."

This is the most DIFFICULT of conquests.—Cities may be

taken by fraud or violence. The most cunning man with reckless daring will make the most successful worldly chieftain. A successful soldier must be a great sneak. The difficulty in this conquest arises from the nature of the enemy—subtle and strong. Paul, after wrestling with this enemy, cries out in agony, " O wretched man that I am, who shall deliver me from the bondage of this sin and death?" This difficulty arises from the nature of the weapons. No force can do it. Swords, bayonets, cannons, are all useless here. They cannot reach the enemy within. There must be meditation, prayer, self-denial, unflagging perseverance. This difficulty arises from the unco-operativeness of the campaign. In taking cities and in all material campaigns, men co-operate, not merely individually but regimentally. The spirit of emulation, the love of applause, and the hope of glory urge them on, but in this conquest of the spirit man must go by himself. He must work in solitude and in shame. He must "tread the winepress alone."

It is the most BLESSED of conquests.—First: *It wins the highest trophy.* What are towns, cities, fleets, armies, continents, won by physical warfare, compared to a soul, which is won by self-conquest? "What shall it profit a man, if he gain the whole world and lose his soul?" All that is material will vanish one day as a cloud, but the soul will survive the wreck of all. Secondly: *It awakens the highest applause.* The applause of worldly conquerors is the boisterous shout of a brainless crowd, but the approbation which the self-conqueror gains is the approbation of his own conscience, of the whole universe, and of his God. "The command of one's self," says Drexelius, "is the greatest empire a man can aspire unto, and consequently to be subject to our passions, the most grievous slavery. Neither is there any triumph more glorious than that of the victory obtained of ourselves, where whilst the conflict is so short, the reward shall ever last."

Proverbs 16:33

Life, a Lottery and a Plan

"The lot *is* cast into the lap: but the whole disposing thereof is of the Lord."*

THE lot is anything, whether *drawn* or *cast*, for the purpose of determining any matter in question. The instances of its use mentioned in Scripture are considerably various :† in finding out a guilty person when there was no direct and satisfactory evidence; in dividing and appropriating land; in the choice of an official functionary; in assigning departments of duty; in deciding controversies. Some translate " *lap*," " urn," into which the lots were cast.

The verse suggests two things—

That the HUMAN side of life is a LOTTERY.—Much connected with our circumstances in this world, seems to be as much the result of chance as the " casting of the lot." We are struck with the apparent casualty when we look at men's circumstances in connection with their *choice*. None of us have any choice as to the condition, the place, the time, in which we are to be born or brought up. We are struck with the apparent casualty also when we look at men's circumstances in connection with their *merits*. How often we find feeble-minded men in eminent positions, and men of talent and genius in obscurity; some by what is called a " hit," making fortunes and earning fame, whilst honest industry plods on with little or no success; vice in mansions, and virtue in the pauper's hut. Verily " the race is not often to the swift, nor the battle to the strong." It is not, however, all casualty. There is some amount of certainty; and these two opposing elements in life are highly disciplinary. The *casual* teaches us to exercise dependence on God, and the *certain* stimulates us to work our own faculties.

* See Readings on chap. xix. 11., xvi. 1.
† 1 Sam. xiv. 38—43, Jonah i. 7, Numbers xxvi. 52, Acts i. 26, 1 Chron. xxiv. 45, Prov. xxii. 18.

The verse suggests again—

That the DIVINE side of life is a PLAN.—"The whole disposing thereof is of the Lord." All that appears chance on the human side is settled law on the Divine. That God controls and disposes of the most trivial contingencies of life may be argued,—First: *From His character.* He is all-present, all-seeing, almighty, all-wise, all-good. There is nothing great or small to Him.—Secondly; *From the connection of the most trivial events with the vastest issues.* Providence is a machine. The most insignificant circumstance is an essential pin, screw, or wheel in the works of the engine. Thirdly: *From the history of the world.* The meeting of the Ishmaelites on their journey to Egypt at the pit the very moment Joseph was cast into it seemed a trifling casualty. But God disposed of it. Indeed, the story of Joseph, as Dr. South remarks, "seems to be made up of nothing else but chances and little contingencies, all tending to mighty ends." Pharaoh's daughter comes to the Nile just when the babe Moses was committed to the ark on the banks of the rolling stream. But God disposed that little incident, and brought wonderful results out of it. A whale meets the vessel in which Jonah sails, at the moment he is thrown into the sea. God disposed of that incident. Examples of this are countless. Every man's life supplies him with many such. The most trivial incidents have often led in our history to the most important issues. "Whatever *will* thou makest," says an old divine, "God is sure to be the *executor.*" An architect holds in his hand the plan of a magnificent cathedral. He has signed the contract to complete the edifice, and hundreds of men are set to work—some at home and some abroad; some to work in timber, some in stone, some on iron and some on brass. Few, if any, know his plan; yet his plan unconsciously rules them all, and all are co-operating towards its ultimate realization. They are all free, yet controlled by the master thought of another. It is so with God and His moral creatures. His plan runs through all their activities, and shapes their destiny, though they know it not, and feel no restraining or constraining force. "The lot is cast into the lap; but the whole disposing thereof is of the Lord."

Proverbs 17:1-2

Family Scenes

> "Better *is* a dry morsel, and quietness therewith, than an house full of sacrifices *with* strife. A wise servant shall have rule over a son that causeth shame, and shall have part of the inheritance among the brethren"

A PROVERB like that in the first verse, has already come under our notice. "Better is a dinner of herbs where love is, than a stalled ox and hatred therewith."* We may take the two verses together because they alike point to domestic life, and they give us three things which are often found in households.

A DISCONTENTED TEMPER.—"Better is a dry morsel and quietness therewith, than a house full of sacrifices with strife." The word "*sacrifices*" refers to the practice of feasting on the flesh of slain victims when they were not holocaust to be entirely consumed on the altar.† The margin gives the true idea. "A house full of good cheer with strife—plenty with discontent." The idea of Solomon is that domestic poverty with content is better than plenty with discontent. These things are often found in association. There is many a pauper home where the spirit of contentment reigns supreme, and many a wealthy mansion, where there is nothing but brawls and contention. And who, that knows life, will not say, that the former is the preferable condition? A contented mind is a continual feast. "It produces," says Addison, "in some measure all those effects which the alchemist usually ascribed to what he calls the philosopher's stone, and if it does not bring riches, it does the same thing by banishing the desire of them." If it cannot remove the disquietudes arising from

---

* See Reading on chap. xv. 16, **17.**
† 1 Samuel ix. 12, 13, 20—24.

a man's mind, body, or fortune, it makes him easy under them.

> "Lord, who would live turmoil'd in court,
> And may enjoy such quiet walks as these?
> This small inheritance my father left me
> Contented me, and's worth a monarchy.
> I seek not to wax great by others' waning,
> Or gather wealth, I care not with what envy;
> Sufficeth that I maintain my state,
> And send the poor well pleased from my gate."
>
> SHAKESPEARE

We have here—

A WORTHLESS SON.—"A son that causeth shame." Who is the son that causeth shame? He, who with the means of knowledge is destitute of information and culture; he who degrades his position by indolence, intemperance, and profligacy; he who for his own gratification and indulgence, violates the rights and does outrage to the feelings of those whom he is bound to love and obey. The gross voluptuary, the empty sot, the jewelled dandy, "causeth shame,"—shame to his parents, to his brothers, his sisters. He is a disgrace to an intelligent and high-minded family. Many such sons, alas, there are in English homes, and they cause shame.

We have here—

A VALUABLE SERVANT.—"The wise servant shall rule over a son that causeth shame, and shall have part of the inheritance among the brethren." A well tried servant gets moral influence in a house. He rules over a son. A servant, who for many years has industriously and honestly administered to the comfort of a family, seldom fails to gain power. In the olden times, as in the case of Abraham, servants were born in a family, and when they conducted themselves well, their influence became great. A well tried servant sometimes shares the fortunes of the house. "Shall have part of the inheritance among the brethren." Instances sometimes occur even in modern times of such servants becoming the legatees of their masters. Jacob by marrying Laban's daughter was portioned with an inheritance.

From the whole we may infer—

First: *That the temper of a man's soul is more important to him than his temporal condition.* A cot with contentment is a far better home than a castle with an ill-satisfied soul. The quiet mind is better than a crown. Contentment is a pearl of great price, and whoever procures it at the expense of ten thousand desires makes a wise and happy purchase. Secondly: *That the power of character is superior to the power of station.* A man may have the station of being "the son" and heir of a wealthy house, and yet be disgraced. Another may occupy a menial position, yet by force of noble character, get a sovereignty in his circle. "It is the man who adorns the station, not the station the man."

Proverbs 17:3

Divine Discipline

"The fining pot *is* for silver, and the furnace for gold: but the LORD trieth the hearts."

A COMPARISON is here intended. "As the fining pot is for silver, and the furnace for gold, so the Lord trieth the hearts." There are two things to be noticed here:

THE VALUABLE AND WORTHLESS IN CONNECTION WITH MAN.—The ore which the refiner puts into the crucible, or furnace, has the precious metal in connection with extraneous and worthless matter, mere dross. First: In man there is the valuable in *essence* in connection with the *comparatively worthless.* The soul is man's essence, his self, the offspring, the image, the servant of God, and how valuable is this! The material organization in which that soul lives is but "dust," and the secular conditions that surround it are of little worth. The soul is the "gold," all else dross. Secondly: In man's character there is the valuable in *principle* in connection with the *most worthless*

There are some good things in all men, even the most corrupt, some true idea, some generous impulses, some virtuous feelings. But these are found combined with and overlaid by selfishness, pride, carnality, and practical infidelity. With impure loves, false hopes, erroneous ideas, and wicked purposes, man appears here as the ore in the refiner's hand just before it has dropped into the furnace. He is as gold combined with dross, the valuable with the worthless. As in some lumps of ore there is more gold in connection with less worthless matter than with others, so with men. There are some with far less gold in connection with less worthless matter than others, both constitutionally and morally.

The other thing to be noticed here is—

THE PURIFYING PROCESS EMPLOYED BY GOD.—"The Lord trieth the hearts." He tries not, as the refiner the ore, to *ascertain* how much good metal there really is, for He knows all that, but in order to separate it from the dross. First: The purifying process is *painful*. It is by "fire." The fire to purify must be raised to the utmost intensity. "The fire shall try every man's work of what sort it is."* Physical suffering, secular disappointments, social bereavements, moral convictions, constitute that furnace in which God tries man. "He knoweth," says Job, "the way I take: when He hath tried me I shall come forth as gold."† Secondly: The purifying process is *constant*. The dispensation under which we live is disciplinary. "And He shall *sit* as a refiner and as a purifier of silver, and He shall purify the sons of Levi, and purge them as gold and silver, that they may offer unto the Lord an offering in righteousness." A correspondent of the *Wesleyan Methodist Magazine* relates that, "A lady, apprehending there was something remarkable in the expressions of this text, determined to call on a silversmith and make enquiries of him, without naming her object. In answer to her enquiries the process of silver refining was fully explained to her. 'But, sir,' said she, 'do you sit while the work of refining is going on?' 'O yes, madam,' replied the silversmith, 'I must sit

* 1 Cor. iii. 13. † Job xxiii. 10.

with my eyes steadily fixed on the furnace, for, if the time necessary for refining be exceeded in the slightest degree, the silver is sure to be injured.' At once, we are told, she saw the beauty and comfort too of the expression. As she was going, the silversmith called her back to mention the further fact that he only knew when the process of purifying was complete *by seeing his own image reflected in the silver.* Beautiful figure!" When Christ sees His own image in His people, His work of purifying is accomplished. Heaven grant that the trial of " our faith being much more precious than of gold that perisheth, though it be tried with fire, might be found unto praise and honour and glory, at the appearing of Jesus Christ!"

Proverbs 17:4

Conversational Likings of Bad Men

"A wicked doer giveth heed to false lips : *and* a liar giveth ear to a naughty tongue."

MEN'S characters may be known by the conversations they most relish. The talk of the holy and the devout is always most distasteful to those whose hearts are in sympathy only with the vanities of the world—the pursuits of wealth, the gratification of the senses. This verse enables us to see the kind of conversation that bad men like.

They like FLATTERY.—" A wicked doer giveth heed to false lips." The flatterer is a man of false lips. The more corrupt men are, the more blindly credulous to everything that makes them appear better than they are. The truth concerning them would disturb perhaps their sleeping consciences, and fill them with distressing feelings, and this they shun. He who compliments them palliates their offences, gives them credit for virtues they possess not, is their favourite companion, and they ever "give heed" to his lips. The more corrupt a circle, the more popular a flattering member. The more corrupt a congregation, the more acceptable a flattering preacher. "A wonderful and horrible thing is committed in the land: the prophets prophesy falsely, and the priests bear rule by that means; and my people would have it so." The worse men are, the more anxious they are to be thought good. Hence the ready heed they give to flattering lips. One of the best things recorded of George III. is, that one of his first acts after his ascension to the throne was to issue an order prohibiting any of the clergy who should be called to preach before him from paying him any compliment in their discourses. His Majesty was led to this form from the fulsome adulation which Dr. Thomas Wilson, Prebendary of Westminster, thought proper to deliver in the Chapel Royal, and for which, instead of thanks, he received from his royal auditor a pointed reprimand, His Majesty observing, "that he came to chapel to hear the praises of God, and not his own."

> "A man I knew, who lived upon a smile,
> And well it fed him; he look'd plump and fair,
> While rankest venom foamed through every vein.
> Living, he fawned on every fool alive;
> And dying, cursed the friend on whom he lived."—YOUNG

What is the kind of conversation that bad men like? The verse shows that—

They like CALUMNY.—"A liar giveth ear to a naughty tongue." The "liar" is also the "wicked doer." The "naughty tongue," while it speaks flatteries and falsehoods of all kinds, speaks *calumnies* also, and the worse the man is the more welcome to his depraved heart are the reports of bad things concerning others. Calumny gratifies the *pride* of evil men. It helps them to cherish the thought that they are not worse than others, but perhaps better. Calumny gratifies the *malignity* of evil men. The worse a man is the more malevolence he has in him, and the more gratified he is at hearing bad things concerning other men. "If," said Bishop Hall, "I cannot stop other men's mouths to reprove it, I will stop mine ears from hearing it, and let him see in my face that he hath no more room in my heart." Bad men constitute the audience to which both flattery and calumny address themselves. Convert this audience into vital sympathy with truth and goodness, and these lying spirits will quit the world.

Proverbs 17:5

The Unfortunate Poor

"Whoso mocketh the poor reproacheth his Maker: *and* he that is glad at calamities shall not be unpunished."

A SIMILAR sentence to this we have had before :* "He that oppresseth the poor reproacheth his Maker; but he that honoureth him hath mercy on the poor." On this verse we have already offered some remarks. There is a poverty that is a crime. It arises from indolence, intemperance, extravagance, stupidity, and other culpable causes. And there is a poverty that is a calamity—a poverty that has come on men irrespective of their choice and against their honest and resolute efforts. These poor may be considered as planted by God in the earth, and they serve most useful purposes in the discipline of the world. These are the poor referred to here, and two facts are stated—

That contempt for such is IMPIOUS.—"Whoso mocketh the poor reproacheth his Maker." Mocking is more than disrespect, more than neglect, it is disdain. This feeling is impious. He who has it "reproacheth his Maker." This mocking implies a disregard to *God's ordinance.* The existence of the poor in the world is not a casualty, it is a divine purpose. "The poor shall never cease out of the land." Were there no poor, there would be no opportunity for the development of social compassion and beneficence. This mocking implies a disregard to *the relationships that He has established.* The poor are our brethren, offsprings of the same parent, partakers of the same nature, subject to the same conditions of being. To feel disdain towards them is to disregard relationships that our Maker has

* See Reading on Prov. xiv. 31.

established. This mocking implies a disregard *to the earthly condition of His Son and His disciples.* Christ was poor, "He had nowhere to lay His head." His disciples also were men devoid of wealth and power. "Not many wise men after the flesh, not many mighty, not many noble are called." This mocking implies a disregard *to the Divine grounds of social respect.* God's will is that man's respect to man should not be ruled by physical condition, but by moral character. The good man, though a pauper, should be honoured; the wicked man, though a prince, should be despised. To pour contempt on the current coin with the king's image upon it, is treason against the sovereign. Man, however poor, has the stamp of God's image on him, and to despise that image is a contempt for the Divine majesty. Another fact referred to here concerning the poor is—

That contempt for such is PUNISHABLE.—He that is glad at the calamities of others indicates a fiendish malignity. "Woe unto them that decree unrighteous decrees to turn aside the needy from judgment, and to take from the poor of my children. The Lord will plead their cause, and spoil the souls of those that spoil them." In the day of judgment He will take our conduct towards the poor into account. "Inasmuch as ye did it unto the least of these little ones ye did it unto me." Cruelty to the poor is certain of punishment. "Go to now, ye rich men, weep and howl, for your miseries that shall come upon you. Your riches are corrupted, and your garments are moth-eaten. Your gold and silver is cankered ; and the rust of them shall be a witness against you, and shall eat your flesh as it were fire. Ye have heaped treasure together for the last days. Behold the hire of the labourers which have reaped down your fields, which is of you keep back by fraud, crieth, and the cries of them which have reaped are entered into the ears of the Lord of Sabaoth. Ye have lived in pleasure on the earth, and been wanton ; ye have nourished your hearts as in a day of slaughter!"

Proverbs 17:6

Posterity and Its Ancestors

"Children's children *are* the crown of old men : and the glory of children *are* their fathers."

WE have two things in this passage—

A POSTERITY that is the glory of its ANCESTRY.—"Children's children are the crown of old men." Posterity is not always a "crown" to its ancestors. There are children not a few who disgrace the fair fame of their forefathers. Though they wear their brilliant titles and hold their vast estates, they are, to say the least, but miserable shadows of illustrious progenitors. When "children's children" are a "crown" an honour to their fathers, two things have taken place. First: *Their fathers have rightly fulfilled their mission.* The presumption is that they have, by their example, instructions, and prayers, trained up their children in the "nurture and admonition of the Lord." Where this is not the case, and the children have grown up in godly virtues, no credit of course is due to the parents. On the contrary; the virtues of such children are their condemnation. However great the influence which parents have in the formation of the character of their children, that influence is not absolute. There is a power in the child to counteract it, and by the grace of Heaven many a child brought up in ignorance and depravity has found its way into spiritual light and holiness. The other thing that has taken place when children become a "crown" to their ancestors is, Secondly: *The children have rightly used the privileges they have enjoyed.* They have copied parental example, and have applied parental admonitions, and as they have grown in years, they have advanced in goodness. Let no parents hope that their posterity will be an honour to them, if they have not maintained a godly character themselves, and trained their children in the way in which they should go. And let no children imagine that they can honour their pious ancestors unless they walk in the way of their commandments. Were not Rehoboam and his son a disgrace to their fathers? What a "crown of glory" encircles the brow of that old man whose children's children gather round him, exemplifying the virtues that he embodied in his life and inculcated in his teaching! "Children by their conduct may either weave a garland of honour for the brow of their parents, or encircle their brows with a crown of thorns, and bring down their grey hairs with sorrow to the grave." What an honour was young Timothy, who "from a child knew the holy scriptures," to his grandmother Lois and his mother Eunice! And what a stain upon his reputation—a sword in his bones—a weight of oppressive sadness on the spirit of old age, were the profligate sons of Eli, who himself was to blame, for it is said, his sons "made themselves vile, and he restrained them not."

We have here—

An ANCESTRY that is the glory of its POSTERITY.—"And the glory of children *are* their fathers." It is a great thing to be born of parents healthy in body, strong in intellect, and holy in character. How many come into life inheriting a diseased constitution, an enfeebled brain, and proclivities to the selfish, the mean, and the carnal. Worthy children may well be proud of noble sires. Some fathers disgrace their children's children, and attach infamy to their posterity. Others by their virtues brighten the life of their children's children with a halo of imperishable glory. David, notwithstanding his imperfections, was the glory of his children's children. He preserved to them the throne of Judah for seventeen generations.

> " My boast is not that I deduce my birth
> From loins enthroned and rulers of the earth;
> But higher far my proud pretentions rise:
> The son of parents pass'd into the skies."—COWPER

In conclusion, the subject suggests two thoughts. First: *The physical succession of the race.* Here we read of "fathers," "children," "children's children." "One generation cometh and passeth away." One generation is buried in the dust of another, and future generations will be entombed in our ashes; but though men depart, *man* remains. Generations like waves, rise and break on the eternal shore; but humanity, like the ocean, rolls on in undiminished plenitude and power. The world can do without us. Secondly: *The moral connection of the race.* Men are either an honour or a disgrace to members of their own species, especially to their own lineage. "No man liveth unto himself." Adam's sin has rolled its influence through the souls of all ages, in all climes, and pulsates in the spirit of this generation.

> " 'Tis poor, and not becoming perfect gentry,
> To build their glories at their fathers' cost;
> But at their own expense of blood or virtue
> To raise them living monuments. Our birth
> Is not our own act: honour upon trust
> Our ill deeds forfeit: and the wealthy sums
> Purchased by others' fame or sweat, will be
> Our stain; for we inherit nothing truly
> But what our actions make us worthy of."—CHAPMAN

Proverbs 17:7

Speech, Incongruous and False

"Excellent speech becometh not a fool: much less do lying lips a prince."

IN the first clause of this proverb we have INCONGRUOUS speech.—speech which is inconsistent with the speaker's sentiments, spirit, and character.—" Excellent speech " or, as the margin has it " lips of excellency,' " becometh not a fool." How often do we hear corrupt men using excellent speech. They do it to disguise their own character, and to impose upon their fellow men. There is benevolent speech from the lips of the selfish. This is frequently heard. As a rule the more selfish a man is the more are his words loaded with the generous and the disinterested.

There is tender speech from the lips of the hardened. Obdurate natures can speak soft words of symyathy, and weep feigned tears. There is spiritual speech from the lips of the carnal. Men deeply sunk in the mercenary and the sensual often use devout language; they always do so when they join in the beautiful Liturgy of the Church. All this is sadly incongruous. Such speech in the lips of a fool is, to use the words of another proverb, like "jewels in a swine's snout." Such speech is, of course, hypocritic: it misrepresents both the spirit and character of the speaker. It has no influence for good. However generous, tender, and devout, it is hollow. "When," to use the language of another, "a fool utters a curse, or a wicked man good advice, he to whom it is given, thinks himself, by the very circumstance of its coming from such a person, at liberty to disregard it. The advice having no worth of character to support and recommend it, goes for nothing and falls lifeless and pithless to the ground. It well becomes the public teachers of religion to lay these thoughts to heart. More "excellent speech" cannot be uttered than the doctrines and precepts, the counsels and warnings of the Word of God. But if the character of him who utters them is notoriously at variance with his instructions, the incongruity shocks, disgusts, and revolts the hearer. It draws tears from the pious, and mockery from the profane. The latter feel the admonitions from others. Good they may be, but they are blunted by the character of the speaker. They scoff and exchange the sly wink with each other, or they are provoked at the thought of their being schooled by such a man, and with the one feeling or the other they leave the sanctuary whispering or exclaiming with a careless shrug, 'physician, heal thyself.'"

Here we have, in the second clause of this proverb—

FALSE SPEECH.—"Much less do lying lips a prince." Incongruous speech is of course always false, but false is not always incongruous, it may be in keeping with the character of the speaker who is known to be a false man. The falsehood here is most flagrant, for the prince ought to be the guardian of truth and honesty in the community, and as their guardian he should be their example. Louis IX. of France said, " If truth be banished from all the rest of the world, it ought to be found in the breast of princes." It is a sad reflection upon Plato that he sanctioned falsehoods in princes on the ground that they governed for the public good. Lying men are bad, but lying princes are worse, they shake public confidence, and by their example they dispose the nation to falsehood.

> " This, above all, to thine own self be true ;
> And it must follow, as the night the day,
> Thou canst not then be false to any man."—SHAKESPEARE

" A lie," says Carlyle, "should be trampled on and extinguished wherever found. I am for fumigating the atmosphere when I suspect that falsehood, like pestilence, breathes around me."

> " Let falsehood be a stranger to thy lips.
> Shame on the policy that first began
> To tamper with the heart, to hide its thoughts!
> And doubly shame on that unrighteous tongue
> That sold its honesty, and told a lie!"—HAVARD

Proverbs 17:8

The Power of Patronage

" A gift *is as* a precious stone in the eyes of him that hath it : whithersoever it turneth, it prospereth."

PATRONAGE is one of the mightiest forces in social life ; it is indeed a " precious stone in the eyes " of men.

Patronage is power in the HANDS of the GIVER.—The man " that hath it " to bestow, hath what is a " precious stone" in the eyes of society. It would so operate on his behalf in his neighbourhood or country that " whithersoever he turneth he prospereth." Money is might, it " answereth all things," gifts govern. First : There is a *lawful* use of this power. The man who uses it to increase his own influence for the good of society, to encourage the arts and the sciences, to raise intellectual and moral merit to its right social position, uses this "precious stone" in a praiseworthy way. Patronage is a great talent, which, rightly used, may render high service both to church and state. In truth, a man by patronage may win a bloodless conquest over the malignant passions of personal antagonists. Thus Jacob triumphed over Esau. "I will appease him with a present that goeth before me, and afterwards I will see his face." This "precious stone" rightly used, can achieve sublimer triumphs than all the armies of Europe; it can subdue the enmity of the soul. Secondly: There is an *unlawful* use of this power. It is wrongly used when, for selfish ends and personal aggrandisement, it *bribes* men to act either without or against their consciences. Thus, alas! it is often used both in ecclesiastical and political matters. This "precious stone" held up on the hustings, and sparkling in the eyes of the electors, has cleared the path of many a worthless man for parliamentary honours. Heathens felt the power of this. Philip of Macedon said that there "was no fortress so strong but it might be taken if an ass laden with gold was brought to the gate." "A golden key," said an old author, "can open any prison gate, and cast the watchman into a deep sleep. Gold will break open gates, as well as silence the orator's voice and blind the judge's eyes. It will bind the strong man's hands, and blunt the edge of the sword. It makes war, and it makes peace."

Patronage is power in the LIFE of the RECEIVER.—"Whithersoever it turneth it prospereth." Some suppose the reference is rather to the receiver of the gift than to the bestower. First: It is a power *which binds him in gratitude to his patron*. He who receives a gift from generous impulses of another, if he has within him the true heart of a man, comes under the reign of gratitude; he feels bound to serve the donor whenever he can consistently with his own conscience and duties. Sometimes indeed the force of gratitude will tempt a man even to do the wrong in order to serve his patron. Secondly: It is a

Proverbs 17:9 / 349

power *which serves to increase his own social credit*. He who has received the "precious stone" from an honourable minded patron as a recognition of personal excellence, and as a reward of merit, will find the fact so operating on the social mind around him, that "whithersoever he turneth it prospereth." His compeers will think the more of him on account of the favours he has received. Thus patronage, this "precious stone," is as a power both to the bestower and the recipient. Let us give and receive in a right spirit; let us neither bribe nor be bribed by this "precious stone."

> "Judges and senates have been bought for gold:
> Esteem and love were never to be sold."—POPE

Proverbs 17:9

The Right Concealment and the Wrong Revealment of Offences

"He that covereth a transgression seeketh love: but he that repeateth a matter separateth *very* friends."

TWICE at least before the sentiments of this verse have come in a somewhat different aspect under our notice.*

Here we have—

THE RIGHT CONCEALMENT of offences.—"He that covereth a transgression seeketh love." The writer is, of course, speaking of a *right* covering of a transgression. Our transgressions should not be hidden from God. We should frankly confess our sins to Him, for he that covereth his sins shall not prosper. Nor should our transgressions be covered from our fellowmen against whom they have been committed. We should "confess our faults one to another." We should tell the man we have wronged of the wrong we have done him. The right concealment, or the concealment of him who "seeketh love," includes—
First: Hiding as much as possible *the injuries we*

* See Readings on chap. x. 12, xvi. 28.

have received from others. There is a disposition prevalent in most men to recall, exaggerate, and reveal the injuries they have received. The mother of this is revenge, and it tendeth to social discord, not to friendship. When an injury has been inflicted on us, and the offender has regrettingly confessed the same, it should be entombed—should never rise from its grave or speak again. He that doeth that "seeketh love," his conduct tends to the growth of social love. Secondly: Hiding as much as possible *the offences we discover in others.* A generous nature will throw a mantle of charity over the imperfections, irregularities, and offences of men. "Charity is not easily provoked . . . beareth all things, believeth all things, hopeth all things. It covereth a multitude of sins." Christ never paraded the injuries he received from others, nor did he ever, except when duty forced him, expose the crimes of men about him. The man who treats the offences of his fellow men with a generous, forbearing, and loving spirit, "seeketh love." Dr. South has well said, "It is a noble and great thing to cover the blemishes and to excuse the failings of a friend; to draw a curtain before his stains, and to display his perfections; to bury his weaknesses in silence, but to proclaim his virtues upon the house top."

Here we have also—

The WRONG REVEALMENT of offences.—"He that repeateth a matter separateth very friends." There are those in society whose greatest pleasure it is to detail the story of their own grievances and also of the mistakes and immoralities of their fellow-men. They, to use the language we have elsewhere employed, "open the graves of old disputes and crimes, bring up their ghastly skeletons, and endeavour to put new life in them." Such men "separate very friends." Discord is their music. From this subject we infer, First: *That social harmony is a good that all should seek.* It is the will of Heaven that men in neighbourhoods and nations should live in the loving bonds of brotherhood and peace. This will be the millennium state of the world. The Gospel tends to this. "Peace is the proper result of the Christian temper. It is the great kindness which our religion doth us, that it brings us to a settledness of mind, and a consistency within ourselves." Secondly: *That social offences are opposed to social harmony.* Every offence that man commits against his brother or against his God is a blow against social order, it irritates and disturbs. Thus the very treatment of social offences has much to do with the weal or woe of social order. The generous concealer of social offences is a blessing, the ill-natured revealer is a social curse. The one breathes a spirit of Divine serenity through the world, the other wakes up tempests and forges thunderbolts.

> "I desire
> To reconcile me to his friendly peace.
> 'Tis death to me to be at enmity:
> I hate it, and desire all good men's love."—SHAKESPEARE.

Proverbs 17:10

Moral and Corporeal Chastisement

"A reproof entereth more into a wise man than an hundred stripes into a fool."

THERE are two kinds of chastisement referred to in this passage; moral—"reproof," that which has to do with man's reason, conscience, heart; and corporeal—"stripes," that which deals with man's physical sensibilities. The one afflicts the soul, the other the body. The proverb suggests two remarks concerning these two kinds of chastisement—

The one in its sphere is AS LEGITIMATE as the other. —Solomon assumes that both are right in principle. Notice, First: The sphere of the *moral.* It is for the "wise." The "reproof" is for men open to reason and impression—men whose natures are susceptible to moral arguments and appeals. The sphere of the moral is the sphere where intelligence and argument are appreciated. Secondly: The sphere of the *corporeal.* It is for the "fool," —men who are either incapable of reasoning, brainless louts, or who are stolidly indisposed to attend to any moral appeal. "Stripes" for them. Now, these two kinds of chastisement are exactly suited to their subjects. "Stripes," corporeal inflictions, to the wise, would be a flagrant injustice, an egregious folly, and a serious injury. On the other hand, "reproofs," moral appeals, would be utterly ineffective to all who either could not or would not reason or feel. Of what service is an argument to an ox, or a whip to a soul? Parents and tutors often make fearful mistakes here, they use "stripes" where there are souls, and sometimes "reproofs" where there are only bodies. You may as well endeavour to break stones with argument, or thaw ice with love, as to correct some men by moral means. Flagellation and nothing but flagellation for fools. The proverb suggests that—

The one in its sphere is MORE THOROUGH than the other. —" A reproof entereth more into a wise man than a hundred stripes into a fool." First: The one is more *painful* than the other. The one is spiritual, the other mere physical pain. What is pain arising from a few lashes on the body, compared with the pain arising in the soul from a conviction of moral wrong? "A wounded spirit who can bear?" What pain did reproof give David!* What agony did the reproving look of Christ strike into Peter! Moral chastisement pains the man himself, gives agony to the central nerves of his being: whereas "stripes" give pains only to the body, and the body is the man's not the man. Secondly: The one is more *corrective* than the other. Corporeal chastisement will never do the fool any moral good. You cannot whip the moral devil out of men. "Though thou shouldest bray him in a mortar amongst wheat with a pestle, yet will not his foolishness depart from him."† But moral chastisement correct the wrongs of the soul. The fires of moral conviction separate the gold from the dross.

* Psalm li. † Chap. xxvii. 22.

Proverbs 17:11-13

The Genius and Punishment of Evil

" An evil *man* seeketh only rebellion: therefore a cruel messenger shall be sent against him. Let a bear robbed of her whelps meet a man, rather than a fool in his folly. Whoso rewardeth evil for good, evil shall not depart from his house."

NOTICE here—

The GENIUS of evil.—What is the spirit of evil? It is here represented. First: As lawless. "An evil man seeketh only rebellion." In all the different renderings of this clause, the same general sentiment is brought out. It expresses the wayward, refractory, and unruly spirit of evil. Its instinct is always against law, order, and God; it stands in antagonism to the Divine throughout the universe. It is here represented, Secondly: As furious. "Let a bear robbed of her whelps meet a man rather than a fool in his folly." A strong, terrible figure this of the savage wrath that is in evil when excited. The rage of the "bear robbed of her whelps" is but a faint emblem. See it in Jacob's sons putting a whole city to fire and the sword for the folly of one man.* See it in Saul's massacre of innocent priests. See it in the furnace, "seven-fold heated," of Nebuchadnezzar. See it in Herod murdering the children in Rama. See it in Saul breathing out threatenings and slaughter against the disciples of the Lord. See it even in David binding himself by oath to massacre a whole family. See it in the political tyrannies and the religious persecutions that have afflicted humanity. See it in the barbaric cruelties inflicted on wife and children recorded almost daily in the journals of England. Aye, aye, the instinct of evil is ever furious. It is savage as a "roaring lion." It is here represented, Thirdly: As ungrateful. "Whoso rewardeth evil for good, evil shall not depart from his house." Sin is bad when it returns evil

* Gen. xxxiv. 25, 1 Sam. xxii. 18, Dan. iii. 19, Matt. ii. 18, Acts vii., 1 Sam. xxv. 33.

for evil; it is worse when it returns evil for good. It is a heartless ingratitude combined with a malignant resentment. The genius of evil is ingratitude. "He," says Swift, "that calls a man ungrateful, sums up all the evil that a man can be guilty of."

> "I hate ingratitude more in a man
> Than lying, vainness, babbling, drunkenness,
> Or any taint of vice, whose strong corruption
> Inhabits our frail blood."—SHAKESPEARE

Notice here also—

The PUNISHMENT of evil.—The punishment is stated here in two forms. First: As the advent of a ruthless officer. "Therefore a cruel messenger shall be sent against him." Nemesis is ever wending his steps toward the wicked, always as close to the sinner as his shadow, as venomous as a serpent, and as cruel as a ravenous beast of prey. The punishment is stated here—Secondly: As a permanent resident in the house. "Evil shall not depart from his house." Wherever sin is, there will be the avenger. "Be sure your sins will find you out." What a wretched thing is evil! It is bad in essence, influence, and issues. "Sin and hell," says an old author, "are so turned and twisted up together, that if the power of sin be once dissolved, the bonds of death and hell will also fall asunder. Sin and hell are of the same kind, of the same lineage and descent; as (on the other side) true holiness or religion, and true happiness are but two several notions of one thing, rather than distinct in themselves. Religion delivers us from hell by instating us in a possession of true life and bliss. Hell is rather a state than a place; and heaven cannot be so truly defined by anything without us, as by something that is within." What is hell? Thy gangrened heart, stripped of its self-worn mask, and spread at last bare, in its horrible anatomy, before thine own excruciated gaze!

Proverbs 17:14

Strife

"The beginning of strife *is as* when one letteth out water: therefore leave off contention before it be meddled with."

CRABB makes a difference between *discord* and *strife*. He says, "*Discord* evinces itself in various ways—by looks, words, or actions; *strife* displays itself in words, or acts of violence. *Discord* is fatal to the happiness of families; *strife* is the greatest enemy to peace between neighbours; *discord* arose between the goddesses on the apple being thrown into one assembly. Homer commences his poem with the *strife* that took place between Agamemnon and Achilles."

The passage suggests three ideas concerning strife.

It is an evil OF TERRIFIC PROGRESS.—At first it is like the dropping of water oozing through a mound that encloses a sea. Every drop widens the channel until the drops become a stream, and the stream a torrent. Thus strife spreads. One angry word leads to another, one look of revenge, one act of resentment, will kindle a fire that may set a whole neighbourhood or a nation into conflagration. A drop of strife soon becomes a river, and the river a torrent.

> "Contention, like a horse
> Full of high feeding, madly hath broke loose,
> And bears all before him."—SHAKESPEARE

Another idea suggested by the passage concerning strife is—

It is an evil THAT SHOULD BE CHECKED.—"Therefore leave off contention before it be meddled with." Every lover of his race should suppress it. It is a desolating fury—it makes sad havoc in families, creates divisions in those whom nature has bound together; it produces unhappy contentions in churches, and makes nations mad with the spirit of bloody war. "Blessed is the peace-maker." A true peace-maker should be inspired with the spirit of peace, maintain the character of peace, use the argument of peace. Thus he will check the spirit of strife. The disposition of a peace-maker is a blessed one : it implies self-control, a generous sympathy with the conflicting parties, a calm, moral, mediating power, equal to the subjugation of antagonistic souls. The peace-maker has far higher attributes than the warrior. A man has only to have the low cunning of the fox, and the savage daring of the lion, to become famous on the battle-field ; but he must have the philosophy of a sage, and the love of a saint, to act effectively the "day's-man," put his hand on contending parties, and of the "twain make one." Such shall be called the "children of God." The peacemaker is like the "God of peace," and filiation to that God consists in moral assimilation to His character.

Another idea suggested by the passage concerning strife is—

It is an evil WHICH CAN BE EASILY CHECKED AT THE BEGINNING.—" The beginning of strife is as when one letteth out water." You may mend the embankment with tolerable ease at the stage when it emits only a few oozing drops ; the mightiest and most furious beasts of prey you can easily destroy at their birth ; the most majestic and resistless river you can stop at its spring head. So it is with strife. In its incipient state you may easily crush it. The first angry thought, the first malevolent desire, by serious reflection, resolute will, devout prayer, these may be overcome. Crush the upas in the germ, tread out the conflagration in the spark. Let the only strife we know be a strife against evil and in favour of good. May we strive with others, to use a figure of Lord Bacon, "as the vine with the olive, which of us shall bear the best fruit ; but not as the briar with the thistle, which is the most unprofitable."

> " A peace is of the nature of a conquest :
> For there both parties nobly are subdued,
> And neither party loser."—SHAKESPEARE

Proverbs 17:15

Perverse Treatment of the Characters of Men

"He that justifieth the wicked, and he that condemneth the just, even they both *are* abomination to the Lord."

THE evil referred to in the proverb, namely, that of justifying the wicked and condemning the just, is by no means uncommon. On the contrary, it is—

PREVALENT IN SOCIETY.—The prevalency arises from various causes. There is mental servility. The doings of a wicked man, especially if he be wealthy and influential, will always find, amongst the servile in society, numbers to justify and defend. On the contrary, they will represent the virtues of the just, if poor, as worthless and even reprehensible. Sycophancy is ever justifying the wicked and condemning the just. Another cause is, self-interest. When the wicked are customers or patrons, their crimes will be readily extenuated; whilst the just who sustain no such relationship become subjects of calumny and blame. Add to this spiritual infirmity. The eye of the conscience is either too dim to discern moral distinctions, or the heart is too cowardly to avow them. Thus this perverse treatment of character is prevalent. The world abounds with unjust judges, and justice is everywhere perverted, even in temples consecrated to her name. The proverb states that this evil is—

OFFENSIVE TO GOD.—"They both are abomination to the Lord." *It is repugnant to His character.* "He is light and in Him there is no darkness at all." Sin is the abominable thing which He hates. Men, therefore, who not only are regardless of justice but perpetrate unrighteousness, are to the last degree repugnant to His holy nature. *It is dangerous to His universe.* To defend the wrong and condemn the right is the way to spread anarchy throughout the moral realm of God. Observe from this—

First: The sad state of human society. Here are not only wicked men, but men justifying wickedness, and even condemning goodness. How obvious it is that we are morally lost. "The crown is fallen from our head. Woe unto us that we have sinned." Secondly: The value of Christianity. This is Heaven's instrument, designed and adapted to effect a true moral reformation in human society.

Brothers, let us stand up ever for the right. "The right," as Archdeacon Hare has well said, "is might and, ever was, and ever shall be so. Holiness is might, meekness is might, patience is might, humility is might, self-denial and self-sacrifice is might, faith is might, love is might, every gift of the Spirit is might. The cross was two pieces of dead wood, and a helpless unresisting man was nailed to it; yet it was mightier than the world, and triumphed, and will ever triumph over it. Heaven and earth shall pass away, but no pure, holy deed, or word, or thought. On the other hand, might, that which the children of earth call so, the strong wind, the earthquake, the fire, perishes through its own violence, self-exhausted, and self-consumed; as our age of the world has been allowed to witness in the most signal example. For many of us remember, and they who do not have heard from their fathers, how the mightiest man on earth, he who had girt himself with all might, except that of right, burst like a tempest-cloud, burnt himself out like a conflagration, and only left the scars of his ravages to mark where he had been. Who among you can look into an infant's face and not see a power in it mightier than all the armies of Attila or Napoleon?" "A man," says Carlyle," is right and invincible, virtuous, and on the road towards sure conquest, precisely while he joins himself to the great deep law of the world, in spite of all superficial laws, temporary appearances, profit and loss calculation—he is victorious while he co-operates with that great central law—not victorious otherwise."

Proverbs 17:16

Capacity Without Will

"Wherefore *is there* a price in the hand of a fool to get wisdom, seeing *he hath* no heart *to it*."

IN these words we have three things.—

A GREAT PRIVILEGE.—The privilege is this, "a price in the hand" to get wisdom. The "price in the hand" may be regarded as representing the possession of all the necessary means for the attainment of knowledge. What are the means? *Leisure*. Many men have not the "price," for lack of time. They are so absorbed in other engagements, that they are unable to seize even one hour a day for mental pursuits. What are the means? *Books*. The man who has in his possession the works of one great author has a "price in the hand" for wisdom. Thousands are destitute of such productions as are necessary to stimulate the faculties, to guide the judgment, and to inform the understanding. What are the means? *Companions*. Enlightened and thoughtful society is amongst the best means of knowledge. "He that walketh with wise men shall be wise." He that hath intelligent companions hath the "price in the hand" for "wisdom." What are the means? *Travellings*. To visit distant scenes, mingle with different tribes and classes of men, and to come under the influence of different laws, manners, customs, are all valuable means of mental culture. All these may be said to form the "price" of wisdom. The man who has these has the purchase money in his hand. With it he may unlock the gate of universal science, and revel in the sunny realm of wisdom.

Here we have—

A UNIVERSAL PRINCIPLE.—The principle is this, the man who has not the heart for knowledge,—the "price," though he has all the facilities—will never get it. Indeed a man must have a *heart* for a thing before he seeks to attain it. The man who would succeed in his business or profession must have a heart for it, and the man also who would succeed in the acquisition of knowledge, and in the attainment of godliness, must have a "heart for it." Without the heart there will not be that persistency which is necessary. "He must agonize to enter in at the strait gate" of intelligence and goodness. Men's failures in all the varied avocations in life, generally arise from the lack of heart. When a man puts his whole soul to a thing he generally succeeds. To him all things become possible.

Here we have—

A DIFFICULT PROBLEM.—The whole verse states the problem. "Wherefore is there a price in the hand of the fool to get wisdom, seeing he hath no heart to it?" The question is, why should a man who has no heart for knowledge, be in possession of all necessary means? These two things are often found together. Plenty of opportunities with a soul indisposed. What thousands have access to universities, libraries, cultured society, foreign countries, who have no heart for knowledge, and they remain fools amidst all! Why should such fools have the means? This is the difficult question that was asked. "Wherefore?" Though I do not presume to reach the grand reason in the mind of God, I can see enough to hush complaints. It is far better to have the heart without the means, than the means without the heart. All men may have the heart, and all who have the heart have their mental eyes open, their mental faculties in good health, and their mental horizon enlarging and destined still to brighten and expand. "The more we know," says Coleridge, "the greater our thirst for knowledge. The water lily in the midst of waters, opens its leaves and expands its petals at the first pattering of showers, and rejoices in the rain drops with a quicker sympathy than the parched shrub in the sandy desert."

Proverbs 17:17; 18:24

Degrees and Duties of True Friendship

"A friend loveth at all times, and a brother is born for adversity."

"A man *that hath* friends must shew himself friendly: and there is a friend *that* sticketh closer than a brother."

ONE of the greatest needs of man is that of friendship. Without friendship he would die in the first dawn of infancy. He needs friendship to nurture his body, and educate his mind. Friendship is his shield in danger, his guide in perplexity, his strength in weakness, his succour in sorrow. He needs the hand of friendship to receive him into the world, and to help him out; and through all the intervening stages, from the cradle to the grave, he requires its presence and its aid. What sun, and air, and dew, are to the seed, friendship is to him, that which quickens, nurtures, develops, and perfects his being. These proverbs lead us to notice the degrees and duties of that *true* friendship, which Aristotle describes as " composed of one soul in two bodies."

THE DEGREES OF TRUE FRIENDSHIP.—Three degrees of true friendship are suggested by these words. First: *A constant* love. " A friend loveth at all times." *Constancy* in love is an essential element in all genuine friendship. There is a thing called friendship, very warm, very demonstrative, but very mutable; it changes with circumstances. When its object is in prosperity, it keeps by his side, cheers him with sunny looks and approving words, but when adversity comes, it skulks away, and keeps out of sight. Unlike this, genuine friendship comes to us in prosperous days only by invitation, but hastens to our side unasked when sorrow darkens our homestead. A modern writer has well described the true friend: "Concerning the man you call your friend—tell me, will he weep with you in the hour of distress? Will he faithfully reprove you to your face, for actions for which others are ridiculing or censuring you behind your back? Will he dare to stand forth in your defence, when detraction is secretly aiming its deadly weapons at your reputation? Will he acknowledge you with the same cordiality, and behave to you with the same friendly attention, in the company of your superiors in rank and fortune, as when the claims of pride and vanity do not interfere with those of friendship? If misfortune and losses should oblige you to retire into a walk of life in which you cannot appear with the same distinction, or entertain your friends with the same liberality as formerly, will he still think himself happy in your society, and, instead of gradually withdrawing himself from an unprofitable connection, take pleasure in professing himself your friend, and cheerfully assist you to support the burden of your affliction? When sickness shall call you to retire from the gay and busy scenes of the world, will he follow you into your gloomy retreat, listen with attention to your 'tale of symptoms,' and minister the balm of consolation to your fainting spirit? And lastly, when death shall burst asunder every earthly tie, will he shed a tear upon your grave, and lodge the dear remembrance of your mutual love in his heart, as a treasure never to be resigned?" The man who will not do all this, may be your companion, your flatterer, your seducer, but, depend upon it, he is not your friend. False friends are like chaff, they fly away before the first blast of adversity; the true are the precious grain that lie at our feet.

The other degree of friendship suggested here is, Secondly: A *brotherly* love. "A brother is born for adversity." Some regard the expression as indicating the writer's idea that a friend that "loveth at all times," is yet to be born. He does not at present exist. Whatever might be Solomon's exact idea, his words suggest the fact that brotherly affection is of higher worth than ordinary genuine friendship. Genuine affection may exist, and does exist where there is no blood relationship, but where the blood relationship of brothers exists in connection with it, its value is increased, it takes a higher type. True brotherliness gives a wondrous tenderness, depth, and energy to friendship. Kindred blood coursing through the veins, hearts centering their affections upon the same parents, and spreading their sympathies over the same relations and interests, a thousand thoughts, impressions, hopes, and memories, which the loving intercourse of early years have given them in common, cannot fail to impart a priceless worth to genuine friendship. A true brother is indeed a man "born for adversity." It is when the sky of adversity is darkest over brethren and sisters, and its storms beat most furiously upon them, that he is most strong and constant in his love, he is there like a bright angel, and will not depart until the breaking of the darkness and the hushing of the tempest. Thank God for all true brotherliness in the world.

Another degree of friendship suggested here is, Thirdly: A *super*-brotherly love. "There is a friend that sticketh closer than a brother." Here we have genuine friendship in its highest degree. Constancy is its first stage, brotherliness is the next, super-brotherliness is the highest. But who is this "friend that sticketh closer than a brother?" Jonathan stuck to David, but not closer than a brother. We know One, and only One, Who answers to this description. It is the Son of God. "He that loved us and gave Himself for us." "He is not ashamed to call us brethren." "He is touched with the feeling of our infirmities." "He is afflicted in all our afflictions." What a friend is He! How disinterested, self-sacrificing, tender, constant, infinite, His love! He "sticketh closer than a brother." A brother must leave us sooner or later. He dies, or we die, and we part. We cannot go with him into the "valley of the shadow of death," nor he descend with us. We part. But Christ is ever with us. "Lo I am always with you, even unto the end."

Here we have also:

THE DUTY OF TRUE FRIENDSHIP.—"A man that hath friends must show himself friendly." What is our duty to genuine friends? First: We must justify their friendship. We must show by the purity of our love, the excellence of our principles, the nobleness of our spirit, the loftiness of our aims, that we are worthy of the affection and confidence that are bestowed upon us. To be genuinely loved we must be morally lovable, and to be morally lovable we must be good. One mean unworthy act of mine is enough to burn the golden thread that links my friend to me. To shew yourselves friendly, you must show that in your life which will justify the friendship you enjoy. Secondly: We must honour their friendship. Men must see in our character that which will give them a virtuous pride in calling us friends, however obscure our lives, humble our homes, or unfortunate our circumstances. Let us be great in character, however obscure in position. Thirdly: We must reciprocate their friendship. Their offices of love, their acts of kindness, their expressions of tenderness we must requite, if not with material gifts through poverty, with strong gratitude and high devotion. He who does not reciprocate love will soon lose it, he who receives all and gives nothing in return will soon block up the river of favours. "He that hath friends must show himself friendly." Whether his friends be unrelated to him by the ties of consanguinity, or related by the bonds of brotherhood, or related by ties more close and tender than those of a brother, "he must show himself friendly," in order to retain the friendship. Heaven give us this generous friendship! A star that breaks the darkest clouds of earth and that will shine on for ever. True friendship is immortal. "The friendship," says Robert Hall, "of high and sanctified spirits loses nothing by death but its alloy; failings disappear, and the virtues of those whose faces we shall behold no more appear greater and more sacred when beheld through the shades of the sepulchre."

> "Smitten friends
> Are angels sent on errands full of love;
> For us they languish, and for us they die."—DR. YOUNG

Proverbs 17:21, 25

The Fool: Negatively and Positively

"He that begetteth a fool *doeth it* to his sorrow : and the father of a fool hath no joy." *

"A foolish son *is* a grief to his father, and bitterness to her that bare him."

"THE joys of parents," says Lord Bacon, "are secret, and so are their griefs and fears: they cannot utter the one; they will not utter the other. Children sweeten labours, but they make misfortunes more bitter; they increase the cares of life, but they mitigate the remembrance of death." A man must be a parent to know the heart of a parent, and he must be cursed with worthless and wicked children in order to know the crushing grief of those who are. There are two ways in which the child who is a "fool"—a fool not by natural incapacity, but by moral depravity—gives sorrow to his parents.—*Negatively*. He is not what a son should be. He neglects all that a son should do. He does not reciprocate the love. What love, self-sacrificing, tender, anxious, ever-toiling love, has been lavished on him, but he returns it no more than a stick or a stone. He does not acknowledge the kindness. What kindness has been expended on him! Yet he knows no gratitude, he manifests no thanksgiving. He recognizes no authority. The parental word is disregarded, the parental will is disobeyed, the parental order is set at defiance. All this is the conduct of a "fool," and in all this there is sorrow to the heart of the father and the mother. The other way in which the child gives sorrow to his parents is *positively*. A wicked son is active in his wickedness. Sometimes the conduct of such children involves their parents in secular ruin. The extravagance, the gambling, the reckless speculations of children, have wrecked the

---

* The subject of the 18, 19, and 20 verses, viz., suretiship, strife, ambition, frowardness of heart, and perverseness of speech, have already engaged our attention. See Readings on chap. vi. 1—5, xvii. 14, xvi. 18, vi. 12—15.

fortunes of many a family, and brought desolation to many a home. Sometimes the conduct of such children brings disgrace upon their parents. By their violation of the laws of chastity, social honour, commercial justice, they have often degraded the character of their families. The son who is a "fool" has often invested with infamy a family name that has shone brightly for many an age.

Household life is so momentous to men individually and socially, that it can never be too frequently examined and too earnestly pondered. Hence it constantly appears in the thoughts of Solomon; and is not unfrequently referred to by other inspired men. It may be well therefore for us to look a little closer into the subject. In these verses we have three things in relation to it.

A REPREHENSIBLE DOMESTIC CHARACTER.—"A foolish son." By a "foolish son" Solomon means not a son destitute of mental capacity—an idiot, but a graceless son, one destitute of that virtue which is in reality the true *reason* of the soul. Immorality is moral madness. First: A son is a fool who disregards his parents. There are those, alas, in families who lose the filial element, and who become indifferent alike to parental feelings and parental claims. They wound parental love and despise parental rule. Is this not foolish? What friends have they so sincere in their love, so strong in their attachment? Secondly: A son is a "fool" who neglects his study. The best interests of a young man consist in the filling of his mind with useful knowledge, the culturing of his heart into pure sympathies, the training of his powers to act virtuously, forcefully, and happily. But he who neglects this, and gives himself up to indolence, self-indulgence, and sensuality, is a "fool." Thirdly: A son is a "fool" who neglects his God. The life and destiny of all are in His hands. To neglect Him, therefore, is the height of folly. But if this disregard, this negative conduct, shows his folly, how much more does this folly appear in the positive evils that grow out of this negative behaviour? Indolence, intemperance, sensuality, roguery, profanity, murder, and such like enormities, flow out of disregard to parents, study, and God.

Alas, how many families there are in England who have such fools as members! The verses present to us—

A QUESTIONABLE DOMESTIC TRAINING. — When such fools as these appear in families there is a presumption that the training has been defective. For is it not said, "Train up a child in the way he should go and when he is old he will not depart from it?" I know what may be pleaded against the certain efficacy of this discipline. *Organisation* is pleaded. It is said that the conformation of some children is bad, that there is a sad lack of the moral in their nature, and that the animal predominates over the mental. *Will* is pleaded. It is said that every child has freedom and independency of mind, and that this prevents the possibility of invariable results. Mind is not like dead matter on which we may produce any impression we please; it is endowed with a resisting and self-modifying force. Against these objections three things are to be observed. First: The power of goodness upon unsophisticated childhood. The Great Maker of our being has established such a relation between the principles of truth, justice, and moral excellence, that the mind in an unsophisticated state not only can see them, but is bound to admire and render them homage. Secondly: The force of parental influence upon the child. The mind of the child in its first stages is to the parent as clay in the hands of the potter, it can be moulded almost into any shape and turned to any service. Thirdly: The promise of God. The Great Father has promised to render efficient a right parental training. On the whole, then, there seems to me no necessity for parents to have moral fools as children. The verses present—

A SAD DOMESTIC EXPERIENCE.—" A foolish son is a grief to his father, and a bitterness to her that bare him." How true this is. To have a son a drunkard, a rogue, a swindler, a murderer, must involve an amount of parental agony, which is not easy to imagine. What agony did Absalom give David! The fact that children bring such misery to their parents suggests two great facts. First: That our greatest trials often spring from our greatest blessings. Every right-hearted parent regards his or her child as one of the greatest blessings that kind Heaven has bestowed. Yet this blessing often becomes a curse. It is so in other things. Secondly: Our greatest devils often spring from ourselves. Who is a greater enemy to the peace and prosperity of the father and the mother, than an undutiful, an unprincipled, a heartless, and a reckless, son? They have no greater fiend than he; he is their torment. In many other ways men create their own devils. Men form engagements, create enterprises, and enter into arrangements in young life which produce devils to torment them to the end of their days.

This subject affords a homily to young parents that cannot be too deeply pondered. There is a discipline which, under God, may deliver them from the curse of a foolish son. It is not passion, violence, rude authority; it is the calm discipline of holy love. "It is a great mistake," says Dr. Bushnell, "to suppose that what will make a child stare, or tremble, impresses more authority. The violent emphasis, the hard, stormy voice, the menacing air only weakens authority; it commands a good thing as if it were only a bad, and fit to be no way impressed save by some stress of assumption. Let the command be always quietly given, as if it had some right in itself and could utter itself to the conscience by some emphasis of its own. Is it not well understood that a bawling and violent teamster has no real government of his team? Is it not practically seen that a skilful commander of one of those huge floating cities, moved by steam on our American waters, manages and works every motion by the waving of a hand, or by signs that pass in silence—issuing no order at all, save in the gentlest undertone of voice? So when there is, or is to be, a real order and law in the house, it will come of no hard and boisterous, or fretful and termagant way of commandment. Gentleness will speak the word of firmness, and firmness will be clothed in the airs of true gentleness."

Proverbs 17:22
Bodily Health Dependent on Mental Moods

"A merry heart doeth good *like* a medicine; but a broken spirit drieth the bones."

So closely connected is the soul with the body, that physical health is ever, to a great extent, dependent on mental states. A dark thought has power to work disease and death into the corporeal frame. This is a fact—First: Recognised by medical science. A wise physician avails himself of this fact and is ever anxious not only to dispel all sad thoughts from the mind of the patient, but to awaken the most pleasurable ideas and emotions. This is a fact, Secondly: Attested by general experience. Who has not experienced the influence of his mental thoughts and feelings on the state of his health? How often has every man in the course of his life felt a distressing thought sickening and shattering his body. David felt it, when he said, " When I kept silence, my bones waxed old through my roaring all the day long. For day and night thy hand was heavy upon thee: my moisture is turned into the drought of summer. Selah."* This is a fact, Thirdly: Suggestive of practical lessons. Is it true that a "broken spirit "—*i.e.*, a spirit saddened and depressed, "drieth the bones," reduces all healthy secretions, enfeebles the energy and destroys the health? Is it true, on the other hand, that a cheerful spirit will act as a medicine to restore an enfeebled body to health? If these things are true, then we may infer three principles.

THE RESPONSIBILITY OF MAN FOR HIS PHYSICAL HEALTH.†—There is certainly no virtue in having a weak and sickly frame. Though it is often a calamity entailed on us by our ancestors, or by circumstances over which we have no control; it always implies sin somewhere, either in ourselves or others. There is no virtue in it, and yet

---
* Psalm xxxii. 3, 4.
† See Readings on chap. xiv. 13—15.

numbers in society speak and act as if there were something meritorious in having a delicate frame. Robust health some, at least, seem to consider not respectable and genteel, and hence they have perennial complaints; they are always "poorly" and delicate. In many cases the physical ailments of these people spring from unhealthy and unvirtuous states of mind. Man is responsible for his mental disposition, whether cheerful or gloomy, and his disposition greatly determines his health. I infer again from this fact:—

THE DUTY OF THE GUARDIANS OF CHILDHOOD AND YOUTH.—If the parents and guardians of childhood and youth would have their charge grow up with robust health, and well developed frames, they should deal rightly with their minds; they should labour to dispel all saddening influences from the young heart, and fill it with the sunshine of cheerfulness and joy. There is much in some families and schools to break the spirit of the young, and thus dry their very bones. Modern medical science talks largely of germs of disease that float in the atmosphere, but what these germs are it cannot tell us, nor can it say how they affect us. But in the atmosphere of an immoral soul there are certain germs of physical disease that are very discoverable—lust, anger, revenge, envy, jealousy, all these impregnate the moral atmosphere of impious minds and they are poison to the corporeal frame. They corrupt the blood, they sap the constitution, they work out dissolution. I infer lastly from this fact:—

THE SANITARY INFLUENCE OF CHRISTIANITY.— The design of Christianity is to fill the human heart with joy. "These things have I spoken unto you that your joy may be full." It is in every way adapted to accomplish this; it never fails in effecting this wherever it is fully received. No other system on earth has ever filled the human heart with joy, no other system can do so. Hence Christianity, by doing so, is the best physician to the body. He who promotes Christianity is the wise philanthropist. To promote it is to promote the well-being of man, body as well as soul. Some people are always trying to keep the body well, and entirely neglect the condition of the soul. This is philosophically absurd. It is like trying to cure a diseased tree by binding up the branches. "People," says Sterne, "who are always taking care of their health, are like misers, who are holding a treasure which they have never spirit to enjoy."

Proverbs 17:23

Bribery

"A wicked *man* taketh a gift out of the bosom to pervert the ways of judgment."

HAVING already noticed a sentiment somewhat similar to these words, our remarks will be very brief.* The verse suggests two remarks about bribery, an evil which Solomon often deprecated, and which Jehovah Himself denounces.†

ITS AIM IS PERNICIOUS.—A bribe is given to "pervert the ways of judgment." "A bribe," says Webster, "is a price, reward, gift, or favour bestowed or promised, with a view to pervert the judgment or corrupt the conduct of a judge, witness, or other person." Perversion is always its aim; it is to induce men to do that which is either without their convictions, or against their convictions. Absalom bribed the people of Judæa in order to get to the throne. The high-priests bribed Judas in order to effect the crucifixion of Christ. Whilst bribery is the canker and disgrace of constitutional governments, it is a crime in whatever department of life, by whomsoever practised. He who presents a bribe perpetrates a moral wrong. He sacrifices truth and justice to his own personal interest, and he endeavours, by exciting the selfishness of others, to deaden in them the sense of right, and muffle the voice of truth. The receiver of the bribe is as bad. He accepts the greatest insult that can be offered to him as a man, and consents to barter away eternal principles for earthly pelf. Too often have the legislators of England won their position by

* See Reading on chap. xvii. 8. † Isaiah i. 23, 24.

bribery. Another remark which the verse suggests concerning bribery is that :—

ITS ACTION IS CLANDESTINE.—"A wicked man taketh a gift out of the bosom." So bad is it, that even the author of it is ashamed. He does it in secrecy. Sin is a shameful thing, all consciences blush at it, its work is evermore in darkness. Secretly and insidiously it effects its purposes. The subject teaches two things. First: The power of money. "Money answereth all things," says Solomon. Money can buy men, and it is doing so on an extensive scale throughout the world. Men are everywhere being bought, not merely their limbs, but their intellects and their souls.

Gold! It is the mightiest amongst the world's autocrats, and the most popular amongst its divinities. No motive in all the world's activities is more universal and resistless, no argument in all its reasonings more cogent and conclusive. "A man," says Addison, "who is furnished with arguments from the mint will convince his antagonist much sooner than one who draws them from reason and philosophy. Gold is a wonderful clearer of the understanding—it dissipates every doubt and scruple in an instant; accommodates itself to the meanest capacities ; silences the loud and clamorous, and brings over the most obstinate and inflexible. Philip of Macedon was a man of most invincible reason this way. He refuted by it all the wisdom of Athens—confounded their statesmen, struck their orators dumb, and at length argued them out of their liberties."

The subject teaches, Secondly : The urgency of a moral regeneration. What is wanted for commercial soundness, social order, and good government is, that moral regeneration which endows the soul with an inflexible adherence to honour, rectitude, and truth. This, also, is the work of Christianity. Parliamentary, administrative, ecclesiastical reformation, are merely things of parchment, but the reformation of Christianity is the reformation of the soul. Let nothing bribe us ever to the wrong. Heaven honours the man who stands against bribes. "He that walketh righteously and speaketh uprightly ; he that despiseth the gain of oppressions, that shaketh his hands from holding of bribes, that stoppeth his ears from hearing of blood, and shutteth his eyes from seeing evil, he shall dwell on high ; his place of defence shall be the munitions of rocks; bread shall be given him, his waters shall be sure."*

Proverbs 17:24

A Double Picture

" Wisdom *is* before him that hath understanding : but the eyes of a fool *are* in the ends of the earth."

HERE are two pictures widely dissimilar, one the picture of a wise man, and the other of a fool. Let us glance at them both.

They differ in FACE.—The one has a meaning, the other an unmeaning face. One translator renders the words—" In the countenance of a wise man wisdom appeareth, but the fool's eyes roll to and fro." It is ever so. God has so formed man that his face is the index to his soul—the dial-plate of the mental clock. If the mind does not modify the features, it alters the expression, and changes the whole style of countenance. By the face is seen whether the soul is cultured or uncultured, coarse or refined, amiable or irascible, virtuous or vicious. A wise man's face looks wisdom—calm, devout, reflective. The fool's face looks folly. As the translucent lake reflects the passing clouds and rolling lights of sky, so does the human countenance mirror the soul. Man is instinctively a physiognomist; even children read our hearts by our faces.

" The cheek is apter than the tongue to tell an errand."
SHAKESPEARE

They differ in MIND.—" Wisdom is before him that hath understanding, but the eyes of a fool are in the ends of the earth." The one has an occupied, the other a vacant mind

* Isaiah xxxiii. 15, 16.

The meaning of Solomon perhaps may be wisdom is before, that is, present, with the man that "hath understanding." The principles of wisdom are in his mind, are ever before his eye. Wisdom is "before" his mind in every circumstance and condition. Its *rule*, the Word of God, is before him. Its *principle*, the love of God, is before him. Thus he has an occupied mind. But the mind of the fool is vacant. His "eyes are in the ends of the earth." He has nothing before him, nothing true, or wise, or good. He looks at emptiness. Alas! how vacant the mind of a morally unwise man! It is a vessel without ballast, at the mercy of the winds and waves. His thoughts are unsubstantial, his hopes are illusory, the sphere of his conscious life a *mirage*. The difference in the soul between a morally wise and a morally foolish man, is as great as that between a well-rooted tree that defies the fiercest tempest, and the chaff that is the sport of every wind. Heaven deliver us from a morally empty mind—a mind without true principles, manly aims, and genuine loves.

They differ in HEART.—The one has a settled the other an unsettled heart. This is suggestively implied. The morally wise man is fixed, wisdom is "before him," and his heart is on it. He is rooted and grounded in the faith. He is not used by circumstances, but he makes circumstances serve him. He has a purpose in life, and from that purpose nothing will turn him. "This one thing I do." But the fool is unsettled, his "eyes are in the ends of the earth." His mind, like the evil spirit, walks to and fro through the earth, seeking rest and finding none. An old writer describes the character thus: "To-day he goes to the quay to be shipped for Rome. But before the tide come, his tide is turned. One party thinks him theirs; the adverse theirs; he is with both, with neither, not an hour with himself. Indifference is his ballast, and opinion his sail; he resolves not to resolve. He knows not what he doth hold. He opens his mind to receive notions, as one opens his palm to take an handful of water. He hath very much, if he could hold it. He is sure to die, but not a religion to die in. He demurs, like a posed lawyer, as if delay could remove some impediments. In a controverted point, he holds with the last reasoner he either heard or read. The next diverts him, and his opinion dwells with him perhaps so long as the teacher of it is in sight. He will rather take dross for gold than try it in the furnace. He receives many judgments, retains none. He loathes manna after two days' feeding. His best dwelling would be his confined chamber, where he would trouble nothing but his pillow. He is full of business at church; a stranger at home; a sceptic abroad; an observer in the street; everywhere a fool."

Proverbs 17:26
Persecution and Treason

"Also to punish the just *is* not good, *nor* to strike princes for equity."

THERE are two kinds of "princes"—official and moral. The former are often contemptible. They are mean-natured, weak-facultied, low-spirited men, born into high positions. They have nothing princely in the blood and bearing of their souls. The latter are real princes. They are princely in their thoughts, sympathies, and aims. They are high-souled men, God's nobles. Which of these does Solomon refer to in the text? Perhaps to neither separately, but to both in combination: the prince not only in office, but in character too. The proverb directs us—

TO A PUNISHMENT THAT IS PERSECUTION. — "Also to punish the just is not good." He means more than this; he means what he has expressed before, that it is not only not good, but that it is "abomination to the Lord."* To inflict punishment upon the *unjust* is often right and imperative. It is God's will that evil doers shall be punished in a certain way and to a certain extent, but to inflict suffering on the just is not legitimate punishment; it is persecution. There is a great deal in society that passes for

* See Reading on verse 15.

punishment, which is nothing but unjust persecution. First: It is seen in domestic discipline. Children are often punished not on account of moral wrong, but on account of idiosyncracies and peculiarities which are not immoral. Every pain inflicted on a child where there is not moral wrong, is a persecution, not a just chastisement. Secondly: It is seen in political governments. The government that inflicts inconveniences and disabilities upon those who are civilly just, persecutes. The enforcement of laws, the exactions of imposts that chime not with the eternal principles of right, are persecution. Thirdly: It is seen in ecclesiastical arrangements. The ecclesiastics that inflict sufferings on account of diversity of creed and conviction, persecute. Ecclesiastics have been the great persecutors. Of all men in history they have done most in punishing the just. The proverb directs us—

TO A REBELLION THAT IS TREASON.—"Nor to strike princes for equity." The strike here does not mean merely physical violence. There are other strokes besides those of the hand—the strokes of the pen, the tongue, the life. These are often more painful and terrible than hand strokes. Now to strike—to oppose princes— "for equity" is *treason*. There is a rebellion that is not treason. To rise up and oppose princes and potentates who have no equity, is a virtue, not a crime. Rebellion, to be treason, must be striking against the equitable. First: Opposition to good government is treason. He who opposes a government conducted on the eternal principles of justice and equity, is a traitor not only in the sight of man, but in the sight of God. Secondly: Opposition to a true enterprise is treason. Schemes founded on benevolence and justice, started and worked in order to advance the right, should be loyally respected. There is as much treason in striking against them, as in striking against a righteous government. Thirdly: Opposition to true men is treason. True men are men of God. They are the shrines, the organs, the representatives, the servants of the Divine. To strike at them is treason; they are God's true princes.

Proverbs 17:27-28

Frugality in Speech

"He that hath knowledge spareth his words: *and* a man of understanding is of an excellent spirit. Even a fool, when he holdeth his peace, is counted wise: *and* he that shutteth his lips *is esteemed* a man of understanding."

How often the same ideas come up in the mind of the most original and fertile thinkers! Few men had souls more fecundant in thought than Solomon. Yet there are certain ideas that are constantly appearing, and that, too, often in the same verbal garb. The idea in this passage we have often met with before, and we shall meet with it again as we go on through the book. The verses suggest two thoughts on frugality in the use of words.

IT IS FREQUENTLY SYMPTOMATIC OF SOMETHING GOOD. —" He that hath knowledge, spareth his words, and a man of understanding is of an excellent spirit." First: It sometimes indicates an enlightened judgment. " He that hath knowledge spareth his words." There is, of course, sometimes a paucity of speech for the want of intelligence. The tongue is silent because the mind is blank. There is nothing to communicate. There is, of course, no virtue in this verbal frugality. But there is a spareness of words which is the result of intelligence. The man has such an impression of the power of words for good or for evil, and the responsibility connected with the faculty of language, that he is conscientiously cautious. He is slow to speak Secondly: It sometimes indicates a good spirit. " A man of understanding is of an excellent spirit." The margin reads instead of "excellent," *cool* spirit. And this seems to me the idea intended. There are some whose natures are so fiery, impetuous, and uncontrollable, that they cannot restrain their words; they flow as a torrent. The ebullition of the apostles who said, " Lord wilt thou that we command fire to come down from heaven and consume them even as Elias did?"* is an illustration of this. But a man of a cool spirit exercises that self-control which commands his tongue. A man powerfully provoked to the use of bad words, standing silent, or speaking a few apt sentences in the calm dignity of self-control, is one of the finest sights in the whole field of human society. Christ amidst the taunts of His judges was silent. "He answered them never a word." There is, however, a taciturnity which does not indicate a good spirit. It is the sullen and the sulky. There are men who are possessed of this "dumb devil." Another thing suggested of frugality of speech is—

IT IS FREQUENTLY FAVOURABLE TO ONE'S REPUTATION. —"Even a fool, when he holdeth his peace, is counted wise: and he that shutteth his lips is esteemed a man of understanding." The fool is a fool whether he speaks or not, but he may not only conceal his folly by his silence, but may even get a reputation amongst a class for wisdom by it. This fact, for fact it is, shows, First: Our liability to be deceived in the character of men. We sometimes judge a fool to be a wise man. We cannot read with accuracy the human character. We often give credit to men for what they have not, and deny to men the excellencies which they possess. We lack the insight into motives necessary to qualify us to sit in judgment on others. This shows, Secondly: That wise men are generally sparing in their use of words. It is the little fussy, shallow brook that rattles. The deep river rolls in silence. Silence being a characteristic of wise men, the fool may pass for a wise man so long as he can maintain it. A modern author has said that "speech is silver, silence is gold." This idea is older than Solomon. There is an old Arabic proverb poetically expressed, that embodies it—

> "Keep silence, then; nor speak but when besought:
> Who listens long grows tired of what is told.
> With tones of silver though thy tongue be fraught,
> Know this,—that silence of itself is gold."

* Luke ix. 54, 55.

Proverbs 18:1-2

A Student's Spirit

"Through desire a man, having separated himself, seeketh and intermeddleth with all wisdom. A fool hath no delight in understanding, but that his heart may discover itself."

OF the first of these verses two views are given by critics and commentators. They are *opposites*. The one makes Solomon refer to a pursuit of knowledge and wisdom that is right and commendable, the other regards him as speaking of what is wrong and censurable. And of this second view of the general meaning there are several varieties. By one critic (Schultens), the intended character is thus described—"A self-conceited, hair-brained fool seeks to satisfy his fancy, and intermingleth himself with all things." Another (Schulz), draws it thus :—" He who has separated himself agitates questions as his desire prompts, and breaks his teeth on every hard point." A third (Parkhurst), thus—" The recluse seeks his own pleasure or inclination : he laughs at or derides everything solid or wise." And a fourth (Hodgson), differently from all these, " He seeks occasions who desires to separate himself from his friends." In the margin we have it thus : "He that separateth himself, seeketh and intermeddleth with all wisdom." Another gives it, like our translators, a general form, without expressing either good or evil in the case :— " A retired man pursueth the researches he delighteth in, and hath pleasure in every branch of science."* We accept the last interpretation, which agrees with our version. In this view the verses may be regarded as expressing the idea that through desire for knowledge, a man separates himself from society, that he may more successfully prosecute his researches. In this sense the verses may be used to illustrate the true student spirit.

It is an ISOLATING spirit.—" Through desire a man having *separated* himself." A man who has a strong desire

---
* Wardlaw's posthumous work on Proverbs.

for knowledge will feel it necessary to withdraw habitually into *solitude* and *silence*. Society is so tumultuous in its career—so absorbing in its concerns, that a successful inquiry after knowledge in its midst would be all but impossible. Hence a strong desire for mental culture, and the attainment of truth, necessitates isolation. The true student has ever been, and must ever be, more or less a recluse. It is in loneliness and quiet that he makes his discoveries, and wins his intellectual trophies. In quest of *spiritual* truth this is *especially* necessary. John the Baptist lived in the desert until his "showing unto Israel." Paul dwelt in the solitudes of Arabia, and even Christ felt it necessary to send the multitude away, and go into a solitary place. "All weighty things," says Richter, "are done in solitude, that is, without society. The means of improvement consist not in projects, or in any violent designs, for these cool, and cool very soon, but in patiently practising for whole long days, by which I make the thing clear to my highest reason."

> "Bear me, some god! oh, quickly bear me hence
> To wholesome solitude, the nurse of sense;
> Where Contemplation plumes her ruffled wings,
> And the free soul looks down to pity kings."—POPE

The true student spirit is—

An INVESTIGATING spirit.—"He seeketh and intermeddleth with all wisdom." A true student is inspired with the importance of *all* truth, is a free enquirer in the highest sense. He knows the truth is ever varied, and he intermeddles with all, searches into all. He searches after wisdom to guide men in their *material* concerns:—wisdom to guide in the affairs of governments, markets, homes. He searches after wisdom to guide men in their *spiritual* concerns. He searches into the way by which the guilty is to be pardoned, the slave enfranchised, the polluted cleansed, the sorrowful comforted, the lost saved. He has not the true student spirit who gives himself to one branch of truth, exaggerates the importance of that, and ignores all else. The true student deals with the whole Book, examines every verse and chapter, and endeavours to ascertain the relations, the unity, and the uses of the whole. He "intermeddleth with all wisdom." The true student spirit is—

A WISE spirit.—It is set here in contrast with that of a fool. "A fool hath no delight in understanding; but that his heart may discover itself." A fool hates knowledge, all his desire is to pour out his own frivolity that "his heart may discover itself." What a discovery is the discovery of a fool's heart! It is a discovery of ignorance, carnality, selfishness, and vanity. He is wise who seeks knowledge. Knowledge gives us a new *world*. How different is the world of a fool from that of a wise man. Knowledge gives us new *sources of pleasure*. Pleasures of contemplation, religion, social usefulness. Knowledge gives us new *faculties of action*. It gives us eyes to see what otherwise lay in darkness, ears to hear what before was silent. He therefore who seeks knowledge in a right spirit and for a right end, is a wise man. "Men," says Bacon, "have entered into a desire of learning and knowledge sometimes upon a natural curiosity and inquisitive appetite; sometimes to entertain their mind with variety and delight; sometimes for ornament and reputation, and sometimes to enable them to obtain the victory of wit and contradiction, and sometimes for lucre and possession; but seldom sincerely to give a true account of their gift of reason for the benefit and use of man, as if there were sought in knowledge a couch whereupon to rest a searching and restless spirit, or a terrace for a wandering and variable mind, to walk up and down with a fair prospect, or a tower of state for a proud mind to raise itself upon, or a fort on commanding ground for strife or contention, or a shop for profit or sale, and not a rich store-house for the glory of the Creator and the relief of man's estate."

Proverbs 18:3

Wickedness, Contemptible and Contemptuous

"When the wicked cometh, *then* cometh also contempt, and with ignominy reproach."

THE words suggest—

That wickedness is a CONTEMPTIBLE thing.—"When the wicked cometh, then cometh also contempt." Wickedness is contemptible in *itself*. Analyze it, and you will find all its elements amongst the despicable in the moral domain. It involves selfishness, and does not universal conscience look down on this with ineffable disdain? It involves falsehood, and who can respect lies? What a toad is amongst animals, a liar is amongst men—a thing to be kicked out of your path. It involves vanity, and a soul inflicted with self-conceit is it not the scorn of every observer? It involves sensuality, and does not universal conscience recoil with loathing from the doings of the voluptuary and the debauchee? All these are some of the many elements of wickedness, and are they not amongst the most contemptible of all things? Aye, verily, though its countenance be painted into the beautiful in feature and expression, its forms robed in comely costume, its tongue speak in tones of music, and artistic genius make it seem beautiful, it is essentially a loathsome and contemptible thing. It is revolting to all consciences and to God. It is not only contemptible in itself, but is so in its *influence*. "When the wicked cometh, then also cometh contempt." It brings the men and things it touches into contempt. When it cometh into political life, it bringeth contempt on the nation. When it cometh into ecclesiastical office, it bringeth contempt upon the Church. When it cometh into friendly circles, it bringeth contempt upon the members. Wickedness is a leprosy, it defiles all it touches.

The words suggest—

That wickedness is a CONTEMPTUOUS thing.—"And with ignominy reproach." It is haughty, supercilious, and essentially contemptuous in spirit. Take its treatment of Incarnate Goodness, as an example. How it insulted Him at His trials by putting on Him the mock robes of royalty, and calling him king! How it insulted Him on the Cross! "And they that passed by reviled him, wagging their heads, and saying, Thou that destroyest the temple, and buildest it in three days, save thyself." The righteous victim of this contempt often feels it deeply, and exclaims —"Reproach hath broken my heart." How contemptuously the wicked have treated the righteous! Their language has always been that of reviling and reproach.

Stand aloof from the wicked. They can have no sympathy with you. Their touch will only degrade you. Heed not their contempt, manfully dare their scorns and sneers! "Contempt," says Dr. South, "naturally implies a man's esteeming of himself greater than the person whom he contemns: he therefore that slights, that contemns an affront, is properly superior to it; and he conquers an injury who conquers his resentment of it. Socrates, being kicked by an ass, did not think it revenge proper for Socrates to kick the ass again."

Proverbs 18:4

The Words of Inspired Wisdom

"The words of a man's mouth *are as* deep waters, *and* the wellspring of wisdom *as* a flowing brook."

THERE are some who regard the two clauses of this verse as antithetic. The former indicating hidden depths of evil in the wicked man. "The words of his mouth are as deep waters." That is, he is so full of guile and deceit that you **cannot reach his** meaning. The latter indicating the transparent communications of the wise and the good. "The wellspring of wisdom as a flowing brook." The communications of the one are guileful,—the words conceal rather than reveal. The words of the other are honest and lucid. There are others who regard the two clauses as a parallelism. The character of the former clause is to be taken from the latter. The "words of a man's mouth," that is, according to the second clause, of a wise man's mouth, "are as deep waters," and the "wellspring of wisdom as a flowing brook." We shall use the proverb thus as a parallelism, to illustrate the words of *inspired wisdom* which are "wise" in the highest sense.

They are FULL.—They are as "deep waters." The world abounds with *shallow* words, mere empty sounds. The words in the general conversation of society, and in the popular literature of the day, are empty, shells without a kernel, mere husks without grain. But the words of inspired men are brimful—full of *light* and full of *power*. *The greatest thinkers have failed to exhaust their meaning.* What volumes of criticism, what libraries of sermons have been published by the ablest scholars and thinkers of past times! And yet who will say that any of the inspired writers have had their meaning fully reached and comprehended? Each has a depth still unfathomed, points unapproached. *Every modern thinker discovers new significance.* The man of vigorous, independent, active intellect, after having read all expositions on the Holy Volume, feels that there is a field yet unexplored. In respect of fulness there are no words like the words of inspired men. Every paragraph has a continent of thought.

> "There lie vast treasures unexplored,
> And wonders yet untold."

Sir William Jones has said: "I have carefully and regularly perused the Holy Scriptures, and am of opinion that the volume, independently of its Divine origin, contains more sublimity, purer morality, more important history, and finer strains of eloquence, than can be collected from all other books, in whatever language they may have been written."

They are FLOWING.—" A flowing brook." The words of eternal truth are always in motion. They pulsate in thousands of souls every hour, and onward is their tendency. They flow from the eternal wellspring of truth, and flow down through human channels. Divine wisdom speaks through man, as well as through other organs. "Holy men spake as they were moved by the Holy Ghost." We have "the treasure in earthen vessels." "God who at sundry times and in divers manners spake in time past unto the fathers by the prophets, hath in these last days spoken unto us by his Son." The highest teacher was a man, Christ, the Logos. The words of His mouth were indeed as "deep waters." Since Heaven has thus made man the organ of wisdom, it behoves him devoutly to realise the honour God has conferred upon his nature, and earnestly to aspire to the high honour of being a messenger of the Eternal. It is for us to become at once its students and revealers, its recipients and its reflectors.

They are FERTILISING.—They are here compared to "waters," and to "a flowing brook." What water is to all physical life, the words of heavenly wisdom are to souls. They quicken and satisfy. It is a *perennial* brook. It has streamed down the centuries, imparting life and beauty in its somewhat meandering course. Wherever in the history of humanity, past or present, spots of moral verdure and loveliness appear, this brook has touched with its quickenstreams. It is an *accumulating* "brook." As brooks in nature swell into rivers by the confluence of contributary streams, so the brook of Divine truth widens and deepens by every contribution of holy thought. And never was it so deep and broad as now. May it speed on, and soon cover the earth as the waters cover over the channels of the deep—

"Till, like a sea of glory,
It spreads from pole to pole."

Proverbs 18:5

Three Bad Things

"*It is* not good to accept the person of the wicked, to overthrow the righteous in judgment."

THE Scripture frequently deprecates "respect of persons." Thus James says, "My brethren, have not the faith of our Lord Jesus with respect to persons." All respect, however, for persons is not wrong. To appreciate those who possess force of intellect, great intelligence, high morality, more than the mentally feeble, ignorant, and immoral, is not only right, but obligatory. The proverb indicates three great evils.

VOLUNTARY CONNECTION WITH WICKED MEN.—"It is not good to accept the person of the wicked." There is a connection in this world which we have with wicked men, that is necessary and unavoidable. We cannot help it. We have to live with them, and often by them, and as godly men for them. But to choose a connection with them is bad. To "accept" them *matrimonially* is bad. Woe to the virgin that enters into conjugal relationship with the wicked man. To "accept" them *mercantilely* is bad. To accept them as partners in commercial enterprise is wrong and often ruinous. To "accept" them *politically* is bad. To accept them as our representatives in Parliament is a crime and a curse. To "accept" them *ecclesiastically* is bad. An ungodly priest, minister, or bishop is a curse. On no ground are we justified in forming a voluntary connection with wicked men. However transcendent their genius, great their intellectual attainments, vast their wealth, or eminent their social position, because they are wicked, they are to be shunned and reprobated. Wickedness is untrustworthy, dissociating, and divinely cursed. "It is not good," therefore, "to accept the person of the wicked" "Come out from among them; be ye separate; touch not the unholy thing." Another evil indicated is—

THE "OVERTHROW" OF GOOD MEN. — "To overthrow the righteous in judgment." The righteous are often in this life overthrown. Sometimes in *social* life. In the judgment of society they are frequently overthrown by falsehood, calumny, and slander. Their bright reputations are sometimes tarnished, and not seldom stained by slanderous tongues. They are overthrown sometimes in the *courts of justice.* By false witnesses and deceptive special pleadings they often lose their righteous cause. The best of men are not unfrequently pronounced criminals and deprived of their rights. The world's noblest men, righteous patriots, holy reformers, godly martyrs, have been "overthrown" in the "judgment." Another evil indicated here is—

The "overthrow" of good men BY THE EMPLOYMENT OF THE WICKED.—"It is not good to accept the person of the wicked to overthrow the righteous in judgment." The wicked in all ages have been thus employed. The Sanhedrim in Judea, in the days of Christ and the apostles, often used them thus. "Now the chief priests and elders and all the council sought false witness against Jesus to put Him to death, but found none; yea though many false witnesses came yet found they none." The Inquisition of Christendom employed such to "overthrow the righteous in judgment." The moral of these remarks is: *Shun the wicked and adhere to the righteous.* The cause of the good, though misrepresented, denounced, temporarily overthrown, is holy, and smiled upon by Heaven. Their apparent "overthrow" is only like the sinking of the sun beneath the cloudy horizon, to rise with refulgent brightness at a destined hour. "The path of the just is as the shining light, that shineth more and more unto the perfect day."

Proverbs 18:6-8

The Speech of a Splenetic Fool

"A fool's lips enter into contention, and his mouth calleth for strokes. A fool's mouth *is* his destruction, and his lips *are* the snare of his soul. The words of a talebearer *are* as wounds, and they go down into the innermost parts of the belly."

How frequently Solomon speaks of the fool! and the fool in his idea was not an intellectually demented man, but a morally bad man; he was not a man destitute of reason, but one who used his reason wrongly. In sooth, a fool and a sinner; folly, and wickedness, were in his mind convertible terms, representatives of the same character. And so, in truth, they are. A sinner is a fool; he acts contrary to the dictates of rationality; he barters away the joys of eternity for the puerilities of an hour. But all fools and sinners are not in every respect alike. They differ in temperament, in modes of thinking, in habits of life, and in degrees of moral turpitude. The fool referred to in the passage is a *splenetic* fool; he is full of gall. The proverb indicates that the speech of such a man—

Is QUERULOUS.—"A fool's lips enter into contention." His ill-nature shows itself in his readiness to pick quarrels, to create frays. He is easily offended. Sometimes a look, a simple incidental act, he will interpret as an insult. His temper is turpentine, which a spark will set ablaze. Alas! how many men there are in society of this miserable temper. They are full of the canine. They are seldom found but with the curled lip, the grin and growl of the cur. "The poison of asps is under their lips." "If," to use the language of Johnson, "they had two ideas in their head they would fall out with each other." Of such Shenstone's remark is good, "I consider your very testy and quarrelsome people in the same light as I do a loaded gun, which may by accident go off and kill me."

The verses indicate that the speech of a splenetic man—

Is PROVOCATIONAL —" His mouth calleth for strokes." He irritates the men he speaks to, and often prompts to acts of violence. He brings on himself the strokes of indignant words, and sometimes physical blows. Whilst a "soft word turneth away wrath," the angry word of a splenetic soul creates it. Domestic and social broils, litigations, duellings, and battles, are the fruits of this miserable temper. "I commend his discretion and valour," says Fuller, "who walking in London streets met a gallant, who cried to him a pretty distance beforehand—'I will have the wall!' 'Yea,' answered he, 'and take the house too, if you can but agree with the landlord.'" The verses indicate that the speech of such a splenetic man—

Is SELF-RUINOUS.—"A fool's mouth is his destruction, and his lips are the snare of his soul." Such speech is self-destructive. It destroys the *man's own reputation*. A querulous man has no social respect or influence; he is shunned, men recoil from him as something noisome and contemptible. Such speech destroys the man's own *social enjoyment*. He has no loving fellowships, no lasting friendships. A free loving intercourse with men, which is one of the blessings of life, is denied him. He finds few to listen to him, fewer still to reciprocate his fiendish spirit. Such speech destroys, moreover, his own *peace of mind*. An ill-tempered man can have no inward satisfaction. Thus it is that his "mouth is his destruction, and his lips are the snare of his soul." "There cannot," says Sir W. Temple, "live a more unhappy creature than an ill-natured old man, who is neither capable of receiving pleasures nor sensible of doing them to others." The verses further indicate that the speech of such a splenetic man—

Is SOCIALLY INJURIOUS.—"The words of a talebearer are as wounds, and they go down into the innermost parts of the belly." The talebearer as a rule is a man with a splenetic temperament; he delights in mischief. The words of such tempers are as deadly as the bite of a viper. Splenetic fools are the mischief-makers in society. They bear tales which, like the envenomed fangs of a serpent, infuse a deadly virus of suspicion and ill-feeling into hearts once united in the ties of loving friendship. True men, however, can dare the calumny of such splenetic bipeds.

> "If I am
> Traduced by ignorant tongues, which neither know
> My faculties nor person, yet will be
> The chronicles of my doing—let me say,
> 'Tis but the fate of place, and the rough brake
> That virtue must go through."—SHAKESPEARE

Proverbs 18:9

Miserable Twinship

"He also that is slothful in his work is brother to him that is a great waster."

WE have so frequently had occasion to remark on slothfulness in passing through this book, that we shall confine our explanatory observations here to the other evil, namely, Wastefulness. Wastefulness may spring from one or two causes, *thriftlessness* or *extravagance*. In the former case there may be no desire to waste, on the contrary, a strong wish to be economical, but for the lack of management and tact resources run to waste. Thriftlessness in housekeeping is a terrible curse. Woe to the husband who has a thriftless wife. He will have to labour hard in order to replenish the resources that are ever running away through the channel of domestic thriftlessness. Extravagance is another cause of waste. The means entrusted to an extravagant person are not duly valued, and are consequently soon squandered away with recklessness. The spendthrift who inherits a fortune, goes through it with a gallop. But the proverb asserts an affinity between the slothful and the waster, and surely they are akin.

They are "brothers" in their SELF-INDULGENT SPIRIT. —Self-indulgence is the spring of each. The lazy man will not work, will not use his limbs, or ply his faculties. He will not give himself industriously to the real duties of life, because he loves ease. His cry is "a little more sleep, a little more slumber, a little more folding of the hands to sleep." The waster, whether from thriftlessness or extravagance, is influenced by the same spirit—self-indulgence. The sense of duty and concern for the good of others are lost in the self-indulgent feeling. The waster, whether he be the thriftless, or the reckless fool, is a brother in spirit to the slothful idler.

They are "brothers" in their MORAL IMPROPRIETY.—Both are morally wrong. Laziness is a sin; a sin against the constitution of our own natures, the claims of society, the arrangements of the universe, and the will of God. Man is made to work, and work is the divine condition of his well-being. Wastefulness is also a sin. What we have, we have on trust; we are stewards, not owners; and it is our duty to use all with conscientious discretion as the Proprietor wills. The man in the Gospel who wasted his goods, and the slothful servant who hid his Lord's talent, were alike held sinful.

They are "brothers" in their RUINOUS TENDENCY.— Slothfulness leads to ruin. To ruin of all sorts. To physical, intellectual, commercial ruin. The lazy man is like a tree diseased in its roots, he must rot. He who through life hides the one talent in a napkin, must ultimately be damned. Wastefulness is also ruinous. It implies a lack of that sense of individual responsibility apart from which there is no virtue. And ruin, if not in a secular, yet in a spiritual sense, is inevitable.

Learn, hence, the importance of combining diligence with economy, industry with careful management. The combination of these is important in *worldly* matters. What in domestic affairs boots industry if there is waste? How many thriftless housewives keep the most industrious husbands in constant poverty! The combination is important in *spiritual* matters too. We should not only be diligent in getting knowledge and attaining to higher experiences, but if we would be useful we must rightly manage our attainments. There is such a thing as waste power and waste influence. There is a true policy required for the management of our intellectual and moral resources.

> " Oh! waste thou not the smallest thing
>   Created by Divinity ;
> For grains of sand the mountains make,
>   And atomies infinity.
> Waste thou not the smallest time ;
>   'Tis imbecile infirmity ;
> For well thou know'st, if aught thou know'st,
>   That seconds form eternity."—EDWARD KNIGHT

Proverbs 18:10-12

The Soul's Tower

"*The* name of the LORD *is* a strong tower : the righteous runneth into it and is safe. The rich man's wealth *is* his strong city, and as an high wall in his own conceit. Before destruction the heart of man is haughty, and before honour *is* humility."

THAT the soul of unregenerate men is in danger is a *fact*, a fact attested by the Word of God, the religions of mankind, and the consciousness of the race. There are seasons when men become terribly alive to this danger, and they cry out with the Philippian jailor, " What shall I do to be saved?" Under this feeling it looks out for a "Tower"— a refuge. The verses direct us to two soul "towers"—the one the true, the other the false.

The soul's TRUE Tower.—This tower is here *described*. It is the "NAME of the Lord." This means not merely His character, attributes, and titles, but Himself. Our name is not ourselves. On the contrary, men's names are not only often unmeaning, but frequently misrepresenting: they give no idea as to what the men who wear them are. God's name is Himself; and He is often spoken of as a tower for souls, a "fortress," a "refuge," a "strong tower," a "high tower." He is, indeed, the refuge of souls. Ever near, impregnable, always accessible. The verses suggest that this soul Tower must be sought. "The righteous"—those who have been rightly enlightened and impressed "runneth into it." They run to it in all their trials, temptations, and dangers, as their only refuge. They look for protection nowhere but in Him, not in churches, theologies, or priesthoods. "They know His *Name*, and they put their trust in Him." They run as a gallant vessel in a storm into a sheltering harbour, or as an affrighted child into the arms of a loving mother. The verse asserts that this soul's Tower is *Safe*. "And is safe," in the margin reads, *is set afloat*. It is so high up as to be beyond the reach of enemies. Storms that shake the earth and lash the ocean with fury, never touch the sun. In undisturbed majesty he travels on his way. High above the sun is the soul's true "Tower." "If God be for us, who can be against us?" "We have a strong city, salvation for walls and bulwarks." Here is safety, and nowhere else. There is no security out of Him. He is the City of Refuge.

The verses direct us to—

The soul's FALSE Tower.—"The rich man's wealth is his strong city." Wealth is one of the false towers referred to here, and this in sooth is a very *common* tower. Everywhere souls are resting in it. On all hands we hear men say, " Soul, thou hast much goods laid up for many years, take thine ease, eat, drink, and be merry." Men are every where in quest of this tower. They are busily and earnestly building up fortunes as a "tower" for their souls. The verse suggests two thoughts concerning this Tower of wealth. Its security is *proudly estimated*. It is a "high wall in his own conceit." The owner fancies it very lofty, great, and strong. Albeit its walls have no real strength. What can wealth do for the imperishable existent within us in the seasons of moral conviction, in the hour of death, in the day of judgment? "Naked came we into the world," &c. Its security is *utterly fictitious*. "Before destruction the heart of man is haughty, and before honour is humility." We have had these proverbs before.* They are here used

* See Reading on chap. xvi. 18, xv. 33.

to show the inevitable ruin of those who are proudly trusting to their own resources, and the blessedness of those who humbly trust in God. Alas! souls are trusting to false towers—such as wealth, self-merit, wisdom, sacerdotal help; all such towers must crumble to dust. Death will shatter them, and judgment will sweep them clean away. "Say unto them who daub it with untempered mortar that it shall fall: there shall be an overflowing shower, and ye, O great hailstones, shall fall, and a stormy wind shall rend it."

Proverbs 18:13

Impetuous Flippancy

"He that answereth a matter before he heareth *it*, it *is* folly and shame unto him."

THE subject of these words is *impetuous flippancy*, a great social evil too common in most circles. Observe—

The evil SKETCHED.—" He that answereth a matter before he heareth it." How often this is done in *ordinary conversation*. Are you making a communication? There are people who are so impetuous and flippant that they will interrupt you before you are half through your statement; they will intrude some remark, they will commence some reply. Are you reasoning out a proposition? They can't hear you to the close; they begin the refutation before they have known your argument. How often this is done *in polemic discussion*. There are those who have answered Renan, Colenso, the "Essays and Reviews," "Ecce Homo!" and works which have recently appeared of a kindred character, before they have half read the pages or measured the argument. This impetuous flippancy, alas! is not confined to the social circle, but appears on platforms, in pulpits, and in the press. Sometimes it shows its ugly head even in courts of justice—a "matter" is not seldom answered there before it is heard. Observe—

The evil CHARACTERISED.—"It is a folly and a shame unto him." And truly it is so if we consider some of the causes from which it springs. First: *Uncontrolledness*. The man who has acted worthily of his being, disciplined his faculties, and brought his nature under self-control, would not act thus. He would hear the matter to its close though it clashed with his views, opposed his interests, and roused his passions. Impetuous flippancy implies inner lawlessness, indicates a mind untrained to self-control, a mind without an inner sovereignty. Another cause is, Secondly: *Prejudice*. The mind is *biassed* on the other side, and the statements of the speaker or writer are so distasteful that a reply is tendered before the matter has been fully heard. Much of this impetuous flippancy springs from unfounded prepossessions. Another cause is, Thirdly: *Laziness*. Sometimes it springs from an indolent, sleepy, lethargic temperament, that can't bear any exertion, and to spare effort will cut the matter short. The listener hears a little, his attention flags, he yawns, and to end the exertion he decides the question. Another cause is, Fourthly: *Vanity*. The self-conceited man has an eye to see the whole in a moment, all the threads of the argument are before him after a few sentences. It is needless for him to listen any more, therefore he interrupts. And so anxious is he to make a display of his great knowledge and power, that he begins his answer at once. Now is not this uncontrolledness, prejudice, laziness, and vanity, from which this evil springs a "shame and a folly"?

Cultivate self-control, free the mind from all prepossessions, shake off all mental sloth, "be not wise in your own conceit," and then you will listen fully to a matter before you will make an answer. Let truth be supreme in your estimation; be swift to hear and slow to speak.

Proverbs 18:14

The Unbearable Wound

"The spirit of a man will sustain his infirmity; but a wounded spirit who can bear?"

THE text speaks of an unbearable wound. What is that? Not mere physical sufferings—they can be borne—but moral. The wound of remorse, self-contempt, self-loathing, self-denunciation. It is the wound of a spirit feeling not only that the universe is against it, and God against it, but that its own conscience is against it. But why is this wound unbearable?

Because the sufferer is DEPRIVED of the ORDINARY MEANS of support.—What are the ordinary means which sustain a man under suffering? There is *a consciousness of rectitude*. When conscience stands by us, and says, "Well done," what suffering can we not bear? But this wounded spirit has conscience against it. There is *a feeling of inevitableness*. If sufferings come upon a man, and he believes, as the old Stoics did, that they come as a resistless necessity, he may console himself by feeling that nothing can be done, and absolute submission is prudence. But in the case of this wounded spirit, the man feels that he has brought the suffering on himself. There is *unshaken confidence in God*. When the sufferer feels confidence in Him, he may exult. Job did. "He knoweth the way that I take. When he hath tried me I shall come forth as gold." Or with Paul, who said, "Our light affliction, which is but for a moment, worketh for us a far more exceeding and eternal weight of glory." But in the case of the wounded spirit there is no confidence in God. All interest in Him is gone, all trust lost, lost for ever. There is *hope in a brighter future*. What power has hope to bear man up under trials? It brings sunshine from the future to break the clouds of the present. But the "wounded spirit" has no hope; the star of hope is blotted from the firmament, and all is midnight. There is *friendly sympathy*.

Human sympathy has a wonderful power to help man under his sufferings. But a soul suffering under moral remorse cannot avail himself of this. In the first place, men cannot sympathise with others on account of their sins; and if they could, the suffering soul would get no comfort therefrom. Another reason that makes this moral wound unbearable is:

Because the sufferer is COMPELLED to use one of HIS CHIEF FACULTIES TO ENHANCE HIS AGONY.—Thought is one of the leading powers of the soul. By it man can deaden his physical agonies and bear himself up above other mental trials. Thought can take the prisoner from the dungeon abroad into the open universe; the pauper into the paradise of God; the martyr in agony into the felicity of Heaven. But this faculty a *guilty* conscience will ever employ for its own torment. Thoughts are governed by different principles. Sometimes intellect controls them, then they take the man into speculation; sometimes imagination, then they take him into poetry; sometimes avarice, then they take him into worldliness; sometimes sensuality, then they take him into a world of lusts. But the "wounded spirit" makes the guilty conscience the master of thought, and this takes the man into hell. When it takes the rein of thought, it directs it to two terrible subjects of contemplation: The crimes of the past and the retributive judgment of the future. Well, then, might Solomon say, "A wounded spirit who can bear?" Brother! the conclusion of all this is, that you must either have a hell, or seek at once a SPECIAL remedy. I say SPECIAL. *Ordinary means of support will not do, as we have seen.* The elements of hell are within. Within are the fuel of the last fires, and the gathering clouds of the last outer darkness. Do you exclaim,

> "Which way shall I fly
> Infinite wrath and infinite despair?
> Which way shall I fly is hell, MYSELF am hell."

Where is the special remedy? "Behold the Lamb of God Who taketh away the SINS of the world." Here is the PHYSICIAN who alone can heal this wound.

Proverbs 18:15-16

The Attainment of Knowledge and the Power of Kindness

"The heart of the prudent getteth knowledge; and the ear of the wise seeketh knowledge. A man's gift maketh room for him, and bringeth him before great men."

THESE verses point to two of the most priceless things in the spiritual world, knowledge and kindness, the light of the intellect and the life of the soul. Christ is the Revealer and the Minister of these two, in their most perfect forms and measure. "Grace and truth came by Jesus Christ." Notice,

THE ATTAINMENT OF KNOWLEDGE.—"The heart of the prudent getteth knowledge." It is suggested that the attainment of knowledge requires two things. First: A heart for it. "The heart of the prudent." Heart here, as in many other places, means the whole mind, and the idea is that this mind in a certain state is necessary to the getting of knowledge. There must be in every "heart," at least, (1) A consciousness of its need. The opiniated, self-sufficient man, who is wise in his own conceit, will never attain it. Though the sun of knowledge shine around him its beams cannot enter his mind. All the shutters of his mental house are so closed by self-sufficiency that no rays can break in. A sense of ignorance is the first step to the attainment of knowledge. A man must feel the darkness before he struggles for the light. (2) A craving for its possession. This grows out of the sense of need. There must be a hungering and thirsting for knowledge. The cry of the soul should be, "Where shall wisdom be found?" Why does ignorance prevail so extensively in this country and in this age? Not for the lack of the means of knowledge, but for the want of heart to receive it. "Wherefore is there a price in the hand of a fool to get wisdom, seeing he hath no heart to it?" The other thing necessary to the attainment of knowledge is, Secondly: An effort for it. "The ear of the wise seeketh knowledge." As the heart is here put for the soul, the ear is put for its receptive faculties. The ear is one of the greatest inlets to the mind. It not only listens eagerly to all the voices of intelligence, but more, it discriminates between them. "The ear trieth the words." Effort is required. Mere desire, however strong, will not do. There must be observation, comparison, generalisation. The endeavour must be honest, strenuous, and persevering. Wisdom does not come into the soul unless it is searched for as a "hidden treasure." Whilst all this is true of general knowledge, it is especially true of spiritual and redemptive. The knowledge that maketh wise unto salvation, men will never get unless they hunger for it and struggle after it. Notice again,

THE POWER OF KINDNESS.—"A man's gift maketh room for him and bringeth him before great men." A similar utterance to this we have already noticed.* There are two kinds of gifts, the gift of selfishness and the gift of kindness. A man sometimes bestows a favour on another in order to get back something of a higher value. This gift is a bribe. Still it may answer that purpose, the giver has "room" made for him by it, and he is brought "before great men." "Great men"—conventional magnates, but moral serfs. But the gift of kindness is the true gift and the real power. It makes "room" for the giver in the heart of the receiver, and it bringeth him before *truly* "great men." Great men recognize and honour the generous. We have many instances in the Bible of gifts thus making room for the giver.* Eliezer's gifts made *room* for him in Rebekah's family. Jacob's gifts made *room* for him in his brother's heart. He sent his present to the governor of Egypt, to bring his sons with acceptance before a great man. Ehud's gifts made room for his errand. Abi-

* See Reading on chap. xvii. 8.
* Gen. xxiv. 30—33; Gen. xxx. 1—11; Gen. xliii. 11; Judges iii. 17, 18; 1 Sam. xxv. 18.

gail's for the preservation of her house. First: Kindness is the mightiest power. It is a power that will subdue the wildest beasts, and has conquered the most savage and hostile souls. In truth it is the only power to conquer mind. Men who will dare the bayonet and the sword have fallen prostrate before the power of kindness. David's kindness made Saul the despot weep. Kindness makes "*room*" for us in human hearts.

> "When I went out to the gate through the city:
> When I prepared my seat in the street!
> The young men saw me, and hid themselves;
> And the aged arose, and stood up.
> The princes refrained talking,
> And laid their hand on their mouth.
> The nobles held their peace,
> And their tongue cleaved to the roof of their mouth.
> When the ear heard me, then it blessed me;
> And when the eye saw me, it gave witness to me;
> Because I delivered the poor that cried,
> And the fatherless, and him that had none to help him.
> The blessing of him that was ready to perish came upon me:
> And I caused the widow's heart to sing for joy."
>
> JOB

Secondly : Kindness is the divinest power. It is indeed the power of God unto salvation. The Gospel is at once its expression and the medium. Christ loved the world and gave Himself for it, and His kindness is that which maketh "*room*" for Him in all souls and lands.

> " A little word in kindness spoken,
> A motion or a tear,
> Has often healed the heart that's broken,
> And made a friend sincere.
> Then deem it not an idle thing
> A pleasant word to speak :
> The face you wear, the thoughts you bring,
> A heart may heal or break."—J. C. WHITTIER.

Proverbs 18:17-19

Social Disputes

"*He that is* first in his own cause *seemeth* just; but his neighbour cometh and searcheth him. The lot causeth contentions to cease, and parteth between the mighty. A brother offended *is harder to be won* than a strong city: and *their* contentions *are* like the bars of a castle."

IDEAL society, or society as it *ought* to be, is an organic unity, a body of which each individual is a member, with a loving sympathy, as the life's blood circulating through every part, and a common purpose like the head working every muscle, faculty, and limb. But *actually* it is anything but this. The whole is not only out of joint but dismembered, and each part is separate and oftentimes a hostile existent. One section grates, jostles, battles against another. It seems to have been so for ages. It was so in the days of Solomon, it is so now. The verses lead us to make three remarks concerning these social disputes.

THEIR SETTLEMENT REQUIRES THE HEARING OF BOTH DISPUTANTS.—" He that is first in his own cause seemeth just; but his neighbour cometh and searcheth him." Social disputes are a great evil. They are injurious to the parties immediately concerned, and injurious in their influence on others. It is therefore very desirable that efforts should at all times be employed for their settlement, and a third person may succeed in bringing this about. He who properly fulfils the duty of this third person as the "Daysman" has the benediction of the "peacemaker." The verses indicate what he must do in order to succeed. He must give a hearing to both parties. The reason for this is, that one may give a wrong impression of the real case. The first " seemeth just," but the second gives a different shape to the point. A fact may be dealt with falsely in a variety of ways. By denial. There may be a positive contradiction of all the essential circumstances of the case. Or by omission. The facts may be stated so partially as to give an utterly wrong showing. What is told is true, but it is not the whole truth, and what is untold is capable of changing the aspect of the told. Or by addition. Something is introduced as connected with the affair, which has no bearing upon it, but which gives it a false character. Or by grouping. Circumstances may be arranged in such an order, the insignificant put in the place of the important and the reverse, as to give an utterly wrong view. Copy a painting with the utmost precision so far as the number, size, colour, attitude of the objects are concerned, but let the figures have a different grouping, and your copy shall give an impression very different from that of the original. It is just so in the narration of facts. Thus he that cometh first in "his own cause" may make his case appear just. Hence the necessity of waiting to hear what his neighbour has to say, and comparing the statements of both, sifting well in order to arrive at the truth. Two historians dealing with the same facts, and both writing conscientiously, give them a widely different aspect. Another remark which the verses suggest concerning the settlement of social disputes is—

THAT THERE SHOULD BE A MUTUAL AGREEMENT TO ABIDE BY A CERTAIN TEST TO TERMINATE THE DISPUTE. —"The lot causeth contentions to cease." We have already noticed the "lot."* It is here referred to as an ordinance for settling disputes. The tribes had their territories settled by "*lot.*" Saul was chosen to his kingdom by "*lot.*" Mathias was numbered amongst the apostles by "*lot.*" Why should it not be used now in the settlements of disputes when other means have failed? Many an international quarrel, ecclesiastical contention, and social litigation may be easily settled by binding the opposing parties to agree to such a test. It is true it may not always secure justice in the particular case, but it would terminate disputes which might involve families, communities, nations, in misery and ruin. Another remark which the verses suggest concerning the settlement of social disputes is—

THAT THE BITTERNESS OF DISPUTES IS OFTEN AGGRA-

* See Reading on chap. xvi. 33.

VATED BY BLOOD RELATIONSHIP.—" A brother offended is harder to be won than a strong city : and their contentions are like the bars of a castle." The closer the relationship in case of dispute the wider the breach, and the more difficult the reconciliation. A really offended brother is often harder to win back to friendship than the taking of a "strong city," or the breaking of the "bars of a castle." Take the cases of Cain and Abel, Joseph and his brethren, Absalom and Abiram, Esau and Jacob. In all these instances nothing less than death was plotted and sought. Why is this? Why is a *brother's* anger so implacable? Several reasons may be suggested. First: Great love has been wounded. The more love you have for a man the greater capability you have of indignation towards him if he does the unrighteous and dishonourable towards you. How strong the love of a real brother! And of such we presume Solomon is here speaking. The wrath of love is a terrible wrath—It is oil in flames. Secondly : Great services have been ill-requited. What attentions a true brother shows, how numerous, how delicate, how self-sacrificing! If the object of all has proved utterly unworthy of them, how intense his chagrin, how poignant his distress! Thirdly: Great hopes are frustrated. The "offended brother" anticipated a brother's sympathy, counsel, friendship, through all the chequered scenes of life. These hopes are shattered and the wreck is vexatious beyond measure. Fourthly: Great reluctance on the offender's side to acknowledge the fault and seek reconciliation. Strange as it may seem, it is yet true, a man would sooner offer an apology to any one than to his relations, especially to brothers. Solomon knew human life. What he speaks is true to man—the world over.

What anarchy and distress sin brings into the social world. When shall Christianity reconcile contending parties, and hush the discords of the race?

Proverbs 18:20-21

The Influence of the Tongue

"A man's belly shall be satisfied with the fruit of his mouth; *and* with the increase of his lips shall he be filled. Death and life *are* in the power of the tongue: and they that love it shall eat the fruit thereof."

THE word "belly" is here used, to represent the *inward* man. Thus it is used* elsewhere.—"The spirit of man is the candle of the Lord; searching all the inward parts of the belly," and again, "Out of his belly shall flow rivers of living water." The words, therefore, may be rendered, "a man's moral self shall be satisfied." And the two verses may be taken to illustrate the influence of the tongue. What is the "fruit of the mouth," and the "increase of the lips," but the expression of the tongue? Notice—

THE INFLUENCE OF THE TONGUE UPON THE SPEAKER.—Solomon says that a certain kind of speech which he calls the "fruit of the mouth" is satisfying to the "belly"—the inner man. What is this soul-satisfying speech? It must have two characteristics. First: It must be conscientiously truthful. Unless a man feels in his heart that the words he has spoken to another are true to fact, true to reality, he can have no moral satisfaction in his utterance. But a communication which he in his conscience believes is true will distil a satisfying influence upon his soul. Secondly: It must be intentionally useful. If the intention is to shake faith, to suggest the impure, to generate strife, to lead astray, it will be far enough from yielding moral satisfaction to the speaker. On the contrary, if he intended it to be useful, though it did not prove so, though perhaps it was not adapted to do good, it will refresh and gratify his inner nature. The fact is, a man's conscience tells him that he is responsible for his words as well as for his works, and that the words that he feels to be right will yield him satisfaction as well as the works which his conscience approves.

* Chap. xx. 27.

Notice—

THE INFLUENCE OF THE TONGUE UPON SOCIETY.—"Death and life are in the power of the tongue, and they that love it shall eat the fruit thereof." This will apply—First: To speech in ordinary conversation. Many a tongue in ordinary intercourse produces death. By slander it kills men's reputation; by obscenity it kills men's purity; by scepticism it kills men's faith; by infidelity it kills men's souls. On the other hand, the ordinary speeches of many tend to life—intellectual, social, spiritual. God alone knows the influence of words upon human souls. Every sentence is a seed that will produce either nightshade or corn. This will apply—Secondly: To speech in courts of justice. The words of a perjured witness, and those of a fallacious pleader may consign an innocent man to the cell or scaffold: or, save the life of one that is guilty and deserves to die. This will apply—Thirdly: To ministers of the gospel. "For we are unto God a sweet savour of Christ in them that are saved, and in them that perish: to the one we are the savour of death unto death; and to the other the savour of life unto life."

CONCLUSION.—"Let us," as St. Chrysostom says, "guard this little member, the tongue, more than the pupil of the eye, and the more cautious we should be because we are of unclean lips." "Set a watch, O Lord, before my mouth. Keep the door of my lips!"

Proverbs 18:22

A Happy Marriage

"*Whoso* findeth a wife findeth a good *thing*, and obtaineth favour of the LORD."

AT the outset these words strike two thoughts on our attention. First: That celibacy is not the best mode of social life. Solomon means to say that it is a good thing to have a wife. Even in the state of innocence it was not good for man to be alone. It is said that the Guardians of the Holborn Union lately advertised for candidates to fill the situation of engineer at the workhouse, a single man was required, a wife not being allowed to reside on the premises. Twenty-one candidates presented themselves, but it was found that as to testimonials, character, workmanship, and appearance, the *best* men were all married men. The Guardians had, therefore, to elect a married man. The other thought which these words strike on our attention is—Secondly: That monogamy is the true marriage. Solomon does not say, "he that findeth wives," but "he that findeth a wife." Though he himself had many wives, he nowhere justifies a plurality. Christ declares that for any woman to marry while she has a husband alive, is adultery; and by parity of reasoning it must be adultery for any man to marry while his wife is alive. The constitution of nature, the baneful results of polygamy, and the teachings of the Bible, clearly demonstrate that marriage life consists of two, and only two. Duality appears everywhere throughout the universe as a law.

The proverb in its completeness teaches—

That a good wife IS A "GOOD THING."—Of a good wife, of course, the writer must be supposed to speak, for a bad wife is a bad thing. Manoah found a "good thing" in his wife. The patriarch of Uz does not seem to have found a "good thing" in his. In the Septuagint version, the text reads "a good wife." What is a good wife? First: A good woman. A woman of chaste loves, incorruptible virtues, godly sympathies and aims. One who has in her nature a power at once to command and reciprocate the highest affections of a man. A good wife must be— Secondly: A suitable companion. A good woman would not be a good wife to all men. There must be a mutual fitness, a fitness of temperament, taste, habits, culture, associations. A full description of a good wife is given in the last chapter of this book. Verily a good wife is a good thing.

The proverb teaches :

That a good wife IS A DIVINE GIFT.—" Obtaineth favour of the Lord." All good things are His gifts. " Every good and perfect gift cometh down from above." But few better gifts can a man have from God, in passing through life, than a good wife. " A good wife," says an old and eloquent writer, " is heaven's last, best gift to a man; his angel of mercy ; minister of graces innumerable ; his gem of many virtues ; his casket of jewels. Her voice his sweetest music ; her smiles, his brightest day ; her kiss the guardian of innocence ; her arms the pale of his safety, the balm of his health, the balsam of his life ; her industry his surest wealth, her economy his safest steward ; her lips his faithful counsellors ; her bosom the softest pillow of his cares, and her prayers the ablest advocates of heaven's blessing on his head. A married man falling into misfortune is more apt to retrieve his situation in the world than a single one, chiefly because his spirits are soothed and retrieved by domestic endearments, and his self-respect kept alive by finding that although all abroad be darkness and humiliation, yet there is a little world of love at home over which he is monarch."

Young men, be cautious in your choice of a companion for life. " When Themistocles was to marry his daughter, there were two suitors, the one rich and a fool, and the other wise but not rich ; and being asked which of the two he had rather his daughter should have, he answered, I had rather she should marry a man without money, than money without a man. The best of marriage is in the man or woman, not in the means or the money."

Proverbs 18:23; 19:4, 6-7

Poverty, Riches and Social Selfishness

"The poor useth intreaties; but the rich answereth roughly."
"Wealth maketh many friends; but the poor is separated from his neighbour."
"Many will intreat the favour of the prince: and every man *is* a friend to him that giveth gifts. All the brethren of the poor do hate him : how much more do his friends go far from him ? he pursueth *them with* words, *yet* they *are* wanting *to him.*"

WE bring those passages together because they are related by common sentiments. They present us with three subjects of thought, the trials of poverty, the temptations of wealth, and the selfishness of society.

THE TRIALS OF POVERTY.—The passages point to three great trials to which the poor are at all times more or less subjected. First: *Degradation.* "The poor useth entreaties." To beg of a fellow-man is a degradation; it is that from which our manhood revolts. Yet the poor, from the necessity of their condition, are forced to this. They have to mortify the natural independence of their spirit. They are subjected to—Secondly : *Insolence.* "The rich answereth roughly." Their sufferings from the pinch of indigence and the humiliation of entreating assistance are aggravated by the haughty heartlessness of those whose aid they implore. They are subjected to—Thirdly : *Desertion.* "The poor is separated from his neighbour." "All the brethren of the poor do hate him." Who in this selfish world will make friends with the poor, however superior in intellect or excellent in character? The poor man is deserted, he must live in his own little hut alone, he is no attraction to any one. A wealthy man will be followed and fawned on by a host of professed friends, but let his riches take wing and fly away, and all will desert him. As the winter brooks filled from the opening springs and showers dry up and vanish in the summer heat, so man's friends desert him in the day of poverty and trial. When the wealthy man with his large circle of friends becomes poor, the poles of his magnet are reversed, and his old friends feel the repulsion. Such is life, such it was in Judea in the days of Solomon, and such it is now here in our England. The verses present to us—

THE TEMPTATIONS OF WEALTH.—Here are presented all the temptations of wealth—its influence. First: Upon the mind of its possessor. It tends to promote haughtiness and insolence. " The rich answereth roughly." The rich, it should be observed, who are most liable to this abominable spirit, are those who have *suddenly* become wealthy. The manufacturer, the merchant, the joint-stock speculator, who have risen rapidly from comparative indigence to opulence, are as a rule the most supercilious, haughty, and insolent. They lack generally the intelligence, the culture, and refinement necessary to control the pride which the gratification of their greed engenders. The influence of wealth is revealed—Secondly: Upon the mind of the wealthy man's circle. " Wealth maketh many friends." " Many will entreat the favour of the prince." Riches tempt those who live around the possessor to cringe, fawn, and flatter. They tend to the promotion of a base servility. "Wealth maketh many friends."—" Friends!"—fawning flatterers—base parasites—snivelling sycophants. The verses present to us—

THE SELFISHNESS OF SOCIETY.—" Every man is a friend to him that giveth gifts." "All the brethren of the poor do hate him; how much more do his friends go far from him? He pursueth them with words, yet they are wanting to him." Here is a revelation of social selfishness! Poor men, however good, deserted because they cannot help us, rich men, however wicked, followed because they have the power to do a service. Does not this spirit of selfishness run through all society? Men are not honoured because of what they are. but because of what they have, not for their character but for their cash, not for their mind but for their money. This selfishness is the curse, the disgrace of our race: it is the essence of sin, the bond of slavery, the fontal source of all our social misery.

Proverbs 19:1

The Better Man

"Better *is* the poor that walketh in his integrity, than *he that is* perverse in his lips, and is a fool." *

THERE is another antithesis implied here that is not expressed. The introduction of the word "rich" will convey, I think, the writer's idea. The verse might be rendered thus, "Better is the poor that walketh in his integrity, than the rich that is perverse in his lips and is a fool." The sentiment is that a poor godly man is better than a wealthy wicked man—a man that is "perverse in his lips" and is a "fool." This may be illustrated by two remarks.

HE IS A "BETTER" MAN IN HIMSELF.—First: He is a better character. A man's real worth is determined, not by his circumstances, but by his character; not by his outward condition but by his inner principles; not by his surroundings, but by his soul. "As a man thinketh in his heart, so is he." So is he in respect to all real worth and dignity in human nature. Contrast the principles of the two. Contrast sensuality with spirituality, falsehood with truth, integrity with dishonesty, practical godliness with practical atheism. Contrast the worth of the two. What is secular to spiritual wealth? The one is contingent, the other is absolute; the one is vital, the other is alienable; the one is an essential blessing, the other may be a bane. The ungodly man leaves his wealth behind, the godly poor carries it with him wherever he goes. Secondly: He has better enjoyments. He has purer loves, higher hopes, and loftier fellowships. His happiness is from within, it springs up as a well of water into everlasting life. The happiness of the ungodly rich, such as it is, is all derived from the contingent, the fleeting and the perishing.

HE IS A "BETTER" MAN TO OTHERS.—He is a "better" *relation*. He is a better husband, son, brother, master, ser-

* The preceding verse we have noticed in a former Reading.

vant. He is a "better" *neighbour*. More considerate, respectful, tender, sympathetic. He is a "better" *citizen*. He has a nobler loyalty, a higher patriotism, a deeper philanthropy. The stability and progress of nations depend upon the virtues which he cultivates, developes, and promotes.

A word to thee, my poor pious friend. Do not repine at thy condition. Banish for ever the idea that because thou hast not wealth thou art dealt hardly with in this world. There are many things, even apart from piety, far better than riches. *Health* is "better." Wouldst thou not sooner be a healthy man in a cottage than a diseased being upon a throne? *Each of the senses* is "better." Wouldst thou not sooner be a humble labourer, enjoying the full use of all thy senses, than dwell in the greatest opulence, without the power of hearing or of vision? *Intellect* is "better" than wealth. Wouldst thou not rather have a mind capable of grasping the universal, and sympathising with the beautiful and good everywhere, than live in palaces and wander on acres of thine own with enfeebled soul? If God has given thee but one grain of good brain more than He has to thy rich neighbour, is not that of more value to thee than all the acres of the globe? *Knowledge* is "better." Wouldst thou not rather have thy intellect richly stored with the facts of universal history, the scenes of various countries, the principles of Divine government, than own a continent, with a weak and empty mind? *Friendship* is "better." To possess the love of a true heart, the sympathy of a noble soul, is better than to be a desolate millionaire. *Godliness* is better than all. Do not therefore envy the rich. Rise to that altitude of spirit that will enable thee to mourn over the poverty of princes, and weep over the degradation of kings.

Proverbs 19:2-3

The Soul Without Knowledge

"Also, *that* the soul *be* without knowledge, *it is* not good; and he that hasteth with *his* feet sinneth. The foolishness of man perverteth his way: and his heart fretteth against the Lord."

THE connection of the two clauses of the first verse above has led critics to attach different senses to the word "knowledge," and has given rise to various translations to convey what each has conceived to be the sense. "It is not good for the soul to be without *caution*, for he that hasteth with his feet sinneth." "Quickness of action, without prudence of spirit, is not good, for he that hasteth with his feet sinneth." "Fervent zeal without prudence is not good, for he that hasteth with his feet sinneth." "Ignorance of one's self is not good, and he that is hasty of foot sinneth." "These various renderings," says a modern expositor, "express respectively correct sentiments and truths of practical value." But there does not appear the least necessity for any alteration of the received version. These two verses present two facts to our notice in relation to ignorance.

That ignorance is NOT GOOD for the soul.—"That the soul be without knowledge it is not good." This will appear if we consider—First: That an ignorant soul is exceedingly confined. The sphere of the mind's operations is the facts and circumstances with which it is acquainted. It cannot range beyond what it knows. The more limited its information, the narrower is the scene of its activities. The man of enlarged scientific information has a range over vast continents, whereas the ignorant man is confined within the cell of his senses. Our souls get scope by exploring the unknown. "Knowledge," says Shakespeare, "is the wing on which we fly to heaven." Secondly: That an ignorant soul is exceedingly benighted. The contracted sphere in which he lives is only lighted with the rushlight of a few crude thoughts and traditional notions. So dark is the atmosphere of the soul, that it knows not how or whither to move. Knowledge is light. The accession of every true idea is a planting of a new star in the mental heavens. The more knowledge the brighter will sparkle the sky of our being. Thirdly: That an ignorant soul is exceedingly feeble. Exercise and food are as essential to the power of the mind as they are to the power of the body. Knowledge is at at once the incentive to exercise and the aliment to strengthen. Mind without knowledge is like a full-grown body, which has never had any exercise or wholesome food; there are all the limbs and organs complete, but there is no walking and no work. "Ignorance," says Johnson, "is mere privation, by which nothing can be produced; it is a vacuity in which the soul sits motionless and torpid for want of attraction. And, without knowing why, we always rejoice when we learn, and grieve when we forget." Truly the soul without knowledge is not good. Of what good are limbs without the power of exercise; what good are eyes without light?

The other fact that the verses present to us is:

That ignorance is PERILOUS to the soul.—Ignorance is more than a negative evil; it is a positive curse. The verses teach that ignorance—First: Exposes to sinful haste. "He that hasteth with his feet sinneth." Men without knowledge are ever in danger of acting incautiously, acting with a reckless haste. As a rule the more ignorant a man is, the more hasty he is in the conclusions of his judgment and the flash of his passions. The less informed the mind is, the more rapid and reckless in its generalisation. The cause of science has suffered not a little from this haste. Impulse, not intelligence, is the helmsman of the ignorant soul. The verses teach that ignorance—Secondly: Exposes to a perversity of conduct. "The foolishness of man perverteth his way." What is foolishness but ignorance? Ignorant men are terribly liable to perversity of conduct in every relation of life, and especially in relation to the great God. The murderers of Christ were ignorant. "They know not what they do," said Christ. And Paul says, "had they known it they would not have crucified the Lord of glory." The verses teach that ignorance—Thirdly: Exposes to impiety of feeling. "His heart fretteth against the Lord." Thus the ignorant Israelites did in the wilderness. And ignorant men are ever disposed to find fault with their Maker. "The way of the Lord is not equal." This has ever been their charge. Ignorance is always petulant and fretful. It is an awful sin to fret against the Lord. "Woe unto him that striveth with his maker! Let the potsherds strive with the potsherds of the earth. Shall the clay say to him that fashioneth it, What makest thou? or thy work, He hath no hands!"

Get knowledge, my brother. A nation of ignorant souls is not only a nation of worthless men, but a nation liable to the commission of flagrant mistakes and crimes. Men should get knowledge for the sake of becoming useful. "I would advise all in general," says Lord Bacon, "that they would take into serious consideration the true and genuine ends of knowledge; that they seek it not either for pleasure, or contention, or contempt of others, or for profit, or for fame, or for honour and promotion, or such like adulterate or inferior ends, but for merit and emolument of life, that they may regulate and perfect the same in charity."

Proverbs 19:5, 9

Falsehood

"A false witness shall not be unpunished, and *he that* speaketh lies shall not escape." *

"A false witness shall not be unpunished, and *he that* speaketh lies shall perish."

THE world abounds in falsehood. Lies swarm in every department of life. They are in the market, on the hustings, in courts of justice, in the senate house, in the

* Verse 4 has been discussed in a previous Reading.

sanctuaries of religion; and they crowd the very pages of modern literature. They infest the social atmosphere. Men on all hands live in fiction and by fiction. Everywhere they walk in a vain show. The general truth contained in the passage before us is, *that falsehood leads to ruin.* "He that speaketh lies shall perish. Falsehood is ruinous to REPUTATION.—A good reputation is to every man a priceless gem. But the "false witness," the liar, endangers this. When his prevarications and falsities are discovered, his reputation perishes. Give a man the brand of a perjurer, or a liar, and what a worthless wretch he appears moving through society! It is ruinous to INFLUENCE. —What influence has a known liar in society? What esteem can he awaken? What confidence can he inspire? What credit can he gain? He is suspected, he is despised! When Aristotle was asked what a man could gain by telling a falsehood, he replied, "Never to be credited when he speaks the truth." It is ruinous to the SOUL.— The virtue and happiness of a moral being depend upon the conformity of his language and life to *reality*. The false man destroys the strength, the freedom, the happiness of his soul; he lives in a house built upon the sand; ruin is inevitable. "Falsehood," says Coleridge, " is fire in stubble. It likewise turns all the light stuff around it into its own substance for a moment—one crackling, blazing moment, and then dies. And all its contents are scattered in the wind without place or evidence of their existence, as viewless as the wind which scatters them."

Proverbs 19:11-12; 19:19

Anger, Controlled and Uncontrolled

"The discretion of a men deferreth his anger; and *it is* his glory to pass over a transgression. The king's wrath *is* as the roaring of a lion; but his favour *is* as dew upon the grass." *

"A man of great wrath shall suffer punishment: for if thou deliver *him*, yet thou must do it again."

ANGER is an affection inherent in our nature. It is therefore not wrong in itself, it is wrong only when it is directed to wrong objects, or to right objects in a wrong degree of amount and duration. Anger in itself is as holy a passion as love. Indeed, in its legitimate form it is but a development of love :—love indignant with that which is opposed to the cause of right and happiness. Albeit like every affection of our nature, it is often sadly perverted, it not unfrequently becomes malignant and furious. The passage presents anger to us in two aspects, controlled and uncontrolled.

CONTROLLED.—" The discretion of a man deferreth his anger; and it is his glory to pass over a transgression." The wise man is liable to this passion, and circumstances in his life frequently occur to evoke it. It rushes up within him, and its instinct is for revenge, but he forbears. Instead of acting under its impulse, he waits until its fires cool down. It is said of Julius Cæsar, that when provoked, he used to repeat the whole Roman alphabet before he suffered himself to speak; and Plato once said to his servant, "I would beat thee but I am angry." It is noble to see a man holding a calm mastery over the billows of his own passions, bidding them to go so far and no farther. The man that cannot control his anger is like a ship in a tumultuous sea with the devil for its pilot. "It is his glory to pass over a transgression." This is something more than postponing its avengement, it is

* Verses 6, 7, 8, 9, 10 have been discussed in other Readings.

checking it. It is blowing out its first sparks, it is crushing it in its very germ. This is "glory." It is a splendid conquest. He who governs himself is a true king.

We have anger here—

UNCONTROLLED.—The verses suggest two remarks in relation to uncontrolled anger. First: It is sometimes terrible. "The king's wrath is as the roaring of a lion." This is the most savage of beasts, and his roar the most terrific of sounds. Shame on the king who gives vent to ungovernable wrath. The office he holds binds him more than others to control his own passions. He who cannot govern himself has no right to attempt the governing of others. He sits as an usurper upon the throne of a nation. It is a lamentable fact that kings have shown less command over their evil tempers than have the ordinary run of mankind. It is implied that their temper affects the nation. Their anger terrifies the people like the "roar of a lion," their favour is as refreshing and blessed as the "dew upon the grass." Secondly: It is always self-injurious. "A man of great wrath shall suffer punishment; for if thou deliver him, yet thou must do it again." Violent passions ever inflict their own punishment upon their unhappy subjects. When a man allows himself to be flooded with angry feelings he injures his own body. They set the blood flowing too quickly for its narrow channels; they tend to disorganize the whole physical frame as the burning cheek, the throbbing temple, and the quivering lip declare. But they injure the soul too in a variety of ways. Well does Pope say, "To be angry is to revenge others' faults upon ourselves." Anger is misery.

> "Anger is like
> A full hot horse, who, being allowed his way,
> Self-mettle tires him."— SHAKESPEARE

There is an old proverb that anger is "like ashes, which fly back in the face of him who throws them." Dr. Arnold, when at Laleham, once lost all patience with a dull scholar, when the pupil looked up in his face, and said, "Why do you speak angrily, sir? Indeed I am doing the best I can." Years after he used to tell the story to his children, and say, "I never felt so ashamed of myself in my life. That look and that speech I have never forgotten." When the frenzy runs high, the "man of great wrath" gores right and left, like a wild bull, all who are within his reach; but, when it has subsided, he is tormented by a remorse from which the brute is free.

Brothers, we are commanded to be angry and sin not, and not to let the sun go down on our wrath. William the Conqueror commanded the English, when the curfew bell rang, to put out their fires and to extinguish their candles. Let us not allow the Sun ever to pass from our horizon with any sparks of anger in the breast.

Proverbs 19:13-14

A Cursed Home and a Blessed Home

"A foolish son *is* the calamity of his father: and the contentions of a wife *are* a continual dropping. House and riches *are* the inheritance of fathers: and a prudent wife *is* from the LORD."

"HOME," says the late illustrious Robertson, of Brighton, " is the one place in all this world where hearts are sure of each other. It is the place of confidence. It is the place where we tear off that mask of guarded and suspicious coldness which the world forces us to wear in self-defence, and where we pour out the unreserved communications of full and confiding hearts. It is the spot where expressions of tenderness gush out without any sensation of awkwardness, and without any dread of ridicule." This is an ideal home. Would that in all families it were realized! The verses before us present to us—

A Home CURSED.—There are many things that curse a home in this sinful world. Two things are mentioned here. First: "A foolish son." We have had occasion more than once to refer to the foolish son. Who is he? A son who does not reciprocate his parents' love, does not acknowledge his parents' kindness, does not recognize his parents' rule. Such a son is "the calamity of his father." "Many," says an old expositor, "are the miseries of a man's life, but none like that which cometh from him who should be the stay of his life." Secondly: A contentious wife. An ill-tempered, irritable, and irritating wife is indeed a curse to a home. It is as a "continual dropping." You are in a house where the rain is constantly dropping from the roof into every room, there is no corner where it does not come, wherever you stand or sit irritating drops descend upon your head, damaging your clothes and furniture too. Your temper is irritated, and your goods are running to ruin. Such is the figure in which Solomon sets forth the baneful influence of a contentious wife. "A continual dropping" is said to be one of the engines which the wit of man contrived when it was put upon the stretch for the means of torturing his fellows. The victim was so placed that a drop of water continued to fall at regular intervals on his naked head. With length of time, and no hope of relief, the agony becomes excruciating, and either the patient's reason or his life gives way. The contentious wife breaks the heart of her husband as well as destroys the comfort of her home.

These two things are undoubtedly a curse to a home. "What shall be said," says a modern writer, "when the two evils of this verse unite? There cannot be a case more pitiable. Under the former alone a man may be sustained and comforted by the cheering society and converse of a fond wife, the sharer and the soother of his sorrows, as he is of hers; and under the latter alone his misery may be not a little mitigated by the prudence, the sympathy, and the aid of a pious and affectionate son. But when the two come together—how deplorable!—the husband and the father alike wretched—neither relation alleviating, but each aggravating the affliction of the other!" We have here—

A Home BLESSED.—First: Blest with wealth as an inheritance. "Houses and riches are the inheritance of fathers." The value of wealth in making a home comfortable, cheerful, and attractive will not be doubted. Wealth is a blessing. When rightly used it adds greatly to our power, our usefulness, and enjoyments. Secondly: Blest with a prudent wife as a "gift from the Lord." "A prudent wife" is elsewhere called a virtuous woman. She is one who loves her husband and her children, is discreet, chaste, a keeper at home, good, obedient to her own husband. Such a woman is "from the Lord." Her goodness is from the Lord, all her useful attributes are His endowments, and His providence brought her into the possession of her husband. It is His gift. Solomon indicates a contrast between these two blessings. He intimates that one is more directly "from the Lord" than the other. "Houses and riches are the inheritance of fathers." They are often transmitted from sire to son. But a "prudent wife" is from the Lord. The blessing is more directly and manifestly His bestowment. "The history of Ruth beautifully illustrates the train of matrimonial Providence. The Moabitess married, contrary to all human probability, a man of Israel, that she might be brought into Naomi's family, return with her to her own land, and in course of filial duty be brought under the eye, and drawn to the heart of Boaz, her appointed husband."

Proverbs 19:8, 16

Goodness and Happiness

"He that getteth wisdom loveth his own soul: he that keepeth understanding shall find good."

"He that keepeth the commandment keepeth his own soul: *but* he that despiseth his ways shall die." *

SOLOMON, like other of the inspired writers, frequently employs different words to represent the same thing. In

---

* The subject of this verse has been discussed in a former Reading.

the verses before us there are no less than three words to represent one thing—religion. "Wisdom," "understanding," "commandment." Religion is a subject of such transcendent importance, and so many sided, that no one term could possibly set it forth. The verses suggest two remarks.

THAT SPIRITUAL GOODNESS IS THE GRAND OBJECT OF LIFE.—In what does spiritual goodness consist? An answer can be got from the verses. First: In getting the true thing. "He that getteth wisdom." It is not a thing which comes into the soul irrespective of our choice and effort. It must be sought after with earnestness and perseverance. "Getteth wisdom."—"With all thy getting get understanding." Secondly: In retaining the true thing. "He that keepeth understanding." There is a possibility of losing it, after having gained it by immense effort. Men have fallen, therefore it must be retained by watchfulness and prayer. "Buy the truth and sell it not." When you have got it hold it with all the tenacity of your being. Thirdly: In acting out the true thing. "He that keepeth the commandment." Religion is not a mere truth, gained by study and retained by holy watchfulness in the soul. It is truth translated into actions, embodied into life. It is keeping the commandment. "If a man love me he will keep my commandments." Such is the sketch of goodness and religion as given in these verses. Elsewhere it is represented in other forms, such as "honouring Christ," "glorifying God," "repenting," and "believing." Our point is that to become religious is the grand end of our existence. Nothing higher than this *can* be aimed at. It is higher than Heaven. What *can* be greater than to become like God? Nothing lower *should* be aimed at. The man who aims at something lower than this, something less than to become religious and godlike, wastes his energies and misses the end of his being. Goodness is the heaven of souls. There is no other Heaven. The verses suggest—

THAT HAPPINESS IS THE OUTCOME OF SPIRITUAL GOODNESS.—We are told here that he who gets, retains, and practises this divine thing " loveth his own soul," "keepeth his own soul," and that he who does it not "shall die." " He who findeth me," says religion, " findeth life." And again it says, " He who sinneth against me, sinneth against his own life; whoso loveth me hateth death." How is a man to get true happiness? Not by seeking it as an end, but by becoming good—out of goodness will bloom this Paradise. " This is life eternal, to know Thee, the only true God, and Jesus Christ whom Thou hast sent." True blessedness is to be found in the true idea, the true affection, the true deed. Who is the man that really " loveth his own soul "? Not the man that is struggling everlastingly after his own happiness, whether in the world or in religion. But the man who is striving after goodness, who is following on to know the Lord, who is " forgetting those things which are behind, and reaching forth unto those things that are before, pressing toward the mark for the prize of the high calling of God in Christ Jesus."

Proverbs 19:17

The Deserving Poor

" He that hath pity upon the poor lendeth unto the LORD: and that which he hath given will he pay him again."

WE are told that the poor shall never cease out of the land. Paley defines a poor man, as he, of whatever rank, whose expenses exceed his resources. It is very clear from this that there may be poverty which has no claim to our commiseration and charity. For bad management, extravagance, and indolence, which are crimes, originate a great deal of a certain kind of indigence. There is, however, in all neighbourhoods, and ever has been, a large amount of *deserving* poverty—poverty that has come on by oppressions, misfortunes, and afflictions. The verses lead us to consider three things in relation to the deserving poor.

MAN'S DUTY towards the deserving poor.—" He that hath pity on the poor." Two things are implied concerning this pity.

First: It must be practical. The text speaks of it as "lending to the Lord." It is pity, therefore, that gives, in order to relieve distress. The pity that goes off in sentimental sighs, or proceeds no farther than words, saying, "Depart in peace, be warmed, be filled," is not true pity—the pity that God demands. It is a practical pity. "Is not this the fast that I have chosen, to deal thy bread to the hungry, that thou bring the poor that are cast out to thy house, when thou seest the naked that thou cover him." Secondly: It must be genuine. The words imply that the pity is accepted of the Lord. He takes it as a *loan*, therefore it must be genuine. The service rendered is from right principles. There is a large amount of charity shown to the poor which is inspired by motives abhorrent to Omniscient Purity. Some give because it is respectable; some because it tends to a little fame; some in the hope of a return in some form or other; some from the feeling of self-righteousness, hoping thereby to secure the favour of God. All this is spurious charity—charity that God will not, cannot accept as a loan. The charity which is a *loan* to the Lord must be a genuine, disinterested, and loving gift to the poor. Again, this verse leads us to consider—

GOD'S INTEREST in the deserving poor.—So deep is His interest in the poor that He regards a genuine gift to them as a *loan* to Him. God's interest in the poor is shown in three ways. First: In the obligation that is imposed on the rich to help them. He denounces all neglect and cruelty of the poor. "Woe unto him that buildeth his house by unrighteousness and his chamber by wrong, that useth his neighbour's service without wages." Again, "Whoso mocketh the poor reproacheth his Maker." Again, "What mean ye that ye beat my people to pieces and grind the faces of the poor?" Again, "Whoso stoppeth his ears to the cry of the poor, he also shall cry himself but shall not be heard." He inculcates practical sympathy for the poor. Secondly: In the earthly condition into which He sent His Son. Christ came of the poor. He descended into "the lower parts of the earth." His parents were poor. His associates were poor. He Himself was poor. "He had nowhere to lay His head." Thirdly: In the class from which He selected His servants. His greatest prophets in olden times were ploughmen and shepherds. His apostles were the fishermen and the tentmaker. He chose the poor of this world to be His disciples and apostles. Once more, this verse leads us to consider—

GOD'S ACKOWLEDGMENT OF SERVICE RENDERED TO THE DESERVING POOR.—"And that which he hath given will He pay him again." Every gift of genuine piety to the poor is a loan to the Lord, and a loan that shall be paid. It is often amply repaid in this world, and it will be acknowledged in the day of judgment. "Inasmuch as ye have done it unto the least of these my brethren, ye have done it unto me."

Let us remember the poor. It is a sacred and religious duty. "It is pure and undefiled religion." "God," says Jeremy Taylor, "is pleased with no music below so much as in the thanksgiving songs of relieved widows, of supported orphans, of rejoicing and comforted and thankful persons. This part of our communication does the work of God and our neighbours, and bears us to heaven in streams made by the overflowing of our brother's comfort."

Proverbs 19:18, 20

Parental Discipline and Filial Improvement

"Chasten thy son while there is hope, and let not thy soul spare for his crying."

"Hear counsel, and receive instruction, that thou mayest be wise in thy latter end." *

THE subject of these words is parental discipline and filial improvement.

* The 19th verse has been discussed in a former Reading.

PARENTAL DISCIPLINE.—The words teach, First: That parental discipline should always be timely. "Chasten thy son while there is hope." There is a period for discipline in the experience of every child. Of all periods it is the most important: it does not extend over many years; it is the character-forming period—the period when there are in the mind no set principles, no favourite notions, no settled habits. The soil is fresh and without weeds; the sapling is tender and can be turned to any shape; the wax is soft and can receive any impression. That is the time for discipline. Woe to the parent who neglects this period; and great the calamity to his child. Secondly: Parental discipline is sometimes painful. "Let not thy soul spare for his crying." It is sometimes painful to the child. The greatest pain is not that inflicted by corporeal punishment: the material rod is not the most painful, nor is it the most effective. It is the rod of truth, the rod of displeased love, the rod that does not touch the flesh but the heart. It is sometimes painful to the parent. No true parent can in his discipline inflict so much pain upon his child as he himself experiences. He who inflicts pain upon his child from passion and revenge may experience some gratification in his unmanly and infernal work; but he who does it purely for the child's good is distressed to the very soul: he stabs his own heart—his love bleeds. Thirdly: Parental discipline should ever be firm. "Let not thy soul spare for his crying." The child's tears may distress you, his shrieks may go to your soul and unman you—still be firm. The evil that you seek to crush must be crushed, or your child will be damned. Calmly keep your object in view. Desist only when the child cries, not on account of the rod, but on account of the fault. There is a parental indulgence that is the greatest curse to children. Eli an example.

> " The voice of parents is the voice of God,
> For to their children they are heaven's lieutenants;
> Made fathers, not for common uses merely,
> But to steer
> The wanton freight of youth through storms and dangers,
> Which, with full sails they bear upon, and straighten

> The mortal line of life they bend so often.
> For these are we made fathers, and for these
> May challenge duty on our children's part.
> Obedience is the sacrifice of angels,
> Whose form you carry."—SHAKESPEARE

FILIAL IMPROVEMENT.—Observe, First: The conditions of improvement. "Hear counsel and receive instruction." Truth speaks everywhere—in nature, in human history, in the Scriptures of God. But men do not hear, they are deaf. The first thing is to listen to her voice. "Receive instruction." Take it into the *understanding*, the *affections*, the *life*. Take it in as the very food of the soul; digest it well, so that it become the very blood of life. Secondly: The purpose of improvement. "That thou mayest be wise in thy latter end." A wise man is one who thinks, feels, and acts wisely in all things—a man that realizes the grand idea of his being—a good man. Now, whilst goodness is always important, its importance will be specially felt in the "latter end"—the end that awaits us all; the end that ends all our connections with this life; that ushers us consciously into the spiritual, retributive and eternal. It is a sad thing to live a fool; it is a sadder thing to die one. Men who were counted wise by the world were fools in their latter end. Voltaire said, "I will give you half of what I am worth if you will give me six months' life." Gibbon said, "All was dark and doubtful." Hobbs said, "I am taking a leap in the dark."

Proverbs 19:21

The Mind of Man and the Mind of God

"*There are* many devices in a man's heart: nevertheless the counsel of the LORD, that shall stand."

THESE words bring under our notice the mind of man and the mind of God. Man has a mind, or rather man *is* mind.

He is spiritual, rational, free, moral, immortal. God is mind. He is a spirit. Man's mind is the offspring of the Divine, and there is a resemblance between them.

The verse implies—

That the mind of man has "MANY DEVICES," the mind of God has but ONE COUNSEL.—"There are many devices in a man's heart." Every man's soul teems with devices, devices concerning pleasure, commerce, politics, religion. These "devices" are often selfish, ambitious, malignant, impious. As they are generated by different dispositions of heart, they have no *unity* amongst themselves; they are often in fierce battle, and fill the soul with confusion. But the mind of God has *one* purpose, "the counsel of the Lord." All God's thoughts are but phases of one eternal purpose, that takes in the universe, and runs through the ages.

The verse implies—

That the mind of man is SUBORDINATE, the mind of God SUPREME.—This is implied here, and fully expressed in many other places of the Bible. "A man's heart deviseth the way, but the Lord directeth his steps." "O Lord, I know that the way of man is not in himself; it is not in man that walketh to direct his steps." First: This is a fact well attested by history. The "devices" of Joseph's brethren He subordinated to His own purpose. The "devices" of Pharaoh to destroy all the babes of Israel were, through the preservation of Moses, subordinated to the working out of God's purpose in the emancipation of the Jews from Egyptian thraldom. The "devices" of the Scribes and Pharisees, leading to the crucifixion of the Son of God, were overruled for the development of His "determinate counsel." The passing of the fugitive law, which required every American citizen to deliver up the fleeing African into the hands of his pursuers, and which was passed in order to strengthen the dominion of slavery, led, under God, to the production of such literature on the question, as snapped the chains of four million human beings, and made them free citizens of the world. Secondly: This is a fact that reveals the greatness of God. I see the greatness of God in controlling the material universe, but I see more of His greatness in controlling the hostile elements of moral mind, than in directing the elements of nature. "He maketh the wrath of man to praise him." It has been said that the 104th Psalm is a hymn to God in material nature, and the 105th Psalm a hymn to Him in human history.

The verse implies—

That the mind of man is CHANGEABLE, the mind of God is UNALTERABLE.—"The counsel of the Lord, that shall stand." However numerous "devices" are, let them be as the sands on the sea-shore, or the drops that make up the ocean, however antagonistic to the Divine mind, however skilfully organized, and backed by all the battalions of hell and earth, they will not shake God's "counsel." They will no more affect His purpose than a whiff of smoke can shake the stars. "There is no wisdom, nor understanding, nor counsel against the Lord."

Learn the *inevitable* fall of all that is opposed to the will of God. Whatever in systems and institutions, whatever in commerce, politics, or religion; whatever in Church or state is opposed to the "counsel of the Lord," must inevitably totter and fall. And learn the *inevitable* fulfilment of all His promises.

Whatever He has purposed shall be accomplished. His eternal counsel moves on, nothing can hinder it. All the volcanoes, thunders, lightnings, tornadoes, united together on this earth, and shaking it to its centre, cannot hinder for one instant the sun in his majestic march, nor can all the opposition of earth and hell united prevent the Eternal accomplishing all the promises of His word.

> "There is a power
> Unseen, that rules the illimitable world;
> That guides its motions, from the brightest star,
> To the least dust of this sin-stained mould;
> While man, who madly deems himself the lord
> Of all, is nought but weakness and dependence.
> This sacred trust, by sure experience taught,
> Thou must have learnt when wandering all alone:
> Each bird, each insect, flitting through the sky,
> Was more sufficient for itself than thou."—THOMPSON

Proverbs 19:22

Kindness

"The desire of a man *is* his kindness: and a poor man *is* better than a liar."

IT is implied in these words—

That kindness is a GOOD THING.—Solomon means to say that kindness even as a "desire" is a good thing. If there were no words to express it, no means to gratify it, still as a desire it is good. It is good in itself. Love is the essence of virtue. It is what God approves, it is like Himself. It is good in its influence upon the possessor. The mind under the influence of love is free, cheerful, sunny. It is good in its bearing upon society. The society of a kind and loving soul is congenial and useful.

It is implied—

That this good thing may exist ONLY IN DESIRE.—"The desire of a man is his kindness." The meaning is that *kindness* must be measured by the amount of a man's *desires* to do good, rather than by the amount of his *ability*. There are cases when it can only exist as a "*desire.*" There are thousands who have kindness towards the suffering and distressed, but who are entirely destitute of the means to render help. Our Great Master appreciates kindness in this form. "If there be a willing mind it is accepted according to that a man hath, and not according to that he hath not." David's desire to build the Temple was as acceptable to God as if he had actually reared the magnificent edifice.

It is implied—

That kindness as a desire WITHOUT MEANS, is "better" than as WORDS with ABILITY.—"A poor man is better than a liar." The poor man here must be regarded as the man who has kindness in his heart, but is destitute of ability, and "the liar" as the man who has plenty of ability, and whose kindness is merely in generous talk. There are many such. There are many who talk as if their hearts were full of love. Their language would lead you to infer that their love was strong enough to remove all misery from the world if they had the means, but it is all talk. Their kindness is a blossom that never turns into fruit.

These men are the hollowest shams, they are living lies. Far better is the poor man who has kindness in his heart than such a "liar." He is better in himself, better in the eye of the good, better in the estimation of Heaven.

> "It is a little thing,
> To give a cup of water; and yet its draught
> Of cool refreshment, drained by feverish lips,
> May send a shock of pleasure to the soul
> More exquisite by far than when nectarious juice
> Renews the life of joy in happiest hour."—TALFOURD.

Proverbs 19:23

The Fruits of Personal Religion

"The fear of the LORD tendeth to life: and he that hath it shall abide satisfied; he shall not be visited with evil."

THE expression, "he that hath it" is not in the original; it has been supplied by our translators. The words have been rendered thus, "The fear of the Lord is life, and who hath it shall rest; he shall not be visited with evil." We do not see that this rendering has any idea more than what is in our version. The subject is the fruits of personal religion. "The fear of the Lord," here, as elsewhere, stands for religion. It is a loving, loyal, reverence for God. And this has threefold fruit.

VITALITY.—It "tendeth to life." It is conducive to bodily life. Intelligent religion leads its possessor to attend to the laws of physical health and happiness. It is conducive to intellectual life. Love to God stimulates the intellect to study Him and His works. It is conducive to spiritual life—the life of pure affections, high aims, and virtuous deeds. Another fruit is—

SATISFACTION.—"Shall abide satisfied." It pacifies the conscience. The sense of guilt, which gnaws and distresses the soul, it removes, and infuses in its place "joy and peace in believing." It reconciles to providence. It makes a man acquiesce in his lot, to say, "Not my will, but Thine be done." It causes him to rejoice in hope of the glory of God. Another fruit is—

SAFETY.—"He shall not be visited with evil." He may have sufferings, but sufferings in this case will not be evils, they will be blessings in disguise. "His light afflictions will work out a far more exceeding and eternal weight of glory." They will not separate him from the love of God. In all tribulations he will rejoice. He will not be *visited* with any event that will damage his interests or endanger his soul. "God is his refuge and strength." A high, secure, impregnable fortress this!

Proverbs 19:24

Laziness

"A slothful *man* hideth his hand in *his* bosom, and will not so much as bring it to his mouth again."

MOST critics substitute the word *dish* for bosom here. "A slothful man hideth his hand in his dish." This certainly makes the description of the lazy man more graphic. His repast is provided for him. It is spread before him, but he is too lazy to take it; he drops his hand in the dish. He is not only too lazy to earn his food by honest labour, and to prepare it for his own use, but when it is there he is almost too indolent to raise it to his mouth. He who is "slow at meat is slow at work." Indolence becomes more and more strong as it is yielded to. Sloth in some natures is nursed to a sovereignty. The less a man exerts himself, the more indisposed he becomes to exertion, until at last the slightest effort becomes a felt inconvenience. This laziness may be seen in different departments of life. IN WORDLY CONCERNS.—There are men before whom Providence has brought the "dish," containing all the conditions of affluence and social prosperity, but the man is too lazy to put his hand to it. He sits and yawns and says,—it is time enough to begin. Laziness has brought many a man, who might have been in affluence, to wretched pauperism. It may be seen—IN INTELLECTUAL MATTERS.—The "dish" of knowledge is laid before a lazy man; he has books, leisure, money, everything in fact to enable him to enrich his mind with knowledge, and train his faculties for distinguished work in the realm of science, but he is too lazy.

His mind becomes enfeebled and diseased for the want of exercise. It may be seen—IN SPIRITUAL INTERESTS.—Gospel provisions are laid before the lazy man. There are the "unsearchable riches of Christ;" there is the "crown of glory;" but he is too indolent to make any exertion to participate in the heavenly blessings. "Go thy way for this time," he says, "and when I have a convenient season I will send for thee." Pollock has well described the indolent soul:

> " Sloth lay till mid-day, turning on his couch,
> Like ponderous door upon its weary hinge;
> And having rolled him out, with much ado,
> And many a dismal sigh, and vain attempt,
> He sauntered out accoutred carelessly,
> With half-op'd, misty, unobservant eye,
> Somniferous, that weighed the object down
> On which its burden fed – an hour or two;
> Then, with a groan, retired to rest again."

Proverbs 19:25

Man Chastising the Wrong

"Smite a scorner, and the simple will beware: and reprove one that hath understanding, *and* he will understand knowledge."

THESE words imply certain truths that are worthy of note.

Wrong may exist in very DIFFERENT CHARACTERS.—There are three characters mentioned in the passage—(1) "The scorner." The scorner is a character made up of pride, irreverence, and cruelty. He mocks at sin; he scoffs at religion. He looks with a haughty contempt upon those opinions which agree not with his own. (2) "The simple." The simple man is he who is more or less unsophisticated in mind, and untainted by crime. One who is inexperienced, unsuspicious, confiding, and impressible. (3) "One that understandeth knowledge." This is a character whom Solomon represents in other places as the just man, the wise man, the prudent man, expressions which with him mean *personal religion*. These three characters, therefore, may comprise;—the man *against* religion, the man *without* religion, and the man *with* religion. And it is implied here that there may be wrong in connection with all. The "scorner" is thoroughly wrong. The simple is potentially wrong. He that "hath understanding" is occasionally wrong, or he would not require "reproof."

It is implied—

That wrong in all characters SHOULD BE CHASTISED.—" Smite a scorner and the simple will beware, and reprove one that hath understanding and he will understand knowledge." It is not only the duty of *rulers* to punish crime, but it is the duty of every *honest man to inflict chastisement* upon wrong wherever it is seen. He can do so in many ways, without violence, without breaking the public peace, without the infringement of any human rights. The withdrawal of patronage, separation from the offenders' society, social ostracism, the administration of reproof, and the expression of displeasure, are amongst the means by which an honest man, even in his private capacity, can chastise the wrong. Every honest man not only can but should punish wrong whenever he sees it. "Do not I hate them, O God, that hate thee. Gather not my soul with sinners."

It is implied—

That the kind of chastisement should be ACCORDING TO CHARACTER.—"The scorner" is to be *smitten*. "Smite a scorner." The man of "understanding" is to be reproved. Reproof to an inveterate scorner would be useless. "Give not that which is holy unto the dogs, neither cast ye your pearls before swine, lest they trample them under their feet and turn again and rend you." "He that reproveth a scorner," says Solomon, in another place, "getteth unto himself shame." The scorner requires the smiting of silent contempt, withering sarcasm, slashing invective. It was by silent contempt that the holy Jesus smote the scorning Pilate. But whilst the scorner requires smiting and not reproof, the man of understanding requires reproof and not smiting. He has fallen into error, and what he requires is to have the error pointed out—its moral enormity exposed. His wrong is not the *rule* but the *exception* of his life. He has fallen into it, he has been overcome of evil, and he must be dealt with by justice tempered with kindness. "Brethren, if a man be overtaken in fault, ye that are spiritual restore him."

It is implied—

That the EFFECTS of the chastisement will vary according to the character.—First: The chastisement inflicted upon the scorner will be rather a benefit to others than to himself. "Smite a scorner, and the *simple* will beware." He is to be punished not merely for his own sake, but as a warning to others—to put the simple and unsophisticated on their guard. Severity towards the incorrigible may act as a warning to others. Secondly: The chastisement inflicted on the man of understanding is of service to himself. "Reprove one that hath understanding, and he shall understand knowledge." He takes it in good part. He renounces the evil, he resolves to improve. He says, "Let the righteous smite me, and it shall be a kindness: and let him reprove, it shall be an excellent oil which shall not break my head."

Brothers, wrong exists everywhere around us. Evil fronts us in almost every man we meet. It is for us to set ourselves in strong antagonism to it wherever it appears. Let us feel that it is for us in our measure to do what Christ came into the world to accomplish—to "condemn sin in the flesh," to condemn it everywhere and at all times

> "Reprove not in their wrath incensèd men,
> Good counsel comes clean out of season then;
> But when his fury is appeased and past,
> He will conceive his fault, and mend at last."
>
> RANDOLPH

Proverbs 19:26-27

Filial Depravity and Parental Warning

"He that wasteth *his* father, *and* chaseth away *his* mother is a son that causeth shame, and bringeth reproach. Cease, my son, to hear the instruction *that causeth* to err from the words of knowledge."

AGAIN and again does Solomon refer to family life, and touch on the vices and virtues of home. He knew that no relationship was so vital to the race as that subsisting between parents and children. These verses give us two things:

FILIAL DEPRAVITY.—Here is a depraved son described. First: As wasting his father. There are many ways in which a reckless and wicked son "wasteth his father." Sometimes he wasteth his *property*. Many a son, by his expensive habits, gambling propensities, and reckless extravagance, has reduced his father from opulence to beggary, from a mansion to a pauper's hovel. Sometimes he wasteth his *health*. The conduct of a depraved son has shattered the health of many a father, and brought down his grey hairs with sorrow to the grave. A depraved son is described, Secondly: As repelling his mother. "He chaseth away his mother." She appears before him, perhaps with her bosom swollen with the tenderest sympathies of love, her eyes suffused with tears, and in the agony of affection expostulates with him, seeking to turn him from his evil habits, but he repels her, he chaseth her away. The depraved son is described, Thirdly: As disgracing his family. "He causeth shame, and bringeth reproach." Such is the constitution of society, that a whole family is often disgraced by the atrocities of one of its members. Such is the sketch here of filial depravity. Does such a son exist? Is not this a visionary picture? Alas! such sons have always been, and they abound even in Christian England. The character was a reality in Solomon's time, it is a reality now. We talk of monsters in nature, but a greater moral monster know I not than a son like that which is indicated here. He is without "natural affection," and the sorrows of his parents go before him as a terrible cloud to break in thunder upon his conscience in eternity.

The verses gives us—

PARENTAL WARNING.—"Cease, my son, to hear the instruction that *causeth* to err from the words of knowledge." First: Children are the subjects of instruction. All children are learning animals. They have learning instincts and capacities. Whether they go to school or not, they learn. They learn in the streets and alleys. There is a great public school which nature has established, and in which, alas, the devil works to corrupt the morals of the people. Secondly: Their instruction has a connection with their conduct. This is implied. Our first ideas root themselves in our being, and become the germs of future conduct. A bad creed must lead to vicious conduct. Hence the importance of sound doctrine. Thirdly: There is an instruction that leads to wrong. "Instruction that causeth to err from the words of knowledge." The instruction of the materialist, who teaches that there is no soul, no future life, "causeth to err from the words of knowledge." The instruction of the fatalist, which teaches that all things are so settled by an eternal necessity, as that free agency and responsibility cannot possibly exist, "causeth to err from the words of knowledge." The instruction of the sacramentalist, which teaches that you are to be saved by attending to rites and ceremonies, "causeth to err from the words of knowledge." Such instructions as these are rife in our country in these days. It is right, therefore, for the father to say to the son, "Cease, my son, to hear the instruction that causeth to err," believe not every spirit, but "try the spirits whether they are of God, because many false prophets are gone out into the world."

Proverbs 19:28-29

The Character and Doom of the Wicked

"An ungodly witness scorneth judgment: and the mouth of the wicked devoureth iniquity. Judgments are prepared for scorners, and stripes for the backs of fools."

THE "ungodly witness" is in the margin called "witnesses of Belial." "Sons of Belial" is a common appellation for impious and wicked men. Observe—

The CHARACTER of wicked men.—They are described here, First: As the witnesses of the devil. In their words, conversation, manners, spirit, they represent that which is ungodly. "They are witnesses of Belial." Their whole life is *one great lie*, and they are of their father, who was "a liar from the beginning." They are described—Secondly: As scorners of judgment. They are fools that make a mock of sin. They ridicule the most serious things, they scoff at the solemnities of death and eternity. The spirit of seriousness has forsaken them. They are irreverent and profane. They are described—Thirdly: As ravenous after iniquity. "The wicked devoureth iniquity." Sin is the one tempting thing to them. It is that one apple in the garden of life which makes their mouths water. Their appetite for it is whetted to the highest edge, and with voracity the "mouth of the wicked devoureth iniquity." What a picture is this! Alas, that it should be the life-like image of many. How many there are whose life is a "witness" to the false, who scoff at the serious; and whose strongest appetite is for that upon which sacred heaven has put its interdict. Observe again—

The DOOM of the wicked.—"Judgments are prepared for scorners, and stripes for the backs of fools." The punishment is *prepared*. All the anguish is arranged. The full cup is waiting. Judgment will not befal them as an accident. It is arranged and ready. Who shall describe the judgment? Who shall number the soul-lacerating stripes that wait the wicked in the penal settlements of eternity? "Our sin," said Bishop Hall, "is our own, and the wages of sin is death." He that doeth the work earns the wages. So then the righteous God is cleared both of our sin and our death. Only His justice pays us what our evil deeds deserve. What a wretched thing is a wilful sinner, and that will needs be guilty of his own death!

Proverbs 20:1

An Intemperate Use of Strong Drink

"Wine *is* a mocker, strong drink *is* raging: and whosoever is deceived hereby is not wise."

AT the outset we may observe that the proverb of itself is sufficient to expose the absurdity of those who, with an ignorant zeal endeavour to show that the wine of the Bible is not intoxicating. Though of course it was not like the brandied wine of this age, it was obviously alcoholic.

The intemperate use of strong drink is DECEITFUL.— "Wine is a mocker." It deceives men in many ways. Not only does it deceive the drunkard by beguiling and befooling him, but it deceives others as to its advantage. That it strengthens the system is a deception; chemistry has shown that it contains no nourishment for the body. That it enriches the national revenue is a deception. It is true that the taxes on alcoholic drinks bring millions annually into the national exchequer, but how much of the wealth of the nation does it exhaust by the pauperism and crime which it creates? Alcoholic drink is the great false prophet in England. A prophet working busily in every district, under the inspiration of hell. It may be said of many a civilized community, "they erred through wine, and through strong drink are out of the way; the priest and the prophet have erred through strong drink, they are swallowed up of wine, they are out of the way through strong drink; they err in vision, they stumble in judgment." The verse teaches—

The intemperate use of strong drink is ENRAGING.—
"Strong drink is raging." It excites the worst passions of human nature. Hence the quarrels, brawls, and murders that spring from it. It often kindles in men the very fires of hell. It fills our prisons with culprits, and supplies our judges with the chief part of their work. The verses teach—

The intemperate use of strong drink is FOOLISH.—
"Whosoever is deceived thereby is not wise." Nothing is more foolish than to indulge in alcoholic drinks. It injures the health, it enfeebles the intellect, it deadens the moral sensibilities, it destroys reputation, it impoverishes the exchequer, it disturbs friendship, it breeds quarrels, it brings misery into the family, it is fraught with innumerable curses. "Whosoever is deceived thereby is not wise."

"A drunken man is like a drowned man, a fool or madman: one draught above heat makes him a fool; the second mads him, and the third drowns him."
SHAKESPEARE

"There is no sin," says a divine of 1662, "which doth more deface God's image, than drunkenness, it disguiseth a person, and doth even unman him. Drunkenness gives him the throat of a fish, and the belly of a swine, and the heart of an ass. Drunkenness is the shame of nature, the extinguisher of reason, the shipwreck of chastity, and the murderer of conscience."

Proverbs 20:2

The Terrific in Human Government

"The fear of a king *is* as the roaring of a lion: *whoso* provoketh him to anger sinneth *against* his own soul."

I TAKE the king here as representing government, whether democratic, aristocratic, monarchical, or the three combined, as in the government of our country. The supreme judicial, and executive authority is the king. The verse implies three things concerning human governments.

Human governments contain in them the TERRIFIC.—"The fear of a king"—a government. Government implies laws, and laws imply punitive sanctions. Behind all governments there is the power to take away the property, the comfort, the liberty, the rights, the existence of the disobedient. Terrible power this, and it is held by all constitutional governments. A true king is "a terror to evil doers." The terrific in human government can be provoked INTO ACTION.—"Whoso provoketh him to anger." Disobedience and disloyalty bring out the terrible in human governments. The dark dungeons, the clanking chains, the penal inflictions, the scaffold and the gallows, are all brought forth by disobedience. Transgression wakes the thunder. The ruler "beareth not the sword in vain." He that provokes it into action brings RUIN ON HIMSELF.— He rouses the lion whose "roar" is overwhelming. It roars for destruction. No one man can stand before it. It will require an army to capture and overcome the roaring lion of an offended government. The British Lion, when excited, can strike terror through the world and tear a nation into pieces. The man ruins himself, who by his disobedience brings out this lion of retribution. He "sinneth against his own soul."

Proverbs 20:3

Unlawful Strife

"*It is* an honour for a man to cease from strife : but every fool will be meddling."

THERE is a lawful strife. Strife against the false, the selfish, the impure, the unrighteous, the ungodly, is lawful, is incumbent. The conquest of wrong is essential to the dignity and blessedness of Heaven. "He that overcometh and keepeth my words unto the end, to him will I give power over the nations."

The verse leads us to notice—

The HONOUR OF CEASING FROM UNLAWFUL STRIFE.—"It is an honour for a man to cease from strife." To be honourable, the ceasing must, First: Be voluntary. If a man ceases from strife because he is so baffled, disabled, crushed, that he could not but desist, there is no honour in it. He must withdraw voluntarily. Secondly: It must be self-denying. If there are no insults to avenge, no wrongs to resent, no rights to demand, what honour would there be in desisting? The honour is in giving up when on the right side. Thirdly: It must be forgiving. If in ceasing there remains ought of rancour or revenge in the breast there is no honour in it. Wherever strife is voluntarily, self-denyingly, and forgivingly withdrawn from, there is honour. The honour of self-conquest. The man who has done so has conquered his own passions. The honour of divine magnanimity. Such ceasing from strife is God-like.

The verse also teaches—

The FOLLY OF CREATING SOCIAL STRIFE.—"Every fool will be meddling." "Meddling" is the parent of strife. An officious interference with the business of others, a prying into their concerns create discords. All strifes, domestic, social, ecclesiastic, and political, may be traced to meddlesomeness. The meddling man is a "fool," because he gratifies his own idle curiosity at the expense of his own well-being and the happiness of society. "Put on, therefore, as the elect of God, holy and beloved, bowels of mercies, kindness, humbleness of mind, meekness, long-suffering, forbearing one another and forgiving one another. If any man have a quarrel against any, even as Christ forgave you, so also do ye. And above all these things put on charity, which is the bond of perfectness. And let the peace of God rule in your hearts, to the which also ye are called in one body; and be ye thankful."

Proverbs 20:4

Indolence

"The sluggard will not plow by reason of the cold: *therefore* shall he beg in harvest, and *have* nothing."

No evil does Solomon more frequently describe and denounce than indolence. We have already met with his views several times on the subject, and we shall frequently meet with them again as we proceed with this book.* The words suggest two remarks concerning indolence:—

It PLEADS WRETCHED EXCUSES.—"The sluggard will not plow by reason of the cold." What a futile reason is this! Cold weather was the time for ploughing. In summer heat it is too late to upturn the soil and prepare it for the seed—nature's germinating power has then gone for the year. Besides, no better means could be found to overcome the cold than by ploughing. There is no better way to counteract the chilly influence of the atmosphere, to send a healthful glow through the whole body, than physical exercise. No fire on the hearth could ever warm the human frame so effectually as the fire that bodily activity kindles within. This is only a specimen of the miserable excuses that indolence pleads. It has always some lion in the way, some thorn in the hedge. Indolence, sterile in goodness, is fertile in excuses. The indolent man will not work, either because the work is too mean or too important, the season too early or too late, the temperature too hot or too cold.

It ENTAILS GREAT MISERY.—Beggary. "Therefore shall he beg." What greater degradation for a man than to become a mendicant? Indolence leads to pauperism. Thomson wrote a poem on the "Castle of Indolence." He locates the castle in a dreamy land, where every sense is steeped in the most luxurious though enervating delights.

* See Readings on chap. x. 24; xii. 11, 24, 27; xiii. 4, 23; xv. 19; xvi. 26; xviii. 9; xix. 15, 24.

The lord of the castle was a powerful enchanter, who, by his arts, enticed thoughtless travellers within the gates, that he might destroy their strength and ruin their hopes by a ceaseless round of voluptuous pleasures.

Beggary in harvest. Beggary at the season when others have plenty, and when he too ought to have plenty. Beggary without success. "He shall beg in harvest, and have nothing." Because none can pity laziness, his petitions are rejected. There is a great harvest before us all. Those who have been spiritually indolent, neglecting the cultivation of their souls, will then be found begging, and begging in vain. "They that were foolish took their lamps, and took no oil with them: but the wise took oil in their vessels with their lamps. While the bridegroom tarried, they all slumbered and slept. And at midnight there was a cry made, Behold the bridegroom cometh, go ye out to meet him. Then all those virgins arose, and trimmed their lamps. And the foolish said unto the wise, Give us of your oil, for our lamps are gone out. But the wise answered, saying, *not so ;* lest there be not enough for us and you; but go ye rather to them that sell, and buy for yourselves."

Proverbs 20:5

The Getting of Wisdom from the Wise

"Counsel in the heart of Man *is like* deep water; but a man of understanding will draw it out."

WE take the word "counsel" here to mean wisdom. The distinction which Cowper draws between knowledge and wisdom is philosophic and important :

" Knowledge and wisdom, far from being one,
  Have ofttimes no connection. Knowledge dwells
  In heads replete with thoughts of other men,
  Wisdom in minds attentive to their own.

> Knowledge, a rude unprofitable mass,
> The mere materials with which wisdom builds,
> Till smoothed and square, and fitted into place,
> Does but encumber what it seems t'enrich.
> Knowledge is proud that he has learned so much,
> Wisdom is humble that he knows no more."

From the proverb four remarks may be drawn.

WISDOM TO MAN IS A VERY VALUABLE THING.—It is here represented as "water" which "a man of understanding" will strive to get at. We have had occasion frequently to sketch the advantages of knowledge. Without repeating ourselves, we may here say, that knowledge does two things for man. First: It improves the sphere of his being. The sphere of man's mental existence, large or small, bright or gloomy, sterile or fruitful, happy or otherwise, depends entirely upon the kind and amount of his intelligence. An ignorant soul has a wretchedly small and cloudy circle to move in. There is as much difference between the sphere of an intelligent man and that of an ignorant one as there its between a dungeon and a palace. Another thing which knowledge does for man is, Secondly: It improves the powers of his being. It brightens the eyes of the intellect, and gives to imagination pinions for a loftier and happier flight; it gives to thought a wider reach and a firmer grasp, and unseals in the soul new fountains of delicious sentiment and thought.

SOME MEN ARE FAVOURED WITH MORE WISDOM THAN OTHERS.—This is implied; Solomon supposes that in some men it lies as "deep" as "water." So it does. The difference in the amount of men's intelligence arises from the difference in their capacities, proclivities, and opportunities for mental improvement. There are men of genius, men of strong philosophic tendencies, men of leisure, men with splendid libraries; such men are in a position to get more knowledge than the millions who are less favoured. Hence it comes to pass that in all circles there are those with valuable intelligence, like "*deep water*" within them; and these waters are ever deepening, for it is a law that the more knowledge a man has the more flows into him. "The more we know," says Coleridge, "the greater our thirst for knowledge. The water lily in the midst of waters opens its leaves and expands its petals at the first pattering of showers, and rejoices in the rain drops with a quicker sympathy than the parched shrub in the sandy desert."

THOSE WHO HAVE THE MOST WISDOM ARE GENERALLY THE MOST RESERVED.—This is manifestly implied from the expression "will draw it out." It will not run out spontaneously; it has to be *drawn* out. Where knowledge dwells in large quantities, it is not like water on the surface, that you can get at easily; it is rather like water that lies fathoms under the earth, clear, beautiful, and refreshing, got at only by the pump, or the windlass and bucket. It has to be *drawn* out. It is, has always been, and perhaps ever will be, that the most intelligent men are the most modest and reserved. The superficial are talkative; the profound are taciturn. The fluent in speech is ever the shallow in thought. Great knowledge is always reticent.

In consequence of this reservedness of the most wise, it REQUIRES SAGACITY IN OTHERS TO DRAW IT FORTH.—"A man of understanding will draw it out." Would you draw knowledge out of the wise man in your circle? There is a way to do it. Not by flippant questionings, but by modest enquiries, propounded in a truth-loving spirit. Would you draw knowledge out of your teacher? You must so study the lessons that he gives you, as to bring his mind into a constant flow to supply your cravings after knowledge. Would you *draw* knowledge of the highest kind from your minister? Then let him feel that you have come to "enquire in the temple of the Lord."

Some pulpits are filled with thoughtless men, because congregations will not think. Even Christ Himself felt that He could not unfold what was in Him on account of the ignorance and prejudice of His auditory.

Proverbs 20:6-7

A Prevalent Vice and a Rare Virtue

"Most men will proclaim every one his own goodness: but a faithful man who can find? The just *man* walketh in his integrity: his children *are* blessed after him."

HERE is—

A PREVALENT VICE.—"Most men will proclaim every one his own goodness." Here is that abominable thing which we designate *vanity*, an ostentatious parading of one's own imaginary merits. This evil meets you almost everywhere, and it often exhibits itself indirectly, and under the forms of feigned humility. It is seen in the religious world, in the way in which certain men get their subscriptions trumpeted in reports, and their charitable doings emblazoned in journals. It is seen in the political world. In the House of Commons some of the men who are reputed as great orators through the eternal parading of their own doings, are making their names synonymes for vanity and conceit. They proclaim their "own goodness." They are the just men, the philanthropists, the true reformers, and they would have the world believe that what England is, she owes to them. First: This vice is an obstruction to self-improvement. The man who prides himself on his own cleverness, will never get knowledge—who exults in his own virtue, will never advance in genuine goodness. Vanity is in one sense the fruit of ignorance. It has been said that it thrives most in subterranean places, never reached by the air of heaven, and the light of the sun. It is the cause as well. Vanity in the plenitude of self-sufficiency sits down in its own chamber, draws its curtains, shuts out the sun, and sees things only by the glimmerings of its own little rushlight. Secondly: This vice is socially offensive. Nothing is more distasteful in society than vanity. "Wouldest thou not be thought a fool," says old

Quarles, "in another's conceit, be not wise in thine own; he that trusts to his own wisdom, proclaims his own folly: he is truly wise, and shall appear so, that hath folly enough to be thought not worldly wise, or wisdom enough to see his own folly." Vanity is an unsuccessful agent; it never gets what it seeks; it works for praise, but never fails to create disgust. Thirdly: This vice is essentially opposed to Christianity. What says Paul? "For I say through the grace given unto me, to every man that is among you, not to think of himself more highly than he ought to think; but to think soberly, according as God hath dealt to every man the measure of faith." What says Christ? "Let not thy left hand know what thy right hand doeth." What was the doom of the self-parading Pharisee in the temple? How humble was Christ. "He made Himself of no reputation, but took on Him the form of a servant." Here is—

A RARE VIRTUE.—"But a faithful man who can find?" What is faithfulness? The man who in the verse is called faithful, is in the next represented as just, "walking in his integrity." Each of the three terms represents the same thing. To be faithful is to be practically true to our own convictions. Never acting without or against them. Practically true to our own professions. Never breaking promises or swerving from engagements. Now this is a rare virtue. The great mass of men are time serving, mere devotees of expediency. A "faithful man" is a man showing good fidelity in all things. Mark what is said of this "faithful" and just man, who "walketh in his integrity." "His children are blessed after him." The destiny of children greatly depends upon their parents. The sap in the roots shapes the branch, and gives its character to the fruit. Whilst it is a terrible calamity for children to be born of the ill-bred, the ill-formed, the ill-fed, the prostitute, and the debauchee; it is a blessed thing to be born of parents healthful in body and noble in character. The children are blessed with their health, with their spirit, with their habits. "Train up a child in the way he should go, and when he is old he will not depart from it." It is said that Plato seeing a child doing mischief in the street, went forth and corrected his father for it.

Proverbs 20:8

The Picture of a Noble King

"A king that sitteth in the throne of judgment scattereth away all evil with his eyes."

WE have before met with the subject of these words, under other forms of expression,* and the remarks which we have now to offer should be regarded in connection with observations upon those cognate passages. This verse gives us the picture of a noble king.

HIS OFFICIAL POSITION.—He "sitteth on the throne of judgment." The word "judgment" may stand for justice or rectitude. A true king is on his throne. He is there *by* right. What gives a man right to become the king of others? We mean the moral right. Not conquest, birth, or suffrage, but *fitness*. That man in any community who has the most brain, heart, intelligence, conscience, divinity, is the one most entitled to kingship. He is a God-made king. He is there *for* right. He is there to see justice done. He does not rule for the interest of a class, but for the good of all. His laws are equitable. Partialities and predilections which govern plebeian souls have no sway over him. "He is just, ruling in the fear of God." "He is a terror to evil doers, and a praise to them that do well."

> "He's a king,
> A true, right king, that dare do aught save wrong;
> Fears nothing mortal but to be unjust:
> Who is not blown up with the flattering puffs
> Of spongy sycophants: who stands unmoved,
> Despite the jostling of opinion."—MARSTON

* See Readings on chap. xvi. 14, 15; xix. 12; xx. 2.

The verse gives us—

HIS MORAL INFLUENCE.—He " scattereth away all evil with his eyes." A man with a true, royal character has a nobler power than official kingship. Legislation, though backed by the invincibility of arms, is in respect to true power in an empire, not to be compared with a life embodying divine principles, and animated with the divine spirit. Before such a life evils melt away quietly, as mists before the morning sun. He " scattereth away all evils with his eyes." Before the glance of such a king the corrupt would flee from his cabinet and the unchaste from his court. What a king might do and *ought* to do is to purify the morals and exalt the character of his people. In this so-called Christian land there are people who justify worldliness, pleasures, frivolities, and empty amusements in royal life. Of all men in the kingdom the man who is on the throne should be the most moral, the most Christian, the most earnest and indefatigable in his endeavours to expel the false and the filthy, the immoral and the ungodly from the land. Hail the time when the throne of our England shall be occupied by such kings, " when the saints shall take it and possess it for ever." " A king," says Lord Bacon, " must have a special care of five things if he would not have his crown to be but to him 'unhappy felicity.' That pretended holiness be not in the Church, for that is twofold iniquity; that useless equity sit not in the chancery, for that is 'foolish pity;' that useless iniquity keep not the exchequer, for that is cruel robbery; that faithful rashness be not his general, for that will bring, but too late, repentance; that faithless prudence be not his secretary, for that is a snake between the green grass." I will venture to add two more to the philosopher's list: That self-indulgence and arrogance have no place in his heart, and that his idea of nobility should be the moral grandeur embodied in the life of Jesus.

Proverbs 20:9

Moral Purity

"Who can say, I have made my heart clean, I am pure from my sin?"

OUR subject is moral purity, and the verse represents it in two aspects.

As TRANSCENDENTLY IMPORTANT.—First: It is essential to peace of conscience. Through the depravity of our lives from the earliest date of moral consciousness our souls are stained with corruption. The eye of conscience looking at this broad, deep stain gives that anguish of spirit under which we exclaim, "O wretched man, that I am." An unclean heart must ever have an unquiet conscience. Secondly: It is essential to the growth of soul. Moral uncleanness is an atmosphere of mind that prevents germination and growth. It obstructs the quickening sunbeam, the refreshing dew, and the fertilising shower. Moral uncleanness makes the inner heavens as brass. Thirdly: It is essential to social love. Our happiness consists in loving and being loved, but no one can really love the morally unclean. The deepest things in human nature recoil with disgust from the spiritually impure. Fourthly: It is essential to fellowship with God. "Blessed are the pure in heart, for they shall see God." "Without holiness no man shall see God." Fifthly: It is essential to usefulness. "Holiness," says Dr. T. W. Jenkin, "is the only means by which holiness can be diffused. It is like salt, its usefulness to others must begin with itself. The man who fails to persuade himself to be holy is sure to be unsuccessful with others. It is the wise man that can impart wisdom to others, it is the good man that can diffuse goodness, and it is only the holy man that can diffuse holiness. Every man can bring forth to others only out of the treasures deposited first in his own heart. He who undertakes to restore mankind to clear-sightedness, must be of clear and accurate vision himself, for he who has a beam in his own eye is not likely to remove either beam or mote from the eye of the world. The physician who is to restore health to others must not himself be fretting with the leprosy." Sixthly: It is essential to the realization of Christ's mission. He came to open a fountain for the washing away of sin. He came to put away sins by the sacrifice of Himself. He came to purify unto Himself a peculiar people, zealous of good works. His biographic influence taketh away all sin.

The verse represents moral purity—

AS LAMENTABLY RARE.—"Who can say, I have made my heart clean, I am pure from my sin?" This is God's challenge. "Gird up thy loins like a man, for I will demand of thee, and answer thou me. "Who?" Not the ungodly, the worldling, the intemperate, the selfish, the self-righteous, the hypocritical, none of these can say it. Who? Not even the genuine Christian on earth. So imperfect are the best here, that the more pure they become, the more they feel their pollution. One good man says, "I abhor myself in dust and ashes." Another, "Woe is me, I am a man with unclean lips." Another, "I am the least of all saints, and the chief of sinners." Who? Only holy angels and the perfected saints in Heaven can say it, "We are without spots, or wrinkles, or any such thing." Dr. Livingstone once asked a Bechuana what he understood by the word "holiness"? He answered, "When copious showers have descended during the night and all the earth, and leaves, and cattle are washed clean, and the sun rising shows a drop of dew on every blade of grass, and the air breathes fresh—that is holiness."

> "Not all the pomp and pageantry of worlds
> Reflect such glory on the Eye Supreme,
> As the meek virtues of one holy man."—MONTGOMERY

Proverbs 20:10, 23

The Market

"**Divers weights *and*** divers measures, both of them *are* alike abomination to the LORD. . . . Divers weights *are* an abomination unto the LORD; and a false balance *is* not good."

MAN is by his instincts and necessities a trader. He has a bartering power. Visit the darkest regions of barbaric life, and you will find the wild and savage natives driving some species of trade. They may only exchange feathers, shells, or some petty toys; still it is commerce. Our missionaries often introduce themselves to heathen scenes and ingratiate themselves with heathen hearts by first appealing to this mercantile instinct.* Hence commerce is as old and universal as man. In the original, as intimated in the margin of our English Bible, the terms of the passage before us are a "stone and a stone," or a weight and a weight—an ephah and an ephah. The idea probably is that there is one set of weights and measures to sell with, another to buy with, one for the inspector, and another for the buyer, one for the inexperienced and confiding, and another for the shrewd and suspecting. The verse lead us to consider the market in two aspects.

AS THE SCENE OF DISHONEST TRICKS.—"Divers weights and divers measures." In the days of Solomon, as now, men in the market had different sets of weights and measures for different occasions, to gratify their greed. Chicanery was perhaps never more rife in the markets of the world than now, and never played a more subtle, powerful, and disastrous part than in British emporiums. Men are cheated in a thousand ways. False standards, adulterations, fallacious representations, are some of the methods which dishonest men employ to impose upon their customers and clients. There are swindling companies in our midst legalized, working ruin amongst the least en-

* See Philosophy of Happiness, published by Dickenson, Farringdon Street.

lightened and least suspicious of our countrymen. Our commercial immorality has gained proportions hideous and portentous. Our national credit is decaying, and men are being swindled in so many ways that multitudes are constantly seeking homes on other shores. Heaven only knows what will be the end!

The verses lead us to consider the market—

AS THE SCENE OF DIVINE INSPECTION.—"Divers weights are an abomination unto the Lord and a false weight is not good." The Omnipresent One is as truly in the market as in any other part of His universe. His eye is everywhere, and what He sees He feels. "Atoms," says Secker, "which are invisible in the candle-light of reason are all made to dance naked in the sunshine of Omniscience" The wrong is an "abomination" to Him wherever it exists. First: He prohibits dishonesty in trade. "Just balances, just weights, a just ephah, and a just hin shall ye have: I am the Lord your God, which brought you out of the land of Egypt."* Secondly: He enjoins social justice. "Therefore all things whatsoever ye would that men should do to you, do ye even so to them; for this is the law and the prophets." Thirdly: He abhors dishonesty. "Thou shalt not have in thy bag divers weights, a great and a small. Thou shalt not have in thine house divers measures, a great and a small. But thou shalt have a perfect and just weight, a perfect and just measure shalt thou have; that thy days shall be lengthened in the land which the Lord thy God giveth thee. For all that do such things, and all that do unrighteously, are an abomination unto the Lord thy God." Dishonesty in trade brought ruin upon Israel. Merchants and tradesmen, look well to this. Not only never use, but don't have on your premises false weights and measures; that which is the rule of justice must be just. Honesty is the best policy. "I tell thee," says Thomas Carlyle, "there is nothing else but justice: one strong thing I find here below—the just thing, the true thing. My friend, if thou hadst all the artillery of Woolwich marching at thy back in support of an unjust

* Lev. xix. 36; Matt. vii. 18; Deut. xxv. 13—16; Amos viii. 5.

thing, and infinite bonfires visibly waiting ahead of thee to blaze centuries to come for thy victory on behalf of it, I would advise thee to call 'Halt!' to fling down thy baton and say, 'In God's name, No!' What will thy success amount to? If the thing be unjust thou hast not succeeded though bonfires blaze from north to south, and bells rang, and editors wrote leading articles, and the just thing lay trampled out of sight to all mortal eyes, an abolished and an annihilated thing."

Proverbs 20:12

The Hearing Ear and the Seeing Eye

"The hearing ear, and the seeing eye, the LORD hath made even both of them." *

WHY does Solomon say this? Has not the Lord made everything? Is He not the Creator of "heaven and earth and all things that are therein?" Who but the sensuous and unphilosophic doubt this? Verily, the royal sage here utters a common-place truism. From the obvious fact, however, we draw two practical conclusions.

That God should be STUDIED IN these organs. "This famous town of Man-soul," says Bunyan, "had five gates in at which to come, out at which to go; and these were made likewise answerable to the walls—to wit, impregnable, and such as never could be opened nor forced but by the will of those within. The names of the gates were these—Ear-gate, Eye-gate, Mouth-gate, Nose-gate, and Feel-gate." Of these five, the "hearing ear" and the "seeing eye" would be popularly and perhaps accurately considered the chief gateways to the soul. First: In them Divine wisdom is manifest. Take the mechanism of these organs. The human frame is "fearfully and

* The eleventh verse has been noticed in a previous Reading.

wonderfully made;" but no parts in the frame are more wonderful in their execution than these. "The eye," says one, "by its admirable combination of coats and humours, and lenses, produces on the retina, or expansion of nerve at the back of the socket or bony cavity, in which it is so securely lodged, a distinct picture of the minutest or largest object; so that, on a space that is less than an inch in diameter, a landscape of miles in extent, with all its variety of scenery, is depicted with perfect exactness of relative proportion in all its parts."

> "The eye takes in at once the landscape of the world,
> At a small inlet which a grain might close,
> And half creates the wondrous world we see."—YOUNG

Nor is the *ear* less wonderful. It is a complicated mechanism, lying wholly within the body, showing only the wider outer porch through which the sound enters. It conveys the sound through various chambers to the innermost extremities of those nerves which hear the messages, to the brain. So delicate is this organ, that it catches the softest whispers, and conveys them to the soul, and so strong that it hears the roll of the loudest thunders in the chamber of its mistress.

Volumes have been written on the mechanism of these organs. Take the adaptation of these organs. How exquisitely suited they are to the offices they have to fulfil. "Conveying the impressions of the outer universe to the spiritual dweller within, we can," says an eminent author, 'by attending to the laws of vision and sound, produce something that, in structure and in mechanism or physical effect, bears some analogy to them. But this is not *sight*; this is not *hearing*. These imply perceptions. And to perception there are requisite an auditory and an optic nerve, that convey the sensation of sound and vision to the brain; and a *perceiving mind*—an immaterial, spiritual, thinking substance, essence, element—or what else shall we call it? that thus perceives its perceptions of things heard and things seen! Oh, this is the highest and deepest wonder of all! The mechanical structure we can trace out and demonstrate. We can show how by the laws of transmission and refraction, the picture is made on the retina of the eye; and how, by the laws of sound, the yielding, tremulous, undulating air affects the *tympanum* or drum of the ear. But we can get no farther. *How* it is that the mind receives its perceptions, how it is that it is affected, what is the nature of nervous influence, or of the process by which, through the medium of the nerves and brain, thought is produced on the mind—of all this we are profoundly ignorant." The celebrated Galen is said to have been converted from atheism by an attentive observation of the perfect structure of the eye. Secondly: In them divine goodness is manifest. They give us the outward world. Without these what would the glorious heavens, the lovely landscape, and the melodies of the world be to us? Nothing. They convey to us happiness from the outward world. The Almighty might have provided the hideous and revolting for the eye, the disharmonious and the discordant for the ear. But not so, there is beauty, sublimity, and music. Thirdly: In them the Divine intelligence is symbolised. " He that planteth the ear, shall he not hear: he that formed the eye, shall he not see?"

On these words we offer another remark, namely:

That God should be SERVED in these organs.—We should use them for the purpose for which He gave them. These organs are given to man for a higher purpose than that for which they are given to brutes. Brutes have them, and in some cases have them in higher perfection than we have. But in brutes they fulfil their mission when they convey *sensation*, and nothing more. The service for which God intends us to use them is to *convey into our understandings His ideas*, into our *hearts His spirit*. With these eyes we should read the volumes which He has written, both in nature and in Holy writ—read them accurately, devoutly, practically. With these ears we should hear the discourses which He delivers in the voices of the world, and in the ministry of His servants. Alas! men don't use these organs in God's service. The great multitude "seeing, see not, and hearing, hear not, neither do they understand." Two things at least, we should do with them. First: Translate the sensations they convey to us into Divine ideas. All outward forms and sounds are redolent with the thoughts of God. For His great thoughts our souls are made, and crave. Secondly: Apply the Divine ideas to the formation of our characters. God's ideas should become at once the *spring* and *rule* of all our activities. Remember, that these organs are the gifts and emblems of the Eternal Mind.

Proverbs 20:13

Early Rising

"Love not sleep, lest thou come to poverty; open thine eyes, *and* thou shalt be satisfied with bread."

WE have so frequently met with the subject of indolence, and made reflections upon it, that we need do nothing more than record a few striking examples of the advantages of early rising. Sleep in itself is a blessing; it is strength to the exhausted; it is medicine to the diseased; it is solace to the sorrowing. But the love of sleep implies a drowsiness of nature, which makes the very blessing a curse. The man who over indulges in it, as a rule, does "come to poverty." The natural tendency of indolence is destitution; destitution temporal, intellectual, and spiritual follows laziness. "Open thine eyes," then. Open them at the dawn of morning, and watch profitable opportunities for profitable labour. Our subject is the reward of early rising. "Thou shalt be satisfied with bread." Most men who have distinguished themselves in any department of labour, have been early risers. "You rise late," says Todd, " and, of course, commence your business at a late hour, and everything goes wrong all day." Franklin says, "that he who rises late may trot all day, and not have overtaken his business at night." Dean Swift avers that he "never knew any man come to greatness and eminence who lay in bed of a morning." "I would," says Lord Chatham, "have inscribed on the curtains of your bed, and the walls of your chamber, 'If you do not rise early, you can make progress in nothing. If you do not set apart your hours of reading, if you suffer yourself or any one else to break in upon them, your days will slip through your hands unprofitable and frivolous, and unenjoyed by yourself.' The man who rises early, not only drinks in the most invigorating influences of the day, but adds to the length of his life." "The difference," says Doddridge, "between rising at five and seven o'clock in the morning, for the space of forty years, supposing a man to go to bed at the same hour at night, is nearly equivalent to the addition of ten years to a man's life."

We subjoin here a few examples of those who acknowledge the advantage of early rising :

John Milton says of himself, that he was at his studies "in winter often ere the sound of any bell awoke men to labour or devotion : in summer as oft with the bird that first rouses, or not much tardier, to read good authors till attention be weary or memory have its full fraught : then with useful and generous labours preserving the body's health and hardiness." Wesley repeatedly ascribes his own health and prolonged life to the practice of rising at four. When seventy-eight years old, he writes : "By the blessing of God I am just the same as when I ended my twenty-eighth year. This hath God wrought chiefly by my constant exercise, rising early in the morning." "In my youth," says Buffon, one of the most famous writers and naturalists of the eighteenth century, "I was very fond of sleep ; it robbed me of a great deal of my time ; but my poor servant, Joseph, was of great service in enabling me to overcome it. I promised to give Joseph a crown every time that he would make me get up at six. Next morning he did not fail to wake and torment me ; but he only received abuse. The next day he did the same with no better success, and I was obliged to confess at noon that I had lost my time. I told him that he did not know how to manage his business; he ought to think of my purpose, and not mind my threats. The day following he employed force; I begged him for indulgence, I bid him be gone, I stormed, but Joseph persisted. I was, therefore, obliged to comply, and he was rewarded every day for the abuse which he suffered at the moment when I awoke by thanks, accompanied by a crown, which he received about an hour after. Yes, I am indebted to my poor servant for *ten* or a *dozen* of the volumes of my works."

> " Rise with the lark, and with the lark to bed:
> The breath of night's destructive to the hue
> Of ev'ry flower that blows. Go to the field,
> And ask the humble daisy why it sleeps
> Soon as the sun departs? Why close the eyes
> Of blossoms infinite, long ere the moon
> Her oriental veil puts off? Think why,
> Nor let the sweetest blossom Nature boasts
> Be thus exposed to night's unkindly damp.
> Well may it droop, and all its freshness lose,
> Compelled to taste the rank and poisonous steam
> Of midnight theatre and morning ball.
> Give to repose the solemn hour she claims,
> And from the forehead of the morning steal
> The sweet occasion. Oh, there is a charm
> Which morning has, that gives the brow of age
> A smack of earth, and makes the lip of youth
> Shed perfume exquisite. Expect it not,
> Ye who till noon upon a down-bed lie,
> Indulging feverous sleep."—HURDIS

Proverbs 20:14

Chicanery

"*It is* naught, *it is* naught, saith the buyer: but when he is gone his way then he boasteth."

MR. BRIDGES says, "that Augustine mentions a somewhat ludicrous but significant story. A mountebank publishes in the full theatre that in the next entertainment he would show to every man present what was in his heart.

An immense concourse attended, and the man redeemed his pledge to the vast assembly by a single sentence, '*Vili vultis emere, et caro vendere*,' 'You all wish to buy cheap, and to sell dear,' a sentence generally applauded; every one, even the most trifling (as Augustine observes) finding the confirming witness in his own conscience." There is no harm in buying in the cheapest market and selling in the dearest. In fact, this is both wise and right in the vendor. Some regard the word "*buyer*" here in the sense of possessor, and thus the idea of the passage is changed, and it is this—that a man attaches greater value to a thing after he has lost it than before. When he has it in his possession he does not think much of it, but when it is gone, it appears to him of great value. This is a law of human nature. Our Saviour recognises it, and uses it to illustrate the value that the Great Father of Spirits sets upon a lost soul, which He represents under the figures of the lost piece of silver, the lost sheep, the lost son. But it is more like Solomon to regard the text as meaning what the "buyer" says.

We offer two remarks upon the passage.

That it reveals A COMMON commercial practice.—" It is naught, it is naught, saith the buyer." What is here stated concerning the "buyer" in Judæa, hundreds of years ago, has always and everywhere been true in human merchandize. The "buyer" depreciates the commodity in the process of purchase. He says, " It is naught, it is naught." He finds fault with the material, the texture, or the workmanship of the article. He does this in order to get it at a price below its worth. And when he succeeds, and it comes legally in his possession, the value of the article is not only properly estimated, but greatly exaggerated. "He boasteth." Why? Because his *vanity* has been gratified. He feels that he has done a clever thing. By the skill of his depreciating argument he has conquered the vendor and brought him down to his own mark. "He boasteth." Why? Because his *greed* has been gratified. He has procured property for a consideration beneath its value, and he is thereby enriched.

The other remark we offer on this passage is—

That it reveals AN IMMORAL commercial practice.— First: There is falsehood. If the article is "*naught*," why does the buyer want it at all, and why, when he gets it, does he esteem it of high value? It is a lie, and "lying lips are an abomination to the Lord." The commercial atmosphere of England is so infested with lies, that without a speedy moral fumigation, our mercantile credit, I trow, will be ruined. Secondly: There is dishonesty. He who gets from another property for a consideration beneath its worth, is a thief. "The cheat," says old Thomas Fuller, " spins like a spider out of his own entrails to entrap the simple and unwary that light in his way, whom he devours and feeds upon." It is a violation of the Divine rule, "Whatsoever ye would that men should do to you, do ye unto them."

O, ye Traders, who thus transact your business, there is no room for boasting; your secular profits represent terrible moral losses! Though ye are prosperous traders, ye are gazetted in the universe as moral bankrupts.

Proverbs 20:15

Material Wealth and Intelligent Speech

"There is gold, and a multitude of rubies: but the lips of knowledge *are* a precious jewel."

THERE is evidently a comparison here between material wealth and enlightened speech. "Gold," and "rubies" here represent worldly riches, and the "lips of knowledge," represent the speech "that ministereth grace unto the hearers." We offer three remarks on the comparison in the verse—

One is RARER than the other.—This seems to be implied, for it is said, "There is gold and a *multitude* of rubies." In the days of Solomon there seemed to be plenty of material wealth, for we read that "the king made silver to be in

Jerusalem as stones, and cedars made he to be as the sycamore trees that are in the vale for abundance." And wealth is pretty abundant here in England. But intelligent speech is rare. Where wealth counts its thousands, wisdom can only count its tens. "Where shall wisdom be found, and where is the way of understanding?" One is MORE INTRINSICALLY VALUABLE than the other.—There is no more intrinsic worth in "gold" and "rubies" than in brass and stones. They are valuable only on account of their scarcity. But in wise words of truth and soberness there is an intrinsic worth. They are the embodiments and the vehicles of those treasures which enrich immortal spirits, are appreciated by God, and are counted valuable by all holy minds in all times and worlds. They are indeed "a precious jewel." Their lustre no time can dim, their worth no change can deteriorate. One is MORE SERVICEABLE than the other.—"Gold" and "rubies" can only serve men temporally and for a short time. Wise words will serve men for ever. What thousands have felt the value of such words. "Such was the delight of hanging upon the lips of the golden-mouthed Chrysostom, that the common proverb was—'Rather let the sun not shine than Chrysostom not preach.'" Such words convert, purify, ennoble, and save men. "The "lips of knowledge" are the organs through which God pours the highest blessings of his grace.

Value spiritual wisdom as the great thing. "It cannot be gotten for gold, neither shall silver be weighed for the price thereof. It cannot be valued with the gold of Ophir, with the precious onyx, or the sapphire. The gold and the crystal cannot equal it, and the exchange of it shall not be for jewels of fine gold. No mention shall be made of coral, or of pearls, for the price of wisdom is above rubies. The topaz of Ethiopia shall not equal it, neither shall it be valued with pure gold."

Proverbs 20:16, 18, 21

Business Economics

"Take his garment that is surety *for* a stranger: and take a pledge of him for a strange woman. Bread of deceit *is* sweet to a man; but afterwards his mouth shall be filled with gravel. *Every* purpose is established by counsel: and with good advice make war. . . . An inheritance *may be* gotten hastily at the beginning: but the end thereof shall not be blessed."

THE book of Solomon deserves, and will repay, the study of all young men who intend to embark, or have embarked, in mercantile pursuits. It abounds with those maxims which will stimulate diligence, insure integrity, and promote success. The author of the book was not only an ethical philosopher, but a shrewd man of business. He understood not only the moral laws that should rule men in all their intercourse with each other, but also the necessary conditions of real success in all business undertakings. In the verses before us there are no less than four maxims for business expressed with more or less clearness and force. There is—

CAUTION IN CREDIT.—" Take his garment that is surety for a stranger." The question of suretiship has engaged our attention several times already.* The man here sketched is recklessly imprudent and morally profligate. He becomes "surety for a stranger," and is addicted to vicious indulgences, for he is represented as in association with a "strange woman." Such a man is not to be trusted in business without the strongest security. "Take his garment." Under the Jewish law the garment was the very last thing which was to be taken in pledge, and could not be retained beyond the passing day.† The advice of Solomon amounts to this: Have nothing to do with such men in business; don't give credit to the reckless and the profligate; see that men are trustworthy in character and

* See Reading on Prov. vi. 1, 2; xi. 15; xvii. 18.
† Exodus xxii. 26, 27.

in means before you trust them. Half the failures in business probably arise from trusting corrupt and fraudulent men. There is—

HONESTY IN DEALING.—" Bread of deceit is sweet to a man; but afterwards his mouth shall be filled with gravel." The fact implies, First : That property may be obtained by fraud. How much worldly wealth is acquired every day in the world by cozenage and deceit! Fraud is, perhaps, the most active architect in the building up of fortunes. Secondly: That property so obtained may for a time be very pleasant. It "is sweet to a man." Public opinion gives its owner credit for industry and skill, and knows nothing, for a time, of his fraudulent measures. Conscience, too, sleeps in the lap of luxury, and whatever can minister pleasure to appetite, taste, vanity, or ambition, stands at his side and awaits his bidding. He feels it "is sweet." Thirdly: That the pleasure attending such property must end in suffering. " Afterwards his mouth shall be filled with gravel!" What more emphatic expression of chagrin and bitter disappointment than the idea of a hungry man putting in his mouth with an eager hand the bread that should relieve his appetite, and finding it turn to sand and gravelly stone ? What examples have we here in this country recorded in almost every day's journals, of fortunes once sweet turning to gall, bread once sweet becoming " gravel"! Convicted swindlers feel it so. It was so with Achan and his wedge of gold ; with Gehazi and his talents of silver, with Judas and his thirty pieces,—with all such the "bread" once "sweet" became "gravel." There is—

DELIBERATION IN EMBARKING. — " Every purpose is established by counsel, and with good advice make war." " With good advice make war!" Then we think war would seldom be made, if at all. " Good advice" must be advice in harmony with Divine law, and those laws are dead against wars :

> " War is a game which, were their subjects wise,
> Kings should not play at."

The general idea of the passage is this:—Well consider every undertaking before you embark in it. Two questions should be settled before you start on an enterprise. First: Whether the enterprise in itself is lawful. Is it a right thing? There are sinful enterprises. The manufacture and sale of intoxicating drinks, the publication and sale of immoral and worthless literature, and military life in all its departments. Men who take true "counsel" will never embark in such enterprises as these. Secondly: Whether the means to be employed are good: that is, whether they are in harmony with rectitude and adapted to the end. Christ Himself urges this deliberation before embarking in our undertakings. "What king going to make war against another king sitteth not down to count the cost." There is—

TEMPERATENESS IN ACCUMULATING.—"An inheritance may be gotten hastily at the beginning, but the end thereof shall not be blessed." Solomon does not mean by this that all the property that comes suddenly to a man is necessarily unblessed. A poor man may by legacy or lineage come into possession of a lordly "inheritance" in a single day: in this he would be fortunate and not criminal, and if he used it rightly it would be a blessing to him in the end and for ever. Nor does he mean that a man who through a signally wise and assiduously diligent application of means to ends, and in all with strict honesty and devout spirit, accumulates wealth speedily, is not blessed in his possessions. He points, undoubtedly, to the man who with a voracious greed for wealth, seizes every opportunity to attain it, regardless of truth, honour, and justice, and thus becomes rich in a short time. Our country abounds with instances of men who in this way bound from poverty to opulence in a few days. But the end is not "blessed." Anything but blessed. Discovery comes and clothes them with infamy; conscience is roused and torments them. The curses of the defrauded and the frowns of the Almighty are over them.

Young men, ponder well these maxims, which all your

business undertakings require. Caution in credit, honesty in dealing, deliberation in embarking and temperateness in accumulating.

Proverbs 20:19-20

The Idle Talebearer and the Wicked Son

"He that goeth about *as* a talebearer revealeth secrets: therefore meddle not with him that flattereth with his lips. Whoso curseth his father or his mother, his lamp shall be put out in obscure darkness."

EACH of these verses presents a bad character—the mischievous tattler and the unnatural child. Solomon has referred to them more than once before, and never does he point to them without an indignant scorn.

Here is—

THE IDLE TALEBEARER.—"He that goeth about as a talebearer revealeth secrets; therefore meddle not with him that flattereth with his lips." A talebearer is one who "officiously tells tales: one who impertinently communicates intelligence or anecdotes, and makes mischief in society by his officiousness." We gather from Solomon's description here, First: That he is insidious. He gets hold of the "secrets" of men. By his soft words and bland manners he ingratiates himself into the confidence of the unsuspecting, and gets hold of things connected with their experience which they would not on any account make public. All men have some secrets—things which they would not willingly allow to fall from their own lips, still less from the lips of others; yet at times they are tempted to entrust them to those in whom they have confidence; the talebearer gets hold of them. Secondly: He is treacherous. He "revealeth secrets." Sometimes he may do it wantonly, for the mere love of gossip; sometimes from vanity, to show what confidence men repose in him; sometimes maliciously, in order to disturb old friendships, to create social broils. In any case, he is a traitor.

He has betrayed those who trusted to him that which they regarded as amongst the sacred things of their experience. Thirdly: He is fawning. He "flattereth with his lips." Those to whom he betrays the secrets, he flatters; he gives them to understand that he will tell no one else, that were it not for their intelligence and integrity, he could not make to them such communications. He is a base fawning parasite. Fourthly: He is dangerous. "Meddle not with him." The man that will flatter you, vilify the absent, betray the "secrets" of others, is to be shunned. Have nothing to do with him. He goeth about from family to family, from circle to circle, retailing his secrets, making his comments, insidiously striking at reputations, creating wounds, and leaving them to rankle in the hearts of men. His mouth is a lethal weapon, with which he murders the good names of men. "Meddle not with him." Dean Swift has well described such tale-bearers :

> " Nor do they trust their tongues alone,
> But speak a language of their own:
> Can read a nod, a shrug, a look,
> Far better than a printed book;
> Convey a libel in a frown,
> And wink a reputation down;
> Or by the tossing of a fan
> Describe the lady and the man."

Here is—

THE WICKED SON.—"Whoso curseth his father or his mother, his lamp shall be put out in obscure darkness." First: Here is a horrible crime. To curse is to imprecate evil on any one. How appalling the crime of cursing father or mother, the instrumental authors of our being, the tender preservers of our infancy and childhood, and the loving guardians of our youth! Yet such monsters are to be found. The law of Moses required that such children should be put to death.* Secondly: Here is a terrible doom. "His lamp shall be put out in obscure darkness." The lamp is often used as a figure of prosperity. Such a wicked child shall not prosper. The laws of the moral

* Exod. xx. 17; Lev. xx. 9; Jno. xiii. 9; Job xviii. 16.

universe prevent his success. "His lamp shall be put out." He shall be wrapped in the darkness of poverty, disappointment, and remorse.

Proverbs 20:22

The Duty of Man Under a Sense of Injuries

"Say not thou, I will recompense evil; *but* wait on the Lord, and he shall save thee." *

THE verse suggests two remarks at the outset. First: That men in passing through this life are subject to injuries from their fellow men. Through sin men, instead of being the loving brothers of each other, are become to an awful extent the deceivers, the plunderers, the oppressors, and the devils. Hence men are everywhere found groaning under the injuries they have received from their fellowmen. Secondly: That men under a sense of injury crave for the punishment of their enemies. There is a sense of justice placed in every human soul: injuries kindle this sense of justice into a fiery passion, and this passion is revenge, and this revenge cries for the destruction of the enemy. "Revenge," says Bacon, "is wild justice." Yes, it is justice maddened into fury. Few passions get such power over men as revenge: it is often implacable.

> "I'll have my bond: I will not hear thee speak:
> I'll have my bond; and therefore speak no more.
> I'll not be made a soft and dull-eyed fool,
> To shake the head, relent, and sigh, and yield
> To Christian intercessors."—SHAKESPEARE

Now the Bible legislates for man under a sense of injuries. The verse requires him to do two things.

CEASE FROM THE WORK OF AVENGING HIMSELF.—"Say not thou I will recompense evil." There is a great

* Verse 21 has been noticed on page 464.

temptation under the injury to "say" so, a great temptation to grasp the iron rod of retribution and pursue the offender even unto death, but this must not be done. There are several good reasons for this. First: The injured man is disqualified for the infliction of just punishment. He is himself a criminal, living under the ban of eternal justice, and his own sense of rectitude is perverted. He has therefore neither the right nor the capacity to deal out retribution to any one. Has a criminal a right to the seat of the judge?

> "Use every man after his deserts, and
> Who shall 'scape whipping?"

Every man would, in this case, be engaged in whipping his brother, and the world would become a pandemonium reeking with blood. Secondly: The punishment he inflicts is an injury to himself. "Revenge is sweet," it is said; but if there is gratification in it, it is only momentary. When the final stroke has been given, the season of reflection sets in, and conscience comes up and makes the avenger its own victim. Thirdly: The Bible prohibits the attempt. It is prohibited even in the Old Testament, Exod. xxiii. 4, 5; Lev. xviii. 19; Prov. xviii. 13; xxiv. 29. The New Testament abounds with interdicts. Matt. v. 36, 45; Rom. xii. 17, 21. The verse requires him to—

COMMIT THE AVENGEMENT TO GOD.—"Wait on the Lord and he shall save thee." Is my enemy to be allowed to perpetrate his enormities on me with impunity? No, he will be punished; punished far more effectively than I can do if I leave it in the hands of Him Who judgeth righteously. He is Omniscient. We know but imperfectly. He is without passions. We are blinded by selfishness. He is without partiality. We are prejudiced on our own sides. "Vengeance is mine; I will repay, saith the Lord." He will avenge us of our enemies. By the dispensations of His providence, by the compunctions of conscience, by making the injuries we have received spiritually useful to ourselves.

Hear the Divine word on the subject. "See that none

render evil for evil unto any man; but ever follow that which is good, both among yourselves and to all men." "Recompense to no man evil for evil. . . . Dearly beloved, avenge not yourselves: but rather give place unto wrath; for it is written, Vengeance is mine: I will repay, saith the Lord. Be not overcome of evil, but overcome evil with good." "Wherefore let them that suffer according to the will of God, commit the keeping of their souls to Him in well doing, as unto a faithful Creator." "Commit thy way unto the Lord; trust also in Him, and He shall bring it to pass. . . . The Lord shall help them and deliver them: He shall deliver them from the wicked and save them, because they trust in Him."

Proverbs 20:24

A Providence Over Man

"Man's goings *are* of the LORD; how can a man then understand his own way?" *

THE doctrine of these words pervades the Bible, is frequently stated by Solomon, and accords with the reason and experience of mankind. The words lead us to consider providence—

AS A REALIZED FACT.—"Man's goings are of the Lord." We are not left to chance, we are neither the creatures of caprice, nor the absolute masters of our own destiny. The life of every man may be divided into two chapters. The first embracing all connected with his being, which has taken place irrespective of his own will. How much there is here. We had nothing to do with the questions whether we should exist at all, or if we existed what should be the peculiar attributes of our being, who should be our parents, in what country we should be born,

* Verse 23 is noticed on page 453.

in what period of the world's history our lot should be cast, under what circumstances we should be nursed and educated. All these things were absolutely ordered "of the Lord." We had no voice whatever in the connexion with them, we were absolutely passive. The other chapter in man's history embraces, Secondly: All that is connected with his history as a voluntary agent. A period dawns when we all begin to act as free workers. We choose and reject, we adopt this course and eschew that, we create some circumstances and subordinate others, and in all we fancy and feel ourselves to be unrestrained and free. But in all these "goings" of ours we are under the control "of the Lord." The good in us He originates. Whatever we do that is true, noble, and God-like, He inspires. The evil in us He controls. He subordinates it to His own purposes, and makes it subserve the interest of the universe. "Surely the wrath of man shall praise Thee; the remainder of wrath shalt thou restrain." The cases of Joseph, Jeremiah, John the Baptist, and the Apostles illustrate this. The crucifixion of Christ stands out above all other facts in history as a demonstration of God's overruling power of evil. "Modern history also abounds with examples. Luther was violently carried off and confined in Wartburg Castle, and there he translated the Scriptures, wrote upon the Galatians, and preached every Sunday in the castle. Bunyan was twelve years in Bedford jail, and wrote the "Pilgrim's Progress." Rutherford, in Aberdeen Castle, wrote his beautiful "Letters." John Welsh, in Blackness Castle, Madame Guion, in the Bastile, where she remained fourteen years, and wrote some of her sweetest poetry—the prisons of the inquisition, "the" day only can reveal their silent sorrows and patient courage. The inscriptions on the walls alone are glorious witnesses." The words lead us to consider God's overruling providence.—

AS A DIFFICULT PROBLEM.—"How can a man then understand his own way?" First: How can he understand the freedom of his own way? If all the good in him is divinely inspired, and all the evil overruled and subordinated, how can he be free? Must he not be in the hands of his Maker as clay in the hands of the potter? A philosophic reconciliation of man's moral freedom with God's comprehensive and unalterable plan is impossible. All that we know is, that we are conscious that we are free, that heaven holds us as responsible, and that our deepest nature acquiesces. Secondly: How can he understand the *future* contingencies of his own way? Whilst there are certain things in his future that are pretty clear to him, such as death and retribution, there are other things that lie in impenetrable gloom. "We know not what a day may bring forth." Our future may turn out the very reverse of what we intend. It is often so. "The Babel builders," says Bridges, "raised that proud tower to prevent their dispersion; and it was the very means of their dispersion." Pharaoh's "wise dealing" for the aggrandisement of his kingdom, issued in its destruction. Haman's project of his own glory was the first step of his own ruin. Often, also, is the way, when not counter, far beyond our own ken. Little did Israel *understand* the reason of their circuitous way to Canaan. Yet did it prove in the end to be the "*right way.*" As little did Ahasuerus *understand* the profound reason why "on that night could not the king sleep." A minute incident, seeming scarcely worthy to be recorded, yet a necessary link in the chain of the Lord's everlasting purposes to His Church. Little did Philip understand his own way when he was moved from the wide sphere of preaching the Gospel in Samaria, to go into the desert, which ultimately proved a wider extension of the Gospel. As little did the great apostle understand that his "*prosperous* journey" to see his beloved flock at Rome would be a narrow escape from shipwreck, and to be conducted in chains. Little do we know what we pray for. "By terrible things wilt thou answer us in righteousness, O God of our salvation." We go out in the morning not understanding our way, "not knowing what an hour may bring forth." Some turn, connected with our happiness or misery for life, meets us before night. Joseph, in

* Gen. xi. 4—9; Esther vi. 6—13; Esther vi. 1; Psalm lxv. 5; chap. xxvii 1; John iv. 7.

taking his walk to search for his brethren, never anticipated a more than twenty years' separation from his father.*
And what ought those cross ways or dark ways to teach us? Not constant, trembling anxiety, but daily dependence. "I will bring the blind by a way that they know not: I will lead them in paths that they have not known." But shall they be left in dark perplexity? "I will make darkness light before them, and crooked things straight. These things will I do unto them, and not forsake them." Often do I look back amazed at the strangeness of my course, so different, so contrary to my way. But it is enough for me that all is in Thine hands, that "my steps are ordered of thee." I dare trust Thy wisdom, Thy goodness, Thy tenderness, Thy faithful care. Lead me, uphold me, forsake me not. "Thou shalt guide me with Thy counsel, and afterwards receive me to glory."

Proverbs 20:25

Selfishness in Religion

"*It is* a snare to the man *who* devoureth *that which is* holy, and after vows to make enquiry."

THERE were under the Levitical dispensation certain things prescribed by the law as consecrated to God, such as tithes, first-fruits, firstlings of the herds and the flock. There were also things that were voluntarily consecrated or set apart as free-will offerings to Jehovah. It is to these, perhaps, that Solomon here specially refers. The expression "to devour that which is holy," characterizes the conduct of those who appropriate that to their own use which had been either by themselves or others consecrated to the service of God.

The subject leads us to consider selfishness in religion.

* Gen. xxxvii. 14; Isaiah xlii. 16; Psalm xxxvii. 23.

Selfishness everywhere is bad, it is the tap root of our wickedness, it is the stronghold of the devil, it is the chief of all the "principalities and powers of darkness." But when selfishness intrudes into the temple of religion it is peculiarly hideous. It is then the serpent amongst seraphs, the devil in the presence of Christ. Alas, it often does this. Selfishness is frequently found as operative in sanctuaries as in shops, in temples as in theatres. The verse indicates its twofold working.

THE APPROPRIATING OF THE CONSECRATED TO PERSONAL USE.—The verse speaks of the man who "devoureth that which is holy." This was the sin of Achan; he robbed the treasury of the Lord. * In truth this was the sin of the whole Jewish nation. "Will a man rob God? Yet ye have robbed me. But ye say, wherein have we robbed thee? In tithes and offerings. Ye are cursed with a curse, for ye have robbed me, even this whole nation." This is done now in many ways. First: In the personal appropriations of ecclesiastical endowments. Our forefathers, whether wisely or not, devoted immense properties to posterity for the promotion of divine ideas and divine virtues in this country. The ecclesiastics who appropriate thousands of this property to their own use, and by it live in palaces, fare sumptuously every day, and roll amongst their contemporaries in chariots of wealth and forms of splendour,—what do they? Do not they "devour that which is holy?" Are they not pampering their appetites and feeding their vanity by that which is consecrated to God? Secondly: In the assumption of sacred offices for personal ends. Those who enter on the office of the ministry, whether in or out of the Episcopal Church (and it is to be feared the number is legion), in order to gratify the greed for wealth, or ease, or social power, what do they do but "devour that which is holy"? They are turning to their own use an institution consecrated to the service of humanity. Thirdly: In the adoption of the Christian profession from motives of personal interest. There was a time when men made a secular sacrifice to unite with congre-

* Joshua vi. 19; vii. 1; Mal. iii. 8, 9.

gations, and identify themselves with Christian Churches. It is not so now. Those who join a church in order to get clients, customers, or patrons, what do they do but "devour that which is holy"? They use the Christian name, the divinest and most sacred thing in the world, for selfish and sordid ends.

The verse indicates the working of this selfishness in religion by—

THE ENDEAVOURING TO AVOID THE FULFILMENT OF RELIGIOUS VOWS.—"And after vows to make enquiry." There are three things that must be remembered in connection with this expression. First: The idea that it is wrong to make religious vows is not here. A "vow" means a solemn promise or engagement before God to render some service or make some sacrifice. And such vows are not only right, but binding and necessary. It is only as the soul makes a firm resolve to accomplish true and noble things that it can rise from its degradation and depravity. Nothing great is done without solemn determination. Secondly: The idea that it is wrong to break improper vows is not here. There are vows which never should be made, such as the vows of celibacy, and the vows of sponsors in episcopal baptisms, and the vows of priests in their ordination to adhere for ever to the same creed and polity. The man who solemnly vows to retain the same beliefs for ever, forswears his own progress, arrogates his own infallibility, and is a fool. The sooner a wrong vow is broken the better. Thirdly: The idea that it is wrong to think upon the vow after it is made is not here. No amount of thinking, however deep and earnest before it was made, precludes the propriety, obligation, or necessity of thinking about it afterwards. If the reasons for its formation are morally sound, the more they are thought upon the stronger they will become. If not, the more they are thought upon, the stronger will appear the obligation for revocation. But the idea here is not to think "after" a religious or generous vow is made, in order to escape its fulfilment. Selfishness often puts the mind to think afterwards in this direction and for this purpose.

One man under high spiritual excitement, produced, it may be, by a providence, a book, a conversation, or a sermon, vows to consecrate so much of his property to the cause of humanity and Christ. The excitement passes away, the vow is felt by conscience to be binding, and selfishness urges the mind to contemplate methods for a satisfactory release. How often this is done! Another man loses his health, is laid on the bed of languishing, and death seems close at hand. He feels the touch of his icy fingers upon his heart. He makes a vow to God, he utters it in the presence of the minister and those about his bed, that should he recover, his life and property shall be consecrated to holiness. He is restored to all the robustness and buoyancy of former years. He remembers his vow; its binding power is felt on his conscience, and selfishness sets him to think upon such methods as shall free him from its obligation, and enable him to live again according to his likings. In such ways as these selfishness urges men " after vows to make enquiry."

God deliver us from selfishness. How graphically one of our poets paints a selfish man :-

> " He pours no cordial in the wounds of pain ;
> Unlocks no prison, and unclasps no chain.
> His heart is like the rock where sun nor dew
> Can rear one plant or flower of heavenly hue.
> No thought of mercy there may have its birth,
> For helpless misery or suffering worth.
> The end of all his life is paltry pelf,
> And all his thoughts are centred on—himself.
> The wretch of both worlds ; for so mean a sum,
> First starved in this, then damned in that to come."

Proverbs 20:26, 28

A Strong Government

"A wise king scattereth the wicked, and bringeth the wheel over them. . Mercy and truth preserve the king: and his throne is upholden by mercy."

THESE two verses indicate the elements of a strong human government, and these are severity, truth, and mercy.

SEVERITY.—"A wise king scattereth the wicked, and bringeth the wheel over them." The allusion is here to the way of threshing in the East. One mode was by a wain, which had wheels with iron teeth like a saw. The axle was armed with serrated *wheels* throughout. It moved upon three rollers armed with iron teeth, or wheels, to cut the straw. The figure conveys two ideas. First: Separation. The old agricultural wheel cut the straw and separated the chaff from the wheat. The policy of a good government must ever be not only to separate the wicked from the true and virtuous citizen, but to separate the wicked from one another, and thus prevent them from leaguing together for spoliation and rebellion. The figure, Secondly: Conveys the idea of disablement. "Bringeth a wheel over them." This does not necessarily mean the destruction of their lives (we question the right of human government to take away life), but the crushing of the rebellious power, and disabling criminals from working out their lawless and dangerous aims. Now, it is to be observed, that it is against the "wicked" that these severities are to be employed. Not against the reformer of public abuses, or believer in improper creeds, but the *wicked*, those whose hearts are not only out of sympathy with the laws of God and man, but who are in direct antagonism to all that is morally and politically right. Another element of strong government indicated in these words, is

TRUTH.—"Mercy and truth preserve the king." A good government should be true. First: In its legislation. Its laws should be in harmony with eternal facts. They should agree with the claims of God, and with the rights of universal man. A government that is not true in its laws is not sound, and cannot long stand. Secondly: In its administration. It must be truthful in all the operations of executive. There must be no respect of persons. Similar transgressions must meet with similar penalties. Thus there must be reality in all. The king must not be pusillanimous, truculent, or changeable; he must be firm as granite, inexorable as justice. Another element of strong government is

MERCY.—"His throne is upholden by mercy." Mercy should be the genius of all. Mercy should temper severity and mellow law. The severity should be merciful, the just should be merciful. The whole government should be shaped and worked in order to prevent potential and remove existing misery. Where there is not this "mercy" the government will not be strong. "The throne of a tyrant," says one, "may be maintained in temporary stability by the force of terror, by the dread of civil or military executions. He may surround his throne by myrmidons of his power; he may prolong his reign by fear; but after all his is power that hangs upon a breath. All tremble to give expression to the feeling which yet universally prevails—the feeling of discontent, of alienation, of rebellion. One sentence may be enough to wake the thunders of a general rebellion. The utterance is responded to from every corner of the land, the spell is broken, every eye flashes the long suppressed resentment, every lip quivers in giving vent to the pent-up murmurings, man, woman, and child are all on the alert, hands are joined, conspiracies are formed, weapons are brandished, the tyrant is hurled from his throne."

Proverbs 20:27

Conscience

"The spirit of man *is* the candle of the LORD, searching all the inward parts of the belly."

By the "spirit" here I understand not the intellectual but the moral mind of man—the conscience. That which Byron calls "the oracle of God," and Coleridge "the pulse of reason;" but that which I regard as the very heart of humanity, that without which we may be thinking animals, but not men. Conscience is not an attribute of man—but the substratum, not a branch—but the root from which all the branches of his being spring.* The verse leads us to make two remarks about this conscience.

It is a divine light in man.—"The candle of the Lord." Culverwell has written a masterly treatise on this lamp within us. Conscience has been well called "God's vicegerent in the soul." It is to God what the moon is to the sun, reflecting his beams. Concerning this inner light, two things should be noted. First: It is clouded. Whilst it is in every man, it is in most men encircled with such a dense atmosphere of carnality, selfishness and sin, that its beams are scarcely seen. It is like the moon in an eclipse. It is there in its own grand orbit, but the earth has come between it and the great central orb. Secondly: It is inextinguishable. Though sin has clouded it so that it is all but hidden it cannot be extinguished. Hell's hurricanes, through a thousand centuries, have failed to extinguish one conscience. The lunar orb may be eclipsed, but it remains intact, holds its own orbit, and retains unaltered its relation to the eternal sun.

Another remark which the verse leads us to make concerning conscience is—

It is a self-revealing light.—"Searching all the

---

* For remarks on conscience, see HOMILIST, vol. iii., second series, pp. 488 and 535. See also vol. ii., first series, p. 227.

inward parts of the belly." The word "belly" here stands for the inmost depths of the soul, and the idea is, that conscience is a light that pours its beams into the central abysses of our being. So it does. It reveals to us our *motives*. Motives are the springs that set the whole of our machinery at work, and conscience concerns itself with these, sheds light upon the rightness and the wrongness of motives. In this way. First: It reveals the responsibility of actions. It is that power in us which shatters all the arguments of the intellect against our accountability. It holds us responsible for our likings and dislikes, for our affinities and antipathies. Secondly: It reveals the moral character of actions. Under its light man can have no doubt as to what action is wrong. "When the Gentiles, which have not the law, do by nature the things contained in the law, these having not the law, are a law unto themselves, which show the work of the law written in their hearts, their conscience also bearing witness, and their thoughts the meanwhile accusing or else excusing one another."

Let every man look well to his inner light. It is the divinity within him. Though it cannot be quenched, it may be so enrapt with the clouds of sin as to obscure its light. To go on in life with a darkened conscience, is to walk a road, of malignant foes and terrific precipices. "Every one that doeth evil hateth the light, neither cometh to the light lest his deeds should be reproved."

Proverbs 20:29

The Glory of Godliness, Both in Youth and Age

"The glory of young men *is* their strength: and the beauty of old men *is* the grey head." *

NEITHER of these clauses can be accepted without a qualification. There is no glory in the "strength" of a

* Verse 28 has been discussed on page 478.

young man, muscular or mental, if that strength is wrongly inspired and directed. Nor is there any "beauty" connected with the "grey head" if the old man has spent his years in debauchery and vice. Indeed, a dissolute old man is one of the most unbeautiful and hideous objects on which the eye can rest. Attach godliness to the strength of the young and to the "grey head" of the old, and then both clauses are full of truth.

GODLINESS IN YOUTH MAKES STRENGTH GLORIOUS.—Strength is one of the choicest gifts of our being. Muscular strength is a good thing, mental strength is a better thing; moral strength—strength to brave the wrong and do the right—is the best of all. But why is strength in a godly youth a glorious thing? First: Because it is inspired by a glorious spirit,—the spirit of love, unselfish and devout. Of all the objects in the universe, love is the most loveable. It is the glory of God Himself. Take from Him His love, and you will strip Him of His glory. Secondly: Because it is directed to a glorious object. What is the object to which it is directed? The destroying of the dark empire of ignorance, sin, and misery, and the establishment of the empire of intelligence, virtue, and blessedness. Truly the "glory" of such "young men is their strength."

GODLINESS IN AGE MAKES THE GREY HEAD LOVELY.—"The beauty of old men is their grey head." In a previous chapter it is said, "The hoary head is a crown of glory, if it be found in the way of righteousness."* There are three things in a truly godly old man which give beauty to his grey head. First: Affluent experience. He has travelled the winding path of life almost to its end, and can tell many a useful and inspiring anecdote of defeats and triumphs, of sorrows and joys, of hopes and disappointments, of gains and losses. The experience of a human life, devoted to the true and the good, is of all the valuable things on this earth the most valuable. It is one of God's best bibles. Secondly: Mellowness of character. The fruitful tree is beautiful in all seasons; beautiful in the buddings

* See Reading on page 328.

and blossoms of early spring; beautiful in the opening summer, with the unripened fruit clustering on its branches; but never so beautiful as when autumn has given the bloom of ripeness to the rich produce of its strength. How glorious is a human character ripe for heaven! Thirdly: Calm waiting. The work is done. Did man ever appear more beautiful than "Paul the aged," when he exclaimed, "I have fought the good fight, I have finished my course"? Who does not see beauty in such a character? "Verily thou shalt rise up before the hoary and the honourable old men."

Youth and age may both be beautiful and glorious in their own way and measure. Indeed, there must be a something common to both to make them beautiful. Cicero says, "As I approve of the youth that has something of the old man in him, so I am no less pleased with an old man who has something of the youth." The godly old man has much in him of the freshness of youth, and the godly youth possesses not a little of the gravity of age.

Proverbs 20:30

God's Discipline of His Children

"The blueness of a wound cleanseth away evil: so *do* stripes the inward part of the belly."

"It is not easy," says Dr. Wardlaw, "to attach a definite meaning to these words. Suppose with some the blueness of a wound to be a symptom of its healing, what comparison can there be between a mere symptom or indication of healing and the severity of chastisement or discipline? Suppose with others the *blueness* or *lividness* of the wound to be the effect or mark of its severity; then, properly speaking, there can hardly be a comparison between the effects, whatever they are conceived to be, of severe wounds and severe stripes, they are so nearly one and the same thing.

I know not indeed how the original word came to be rendered 'blueness.' The one word as well as the other is given in lexicons as signifying, among other meanings, '*a wound.*' But '*the wounds of a wound*' would, of course, be inadmissible. The following translation has been given by one critic of eminence :—' The bruises or contusions of a blow are a cleanser to the wicked man, and stripes cleanse the inward parts of the belly.' But this is liable to the same objection with the last-mentioned view, namely, that the two things in the comparison are too nearly the same, for what difference is there between the contusions of a blow cleansing the wicked, and 'stripes cleansing the inward parts of the belly'? The idea in either case is almost, if not altogether, *identical*. The following translation has been suggested, ' Surely the compression of a wound cleanseth away evil, and so do stripes the inward part of the belly.' The radical meaning of the word here translated *blueness*, means to unite, to join together. The pressing of the wound is often necessary, in order to cleanse it of that purulent and peccant humour, which prevents its healing."

The passage thus explained presents two thoughts concerning God's discipline of His children.

It is sometimes SEVERE.—It is as the compression of the wound. The squeezing of a wound in order to extract the virus is sometimes agonizing, yet it must be done. How painful often are God's dispensations with His people! Sometimes He takes from them the most *loved ones*, husband, wife, children, parents. Sometimes their *property*. He brings them from opulence to poverty. Sometimes their *health*. He sends diseases into their bodies to render existence all but intolerable. How severely did He try Abraham, and Job, Daniel, and Paul! There is so much dross in the gold that it requires the furnace to purify it. So many worthless branches wasting the life of the tree, that it requires the pruning knife to lop them off. " Whom the Lord loveth He chasteneth, and scourgeth every son whom He receiveth."

It is sometimes USEFUL.—" So *do* stripes the inward

parts of the belly." The idea is that as the compression of the wound presses out the humour that prevents the healing, so providential discipline tends to the good of our inmost soul. Trials are useful to spiritual character in many ways. They lead to serious thoughtfulness; they weaken our affections for earth; they deepen our sense of dependence on God. "Though no chastening for the present seemeth to be joyous, but grievous, nevertheless, afterward it yieldeth the peaceable fruit of righteousness unto them which are exercised thereby." " Trials," says Frederick Robertson, "bring man face to face with God—God and he touch; and the flimsy veil of bright cloud that hung between him and the sky is blown away; he feels that he is standing outside the earth with nothing between him and the Eternal Infinite. Oh! there is something in the sick-bed, and the aching heart, and the restlessness, and the languor of shattered health, and the sorrow of affections withered, and the stream of life poisoned at its fountain, and the cold lonely feeling of utter rawness of heart which is felt when God strikes home in earnest, that forces a man to feel what is real and what is not."

Proverbs 21:1-3

God and the Human Race

"The king's heart *is* in the hand of the LORD, *as* the rivers of water: he turneth it whithersoever he will. Every way of a man *is* right in his own eyes: but the LORD pondereth the hearts. To do justice and judgment *is* more acceptable to the LORD than sacrifice."

IN these verses we have God unfolded to us—

AS THE CONTROLLER OF HUMAN HEARTS.—"The king's heart is in the hand of the Lord as the rivers of water: he turneth it whithersoever he will." Some suppose there is an allusion to a gardener directing the rills of water through the different parts of his ground, and that the comparison is between the ease with which the gardener does this, and the ease with which the Almighty controls the purposes and volitions of the human soul. First: This is an undoubted fact. *A priori* reasoning renders this obvious. The God of infinite wisdom must have a purpose to answer in relation to the existence and history of the human race. He has a purpose not only in the rise and fall of empires, but in all the events that happen in the individual history of the obscure as well as the illustrious. But unless He has a control over the workings of the human heart and the volitions of the human soul, how could this purpose be realized? If He controls not the thoughts and the impulses of the human mind, He has no control over the human race, and His purposes have no guarantee for their fulfilment. But God says, "My counsel shall stand, and I will do all my pleasure;" and hence He must be the Master of the Human soul, turning all its rills of thought and feeling at His pleasure. History demonstrates the truth. Abimelech's heart was in the hand of the Lord for good. Pharaoh's heart was turned towards Joseph. The heart of the Babylonish despot was turned toward Daniel and his captive brethren. The hearts of the Jews in relation to Christ were under Divine control. Secondly: This fact interferes not with human responsibility. Though the Creator has an absolute control over all the workings of our minds, yet we are conscious that we are free in all our volitions and actions. Though the reconciliation of these two facts transcends our philosophy, they involve no absurdity. Suppose a man of great insight into character, and great experience as to how certain circumstances affect certain organizations, predicted that if a certain person whom he thoroughly understood was placed in certain conditions, a certain course of conduct on his part would be the inevitable result: that person, without knowing the prediction, falls into those circumstances and pursues a course of conduct identical with that foretold. Did the knowledge of the prophet exercise any coercion at all upon the mind of this individual? Certainly not. It is therefore not impossible to conceive of Him Who knows all men's organizations, and all the circumstances through which they are to pass, carrying on His purposes and yet leaving them in perfect possession of their freedom and accountability.

In these verses we have God unfolded to us—

As the JUDGE OF HUMAN CHARACTER.—" Every way of a man is right in his own eyes: but the Lord pondereth the hearts." There is in all probability a connection between this verse and the preceding one. And its connection suggests—First: That God judges men's characters not according to their own estimate. Men generally are so vain that they form a high opinion of themselves, but this estimate may be the very reverse of God's. Secondly: That God judges men's characters not according to the result of their conduct. Though they may unwittingly work out His plans, they do not approve themselves to Him on that account. The cruel treatment which Joseph's brethren inflicted on him subserved the Divine purpose; still it was not less wicked on that account. The crucifixion of Christ by the Jews was according to the Divine plan; yet the deed was the most heinous of all crimes. Thirdly: That God judges men's characters by the heart. "The Lord pondereth the hearts." The essence of the character is in the motive. "The Lord weigheth the spirits."

In these verses we have God unfolded to us—

As the APPROVER OF HUMAN GOODNESS.—"To do justice and judgment is more acceptable to the Lord than sacrifice." This sentiment is frequently expressed in the Bible.* "Sacrifice," at best is only circumstantially good —rectitude is essentially so. Sacrifice, at best, is only the means and expression of good—rectitude is goodness itself. God accepts the moral without the ceremonial, but never the ceremonial without the moral. The universe can do without the ceremonial, but not without the moral. "Justice and judgment" are the everlasting foundations of God's throne.

How great is God! He controls all hearts, and ap-

---

* 1 Sam. xv. 22; Isa. i. 11—15; lxvi. 3, 4; Jer. vii. 21—23; Hosea vi. 6; Micah vi. 6—8; Matt. xxiii. 33.

proves of all goodness. In all, and over all, He is THE GOOD.

> " Let all the air be lightnings, the dark blue
> Of ever-stretching space substantial fire;
> Still God is good, still tends o'er those He loves."— *Festus*

Proverbs 21:4
The Prosperity of the Wicked is Sin

" An high look, and a proud heart, and the plowing of the wicked, is sin."

THE word "plowing" in the margin is rendered "light." "The light of the wicked." The marginal references, of course, have precisely the same authority as those in the text, and are not unfrequently more faithful to the original. "The verse," it has been observed, "is remarkably laconic—the loftiness of eyes—pride of heart—the light of the wicked, sin." The meaning seems to be that in the prosperity of the wicked (for light is the symbol of prosperity) there is sin. This is the subject. The words teach—

That the wicked are PROUD.—" An high look and a proud heart." The first of these is but the expression of the second, the " high look," or, as in margin, " haughtiness of eyes." Pride arises from ignorance. First: From an ignorance of *self*. The man who knows himself even as a creature, who knows how insignificant he is as compared with the universe, will be humble; and much more the man who knows himself as a sinner, and who understands his moral wretchedness and dangers. Secondly: From an ignorance of *God*. Who that has any conception of the Infinite, could be proud in His presence? He who has a glimpse of Him will fall down like Isaiah, and exclaim, " Woe is me, I am a man of unclean lips." Pride and wickedness go together, and both are an " abomination to the Lord." The words teach—

That the wicked SOMETIMES HAVE PROSPERITY.—" The plowing—or rather the light—of the wicked." Light in the Old Testament is the symbol of prosperity. The wicked often prosper in the world. They amass fortunes, and take the leading positions in social life. This is often a perplexity to the good. "Wherefore do the wicked prosper?" In all ages true souls have thus cried out: and this also reveals the wonderful patience of God. How great the forbearance of Him Who allows His enemies to revel in palaces and sit on thrones! And this, moreover, prophesies a future retribution. There must come a reckoning day, a period for balancing all human accounts.

The words teach—

That the prosperity of the wicked IS WRONG.—"The plowing of the wicked is sin." Indeed, everything a wicked man does is sin, whether he ploughs, sows, or reaps, whether he buys or sells, whether he prays or swears, every act is sin. "Every thought in the imagination of his heart is evil continually." As he that is born of God cannot sin, so he that is wicked cannot but sin: he has no good intentions, and he can do no good acts. "Holy intention," says Bishop Taylor, "is to the actions of a man that which the soul is to the body, or form to its matter, or the root to the tree, or the sun to the world, or the fountain to the river, or the base to a pillar. Without these the body is a dead trunk, the matter is sluggish, the tree is a block, the world is darkness, the river is quickly dry, the pillar rushes into flatness and ruin, and the action is sinful, or unprofitable and vain." As the sinner has not these good intentions he is sinful in everything. "The evil spirit called sin," says Dr. Bushnell, "may be trained up to politeness, and made to be genteel sin; it may be elegant, cultivated sin; it may be very exclusive and fashionable sin; it may be industrious, thrifty sin; it may be a great political manager, a great commercial operator, a great inventor; it may be learned, scientific, eloquent, highly-poetic sin! Still it is sin, and being that, has in fact thes ame radical or fundamental quality that, in its ranker and less restrained conditions, produces all the most hideous and revolting crimes of the world."

Proverbs 21:5-7; 22:29

The Right and Wrong Road to Plenty

"The thoughts of the diligent *tend* only to plenteousness; but of every one *that is* hasty only to want. The getting of treasures by a lying tongue *is* a vanity tossed to and fro of them that seek death. The robbery of the wicked shall destroy them; because they refuse to do judgment."

"Seest thou a man diligent in his business? he shall stand before kings: he shall not stand before mean *men*."

To have *plenty* of a good thing is felt by all to be desirable. Money is a good thing: it increases not only man's means of enjoyment, but man's power of usefulness. Knowledge is a good thing; the mind without it is in a cell, narrow, and dark. Great is the blessing of plenteous knowledge. The "plenteousness" in the verses, however, refers to worldly wealth, and points to the right and wrong way of gaining it. Observe:

The RIGHT road.—"The thoughts of the diligent tend only to plenteousness." Diligence stands opposed—First: To laziness. Frequently have we had occasion to notice Solomon's reprobation of idleness. Idleness has been called Satan's seed-time—the mother of wanton children—the rust and canker of the soul—the devil's cushion and pillow. Diligence is the opposite of this. It is industrious activity. It stands opposed—Secondly: To rashness: It is here put in contrast with hastiness. "But of every one that is hasty only to want." The hasty man has no *plan*. When he works it is desultory and spasmodic. The hasty man has no *perseverance*. To-day he is all enthusiasm in his labour, both his hands are stretched out, and with might and main he struggles for plenty; to-morrow he is in a state of collapse. The "diligent" man in opposition to this works by a plan, and works with perseverance. He begins in earnest, and goes on to the end in earnest, conquering difficulties, and reaping rewards; thus he gets rich. "Seest thou a man diligent in business? he shall stand before kings; he shall not stand before mean men." Observe:

The WRONG road.—First: *Falsehood* is a wrong road. "The getting of treasures by a lying tongue is a vanity tossed to and fro of them that seek death." It is often the shortest road to wealth, and hence the most popular; it is crowded with travellers. The commercial atmosphere is infested with fallacies; shops swarm with lies. Falsehood is a great fortune maker here in our England, and although it is a short and popular road, it is ultimately a ruinous one. It "is a vanity tossed to and fro of them that seek death." What is "tossed to and fro"—the treasure or the falsehood that obtained it? The latter, I think. A lie is a prolific thing. One falsehood creates many, one cheat produces another. There is a tossing to and fro. The time comes when the swindle is discovered, and then there is ruin. The men who gain wealth by falsehood are "seeking death." Secondly: *Dishonesty* is a wrong road. "The robbery of the wicked shall destroy them." Falsehood and fraud are twins; lies and robbery go together. Dishonesty, like falsehood, is a rapid, and, alas! a very common road to wealth. But this also leads to ruin. "The robbery of the wicked shall destroy him." It often does so here, when the swindle is discovered and brought into the court of justice: and it will inevitably do so at last when the Great Judge shall call every man to an account. "Know ye not that the unrighteous shall not inherit the kingdom of God." Unrighteous gain is a dear bargain. Money got by fraud and dishonesty will one day ruin its possessor, as the thirty pieces of silver did the foul betrayer of our Lord. Be honest, not because "honesty is the best policy," for I agree with Archbishop Whately, that he who acts on this principle is not an honest man—but because honesty is right.

"Dishonour waits on perfidy. A man
Should blush to *think* a falsehood: 'tis the crime
Of cowards."—JOHNSON

Proverbs 21:8

The Unregenerate and the Regenerate

"The way of man *is* froward and strange: but *as for* the pure, his work *is* right."

THE verse evidently expresses a contrast between the bad man and the good man. Its first clause may be read—"The way of the unregenerate man is froward and strange." Paul, in writing to the Corinthians* says, "For ye are yet carnal: for whereas there is among you envying and strife, and divisions; are ye not carnal and walk as men?" By "walking as men," he means walking as unconverted men, and by "the way of man," in this verse, we are to understand the way of the unrenewed. Notice then:

The way of the UNREGENERATE.—First: The way of an unconverted man is here called a "froward" way. The word "froward" means refractory, rebellious; and what is sin but frowardness? "Lo this only have I found, that God hath made man upright: but they have sought out many inventions." The state of the unrenewed heart is that of rebellious insubordination. "Who is the Lord that I should obey Him?" Secondly: The way of an unconverted man is here called a "strange" way. It is "strange"—it is not the original way. Man was made to walk in the path of virtue and piety. It is "strange"—it is not the authorized way. It is not the high road sanctioned by Divine authority, it is a by-path which the foot of the transgressor has made. It is "strange"—it is a perplexing way, it is labyrinthian, misty, and perilous. Notice also:

The way of the REGENERATE.—"But as for the pure his work is right." First: The regenerate are "*pure.*" They are cleansed by the washing of regeneration and the renewing of the Holy Ghost: their consciences "have been purged from dead works to serve the living God." Secondly: The regenerate *work well.* "His work is

* 1 Cor. iii. 2.

right." The rectitude of "his work" is at once the effect and evidence of his purity. A right work implies two things: A right standard. What is the right standard? Not the laws of man, not the customs of society, not the example of the holiest creature, but the *will* of God. His character is the foundation, and His Will the rule of virtue in all worlds and for ever. A right work implies also a right motive. He only does the right who obeys that will from the right motive, and the right motive is supreme love to God.

If we are regenerate, *right* is our watchword, right is our goal. "It is common," says Burke, "for men to say that such and such things are perfectly right, very desirable; but, unfortunately, they are not practicable. Oh, no. Those things which are not practicable are not desirable. There is nothing really beneficial that does not lie within the reach of an informed understanding and a well-directed pursuit. There is nothing that God has judged good for us that He has not given us the means to accomplish, both in the natural and moral world. If we cry like children for the moon, like children we mus cry on." A more common and disastrous sophistry know I not than that which asserts a course of action to be right in itself but impracticable under existing circumstances. What is right is evermore expedient, binding, and performable. Right stands for ever as the thing to be done, the goal to be aimed at.

> "Powers depart,
> Possessions vanish, and opinions change,
> And passions hold a fluctuating seat;
> But, by the storm of circumstances unshaken,
> And subject neither to eclipse nor wane,
> Duty exists: immutably survives
> For our support, the measures and the forms,
> Which an abstract intelligence supplies:
> Whose kingdom is where time and space are not."
>   WORDSWORTH.

Proverbs 21:9, 19; 25:24

Matrimonial Misery

"*It is* better to dwell in the corner of the housetop, than with a brawling woman in a wide house. . . . *It is* better to dwell in the wilderness, than with a contentious and an angry woman."

"*It is* better to dwell in the corner of the housetop, than with a brawling woman and in a wide house."

HERE is a wife the very opposite of that described by old Ben Jonson:

"She who ne'er answers till a husband cools,
Or, if she rules him, never shows she rules;
Charms by accepting, by submitting sways,
Yet has her humour most when she obeys."

These verses lead us to consider—

THE TORTURING POWER OF A BRAWLING WIFE.—"It is better to dwell in the corner of the housetop than with a brawling woman in a wide house." Solomon states two very uncomfortable positions as preferable to the company of a "brawling woman." First: "The corner of a housetop." The roofs of the houses in the East were flat, and when solitude was courted the housetop was the resort. To dwell, however, in a corner of the housetop alone, exposed to the scorchings of a tropical sun, and the fury of tropical storms, was by no means a desirable thing. Yet far better would it be for a man to dwell in solitude amid the fury of the elements, than to live among the snarls, yells, groans, and curses of a fiendish virago. In the one case his temper might remain calm and unruffled, in the other it would be in a state of perpetual irritation. The other uncomfortable position is—Secondly: "The wilderness." This is a position more undesirable even than the "housetop." The wilderness, away from communications of society. Alone in dreariness and danger. "I had rather," says the wise son of Sirach, "dwell with a lion and a dragon, than to keep house with a wicked woman." "Every one," says Arnot, "has known some pair chained together by human laws where the heart's union has either never existed or been rent asunder. Two ships at sea are bound to each other by strong short chains. As long as the sea remains perfectly calm, all may be well with both; though they do each other no good, they may not inflict much evil. But the sea never rests long, and seldom rests at all. Woe to these two ships when the waves begin to roll. There are two conditions in which they might be safe. If they were either brought more closely together, or more widely separated, it might yet be well with them. If they were from stem to stern rivetted into one, or if the chain were broken, and the two left to follow independently their several courses, there would be no further cause of anxiety on their account. If they are so united that they shall move as one body, they are safe; if they move far apart they are safe. The worst possible position is to be chained together, and yet have separate and independent motion in the waves. They will rasp each other's sides off, and tear open each other's heart, and go down together." The verses lead us to consider—

THE DEMORALIZING POWER OF SIN.—"A brawling *woman*." What a monstrosity! What an unnatural object! The ideal of womanhood includes the tender, the gentle, the graceful, the reticent, and retiring. A "brawling" *wife* is still more unnatural. Pledged to bestow her strongest affections, and to render loyal services to the man of her choice, she should ever appear before him as his ministering angel. To minister to his comforts, and to stimulate him to the pure and the noble. Her calmness should soothe his temper, when ruffled by the cares and struggles of secular life; her tenderness should mollify the heart, which the rough influences of the world tend to petrify into granite. Shakespeare's description of a true wife is not far from the Divine ideal:

496 / Book of Proverbs

> " Heaven witness
> I have been to you a true and humble wife,
> At all times to your will conformable :
> Ever in fear to kindle your dislike ;
> Yea, subject to your countenance, glad or sorry,
> As I saw it incline. When was the hour
> I ever contradicted your desire,
> Or made it not mine too ? Or which of your friends
> Have I not strove to love, although I knew
> He were mine enemy ? What friend of mine
> That had to him derived your anger, did I
> Continue in my liking ? nay, gave notice
> He was from thence discharged ? Sir, call to mind
> That I have been your wife, in this obedience,
> Upwards of twenty years, and have been blest
> With many children by you : if, in the course
> And process of this time, you can report,
> And prove it too, against mine honour aught,
> My bond to wedlock, or my love and duty,
> Against your sacred person, in God's name
> Turn me away, and let the foul'st contempt
> Shut door upon me, and so give me up
> To the sharpest kind of justice."

What has effected this transfiguration ; what has transformed the calm angel into a brawler, the loving wife into a fiend and virago ? What ? Sin. Sin dehumanizes humanity. The verses lead us to consider—

THE CAUTION REQUIRED IN MATRIMONIAL ALLIANCES.—If a wife has power to embitter a man's whole life, to render it almost intolerable, with what caution should he enter the connubial relationship ! And yet, strange to say, men, aye and women too, are less cautious in choosing their companions for life than they are in choosing objects of most inferior description. People often bestow more care in selecting a fabric for their garment than in selecting their partner for life. Men often make more searching enquiries into the qualities of a cow, a dog, or a horse, which they intend to procure, than into the qualities of a woman whom they purpose to make their companion. No wonder there is so much matrimonial misery in the world when alliances are formed either from blind impulse or mercenary considerations. The man who without the exercise of his best judgment enters this, of all relationships the most endearing and Divine, either for lucre, or from lusts, justly deserves the pitiless peltings of a termagant through the whole of his life. And the same may be said of a woman. There are "brawling" men as well as "brawling" women; men who become the tormenting devils of those they swore to succour and bless.

"It is not good that the man should be alone." So saith the Almighty; so say the deepest instincts of our nature; so saith human experience. Yet better a thousand times be alone, better be on "the corner of a housetop," better in the howling "wilderness" amongst the prowling beasts of prey, better anywhere than with a "brawling" wife. Yet many wise and noble men have had to endure this. When Socrates was asked, "Why he endured his wife?" "By this means," he replied, "I have a schoolmaster at home, and an example how I should behave myself abroad. For I shall be the more quiet with others, being thus daily exercised and taught in the forbearing of her."

Proverbs 21:10-12

The Wicked

"The soul of the wicked desireth evil: his neighbour findeth no favour in his eyes. When the scorner is punished, the simple is made wise: and when the wise is instructed, he receiveth knowledge. The righteous *man* wisely considereth the house of the wicked: *but God* overthroweth the wicked for *their* wickedness."

HERE is another of the many descriptions of the wicked that have in this book gone before, and have yet to follow. Solomon is constantly hitting off sketches of the characters of the two great moral classes of mankind. As new phases of wickedness or goodness come under his eye, or start from his imagination, he portrays them. Here we have wicked men presented to us:

AS ANIMATED BY THE WORST OF DISPOSITIONS.—

Two dispositions of mind are here indicated. First: *Malignity*. "The soul of the wicked desireth evil." The "evil" here is injury to his neighbour. "His neighbour findeth no favour in his eyes." He injures his neighbour to gratify not merely his greed and ambition, but his malice. He delights in suffering for its own sake. The throes of anguish are music in the ear of the wicked. "The poison of asps is under their lips: whose mouth is full of cursing and bitterness. Their feet are swift to shed blood." This is the very spirit of hell—this is Satanic sin. Sin is malevolence. Secondly: *Derision*. "The scorner is punished." We have frequently met with the "scorner" before. The "scorner" is one destitute of all sense of reverence, of every sentiment of humility. He is haughty, profane, and heartless. "Fools make a mock at sin." Wickedness scoffs at the sacred and the divine. Here we have wicked men presented to us—

AS SUBJECT TO DIVINE PUNISHMENT.—"The scorner is *punished*." "God overthroweth the wicked for their wickedness." The certainty that unrepentant wickedness will be punished may be argued—First: From the principle of moral causation. God has established such a connection between character and condition that misery must ever spring from sin, and blessedness from virtue. Our present grows out of the past, hence our sins must find us out. What we morally sowed yesterday, we reap in experience to-day, and so on for ever. Secondly; From the operations of moral memory. Memory recalls sins, places them before the eye of conscience, and sets the soul aflame. Thirdly: From the declarations of Scripture. "The wicked shall not go unpunished." "The wicked shall be turned into hell, with all the nations that forget God." Fourthly: From the history of mankind. Nations are an example. The Antediluvians, the Sodomites, the Jews. Individuals are an example. Moses, David, Judas. Here we have wicked men presented to us—

AS STUDIED BY THE GOOD.—First: The influence of their punishment when studied by the simple. "The simple is made wise." Elsewhere Solomon has said,

"Smite a scorner and the simple will beware." By the "simple" is to be understood the inexperienced; those who are comparatively innocent. When they see the wicked punished, they are "made wise." They see what comes of sin, and they learn to shun it. Secondly: The influence of their punishment when studied by the wise. "And when the wise is instructed he receiveth knowledge." The "simple" become wise, and the wise increase in knowledge by it. Even David learned wisdom by the punishment of the wicked. "Thou puttest away all the wicked of the earth like dross: therefore I love thy testimonies. My flesh trembleth for fear of Thee, and I am afraid of Thy judgments." Thirdly: The influence of their punishment when studied by the righteous. "The righteous man wisely considereth the house of the wicked; but God overthroweth the wicked for their wickedness." Dr. Boothroyd thus translates the verse: "The righteous man teacheth or gives instruction to the house of the wicked, to turn away the wicked from evil." An able expositor's remarks on this rendering are as follows: "A forced and unnatural supplement is thus avoided, and the difficulties, in a simply critical view, are at least greatly lessened. In the Vulgate Latin version the same turn is given to the second part of the verse. 'The just man thinks maturely concerning the house of the wicked, that he may draw away the wicked from evil.'" Thus the wicked, in their malignant and scoffing spirit, and the punishment that follows them, become useful to the simple, the wise, and the righteous, as they are made subjects of serious and devout reflection. Good men can get good out of the wicked, by devout thought they can make the devil himself render them service.

Proverbs 21:13

The Cry of the Poor

"Whoso stoppeth his ears at the cry of the poor, he also shall cry himself, but shall not be heard."

THE text leads us to consider social distress, social heartlessness, and social retribution.

SOCIAL DISTRESS.—"The cry of the poor." The poor have ever existed, and we are told that "they shall never cease out of the land." The poor may be divided into two classes. First: The deserving. There is a poverty that comes on men by circumstances over which they have no control: infirm bodies, diseased faculties, social oppression, untoward events. Such poverty deserves and demands commiseration and help. Such poverty is often associated not only with great intelligence, but with virtue and piety of a high order. "I have read," says Sir Walter Scott, "books enough, and observed and conversed with enough of eminent and splendidly cultivated minds, too, in my time; but I assure you I have heard higher sentiments from the poor, uneducated men and women, when exerting the spirit of severe yet gentle heroism under difficulties and afflictions, or speaking their simple thought as to circumstances in the lots of friends and neighbours, than I ever yet met with, except in the pages of the Bible." Secondly: The undeserving. A large number of the poor in all countries have brought poverty on themselves. From laziness, extravagance, intemperance, have sprung their indigence and their woes. Far be it from me to suggest that all those who have got into penury and want by their own conduct, have no claims upon our compassion. There are many whose grief for their past conduct greatly intensifies the wretchedness of their poverty. Many who fruitlessly struggle to relieve themselves of their indigence with the determination to adopt a new course of life in the future. Such call for our pity and claim our helping hand.

SOCIAL HEARTLESSNESS.—" Whoso stoppeth his ears." There are those who stop their ears at "the cry of the poor." At this moment pauperism in England (where it should scarcely have any existence at all) has reached an extent greater than in any past period of her history, and it is increasing every week. "The cry of the poor" is deeper and louder here than ever, and getting new volume every day. There are two classes of men that should regard this "cry." First: The wealthy. Material good is limited, the material universe itself is finite. The more one man has of this world's goods the less remains for others. In this country there are tens of thousands who have appropriated to their own use more than their own moral share. Justice, to say nothing of mercy, demands that they should distribute of their abundance to the relief of the distressed. Secondly: The legislating. The resources of the country are in a great measure in the hands of our rulers. They can enrich them and impoverish them, they can develop and direct them, and their grand object should be so to manage imperial matters that there should be no want and complaining within our borders. It is for them, by the cultivation of waste lands, and the promotion of emigration, to provide for the working classes fields of remunerative labour. This, however, they have shamefully neglected. Even the members of our present Government, notwithstanding the wonderful philanthropic profession which before they obtained power they rung into the ear of the country, are doing nothing to check poverty. What are those in the House of Commons, who for upwards of a quarter of a century have been dealing in that tall philanthropic talk by which they have won their popularity and power, doing to mitigate our growing pauperism? Our statesmen talk of retrenchment, and what do they retrench? Do they demonstrate to the nation the honesty of their professions by voluntarily surrendering a portion of the enormous incomes which they themselves derive from the State? No. They discharge poor labourers from the dockyards, and humble clerks with large families, and thereby only augment the poverty of the land. In the name of Heaven, what is the good of a Government if it cannot overcome pauperism?

SOCIAL RETRIBUTION.—The text tells us, "whoso stoppeth his ear at the cry of the poor, he also shall cry himself, but shall not be heard." Alas, there are many of the rich and the ruling who stop their ears. Their ears are opened to fawning flattery and panegyric adulations. The cheers of platforms and the laudations of journals are music to their souls. But the long, deep wail of the poor, which not only comes up from all the alleys of the towns and cities of England, but from thousands of the wretched hovels in rural scenes, they cannot hear. For such, retribution will come. "With what measure they mete it shall be meted to them again." They shall one day cry, "but shall not be heard." "He shall have judgment without mercy that has showed no mercy." This retribution often occurs in this life; it is certain to occur at last. "Inasmuch as ye have not done it to the least of these my brethren, ye have not done it unto me." "Go to now, ye rich men, weep and howl for your miseries that shall come upon you."

Heaven forbid that we should stop our ears at "the cry of the poor." Let us commiserate them, let us help them to the utmost of our ability. Howard's rule is this, a rule which he embodied in his noble life, "That our superfluities give way to other men's convenience, that our conveniences give way to other men's necessaries, and that even our necessaries sometimes give way to other men's extremities." "Charity," says Chrysostom, "is the scope of all God's commands."

Proverbs 21:14

Social Anger

"A gift in secret pacifieth anger: and a reward in the bosom strong wrath."

THE subject of these words is *social anger*. Next to the evil of having anger burning as a flame in our *own* hearts, is that of its existing in the hearts of others toward us. To have a man within the circle of your social life crying out in the language of Shakespeare—

> "Oh, that the slave had forty thousand lives;
> One is too poor, too weak for my revenge!
> I would have him nine years a killing!"

is a terrible calamity. The verse exhibits anger in two aspects.

AS UNRIGHTEOUSLY PROVOKED.—The anger spoken of here is an anger that ought not to have been excited, otherwise its pacification would not be referred to as proper and desirable. There is a righteous excitation of anger in the minds of our contemporaries. When we rouse indignation because we deal out honest reproofs, expose corrupt motives, and thwart immoral schemes, we are not chargeable with any blame on account of the anger. Christ Himself set the souls of the men about Him aflame with indignation. But when by an *unjust* impugning of motives, a slanderous expression, a false charge, or a dishonourable act, we awaken anger, we are justly blameable for its existence, and we are bound to use every justifiable means to put an end to it. We should not allow the fire to burn on without efforts for its extinction.

AS GENEROUSLY OVERCOME.—"A gift in secret pacifieth anger: and a reward in the bosom strong wrath." What kind of gift can put out the flame of anger? First: It must be obviously *disinterested*. If I present the most costly gift to my enemy in order to appease his wrath, unless he sees convincingly that the gift is free from all selfishness and fear, and perfectly disinterested, he may accept it and be silenced by it, but his anger will be unsubdued. Love alone can overcome anger. The waters to quench the fires of revenge must be drawn from the fountains of a loving heart. Secondly: It must be obviously *unostentatious*. It must be "a gift in secret"—"a reward in the bosom." A gift loses its moral value, its moral power as an atonement, when it is offered in an ostentatious spirit. It is an instinct of virtue to shrink from parade; it wishes to make itself known by silent deeds, not by trumpet sounds.

Do not let anger which you have unrighteously excited burn on in human breasts without earnest effort for its extinguishment, for verily anger is a terrible thing. "If you look into this troubled sea of anger," says good old Thomas Adams in his quaint way, "and desire to see the image of a man, behold you find fiery eyes, a faltering tongue, gnashing teeth, a heart boiling in brine, and drying up the moisture of the flesh till there be scarce any part left of his right composition." "If thine enemy be hungry, give him bread to eat; and if he be thirsty, give him water to drink; for thou shalt heap coals of fire upon his head, and the Lord shall reward thee."

Proverbs 21:15

Moral Contrasts

" *It is* joy to the just to do judgment: but destruction *shall be* to the workers of iniquity."

HERE is a twofold contrast.

A contrast in CONDUCT.—First: Here is a doing of judgment. "It is a joy to the just to *do* judgment." The whole of man's duty may be comprehended in two words —do justice. Do justice to *yourself*, respect your own nature, train your own faculties, promote your own rights.

Do justice to *society*—"whatever ye would that men should do unto you, do even so to them." Do justice to your *Maker*—"render unto him the glory due unto His name." Secondly: Here is a working of wrong. "Workers of iniquity." This is the very opposite conduct to the former. To work iniquity is to act in opposition to all the duties we owe ourselves, society, and God. All men on earth are found pursuing one of these two courses: all are doing the just or the unjust. Here is—A contrast in DESTINY.—Here is blessedness. "It is joy to the just to do judgment." "Virtue is its own reward." As heat issues from the fire, and light flows from the sun, joy springs from righteous doings. The ways of rectitude are ways of pleasantness and peace. Every true act of justice swells the melody of the heart's true joy. "The work of righteousness shall be peace, and the effect of righteousness, quietness and assurance for ever." Secondly: Here is ruin. "Destruction shall be to the workers of iniquity." "Destruction" of what? Not of existence, not of consciousness, not of moral obligations, but of all that can make existence happy. The "workers of iniquity" are working their own ruin. Destruction and misery are in their way, and the ways of peace they have not known.

Proverbs 21:16

Hopeless Apostasy

"The man that wandereth out of the way of understanding shall remain in the congregation of the dead."

APOSTASY is of *two* kinds, good and bad. The man who renounces a false creed, or abandons a wrong course of life, is a praiseworthy apostate. But he who renounces the true and the right, is an apostate morally censurable. All sinners in the universe are apostates in this sense, they have forsaken the true and the good. All sin is an apostasy. There are *two* classes of criminal apostates in the universe—those whose condition is hopeless, and those who may yet be restored to the true and the good. Fallen angels, and finally impenitent men, belong in all probability to the former class; those who are redeemable by Christianity belong to the latter.

The verse points us to the *hopeless* apostate.

HIS CONDUCT.—He "wandereth out of the way of understanding." First: All apostates were once in "the way of understanding." "The way of understanding" is the way of rectitude, religion, godliness. The Infinitely Holy One never created a soul that He did not put in that way at first. All the lowest fiends in the universe were once in "the way of understanding." To suppose otherwise would be to make God the author of sin. "Lo, this only have I found, that God hath made man upright: but they have sought out many inventions." Secondly: All apostates are now wandering from that way. "All we like sheep have gone astray." All sinners are prodigals that have wandered from their Father's house—homeless, benighted, hell-exposed wanderers. They are lost, and every step makes their condition worse. Fallen spirits are stars that have wandered from their orbit, to whom is reserved "the blackness of darkness for ever."

HIS RUIN.—"Shall remain in the congregation of the dead." The word here translated "dead" is elsewhere rendered "giants." But it is also rendered "dead" in many other passages. Parkhurst and most critics consider intensity to be implied in the word, and would represent the idea by the expression "mighty dead." The language implies, First: Utter ruin. "Dead." The death of the hopeless apostate is not annihilation, but something infinitely worse; it means the wreck of all that can make existence worth having. Secondly: Collective ruin. "The congregation of the dead." There is a vast assemblage of ruined souls somewhere in the universe. They are together, yet they have no fellowship, for they lack mutual sympathy and confidence. "Devil with devil damned." What a "congregation!" Who can tell their number? Who can fathom the depth of their anguish? Conscience their preacher, and groans their psalmody. But on this earth is not the vast assemblage of corrupt men, "a congregation of the dead?" Thirdly: Interminable ruin. "Shall remain." "Remain"—how long? Will there ever come a period to the misery of their condition? I know not. The following passages are terrible answers to the problem. "For if we sin wilfully after that we have received the knowledge of the truth, there remaineth no more sacrifice for sins, but a certain fearful looking for of judgment and fiery indignation, which shall devour the adversaries." "For if after they have escaped the pollutions of the world through the knowledge of the Lord and Saviour Jesus Christ, they are again entangled therein, and overcome, the latter end is worse with them than the beginning."

Proverbs 21:17

Self-indulgence, a Source of Poverty

"He that loveth pleasure *shall be* a poor man: he that loveth wine and oil shall not be rich."

SELF-INDULGENCE is prevalent amongst all classes. There is a strong tendency in all to pamper appetite, and to gratify the flesh. Wealth, where it is possessed, is employed for this purpose. It is used to bring the choicest viands from every shore, and to procure those arts that can please the senses, and charm the imagination. Where it is not possessed, it is struggled after with the hope of its ministering to self-gratification. Self-indulgence is not human happiness; it is a delirium, not a delight. It is a mere titillation of the dying nerves, not a Divine thrill of our imperishable sensibilities and powers. Its music is the notes of a maniac, not the strains of a seraph.

The verse teaches that this self-indulgence tends to poverty, but how?

It involves an EXTRAVAGANCE OF EXPENDITURE.—A man that "loveth pleasure" and "wine and oil," who gives himself up to self-indulgence, is generally tempted to lavish expenditure of his means. Pleasure is an expensive divinity. It demands the most costly sacrifices. The largest fortunes must often be laid upon its altar. How frequently in our journals do we read of historic families ruined, and lordly estates bartered away, for the mere love of pleasure! Profligate voluptuousness, with its expensive viands, its luxurious refinements, its costly establishments, and its foolish pastimes, makes light work with fortunes.

It involves a FOSTERING OF LAZINESS.—The self-indulgent man becomes such a lover of ease, that effort of any kind becomes distasteful and repulsive; the spirit of industry forsakes him, and all his energies sleep in the lap of self-indulgence. And indolence, as Solomon has often told us, and as all history shows, tends to poverty. "He that loveth pleasure, shall be a poor man; he that loveth wine and oil shall not be rich." But whilst it is true that self-indulgence leads to *material* poverty, it also leads to a poverty of a far worse description. It leads to *intellectual* poverty. The self-indulgent man, if he reads at all, reads not those productions which inform the judgment, challenge thought, and stimulate inquiry, but tales that are the foulest froth of literature. If he thinks, he does not think upon those great subjects which quicken, refine, and ennoble the soul, but on such as constitute the gossip of the hour. Consequently, his intellect is pauperized. It leads to *spiritual* poverty. The man who would get his soul strong in holy resolves and righteous principles, must agonize to enter in at the "strait gate" of habitual reflection, holy labour, and earnest worship. This the self-indulgent man will not do.

Proverbs 21:18

The Wicked, a Ransom for the Righteous

"The wicked *shall be* a ransom for the righteous, and the transgressor for the upright."

THE sentiment expressed in these words is God's *special* regard for the interest of His people. He uses even wicked men as a "ransom" for them. The sentiment is expressed elsewhere—" For I am the Lord, thy God, the Holy One of Israel, thy Saviour : I gave Egypt for thy ransom, Ethiopia and Seba for thee. Since thou wast precious in my sight, thou hast been honourable, and I have loved thee : therefore will I give men for thee, and people for thy life." *
" How was Egypt a 'ransom'?" says an able expositor. " Not in the strict and proper sense of the word ; but when Israel was to be delivered, and Egypt, the oppressor, stood in the way, the deliverance was effected at the cost of Egypt,—by plagues on her people and land, and the destruction of her armies. Thus, in after times, was the army of Sennacherib sacrificed for the deliverance of good King Hezekiah and his people, when in the time of their perplexity and peril, they cried unto the Lord. Thus did the plots of the wicked Haman for the destruction of Mordecai and the Jews come back upon himself. In the end, " all the wicked " that have opposed " the righteous," and done what they could to frustrate their salvation, shall become, for their sakes, the victims of the Divine displeasure." The wicked are a " ransom " for the righteous in many ways. Their history is a *warning* to the righteous. However secularly grand in life, their end is ever lamentable. " Like sheep they are laid in the grave." They act as beacons to the good. " I have seen the wicked in great power, and spreading himself like a green bay tree : yet he passed away, and, lo, he was not; yea, I sought him, but he could not be found."† Their antagonism is a *test* to

---

* Isaiah xliii. 3, 4. † Psalm xxxvii. 35.

the righteous. Principles, to grow in purity and strength, require testing. As trees require storms to strengthen their roots, righteous souls require opposition to deepen their hold on truth and God. Their productions are often of *service* to the righteous. The discoveries they make, the arts they invent, the enterprises they accomplish, are often turned by the good to their own account. God makes the wicked serve the good. Whatever the wicked in the midst of their pride and pomp may think, they are mere *sacrifices* for the good and the true. This is God's plan. Several remarks rise out of this fact:

THE WICKED ARE NOT TO BE ENVIED.—What though they have the wealth and power of the world, they are the mere servants of the righteous; and what is worse, they serve the righteous not only without a will, but *against* their will. Serve them by their very opposition; serve them as Joseph's brothers served him, as the Jewish Sanhedrim in the Crucifixion of Christ served the highest interests of humanity. Do not envy the wicked. THE GOOD ARE NOT TO BE PITIED.—They may be poor, despised, oppressed; what of that? "All things work together for their good." Heartless despots and proud aristocracies are but spokes in the wheels of that providential chariot which rolls the good triumphantly onward to sublimer experiences. THE WORLD'S RULER IS NOT TO BE MISTRUSTED.—He has promised, what the purity, the justice, and the love of His character demand, that the saints shall rule the earth one day, that the right with the might shall prevail. Since He is such a Master of wicked men and even devils, too, as to make them unwittingly minister to the good of His people, shall we doubt Him? Hell itself is an instrument by which He works out His vast and beneficent designs. The arch-fiend, the head and leader of all wicked principalities and powers, is not only chained to His car, but made to bear it onward according to His Eternal Will.

Proverbs 21:20

Wealth in Relation to Character

"There is treasure to be desired and oil in the dwelling of the wise: but a foolish man spendeth it up"*

MEN make a great mistake when they suppose that things which are good for some are equally good for others. It is the character of the man that determines the value of things to him. What would be a blessing to one man would be a curse to another. Intellect, genius, wealth, these are of no service to a man without pure love and noble aims, but the reverse. What boots a musical instrument in a man's house if neither he nor his household have either the science or the soul of music? These remarks are suggested by this verse, which implies that wealth is desirable for the good, but undesirable for the wicked.

It is DESIRABLE for the GOOD.—"There is treasure to *be desired* and oil in the dwelling of the wise." Wealth "in the dwelling of the wise" is a good thing, a thing to be rejoiced in, not only by its possessor, but by his neighbours and the world at large. First: He will get out of it good for his own soul. To him it will not be a golden chain fastening him to the material, but a pinion to bear him into the sunny realms of spiritual freedom. It is said that the Duke of Brunswick is confined in Paris by the fear of losing his wealth, which consists of an extraordinary collection of diamonds, valued at nearly half-a-million. These diamonds keep him in chains. He does not sleep away a single night. There he lies, in a house constructed not so much for comfort as security. It is burglar-proof, surrounded on every side by a high wall; the wall itself is surrounded by a lofty iron railing defended by innumerable sharp spear heads, which are so contrived that if any person touches one of them, a chime of bells begins instantly to

* Verse 19 has been noticed in a previous Reading.

ring an alarm. This iron railing cost him £2,821. He keeps his diamonds in a wall; his bed is placed against it, that no burglar may break into it without killing, or, at least, waking him, and that he may amuse himself without leaving his bed. The safe is lined with granite and with iron; if it is opened by violence, a discharge of firearms, which will inevitably kill the burglar, takes place, and at the same time a chime of bells in every room in the house is set ringing. He has but one window in his bedroom, the sash of the stoutest iron, and cannot be entered unless one be master of the secret combination of the lock. A case of a dozen six-barrelled revolvers, loaded and capped, lies upon a table within reach of his bed. "A good fortune," says Seneca,—and he spoke from experience, for he is said to have been worth £3,000,000—"is a great slavery." To the true, generous, and godly soul, however, wealth has no such manacling power; on the contrary, it becomes the means of widening the soul's sphere of action, and stimulating its love of freedom. His gold is not a prison to confine him, but a vessel to bear him abroad into new climes. Secondly: He will use it for good to others. He will employ it to ameliorate the material distresses of men. With it he will feed the hungry, clothe the naked, and heal the sick. With it he will promote the mental advancement of men. He will rear schools, employ teachers, and multiply agencies for advancing the mental culture of the race. He will not neglect the spiritual interests of mankind. He will build churches, multiply copies of the scriptures, and promote the ministry of the Holy Word. In a world like ours what good a rich man may do with his wealth! Hence "treasure is to be *desired*, and oil in the dwelling of the wise."

The verse implies that wealth—

Is UNDESIRABLE for the WICKED.—"But a foolish man spendeth it up." "Foolish" is the synonym for wicked. It is implied that the wicked often come into the possession of wealth, for they cannot spend it unless they have it. As a rule, perhaps, the wicked in the world possess a larger amount of wealth than the good. They get it by fraud and violence, and sometimes by fortune. Not unfrequently, indeed, do they come in possession of the property once held by the good. Perhaps Solomon here has a reference to that. Elsewhere, at any rate, he alludes to it. "Yea, I hated all my labour which I had taken under the sun: because I should leave it unto the man that shall be after me. And who knoweth whether he shall be a wise man or a fool? Yet shall he have rule over my labour wherein I have laboured, and wherein I have shown myself wise under the sun. This is also vanity."* But however he may come in possession of it, it is of no real service to him. "He spendeth it up." This may mean either, First: That he spendeth it upon himself. This he generally does. He lays it out to pamper his appetites, and gratify his lusts. He often spends it all upon himself, and thus buries his soul in bloated animalism. This may mean, Secondly: He squanders it away. How often do wicked men by their extravagancies and gamblings dissipate large fortunes! And sometimes by their very greed they do so. "As Æsop's dog, who, having a piece of meat in his mouth, and espying the shadow thereof in the water, thinking it had been another piece of flesh, snatched at it, and, through his greedy desire, lost that which he had before. Even so rich men, who might peaceably and quietly enjoy the goods they have, and taste with pleasure the fruits of their labours, by their covetous humour deprive themselves wholly thereof, and setting before their eyes a fraudulent and deceitful hope of things that seem to be good, forget for the most part those things that are good indeed."

Rejoice in the wealth of the good, covet not the wealth of the wicked. "If a rich man," says Socrates, "is proud of his wealth, he should not be praised until it is known how he spends it."

> "Young was I once, and poor; now rich, and old.
> A harder case than mine was never told:
> Blest with the power to use them, I had none;
> Loaded with riches now, the power is gone."
> ANTIPHILUS

---

* Eccles. xi. 18, 19.

Proverbs 21:21

The True Pursuit of Mankind

"He that followeth after righteousness and mercy findeth life, righteousness, and honour."

MAN is made for action; his health and his happiness depend upon the development of his activities. Inaction is *ennui*, is death. The development of his active powers requires an object of pursuit set before him calculated to stimulate his desires, and at the same time to command the approval of his conscience. An object of pursuit sufficient to excite and harmoniously develop all the activities of human nature must be characterized at least by three qualities. It must agree with the sense of right. Men will not throw their full being into a work that clashes with that imperishable sense of rectitude which Heaven has planted in human nature. It must agree with the necessary conditions of physical comfort. The object must be great enough to allow a man full scope for that industry and skill by which physical subsistence and secular comforts are attained. It must be everlastingly interesting. The object must keep up man's interest from day to day, year to year, age to age, as long as he exists. If the interest wanes, his energies will collapse. Where is such an object of pursuit to be found? It is in the Bible, it is in the verse.

GOODNESS IS THE OBJECT.—"He that followeth after righteousness and mercy." These two words represent universal excellence. "*Righteousness*" means giving one his due, doing justice to all. There is a justice man owes himself. He should properly train his own faculties, discipline his own affections, guard his own rights. There is a justice which a man owes his fellow-creatures; and there is a justice which he owes his God. He is bound to love Him with all his heart, and to serve Him with all his energy. "*Mercy*" is love. There may be love without mercy, because it may exist without knowledge of suffering; but there is no mercy without love—and "love is the fulfilling of the law." "God is love," and without love or charity, "we are nothing." Now this goodness consisting in rectitude and love, is to be the grand object of human pursuit. We are to follow after this, First: Supremely. It is to be the greatest thing in our horizon; it is to be the goal in the race of life. "I follow after," says Paul, "if that I may apprehend that for which also I am apprehended of Christ Jesus. Brethren, I count not myself to have apprehended; but this one thing I do, forgetting those things which are behind, and reaching forth unto those which are before, I press toward the mark, for the prize of the high calling of God in Christ Jesus."* We are to follow after this, Secondly: Constantly. It must be pursued, not occasionally, but always; not on the Sundays, but on the week-days as well; not in occasional seasons of worship, but in all departments of business. It is to be the *one thing*. As the motherly life runs through all the various departments of motherly history, so this moral life must permeate and rule all our daily activities.

HAPPINESS IS THE ATTENDANT.—"Findeth life, righteousness and honour." "He findeth life." Life stands for happiness frequently in the Bible. "Eternal life," in the New Testament, means eternal blessedness. The unregenerate has no true life; to have true life is to have true happiness. He "findeth righteousness." The righteous man will be righteously dealt with. The measure he has meted to others will be measured to him again. He "findeth honour." God has established such a connection between excellence and conscience, that conscience must reverence it wherever seen. Take the three words, "life, righteousness, honour," as representing *happiness*, then you have the idea that happiness comes as goodness is pursued. It does not come because the man is seeking it, but because he is seeking goodness as an end it flows in upon him at every step. This is the true doctrine. Hap-

* Phil. iii. 12—14.

piness never comes to man when he seeks it as an end. The constitution of our nature shows this. Happiness, whence comes it? It wells out of those activities which spring from generous self-oblivious love. The experience of man shows this. Who have been the truly happy men? The unselfish and the loving. The word of God shows this. "He that loseth his life shall find it." "The pure in heart shall see God." The man is "blessed in his deeds." Is not happiness the end of the universe? Yes. Did not God intend us to be happy? Yes. But He has ordained that our happiness shall grow out of our goodness. To be happy is to be good; to be good is to be like Himself.

Proverbs 21:22

The March of the Good

"A wise *man* scaleth the city of the mighty, and casteth down the strength thereof."

THE sentiment of this verse Solomon expresses more than once in the book of Ecclesiastes.—" Wisdom strengthened the wise more than the mighty men which are in the city." "Wisdom is better than strength." The superiority of mental to muscular force is everywhere manifest. It is seen in man's control in the world about him. By intelligence he brings the wildest and strongest beasts of the field into subjection to himself. It is seen in human governments: it is the few wise men of an age that control the millions: the few civilised souls that lead a nation of barbarians captive at their will. A few thinking men in England control 150,000,000 of the human race in India. "Wisdom is better than strength." The superiority of mental over muscular force has often been seen in *human warfare*. The proverb has had at times a literal fulfilment. Look at ancient Babylon, with its insurmountable walls and bulwarks; it seemed secure, and its monarch could smile in proud defiance at the power of the mightiest assailants. But Cyrus had something besides military forces. He had *wisdom*; and the turning of the course of the Euphrates, and entering by its channel, accomplished what force could not in any way effect. In an unexpected moment, a moment of careless and fearless mirth and revelry, while it was glorying in the impregnable security of its lofty and massive muniments, "the strength of the confidence" of Babylon was "cast down." The superiority of mental over muscular force is seen every day in commerce. Who are the men who do the most business in the world's great mart? Not the men whose muscular power is always on the stretch, all hurry, bustle, and almost out of breath; but those who, with superior mind, forecast, arrange, direct. It is not in the shop where the greatest bustle is that the most business is done. "Strength, wanting judgment and policy to rule, overturneth itself." *(Horace).* The superiority of mental over muscular force is seen in religion. Mere force, alas, has often been employed by governments to secure religion, but it has signally failed; coercion cannot travel to a man's soul. It is the power of mind alone, in the form of argument, suasion, example, that spreads truth. We shall now look on the text as suggesting the march of the good. "A wise man," in Solomon's meaning, is a good man, and the words therefore may express, that a good man overcomes difficulties.

A good man in his progress SURMOUNTS OBSTRUCTIONS.—"A wise man scaleth the city of the mighty." The march of a good man may be compared to that of an aggressive soldier; one who has to go forth to subdue fresh enemies and win new conquests, one who, like him in the Apocalyptic vision, has to go forth "conquering and to conquer." Everywhere, however, he meets with difficulties—"the city of the mighty." Political institutions, social customs, secular interests, and religious prejudices. These rear their formidable heads before him like the "city of the mighty." In the strength of God he goes on. He "scaleth the city."

"He casteth down imaginations, and everything that exalteth itself." By his faith he overcomes difficulties; he says to the mountain, "Depart," and his behest is obeyed. Thus Paul marched on. A good man in his progress CONFOUNDS OBSTRUCTIONS.—"He casteth down the strength of the confidence thereof." He becomes more than a conqueror. The Christian warrior destroys the confidence of his opponents; he strikes into their souls the arrows of his convictions, and in their terror, they exclaim, "Men and brethren, what shall we do?" The confidence of the wicked is based on falsehood, and as truth advances it gives way; is based on ignorance, and as intelligence advances it must yield; is based on selfishness and injustice, and as benevolence and rectitude advance it must totter to the fall. Let not force, though organized by governments and backed by battalions, depress the good man with alarm.

> " What is strength, without a double share
> Of wisdom? Vast, unwieldly, burthensome;
> Proudly secure, yet liable to fall
> By weakest subtleties: strength's not made to rule,
> But to subserve where wisdom bears command."
>
> MILTON

"My brethren, be strong in the Lord, and in the power of his might. Put on the whole armour of God, that ye may be able to stand against the wiles of the devil."

Proverbs 21:23

The Government of the Tongue

" Whoso keepeth his mouth and his tongue keepeth his soul from troubles."

I HAVE somewhere read of a plain, ignorant man, who came to a learned man and desired him to teach him some one Psalm or other. He began to read to him Psalm xxxix., *Dixi custodiam, &c.,* " I said, I will look to my ways that I offend not with my tongue." Having passed this first verse the poor man shut the book and took his leave, saying that he would go and learn that point first. When he had absented himself for the space of some months, he was demanded by his teacher when he would go forward. He answered that he had not learned his old lesson, and he gave the very same answer to one that asked the like question forty-nine years after. Such a hard thing is it to rule this unruly member of the tongue, that it must be kept in with a bit and a bridle, bolts and bars. Our subject is the government of the tongue.

Such a government is NECESSARY. "Whoso keepeth his mouth and his tongue, keepeth his soul from troubles." What *troubles* come through an ungoverned tongue? First: Troubles on self. The troubles of moral remorse have often been brought into the soul through unguarded language. When a word unkind, untruthful, or unjust, has slipped from the lips thought begins its work, and the conscience gets painfully excited, and the soul thunders with self-denunciation. Such a word would be recalled, but it cannot be. It has gone forth, and its march will be as interminable as the march of the stars. The troubles of social distress have often come upon a man through unguarded language. Friends have been sacrificed, enemies created, litigations commenced, and fines and penalties enacted. Truly an ungovernable tongue is like an unbridled steed or an unruddered vessel. It will bear to ruin. Secondly: Troubles on others. An ungoverned tongue is like a river whose embankments have given way, spreading disasters through a whole neighbourhood. Half the law suits and wars in the world have been brought about through unguarded speech. In America, the Indians strike a spark from flint and steel, and thus set fire to dry grass, and the flames spread and spread until they sweep like a roaring torrent over a territory as large as England, and men and cattle have to flee for their lives. An unguarded word can produce a social conflagration greater far. "Behold how great a matter a little fire kindleth," and the tongue is a fire.

Such a government is PRACTICABLE.—This is implied in the expression, "Whoso keepeth his mouth." St. James makes it incumbent, by showing that it is essential to religion. "If any among you seem to be religious, and bridleth not his tongue, and deceiveth his own heart, this man's religion is vain." The tongue is not an involuntary organ, an organ that works irrespective of the will, like the heart and lungs; it is always the servant of the mind, it never moves without volition. Heaven has endowed us with a natural sovereignty, equal not only to the government of the tongue, but to all the lusts and passions that set it in motion. A finer manifestation of moral majesty you can scarcely have than in reticence under terribly exciting circumstances; and such a reticence Christ displayed when He stood before His insulting judges. Do not let this steed ride without a bridle, do not let this vessel move without a rudder. "Give not thy tongue," says old Quarles, "too great a liberty, lest it take thee prisoner. A word unspoken is like the sword in the scabbard, thine; if vented, thy sword is in another's hand. If thou desirest to be held wise, be so wise as to hold thy tongue."

Proverbs 21:24

The Infamous

"Proud *and* haughty scorner *is* his name, who dealeth in proud wrath."

THERE are two very abhorrent things in the text, an infamous name and infamous conduct.

An infamous NAME.—"Proud and haughty scorner is his name." The first element in an infamous name is pride, and this is an ignominious thing. What is pride? Exaggerated self-esteem. The proud man is one who has grossly overrated his own merits, and who lives and acts in the absurd fiction. The next element in an infamous name is haughtiness. Haughtiness is pride in its last stage of moral absurdity. It is pride run into arrogance and imperious contempt. The third element in an infamous name is scorn. Scorn is extreme haughtiness. The "scorner" is a man that despises everything that does not tally with his own notions, and recognize his own imaginary superiority. A more odious character than a "scorner" is not to be found in any of the ranks of infamy. The man to whom this name applies must be characterized, First: By untruthfulness. The proud man lives in falsehood. He is inspired with ideas concerning himself that are so outrageously untrue to fact, that men laugh at him and despise him. Secondly: By inhumanity. To the "proud" and "haughty" self is so important that the claims of others are ignored or outraged. The haughty spirit will tread the interests of families, communities, and nations in the dust, in order to aggrandize self. Thirdly: By irreligion. The "scorner" has no reverence either for virtue, truth, or God. Such is the infamous name that we have here, a name abhorrent to God and man. There are certain names in law which, if you apply to men, will render you liable to an action for libel; but here are names worse than any of them, which civil law does not touch. Tell me that a man is "proud" and "haughty," and scorning, and you will tell me that he is allied to the infernal, and that he is a child of the devil. Pharaoh, Sennacherib, and Haman are amongst the men that stand forth in history as the representatives of this infamous name. Here is—

An Infamous CONDUCT.—"Dealeth in proud wrath." This is the conduct of the man who deserves the infamous name. He is not only angry. Most men are angry at times. And there is a righteous anger; but he "dealeth" in wrath, "proud wrath." Insolent and haughty indignation. He *dealeth* in it. His wrath does not come up occasionally as a gust of wind and then pass away, but he deals in it; it is his trade. Malignity is his inspiration; it gratifies him to inflict suffering; the groans of anguish are music to his ears. There have ever been monsters of this class. The Neros and the Julians of history. Malice, it has been said, is the devil's picture. Lust makes a man brutish, malice makes him devilish. Malice is mental murder: you may kill a man and never touch him.

Let us studiously, earnestly, and prayerfully eschew the evils that make up the infamous character in the text. Let us cultivate humility, that low, sweet root from which all heavenly virtues shoot. "Humility," says Sir Thomas More, "to superiors is duty; to equals courtesy; to inferiors nobleness, and to all it's safety." It is safety, because it always keeps the soul at anchor, however high the seas or boisterous the winds.

Proverbs 21:25-26

Sloth

"The desire of the slothful killeth him; for his hands refuse to labour. He coveteth greedily all the day long: but the righteous giveth and spareth not."

SOLOMON here strikes another blow at sloth. It is one of his Apollyons. We have found him battling with it many times before. Here he deals out to it another stroke as he passes on. He seems to attach to it here several evils, suicide, greed, and unrighteousness.

SUICIDE.—"The desire of the slothful killeth him." The man who is too lazy to move his limbs or open his eyes is not too lazy to have a "desire." Within the bosom of his lazy carcase he hatches swarms of desires, he covets social prestige, mental furniture, perhaps moral goodness; but he is too indolent to make the necessary efforts to gain them. "His hands refuse to labour." These desires kill him. There are several things that tend to kill such a man. First: Ennui. This is what Byron calls "that awful yawn which sleep cannot abate." In all life there is not a more crushing power than lassitude. It breeds those morbid moods that explain half the diseases of the rich and would-be gentry, "the lounging class." Secondly: Disappointment. There is the desire for what is considered a good, some little effort perhaps is made, but the effort is insufficient, and it succeeds not, and then comes disappointment, and disappointment kills. Thirdly: Envy. The slothful sees others succeed, coming into possession, and enjoying the very blessings he desired; this brings with it that envy which Solomon says is the "rottenness of the bones." The poet says,

> " O envy, hide thy bosom; hide it deep!
> A thousand snakes, with black envenomed mouths,
> Nest there, and hiss and feed through all thy heart."

Fourthly: Poverty. How much of that pauperism which slays its thousands in England every year is brought on through slothfulness! Sloth fills our workhouses with paupers, our prisons with criminals, our army with recruits. Fifthly: Remorse. When the good desired is virtuous in its character, its non-possession fills the slothful with self-accusation and remorse, for he knows that he might have had it had he worked. How true it is, then, that "the desire of the slothful killeth him, for his hands refuse to labour." Another evil is—

GREED.—" He coveteth greedily all the day long." He sees others in the possession and enjoyment of what he wants. He longs after the same but he will do nothing to obtain it. " He sets his heart on all he sees, and pines away in that " envy which is the rottenness of the bones." In the Paris French translation the word stands thus—" All the day long he does nothing but wish." How very expressive at once of the unconquerable indolence and the fretful, envious, pining unhappiness of the sluggard! And in his wishing he may at times, by the power of a sanguine imagination, work himself into hope. And then, disappointed, he only embitters the cup of his own mingling—aggravates the misery which he is painfully conscious is self-inflicted." The slothful are generally greedy, and covetousness lies at the root of all crime; it is against the Decalogue of Jehovah, the Gospel of Jesus, and the moral order of the universe. Paul classes it amongst the damnabilities of the moral world.

UNRIGHTEOUSNESS.—"But the righteous giveth and spareth not." This implies that the slothful are neither righteous nor generous. The "righteous" are industrious. But the slothful are the reverse. An indolent man is living the life of practical injustice; he consumes the product of other men's labours, he takes from the common stock and adds nothing to it. The idler, whether in the higher or lower ranks of society, is a social felon, and should be dealt with accordingly. Because he is slothful he has neither the heart nor the power to give—not like the righteous, "who giveth and spareth not." Diligence not only brings power to give, but often the disposition to do so. Avoid sloth, cultivate habits of industry; diligence is at once the condition of getting and enjoying good. He who knows not what it is to labour, knows not what it is to enjoy. "Recreation is only valuable as it unbends us; the idle know nothing of it." "It is only by labour," says Ruskin, "that thought can be made healthy, and only by thought that labour can be made happy, and the two cannot be separated with impunity." Avoid sloth as you would a fiend.

> " See the issue of your sloth :—
> Of sloth comes pleasure, of pleasure comes riot,
> Of riot comes disease, of disease comes spending,
> Of spending comes want, of want comes theft,
> And of theft comes hanging."—BEN JONSON

Proverbs 21:27

Wickedness

"The sacrifice of the wicked *is* abomination : how much more, *when* he bringeth it with a wicked mind?"

THE first clause of the verse is a repetition of one already noticed.* We shall therefore only offer two remarks on it.

* See Reading on chap. xv. 8.

That the BEST services of the wicked are always an "abomination" to the Lord.—Sacrifices are the highest services that men can render. They are always of two kinds—offerings to God as an expression of love and homage, and offerings to men, as expressions of goodwill and compassion. There are no higher services than these for man; it is ever "more blessed to give than to receive." The highest happiness of all intelligent creatures consists in giving—giving to God and His creation. The "wicked" engage sometimes in this high service. They "sacrifice." They offer prayers, they sing hymns, they subscribe to religious institutions, and sometimes give gifts to men; but these services in them in all cases are an "abomination" to the Lord. Why? Because the amount offered has not been large enough, or because it has not been presented in those forms which the laws of religion and benevolence prescribe and sanction? No. But because the heart is wrong. God abhors the sacrifice where the heart is not found. The wicked man is one who keeps his heart from God, and if he keeps his heart from Him, though he gave his all beside, though he gave his body to be burned, his offerings would be an "abomination."

The abomination of the best services of the wicked is SOMETIMES INCREASED. — "How much more when he bringeth it with a wicked mind." "The mind," says Bridges, "under the dominant power of sin, is like a pestilential atmosphere, which infests all within its sphere of influence. Such was it when Balaam brought his sacrifice that he might curse Israel; Saul, in wayward disobedience; the adulteress, as a lulling to her unwary prey; the Pharisees, as a handle to their covetousness; Antinomian professors, for the indulgence of their lusts! What an abomination must their service be before Him, Who is 'of purer eyes than to behold evil, and cannot look on iniquity!'" "There are degrees in sin," says a modern writer, "there are aggravating circumstances in the same kinds of sin. There is wickedness in all hypocrisy—in all religious dissimulation,—there being no one thing in which 'simplicity and godly sincerity' are more imperatively required than the services of religion; but of all religious dissimulation, that must be the most heinous in which an act of worship is performed expressly to cover and facilitate the execution of an act of villany: when a worshipper bows before the God of mercy and truth, with the assassin's dagger under his garment, or confesses and prays 'to the righteous Lord who loveth righteousness,' to preclude suspicion—to inspire confidence in his holy character, that he may more easily succeed in pillaging the poor."

How much, in the churches of Christendom, which passes for worship every Sunday, is an "abomination"? How much? All that is not sincere.

> "Oft, neath
> The saintly veil, the votary of sin
> May lurk unseen, and to that eye alone
> Which penetrates the inmost heart, revealed."
>
> BAILEY

Proverbs 21:28-29

Moral Qualities and Their Results

"A false witness shall perish: but the man that heareth speaketh constantly. A wicked man hardeneth his face: but *as for* the upright, he directeth his way.'

IN these two verses we discover four moral qualities, and an intimation of their issues—falsehood and ruin, veracity and safety, wickedness and effrontery, righteousness and self-control.

FALSEHOOD AND RUIN.—"A false witness shall perish." In the margin, for "false witness'" we have a "witness of lies." There are witnesses of lies in various departments of life. In courts of justice. How many there are who, in the witness-box, are constantly found giving in evidence inventions of their own, stating what they know to have no foundation in fact. In social circles. There are those who are so accustomed to falsehood, that their conversation is mythological. They coin falsehoods and put them into circulation. In literary paths. How many things that are recorded every day in the journalism as facts, are utterly unfounded! There are scribblers that live by falsehood. How much of the authorship of the present day consists of fabrication! The most popular writers are the greatest liars; the books that have the largest circulation are fiction. In religious teaching. What errors stream from the pulpits of Christendom; things are propounded as Divine doctrine that contradict eternal fact, insult the human intellect, and calumniate the Infinitely Good. But "false witnesses" of all descriptions "shall perish," their influence "shall perish," their peace of mind "shall perish."

VERACITY AND SAFETY.—"But the man that heareth speaketh constantly." "The man that heareth" stands opposed to the "false witnesses." He does not speak from his own deceitful imaginations, but from well authenticated testimony. He is the man that "heareth." He does not speak until he has well tested the matter. Tested it by the laws of probability, and the laws of reason. He is a truthful man. His veracity is scrupulous and religious. What is the result of his conduct? He "speaketh constantly." The meaning is, that he sustains his statements; cross-question him, and you can elicit no incoherence, no contradiction. Moses Stuart thinks that the meaning of the expression is—" That the sincere listener to the Divine commands will ever be at liberty to speak and find confidence put in what he says." The man of truth stands constant to his position. Moral realities are immutable, and a true man is true to them.

WICKEDNESS AND EFFRONTERY. — "A wicked man hardeneth his face." This man we have often described. We have only to do here with the result of his conduct. He "hardeneth his face." He has good cause to be ashamed—blushes, blood-red, should suffuse his countenance. But he gets impudent, granite-hearted, and brazen-faced. Sometimes the wicked man, bent upon his way, hardens his face against the most distinct warning and intimations of the will of God.

Nothing would hinder Balaam from his own "perverse way." He even anticipated the conditional permission of God, lest it should ultimately stand in his way. Ahab determinately hardened his face against the clear prohibitions of God. Jehoiakim, before his whole council, set Him at defiance. His people ran with the bravery of madmen "upon the thick bosses of his buckler." And does not sin stand out before us with a brazen face?* The drunkard reels at noon-day. The swearer pours out his wickedness in the open crowd. The sensualist glories in his shame."†

UPRIGHTNESS AND SELF-CONTROL.—"As for the upright he directeth his way." The "upright man" stands opposed to the wicked man, and he "directeth," or, as it is in the margin, considereth, "his way." He does not harden his face, and go recklessly forward. But he considers his way—takes heed to his steps. He endeavours to ascertain what the path of duty is, and resolves that his feet shall never swerve therefrom. He would rather be innocent, and be thought guilty, than be guilty and thought innocent.

Mark well the evils to avoid—falsehood, wickedness; these lead to ruin and to reckless daring. Mark well the excellencies to imitate—veracity and uprightness; in these are safety and self-control. Heaven and hell are both in the qualities of soul we cultivate. Blessed be this state, damned be that!

> "The mind is its own place,
> And in itself can make a heaven or hell."
> MILTON

Proverbs 22:1

Reputation and Riches

"A *good* name *is* rather to be chosen than great riches, *and* loving favour rather than silver and gold."

THE verse must not be supposed to mean either of the two following things: That mere renown is a good thing

* Isaiah iii. 9.   † Phil. iii. 19.

in itself. The love of fame is not the love of virtue, nor has it any virtue in it. And when it becomes a passion, as it often does, it is a heinous evil. It tramples on the rights of humanity, and often sheds the blood of nations. Even our great dramatist seems to have had this strong love within him. "I am not covetous for gold; but if it be a sin to covet honour, I am the most offending soul alive." Nor must the verse be supposed to mean—That mere renown is a better thing to work for than wealth. Of the two things, mere fame and mere wealth, the latter is to be preferred as an object of pursuit. Wealth, uncertain as it is, is more steadfast, and, transient as it is, is more enduring, than mere fame. Even Byron, who sought the latter, and found it too, pronounced it worthless.

> " 'Tis as a snowball, which derives assistance
> From every flake, and yet rolls on the same,
> Even till an iceberg it may chance to grow;
> But, after all, 'tis nothing but cold snow."

The fact is, the verse does not point to mere fame at all, but to a *good* reputation; for though the word "good" is not in the original, it is evidently implied. What the writer means to say is, that a good reputation is better than wealth. The words suggest :—

THAT GREAT WEALTH IS GOOD.—"A good name is rather to be chosen than great riches." He does not say that to choose great riches is not good—the opposite is implied. Great wealth is a blessing when rightly used. Its value is more frequently denounced from envy than from conviction. Wealth increases man's sources of pleasure, and happiness is a good thing. The happy God made his universe to be happy. Wealth increases man's means of improvement. It puts at his service books, leisure, halls of science, galleries of art, and other facilities for true development. Wealth increases his power of usefulness. It enables him to mitigate poverty, to dispel ignorance, ameliorate suffering, and advance all the interests of man. With it he can rear asylums, hospitals, schools, churches, and other institutions helpful to the world. Don't despise wealth—get it if you can. In itself it is a good thing, and, rightly used, it is an immense blessing. The words suggest—

THAT A GOOD REPUTATION IS BETTER.—"A good name is rather to be chosen." Why? Because a good reputation implies the possession of something more valuable than secular wealth. That cannot be a valuable reputation which is undeserved, and contrary to the facts of a man's moral life. It is a fiction—an imposture. A good reputation implies a good character—a character in harmony with the will of God. Such a character is infinitely more valuable than the wealth of millionaires—or the splendour of kingdoms. It is intrinsic, imperishable wealth. Why? Because a good reputation answers higher purposes than secular wealth. It yields higher pleasure to the possessor. A man who knows that he is universally respected, and feels that he deserves the world-wide fame he has obtained, has a pleasure that no worldly wealth can give him. General credit for what we do not possess is rather painful than pleasant; but credit for excellence of which we are conscious is indeed a pleasing thing. Next to the happiness of being good is the happiness of being recognised as such. The "loving favour" which goodness ensures, transcends all the pleasures that "silver and gold" can possibly procure. A bad man may have great riches, but a good man only can have a truly "*good* name." Why? Because a good reputation can render us more useful than secular riches. The good man, who is universally respected because of his goodness, has a free access to the souls of men. His opinions have authority and force. "The loving favour" which men have for him gives his thoughts and counsels a ready entrance to our hearts. Secular wealth does not do this. It often bolts the souls of men against its possessors. Why? Because a good reputation is more inseparably connected with its possessor than secular wealth. Secular wealth has no vital connection with the man. The connection which it has is extrinsic and fleeting. It must leave him sooner or later. Such service as it renders is limited to earth. It is worthless beyond the grave. But a good reputation—a reputation founded on moral excellence of character—

is inseparable from man. The memory of the just is blessed. "The righteous shall be had in everlasting remembrance."

Proverbs 22:2-3

Contrasts in Conditions and Characters

"The rich and poor meet together: the LORD *is* the maker of them all. A prudent *man* foreseeth the evil, and hideth himself: but the simple pass on, and are punished."

THESE verses present to us—

The GRAND AGREEMENT BETWEEN THE RICH AND THE POOR.—First: They have a common meeting place. The "rich and the poor" appear in society to walk at a great distance from each other. In the circumstances of their *birth* they seem to be very distant. The one is down in the region of indigence, the other is up in the sphere of plenty. In the circumstances of *education* they seem distant. The poor are not allowed to mingle with the rich in schools. In the circumstances of their *daily avocation* they are distant. The poor are down in the valleys of manual and servile labour, often working as beasts of burden. The rich are at their lucrative professions and recreative amusements. In the circumstances of their *death* they seem to be distant. How different the external scenes of their death-bed! How different, too, the grave in which they are interred! The difference between them is marked, even in the churchyard and cemeteries. In the circumstances of their *worship* they seem to be distant. The poor must sit in a free seat, whilst the man with the "gold ring" lounges in his cushioned pew. Aye, aye, circumstantially the rich and the poor are very distant from each other in this world.

But notwithstanding this they have a meeting place.—"They meet together." Where do they meet? They meet —in the cardinal necessities of their being. The essentials of life and health—air, water, food, light—are common to all. All meet at the common fountain of necessities. They meet in the common trials of human nature. Sickness, disease, infirmities, decay, death—they all meet here. The small and the great meet in the grave. They descend the same region of darkness, loneliness, putrefaction. They meet in the necessary conditions of intellectual improvement:—observation, comparison, research, reflection. There is no separate path—no royal road to intellectual eminence. In the conditions too of spiritual improvement they meet. "Repentance towards God, and faith in our Lord Jesus Christ," are the necessary means to spiritual culture. There is only one way of salvation. They meet *at the bar of their Judge*. The rich and the poor must stand alike at last before the great tribunal of the judge of quick and dead. Secondly: They have a common relationship. "The Lord is the maker of them all." They have not the same fathers, mothers, sisters, teachers, ministers, masters, but they have the *same Creator*. Before this common relationship all circumstantial distinctions vanish. The greatest monarch on earth in the presence of the Creator is as insignificant as the meanest pauper. Before this common relationship all souls should blend in worship. The poor and the rich are alike bound to love Him supremely, to serve Him devotedly, to praise Him enthusiastically, and for ever.

The verses present to us—

The ESSENTIAL DIFFERENCE BETWEEN THE WISE AND THE FOOLISH.—Observe here, First: The prevision and providence of the wise. "A prudent man foreseeth the evil and hideth himself." True wisdom is always associated with forecast. It descries the future, foresees the evil and the good. The wise man does not live in the past, nor is he absorbed in the present, but he has regard to the approaching. He provides for the secular evils which he foresees, such as commercial panics, bankruptcies, failing health, and for all he makes timely preparations. He provides for the moral evils which he foresees —temptations, trials, death, judgment, and he "hideth himself." He hastens to the true Refuge. Observe,

Secondly: The recklessness and the ruin of the foolish. —"The simple pass on and are punished." Whilst the wise are like Noah, who, foreseeing the impending calamity, prepared an ark and saved himself and house. The foolish are like his contemporaries, pass heedlessly on, and are punished.

All men spiritually are acting the character either of the prudent or the simple. They are either foreseeing the evils in the future and preparing to meet them, or else they pass carelessly on to destruction. "Neglecting preparation for eternity," says one, "is like the traveller across the desert, or through a hostile wilderness, who provides nothing for his journey; like the ambassador to a far country who forgets his message; like the invited guest who puts not on the wedding garment; like the fool who counselleth his soul to take its ease, while God's voice called him to judgment."

Proverbs 22:4-5

Life, Prosperous and Perilous

"By humility *and* the fear of the LORD *are* riches, and honour, and life. Thorns *and* snares *are* in the way of the froward: he that doth keep his soul shall be far from them."

THESE two verses present to us human life in this world in two phases, a prosperous and a perilous one. Here we have one—

A PROSPEROUS phase.—"By humility and the fear of the Lord are riches, and honour, and life."

First: Here are the *elements* of a prosperous life. What are they? (1) Humility. What is humility? Not *weakness*. There are those who are sometimes considered humble who are too infertile in nature to grow ambition. They have just power enough to crawl, they have no wings to fly. Not *servility*. Those who are destitute of self-respect, who are mean and cringing in their instincts and habits, like Uriah Heep in "David Copperfield," are not humble, but mean and base. Not *sanctimoniousness*. There is much mock humility both in the world and in the churches: humble speeches throbbing with pride; humble dresses covering hearts beating with vanity and ambition. The poet says—

> "There are some that use
> Humility to serve their pride, and seem
> Humble upon their way, to be prouder
> At their wish'd journey's end."

The following anecdote was given by Robert Newton, the celebrated Wesleyan preacher. He says, "An instance of false humility was lately mentioned to me by the Deacon of a Christian Church. One of the members was indulging freely in this strain; 'What a poor, short-coming creature I am!' This minister sighed and said, 'Indeed you have long given me painful reason to believe you.' Whereupon the member, being taken at his word, replied in a tone of anger, 'Who told you anything about me? I am as good as you. I will not come to hear you any more; I will go somewhere else.' And so he did." For examples of true humility from Scripture see below.* Another element of a prosperous life here mentioned is— (2) Reverence. "Fear of the Lord." In this fear there is not a particle of servility or terror. It is the fear of love. If there be aught of dread in it, it is the dread not of suffering but of wrong. It means godliness. The two things, humility and the fear of the Lord, are indissolubly associated.

Secondly: Here are the *characteristics* of a prosperous life. What are they? Three are mentioned—"Riches," "honour," "life." The first, secular "riches," sometimes

* Abraham (Gen. xviii. 27); Jacob (Gen. xxxii. 10); Moses (Exod. iii. 2, iv. 10); Joshua (Jos. vii. 6); Gideon (Judges vi. 15); David (1 Chron. xxix. 14); Hezekiah (2 Chron. xxxii. 26); Manasseh (2 Chron. xxxiii. 12); Josiah (2 Chron. xxxiv. 27); Job (Job xl. 4, xliii. 6); Isaiah (Isa. vi. 5); Jeremiah (Jer. i. 6); John the Baptist (Matt. iii. 14); Centurion (Matt. viii. 8); Woman of Canaan (Matt. xv. 27); Elizabeth (Luke i. 43); Peter (Luke v. 8); Paul (Acts xx. 19).

attend religion. "Godliness is profitable unto all things." But such riches are of the lowest kind. The real riches, the wealth of holy thoughts, lofty sentiments, high hopes, are ever associated with genuine religion. "Honour" is also mentioned. True spiritual excellence will always command the honour and confidence of all consciences both in this world and the world to come. It receives the honour that cometh from above. Again, "life" is mentioned. Not, of course, mere existence, but existence in its highest and happiest developments. Existence in connection with all that can make it valuable and blessed. Such is human prosperity. Wealth, honour, and life, all growing out of humility and the fear of the Lord. Here we have another phase of life—

A PERILOUS phase.—"Thorns and snares are in the way of the froward." Observe—

First: The perils of life *described*. "Thorns and snares." There are lives vexed, fretted, wounded, lives of entanglements, and risks, lives, in fact, in which men seem to be walking every step on prickling thorns beneath which lie hid serpents, precipices, and ravenous beasts of prey. Life to some men is nothing but annoyances, pains, and perplexities.

Secondly: The perils of life *incurred*. Who are the men exposed to them? The text answers the question. "Thorns and snares are in the way of the *froward*." The "froward" man stands in contrast to the man of humility and the "fear of the Lord." He is the man of unbridled will, stubborn, and headstrong. Self-willed stubbornness has always led men into perplexities. Sarah, Jacob and Balaam found the way of stubbornness full of "thorns and snares," pains and perplexities. What a wretched destiny is that of a sinner: his footway is distressing, his end is ruinous.

Thirdly: The perils of life *avoided*. "He that doth keep his soul shall be far from them." The word "them" may refer either to the "froward" character or to the "thorns and snares." Either sense gives the idea that the man who keeps his soul, keeps it in humility in the "fear of the

Lord," keeps it in holy fellowship and love, will avoid the perils to which the wicked are exposed.

What a solemn yet glorious thing is life!

> "'Tis not for man to trifle! Life is brief,
> And sin is here.
> Our age is but the falling of a leaf,
> A dropping tear:
> We have no time to sport away the hours;
> All must be earnest in a world like ours.
>
> "Not many lives, but only one have we—
> One, only one!
> How sacred should that one life ever be,
> That narrow span!
> Day after day filled up with blessed toil,
> Hour after hour still bringing in new spoil."
>
> DR. BONAR

Proverbs 22:6

Child-training

"Train up a child in the way he should go: and when he is old he will not depart from it."

FOUR important subjects are implied in this verse.

THE SPECIAL TRAINABILITY OF CHILDHOOD. — "Train up a child." What is training? Not mere teaching. A child may be taught the art of reading and writing, and the elements of general knowledge, and yet be untrained. Instruction is one thing, education is another. There are many well instructed, who are miserably educated, who are in fact not educated at all. Training and education mean the development of the intellectual and moral powers of the soul, the bringing out into right and vigorous action the germinant elements of the mind and heart. Now childhood is the special period for this. If you will turn the river into a new direction, do not wait until it approaches the ocean, and the waters become a volume of resistless force. Begin as near to the fountain head as possible. If you will train a tree, do not wait until its trunk has grown stiff and bulky with years. Begin when it is in a sapling stage. If you train a horse, you must begin with the colt. Youth is the period for training. Indeed all life is trained in youth, children are trained, either rightly or wrongly, the process is ever going on. The soul is constantly running into hideous crookedness and deformity or into stately forms of strength. It is not a question with parents and guardians whether those committed to their charge shall be educated or not, educated they will be in some form or other.

Another subject implied in this verse is—

THE RIGHTEOUS PATH OF LIFE.—" In the way he should go." Not in the way in which a child *would* go. That would in all probability be in most cases a false and wicked way, the way of error and ruin. Not the way in which the world would have him go, the way of selfishness, carnality, and pride. But in the way in which he "*should* go." What is the way? The way of Christ. He is the example. "Follow me" comprehends the totality of man's moral obligation. To follow Him is to follow *truth, benevolence, happiness*. This is *the* way, the *only* way.

Another subject implied in this verse is—

THE TERRIBLE FORCE OF HABIT.—" When he is old he will not depart from it." If the way in which the child has been trained is evil, when old he will not leave it. " Can the Ethiopian change his skin or the leopard his spots?" The statistics of conversions show that but few bad men turn into the ways of rectitude and religion after forty years of age. The tree is too stiff, and too gnarled to bend, the river of influence has become too voluminous, too near the ocean to be turned in another direction at that period of life. But where the course has been right in youth, the improbability of a change, we think, is greatly increased. Conscience does not back the bad man in his habits, however strong they become. Conscience, this divine faculty, is ever against him. But the good man in his habits is always borne on by the whole might of his moral nature, and a conversion from goodness in old age grows almost into an impossibility.

Another subject implied in this verse is—

THE SOLEMN ACCOUNTABILITY OF PARENTS.—The great duty of training children devolves upon their parents. If they have not the capacity and the time to give the necessary amount of their personal attention to the work, they should use their best judgment in the employment of substitutes. The parent, in consequence of the moral power which he exerts upon the susceptible nature of his children, becomes almost as much the author of their character as he is the instrument of their existence. What, then? Is the child mere passive entity, possessing no moral spontaneity, no resisting force? Little, if any, in the first stages of being. Must we in all cases of immorality and wickedness in children ascribe culpable neglect, if nothing worse, to parental conduct? We are bound to think so from such a passage as this. The great philosopher Locke says, "That of all the men we meet with, nine parts out of ten are what they are, good or bad, useful or not, according to their education."

This subject presents—First: *A lesson to the young*. Let youth avoid the wrong, and cultivate those habits which are in accordance with morality and religion. Second: *A warning to the guardians of youth*. Let parents, Sunday-school teachers, public instructors, and statesmen, look well to the rising generation. If parents would certainly know that their little child would, in the course of seven or eight years, fall into a deep river alone, would they wait until that catastrophe occurred before they taught him to swim? In the course of that period the infants now born will be thrown into the great social river of depravity and corruption; and should they not, in the earliest stages, be taught the moral art of keeping the current beneath them, and making it bear them to scenes of safety and peace?

> " Oh, for the coming of that glorious time,
> When, prizing knowledge as her noblest wealth,
> And best protection, this imperial realm,
> While she exacts allegiance, shall admit
> An obligation, on her part, to *teach*
> Them who are born to serve her and obey;
> Binding herself by statute, to secure

For all the children whom her soil maintains,
The rudiments of letters, and inform
The mind with moral and religious truth,
Both understood and practised—so that none,
However destitute, be left to droop,
By timely culture unsustained, or run
Into wild disorder; or be forced
To drudge through a weary life without the help
Of intellectual implements and tools;
A savage horde among the civilized,
A servile band among the lordly free."
                                WORDSWORTH

Proverbs 22:7

The Social Rule of Wealth

"*The rich ruleth over the poor, and the borrower is servant to the lender.*"

WEALTH not only invests its possessor with the power to gratify his appetites, tastes, and ambition, to cultivate his intellect, and to furnish his mind with stores of choicest knowledge, to ameliorate human woe, and to promote general happiness; but invests him at the same time with a *regal* influence. A wealthy man is the king of his dependants. Indeed wealth rules commerce, and commerce rules the parliaments of the world. In relation to this subject we offer three remarks.

That this rule of wealth should ALWAYS be a GENEROUS rule.—When we see a wealthy man loved, honoured, and loyally served, because of the benefits that he has conferred upon his fellows, his sovereignty is a matter for rejoicing. Such was the sovereignty which Job, in the days of his prosperity, enjoyed. "The young men saw me and hid themselves: and the aged arose and stood up. The princes refrained talking and laid their hand on their mouth. The nobles held their peace, and their tongues cleaved to the roof of their mouth. When the ear heard me, then it blessed me, and when the eye saw me it gave witness to me. Because I delivered the poor that cried, and the fatherless, and them that had none to help him." Again :—

This rule of wealth is FREQUENTLY TYRANNIC.—To how many rich men of all ages do the thundering denunciations of St. James apply, "Behold the hire of the labourers who have reaped down your fields, which is of you kept back by fraud, crieth: and the cries of them which have reaped are entered into the ears of the Lord of Sabaoth. Ye have lived in pleasure on the earth, and been wanton : ye have nourished your hearts as in a day of slaughter. Ye have condemned and killed the just ; and he did not resist you." How often does the wealthy master exercise tyranny over his servants, the wealthy landlord over his tenants, the wealthy merchant over his customers, the wealthy nation over poorer countries. The rule of wealth is oft tyrannic Moreover—

This rule of wealth is EVER TEMPORARY.—There is an empire which a man may establish here over his fellows that might be permanent and ever extending; the empire of superior thoughts, pure sympathies, divine aims and deeds. By these men may become kings for ever under God. But the reign of mere wealth is always uncertain, and at most very brief. Riches lose their power the moment their possessor dies. The rich man's crown falls from his head, and his sceptre from his hand, with his last breath.

From this subject we are reminded of *the responsibility of the rich*. How great the power of wealth! In this world it is a talent often more influential than intellect or genius. Every man is responsible to God for all the good his wealth is *capable* of accomplishing. We are reminded also of *the temptation of the poor*. What is the temptation ? To become servile, cringing in spirit. Sycophancy is the greatest curse of the people. It is a cancer in the heart of England. The men that bow down to wealth are in the majority everywhere, and they are parasites that devour the moral nobleness of nations. We are further reminded of the *wisdom of the diligent.* The diligent man is a wise man. Why? Because the more industrious he is, the more independent he becomes of wealthy men. Though he may bow at first, and thus become for a time a servant, he will soon by assiduous labour pay back his loan, and stand erect before his own master as an independent man.

> " Thy spirit, independence, let me share,
> Lord of the lion-heart and eagle eye;
> Thy steps I follow with my bosom bare,
> Nor heed the storm that howls along the sky."
> SMOLLETT

Proverbs 22:8

Human Life

" He that soweth iniquity shall reap vanity: and the rod of his anger shall fail."

THE words point out:

The INEVITABLE WORK of human life.—What is the work? It is that of moral agriculture—*sowing and reaping*. Every man in every act of life is doing this. Every volition, whether it takes the form of a thought, a word, or a muscular act is a *seed*. There is a germ of imperishable life in it. No frost is cold enough, no fire is hot enough, no weight is heavy enough to destroy this germ. It is *essentially incorruptible*. What seeds men sow every day! What bushels they deposit in the moral soil of their being! But they *reap* as well as sow every day. What was sown yesterday they reap to-day. " Men are living in the fruits of their doings." The law of causation is inviolate and ever operative within us. Out of our moral yesterday has grown our to-day, and thus on for ever. We are *sowers* and *reapers* all of us. Observe again:

The RETRIBUTIVE LAW of human life.—*What* you sow you will reap. First: What you sow in *kind* you shall reap. " He that soweth iniquity shall reap vanity." Job says

"They that plough iniquity and sow wickedness reap the *same*."* Paul says, "Be not deceived; God is not mocked: for whatsoever a man soweth, that shall he also reap. For he that soweth to the flesh shall of the flesh reap corruption; but he that soweth to the spirit shall of the spirit reap life everlasting."† The man whose actions are carnal, selfish, profane, ungodly, will reap a terrible harvest of misery. It cannot be helped. God will not reverse the law, "Whatsoever a man soweth that shall he reap." Secondly: What you sow in *measure* you shall reap. Not a grain will be lost. Sometimes the seed which the husbandman commits to the soil rots. The spring comes round and it appears not above the ground—it is dead. But not a grain in the harvest of life is lost. The more blessed deeds sown, the more blessed life enjoyed, and the converse. He will reap the richest harvest of blessedness who is most active in deeds of love and godliness. Observe again:

The TERRIBLE MISTAKE of human life.—What is the mistake? Sowing iniquity. *This is a general mistake.* The unregenerate millions in all lands are doing this.

This is a mistake which men are slow to learn. Though conscience, the Bible, experience, and the Divine Spirit are all co-working to convince men of this mistake, they blunder on. *This is a mistake whose ultimate consequences will be terrific.* "And the rod of his anger shall fail;" or as in the margin, "With the rod of his anger he shall be consumed." Perhaps this expression refers to the tyrannic power exercised by wealthy men, as referred to in the preceding verse. The rod by which he oppressed and smote the poor for his own selfish ends, that rod "shall fail." Death shall wrest it from his hands. God shall break it in pieces; and his tyranny and iniquity shall leave him nothing but shame, remorse, and the fruits of his immoral life. "Such," says Mr. Bridges, "was Sennacherib in olden time, such was Napoleon in our own day. Never had the world so extensive a *sower of iniquity*, never one reaped a more abundant harvest of *vanity*. The rod of

* Job. vi. 1—3. † Gal. vi. 7, 8.

anger was he to the nations of the earth. But how utterly was the rod suffered to *fail*, when the purpose was accomplished! despoiled of empire, shorn of greatness, an exiled captive."

Proverbs 22:9

Genuine Philanthropy

"He that hath a bountiful eye shall be blessed; for he giveth of his bread to the poor."

SINCE philanthropy in England the last few years has become a *profession*, its name is fast losing its divine significance and its soul-captivating charms. There are hirelings and charletans itinerating the land, and canting in every town in the empire in its sacred name. They wrap themselves in its robes, and use its sacred language, in order to gratify more effectually their ambition and their greed. The verse leads us to notice three things concerning genuine philanthropy—

THE KINDLINESS OF ITS DISPOSITION.—"He that hath a bountiful eye," shall be blessed. "In the Hebrew," says an expositor, "the expression is—"He that is *good of eye*." The opposite phrase—"an *evil eye*"—is frequent in Scripture, and is used in various senses. It is applied, for example, in a general way, to *duplicity of principle*, in which sense it stands opposed to what our Lord calls "having *the eye* single." It is applied also to a *perverted state of the affections* towards any of these objects—supposed, of course, to be indicated by the looks. (Deut. xxviii. 54, 56.) It is further used for envy (Matt. xx. 15; Mark vii. 22); and further still for a principle closely allied to envy—*covetousness*—eagerly looking at the object desired, and grudging every expenditure of it. (Prov. xxiii. 6; xxviii. 22; Deut. xv. 9.) This meaning is illustrated by the use of the corresponding expression, in the verse before us,—"*a good eye.*" It means the eye of compassionate and generous tenderness,—that looks, with a desire to relieve the wants and woes of others; and that, at the same time, does not merely weep—shedding unavailing tears—but, affecting the heart, opens the hand—"for he giveth of his bread to the poor." As the heart looks out through the eye, it appears in the eye. Man's dispositions are reflected in his looks. What a blessed thing to have a bountiful heart! A thousand times better to have a bountiful heart with scanty provisions, than a niggardly heart with boundless affluence. "The liberal deviseth liberal things, and by liberal things he shall stand." The verse leads us to notice—

THE BENEFICENCE OF ITS ACTIVITY.—"He giveth of his bread to the poor." Genuine philanthropy is practical. It does not live on mere sentiment or speech. It goes out in useful deeds. The true philanthropist is ready to distribute and willing to communicate. He gives not as a duty but as a privilege.

> " Give! as the morning that flows out of heaven!
> Give! as the waves, when their channel is riven!
> Give! as the free air and sunshine are given:
> Lavishly, utterly carelessly give!
> Not the waste drops of thy cup overflowing:
> Not the faint sparks of thy hearth overglowing:
> Not a pale bud from the June rose's blowing:
> Give as He gave thee Who gave thee to live!
> Pour out thy love like the rush of a river
> Wasting its waters for ever and ever
> Through the burnt sands that reward not the giver."
>
> *Household Words*

The verse leads us to notice—

THE REWARD OF ITS SERVICE.—It "shall be blessed." "Blessed is he that considereth the poor." He shall be blessed with the commendation of his own conscience, with the grateful affection of the poor, and with the approbation of his God. "If thou draw out thy soul to the hungry, and satisfy the afflicted soul, then shall thy light rise in obscurity, and thy darkness be as the noonday; and the Lord shall guide thee continually, and satisfy thy soul in drought, and make fat thy bones: and thou shalt be like a watered garden, and like a spring of water whose waters fail not." " Verily I say unto you, Inasmuch as ye have done it unto one of the least of these my brethren ye have done it unto me."

The language of Quarles on giving is worth recording. " Proportion thy charity to the extent of thy estate, lest God proportion thy estate to the weakness of thy charity : let the lips of the poor be the trumpet of thy gift, lest in seeking applause thou lose thy reward. Nothing is more pleasing to God than an open hand and a close mouth."

Proverbs 22:10

The Scorner

" Cast out the scorner, and contention shall go out ; yea, strife and reproach shall cease."

THE scorner is a character to which Solomon has frequently called our attention in preceding chapters. Few characters in society are more despicable in spirit or pernicious in influence. He is profane, contemptuous, insolent, flippant, and splenetic. He deals in jeers and gibes, in sneers, satire, and lampoon. Himself the most contemptuous to others, the most contemptible in himself. He sneers at the sacred, he mocks at the momentous. The verse presents him—

As a social DISTURBER.—"Cast out the scorner and contention shall go out." This implies that he is the breaker of harmony, the creator of ill-feeling and confusion. And so he is. He is a disturber in the *family*. The domestic circle to which he belongs, or with which he has any connection, he is sure to agitate with heartburnings and jealousies. He is a disturber in the *church*. When by hypocrisy he sometimes happens to gain admission into a Christian community, he soon makes his pernicious influence felt. His irony creates wounds, his jests shock the serious, his inuendos shake confidence and create suspicions. He is a disturber in the *nation*. If he takes up with politics, aspires to popularity and has oratoric power, he is a demagogue, a firebrand. His object will be to disparage his superiors, to undermine authority, to set class against class. He is, in fact, a disturber in all his social relations. The verse represents him—

As a social PEST.—"Cast out the scorner." He should be thrust from the circle in which he is found. Excommunication is his righteous doom. Sometimes the scorner gains great influence as a politician, and temporising governments, instead of casting him out, take him into office and bribe him by voting him a princely income. For a time the miserable hireling is silenced and the country is rid of his mischievous agitations. But the spirit is still in him, only pampered into plethoric indolence. He should be expelled, be cast out from all places of public trust, from all confidential intercourse, and treated as a social pest. Society should throw on him the eye of dignified contempt. Whether he is the member of a family, a church, or a cabinet, he should be cast out. Never place confidence in the man of a scoffing spirit. He is a canker worm in the social garden and he must be crushed. He is a Jonah on the social bark, and the sea will "not cease from its raging" until he is thrown overboard. "But what," says Bridges, "if we should not be able to cast him out? He may be a husband or a child. At least give a protest. Show that you stand not on the same ground. Turn away from his scorning. This will mortify if not silence. Turn from him to your God. This will bring peace. Dwell with him, sighing as David in Mesech.* One greater than David teaches us by His example. Honour your Divine Master by enduring as he did year after year the contradiction of sinners.† And who knoweth, but this meek and silent endurance with a loving, bleeding heart, may have power to cast out the scorning, and to mould the scorner into the lowliness of the cross? Then would he be a more welcome member of the family

* Psalm cxx. 5—7. † Heb. xii. 3.

or of the church. 'Strife and reproach' would cease in both should the persecutor of the faith become a monument of grace, a shining witness to the truth."

Proverbs 22:11-12

The Good Man

"He that loveth pureness of heart, *for* the grace of his lips the king *shall be* his friend. The eyes of the LORD preserve knowledge, and he overthroweth the words of the transgressor."

THIS passage leads us to consider the heart, the speech, the influence, and the blessedness of a good man.

The HEART of the good man.—"He that loveth pureness of heart." Not merely does he love the pure in language, in manners and habits, in outward deportment, but the pure in heart, pureness in the very fountains of moral life and action. "Pureness of heart" in man's case implies—First: *A moral renewal.* All men in an unregenerate state are defiled by sin. The very well-springs of their life are polluted. "The heart is deceitful above all things, and desperately wicked." It implies—Secondly: *An urgent necessity.* Without pureness of heart there is no true knowledge of God or fellowship with Him. "Blessed are the pure in heart for they shall see God." "Without holiness no man shall see the Lord." A good man then is a man who loveth "pureness of heart," he possesses and promotes it. For such a heart David prayed, "Create within me a clean heart, O God, and renew a right spirit within me."

The SPEECH of the good man.—"For the grace of his lips the king shall be his friend." By "the grace of his lips" we are to understand something more than grammatic accuracy, or elegant diction—something more than logical correctness or strict veracity. It means speech that is *morally* pure—pure in sentiment, and in aim. It is said of Christ that the people wondered at the gracious words which proceeded out of His mouth. The man of a pure heart will have lips of grace. "If the tree is made good, the fruit will be good." " Out of the abundance of the heart the mouth speaketh." His speech will be seasoned with salt, and he will minister grace unto his hearers. Gracious speech is the antithesis of untruthful, malicious, and unchaste language.

The INFLUENCE of the good man.—"The king shall be his friend." Solomon here speaks probably of his own determination. He meant to say that he would give his friendship to such men. "This," says an able writer, "had been his father's resolution" (Psa. li. 6, cxix. 63). This character smoothed the way to royal favour for Joseph (Gen. xli. 37—45), for Ezra (Ez. vii. 21—25), and Daniel (Dan. vi. 1—3, 28). Nay, we find godly Obadiah in the confidence of wicked Ahab (1 Kings xviii. 3, 12 ; 2 Kings xiii. 14). So powerful is the voice of conscience, even when God and holiness are hated! Yet this choice of the gracious lips is too often rather what ought to be, than what is (chap. xvi. 12, 13). Well is it for the kingdom when the sovereign's choice is according to this rule. (Chap. xxviii. 2 ; xxv. 5). Such alone the great *King* marks as *His friends*. Such He embraces with His fatherly love. (Chap. xv. 9.) Such He welcomes into His heavenly kingdom. (Psa. xv. 1, 2 ; xxiv. 3, 4). " Blessed are the pure in heart for they shall see God" (Matt. v. 8).

The BLESSEDNESS of a good man.—"The eyes of the Lord preserve knowledge." Three different interpretations have been given to this expression. First : *That the Lord vigilantly watches over His truth in the world.* This is a fact, although we are not disposed to accept it as an interpretation of the passage. It is a glorious and elevating truth—That the Great God has ever exercised a watchful care over His cause in the world. Secondly : *That what the eyes of the Lord see He remembers for ever.* "The eyes of the Lord *preserve* knowledge." He retains his knowledge. What we see often passes away from our memory. We do not "preserve" it. We forget far more than we retain. Not so with the Lord. He observes everything, and everything He observes remains with Him for ever. But we are not disposed to accept this as the idea of the passage. Thirdly: *That the Lord exercises a protecting superintendence over those who possess His knowledge.* That it means, in fact, the same as the expression elsewhere, "The eyes of the Lord are upon the righteous." This we accept as the true idea. It, therefore, expresses the blessedness of a good man. He has an all-wise, an all-constant, all-mighty Keeper. Whilst the Lord keeps the good man, He "overthroweth the words of the transgressor."

Let us mark well then the heart, the speech, the influence, and the blessedness of a good man. How pure in sentiment, how excellent in speech, how salutary in influence, how guarded by Heaven! The eyes of the Lord are ever upon him.

> "Though in the paths of death I tread,
> With gloomy horrors overspread,
> My steadfast heart shall fear no ill,
> For thou, O Lord, art with me still:
> Thy friendly crook shall give me aid,
> And guide me through the dreadful shade."
>
> ADDISON

Proverbs 22:13

The Excuses of Laziness

The slothful man *saith, There is* a lion without, I shall be slain in the streets."

To Solomon slothfulness was one of the greatest evils in the character of man. How frequently does he depict it with graphic force! How often does he denounce it with fiery energy! "Idleness," says Colton, "is the great Pacific ocean of life, and in that stagnant abyss, the most salutary things produce no good, the most obnoxious no evil. Vice, indeed, abstractedly considered, may be, and often is, engendered in idleness; but the moment it becomes sufficiently vice, it must quit its cradle and cease to be idle." Two of the evils connected with indolence are suggested in the verse.

It creates FALSE excuses.—"There is a lion without." The streets are very *unlikely* places for lions to resort to. Their home is the secluded glens—in desolate forests and untrodden deserts. If ever they are found in streets, it is by rare accident. The excuse, therefore, which the slothful man urges, is purely imaginary. The lion in the streets is a fiction of his own lazy brain. The slothful man is ever acting thus in the *secular* sphere. Is he a farmer, he neglects the cultivation of his fields, because the weather is too cold or too hot, too cloudy, too dry or too wet. Is he a tradesman, he finds imaginary excuses in the condition of the market: commodities are too high or too low. Is he an artizan, he finds difficulties in the place, the tools, or the materials. The industrious farmer seldom finds insurmountable difficulties in the weather; the industrious tradesman in the market, or the industrious artisan in the work marked out for him to do. The difficulties are purely imaginary—the dreams of idleness. The slothful man also makes excuses in the *spiritual* sphere. When the unregenerate man is urged to the renunciation of his own principles and habits, and the adoption of new spirit and methods, slothfulness urges him to make imaginary excuses. Sometimes he pleads the decrees of God, sometimes the greatness of his sins, sometimes the inconvenience of the season—too soon or too late. The slothful man lives in falsehood. He says there is a "lion without, I shall be slain in the streets," when the imperial beast is leagues away prowling in the boundless forest. Another evil connected with indolence is—

It creates UNMANLY excuses.—The very excuse he pleads, though imaginary, if true would be a strong reason for immediate action. "A lion in the streets!" Why, if he had a spark of manhood in him, a bit of the stuff that makes heroes, he should rouse every power. The lives of the helpless women and children in the town are in danger when the ravenous beast treads the pavement, and humanity urges action. Laziness and cowardice are vitally associated. There is no heroism in the heart of indolence.

To true souls difficulties are a challenge, not a check to action. They are made to be conquered. It is only as they are conquered that man's faculties are developed and his nature ennobled. "Difficulties," says a modern writer, "are God's errands; and when we are sent upon them we should esteem it a proof of God's confidence—as a compliment from Him. The traveller who goes round the world prepares himself to pass through all latitudes, and to meet all changes. So a man must be prepared to take life as it comes; to mount the hill when the hill swells, and to go down the hill when the hill lowers; to walk the plain when it stretches before him, and to ford the river when it rolls over the plain." "I can do all things through Christ, which strengtheneth me."

Proverbs 22:14

The Influence of a Depraved Woman

"The mouth of strange women *is* a deep pit: he that is abhorred of the LORD shall fall therein."

SOLOMON here speaks from experience. Elsewhere he says, "And I find more bitter than death the woman whose heart is snares and nets, and her hands as bands. Whoso pleaseth God shall escape from her, but the sinner shall be taken by her." We have already had occasion to refer more than once to this execrable character.* There are two things in the text concerning the influence of a depraved woman.

IT IS DANGEROUS.—"It is a deep pit." This pit is *artfully concealed*. She does not leave its dark mouth

* See our Readings on chap. ii. 16—19; v. 3—12.

yawning before the eye. In the garden of her fascinations it is concealed in a nook, encircled with lovely shrubs and sweetest flowers. The victim sees it not until his foot has slipped and he falls. This pit is *morally dark*. He who falls into it loses all moral light—the light of God's countenance, the light of pure love, the light of holy hope, the light of approving conscience. He is enwrapt in the gloom of sensuality and vice. This pit is *terribly crowded*. What millions of young men fall into it every age and are ruined. They fall into the pit and are lost to their age. Young men, avoid this artfully concealed, morally dark, terribly crowded pit. "Dark deeds," says Dr. Farrer, " are done in secret; drag them into the light, and they cannot stand it. A debased soul, brought into open daylight and not rushing from it, is naturally purified; that which was darkness in the dark becomes light in the daylight. Therefore to see God's face is to be pure from every shame. And it is to be elevated above all earthliness. A Russian empress once built a palace of ice, and her guests danced and banqueted within its glimmering walls. But when the sun shone it vanished and melted into cold and dripping mud. Even so it is with the aims men toil for most. Death comes, and all they have longed for looks no better than a palace of icicles, which shone with opal colours under the moonbeams, but melts into hideous ruin before the light of God. Therefore to see God's face is to distinguish the real from the illusory, the true from the false. And it is to be at peace. For as the chaos became order and beauty under the wings of the Spirit of God, and as the troubled waves of Galilee sank into calm beneath the Saviour's feet, so there can be no disquietude in His presence, where the wicked cease from troubling, and the weary are at rest!"

IT IS DAMNING.—" He that is abhorred of the Lord shall fall therein." " Her feet," says Solomon in another place, "go down to death, her steps take hold on hell." Those that give themselves up to her influence are " abhorred of the Lord." " He is of purer eyes than to behold iniquity." Solomon had fallen into this pit.

And, oh! the agony of awakened conviction and felt abandonment! "To what do the fearful words amount? To this, that in His righteous displeasure there is not a heavier curse which offended God can allow to fall upon the object of His wrath, than leaving him to be a prey to the seductive blandishments of an unprincipled woman—that if God held any one in abhorrence, this would be the severest vengeance He could take. Oh! let the youth hear that and tremble! There are few vices—if, indeed, there be any—more sadly prevalent; and there are few—if, indeed there be any—more miserably destructive of soul, body and estate. The abhorrence and the curse of God are in the haunts, whether open or secret, of profligacy and lewdness. Wish you to have proof of your being '*abhorred of the Lord*'? Court the company of the 'strange woman.' If not, flee from the temptation, as you would from the opening mouth of hell!"

"Wherewithal shall a young man cleanse his way, by taking heed thereto according to thy word." Let the Word of God, my young brother, be the "lamp to thy feet." "By the words of my lips," says the Psalmist, "have I kept thee from the paths of the destroyer." Cultivate purity in every faculty of being, in every act of life. Let the heart be clean and the life stainless. One hour's pollution may stain a whole life. Life is made up of littles. The pasture land of a thousand hills is but separate blades of grass. The bloom that mantles the prairies is but a combination of separate flowers.

Proverbs 22:15

A Terrible Evil and a Severe Cure

"Foolishness *is* bound in the heart of a child; *but* the rod of correction shall drive it far from him."

HERE we have—

A TERRIBLE EVIL.—"Foolishness is bound in the heart."

By foolishness is meant moral depravity, which, though negative in a child, is positive in an adult. It is in its various forms a liability, a tendency, and a habit of going wrong. How is this depravity bound in the heart of a child? Three facts are noteworthy concerning it—

First: *It is deprivation of goodness in the first stage of life.* It exists in the heart of a child in a negative form, and this is bad enough. The deprivation of the means of life leads to death, the deprivation of good leads to evil. So it turns out that as sure as the child grows up it develops evil in its most positive forms. Where benevolence is not rooted, selfishness grows, and from its roots spring all the branches of evil that curse the universe. Observe—

Secondly: *The abnormal condition of parents.* A man's physical constitution, temper and propensities, are undoubtedly modified by his moral character. The drunkard, the glutton, the debauchee, changes, to a great extent, the constitutional powers and tendencies of his being. Whatever is constitutional he transmits to his offspring. The tendency to drunkenness, gluttony, sensuality, is obviously transmitted:—thus they are "bound in the heart of a child." Observe—

Thirdly: *The corrupt social influence under which the child is trained.* The human infant comes into a world where the social atmosphere is full of the elements and seeds of moral corruption. Thus it is that moral evil extends over the race, runs down from generation to generation, and is found bound up in the life of our earliest childhood. Here we have for this terrible evil—

A SEVERE CURE.—"The rod of correction shall drive it far from him." The rod does not necessarily mean corporeal punishment. This is not the most painful rod, nor is it the most effective for spiritual ends. The corrective rod must be marked by two things:—First: The infliction of *pain*. Pain in some way or other is the rod. It may be pain arising from the restraint of liberty, the want of food, the denial of pleasure, the disapprobation of love. The frown of a loving father is often a severer lash than any material rod. Or it may be pain arising from moral conviction.

The child's conscience may be touched with a sense of the sinfulness of his conduct. Or it may be pain arising from the afflictive dispensations of Providence, such as bodily afflictions and social bereavements. Pain in all cases is the rod of discipline. Secondly: The infliction of pain *from a benevolent disposition*. The infliction of pain, whether corporeal or moral, from caprice or revenge, is not corrective, but the reverse. It deepens and strengthens the evil. The child must be chastened not for our pleasure, but for the child's profit. Injudicious chastisement, ill timed, ill tempered, ill adapted to the case, and ill proportioned in measure, will effectively frustrate the ends of spiritual correction. It is said of those who have reached heaven, that " they came out of great tribulation, and have washed their robes and made them white." Pain, then, administered by love is the Divine rod to bring out depravity from the heart. Pain is a strong breeze that bears away the chaff from the grains of virtue: the gale that urges the bark away from the shores of depravity and vice: the chisel by which the Divine Sculptor cuts out from the rough and shapeless stone an image of beauty fit for the halls of Heaven.

Proverbs 22:16

The Evils of Avarice

"He that oppresseth the poor to increase his *riches, and* he that giveth to the rich, *shall* surely *come* to want."

DRYDEN has graphically described the aim of avarice: " Had covetous men, as the fable goes of Briareus, each of them one hundred hands, they would all of them be employed in grasping and gathering, and hardly one of them in giving or laying out, but all in receiving, and none in restoring: a thing in itself so monstrous, that nothing in nature besides is like it, except it be death and the grave, the only things I know which are always carrying off the spoils of the world, and never making restitution. For otherwise, all the parts of the universe, as they borrow of one another, so they still pay what they borrow, and that by so just and well balanced an equality, that their payments always keep pace with their receipts." The verse refers to three evils connected with avarice—

OPPRESSION.—" He that oppresseth the poor to increase his riches." Everywhere do we see avarice working out its designs, and building up its fortunes, by oppressing the poor. The poor are used as beasts of burden. They have to cross the seas, to delve in mines, to toil in fields, to work in manufactories, to slave in shops and counting-houses, in order to enrich the coffers of the avaricious. Avarice cares nothing for the health, the liberty, the pleasure, the intellectual and social advancement of the poor, so long as it can get from their aching limbs and sweating sinews the object of its greed. Avarice fattens on the miseries of poverty. The interest of others, of the universe itself, are nothing to the avaricious man in comparison with his own. He would be ever receptive, never communicative. He would receive all, give nothing, unless it be with the hope of his contribution flowing back in some form or other with interest to his coffers. He would monopolize universal goodness. The labourer may sweat out his strength, the shopman wear away his health, the mariner hazard his existence, the warrior dye continents in blood, and tread empires in the dust, his selfish heart would exult in all if the smallest benefit would accrue to him therefrom. Is there a crime on the black scroll of human depravity that may not be traced to this source? The mighty flood of evil, that for six thousand years has been rolling its turbid and foaming billows through the heart of groaning humanity has its fountain down in the selfish soul. Selfishness is the head of all wicked "principalities and powers." Another evil which the text refers to connected with avarice is—

SYCOPHANCY.—" He that giveth to the rich." Avarice, whilst tyrannic to the poor, is servile to the rich. The wealth it gets it employs with a miserable crawling baseness, to win the favour and command the smiles of the wealthy and the great. Tyranny and flunkeyism generally go together. Both are the children of avarice. He that proudly domineers over the poor will servilely bow his knee to the rich. A fawning sycophancy is eating out not only the true manhood of England, but of the civilized world. Souls are everywhere bowing down before the glitter of wealth and the pageantry of power. The other evil connected with avarice to which the verse refers, is—

RUIN.—" Shall surely come to want." If not to secular want, a want far worse, the want of an approving conscience, a manly soul, social love, the Divine approbation. Avarice, like every other evil passion, leads to moral pauperism. " Trust not," says Sir T. Browne, "to the omnipotency of gold, and say not unto it, Thou art my confidence. Kiss not thy hand to that terrestrial sun, nor bore thy ear with its servitude. A slave unto mammon makes no servant unto God. Covetousness cracks the sinews of faith, numbs the apprehensions of anything above sense, and, only affected with the certainty of things present, makes a peradventure of things to come; lives but unto one world, nor hopes, but fears, another; makes their own death sweet unto others, bitter unto themselves; brings formal sadness, scenical mourning, and no wet eyes at the grave."

Proverbs 22:17-21

Spiritual Verities

" Bow down thine ear, and hear the words of the wise, and apply thine heart unto my knowledge. For *it is* a pleasant thing if thou keep them within thee; they shall withal be fitted in thy lips. That thy trust may be in the LORD, I have made known to thee this day, even to thee. Have not I written to thee excellent things in counsels and knowledge, that I might make thee know the certainty of the words of truth; that thou mightest answer the words of truth to them that send unto thee?"

THESE verses begin the third of the five sections into which critics have divided the whole book.

The first section comprises the first nine chapters, is introductory and principally addressed to youth. The second comprises the tenth chapter, up to the verses which contain proverbs generally, though not always, detached. The third comprises those verses to the end of the twenty-fourth chapter, and is more connected and paragraphic in its style. The fourth section includes the twenty-fifth and all the chapters up to the twenty-ninth inclusive, this section is like the first, proverbial and sententious. The fifth section extends from the thirtieth chapter to the close, the authorship of which is still unsettled in the region of controversy.

The subject of these verses (which begin the third section of the book) is *spiritual verities*, and these are here called "excellent things." By spiritual verities we mean truths relating directly to man's spiritual nature—its moral condition, interests, and obligations. They are the greatest realities in the universe, of greater moment to man than the whole of the material creation. The passage leads us to make two remarks concerning the personal knowledge of these spiritual truths.

The experimental knowledge of them is a TRANSCENDENT BLESSING. — They are "excellent things" in themselves—things that reveal a spiritual universe, a glorious Redeemer, and an ever-blessed God. But the verses teach that a knowledge of them is a transcendent good. They teach First : That such a knowledge *affords pleasure*. It is a "a pleasant thing." An experimental acquaintance with spiritual truths has ever been felt delectable; it is, to the spiritual tastes of man, sweeter than "honey and the honeycomb;" it fills the soul with joy unspeakable and full of glory. What said Paul ? " I count all things but loss for the excellency of the knowledge of Christ Jesus my Lord." The verses teach, Secondly : That such a knowledge *enriches speech*. "They shall withal be fitted in thy lips." It will give thoughts worthy of the lips, thoughts which the lips can speak with a natural gracefulness and dignity. "The lips of the righteous feed many." The words of a man enriched with heavenly wisdom are pearls that sparkle with the rays of God. The verses teach, Thirdly: That such a knowledge *inspires trust in God.* " That thy trust may be in the Lord." Man's fall and misery consist in the trustlessness of his heart in relation to his Maker. For the want of confidence in Him, human souls, like Noah's dove, flutter over the surging abysses of life, finding no rest for the soles of their feet. This knowledge brings man back to God, and centres him in the *absolute.* " Blessed is the man that trusteth in the Lord." The verses teach, Fourthly: That such a knowledge *establishes the faith of the soul.* " Have I not written to thee excellent things in counsels and knowledge, that I might make thee know the certainty of the words of truth?" The more a man knows of these spiritual verities, the more settled and unwavering is his faith. He has the witness in himself that God is true. He knows in whom he has believed. A man to whom these spiritual verities are an experience is not like a feather tossed by every wind of doctrine, but like a tree, so rooted and grounded in faith as to stand firm amidst the fiercest hurricanes that blow. Such a man's faith stands not in the wisdom of man, but in the power of God. The verses teach, Fifthly: That such a knowledge *qualifies for usefulness.* " That thou mightest answer the words of truth to them that send unto thee." Men in all circles of life have questions put to them about the soul and God, duty and destiny; but he only can satisfactorily solve those mysteries who has an experimental knowledge of spiritual verities. Neither scholarship nor sageship can do it. Genuine saintship alone can give the satisfactory answer. The "fear of the Lord," that is wisdom. Another remark suggested by the verses concerning these spiritual verities is that :

The experimental knowledge of them is ATTAINABLE.— After indicating the transcendent blessings of this knowledge, the question comes with urgency, Is it attainable? We look to the verses for information, and we find that the method for attainment involves four things— First: *Communication.* These spiritual verities come to the soul in the " words of the wise." " Have not," says the writer of these verses, "I written to thee excellent things in counsels and knowledge?" Men do not reach this knowledge as they reach a knowledge of scientific truth, by their own researches and reasoning. It is brought to them in a communication—in a communication from holy men who "spake as they were moved by the Holy Ghost." The "excellent things," the subject of this knowledge, are contained in *The Book*. Secondly: *Attention*. "Bow down thine ear and hear the words of the wise." What boots the utterance of the inspired orator, if he is not listened to? What boot the doctrines of the inspired writer, if they are not studied? There is such a moral deafness in the ear, and it is so dinned with worldly noises, that unless there is a bowing down and earnest listening the spiritual sounds will not be caught. Hence, listen. "Hear, and your soul shall live." Thirdly: *Application*. "Apply thine heart unto my knowledge." You may catch the sound and even interpret its meaning, and yet not attain to its experimental knowledge. There must be application—application of the heart. All the sympathies of the heart must be interested in it; it must be felt to be the *one* thing. Fourthly: *Retention*. "It is a pleasant thing if thou keep them within thee." These spiritual verities may come in *sounds* to the ear, but the sound may die away—may come in *idea* to the intellect, but the idea may vanish from the memory, may come in an *impression* on the heart, but the impression may evaporate as the morning dew; it must be *retained* in order that the transcendent blessings may be enjoyed. "Keep them within thee." There are many things to drive them from thee; hold them with all the tenacity of thy being.

Get this knowledge, brother, whatever other science thou neglectest, get this for thyself. "I have made known to *thee*," says Solomon. The possession of it by others will be of no avail to thee; thou must get it for thyself. Get it *now*. "I have made known this *day* even to thee." There is no time to lose.

Proverbs 22:22-23

The Oppression of the Poor

"Rob not the poor, because he *is* poor: neither oppress the afflicted in the gate: for the LORD will plead their cause, and spoil the soul of those that spoiled them."

AFTER the solemn preface in the preceding verses," says an old author, "one would have expected something new and surprising: but no, here is a plain and common but very needful caution against the barbarous and inhuman practice of oppressing poor people." Observe—

THE CRIME PROHIBITED.—It is the oppression of the poor. This is a *common* crime. The poor have always been oppressed. They do the hard and the trying work of the world. In *trade*, they build our houses, construct our vessels, weave our fabrics, man our vessels over the perils of the deep, and thus produce the wealth of the country. The fortunes of our rich men are trees that have been planted by the hand of the poor man and watered by the sweat of his brow. From the fruit of that tree he is kept off by the hand of haughtiness and violence. The single grape that falls from its clustered branches to the ground shall sooner be allowed to rot in the earth than be put kindly into his hands. In *agriculture*, the poor man toils as a beast of burden in the hot suns of summer and the bleak winds of winter, in order to convert sterility into fruitfulness. His labours give value to the estates of the landlord, and cover the fields with golden crops in autumn; yet out of all he can scarcely get the meanest shelter for his head, the humblest wrappage for his clothing, and the scantiest fare for his support. In *war*, he fights the battles of despots and nations, he falls with millions of his class on the field of slaughter and blood; he builds thrones and constructs crowns, yet he gets no honour or reward; others wear the laurels and gain the prizes. Thus the oppression of the poor man is, alas! a common crime. This is a *heinous* crime. To "rob the poor because he is poor" is a great enormity. To rob any man is wrong, to oppress the richest brother is a crime, but to rob the poor "because he is poor," is of all oppressions the worst. Rich men will not suffer themselves to be wronged, poor men cannot help themselves; and therefore justice requires that we should be more careful to guard their rights. In this crime there is the basest *cowardice*, and the most heartless *cruelty*. Cowardice, because the victim is powerless; cruelty, because the victim is already in distress. Observe—

THE PUNISHMENT THREATENED.—"The Lord will plead their cause, and spoil the soul of those that spoiled them." No crime is more frequently denounced in the Bible as abhorrent to the Eternal Father than that of oppressing the poor "What mean ye that ye beat my people to pieces, and grind the faces of the poor, saith the Lord God of Hosts." (Isaiah iii. 15.) The accumulation of Divine vengeance is heaped upon this sin. (Ps. cix. 6, 16.) Ahab's judgment testified to the fearful spoiling of those who spoil the poor. (1 Kings xxi. 18—24, comp. Isa. xxxiii. 1, Hab. ii. 8.) The captivity in Babylon was the scourge for this wickedness. (Ezek. xxii. 29—31, comp. Jer. xxi. 12). And when the deeds of secrecy shall be brought to light, how black will be the catalogue of sins of oppression! How tremendous the judgment of the oppressor! (Mal. iii. 5). God is the *counsel* of the poor. He "will plead their cause." In courts of human judicature there are sometimes barristers generous enough to stand up and gratuitously defend a poor and unprotected prisoner. This God does for all the poor. If they have no friends amongst men, they have one Great Friend Who will ever be true to them. God is the *avenger* of the poor. He is not only the counsel, but the judge. "He will spoil the soul of those that spoiled them." "He that robs the poor," said an old author, "will be found in the end the murderer of himself."

Proverbs 22:24-28

Interdicted Conduct

"Make no friendship with an angry man; and with a furious man thou shalt not go: Lest thou learn his ways, and get a snare to thy soul. Be not thou *one* of them that strike hands, *or* of them that are sureties for debts. If thou hast nothing to pay, why should he take away thy bed from under thee? Remove not the ancient landmark, which thy fathers have set."

THESE verses point out:

An interdicted FRIENDSHIP.—" Make no friendship with an angry man, and with a furious man thou shalt not go." There are men of malign natures. They are "angry" and "furious." One of the greatest perplexities to me connected with the Divine procedure is the constitutional malignity of some men. Why the benevolent God should send men into the world with natures temperamentally unkind and malicious astounds me. That there are such men must be obvious to all who have any extensive acquaintance with their race. Men without honey, and full of gall; waspish, whose delight is in stinging; canine, whose language is a snarl. Friendship with such men must be avoided. Indeed, real friendship there cannot be; but there may be such an intimate association as to be very pernicious. There are two reasons why this friendship is interdicted. The bad temper of such may *infect his companion*. "Lest thou learn his ways." Such are the susceptibilities of our nature that we catch the temper of those with whom we mostly associate, whether it be good or bad. Ill-temper is as propagating as good, the seed of hemlock will multiply as well as that of wheat. A malign and furious-tempered man will, by his words and manners, so irritate and chafe the soul of his companion that he be-

564 / Book of Proverbs

comes ultimately infected with the same foul disease. The other reason why this friendship with men of malign nature is interdicted is, that the bad temper of such may *endanger his soul*. To catch such a temper is moral ruin. A disposition to anger and revenge is an incipient devil within, a devil that will snare and ruin our spiritual nature. These verses give us also—

An interdicted CONTRACT.—" Be not one of them that strike hands, or of them that are sureties for debts." Solomon has more than once before prohibited suretiships.* "The language," says a distinguished theological writer, " evidently implies not a universal prohibition of suretiship as of a thing wrong in itself and under whatever circumstances, but an advice and admonition to special caution and circumspection. There may be cases in which it is more than justifiable—in which every claim of necessity and mercy renders it an imperative duty. But still we are not entitled for the sake of one to expose others to risk. We are not entitled to overlook and disregard either the risks and rights of other creditors or the interests of a dependent family. The reason, too, assigned here for the caution shows us that in our dealings with others a prudent regard to our interests is a perfectly legitimate motive. ' If thou hast nothing to pay'—that is, if on the failure of the party for whom you have become responsible you have not enough to make good your suretiship—' why should he take away thy bed from under thee?' This may seem a very rare case, yet such creditors there have been, and may still be, whose selfishness and resentment drive to the extreme of harshness, and whose irritation perhaps is exasperated by their seeing that but for the said suretiship the party would have come to a stand and to a settlement earlier, and with so much the less loss, to those whom he has involved. We are commanded 'to love our neighbours as ourselves;' but to do for him what might expose us to having our very bed sold from under us, is to love him better than ourselves, which is a step beyond the Divine injunction. And so many are the cases in which it is

* See Readings on chap. vi. 1—5; xi. 15; xvii. 18.

most difficult for us to get at the precise state and prospects of the person—friend though he may be—who makes the application, that there is hardly anything that calls for greater care, or warrants, in the eyes of all sensible and candid people a larger measure of reserve, and even, generally speaking, of more "steady refusal." These verses give us again—

An interdicted ACTION.—" Remove not the ancient landmark, which thy fathers have set." There is probably a reference here to the divisions of the land of Canaan. When the Most High divided the nations their inheritance, when He separated the sons of Adam, He set the bounds of the people according to the number of the children of Israel.* The verse suggests First: All men have certain rights. They have personal, social, religious, political rights. They have rights that are inalienable, and rights that have been obtained—primary and secondary rights. Secondly: There are standards set up by our fathers by which the rights of man are to be determined. They have been set up in the works of our best ethical writers, in the works of our legal authorities, of which Blackstone is the chief: and above all, in our Bible. Thirdly: These standards are to be respected. They are not to be removed. We must not go beyond the boundary, and encroach upon the rights of others. We have plenty of liberty in the sphere allotted to us. Some have given these words an application too absolute and universal. The stereotyped Conservatives, both in politics and religion, would have them to mean that we must bind ourselves for ever to precedents, be eternally loyal to old usages, and keep things as they have ever been. This is absurd, and contrary to the tenour of the Bible and progressive instincts of the human soul.

* Deut. xxxii. 8.

Proverbs 23:1-3

The Epicure: or Gastric Temptation

"When thou sittest to eat with a ruler, consider diligently what *is* before thee: and put a knife to thy throat, if thou *be* a man given to appetite. Be not desirous of his dainties; for they *are* deceitful meat."

THE temptations to which men are exposed in passing through this life are many and varied. They meet men in every department of life; they touch them at every susceptibility of their natures. There are the temptations of the market, the temple, the chamber, the field, the library, the table; to the last the verses refer. The great tempter, perhaps, is never more active and successful than at banquets; he gets at the brain, heart, and being of man through his stomach. When he gets the gastric faculty he gets the man. Hence, against no temptation does man require warnings more forcible and frequent, and yet the pulpit is comparatively silent on the point. Where it ought to thunder it is mute. The words leads us to consider concerning this gastric temptation:—its *elements* and *resistance*.

ITS ELEMENTS.—What constitutes the temptation to go wrong at the table? The two things which are referred to in the passage. First; *A sumptuous banquet.* "When thou sittest to eat with a ruler." The scene suggested is the table of a prince bespread with all the luxuries and delicacies calculated to raise the appetite to its highest excitement. Secondly: A *keen appetite.*—"If thou be a man given to appetite." The expression "given to appetite," means something more than being hungry, something more than a craving for mere natural food, it means that craving for "dainties" which has been cultivated by a regaling on delicacies. These two things constitute the temptation; the one without the other would be powerless to tempt. Let the table be covered with the choicest delicacies, if there be no appetite there will be no temptation; and on the other hand, let the appetite be ever so strong, if there be nothing on the table there will be no temptation. The two things coming together, the sumptuous fare and the strong appetite, create the temptation. These two elements of temptation civilization has wonderfully strengthened, and continues to do so every day. The brute has an appetite, and he takes from the table of nature provisions in their simplest form, but man employs his imagination both upon his food and his appetite. He brings the fruits of nature into new combinations, and thus gives them new and exciting power over his palate; and in this way he comes into possession of artificial tastes and cravings. The other thing which the words lead us to consider concerning this gastric temptation is—

ITS RESISTANCE.—Here observe—the manner and reason of resistance. First: *The manner.* "Put a knife to thy throat." The idea is, resist with the most resolute determination. So powerful is the temptation which the table exerts on some guests, that if there is to be resistance, it must be with the utmost resolve. The whole force of the soul must be exerted. Perhaps, Solomon means to say it is better to cut your throat with the knife than to use it for feeding on the stimulating viands. Better it would be that the body should die than it should be so pampered as to bury the soul in plethora. Observe— Secondly: *The reason.* "Be not desirous of his dainties, for they are deceitful meat." Those dainties prepared by culinary science are generally deceitful; they promise good, but bring evil both to body and soul. "When you see a number of dishes," says an expositor, "of different kinds, think with yourself—here are fevers, and agues, and gouts in disguise. Here are snares and traps spread along the table, to catch my soul and draw me into sin. *Sense* gives a good report of this plenty; but *reason* and *religion* tell me to take heed, for it is deceitful meat." "If I see," says Bishop Hall, "a dish to please my appetite, I see a serpent in that apple, and will please myself in a wilful denial." The productions of culinary art and confectionery skill are injurious alike to the bodies and souls of men. How much need have we to use the prayer of the Church of England—"Grant unto us such abstinence, that our flesh being subdued unto the Spirit, we may ever obey the godly motions." Are not, it may be asked, all these things given for our enjoyment? Are we not justified in seeking pleasure in the fruits of the earth? Our reply is, that our benevolent Creator has so arranged that the food we require should give pleasure to the hungry man, that the appropriation of the aliment into the system it requires, is pleasant to the senses. But this does not justify us in seeking pleasure *in* them. All bodily appetites should be attended to for purposes of *relief*, not *gratification*. The very moment we seek gratification in any organ or appetite of the body, we degrade our nature and dishonour our Creator. Our happiness is not in the body but in the soul, not without but within, and ought never to be sought for as an end, it comes only in self-consecration to duty and to God. The men who make a "god of their belly" are, for the most part, the most wretched in mind and contemptible in character. The epicure drags his soul in the pool of materialism, and buries its wings in mud.

Proverbs 23:4-5

Riches Not to be Labored for as an End

"Labour not to be rich: cease from thine own wisdom. Wilt thou set thine eyes upon that which is not? for *riches* certainly make themselves wings; they fly away as an eagle toward heaven."

THESE words are to be taken of course in a qualified sense, the sense in which some of the words of our Saviour are to be accepted. Christ says: "Labour not for the meat that perisheth." Obviously He does not mean that we are not to work for our livelihood; this would be contrary alike to the injunctions of the Bible, the arrangements of nature, and the necessities of mankind. He means that we are not to labour solely or chiefly for our temporary wants, but for good of a higher and more enduring kind: " The bread of everlasting life." So the philosoher here means, not that we are to be utterly regardless of worldly wealth and make no efforts for its attainment, but that such must not be our end. The man who despises riches is either a hypocrite or a fool. Wealth is not only a power to aggrandize self, but to bless the world. The annihilation of pauperism, the education of humanity, and the evangelization of the world are greatly dependent on money. There are two reasons suggested, however, why wealth should not be laboured for as an end.

To do so is to pursue YOUR OWN WISDOM.—This is implied in the prohibition, " Cease from thine own wisdom." A man's own wisdom, the wisdom he reaches by an intellect under the government of a corrupt and selfish heart, is a false and dangerous light. It leads right away from truth and holiness and God; it is called a "fleshly" wisdom, it is the child and servant of the senses; its science is fleshly; its literature is fleshly; its art is fleshly; its religion is fleshly; it lives in materialism. It is called foolish wisdom; " the wisdom of this world is foolishness with God." Foolish, indeed; it prefers the shadow to the substance, the form to the spirit, the transient to the imperishable, the devilish to the Divine. Now it is this miserable wisdom that inspires man to labour for riches as an end. The wisdom from above directs him to higher wealth, calls upon him to lay up treasures in heaven, " where no moth can corrupt and no thief break in and steal." Another reason suggested why wealth should not be laboured for as an end is that—

To do so is to pursue A VERY INFERIOR GOOD.—" Wilt thou set thine eyes upon that which is not? For riches certainly make themselves wings: they fly away as an eagle toward heaven." The words here given concerning riches suggest, First: Their *unsubstantial* character. " Upon that which is not." Wealth at best is a most unsubstantial thing; it is a mere air bubble rising on the stream of life, glittering for a moment, and then departs for ever. Great fortunes are but bubbles: they vanish before a ripple on the stream, or a gust in the atmosphere. The words suggest, Secondly: Their *fleeting* character. "They make themselves wings: they fly away as an eagle toward heaven." The fortunes of all men grow wings, some grow them more quickly than others; with some, fortunes are fledged in a night, and in the morning, like an eagle, they are gone—they are vanished from the horizon. How swiftly the wealth of Job fled away!* The words suggest, Thirdly: Their *unworthy* character. They are unworthy of human love. "Wilt thou set thine eyes upon that which is not?" The "eyes" mean heart. Wilt thou regard them with avidity and fond desire? If so, what a fool to give the love of an immortal nature to that which is so unsubstantial and fleeting. "We brought nothing into this world, and it is certain we can carry nothing out."

"Riches, like insects, while conceal'd they lie,
Wait but for wings, and in their season fly.
To whom can riches give repute and trust,
Content or pleasure, but the good and just?
Judges and senates have been bought for gold:
Esteem and love were never to be sold."—POPE

Proverbs 23:6-8

A Spurious Hospitality

"Eat thou not the bread of *him that hath* an evil eye, neither desire thou his dainty meats: for as he thinketh in his heart so *is* he: Eat and drink, saith he to thee; but his heart *is* not with thee. The morsel *which* thou has eaten shalt thou vomit up, and lose thy sweet words."

TRUE hospitality is a social virtue of no ordinary worth. It gives a glow to the social atmosphere, but like all good things it has its counterfeit. There is much spurious hospitality. Much passes for it which in substance is as foreign to it as brass to gold. The verses indicate that this spurious hospitality—

* Job. i. 14—17.

Is SORDID.—"Eat thou not the bread of him that hath an evil eye." The "evil eye" here means covetousness; it is a symbol of the penurious, the stingy, the grudging. Strange that lean-natured miserly souls should make feasts at all, yet they do. Perhaps their banquets are as numerous and magnificent as those whose generous natures are ever aglow with social love. They do it, however, not for the happiness of their guests, or the gratification of their own natures, but for ulterior reasons lying in the region of the mean and the selfish. Sometimes *vanity* is the acting motive. To have around their board guests that will flatter and fawn, yields their selfish natures pleasures of a certain kind. Many stingy souls make feasts for men of popularity and fame in order to gratify their own vanity. Simon the Pharisee of old entertained Jesus of Nazareth probably for this reason; he had no sympathy with Him, but the star of the Galilean was rising, and he wished to participate in the renown. Sometimes *greed* is the acting motive. These men make feasts for clients and customers. They often do fine strokes of business at their dinner-table, in the presence of steaming viands and sparkling glasses. They make feasts for matrimonial ends: they invite to their table those whose connubial connexion with their own sons or daughters they regard as an object devoutly to be wished. They make feasts for secretarial ends. How many feasts are made both in the mercantile and religious world in order to gain funds for companies and societies, in which managers and secretaries have a vital interest: men often make feasts to fill their own pockets at the public expense.

The verses indicate that this spurious hospitality is HYPOCRITICAL.—"For as he thinketh in his heart, so is he: Eat and drink, saith he to thee, but his heart is not with thee." The eye belies the lips; as a host he says one thing and looks another. His words are generous, whilst every mouthful swallowed by the guest gives him a twinge of fretful regret; all the while he thinks more of his purse than of the pleasure of his guests. The kind, sweet words which he uses at the banquet are succeeded by groans and curses in his heart when you retire. The selfish host is a hypocrite at his table; his words belie his heart. The verses indicate that this spurious hospitality—

Is ABHORRENT.—"The morsel which thou hast eaten thou shalt vomit up, and lose thy sweet words." If thou hast insight enough at the time to discern spirits, thou wilt feel an inner disgust for thy host. The discrepancy between the words and heart of the host will disgust thee, the very "morsel which thou hast eaten" thou shalt be ready to "vomit up." Or if at the time the discrepancy is not discovered and felt, it will show itself on some future occasion: he will remind thee of it by some hint or act. He will give thee to understand that that dinner laid thee under some obligation to him which thou shouldest practically recognise. He made that dinner not for thy sake but for the sake of himself, and unless he reaps the anticipated profits out of thee, he will show his displeasure, and this will make thee sick. "The morsel thou hast eaten thou shalt vomit up." That dinner will always be a disgust to thee; notwithstanding all the "sweet words" that were spoken on the occasion, the words of flattery for his fine dishes and wines, his magnificent style aud princely abundance, all such words will be lost words.

Avoid then such feasts. "Desire not thou his dainty meats." Keep away from his table. Paul says: "I have written unto you not to keep company, if any man that is called a brother be a fornicator, or covetous, or an idolater, or a railer, or a drunkard, or an extortioner; with such an one no not to eat."* The covetous man is here classed with the fornicator, the drunkard, the idolater, the extortioner, the railer. Don't sit at the table of a covetous man. Genuine hospitality very soon makes itself manifest wherever it is. "It breaks," says Washington Irving, "through the chills of ceremony and selfishness, and thaws every heart into a flow. There is an emanation from the heart in genuine hospitality which cannot be described, but is immediately felt, and puts the stranger at once at his ease."

* 1 Cor. v. 11.

Proverbs 23:9

The Incorrigible Sinner

" Speak not in the ears of a fool: for he will despise the wisdom of thy words."

WE often speak of retribution as if it always lay beyond the grave, and the day of grace as extending through the whole life of man; but such is not the fact. Retribution begins with many men here, the day of grace terminates with many men before the day of death. There are those who reach an unconvertible state, their characters are stereotyped and fixed as eternity. The things that belong to their peace are hid from their eyes. They are incorrigible. Such is the character referred to in the text—" Speak not in the ears of a fool: for he will despise the wisdom of thy words." Who are the incorrigible?

They are those who ARE not to be taught. "Speak not in the ears of a fool." Here is a prohibition to teachers. There are certain men they are not to address. Elsewhere Solomon gives the same prohibition.* "Reprove not a scorner lest he hate thee: rebuke a wise man and he will love thee." Our Saviour gives the same injunction: "Give not that which is holy unto the dogs, neither cast ye your pearls before swine, lest they trample them under foot, and turn again and rend you." (Matt. vii. 6.) There are men whom God has given up teaching. There was Saul: "The Lord answered him not with dreams or visions, or prophets." He was left to himself, and he went at night to Endor. There was Herod: Christ declined speaking a word to Herod. (Luke xxiii. 9.) There are men to whom a wise teacher should not direct his counsels. Such men are not difficult to recognise; there is a callousness, a profanity, a recklessness, and a scorn which mark them as incorrigible reprobates. Don't speak to them, pass them by with a dignified silence,

* See Reading on chap. ix. 8.

enter into no discussion with them on sacred themes. Who are the incorrigible?

They are those who WILL not be taught. "He will despise the wisdom of thy words." A man who despises wise words has not the spirit for learning: the moral soil of his nature is not that which can receive the seed of spiritual wisdom. It is craggy granite, not seasoned loam. The man has no *docility*; he is too proud and haughty to be taught. He has no *reverence*; to him there is nothing greater than himself. His spirit for receiving counsels of wisdom is as foreign as that of the lion or the wolf.

> "Beware of too sublime a sense
> Of your own worth and consequence:
> The man who dreams himself so great,
> And his importance of such weight,
> That all around, in all that's done,
> Must move and act for him alone,
> Will learn in school of tribulation
> The folly of his expectation."—COWPER

Proverbs 23:10-11

Social Injustice

"Remove not the old landmark; and enter not into the fields of the fatherless: for their redeemer *is* mighty; he shall plead their cause with thee."

AN expression identical with the first clause of this text has recently engaged our attention.* In these words we have three things concerning social injustice.

Social injustice INDICATED.—"Remove not the old landmark." What are the landmarks? The *rights* of man as man. For example, every man has a right to *personal freedom*. He has an inalienable right to the free use of his faculties and his limbs. By wrong-doing, of course, he may forfeit this right to society, but naturally it belongs

* See Reading on chap. xxii. 24—28.

Proverbs 23:10-11 / 575

to him. Every man has a right to *the produce of his own labour*. Whatever a man produces is his; his in a sense in which it can belong to no other. It never would have been had he not existed and laboured. His power over it, if honestly produced, is absolute, so far as society is concerned. Every man has a right to *freedom in religion*. He has a full right to form his own religious convictions, and freely to express them, so long as he does not invade the rights of others. He has a right to worship his own God in his own way, and in his own time. These are some of his rights. They are the "landmarks" marking the field of his own prerogatives. None should touch those landmarks. Woe to those who destroy them! In these words, we have—

Social injustice PERPETRATED ON THE HELPLESS.— "Enter not into the fields of the fatherless." How many orphans there are in the world. Children left desolate, unprotected, and unprovided for. These orphans have their rights. Sad to say, there are villains in society who perpetrate outrages on orphans. This is cowardly, cruel, and common. The case of the "Oliver Twist" of Charles Dickens, though, perhaps, a little exaggerated, indicates the outrages to which helpless children are subjected even in this England of ours. In these words we have—

Social injustice perpetrated on the helpless, JUDICIALLY REGARDED BY GOD.—"Their redeemer is mighty: he shall plead their cause with thee." The word "redeemer" here means "next-of-kin," one appointed by the law of Moses to look after the concerns of his poor relations, and with whom lay the avenging of their blood in cases of cruelty. It was on this principle that Boaz called upon the next-of-kin to come forward and redeem the inheritance of Elemilech at the hands of Naomi. The mighty God is the Protector of the helpless. He will plead their cause, and He will one day redress their wrongs, and punish their oppressors. It is for the rulers of a kingdom to see that their subjects are not oppressed, to see that the rights of none are outraged, and none either young or old are the victims of tyranny, domestic, social, political, or ecclesiastic. It is recorded of Cambyses, King of Persia, who was remarkable for the severity of his government and his inexorable regard to justice, that he had a particular favourite whom he made a judge, and this judge reckoned himself so secure in the credit he had with his master that, without ceremony, causes were bought and sold in the courts of judicature as openly as provisions in the market. But when Cambyses was informed of these proceedings, enraged to find his friendship so ungratefully abused, the honour of his government prostituted, and the liberty and property of his subjects sacrificed to the avarice of this wretched minion, he ordered him to be seized and publicly degraded, after which he commanded his skin to be stripped over his ears, and the seat of government to be covered with it as a warning to others. At the same time to convince the world that this severity proceeded only from the love of justice, he permitted the son to succeed his father in the honours and office of prime minister.

Proverbs 23:12

Spiritual Knowledge

"Apply thine heart unto instruction, and thine ears to the words of knowledge."

FREQUENTLY have we met with this counsel before, under varied forms of expression. It is undoubtedly "instruction" and "knowledge" of the highest kind that is here indicated—the knowledge that makes man wise not only for this life, but for the life to come. Why should Solomon be so earnest on this question? In other words, why should the attainment of spiritual knowledge be so strongly enforced upon man?

Because of its own WORTH.—A knowledge of the creation, its elements, laws, objects, extent, is valuable, but a knowledge of the Creator is infinitely more so. The poor, illiterate man, who experimentally knows God, has a sublimer knowledge than the most enlightened sage that ever lived. "This is life eternal, to know Thee, the only true God, and Jesus Christ, whom Thou hast sent." This knowledge not only heals the diseases, cleanses the impurities, removes the evils, crushes the enemies of the soul, but lifts it into fellowship with the great God Himself. Another reason why the attainment of this knowledge is enforced is—

Because man is NOT IMPRESSED WITH ITS IMPORTANCE.—He is, in his unregenerate state, more desirous of obtaining any other knowledge than this; nay, he has a repugnance to this; he does not like to retain God in his thoughts. Hence the need to him of precept upon precept and line upon line. It is sad that the knowledge which man requires most, he cares least for, that the most priceless treasure is least valued. How wise, as well as gracious, was Christ, in instituting a Gospel ministry, whose great work it is to urge man to search after this knowledge! Preaching is no unnecessary service; it is the most urgent work in the world. It cannot be dispensed with. The other reason why the attainment of spiritual knowledge is enforced is—

Because to ATTAIN IT THERE MUST BE PERSONAL APPLICATION.—"Apply thine heart unto instruction." It is a knowledge that cannot be imparted irrespective of the use of man's own faculties. He must apply persistently, earnestly, devoutly. He must "search the Scriptures," and by comparing spiritual things with spiritual, get at a right *conception* of the truth, and when he has got that conception he must cherish it as a principle in his life, and embody it in his conduct. Let the attainment of this knowledge be our great aim in life, and let us struggle after it, for it can only be reached by effort. Never let the present solicit us with its easy indulgence to despair of that sweetest and noblest hope. By aiming at it we shall at last attain. "I have stood," says one, "in an Alpine valley, and still wrapped in the cold and darkness far below, have seen the first sun-

578 / Book of Proverbs

beam smite with its fierce splendour the highest mountain top, and thought it must be impossible by any to reach from our dim low region that encrimsoned height, and yet the sunrise leapt from peak to peak and flowed and broadened in its golden streams down the mountain side, and I have climbed on and on with long toil and under the full daylight have mounted to that topmost crest of the eternal snow heaved high into the regions of blue air. So is it in the moral world." Whoever toils up-hillward, with his eye upon the summit—

> "Shall find the toppling crags of duty scaled
> Are close upon the shining table lands
> To which our God himself is moon and sun."

Proverbs 23:13-14

Parental Discipline

"Withhold not correction from the child; for *if* thou beatest him with the rod, he shall not die. Thou shalt beat him with the rod, and shalt deliver his soul from hell."

IN these verses we have light thrown upon the question of parental discipline; a question second to none in importance; and from them we infer,

That parental discipline MAY SOMETIMES REQUIRE CASTIGATION.—"Withhold not correction from the child; for if thou beatest him with the rod he shall not die." The castigation may be of different kinds. Corporeal infliction. Where reason is undeveloped, the "rod" may be literally applied. This would be the only way by which the parent could make his disapprobation felt. Personal restriction. The child may be denied that which he craves after, such as liberty, gratification of appetite, or wish. This is often more painful than physical suffering. Moral impression. The parent may, by his admonitions and arguments, and by the expression of his feelings, deeply wound the very heart of his child. The moral rod, that makes the heart feel, the conscience smart, is far severer than the material one.

"You may remember," says French, "in one of Æsop's fables, a school boy once stole a horn-book from one of his school-fellows and brought it home to his mother, who neglected chastising him, but rather encouraged him in the deed. In course of time, the boy now grown into a man began to steal things of greater value, till at length being caught in the very act, he was bound and led to execution. Perceiving his mother following among the crowd, wailing and beating her breast, he begged the officers to be allowed to speak one word in her ear; when she quickly drew near and applied her ear to her son's mouth; he seized the lobe of it tightly between his teeth and bit it off. Upon this she cried out lustily, and the crowd joined her in upbraiding the unnatural son, as if his former evil ways had not been enough; but that his last act must be a deed of impiety against his mother. 'But,' he replied; 'it is she who is the cause of my ruin, for if when I stole my school-fellow's horn-book and brought it to her,' she had given me a sound flogging, I should never have grown up so in wickedness as to come to this untimely end.'" We infer again—

That the END of parental discipline SHOULD BE THE SPIRITUAL DELIVERANCE OF THE CHILD.—Why should the parent inflict pain upon his offspring? Not to vent his own passion, gratify his own anger, nor to make the child more thoroughly the creature of his own selfishness. Alas! how often parents inflict sufferings for such miserable ends as these. No, the end should be the spiritual deliverance of the child. "Thou shalt beat him with the rod, and shalt deliver his soul from hell." In all, the parent should strive to deliver his child from the hell of sensuality, selfishness, spiritual wickedness and practical ignobility and impiety. "What if God should place in your hand a diamond, and tell you to inscribe on it a sentence which should be read at the last day, and shown there as an index of your own thoughts and feelings? What care, what caution, would you exercise in the selection. Now this is what God *has* done. He has placed before the immortal minds of your children, more imperishable than the diamond, on which you are about to inscribe every day and every hour, by your instructions, by your spirit, or by your example, something that will remain and be exhibited for or against you at the judgment day."

Proverbs 23:15-23

An Appeal of Parental Piety

"My son, if thine heart be wise, my heart shall rejoice, even mine. Yea, my reins shall rejoice, when thy lips speak right things. Let not thine heart envy sinners; but *be thou* in the fear of the LORD all the day long. For surely there is an end; and thine expectation shall not be cut off. Hear thou, my son, and be wise, and guide thine heart in the way. Be not among winebibbers; among riotous eaters of flesh: for the drunkard and the glutton shall come to poverty: and drowsiness shall clothe *a man* with rags. Hearken unto thy father that begat thee, and despise not thy mother when she is old. Buy the truth, and sell *it* not; *also* wisdom, and instruction, and understanding."

THESE words may be taken as expressing the appeal of pious parents to their children. Notice—

The PURPOSE of the appeal. What is it? Wisdom. "My son, if thine heart be wise." To be wise is to aim at the highest end, to employ the best means to accomplish that end, and to do so at the best time. The approbation of God is the best aim; Christianity is the best means; now is the best time. Another purpose is, that their children may be *truthful*. "Thy lips speak right things." This means something more than veracity, which is the speaking of things true to the conceptions and feelings of the speaker; it means truthfulness in life, it means that the things spoken should be true in themselves, true to eternal facts. A third purpose is, that their children may be *practically pious*. "Be thou in the fear of the Lord all the day long." That is, live the life of filial loyalty and practical reverence. The fear of reverential love. "All the day long." Not occasionally, but habitually. The purpose is further, that their children may be *physically temperate*. "Be not among winebibbers, among riotous eaters of flesh." Temperance consists, not only in the avoidance of drunkenness, but in the avoidance of gluttony as well. Physical intemperance is not only a sin against the body, but against the soul also. Another purpose is, that their children may be *filially loving*. "Hearken unto thy father that begat thee, and despise not thy mother when she is old." The man who has lost his love for his parents, especially for his mother, has lost the last germ of goodness ; or rather lost that moral soil of nature in which alone virtue and piety can take root and grow. Still more, another purpose is, that their children may *acquire the truth*. "Buy the truth, and sell it not." An expression implying that truth is a precious thing ; that truth, to be obtained, must be purchased ; that truth, when once obtained, should never be parted with. Buy it—give everything you have for it : sell it not, not even for life itself. Notice—

The ARGUMENTS of the appeal.—Parents might enforce many arguments to urge their children to follow their counsel. A few only are suggested in these words. First : *Their own happiness*. "My son, if thine heart be wise, my heart shall rejoice, even mine ; yea, my reins shall rejoice." Is it nothing to make happy the instrumental authors of our being, those who have loved us most tenderly, and served us most self-denyingly ? Secondly : *The approaching end*. "Surely there is an end." An end to domestic relations— an end to all means of improvement. Yes, there is an end, and it is not far off. Thirdly : *Freedom from poverty*. "Be not among winebibbers ; among riotous eaters of flesh : for the drunkard and the glutton shall come to poverty, and drowsiness shall clothe a man with rags." The implication is, that where these evils are avoided, and where virtue is practised, there will be no poverty. "Godliness is profitable unto all things. It has the promise of the life that now is and that which is to come." Never can we ponder too profoundly and practically the fact that in genuine religion, or, in other words, Christliness of life, complete well-being is involved and assured. This gives sunshine to the man; his spirit becomes genial, and his conduct glows with a radiant life. Having a soul full of goodness, he sees good in everything. Being harmonious within, he hears music all round him. He beats out melody in every effort; his "soul delights in fatness;" he is blessed in his deed. Like a man marching to music, he treads the path of life with a joyous step. As a Christ-regenerated man, he is satisfied from himself. His happiness springs up from within, as a well of water to everlasting life.

Proverbs 23:26

Man's Heart

"My son, give me thine heart."

"HEART" here, of course, does not mean the bunch of muscles that beats the blood through the veins, nor does it mean merely the emotional part of human nature, the fountain of our affections and sympathies. It stands for the rational nature in its entirety, all that distinguishes us from the brutes. It is the "inner man"—the man of the man. The verse leads us to make two remarks concerning this heart:

It is a property that man HAS TO DISPOSE OF.—This is implied in the expression "Give me thine heart." First: Man has *nothing higher* to dispose of. His heart is given when he sets his strongest affections upon an object. Wherever he centres his strongest love his heart is, and where his heart is, *he* is. Locally the object to whom he has given his heart may be as far as the antipodes, aye, as far as the heavens are from the earth. Albeit, the man is there, though his body may be confined to some small spot on earth. It is characteristic of the human creature that he can live two lives at once—the animal down amongst the vegetating, and the sensuous and spiritual wherever the object of his love may be. When therefore, he gives his heart, he gives more than if he gave all his worldly possessions, than if he parted with a crown or a kingdom. He gives himself. Secondly: Man *is compelled to* dispose of it. He is forced, not by any outward coercion, but by an inward pressure, by the cravings of his nature. It is as necessary for the soul to love as it is for the body to breathe. The deepest of all the deep hungers of humanity is the hunger in the heart to love. Sometimes so ravenous does man's animal appetite for food become, that he will devour with a kind of relish the most loathsome things; and so voracious is the heart for some object to love, that it will settle down upon the lowest and most contemptible creatures rather than not love at all. Thirdly: Man *alone can* dispose of it. No one can take it from him by force. He is the only priest that can present it. Had he no power over his affections he would be at the mercy of circumstances. He would move as a slave, not as a free man in the universe. He would be an engine driven by force, not an agent, responsible to moral law. Although the Everlasting One has a right to his heart, requires it, and commands him to give it, He will not wrest it from him. Another remark which the verse leads us to make concerning the heart is, that—

It is a property URGENTLY CLAIMED.—There are many who claim it. A thousand objects—wealth, fame, pleasure surround man, especially in his youthful stages—asking him for his heart. Alas! without experience, and without thought, he yields to the request and is ruined. His heart has gone to the wrong object, and he is a lost man. There is only one object in the universe to whom it should be given—that is, the Supremely Good. Why? He alone has *a right to* it. "All souls are His." He called them into existence, and endowed them with their fathomless susceptibilities and amazing powers He who gives his heart to any one else is guilty of the most atrocious injustice. Why? He alone *can develop* it. So constituted is the human soul, that there is no possibility of having all its powers quickened and unfolded without supreme love to the Infinite. What the sunbeam is to the earth, love to God is to the soul, that without which all would be barren and beautiless for ever. Still why? He alone *can satisfy* it. "You might as soon," says an old writer, "fill a bag with wisdom and a chest with virtue, or a circle with a triangle, as the heart of man without God. A man may have enough of the world to sink in, but he can never have enough to satisfy him." The soul crieth out for the living God : nothing short of this will satisfy it. It requires more than His works, attributes, or provisions ; it wants Himself.

How rational, how morally befitting, how sublimely simple, is genuine religion! "My son, give me thine heart." Sir Walter Raleigh, who was atrociously sacrificed by the impious James I., and condemned to be beheaded, on a false charge of treason, in reply to the executioner, who asked him which way he should lay his head, said, "So the heart be right, it is no matter which way the head lies."

Proverbs 23:29-35 *

The Drunkard's Effigy Hung Up as a Beacon

"Who hath woe ? who hath sorrow? who hath contentions ? who hath babbling? who hath wounds without cause ? who hath redness of eyes ? They that tarry long at the wine ; they that go to seek mixed wine. Look not thou upon the wine when it is red, when it giveth his colour in the cup, *when* it moveth itself aright. At the last it biteth like a serpent, and stingeth like an adder. Thine eyes shall behold strange women, and thine heart shall utter perverse things. Yea, thou shalt be as he that lieth down in the midst of the sea, or as he that lieth upon the top of a mast. They have stricken me, *shalt thou say, and* I was not sick ; they have beaten me, *and* I felt *it* not : when shall I awake ? I will seek it yet again."

WE have already dealt with a passage treating the same revolting subject as this.† All that we shall do here will

---

* The subject of the 27th and 28th verses we have frequently noticed.
† See Reading on chap. xx. 1.

be to present the rough outlines of the drunkard's picture, and several things are here indicated.

HIS SENSUAL INDULGENCE.—He is one of those that "tarry long at the wine, that go to seek mixed wine." It is clear from this and other passages that the wines used in Judea in ancient times were intoxicating, although, perhaps, by no means to the extent of modern wines, which are brandied and drugged. What are called foreign wines in the English markets are, to a great extent we are told, home manufactures. The drunkard is not one who sips the juice of the grape as God gives it for his refreshment, and then passes on to his work, but he is one who "tarries long at the wine." He seeks pleasure out of it. He pursues it as a source of enjoyment. He has mixed and flavoured it, that it may become more exciting to his brain, more delicious to his palate. What a picture of thousands in this so-called Christian country, who periodically assemble every day in taverns, hotels, and clubs, in order to "tarry long" at the intoxicating beverage! Another thing indicated here concerning the drunkard is—

HIS OFFENSIVE GARRULOUSNESS.—"Who hath contentions? Who hath babbling?" When alcohol excites the brain, that member of the body which James describes as "setting on fire the whole course of nature," is allowed to give full utterance to all the filthy, incoherent, ill-natured, and ridiculous things that spring from the inebriate's heart. In these babblings there may sometimes be some genial and humourous expressions, but more often ill-natured and irritating "contentions." What quarrels, fightings, and murders have grown out of the drunkard's babblings! They supply our police with labour, our judges with occupation, our workhouses with paupers, our jails with prisoners, our gallows with victims. Another thing indicated here concerning the drunkard is—

HIS BLOODSHOT FACE.—"Who hath redness of eyes?" The habits of the man come to be marked by their effects upon his looks. The inflamed and turgid eye, and the blotched, fiery, and disfigured countenance, indicate that the deleterious poison has gone through his frame and has incorporated with, tainted, and set on fire the entire mass of circulating blood. His very looks become the index of his character. His vacant stare shows that all the ideas concerning the great laws and grand mission of human life are crushed within, and that he is left branded with infamy, to stumble on into a blank eternity. Another thing indicated here concerning the drunkard is—

HIS WRETCHED CONDITION.—" Who hath woe? who hath sorrow?" It seems implied that the drunkard gets into a wretchedness for which no equal can be found. The very means of the drunkard's pleasure " biteth like a serpent, and stingeth like an adder?" Whose woe is greater than his? He has the " woe " of ill-health. Drunkenness poisons the blood, saps the constitution, and generates the foulest diseases. He has the "woe" of secular poverty. Drunkenness indisposes and unfits him for those duties by which a subsistence for himself and family can be obtained. The pauperism of England has its chief fountain in drunkenness. He has the "woe" of social contempt. Who can respect the drunkard? Not his neighbours—not even his wife or children. They soon get to loathe and shun him. He has the "woe" of moral remorse. In his sober moments if his conscience is not seared, compunction creeps into him like a serpent, bites and stings him into anguish. Truly a wretched creature is the drunkard. Another thing indicated here concerning the drunkard is—

HIS EASY TEMPTABILITY.—"Thine eyes shall behold strange women." The idea suggested is that a man under the influence of inebriating drinks is easily tempted. is ripe for the crimes of adultery, falsehood, blasphemy, and other enormities. His judgment is clouded, his sense of propriety is gone; the passions are inflamed, and the breath of temptation will bear him away into sin. He stands, or rather reels, ready for any crime. There is a fable of a man, no doubt familiar to many —but though a fable it involves an important truth and an important warning—of a man whom the devil is said to have offered the alternative of a choice between *three sins*, one or other of which, as the means of averting some evil or obtaining some good, he was bound to commit. The three sins were—*murder, incest, and drunkenness.* The man made choice of the last, as, in his estimation, incomparably the least. This was the devil's device; for when he was under the influence of it, he was easily beguiled into both the other two. It is needless to say how insensible the drunkard becomes to all feelings of delicacy and decorum; how he is ready to commit the most shameless indecencies and glory in his shame; and how rapidly, in such a state, he becomes the prey—the wretched and dishonourable prey—of every vile seducer. Another thing indicated here concerning the drunkard is—

HIS RECKLESS STUPIDITY.—"Thou shalt be as he that lieth down in the midst of the sea, or as he that lieth upon the top of a mast." Exhausted by excitement, and blinded by the fumes of his disordered stomach and intoxicated brain, he falls to sleep. He is unconscious of the spot on which he lies down. It may be near a raging fire or on the margin of a terrible precipice; it may be as dangerous as if he had laid himself down in the midst of the raging sea, or on the top of a mast tossed by the wild winds of Heaven. He is utterly dead to all the surroundings of his terrible position. When his nature has overcome the power of the poison within him, and the mist rolls from his brain and his senses return, and he opens his eyes, he is startled at the terribleness of his position, and it appears to him as awful as if he had been in the midst of the sea, or on the mast-head of a storm-tossed bark. What a condition for a rational being to be in! and yet it is the condition into which the drunkard sinks in his miserable debauch! When he has awoke he knows nothing of what has occurred during the period of his intoxication. He knows not how he had come to that terrible spot. He finds himself stricken, but he knows not by whom—beaten, he knows not the hand. He has wounds "without a cause"—that is, he knows not the cause. Struggling into consciousness, yawning with an intolerable depression, he is unable to account for the injuries that have been inflicted upon his person. Another thing indicated here concerning the drunkard is—

HIS UNCONQUERABLE THIRST.—"When shall I awake? I will seek it yet again." However bitter his reflections upon his awaking, and his remorse, on his awaking his burning thirst remains unquenched. He seeks relief in that very cup which has thus far damned him. "As a dog to his vomit he returns to his filth."

Young men, look at this terrible effigy! It is here raised on the eternal Rock of Truth, to warn every mariner of his dangers on the sea of life. "Look not thou upon the wine when it is red, when it giveth his colour in the cup, when it moveth itself aright." Let not the hue or the sparkle attract you. Avoid it as you would poison. At an Episcopal meeting, a discussion on temperance brought up the wine question. An influential clergyman rose and made a vehement argument in favour of wine. When he had resumed his seat, a layman said, "Mr. Moderator, it is not my purpose in rising to answer the learned arguments you have just listened to. My object is more humble, and, I hope, more practical. I once knew a father, in moderate circumstances, who was at much inconvenience to educate a beloved son at college. Here this son became dissipated, but, after he had graduated and returned to his father, the influence acting upon a generous father, actually reformed him. The father was overjoyed at the prospect that his cherished hopes were still to be realized. Several years passed, when, the young man having completed his professional study, and being about to leave his father to establish a business, was invited to dine with a neighbouring clergyman distinguished for his hospitality and social qualities. At this dinner wine was introduced and offered to this young man, who refused, it was pressed upon him and again refused. This was repeated, and the young man was ridiculed. He was strong enough to overcome appetite, but could not resist ridicule. He drank and fell, and from that moment became a confirmed drunkard, and long since has found a drunkard's grave.

Mr. Moderator," continued the old man, with streaming eyes, "I am that father, and it was at the table of the clergyman who has just taken his seat, and my son I shall never cease to mourn."

Proverbs 24:1-2

The Villany and Absurdity of Sin

"Be not thou envious against evil men, neither desire to be with them. For their heart studieth destruction, and their lips talk of mischief."

THESE words lead us to make a remark on two points—

The VILLANY of sin.—Here is a description of sinners :— "Their heart studieth destruction, and their lips talk of mischief." Malignity is its very essence. All sinners are of their father, the devil, whose inspiration is malice. Their study is mischief. "Their heart studieth destruction." Destruction of what? Evil that curses the world? No, of chastity, truth, moral sensibility, spiritual goodness. Every wicked man in his measure is an Apollyon; like his great leader he goes about "seeking whom he may devour." Their speech is mischief. "Their lips talk of mischief." Their conversation tends to destroy social order, to create social broils, and to set man against man, family against family, nation against nation. Sin is a destroyer. This is its instinct. This is its influence. Holy Scripture describes the genius and history of sinners. "Their throat is an open sepulchre; with their tongues they have used deceit; the poison of asps is under their lips." It is said that when Nicephorus Phocas had built a strong wall about his palace for his own security, in the night-time he heard a voice crying to him, "O Emperor! though thou build thy wall as high as the clouds, yet if sin be within, it will overthrow all." The other point which the words lead us to remark is on :

The ABSURDITY of sin.—"Be thou not envious against

evil men, neither desire to be with them." Two things are here implied, showing the absurdity of sin. First: That sin *envies* the most *unenviable* things. Envy is essentially a bad passion. The poets imagine that Envy dwelt in a dark cave, being pale and lean, looking a-squint, abounding with gall, her teeth black, never rejoicing but in the misfortune of others, ever unquiet, and continually tormenting herself. But this feeling is garbed with absurdity when it is directed to evil men. To envy evil men is to envy those whose natures are charged with the elements of misery, over whom the clouds of God's disfavour rest, and whom a terrible retribution awaits. Secondly : That sin *desires* the most *undesirable* things. "Neither desire to be with them." To be in the fellowship of wicked men, to breathe their foetid breath, to listen to their foul talk and bacchanalian song, to join in their senseless revelries, is in every way a most undesirable thing, and yet, alas! it is desired—desired by the thousands of youth that are rising into manhood. The pleasure of sin is ever cloying. "A philosopher," says John Howe, "in an epistle which he writes to a man from the court of Dionysius, where he was forcibly detained, thus bemoans himself:—We are unhappy, O Antisthenes, beyond measure! And how can we but be unhappy, that are burdened by the tyrant every day with sumptuous feasts, plentiful compotations, precious ornaments, gorgeous apparel? And I knew as soon as I came into this island and city how unhappy my life would be." This is the nature and common condition of even the most pleasing and sensible objects. They first tempt, then please a little, then disappoint, and lastly vex. The eye that beholds them blasts them quickly, rifles and deflowers their glory, and views them with no more delight at first than disdain afterwards. Creature enjoyments have a bottom : are soon drained, and drawn dry. Hence there must be frequent diversions, and their pleasures must be sought out and chosen, not because they are better, but because they are new.

Sin is a great deceiver, it is always theatrical ; it puts on dazzling costumes that attract and charm the uninitiated.

We have read of a tree which, like the almond tree, robes itself in blossoms before the foliage appears. Its flowers are a gorgeous ruby, and their splendour attracts to it in teeming crowds the winged insects of the air. The busy bee in quest of nectar is attracted to it, settles down for a moment, and amidst its encircled beauty drinks its cup and falls dead to the root. Around that tree we are told there lie the remains of myriads of insects who have fallen victims to a fatal delusion. Is not sin like that tree? In the great fields of human society how high it lifts its head, how wide its branches, how brilliant its blossoms! Human souls, fascinated by its external glory, and by its promise of delicious nectar, hasten to it, crowd around it, settle on it, sip its juicy flowers and fall dead.

Beware of sin. Flee from it as Lot was told to do from Sodom, and thus escape for your life.

Proverbs 24:3-7

Enlightened Piety

"Through wisdom is an house builded; and by understanding it is established: and by knowledge shall the chambers be filled with all precious and pleasant riches. A wise man *is* strong; yea, a man of knowledge increaseth strength. For by wise counsel thou shalt make thy war: and in multitude of counsellors *there is* safety. Wisdom *is* too high for a fool: he openeth not his mouth in the gate."

"WISDOM" here is to be regarded not only as representing piety, but piety in association with intelligence and skill. Goodness of a certain sort is sometimes found in connexion with great ignorance and stupidity. It possesses mind unenlightened by knowledge and unskilled by discipline. On the other hand, there is often found a kind of "wisdom" altogether detached from goodness and piety. Examples abound in history, and also in living society, of men of great intelligence, high culture, and ingenious aptitudes, who are destitute of any goodness of heart, in the Bible sense. These two should be always wedded, "the twain should be one." Where they are thus united, we have what I have designated—*enlightened piety*. The text suggests some of the advantages connected with this.

It is conducive to WEALTH.—" Through wisdom is an house builded; and by understanding it is established: and by knowledge shall the chambers be filled with all precious and pleasant riches." The three words, "Wisdom," "Understanding," and " Knowledge," seem, in the meaning of Solomon, synonymous; they signify an *enlightened religion*, and this is conducive to secular prosperity. An ignorant piety often leads to destitution, an unsanctified intelligence to ruin and misery. But when both are combined there is the guarantee of secular advancement. It involves all the conditions of worldly success, *temperance, economy, industry, aptness*, and *the favour of Heaven*. The Heavenly Teacher intimated this when he said, " Seek ye first the kingdom of God and His righteousness, and all these things shall be added unto you;" and Paul recognised this when he said, " Godliness is profitable unto all things, having the promise of the life which now is, and of that which is to come." I have somewhere read of a learned philosopher who objected to religion on the ground that if he adopted it he should lose all he had in the world. A Christian friend said no one ever lost anything by serving Christ, and offered to give his bond to indemnify the philosopher for all losses he should suffer on that account. The bond was duly executed, and the philosopher became a praying man. Just before his death, he sent for his Christian friend, and gave him the paper, saying, "Take this bond and tear it up. I release you from your promise. Jesus has made up to me a hundred-fold for all that I ever did or suffered on His account. There is nothing left for you to pay. Tell everybody how true it is that there is great profit in serving Jesus." The verses suggest another fact connected with enlightened piety, that—

It is conducive to POWER.—"A wise man is strong; yea,

a man of knowledge increaseth strength." First: Intelligence *apart from* piety is power. A man who has great information, and knows how to use it, possesses a power superior to any physical force. "Knowledge is power." This is a proposition that has been crystallised into a proverb. It has passed the realm of debate, and lies sparkling in the region of acknowledged certitudes. Secondly: Piety apart from intelligence is a *higher kind of* power. It is the power of patience, endurance, love, compassion, courage; it is a power that will touch men's hearts, move the very arm of Omnipotence, "take hold upon the strength of God." Thirdly: Piety *associated* with intelligence is the *highest creature* power. What power on earth is equal to that possessed by the man of vast intelligence and consecrated affections, the man of sunny intellect and Heaven-inspired sympathies and aims? This is a power that can and does work wonders. Another fact suggested by the verses in connection with this enlightened piety is, that—

It is conducive to SAFETY.—"For by wise counsel thou shalt make thy war; and in multitude of counsellors there is safety." How in times of danger does it conduce to "safety?" The words suggest two ways. *It takes counsel of the wise.* "By wise counsel thou shalt make thy war." Nothing exposes a man to greater peril than such an overweening conceit of his own opinions and such a feeling of self-sufficiency as will prevent him from taking counsel of the wise. Self-willed monarchs have ruined kingdoms and brought destruction on themselves. The men of enlightened godliness take counsel of the holiest men and of the great God Himself. Another way suggested by the words, in which it is conducive to safety is—*It has power at the gate.* "Wisdom is too high for a fool; he openeth not his mouth in the gate." The "gate" here may refer to the place of public assembly or to the entrance into the city. The man of enlightened piety will be powerful in either position. When he opens his mouth and speaks in the assembly, men will listen to his words and bow to his opinion. Or if he stands at the gate when strangers are entering, opens his mouth when the enemy is advancing, the moral majesty of his aspect and the force of his utterances will drive the invader back more effectively than the swords or bayonets of armies.

Proverbs 24:8-9

Aspects of Depravity

"He that deviseth to do evil shall be called a mischievous person. The thought of foolishness is sin: and the scorner is an abomination to men."

THE man who has the Bible in his hand cannot say that he lacks means of knowing what is good and evil; what characters God will accept and what He will reject. In this Book of books the evil and the good are exhibited in such a variety and fulness of aspect as to render it impossible for men to make a mistake on the momentous subject. Depravity is presented to us in the verses—

AS MISCHIEVOUS IN PURPOSE.—" He that deviseth to do evil shall be called a mischievous person." It is bad enough to be *inclined* to evil; it is worse to *yield* to it, it is worse still to *devise* it; to use that intellect which God has given us in constructing schemes of wickedness. This is the work of the devil himself. His gigantic intellect has ever been thus employed, and continues thus engaged. He is everlastingly constructing schemes of wickedness, and we should not be " ignorant of his devices." And to the same work he inspires all his followers. Balaam was a mischievous person. (Numbers xxxi. 16.) Abimelech earned the same reputation. (Judges ix.) Jeroboam's mischief has stamped his name with a black mark of reprobation—"who made Israel to sin." (1 Kings xii. 22—33.) The heathens of the ancient world are represented as "inventors of evil things." (Romans ix.) All wicked men are desirous of mischief. They are everywhere hatching schemes of evil. Depravity is here presented—

AS SINFUL IN THOUGHT.—"The thought of foolishness is sin." The idea is, that every evil thought is corrupt. How can this be? How can such an intangible, subtle, fugitive thing as thought be a sin? Sinful thoughts are of two classes. First: *Voluntary*. These consist in a voluntary meditation on wrong subjects, such subjects as those which tend to incite lust, avarice, revenge, and impiety, and all wrong states of mind. They consist also in a voluntary meditation on right subjects in a wrong way. Those who take up the great facts of nature, Providence, and the Bible, in order to throw discredit on the existence, wisdom, and goodness of God; and those also who study those facts for infidel, sectarian, or selfish ends, are alike guilty of sinful thoughts. Sinful thoughts are, Secondly: *Involuntary*. These come into us, not only irrespective of our choice, but against our very wish. But if so, how can we be responsible for them? Here is the explanation:—they have grown up out of previous voluntary states of mind. And these states of mind constitute the soil from which they have sprung. Involuntary states of mind grow out of a course of previous voluntary ones. Let us be careful of that from which bad thoughts spring. "The cockatrice's egg," says John Howe, "if long enough hatched becomes a serpent, and therefore ought to be crushed in time." Depravity is here presented—

AS ABHORRENT IN CHARACTER.—"The scorner is an abomination to men." Evil devices, sinful thoughts, and a scorning spirit are all elements of depravity. The man who "sits in the scorner's seat" has reached the nearest seat to hell. Such a character, we have been assured elsewhere, is an abomination to God, but here he is also an abomination to men. Men may laugh at his sarcastic wit, applaud his dexterous shafts of ridicule, but inwardly they despise him. Such a man the human soul cannot trust, cannot love, must recoil from with a profound disgust.

Depart from evil and pursue good, flee from sin and escape to the mountain of purity and truth, the only safe refuge and congenial home of soul. "Sin," says John Bunyan:

> "Is the living worm, the lasting fire;
> Hell would soon lose its heat could sin expire."

Proverbs 24:10

The Day of Adversity

"*If* thou faint in the day of adversity, thy strength *is* small."

Two thoughts are here suggested:

THERE IS A "DAY OF ADVERSITY" FOR ALL.—Man is born to trouble as sparks fly upward. He meets a "day of adversity" in every *part* of his life. In his body, physical diseases; in his intellect, distracting problems; in his conscience, moral convulsions. He meets a "day of adversity" in every *relation* of his life. In his secular relations, trials, and disappointments in his business; in his social relations, abused confidence, false friendships, agonising bereavements. He meets a "day of adversity" in the *end* of his life. The day of death awaits all, and a trying day it is! How cloudy, how tumultuous, how frigid, how desolate! We have all the day of adversity. "Men are but a sponge," says an old writer, "and but a sponge filled with tears; and whether you lay your right hand or left hand upon a full sponge it will weep." Another thought here suggested is that—

The "day of adversity" is a TRIAL OF MORAL STRENGTH. —It is by adversity that our moral strength is tried; thus God tried Abraham, and he turned out to be strong in moral faith; thus God tried Peter, and he turned out to be weak, and fell. We want strength for the day of adversity: that strength of faith in God which will make us resigned, patient, invincible.

Brother, the day of adversity awaits thee. If thou hast not strength to bear up, it will overwhelm thee. Prepare for it, repair to the source of strength, God; "He giveth power to the faint; to him that hath no power He increaseth strength." Thy "day of adversity" is not darker or more tempestuous than better men than thou hast had. "Thou thinkest," says an old author, "thou art more miserable than the rest, other men are happy in respect of thee, their miseries are but flea-bites to thine, thou alone art unhappy, none so bad as thyself. Yet if, as Socrates said, all the men in the world should come and bring their grievances together, of body, mind, fortune, sores, ulcers, madness, epilepsies, agues, and all those common calamities of beggary, want, servitude, imprisonment, and lay them on a heap to be equally divided, wouldst thou share alike and take thy portion, or be as thou art? Without question thou wouldst be what thou art." Let us cultivate moral strength, in order to meet the day of adversity with serenity and heroism.

> " A scrip on my back and a staff in my hand,
> I march on in haste through an enemy's land;
> The road may be rough, but it cannot be long,
> And I'll smooth it with hope, and cheer it with song."
>
> H. F. LYTE

Proverbs 24:11-12

The Neglect of Social Benevolence

"*If* thou forbear to deliver *them that are* drawn unto death, and *those that are* ready to be slain; if thou sayest, Behold, we knew it not; doth not he that pondereth the heart consider *it?* and he that keepeth thy soul, doth *not* he know *it?* and shall *not* he render to *every* man according to his works?"

THE subject of these words is the neglect of social benevolence; and we notice—

The neglect DESCRIBED.—"If thou forbear to deliver them that are drawn unto death, and those that are ready to be slain." Two things are here implied. The *existence* of men in distress. There are men "drawn to death;" and "ready to be slain," now, as well as in the days of Solomon; there are men around us who are being slain not by the sword but by diseases, oppressions, poverty, and disappointments. The other thing implied is the *duty towards* men in distress. There should be an endeavour to deliver them, grapple with their diseases, crush their oppressors, mitigate their poverty, stay their starvation. Every man should try, in the midst of so much distress, to act the part of a deliverer, a physician, a redeemer. Another thing which these verses lead us to notice is—

The neglect EXCUSED.—" If thou sayest, Behold, we knew it not." This is an excuse that is now often pleaded for doing nothing. Men say, " We don't know that such misery exists; we are not sure that the case is a deserving one." Their ignorance in this matter is always voluntary, and therefore criminal, they don't wish to know; they shut their eyes to the fact; and when they are told that men have died of want they say, " We knew it not." Such ignorance is no justifiable excuse. The means of knowledge are abundant. Human misery stares us in the face at every turn. The columns of every day's newspaper are laden with intelligence on the subject, Such ignorance is itself a sin. Every man is bound to know the state of society in which he lives; if there is distress, he should find it out. He should act like Job who said, " The cause which I knew not, I searched out." The neglect of social distress is bad, and the excuses for it only increase its turpitude. The verses lead us to notice again—

The neglect PUNISHED.—"Doth not He that pondereth the heart consider it? and He that keepeth thy soul doth not He know it? and shall not He render to every man according to his works?" There are three facts here which the neglecter of social benevolence should solemnly ponder well. God *knows* him. "Doth not He that pondereth the heart consider it; doth not He know it?" Excuses may do for man, but they will not do for Him; He sees their falsehood; He loathes their hypocrisy. God *preserves* him. " He that keepeth thy soul." He knows that a lie is being told. What impious hardihood to lie to Him in "Whose hand thy breath is, and who knoweth all thy ways." God will *recompense* him. " Shall not He render unto every man according to his works?" There is a day of judgment coming, when thy hypocrisy shall be exposed, and thy covetousness visited with the retributions of eternity. On that day Christ will say to all neglecters of social benevolence. " Inasmuch as ye have not done it unto the least of these my brethren ye have not done it unto me."

> " 'Tis written with the pen of heavenly love
> On every heart which skill divine has moulded,
> A transcript from the statute book above,
> Where angels read the Sovereign's will unfolded.
>
> " It bids us seek the holes where famine lurks,
> Clutching the hoarded crust with trembling fingers;
> Where toil, in damp, unwholesome caverns works,
> Or with strained eyeballs o'er the needle lingers.
>
> " It bids us stand beside the dying bed
> Of those about to quit the world for ever :
> Smoothe the toss'd pillow, prop the aching head,
> Cheer the heart broken, whom death hastes to sever.
>
> " And those who copy thus Christ's life on earth,
> Feeding the poor, and comforting the weeper,
> Will all receive a meed of priceless worth,
> When ripely gathered by the Heavenly Reaper."
>
> *Household Words*

Proverbs 24:13-14

Spiritual Science

" My son, eat thou honey, because *it is* good : and the honeycomb, *which is* sweet to thy taste : so *shall* the knowledge of wisdom *be* unto thy soul : when thou hast found *it*, then there shall be a reward, and thy expectation shall not be cut off."

THE subject of these words is *spiritual science*—a subject which we have had frequently to notice in our passage through this wonderful book. There are many sciences, but the science of God is the root science, that which gives life, unity, and beauty to every branch of knowledge, it is the central science. No man has a thorough knowledge of anything, if he is ignorant of God. What is it to know

Him? It is something more than to know the works of His hands, or the facts of His history. To know a man I must be in possession of the man's spirit, I must be influenced by the same motives, susceptible of the same impressions, inspired by the same aims. I may know all about a man's external history, be well versed in every part of his biography, and yet be ignorant of himself. It is so with God. "For what man knoweth the things of a man, save the spirit of man which is in him? Even so the things of God knoweth no man, but the spirit of God." To know Him I must have His spirit, His disposition. I must participate in that love which is the spring of all His actions, the heart of His heart. "He that loveth not, knoweth not God, for God is love." This is *the* knowledge which is essential to our well-being. "This is life eternal, to know Thee, the only true God, and Jesus Christ, whom Thou hast sent." The verse suggests three remarks concerning this spiritual science:

It is WHOLESOME.—"My son, eat thou honey, because it is *good.*" Honey was one of the choice productions of Canaan. It was used by its inhabitants as an article of diet, and it was not only delicious to the palate, but strengthening to the frame. When Jesus appeared to His disciples after His resurrection, it is said that, "When they believed not for joy, He said unto them, Have ye here any meat? and they gave Him a piece of broiled fish and an honeycomb." Solomon says in effect: that what honey is to the body in strengthening it, spiritual knowledge is to the mind—"it is good." Knowledge of God is the aliment for man's spiritual nature. Without it there is no moral strength; our faculties require God Himself to feed upon. The bread of the soul is not any part or the whole of creation, but the Eternal God Himself. Without Him the soul starves. He is the food of the intellect, the affections, the imagination, the conscience. The soul "crieth out for the living God." The verses further suggest concerning spiritual science that:

It is DELECTABLE.—"And the honeycomb, which is sweet to the taste." God's goodness in nature appears in this as well as in all other things: that the provisions essential to man's strength He has made *palatable* to the taste. He might have made the fruits of the earth which we require for our support bitter as gall, abhorrent to our taste, but he has made all pleasant. Honey is not only strengthening but sweet. The pleasures of spiritual knowledge are of the most exquisite kind. It delights every faculty:—imagination, by opening up enchanting realms of beauty; conscience, by bringing on its ears the transporting music of God's approval; hope, by pointing it to the ever-brightening future; taste,—what said David? "How sweet are thy words unto my taste, yea, sweeter also than honey and the honeycomb." But we learn from the verses—that spiritual science is not only wholesome and delectable, but also that

It is SATISFYING.—" When thou hast found it then there shall be a reward, and thy expectation shall not be cut off." What reward? Goodness is its own reward, and the reward is equal to the highest " expectation." It includes a "love that passeth all knowledge," a " peace that passeth all understanding," " riches that are unsearchable," a "joy that is unspeakable and full of glory."

Let us search diligently for this knowledge. Remember that the Gospel of Christ is the Canaan in which this honey abounds, the high rocks in which it is found. This is *the* knowledge to obtain. " He," says an old writer, " is the best grammarian who has learned to speak the truth from his heart: the best astronomer who has conversation in Heaven: the best musician who has learned to sing the praise of his God: the best arithmetician who so numbers his days as to apply his heart to wisdom. He is knowing in ethics who trains up his family in the Lord: he is the best economist who is wise to salvation, prudent in giving and taking good counsel: he is the best politician, and he is a good linguist that speaks the language of Canaan." You can never get too much of this knowledge. A man may eat too much honey; good as it is, an intemperate use of it will produce nausea and feebleness: not so with this science of sciences, the science of God.

Proverbs 24:15-16
The Hostility
of the Wicked Towards the Good

"Lay not wait, O wicked *man*, against the dwelling of the righteous; spoil not his resting place: for a just *man* falleth seven times, and riseth up again: but the wicked shall fall into mischief."

THESE words lead us to make the following remarks touching the enmity of the wicked towards the good.

The wicked WOULD ruin the good.—This seems to be implied in the prohibition: " Lay not wait, O wicked man, against the dwelling of the righteous; spoil not his resting place." From the Fall to this hour there has been in the mind of the wicked an aversion to the truly righteous. "The seed of the serpent is at enmity with the seed of the woman." In every chapter of human history this enmity is revealed. There were times in this country when it manifested itself by the infliction of the most infernal tortures. Those days are gone, but with them the spirit of hostility is not gone—it works still in sneers, inuendoes, slanders, and other ways. It lays "wait against the dwelling of the righteous," it seeks to "spoil their resting-place." Would not those men who repudiate the religion of Christ, and who constitute, alas! the great majority in this country, be delighted to have theatres and scenes of amusement take the place of our churches and chapels, and Shakespeare, Burns, and Dickens, take the place of the grand old Bible ?

The wicked CANNOT ruin the good.—" For a just man falleth seven times, and riseth up again." *Calamity* and not *immorality* is referred to here, and wicked men may cause a just man to fall into difficulties and troubles. Through their malignant endeavours they may darken his reputation, mar the harmony of his social circle, thwart his secular plans, and reduce him to bankruptcy, but, notwithstanding this, he shall " rise again." There is a marvellous buoyancy in goodness. If the just man who has fallen into calamity rises not to his former secular position, he rises in spirit above his trials. His religion, like a life-boat, bears him over the billows, he braves the tempest, and outrides the storm. Besides this elasticity which is in goodness itself, God's providential hand will be outstretched to raise the fallen man. A just man is near to the heart of God. "He that toucheth you toucheth the apple of my eye." "I am Jesus whom thou persecutest." "He shall deliver thee in six troubles, yea, in seven shall no evil touch thee." "Many are the afflictions of the righteous, but the Lord delivereth him out of them all." He that is engaged, therefore, in endeavouring to injure the good, is engaged in a fruitless work. The just man is destined to rise—no sea of persecution is deep enough to drown him; he will rise, and, like his master, walk upon the billows.

The wicked ruin THEMSELVES IN THE ATTEMPT.— "The wicked shall fall into mischief." "He hath also prepared for him the instruments of death; he ordaineth his arrows against the persecutors. Behold, he travaileth with iniquity, and hath conceived mischief, and brought forth falsehoods. He made a pit and digged it, and is fallen into the ditch which he made. His mischief shall return upon his own head, and his violent dealing shall come down upon his own pate."* Those who seek to injure the good often fall into mischief here and are ruined. History abounds with examples of this fact. The ball which the wicked have shot against the righteous rebounds on their own head, and strikes them down: they are hanged on the gallows which they have prepared for others, and at last the mischief that they will fall into will be irretrievable and tremendous. The path of the sinner is a path of self-entrapment.

* Psalm vii. 13—16.

Proverbs 24:17-18

Revenge

"Rejoice not when thine enemy falleth, and let not thine heart be glad when he stumbleth: lest the LORD see *it*, and it displease him, and he turn away his wrath from him."

REVENGE I may define as a perversion of the innate sentiment of repugnance to wrong as wrong. Antagonism to wrong is a primary instinct of our moral nature. Revenge is this instinct, grown into a wild passion, and directed against the *person* who committed the wrong, rather than against the wrong itself. Johnson makes a distinction between vengeance and revenge. Injuries, he says, are revenged; crimes are avenged. The former is an act of passion, the latter of justice. Our definition may be faulty, but we know the thing—know it from sad experience; we have felt its fires ourselves; we have seen its flash, and heard its thunders in others. It is a most implacable passion, a passion that will burn up itself and turn to ashes. It is a heat of vindictive rage that nothing can allay but blood. "A passion that rains hot vengeance on the offender's head."

The verses direct our attention to three things in relation to revenge.

Its OBJECT.—"Thine enemy." Men are enemies to men. This is a fact as saddening as it is unquestionable. That children of the same Great Father, partakers of the same nature, subject to the same administration, pilgrims to the same eternity, should be at enmity with each other, implies that some terrible change has taken place in the moral nature of man. Humanity is not as it came from the hand of the Great Father of mankind. Sin has made the brother a foe. Now it is against the "enemy" that revenge is directed. If man had no enemy, he would have no revenge; its fire would never be kindled within him. In heaven no such passion burns.

Its GRATIFICATION.—" Let not thine heart be glad when he stumbleth." The fall, the ruin of the enemy, is bliss to the revenging soul. Hence revenge is the genius that invents instruments of torture and implements of destruction —the inspiring and presiding fiend in all battles. The mangled frame of the enemy is to its eye a transporting vision, and his shrieks of agony fall as music on its ear. As a rule, the weaker the nature, the stronger the revenge. A man is great only as he rises above it. David wept and chastened his soul in his enemy's affliction. Job deprecated such a miserable passion. " If I rejoiced at the destruction of him that hated me, or lifted up myself when evil found him, neither have I suffered my mouth to sin by wishing a curse to his soul ;" *and—

> " Exalted Socrates, divinely brave,
>   Injur'd he fell, and dying he forgave.
>   Too noble for revenge, which still we find
>   The weakest frailty of a feeble mind."—DRYDEN

But if unmanly, still more un-Christian. " If thine enemy hunger, feed him ; if he thirst, give him drink ; for in so doing thou shalt heap coals of fire on his head."

Its AVENGER.—" Lest the Lord see it, and it displease Him, and He turn away his wrath from him." Man's revenge is displeasing to God. It is opposed to the benevolence of His nature, and contrary to the teachings of His Word. Man's revenge may cause God to interpose and relieve its victim. " He turn away his wrath from him." Coverdale renders the words thus: "Lest the Lord be angry, and turn His wrath from him to thee." Thus it was with the enemies of Samson. " Hath any wronged thee?" says Quarles. " Be bravely revenged ; slight it, and the work is begun ; forgive it, and it is finished. He is below himself that is not above an injury."

> "How hardly man this lesson learns,
>   To smile and bless the hand that spurns :
>   To see the blow, to feel the pain,
>   But render only love again.

* Psalm xxxv. 13, 14; Job xxxi. 29; Judges xvi. 25—30.

> This spirit not to earth is given:
> One had it, but He came from Heaven.
> Reviled, rejected, and betrayed,
> No curse He breathed, no plaint he made;
> But, when in death's deep pang He sighed,
> Prayed for His murderers, and died."
>
> EDMESTON

Proverbs 24:19-20

An Example of the Folly of Envy

" Fret not thyself because of evil *men*, neither be thou envious at the wicked; for there shall be no reward to the evil *man;* the candle of the wicked shall be put out."

ENVY has been defined as " mortification or discontent excited by the sight of another's superiority or success, accompanied with some degree of hatred or malignity." It is a passion bad in itself, as well as in its consequences. It always involves three things:—First: *Conscious inferiority.* Envy is always directed towards those possessions of another of which we feel ourselves destitute. We never envy those whom we feel in every respect inferior to ourselves. Envy is therefore evermore a compliment to its object. The envious man's language concerning the person to whom it is directed, rightly interpreted, means this: " You are superior to me." " We ought," says Pliny, "to be guarded against every appearance of envy, as a passion that always implies inferiority wherever it resides." It always involves, Secondly : *Malice towards the object.* It is, perhaps, ever associated with some amount of unkind feelings towards the man who possesses the enviable thing. It rejoices in the misfortunes and fall of the rival. It has been called the daughter of pride, the author of murder. It always involves, Thirdly : *Pain.* It " frets." The prosperity of the rival is torturing to the envious man. Solomon said that "envy is the rottenness of the bones;" and Socrates has remarked that "an envious man waxeth lean with the fatness of his neighbours;" and he calls envy a "poison that consumeth the flesh, and drieth up the marrow of the bones."

But the verses give us an example of the *folly* of envy': it is directed against the wicked. "Fret not thyself because of evil men, neither be thou envious at the wicked." Solomon's language is addressed to the righteous he has in his eye the good, and to them he speaks. Now, this fiend crawls into the heart even of the just, and good men have in some time and in some degree been envious of the wicked, and the text suggests the folly of such a feeling. Solomon means to say—

Don't be envious of the wicked; they will have no HAPPINESS in the future; you will.—"There shall be no reward to the evil man." All that the wicked have they have for this life only. Their mansions, retinues, chariots, estates, are only for this life, they go out of the world as naked as they came, bearing only with them that corrupt character from which their hell will flame. Why envy the wicked these things which they hold only for a period so brief and uncertain as this life is? To-day they have them, to-morrow they leave them in the hands of others. If you are righteous,—obscure, poor, afflicted, as you are, there is a "reward" for you in the future. "Your light afflictions, which are but for a moment, are working out for you a far more exceeding and eternal weight of glory." Who is the better off? Surely the wicked demand your pity not your envy. He means to say—

They will have no PROSPERITY in the future; you will.— "The candle of the wicked shall be put out." The "candle" is often used in the Bible to represent prosperity. All the success of the wicked departs when they leave this world; the "candle" is out, and they sink into the black and ever blackening abyss of an awful future. "I give," said the infidel Hobbs, "my body to the dust, and my soul to the Great Perhaps. I am going to take a leap in the dark." But your "candle," the candle of the righteous, will begin to burn with an inextinguishable and ever-increasing luminousness, when you leave the world.

O ye godly men, who in temporal matters are sorely tried, whose path is rugged and thorny, whose heavens are cloudy, and whose atmosphere is bleak and boisterous, envy not the lot of the prosperous wicked around you. "I have seen the wicked in great power, and spreading himself like a green bay tree. Yet he passed away, and, lo, he was not: yea, I sought him, but he could not be found."*

Proverbs 24:21-22

Human Government

"My son, fear thou the LORD and the king: *and* meddle not with them that are given to change: for their calamity shall rise suddenly; and who knoweth the ruin of them both."

THE Bible everywhere recognises the existence of human governments. Indeed, it would be impossible for society to exist without laws, and these laws must have their makers and administrators. The verses may be taken as indicating that which human kings and human subjects should be, and from them we may learn.

THAT KINGS SHOULD BE GODLIKE.—Solomon here exhorts his son "to fear the Lord and the king." He inculcates *reverence* towards both. The very fact that he requires the same state of mind towards the king as he does towards the Almighty justifies the inference that the king whom he recognises is godlike. For the human soul can reverence nothing that is not divine, both in character and conduct. Falsehood, dishonesty, corruption, oppression—it is not in the heart of man to reverence these. First: Kings

* Psalm xxxvii. 35, 36.

should be Godlike in *personal character*. Why is the Almighty to be reverenced? Because of His goodness, His moral perfections; and should any being in the universe be reverenced for any other reason? No. If a king is to be honoured, he must be honour-worthy; if a king is to be reverenced, he should be morally great. Secondly: Kings should be Godlike in *their kingly functions*. They should be impartial. God is no " respecter of persons." Earthly rulers should hold an even balance, and deal out justice to the small as well as to the great. They should be generous. How patient, compassionate, tender, is the great God! He is " slow to anger," and abundant in mercy. There is no vengeance in Him. An angry and revengeful king cannot be reverenced, and ought not to be honoured, were it possible to do so. They should be restorative. The great God's penal inflictions are not to crush the sinner, but his sin. "All these things worketh God oftentimes with man, to bring him back from the pit, that he may be enlightened with the light of the living." A human sovereign should act in the same way. Reformation and restoration, not suffering and destruction, should be his grand object in all his criminal laws and chastisements. We infer farther from these words—

THAT SUBJECTS SHOULD BE CONSERVATIVE.—" Meddle not with them that are given to change." The Apostle speaks of those demagogues who, in his day, were found " walking after the flesh, despising governments, presumptuous, self-willed, not afraid to speak evil of dignities." Such men are found in all ages, and in all kingdoms— meddling demagogues. They have a passion for change, and for change they work, and generally with the view to bring themselves into note and power. It is the duty of every citizen to seek the correction of public abuses, the repeal of unjust laws, and the displacement of incompetent and unrighteous officials. But all this is in perfect harmony with true conservatism, and is not against progress. True conservatism is that which retains with a death-grasp the right and repudiates with heart-earnestness the wrong. But revolutionism is often obstructive. There are men that

610 / Book of Proverbs

are given to change, who have a feverish, restless passion for it, and these men are a curse to any country. "For their calamity shall rise suddenly; and who knoweth the ruin of them both?" Korah and Absalom are examples of this.

Proverbs 24:23-26

Social Conduct

"These *things* also belong to the wise. *It is* not good to have respect of persons in judgment. He that saith unto the wicked, Thou *art* righteous; him shall the people curse, nations shall abhor him: but to them that rebuke *him* shall be delight, and a good blessing shall come upon them. *Every man* shall kiss *his* lips that giveth a right answer."

MAN is a social being. He lives in society, by society, and for it should live and labour. His fellow-men constitute the subject of a large amount of his every day thoughts, and the object of a large share of his activities. There are three social acts in these verses—two are bad and the other is good.

Here is PARTIALITY OF JUDGMENT, which is *bad*.—" It is not good to have respect of persons in judgment." Men are often called to arbitrate upon the conduct of their fellow citizens, whose disputes are submitted to their decision. Whatever may be the subject of dispute, political, social, or ecclesiastical, they are bound by the laws of God to *impartiality* in their inquiries and conclusions. The disputants should be regarded not in any other respect but the merits or demerits of their case. The *question* and not the person, is to be respected in their judgments. The "respect of persons" is bad in *principle*, is an outrage of justice. It is bad also in *influence*. It tends to social disorder, and ill-feeling. The principle of impartiality is enjoined both in the Old and the New Testament. In the Old we have such words as these, "Ye shall do no unrighteousness in judgment; thou shalt not respect the person of the poor, nor honour the person of the mighty; but in righteousness shalt thou judge thy neighbour."

And in the New Testament we have these words, " My brethren, have not the faith of our Lord Jesus Christ, the Lord of glory, with respect of persons." Weighty words are those of the great Hooker on this subject. " If they employ their labour and travail about the public administration of justice, follow it only as a trade, with unquenchable thirst of gain, being not in heart persuaded that justice is God's own work, and themselves His agents in this business, the sentence of right, God's own verdict, and themselves His priests to deliver it; formalities of justice do but serve to smother right; and that which was necessarily ordained for the common good is, through shameful abuse, made the cause of common misery."

Here is FLATTERY OF THE WICKED, which is *execrable*.— " He that saith unto the wicked, Thou art righteous, him shall the people *curse*; nations shall abhor him." How often wicked men are treated both in actions and speech, as if they were righteous. If the wicked man be great in wealth, exalted in social influence and political power, there is a wondrous tendency in all the grades below to flatter him as a " righteous man." A small amount of generosity in a secularly great man will transfigure him before the eyes of men as a great philanthropist. A few acts of formal piety will cause him to be regarded as an illustrious saint. This flattery is an accursed thing. It is abhorrent to the moral heart of humanity. The base flatterer the people shall accurse, and the nations shall abhor. Flattery in all its forms is an accursed thing. It always implies *insincerity*. The sycophant does not mean what he says. He is belying his own conscience. It always implies *vanity*. The flatterer looks for a return of his compliments with interest. "When flatterers meet," says Defoe, " the devil goes to dinner." It always implies *servility*. Sycophancy is the child of a base nature. It is called a sneaking heart.

> "No flattery, boy: an honest man can't live by it.
> It is a little sneaking art, which knaves
> Use to cajole and soften fools withal.
> If thou hast flattery in thy nature, out with't,
> Or send it to a court, for there 'twill thrive!"—OTWAY

Here is REPROOF OF THE WRONG, which is *blessed*.—
"But to them that rebuke him shall be delight, and a good
blessing shall come upon them. Every man shall kiss his
lips that giveth a right answer." It is truly a blessed
thing to reprove the wrong wherever found, in pauper or in
prince. There is *a delight* in such work. "To them that
rebuke him shall be *delight.*" What is the delight?
The delight of an approving conscience. And what is
higher than this? There is *Divine favour* in such work.
"A good *blessing* shall come upon them." God will express
His favour to such a man in many ways. In temporal
prosperity, in social happiness, in spiritual enjoyments.
There is *social approbation* in such work. "Every man
shall kiss his lips that giveth a right answer." To kiss
the lips is to pay the homage of love and respect. The
man whose character is transparently truthful, honest, and
generous towards his fellow-man, in whatever position in
life he may be, will gain the homage and respect of every
person. "Every man shall kiss his lips"—will render him
homage. Our reproofs, however, whilst truthful, should
be kind. Feltham says, "To reprehend well is the most
necessary part of friendship. Who is there that does not
sometimes merit a check; and yet how few will endure
one."

Proverbs 24:27

Human Labor

"Prepare thy work without, and make it fit for thyself in the field; and afterwards build thine house."

"A LARGE number," says a learned expositor, "of proverbial sentiments and maxims of practical wisdom, are to be found couched in terms taken from particular departments of life and business. Every one at all acquainted with even the ordinary, but frequently very terse and pithy proverbs of our own country, must be aware of this. It is so in the verse before us. The advice thus given to bring the lands into good condition, and make the estate productive before we lavish large expenditure upon the mansion, is clearly intended to convey a general lesson." The verse suggests two thoughts in relation to human labour :

In all labour there should be FORETHOUGHT.—" Prepare thy work without, and make it fit for thyself." Before you build the house make preparation. Get the place, collect the materials; see the way clear before you lay the first stone for the superstructure. This forethought is most important. First: It is the best security against *waste*. How much waste time, energy, and money often occurs in an enterprise in consequence of not having well deliberated the whole before the commencement. Every part of an undertaking should be so well considered and weighed that in the execution no difficulty occurs that is not foreseen; no effort or expense demanded that had not been duly estimated. The man who acts from forethought will do thrice as much work, with less effort and anxiety, than a man who takes up an enterprise without due consideration. Secondly; It is the best security against *failure*. Nearly all the enterprises that break down, and whose wrecks are strewn in every department of human labour, owe their ruin to want of forethought. Unforeseen difficulties rise up one after another, until they baffle and confound the worker. Hence the world's Great Teacher inculcates this principle of forethought. "For which of you, intending to build a tower, sitteth not down first, and counteth the cost, whether he have sufficient to finish it?"

In all labour the MOST IMPORTANT WORK SHOULD BE DONE FIRST.—"Let those things," says an expositor, "which are obviously most important and necessary be done *first*, and the less urgent afterwards. Let not a man *begin business* by building and expensively furnishing a fine house. Let the land be first cultivated. Let your business, whatever its nature, be faithfully and diligently minded, and well-established, as far as human industry can effect, or human foresight calculate. Be content, in the meantime, with inferior accommodation. There is an ambitious hasting to make little much, that is deeply reprehensible, because it is injurious to *others* as well as to the speculator himself. A man should have property well realised and secured, before he enters on schemes of expensive building. He must not with sanguine infatuation, appropriate the very first proceeds of his trade to the erection of a *palace to live in !*" Our great dramatist has given a splendid description in the following words, of the importance of forethought in all our labour :

> " When we mean to build,
> We first survey the plot ; then draw the model ;
> And when we see the figure of the house,
> Then must we rate the cost of the erection ;
> Which, if we find outweighs ability,
> What do we then, but draw anew the model,
> In fewer offices ; or, at least, desist
> To build at all ? Much more, in this great work,
> (Which is almost to pluck a kingdom down,
> And set another up,) should we survey
> The plot of situation and the model ;
> Consent upon a sure foundation ;
> Question surveyors ; know our own estate,
> How able such a work to undergo,
> To weigh against his opposite ; or else
> We fortify in paper and in figures,
> Using the names of men instead of men ;
> Like one who draws a model of a house,
> Beyond his power to build it ; who, half through,
> Gives o'er, and leaves his part-created cost
> A naked subject to the weeping clouds,
> And waste for churlish winter's tyranny."

The most important of all works, it is generally admitted, is getting our spiritual natures in accord with the plan of the universe and the will of God. This is religion, or Christliness, which is a better word. " Seek first the kingdom of God and His righteousness, and all other things shall be added unto you."

Proverbs 24:28-29
Types of Corrupt Testimony

"Be not a witness against thy neighbour without cause; and deceive *not* with thy lips. Say not, I will do so to him as he hath done to me: I will render to the man according to his work."

THESE words suppose that our neighbour—our fellow man—may be placed in a position where our testimony concerning him may be required: it might be in the social circle, in the Court of Judicature, or in the Church Assembly. The verses point to three kinds of wrong testimony:

A CAUSELESS one.—"Be not a witness against thy neighbour without cause." A man who gives his testimony against his neighbour, when it is not required for either of the three following objects, viz.: the good of society, self-exculpation, or as a matter of public justice, does it "without cause." And there is much of such testimony in society, and what is it less or more than idle *scandal*? There are those who, for no service, either to themselves or others, are constantly testifying of the defects and infirmities of their neighbours. Sheridan has said that "there are a set of malicious, prating, prudent gossips, male and female, who murder characters to kill time; and will rob a young fellow of his good name before he has years to know the value of it." This is a wrong which the Bible reprobates. The verses point to another kind of wrong testimony—

A FALSE one.—"And deceive not with thy lips." If it is wrong to bear testimony to the defects of your neighbour, when it is not really required to do so on moral grounds, it must be still more wrong to bear testimony to conduct of which you know your neighbour is not guilty: and yet men do so. There is a great deal of "bearing false witness against our neighbour" in society. Slander is prevalent in all circles.

> "Slander lives upon succession,
> For ever housed when once it gets possession."
> SHAKESPEARE

"It is," we are informed, "the custom in Africa for hunters, when they have killed a poisonous snake, to cut off its head and carefully bury it in the ground. A naked foot stepping on one of these fangs would be fatally wounded. The poison would spread in a very short time all through the system. This venom lasts a long time, and is as deadly after the snake is dead as before. The Red Indians used to dip the points of their arrows in this poison, so if they made the least wound their victim would be sure to die. The snake's poison is in its teeth; but there is something quite as dangerous and much more common in communities. There is a human snake with poison on its tongue. Your chances of escape from a serpent are greater. The worst snakes usually glide away in fear at the approach of man, unless disturbed or attacked. But this creature, whose poison lurks in its tongue, attacks without provocation, and follows up its victim with untiring perseverance. We will tell you his name, so you will always be able to shun him. He is called slanderer. He poisons worse than a serpent. Often his venom strikes to the life of a whole family or neighbourhood, destroying all peace and confidence." "Slander," says Robinson, "is compared to poison." "The tongue is an unruly member, full of deadly poison." The deadliest poisons are those for which no test is known: there are poisons so destructive that a single drop insinuated into the veins produces death in three seconds, and yet no chemical science can separate that virus from the contaminated blood, and show the metallic particles of poison glittering palpably, and say, "Behold it is there."

> "The world with calumny abounds;
> The whitest virtue slander wounds:
> There are whose joy is, night and day,
> To talk a character away:
> Eager from rout to rout they haste,
> To blast the generous and the chaste,
> And hunting reputation down,
> Proclaim their triumphs through the town."—POPE.

There is another wrong testimony—

A REVENGEFUL one.—"Say not I will do so to him as he hath done to me: I will render to the man according to his work." Revenge is a passion strongly prohibited and reprobated both in the Old and New Testament. " Vengeance is mine, saith the Lord: I will repay."

> "Speak not of vengeance;
> 'Tis the right of God."

Proverbs 24:30-34

Idleness

"I went by the field of the slothful, and by the vineyard of the man void of understanding; and, lo, it was all grown over with thorns, *and* nettles had covered the face thereof, and the stone wall thereof was broken down. Then I saw, *and* considered *it* well : I looked upon *it, and* received instruction. *Yet* a little sleep, a little slumber, a little folding of the hands to sleep: so shall thy poverty come *as* one that travelleth; and thy want as an armed man."

WE have here indolence portrayed by the hand of a master; and, as it stands before us on the canvas, we see that it is *foolish, procrastinating,* and *ruinous.*

IT IS FOOLISH.—Solomon characterises this indolent man as one "void of understanding." Wherein do you see this man's folly? *In the flagrant neglect of his own interests.* Unlike the condition of millions who have not one yard of green sod which they can call their own, this man held a little estate in his possession. He had a "field" and a "vineyard," and upon the cultivation of this depended his bread. But he neglected it, and it was "all grown over with thorns." Morally this vineyard may signify our spiritual natures, with all their faculties and potential powers, and which it is both our manifest interest and bounden duty to cultivate. There is one noticeable point of distinction between material and spiritual cultivation. You may cultivate your *field by proxy,* but you can only cultivate *your soul yourself.*

IT IS PROCRASTINATING.—Solomon observed that indolence in this man led to constant procrastination. "I saw and considered it well: I looked upon it, and received instruction. Yet a little sleep, a little slumber, a little folding of the hands to sleep." To the indolent man duty is always for the morrow. The idea of working is not given up, but postponed from day to day; and the longer it is postponed the more indisposed the mind grows for its performance. It is always "a little sleep," or looking to a "more convenient season."

> " Be wise to-day: 'tis madness to defer:
> Next day the fatal precedent will plead:
> Thus on, till wisdom is pushed out of life.
> Procrastination is the thief of time:
> Year after year it steals, till all are fled,
> And to the mercies of a moment leaves
> The vast concerns of an eternal scene."—YOUNG

IT IS RUINOUS.—First: Consider the wretched condition to which his estate was reduced. "Lo, it was all grown over with thorns, and nettles had covered the face thereof, and the stone wall thereof was broken down." It might have waved with golden grain, it might have been a scene of loveliness and plenty; but instead of this, it is an unsightly wilderness, unprotected, open to the foot of every intruder. It is a solemn fact that ruin comes, not by cultivation, but by neglect. Your garden will soon become a wilderness if you neglect it. Heaven's kind arrangement this, to stimulate labour. It is so with the soul. You need not strive to ruin yourselves—do *nothing* and you will be damned. Secondly: Consider the utter destitution to which it must inevitably conduct. By this indolence, "thy poverty shall come as one that travelleth, and thy want as an armed man." Two things are suggested by the words. *That the ruin is gradual in its approach.* "Thy poverty shall come." It does not burst on you at once, like a thunder-storm. The punishment of the indolent farmer takes all the months from spring-time to harvest to approach him. Full and adequate retribution does not come at once. "There is a treasuring up against the day of wrath." It is coming now "as one that travelleth;" it is on the road. Its footfalls vibrate on the ear of universal reason. The other thing suggested by the words is—*That the ruin is terrible in its consummation.* " Thy want as an armed man." It will seize you as with the grasp of an indignant warrior. From its iron clutch there will be no deliverance. Indolence brings ruin.

Brother, thou hast a momentous work to do; thou hast to cultivate the wilderness of thy nature; thou hast to repair the moral fences of thy soul. In other words, thou hast to rebuild the ruined temple of thy being. Thou hast no time to lose; thou hast slept already too long. "*Resolve and do*" at once.

> " Lay firmly every stone; long years may be,
> And stormy winds may rend, ere all be done;
> But lay the first—thou mayst not live to see
> To-morrow's sun."

Proverbs 25:1

Solomon's Three Thousand Proverbs

"These *are* also proverbs of Solomon, which the men of Hezekiah king of Judah copied out."

" AT this point commences the *fourth* division of this Book, extending to the close of the twenty-ninth chapter. In the first Book of Kings, fourth chapter and thirty-second verse it is said of Solomon, in enumerating the particulars of his extraordinary wisdom, that ' he spoke three thousand proverbs.' The full collection of these sententious maxims of wisdom had been kept, it would appear, in the possession of the house of David, or of the kings of Judah. The selection in the preceding part of the Book had been made by Solomon himself. Those which follow were added in the time of good king Hezekiah; by the direction, there is every reason to suppose, of that exemplary prince, for the religious benefit of his people. ' The *men* of Hezekiah ' stands in the Septuagint translation, ' the *friends* of Hezekiah '—meaning in all likelihood, Isaiah and other inspired men. Like the Proverbs which precede, these must be regarded, by their admission into the Jewish canon of Scripture, as having the sanction, not only of the wisdom and experience of Solomon but of Divine authority : and we owe them the same reverential regard as we owe to other parts of God's Word."

The verse suggests three subjects of thought—

The FERTILITY OF THE HUMAN MIND WHEN ENGAGED IN THE SERVICE OF GOD.—" These are also Proverbs of Solomon." Elsewhere we are told that the Proverbs of Solomon were three thousand in number, besides one thousand and five ; and his various writings on cedars, beasts, fowls, creeping things, and fishes.* Three thousand Proverbs! not mere *words*—This means mental fertility. Mere literature is easy ; writing words in profusion does not mean fruitfulness of soul. Indeed, as a rule, the most fluent in language, the most infertile in thought. Three thousand Proverbs! not mere *ideas*. A man may have a boundless profusion of thoughts and yet a poor soul. But Proverbs are axioms. They mean thought crystallized. One true Proverb may embody the essence of a thousand thoughts. Thoughts are foliage and blossom : Proverbs are clusters. Truly, wonderfully fertile is the human soul, especially when engaged in Divine service. It is not like the fruit tree. The more fruit the tree produces, the more it exhausts itself, and the less capable of producing it becomes, until at last its fruitfulness is entirely exhausted. Whereas the human mind, the more it produces, the more its producing capacity increases.

Every new thought unlocks new treasures of mind. Like the mystic rod of Moses, it smites a fresh Horeb in the soul and opens fresh fountains of ideas.

The verse suggests—

The DEPARTMENTAL SYSTEM IN HEAVEN'S REMEDIAL WORK.—" The men of Hezekiah king of Judah copied out " the thoughts of Solomon. The proverbs which he struck off from the anvil of his genius, they gathered up and

* 1 Kings iv. 32, 33.

enshrined them in literature. This they did three hundred years afterwards. Some men think, and their thoughts are not worth recording, either by themselves or by others; the sooner they are forgotten by the universe the better. Others think, and their thoughts are valuable, but they cannot write; they have neither the aptitude nor disposition for authorship, and the productions of their mind are lost. Some men write, but cannot think; they will scribble off yards of nothing in a few hours. These 'men of Hezekiah,' however, whether they could think or not, laid hold of the thoughts of the thinker, and embodied them in imperishable language; and for this we thank them. God employs both the originator and the copyist —the thinker and the registrar. Would that all great and holy thinkers had faithful scribes as Solomon had, and as One greater than Solomon had. God gives to every man that work which he is best able to accomplish. One man labours and another enters into his work.

The verse suggests—

The CARE OF PROVIDENCE OVER THE DEVELOPMENTS OF DIVINE TRUTH.—Who raised up these men three hundred years after Solomon, to record his thoughts? God! He superintends the universe of true thoughts as well as the universe of matter. He links them to their centre, appoints their orbits, and makes them shine. His Providence is seen in the *production, preservation, collation,* and *publication* of all the manuscripts of Divine thought. Man is great because he can think divinely. "Man is a reed," says Pascal, "and the weakest reed in nature: but then he is a thinking reed. There is no occasion that the whole universe should arm itself for his destruction. A vapour, a drop of water is sufficient to kill him. And yet should the universe crush him man would still be more noble than that by which he fell, because he would know his fate, while the universe would be insensible of its victory." Thus all our dignity consists in thought. It is hence we are to raise ourselves, and not by the aid of space and duration. Let us study the art of thinking well: this is the foundation of ethics!

> " All thoughts that mould the age begin
> Deep down within the primitive soul,
> And from the many slowly upward win
> To him who grasps the whole."—LOWELL

Proverbs 25:2-5

Kinghood

"*It is* the glory of God to conceal a thing: but the honour of kings *is* to search out a matter. The heaven for height, and the earth for depth, and the heart of kings *is* unsearchable. Take away the dross from the silver, and there shall come forth a vessel for the finer. Take away the wicked *from* before the king, and his throne shall be established in righteousness."

THE chief work of a man's life will, as a rule, be the chief subject of his thoughts. Solomon was a king, and the kingly idea seemed to be one of the leading ideas in the procession of his thoughts. He therefore frequently regarded men in their relation to human kings, and even the great Creator of the universe he was prone to look upon in the character of a monarch. He, being a king in fact, was tempted to look upon all objects, human and Divine, from the standpoint of kinghood. The verses are an illustration of this, and it presents to us—

THE DIVINE RULER OF ALL.—The Eternal is here brought into comparison with human kings. "It is the glory of God to conceal a thing, but the honour of kings is to search out a matter." What does this mean? It does not mean, of course, that it is His glory to conceal from His creatures anything connected with His own Being or workmanship. The *secretive* attribute in a human creature we are ever more disposed to condemn than admire, and such an attribute in God we could never associate with "glory." In truth, any effort at concealment on His part would be needless. Who amongst the loftiest intellects in the universe could ever find Him out? He is, and ever will be the Great Mystery, in which all finite thoughts are lost. And it would be unjust as well as needless. He has endowed His creatures with an imperishable and ever-growing desire to know Him: "The heart and the flesh cry out for the living God." Hence for Him to employ any effort to hide himself, or to obscure His doings, would be unjust to the creatures whom He has invested with such craving. What then is meant by it? Does it mean that His glory is His essential *incomprehensibility?* This is a truth. He is eternally mysterious. We are told that "His way is in the sea,"—that "His path is in the great waters, and His footsteps are not known"—that "He dwells in the light which no man can approach unto"—that "His ways are unsearchable, and His judgments past finding out."

But this, we think, is not the idea that Solomon had. We are bound to interpret his words by their connexion; and when he says in the next clause, that it is "the honour of kings to search out a matter," it seems very clear that he meant this: that it was "the glory of God" to be independent of all *enquiry* after knowledge. He means that whilst it was the honour of kings to search for knowledge, it is the glory of God that He does not require to go in quest of it. He has no need to investigate; He has nothing to discover; His knowledge is intuitive, complete, universal, absolute; His *omniscience* is one of His most glorious attributes. The verses present to us in connection with this—

THE HUMAN RULERS OF MEN.—They suggest several things in relation to human kings: That *honest enquiry in them is always an excellency.* It is "the honour of kings to search out a matter." It is not for them to assume the attribute of omniscience, and to pretend to know things without the prosecution of an honest search. They should enquire in order to get at the eternal principles by which their laws should be shaped, and their whole lives controlled. They should seek the best means for improving the physical, the intellectual, the social, and the spiritual condition of their people. "To search out a matter" pertaining to the interests of man, the cause of truth, and the glory of God, is at once the duty and the dignity not only of kings but of people, not only of men but of *all* intelligent creatures. Knowledge, in all beings but God, is to be got by enquiry. Another thing suggested in relation to human kings is—*That secretiveness in them is sometimes very impenetrable.* " The heaven for height, and the earth for depth, and the heart of kings is unsearchable." This language does not mean that a secretive policy in kings is justifiable. There may be occasions when rulers may be strongly tempted to spread a veil over their policy so as to conceal it from their subjects; but we are not sure that they are ever justified in doing so. Kings should be always just, and justice need never fear the day. We have no faith in court or cabinet secrecies. Nor does this language mean that the kingly heart is something so peculiarly mysterious that it cannot be comprehended. Monarchs have always assumed a mysterious grandeur, and ignorant people have ever been disposed to regard them as objects high up, enshrouded in mystic glory. But this is all nonsense. The king's heart is a common heart, clouded with the common ignorances, and beating with the common defects. What, then, does it mean? Solomon undoubtedly refers to oriental despots, who were always robed in mystery, and gave no account of their doings. Like the Emperor of China in the present day: the despot lives in mystery, the people stand in awe, and know not what cloud may appear over them the next minute, and break in thunder over their heads. The subjects of despots may indeed sooner measure the " height of heaven " and " the depth of earth," than penetrate the mysteries of their masters. Another thing suggested in relation to human kings is—*That purity in them depends on the character of their ministers.* All kings, however despotic, have their ministers—men to execute their behests. On these men they are more or less dependent. These men, the occupants of courts and the members of cabinets, have often been in morals most corrupt and vile, and hence Solomon says—" Take away the dross from the silver, and there shall come forth a vessel for the finer." Take away the wicked from before the king, and his throne shall be established in righteousness. "Here is a comparison. As, in order to the production of a beautiful vessel, such as the refiner would approve and commend, the material of which the vessel is to be made must be purged of its alloy, so, in order to the general government of a prince being of a nature to prove conducive to the benefit of his people and the stability of his throne, the wicked must be removed from his presence and from all intimacy with his life and counsels." The moral characters of kings have ever been more or less dependent upon the characters of their ministers, and are becoming more and more so every day throughout Christendom. Let England see that the members of her Government be men of incorruptible purity, unselfish patriotism, and genuine Christliness of life.

Proverbs 25:6-7

A Corrupt Ambition

"Put not forth thyself in the presence of the king, and stand not in the place of great *men*: for better *it is* that it be said unto thee, Come up hither; than that thou shouldest be put lower in the presence of the prince whom thine eyes have seen."

THE subject of these verses is corrupt ambition. Ambition is a natural instinct of the soul; it is a desire for advancement in some distinguishing respect. The Great One implanted it as an eternal stimulant to onwardness in all that is true, virtuous, and Divine. "It is not in man," says Southey, "to rest in absolute contentment. He is born to hopes and aspirations as the sparks fly upwards, unless he has brutified his nature, and quenched the spirit of his immortality which is his portion." But this instinct of the soul, like all others, has been sadly perverted. Instead of being directed to intellectual and moral excellence, to social usefulness and spiritual culture, it has been devoted to the means of personal aggrandisement and despotic force. It has often urged men to outrage justice, violate domestic sanctities, trample on the rights and lives of men, in order to gain their miserable distinction. "Such ambition," says Sir Walter Scott, "breaks the ties of blood, forgets the obligations of manhood." The verses point to a corrupt ambition, and lead us to offer two remarks upon it.—

It is OBTRUSIVELY FORWARD.—"Put not forth thyself"— margin, set not out thy glory "in the presence of the king." We see this obtrusive ambition working perhaps more prevalently and more injuriously in the lower than in the higher types of mind. The small-brained men are generally the most obtrusively ambitious. Who are the men in corporation towns who are ever pushing themselves forward to municipal honours? Who are the men in religious denominations that are ever struggling for the most prominent positions? Who are the men in politics who have the strongest aspirations, and make the most strenuous efforts for Parliamentary work and Parliamentary honour? As a rule, small-brained men. Thank God! there are exceptions, and the exceptions are our social and political salvation. But, as a rule, great men are not ambitious for such distinctions. It is not the "olive tree," or the "fig tree," or the "vine" in the human forest that will struggle much for such prominent positions, but the "bramble."* This obtrusive ambition of small men is a great evil. It puts them in positions whose duties they are incapable of fulfilling with thorough efficiency. How can the "bramble" control the "cedars," the minnows manage the eagles? It also keeps back from office better men. As a rule, the greater a man is, the more modest, the less intrusive, and the more shrinking from responsibility. This intrusive forwardness is a great curse to England at the present moment. It is said that never were there such a number of small-brained men in the House of Commons as now, and small men are, as a rule, the most garrulous, prominent, and persistent. "Stand not in the place of great men,"—either in Church or State it is a great evil.

* See HOMILIST, third series, vol. viii., p. 187.

Another remark suggested by the verse concerning corrupt ambition, is—

It is LIABLE TO HUMILIATION.—" It is better that it be said unto thee, Come up hither, than that thou shouldest be put lower in the presence of the prince whom thine eyes have seen." The Divine Teacher has given the same command, " When thou art bidden of any man to a wedding, sit not down in the highest room, lest a more honourable man than thou be bidden of him; and he that bade thee and him come and say to thee, ' Give this man a place,' and thou begin with shame to take the lowest room. But when thou art bidden go and sit down in the lowest room, that when he that bade thee cometh, he may say unto thee, 'Friend, go up higher:' then thou shalt have worship in the presence of them that sit at meat with thee." Even here in this life such corrupt ambition is exposed to humiliation. Small men, who have pushed themselves into prominent positions, are often humbled by the contemptuous criticisms of their contemporaries. In the Apocrypha both the father and son are represented as provided with wings; whilst the former was safe because he only skimmed the ground; the son soared to mid-heaven, fell and perished.

Cardinal Wolsey is an example of the end to which such ambition leads. What does he say? " Cromwell, I charge thee, fling away thy ambition. By that sin fell the angels. How can man, then, the image of his Maker, hope to win by it? Love thyself last: cherish those hearts that hate thee: still in thy right hand carry gentle peace, to silence envious tongues. Be just and fear not. Let all the ends thou aimest at be thy country's, thy God's, and truth's; then, if thou fallest, Oh, Cromwell, thou fallest a blessed martyr. Serve the King. And pr'ythee, lead me in. There, take an inventory of all I have, to the last penny: 'tis the King's—my robe, and my integrity to Heaven, is all I dare now call mine own. Oh, Cromwell, Cromwell! had I but served my God with half the zeal I served my king, He would not in mine age have left me naked to mine enemies."

Proverbs 25:8-10

The Worst and Best Way of Treating Social Dissensions

"Go not forth hastily to strive, lest *thou know not* what to do in the end thereof, when thy neighbour hath put thee to shame. Debate thy cause with thy neighbour *himself;* and discover not a secret to another: lest he that heareth *it* put thee to shame, and thine infamy turn not away."

THE social dissensions that are rife in our world are incontestable proofs that humanity has fallen from its normal condition. There is society in Heaven, but no social differences or strifes; but here there are constant contentions in families, nations, churches. Man is ever offending his brother, either intentionally or by accident, with malicious or benevolent designs. The words indicate the best and the worst way of treating such dissensions.

The WORST way.—"Go not forth hastily to strive." Precipitant strife *is bad in itself.* Calm, deliberate strife, whether by tongue or fist is bad; it means antagonism to the offender, is inspired with malice and craves for the infliction of punishment. But hasty strife, for some reasons, is worse. It indicates a petulant nature, an irascible temperament, and is often destitute of any just cause. It may start from mistake, malice, or misunderstanding. Men should never be hasty in yielding to a passion. They should make the passion, however strong and tumultuous for the moment, the subject of thought, and by thought should subdue, purify, and direct it. A man who acts in a passion, acts not only beneath but against his higher nature and his God. Precipitant strife *exposes to shame.* "Lest thou know not what to do in the end thereof when thy neighbour hath put thee to shame." Before the mind of Solomon the following scene seems to have presented itself. Something has come to the ears of A, concerning B, which has roused his indignation, and under its influence he rushes forth to meet B, in order to wreak his vengeance. He meets B, and he, conscious of his innocence, stands calmly before him and smiles with a kindly glow, wondering what all this blustering passion means. He speaks a word and A feels that he is under a wrong impression, that the fire within him has been kindled by a miserable fiction; and he is ashamed of himself, ashamed as his imaginary enemy laughs kindly at him. Thy neighbour A "hath put thee B to shame!" The text moreover indicates,—

The BEST way of settling disputes.—"Debate thy cause with thy neighbour himself." The direction here seems to imply the following things. That an interview is to be obtained with the *offender*. "Debate thy cause with thy neighbour *himself*." The man who has injured you should himself be visited by you. You should not go to another first, but directly to him. You have to do with him and him only at first. That an interview is to be obtained in order to *talk the offence over*. "Debate thy cause." What for? Not to gratify anger, not to seek vengeance, not to brawl, but to reason, to talk, to listen to an explanation and the defence (if it admits of defence), to weigh the whole, and respond according to the real merits of the case. Another thing which the direction implies is that the offence must be thus debated before *the secret is divulged to another*. "Discover not a secret to another." Let the man who first listens to the offence be the man who has given it; drop it into no other ear. Strong may be the temptation to deviate from this direction, but it is to be resisted. The other thing which the direction implies is, that should the secret be divulged to another, the *pacific objects of the interview might be nullified*. "Lest he that heareth it put thee to shame, and thine infamy turn not away." Should the offender hear from another your statement of the offence it will give *him* ground of offence, widen the breach, and nullify the desired result. If you trumpet the offence in the ear of others before you meet the offender, you have done the offender a wrong, and exposed yourself to a lasting disgrace. "Thine infamy turn not away."

The direction which Solomon gives here of treating an

offender, agrees with the direction Christ gave. "If thy brother shall trespass against thee, go and tell him his fault between thee and him alone; if he shall hear thee thou hast gained a brother." Were these counsels acted on, how soon all quarrels as they spring up would be hushed! Beautiful words of Richter on this subject—"Nothing is more moving to a man than the spectacle of reconciliation; our weaknesses are thus indemnified, and are not too costly, being the price we pay for the hour of forgiveness; and the archangel who has never felt anger has reason to envy the man who subdues it. When thou forgivest, the man who has pierced thy heart stands to thee in the relation of the sea-worm, that perforates the shell of the mussel, which straightway closes the wound with a pearl."

Proverbs 25:11

The Excellency of Fitly-spoken Words

"A word fitly spoken *is like* apples of gold in pictures of silver."

THE comparison here has undoubtedly an allusion to some old domestic ornament. "The idea," says Stuart, "is that of a garment of precious stuff, on which are embroidered golden apples among picture work of silver. Costly and precious was such a garment held to be; for besides the ornaments upon it, the material itself was of high value." Others think that the allusion is to a kind of table ornament, constructed of a silver basket of delicate lattice-work, containing gold in the form of apples. The basket would, of course, be so constructed as to show off with advantage its precious treasure, the "apples of gold." The ancient Easterns were men of taste and men of art; they loved the beautiful, and had their ornaments: and some of these were as artistically constructed as those of modern times. The subject here undoubtedly is,—*the excellency of fitly spoken words*. "A word fitly spoken is like apples of gold in pictures of silver." But what is such a word? Fitly spoken words must be distinguished as follows:—

THEY MUST EXHIBIT THE TRUTH TO THE BEST ADVANTAGE.—They must be to the truth what the basket was to the apples of gold,—an instrument for showing them off to the best advantage. Truth is the apple of gold; it is sound, complete, precious. A word that does not convey the truth can never be "fitly spoken;" it ought never to have been spoken, and when spoken it is an evil. Words of frivolity, falsehood, obscenity, blasphemy, are not "apples of gold," anything but that. A fit word is a word that shows the golden truth in the most effective way. There are words that *hide* the truth. They are so profuse and luxuriant that they bury the priceless apple in their wilderness. All grandiloquence is words unfitly spoken. There are words that *disgrace* the truth. They are ill-chosen, mean, suggestive of low and degrading associations. "A word fitly spoken" must be clear, natural, strong, exhibiting the truth in the best conceivable light. Again, words fitly spoken must be words—

ADAPTED TO THE MENTAL MOOD OF THE HEARER.—Different men have different mental moods. Some are naturally sombre, imaginative, and practical; others are gay, poetic, and speculative. Words fitly spoken must be adapted to each particular mood; the form in which truth would suit one mood would be inapt to another. Again, the same man has different moods at different times. Circumstances modify the condition of the soul; physical suffering, social bereavement, moral conviction, create in the mind new seasons. Hence "a word fitly spoken" must be a word presenting truth adapted to the soul in its existing mood. It must be a word in "due season," suited to the various experiences, temperaments, and conditions of each. The perfect teacher is gifted with the tongue of the learned, and knows how to speak a word in season. A fitly spoken word comes down upon the heart like rain upon the new-mown grass. Again, words fitly spoken should be words spoken—

IN THE RIGHT SPIRIT.—Words however fitted to exhibit

a truth, if they are spoken from vanity, anger, ambition, sectarianism, bigotry, cannot possibly be regarded as fitly spoken. All words should breathe a kind spirit, the spirit of Christ, and should be spoken for the benefit of the auditors, to enlighten, console, encourage, strengthen. Words that are uttered for sensual, avaricious or sect purposes, however accurate in grammar and beautiful in rhetoric, are not words that God would consider " fitly spoken." Lastly, words fitly spoken must be—

NATURALLY FLOWING WORDS. — This perhaps is the meaning of the marginal reading—"spoken upon his wheels." They must not be forced or dragged words, but words moving flowingly and swiftly on, like the chariot wheels. The ambitious rhetorician manufactures the garments for his thoughts : they are always stiff and formal, although they may appear beautiful to the artistic eye. Men think in words, and the best words are those into which the thoughts run at first. Such words roll upon the wheels, carrying the apples of gold in the silver basket, there is no rattle or effort.

> " If feeling does not prompt, in vain you strive,
> If from the soul the language does not come
> By its own impulse, to impel the hearts
> Of hearers with communicated power ;
> In vain you strive, in vain you study earnestly,
> Toil on for ever, piece together fragments,
> Cook up your broken scraps of sentences,
> And blow with puffing breath, a struggling light,
> Glimmering confusedly now, now cold in ashes—
> Startle the school-boys with your metaphors,
> And, if such food may suit your appetite,
> Win to vain wonder of applauding children ;
> But never hope to stir the hearts of men,
> And mould the souls of many into one,
> By words which come not native from the heart."
> GOETHE.

Let us all endeavour to use the right words in the family, in the market, in the school, in the debate, in the pulpit, on the platform, and in the press. "Words," says old Bunyan, " make truth to spangle and its rays to shine "

Proverbs 25:12

The Beauty of a Reprovable Disposition

"*As* an earring of gold, and an ornament of fine gold, *so is* a wise reprover upon an obedient ear."

IN this comparison," says an able expositor, "as in the preceding verse, ornament and value are united. And as the ornament selected is that of the ear, the comparison may be meant to convey the idea, that an ear that listens obediently to instruction and reproof is more valuably adorned than that which is ornamented with the most costly jewels. When a reproof is both administered in wisdom, and received in humility and in good part, then there is a union of two equal varieties. A reproof well administered is rare; and not less so is a reproof well taken. We may remark, however, that the rareness of the latter arises, to no small extent, out of the rareness of the former. It is because reproof is so seldom well-*given* that it so seldom well-*taken*."

The subject is, the beauty of a reprovable disposition. It is suggested by Solomon, that the ear opened to true reproof is more beautifully ornamented than the ear hung with the most costly jewels. Such a mind includes two beautiful qualities.

HUMILITY.—Peter says, "whose adorning let it not be the outward adorning of plaiting the hair, and wearing of gold, or of putting on of apparel; but let it be the hidden man of the heart, in that which is not corruptible, even the ornament of a meek and quiet spirit, which is in the sight of God of great price." "Humility," says Porteus, "in the Gospel sense of the word, is a virtue with which the ancients, and more particularly the

Romans, were totally unacquainted. They had not even a word in the language to describe it by. The only word that seems to express it, *humilitas,* signifies baseness, servility, and meanness of spirit—a thing very different from true Christian humility; and indeed this was the only idea they entertained of that virtue. Everything that we call meek and humble, they considered as mean and contemptible. A haughty, imperious, over-bearing temper, a high opinion of their own virtue and wisdom, a contempt of all other nations but their own, a quick sense and a keen resentment, not only of injuries, but even of the slightest affronts—this was the favourite and predominant character among the Romans! And that gentleness of disposition, that low estimation of our own merits, that ready preference of others to ourselves, that fearlessness of giving offence, that abasement of ourselves in the sight of God, which we call humility, they consider as the work of a lame, abject, and unmanly mind." Genuine humility is indeed one of the most beautiful ornaments of the soul. Jonathan Edwards describes it as a " little white flower, such as we see in the spring of the year—low and humble upon the ground,—opening its bosom to receive the pleasant beams of the sun's glory; rejoicing, as it were, in a calm rapture, diffusing around a sweet fragrance, standing peacefully and lovingly in the midst of other flowers round about; all, in like manner, opening their bosoms to drink in the light of the sun." Such a mind includes also—

IMPROVABILITY.—The mind that accepts honest and loving reproofs is in an improvable condition. What in nature is more beautiful than an improvable object? The tree advancing from stage to stage towards fruitfulness is beautiful, the child rising towards manhood is beautiful, but the mind rising from ignorance to knowledge, from bondage to freedom, from corruption to purity, from the earthly and the devilish to the spiritual and the Divine, is the most beautiful object under these Heavens. The soul that will not receive reproofs cannot improve, but must inevitably deteriorate.

The Gospel is a reprover, its first lesson is a reproof, and it ceases not to reprove, until it has made the soul perfect in Christ Jesus. Truly, where reproof is well-timed, and well taken, a wise reproof to "an obedient ear is an earring of gold, and an ornament of gold," set out to the best advantage. Such was Eli's word to Samuel, Abigail's and Nathan's to David; Isaiah's to Hezekiah.

The Apostle's reproof to the Corinthian Church worked so efficiently, that in all things they approved themselves clear in the matter. (1 Cor. v. 1; 2 Cor. ii. 1—3; 2 Cor. vii. ii.) There is no ornament like that of a humble and improvable spirit.

> "It moulds the body to an easy grace,
> And brightens every feature of the face.
> It smoothes th' unpolished tongue with eloquence,
> And adds persuasion to the finest sense."
> STILLINGFLEET

Proverbs 25:13

The Value of a Good Messenger to His Employers

"As the cold of snow in the time of harvest, so is a faithful messenger to them that send him : for he refresheth the soul of his masters."

IT is not necessary to imagine that Solomon here indicates the occurrence in Judea of snow in the times of harvest. It is very improbable that a snow storm ever happened in that country during that period. The ancients in the East did as we do, preserved the ice and snow of winter, in order to cool their summer beverages. A cold draught in a hot summer's day was there, as here, most refreshing. What such a beverage was to the thirsty man in the heat of a tropical summer, is a "faithful messenger" to the soul of his master. Our subject is the value of a good messenger to his employer.

His CHARACTER is refreshing to his master.—What more pleasing to an employer than the development of fidelity in his servants :—to see them faithful, not only to their engagements, but faithful to moral truth and to God? The Eternal Master of us all, we are assured, is as pleased with the fidelity of His servants. "For we are unto God a sweet savour of Christ, in them that are saved, and in them that perish: to the one we are the savour of death unto death, and to the other the savour of life unto life." At last He will reward His servants, not according either to the kind or quantity of their service, but according to their faithfulness. "Well done, good and faithful servant. Thou hast been faithful in a few things, I will make thee ruler over many. Enter into the joy of thy Lord."

His INFLUENCE is refreshing to his master.—His service will inspire his master with confidence in him. Instead of being harassed with suspicions and anxieties as to whether his commissions will be executed or not, free from all such solicitude, he calmly relies upon his representative. His service will awaken general respect for his master. A "faithful messenger" can scarcely fail to bring honour to his employer.

In truth a faithful man is a refreshing object to all observant souls.

> "His words are bonds, his oaths are oracles,
> His love sincere, his thoughts immaculate,
> His tears pure messengers sent from his heart,
> His heart so far from fraud as heaven from earth."
>
> SHAKESPEARE

Such men give to history its aroma, they are calm and faithful in trials, and command the respect of their greatest foes. The speech of Eleazer before the tyrant Antiochus, as given by Josephus, breathes the spirit of all faithful souls. "Old age," says the intrepid martyr, "has not so impaired my mind, or enfeebled my body, but when religion and duty call upon me, I feel a youthful and a vigorous soul. Does this declaration awaken your resentment? Prepare your instruments of torture, provoke the flames of the furnace to a fiercer rage, nothing shall induce me to save these silver locks by a violation of the ordinances of my country and my God. Thou holy law! from whom I derive my knowledge, I will never desert so excellent a master. Thou prime virtue, temperance! I will never abjure thee. August and sacred priesthood! I will never disgrace thee. I will bear it to my ancestors as pure and unsullied soul, as free from stain as I stand in this place devoid of fear, amidst the parade of your threatening engines and implements of martyrdom "

Proverbs 25:14

Swaggering Generosity

"Whoso boasteth himself of a false gift *is like* clouds and wind without rain."

THE verse points to a character by no means uncommon. It is a man of prolific promise: he is so bland in aspect: so liberal in speech, that one might think that he was always hailing opportunities, in order to manifest in some practical way his generosity. But into whatever circles such a man enters he brings disappointment, he is "like clouds without rain." His broad and generous talk excites expectations, only to be blasted.

Such a man is found sometimes in the SOCIAL circle.— Who has not had such a character introduced into the circle of his acquaintance? He appeared so genial in sentiment; so deep and broad in sympathy; his conversation so full of benevolent feeling and world-wide philanthropy, that you fancied, at any rate, that for once a friend had entered your sphere, who would be a blessing to every member: that should misfortune happen to any, he would be the first to render relief. But time rolled on and misfortune came. You appealed to him. How did he greet you? All his professions appeared only as "a cloud without rain" on the parched sky: not one rain-drop of help came from that source.

Such a man is found sometimes in the CHURCH circle. He is admitted into fellowship with the professed disciples of Christ; he has made his confession, and it has chimed with love for humanity and God. All the members felt that with his advent a wonderful blessing had come : the poor would be relieved, the ignorant would be educated, the tried and the afflicted would receive sympathy and succour. The minister expected that he had gained a true helper. But what was the result? He soon found, alas, that it was all talk. When claims were submitted to his benevolence, he appeared only as "a cloud without rain," rolling ever under the hot heavens of emergency.

Such a man is found sometimes in the CIVIC circle.—He appears before you as a candidate for some civic office : he wins your suffrage by great promises. If he is sent to the vestry he will economise your parish expenditure; if to the Corporation he will remove local nuisances and wrongs ; if to the Parliament he will retrench expenditure and reform abuses. He goes, and what does he do? He rolls about the heavens as "a cloud without rain."

Let all, especially young ministers, be warned against such characters. Their tree is ever in blossom, but never runs into fruit ; they disappoint your hopes, and cheat you at every turn. "Whoso boasteth himself of a false gift is like clouds and wind without rain." A more contemptible character know I not than the man of a mean and dastardly selfish nature wearing the livery and speaking the language of love, with one hand dropping a farthing into the "urn of poverty," and with the other taking a shilling out.

Proverbs 25:15, 21, 22

The Manifestation and Mightiness of Moral Power

"By long forbearing is a prince persuaded, and a soft tongue breaketh the bone. . . . If thine enemy be hungry, give him bread to eat; and if he be thirsty, give him water to drink ; for thou shalt heap coals of fire upon his head, and the LORD shall reward thee."

THERE are three kinds of power : material, mental, and moral. The power to act on matter, the power to discover and invent, the power to influence the conscience and heart. The second is greater than the first, the last greater than either or both. "Even in war," says Napoleon, "moral power is to physical as three parts out of four. Man possesses the three; he has muscular, mental, and spiritual might." Nothing does a man aspire to with greater intensity than power, nothing does he appreciate more than power.

> " Power, 'tis the favourite attribute of gods,
> Who look with smiles on men
> Who can aspire to copy them."

The verses direct our attention to the manifestation and might of moral power.

The MANIFESTATION of moral power.—The words indicate a threefold manifestation. *Stillness.* "By long forbearing is a prince persuaded." Forbearance implies calm endurance—a patience like that which the Great Heavenly Exemplar exhibited under insults and persecutions, "Who, when He was reviled, reviled not again." Great moral power often shows itself in this stillness in the presence and under the attacks of enemies. It requires more power to sit still before an enemy than to strike him to the dust. God's moral strength is seen sitting still "whilst the heathen rage, and the people imagine a vain thing." Another manifestation of power here is—*Speech.* "A soft tongue breaketh the bone." "A soft tongue,"—not a simpering tongue, not a silly tongue, not a sycophantic tongue, but the "soft tongue" of tender love and forbearing kindness. Such a tongue is might: it "breaketh the bone." This somewhat paradoxical expression indicates the amazing force of kind words; they break the bone, the ossified heart of the enemy. Another manifestation of power here is—*Service.* "If thine enemy be hungry, give him bread to eat; and if he be thirsty, give him water to drink. For thou shalt heap coals of fire upon his head." Here is something more than stillness or speech. It is returning "good for evil," according to the teaching and example of Christ. "In the smelting of metals," says Arnot, "whether on a large or a small scale, it is necessary that the burning coals should be above the ore as well as beneath it. The melting fuel and the rude stones to be melted are mingled together and brought into contact, particle by particle, throughout the mass. It is thus that the resistance of the stubborn material is overcome, and the precious separated from the vile." There are but few hearts so obdurate as not to melt under the fires of love that blaze over and under them. These words direct our attention to—

The MIGHTINESS of moral power.—Moral power showing itself in all this kindness, in patient endurance, tender speech, and beneficent service, can achieve wonders. Its victories here are represented by three expressions. *Persuading*. "By long forbearing is a prince persuaded." This power can turn the mind of a mighty monarch, backed by invincible armies. A prince's mind can be brought down by the arrows of kindness. Thus David brought down Saul, and bowed the heart of Israel as one man. And thus Christ is subduing the heart of the world. Another expression by which its mightiness is here represented is—*Breaking*. "A soft tongue breaketh the bone." A bone is a hard substance; some men have very hardened natures; their hearts are like granite, all attempts to subdue them by force are futile evermore. But loving words can do it; they can mollify the roughest natures. Gideon, with a kind word, pacified the Ephraimites, and Abigail turned David's wrath away. God's word of kindness is a hammer that breaks the rocky heart of man. There is still another expression to represent the mightiness of its power, and that is—*Melting*. "Thou shalt heap coals of fire on his head." "The Americans have a tract on this subject, entitled, '*The man who killed his neighbours.*' It contains, in the form of a narrative, many useful, practical suggestions on the art of overcoming evil with good. It was with kindness—modest, thoughtful, generous, persevering, unwearied kindness,—that the benevolent countryman killed his churlish neighbour: and it was only the old evil man that he kills, leaving the new man to lead a very different life in the same village, after the dross has been purged away."

How sublimely elevated is the moral legislation of the Bible. Love for enemies found no place in the ethical codes of heathen philosophers, poets, or priests. Jesus brought it as a "new commandment" from the Supreme authority of the universe. He inculcated it in His teaching, He exemplified it in His life, He furnished the mightiest demonstration of it in His death. Let this principle be ours, not merely as an element in our written code, but as a spirit in our life. There is in truth no other way of overcoming our enemies. Our enemy will never disrobe himself of the cloak of anger with which he has tightly wrapped himself around, by the north wind of intellectual discussion, or physical force, however bitter, biting, and boisterous. These will only cause him to bind it more tightly about him. Bring the calm sunbeam of love upon him, in all the strength of its heat, and speedily will he unfasten it as an encumbrance and throw it away.

Proverbs 25:16

The World's Honey

"Hast thou found honey? eat so much as is sufficient for thee, lest thou be filled therewith, and vomit it."

THESE words suggest three remarks:

The world HAS ITS HONEY.—Notwithstanding all that mawkish pietists say against the world, it has, nevertheless, in it much felicity. It is *not* "a wretched land, that yields us no supply." It has honey in it. A delicious sweetness pervades it. It has a *gastric* honey. What pleasures can be derived from a participation in the precious fruits of the earth! The world spreads before man a table of delicious viands. It has a *gregarious* honey. How great the pleasure men have in mingling with their kind merely as social animals; the pleasure of mates, parents, children. It has a *secular* honey. What pleasure there is in the pursuit, the accumulation, and the use of wealth! It has *æsthetic* honey. What pleasure is derived from the beautiful in nature, art, and music. It has *intellectual* honey—pleasures derived from an inquiry into, and discovery of the Divine ideas that underlie all the forms and ring through all the sounds of nature. The world has its *honey* and we should be thankful for it. It might have been filled with bitterness; its fruits might have been all wormwood and gall. But it is not so. Its productions are pleasant to the palate, its forms are beautiful to the eye, its sounds are music to the ear, its odours are delicious to the smell; its bodies often impart the most thrilling delight to the touch, and its phenomena are ever suggestive of inspiring truths to the soul. Thank God for all this honey!

The world's honey MAY BE ABUSED.—" Eat so much as is sufficient for thee, lest thou be filled therewith, and vomit it." There are those who eat too much of the honey. Some eat too much of the gastric honey, and they become gourmands, epicures, voluptuaries. Some eat too much of the gregarious honey, and they become profligate debauchees and bloated animals. Some eat too much of the secular honey, and become wretched misers, haunted with a thousand suspicions. Some eat too much of the æsthetic honey, and grow indifferent to everything but what they consider the beautiful and harmonious. Taste is everything to them. They seem to have no life but in the presence of that which, in the cant of their class, they call " High Art." Some eat too much of the intellectual honey, and they have no life but in that of observatories, laboratories, libraries, and cold abstractions. All these eat too much of the honey.

The world's honey abused PRODUCES NAUSEA.—" Lest thou be filled therewith and vomit it." Over-indulgence in any worldly pleasure issues in a moral sickness and disgust. There is what the French call the *ennui* that comes out of it, "that awful yawn," says Byron, "which sleep cannot abate."

The intemperate use of this honey often makes life an intolerable burden.

> " Give me to drink, Mandragora,
> That I may sleep away this gap of time."
> SHAKESPEARE

Well did Solomon know this from experience.—Eccl. ii. Take care how you *use* the world. You may have too much of a good thing. Use the world and not abuse it. " Every creature of God is good, and nothing to be refused, if it be received with thanksgiving." There is a honey, thank God! of which you cannot take too much, which will never surfeit or sicken,—that is the honey of spiritual enjoyment; the enjoyment of studying, imitating, worshipping Him in Whose " presence there is fulness of joy, and at Whose right hand there are pleasures for evermore."

Proverbs 25:17-20

Bad Neighbors

" Withdraw thy foot from thy neighbour's house; lest he be weary of thee, and *so* hate thee. A man that beareth false witness against his neighbour *is* a maul, and a sword, and a sharp arrow. Confidence in an unfaithful man in time of trouble *is like* a broken tooth, and a foot out of joint. *As* he that taketh away a garment in cold weather, *and as* vinegar upon nitre, so *is* he that singeth songs to an heavy heart."

MAN is a social being, and greatly does his prosperity and happiness depend upon those with whom he is brought into most frequent contact. The Bible everywhere recognises this fact, and supplies abundant directions as to the manner in which we should treat our neighbours. In these verses we have four kind of *bad* neighbours indicated,—the intrusive, the slanderous, the faithless, the injudicious. Notice—

The INTRUSIVE.—" Withdraw thy foot from thy neighbour's house; lest he be weary of thee, and so hate thee."

It is pleasant to be visited by a neighbour whose interest in us is genuine. There are some whose visits can never be too frequent; they carry sunshine with them. We hail their knock at the door, we rejoice at their presence at the table and on the hearth. But there are others who are intrusive, the tread of their foot is heard too frequently in the house. And with them indeed "familiarity breeds contempt." Two evils are here suggested as likely to accrue to those neighbours whose visits are intrusive. They *become tiresome*. "Lest he be weary of thee." How soon we become tired of the visits of those who carry nothing fresh with them, whose nature is stale, whose habits are stereotyped, whose thoughts are old drippings from the common mind! The man of genius, whose mind is a fountain of living water, and not the channel of a muddy stream, will never make you weary. They become *disliked*. "And so hate thee." This is almost a natural consequence of irksomeness. If you lose interest in a man you do not want to see him : his presence even once after annoys you, and, repeated, fires your indignation. An old writer, quaintly remarks :—"It is wisdom, as well as good manners, not to be troublesome to our friends in our visiting them, not to visit too often, or stay too long, or contrive to come at meal-time, or make ourselves busy in the affairs of their families : hereby we make ourselves cheap, mean, and burdensome. Thy neighbour, who is thus plagued and haunted with thy visits, will be weary of thee, and hate thee, and that will be the destruction of friendship which should have been the improvement of it. *Post tres sæpe dies piscis vilescit et hospes*.— After the third day fish and company become distasteful. *Nulli te facias nimis sodalem*—Be not too intimate with any. He that sponges upon his friend loses him." Livy remarks, "that the perfection of good behaviour is for a man to retain his dignity without intruding on the liberty of another." Another bad neighbour here indicated is—

The SLANDEROUS.—"A man that beareth false witness against his neighbour is a maul, and a sword, and a sharp arrow." The mischief of a false witness, which is so strongly and universally condemned in the Scriptures, is here represented by three weapons of death:—A " maul." This old English word, which is now obsolete, signifies a hammer or a club, an implement used in the rough and bloody warfare of fighting men in old times. A " sword." Another deadly implement, that by which millions of men have been cut down in all ages. A " sharp arrow." Another weapon of destruction. A slanderous neighbour is as mischievous as any or all of these murderous weapons. He knocks, he cuts, he pierces; he destroys you by his tongue. Not your body, but your plans, your prosperity, your reputation, your happiness. Slander, which one of the poets has called, "the foulest whelp of sin," is generally directed against the best men. "The worthiest people, says Swift," "are the most injured by it, as we usually find that to be the best fruit which the birds have been pecking at." "Slander is fruitful," says Sterne, "in variety of expedients to satiate as well as disguise itself. If these smooth weapons cut so sore, what shall we say of open and unblushing scandal, subjected to no caution, tied down to no restraints? If the one, like an arrow shot in the dark, does, nevertheless, so much mischief, this, like the pestilence which rages at noonday, sweeps all before it, levelling without distinction the good and the bad: a thousand fall beside it, and ten thousand on its right hand: they fall so rent and torn in this tender part of them, so unmercifully butchered, as sometimes never to recover either the wounds or the anguish of heart which they have occasioned." Another bad neighbour here indicated is—

The FAITHLESS.—" Confidence in an unfaithful man, in time of trouble, is like a broken tooth, and a foot out of joint." Few sources of social misery are so prolific and perennial as that springing from confidence in faithless men, It is here suggested—That the unfaithful man *fails* you. Like the "broken tooth" and the "foot out of joint," he fails to fulfil what is required of him. Just when you want to eat, you find that the tooth is broken and useless;

just when you rise to walk, you find that your foot is out of joint. Just so with the faithless man. When you want him he fails you; the hour when you expected him to stand by you and help you he is wanting. All his old promises of friendship prove to be lies, nothing less. It is here suggested that the unfaithful man *pains* you. In the use of the broken tooth and the disjointed foot, when you try them, there is not only disappointment but torture. Such is the mental distress which is caused by the failure of confidence in the proportion to the degree in which you had cherished it. Especially is this felt "in time of trouble," when help is so particularly needed, and when a kind of claim, independently of all professions and promises, is felt to exist, on sympathy and kindness. Then the heart is sensitively alive to aught like neglect and disappointment. To trust and be deceieved is at any time a bitter trial. To trust in "the time of trouble" and be deceived, is the extreme of mental suffering. Few men can be trusted to do all we expect, still less to do all we require. Micah's Levite, and Mephibosheth's trust in Ziba, and Paul's desertion when he said, "At my first answer no man stood by me, but all men forsook me," are illustrations. Another bad neighbour here indicated is—

The INJUDICIOUS.—"As he that taketh away a garment in cold weather, and as vinegar upon nitre, so is he that singeth songs to an heavy heart." When you are in trouble there are neighbours whose attempt to comfort you is as absurd and as ineffective as the taking away from a man his garment in cold weather, and as giving to a thirsty man vinegar upon nitre to drink. "Nitre," says an able expositor, "does not mean the salt so called by us—saltpetre, but rather an alkaline substance which was called by the Romans nitrum, and which, in a particular state of preparation, was used in Judea for soap. Vinegar, or any other acid, poured on this substance, would, from the want of chemical affinity between them, produce effervescence; and this appears to be the similitude intended—the want of affinity between the song of mirth and the spirit of heaviness. It is incongruous, disquieting, agitating." "Miserable comforters are ye all," says Job. First: The injudicious comforter is one who presents incongruous *subjects*. Sometimes he will talk on worldly subjects, subjects of gain, fashion, and amusement, when the distressed mind is sorely agitated with serious thoughts. Sometimes he will discourse on common-place subjects connected with Providence or doctrinal theology, when the distressed soul requires, not talk, but genuine sympathy and holy quiet. To talk on incongruous subjects to a distressed mind is really as absurd as to strip a poor man of his garment in the cold cutting winds of winter. Secondly: The injudicious comforter is one who presents proper subjects *in an incongruous spirit*. He talks of the right things, but talks of them with a spirit unsympathetic, sometimes undevout, canting, cold, and dogmatic. Such a man's comfort is indeed "vinegar on nitre," conflicting, irritating, and painful.

Let us cultivate the spirit of true neighbourliness. Let us be non-intrusive, truthful, trustworthy, and judicious, so that our visits may at all times be dispensations of light, comfort, and peace.

Proverbs 25:23

Righteous Anger

"The north wind driveth away rain: so *doth* an angry countenance a backbiting tongue." *

THE marginal reading, which is, "the north wind bringeth forth rain: so doth a backbiting tongue an angry countenance," gives quite the opposite sense. In Arabia the north wind blew over a long tract of dry land, and, therefore, usually brought dry weather; but in Judea the north wind, including all the winds between the north and north-

* Verses 21, 22, have been noticed in a previous Reading.

west, blew from the Mediterranean Sea, and therefore commonly brought rain. Accepting the marginal version, the idea is, that as the north wind brings forth rain, a backbiting tongue brings forth an angry countenance. But our version, which we think equally faithful to the original, gives an idea equally good and important; it is, that an expression of displeasure in the listener will silence the tongue of the backbiter. He who listens to backbiters encourages them in their sin, and shares their guilt. It is worthy of note that Homer speaks of the north wind bringing fine weather; and this might have been the observation of Solomon also. All men do not put the same interpretation on meteorological phenomena.

The subject which the words serve to illustrate is *righteous anger*. Anger is not essentially sinful; it is only sinful when it is directed to wrong objects, and when it is cherished. We are divinely ordered not to let "the sun go down" on our wrath. We have somewhere read an account of two Grecian bishops, who, having disagreed on some subject of doctrine, parted in mutual anger; but the eldest, in the course of the day, sent to the other a message in these words, "*Sol ad occasum,*"—the sun is about to go down. The other no sooner heard it, but he reflected on the words of the Apostle, "Let not the sun go down upon your wrath," and so they were both friends again. We are commanded to be "angry and sin not." Moses was angry; Christ was angry; the Great God has anger. The anger referred to here is a *righteous* anger; its object is legitimate, its expression is natural, its influence is useful. We say that—

Its OBJECT IS LEGITIMATE.—It is directed against "a backbiting tongue." A backbiter is a clandestine traducer of character. His speech goes to damage another's reputation behind his back. He does it sometimes by telling truth as well as falsehood; he states facts in the history of the man of whom he speaks discreditable to his character; facts which a manly charity should seek to bury in oblivion. A man need not tell lies to be a backbiter; he can do it by parading damaging facts, and such damaging facts may be found in the chapters of every man's life. He does it sometimes *unmaliciously;* he may have no real ill-feeling in his heart towards the person of whom he speaks, no desire to injure him ; yet injure him he does. He may be prompted by *vanity;* he may disparage another in order to set himself off to better advantage. He may do it from *greed;* his objects may be to rob the subject of his talk of some share of his patronage and support. But whilst the backbiter need not necessarily deal in falsehood, he generally does; whilst he is not necessarily malicious, he generally is. He is always a sneak; he stabs in the dark. He is always a coward; he has not the manliness even to hint to a man's face what he fluently and bravely utters behind his back. He is always a despoiler, he robs another of his reputation.

> " Who steals my purse, steals trash ; 'tis something, nothing;
> 'Twas mine, 'tis his, and has been slave to thousands ;
> But he that filches from me my good name,
> Robs me of that which not enriches him,
> And makes me poor indeed."—SHAKESPEARE

Here there is a fit object for anger. When such a character appears before you, let the heavens of your soul rumble in thunder, and flash in lightning.

As to this righteous anger, we may remark that its EXPRESSION IS NATURAL. — " An angry countenance." The countenance is a fuller, more faithful, and forceful revealer of the soul than the tongue. There is often more in a look than you could put into volumes. " The cheek is apter than the tongue to tell an errand." " This man's brow," says our dramatist, " like a tragic leaf, foretells the nature of a tragic volume." An approving look flashes sunshine oftentimes into the hearts of spectators, makes the wife cheerful for the day, and the children sing for joy. An admiring look has often won hearts which no words could enlist. A courageous look in the leaders of campaigns wakes the invincible in battalions. A reproving look has broken hearts, as Christ's broke the heart of Peter. An angry look, not a mere peevish, petulant look, but a look of right down honest anger directed to a backbiter, would send him quailing in mute confusion from your presence. We do not feel so deeply as we ought God's goodness to us in the revealing power of the countenance. The countenance is the language that wins the love and the confidence of our compeers, that is most potent in reproving the wrong and encouraging the right.

Concerning this righteous anger we may remark further, that its INFLUENCE IS USEFUL. — "The north wind driveth away rain, so doth an angry countenance a backbiting tongue." Perhaps, according to the observation of Solomon, a strong north wind always drove away the rain, scattered the clouds, and dried the earth, and, he says, that just as such wind drove away the rain, an angry countenance would drive away the backbiter. Is not this true? Would a backbiter dare to stand, for a moment, clandestinely traducing the character of another, if the man he addressed would throw on him the scathing looks of honest indignation? No, he would flee from his presence as a whelp howling from the lash of his master. He who listens to clandestine calumnies is as foul in guilt as the vile slanderer himself. Augustine's biographer mentions of him that these two lines were written in his dining-room—

" Quisquis amat dictis absentum rodere vitam,
Hanc mensam veritam noverit esse sibi."

It is added, that he said to a bishop, indulging this habit at his table, " Either I will blot out these verses on the wall, or begone from my table." Bishop Burnet, in his Essay on Queen Mary, mentions her effectual rebuke of calumny: if any indulged in it in her presence, she would ask, if they had read Archbishop Tillotson's Sermon on Evil Speaking, or give them other pointed reproof. "Calumny," says Leighton, "would soon starve and die of itself, if nobody took it in and gave it lodging."

Proverbs 25:25

Good News from a Far Country

"*As* cold waters to a thirsty soul, so *is* good news from a far country."

THE condition of the recipient gives value to the blessing. A river of cold water is not half so valuable to a man who feels not its need, as one glassful to him who is parched with thirst. The oriental travellers feel the value of cold water, and Solomon's illustration would have with them a force which it lacks with us. The subject is the gratefulness of good news from a foreign country; and we shall apply it especially to *heaven*—good news from heaven. There are several things that make good news from a far country as grateful as "cold waters to a thirsty soul."

If the country reported is ALTOGETHER UNLIKE OUR OWN.—The human mind is always interested in what is novel and romantic: strangeness has a strange fascination for the soul. What charms have the reports of Captain Cook, Moffatt, Livingstone, for all minds! Such speakers are always heard with interest, and their writings, detailing their observations and relations, are read with avidity by all classes. Man has an appetite for the romantic. If the country reported HAS CONFERRED AN IMMENSE BENEFIT ON US.—Supposing that we had once been in a state of abject slavery, and that the far country reported to us had effected our emancipation and guaranteed our liberty, with what interest should we listen to everything about it: the act that served us would invest all the scenes connected with its history with a special charm. The news would be as "cold waters to a thirsty soul." If the country reported CONTAINED ANY THAT ARE DEAR TO US. — New Zealand, Vancouver's Island, Australia, America, and many other distant countries are extremely interesting to many families in this land, on account of the friends they have living in

* The 24th verse has been discussed in the Reading on Prov. xxi. 9.

them. News from these scenes are received as "cold waters to a thirsty soul." If the country reported IS A SCENE IN WHICH WE EXPECT TO LIVE OURSELVES.—With what interest does the emigrant listen to everything that has reference to that land whither he is about wending his way, and which he is about adopting as his home!

Heaven, as a far country, pre-eminently meets all these conditions of interest. There is the NOVEL.—" Eye hath not seen, nor ear heard, neither have entered into the heart of man, the things which God hath prepared for them that love him." Listen to Paul's account of it. "I knew a man in Christ above fourteen years ago, (whether in the body I cannot tell; or whether out of the body, I cannot tell: God knoweth;) such an one caught up to the third heaven. And I knew such a man, (whether in the body, or out of the body, I cannot tell: God knoweth;) how that he was caught up into paradise, and heard unspeakable words, which it is not lawful for a man to utter." How unlike that country is to ours! Here is a sphere for the play of the romantic. There is the BENEFACTOR.—What benefits that far country has conferred on us! From hence we have received the Great Christ the Redeemer of the world, and also the blessed Spirit of wisdom, purity, and peace. There are our FRIENDS.—How many of those whom we have known and loved are there! How many such are going there every day! Some of us have more friends in heaven than on earth. There we EXPECT TO LIVE.—Yonder is our inheritance, "an inheritance incorruptible and undefiled, that fadeth not away." Let tidings from this far country be to us as "cold waters to a thirsty soul," grateful and refreshing.

> "O, Paradise! O, Paradise
> Who doth not crave for rest?
> Who would not seek the happy land,
> Where they that love are blest.
> Where loyal hearts and true
> Stand ever in the light,
> All rapture through and through
> In God's most holy sight!"—F. W. FABER

Proverbs 25:26

Religious Apostasy

"A righteous man falling down before the wicked *is as* a troubled fountain, and a corrupt spring."

THE possibility of a good man "falling from grace" was one of the grand questions in the theological controversies of past times. That a good man may relapse into depravity is manifestly possible. To prove that either a good man, or a good angel, is bound by the necessity of his nature to continue in the course of holiness, is to prove that he is no longer free and responsible, but a slave and a machine. For a good man to relapse into depravity is not only possible but very easy. The force of the remaining depravity within him and the force of unholy influences about him render it comparatively easy for the best men to fall. Nor is it merely possible and easy, but it is historically proved. Good men in all ages have apostatised,— David, Peter, Demas, and many others have fallen. In truth it is everywhere Biblically implied. The exhortations to perseverance, and the warnings against apostacy which run through the inspired Word imply the fearful liability of righteous men to "fall down before the wicked." The verse presents this apostacy in two aspects :

As a MORAL FALL.—"A righteous man falling down before the wicked is as a troubled fountain and a corrupt spring." Righteousness is true soul elevation. It is the soul "risen with Christ," "setting its affection on things above, sitting down in the heavenly places with Christ Jesus." It is under the control of high principles. Sympathy with truth, devotion to right, compassion for souls, and supreme love for the supremely good, sway the righteous man. It is also in the enjoyment of high fellowship. It is in association with holy men, angels, and God; its fellowship is indeed with the Father, and with His Son Jesus Christ. The apostacy of such a soul may well be considered a *fall*, and how great the fall! Who shall tell the distance between truth and error, selfishness and love, the love of God and the love of the world? Many men who trouble themselves with the question of the possibility of good men "falling from grace," need not be anxious about themselves,—they cannot fall much lower than they are: they are down in the depths of worldliness and practical atheism. The verse presents this apostacy—

As a SOCIAL CURSE.—It is like a "troubled fountain and corrupt spring." It is implied here that a good man's life is as *valuable* as a fountain. In tropic lands, where rains are only periodic and at distant intervals, fountains and springs are of incalculable worth. How the parched traveller yearns for the refreshing spring. But the value of an Eastern fountain is but a faint image of the value of a good man's character. Such a character is a fountain of life,—clear, free, active,—sending forth streams to irrigate the moral desert, and slake the moral thirst of parched souls. It is implied here that a good man's apostacy is as *injurious* as a spring corrupted. When a good man in a neighbourhood falls into sin it is an event more disastrous to the district than if poisons were thrown into all its fountains of water. As a garden once well cultivated will produce more noxious weeds than the untilled wilderness, so the influence of an apostate's life is more pernicious than that of the ordinary sinner. The good man who falls into sin is like the gallant bark that goes down in the mouth of the haven: it becomes more perilous to the sailor than if it had sunk abroad in the open sea.

Beware of backsliding. "Let him that thinketh he standeth take heed lest he fall." None sink so far into hell as those that come nearest heaven. No plants, if they rot, become more offensive and pernicious than those which once appeared in richest foliage and choicest flowers.

"The soul, once tainted with so foul a crime,
No more shall glow with friendship's hallow'd ardour.
Those holy beings, whose superior care
Guides erring mortals to the path of virtue,
Affrighted at impiety like thine,
Resign their charge to baseness and to ruin."
                                                JOHNSON

Proverbs 25:27

Natural Desires Running too Far

It is not good to eat much honey: **so** *for men* to search their own glory *is not* glory."

MAN is a creature of manifold desires. He has animal, social, intellectual, and moral desires; these desires impel him to action; they are the springs that keep in motion the machinery of his being. These desires may be divided into two grand classes. Those that *can never go* too far, and those that often do. There are desires in human nature that can never get too strong, never do too much work, never run too far. Such are the desires for knowledge, holiness, assimilation to God. And there are those that *often run* too far. Such are the desire for wealth, which often runs into avarice; the desire for power which often runs into tyranny; the desire for pleasure which often runs into licentiousness and lust. Here we have running too far—

The desire for ANIMAL PLEASURE.—"It is not good to eat much honey." Honey here stands for pleasure, as we have seen in our remarks on the 16th verse of this chapter. Life has its animal sweetness,—the God of nature intended the five senses to convey pleasurable sensations. A desire for pleasure is natural, but it may run too far; it often does so, and when it does, Solomon says, in the text, it is not good. It is not good for the *body*. The man who gives himself up to animal gratifications undermines his health, inbreathes the germs of physical disease and dissolution. It is not good for the *intellect*. A pampered, plethoric body dims the mental vision, enervates the intellect, clogs the rational faculties. In animal voluptuousness the brain runs into fat, and the intellect into a grub. The rise of the animal is the fall of the mental. It is not good for the *soul*. The pampering of the senses is the death of the soul; it takes from conscience its sensibility, and from the religious element its force; the moral man becomes " carnally sold under sin." How true, then, what Solomon says, "It is not good to eat much honey." Here we have running too far—

The desire for HUMAN PRAISE.—"So for men to search their own glory is not glory." The word "not," which is here in italics, is not in the original; it has been supplied by our translators. In doing so they have evidently expressed the idea intended. A desire for the praise of our fellow-men is natural, innocent, and useful. He who is utterly regardless of the judgment and feelings of others concerning him is a character rather to be despised than commended. It is natural for men to desire the commendation of their circle. It is very true that the praise of corrupt society is seldom of much worth, and often indeed contemptible; for society is so lavish of its praise that it will applaud in thunderous strains the villain, if he will only appear in a little pomp and pageantry. Who has not often seen what Shakespeare describes?

> " Such a noise arose,
> As the shrouds make at sea in a stiff tempest,
> As loud, and to as many tunes; hats, cloaks,
> Doublets, I think, flew up; and had their faces
> Been loose this day, they had been lost."

There are men whose desire for human praise becomes a passion; popularity is the god at whose shrine they are always paying their devotions. We have abundant examples in our own age of authors, artists, preachers, and statesmen doing so. In the days of Christ the Jews loved the praise of men rather than the praise of God. The grand distinction between a great man and a little man is this that popularity follows the former, but attracts the latter; the one walks calmly and majestically before it, the other runs with breathless earnestness after it.

Be master of your desires. Let them be your servants, not your sovereigns. Use them as the mariner uses the winds and the waves, to bear you to the shores of the holy and the blest.

Proverbs 25:28

The Lack of Self-mastery

> "He that *hath* no rule over his own spirit *is like* a city *that is* broken down *and* without walls."

IN Proverbs, chapter xvi., verse 32, it is said, "He that is slow to anger is better than the mighty; and he that ruleth his spirit than he that taketh a city." These words, which point to the important work of self-conquest, we have already examined, and our remarks should be read in connection with the observation suggested by this proverb.* The subject here is the *lack of self-mastery*. The soul that has not obtained a command over itself is here compared to "a city that is broken down and without walls," and the figure suggests two thoughts concerning such a condition:

The condition is UNSIGHTLY.— How unsightly a city appears after it has been besieged, sacked, and plundered by a conquering army! The more architecturally beautiful it had been, the more revolting now. We look at its shattered condition in the light of the memory of its former beauties, and we are shocked with the hideous aspects which the violence of the invader has created. But far more unsightly is the state of the soul that has no mastery over itself. Genius besmeared in the mud of depravity, conscience submerged beneath the foul waves of passion, and intellect becoming the mere creature of sensuality and worldliness, are the most unsightly objects on which an angel's eye can rest. And yet, alas! such unsightly scenes are common. Jerusalem, when Nehemiah wept amidst its ruins, looked most ghastly to his heart; but a soul which has no mastery over its own lusts and passions is an object far more ghastly to behold.

The condition is UNSAFE.—"The walls of the city are broken down." It has no ramparts of defence. Its mani-

---
* See Readings, No. clxvii. p. 231.

fest insecurity invites the entrance and assaults of the invader. It is so with the soul where there is no self-mastery. It is open to every tempter. It "gives place to the devil." A soul destitute of self-control is in a most perilous condition—a mere breath will hurl it from the orbit of order—a mere spark of temptation will set it in flames.

Look well to the fortifications around thy soul, brother! Hold the whole of thy nature in control. "He who reigns within himself," says Milton, "and rules, desires and fears, is more than a king."

> "May I govern my passions with absolute sway,
> And grow wiser and better as life wears away."

"In the little world within the breast," says Dr. Caird, "there are stations of rank, dominion, authority, to which we may aspire, or from which we may fall. There is an inward slavery baser than any bodily servitude: there is an inward rule and governance of a man's spirit, an object of loftier ambition, far—than the possession of any earthly crown or sceptre. For self-government is indeed the noblest rule on earth. The highest sovereignty is that of the man who can say, 'He hath made us kings unto God.' The truest conquest is where the soul 'is bringing every thought into captivity to the obedience of Christ.' The monarch of his own mind is the only real potentate."

Proverbs 26:1, 8
Honor Paid to Bad Men is Unseemly and Pernicious

> "As snow in summer, and as rain in harvest, so honour is not seemly for a fool. . . . As he that bindeth a stone in a sling, so *is* he that giveth honour to a fool."

THE respect which man pays his fellow is often grounded on reasons immoral and absurd. Sometimes man is respected on the ground of his personal appearance, sometimes on the ground of his mental abilities, sometimes on the ground of his worldly possessions, sometimes on the ground of his lineage and social position; but respect for men on any of these grounds *alone* is, to say the least, very questionable in morality. The true and Divinely authorized ground of respect for man is moral goodness. The man who is morally good, however deficient in other things, has a Divine claim to our honour. The man who has not goodness, whatever else he may possess, calls for our contempt rather than our respect. He alone is the honourable man who possesses the nobility of goodness. Notwithstanding this, so corrupt is society that men in abundance are to be found who "honour fools," honour wicked men—honour them, not because they are wicked, for conscience will not allow them to do so, but because they have power, wealth, or high social status. It is against this that Solomon speaks in these verses.

Honour paid to bad men is UNSEEMLY.—It is "as snow in summer and as rain in harvest,"—unseasonable and incongruous. How unseemly nature would appear in August with snow mantling our corn-fields, the air as chilly and the heavens as lowering as in the middle of winter! Solomon means to say it is just as unseemly to see a human soul rendering respect to a man who is "a fool"—that is, a man destitute of moral goodness. Souls are morally constituted to reverence the good, and the good only; to loathe and abhor the morally bad, wherever it is seen, whether in connexion with lordly possessions, kingly power, or, what is higher still, mental genius. So perverted are men's moral tastes that they do not discover this incongruity, otherwise flunkeyism, which is so terribly prevalent everywhere, would be felt to be as far out of keeping with the moral constitution of things as "snow in summer." Bad men, who have neither wit nor grace, are often preferred by princes and hurrahed by peoples.

Honour paid to bad men is PERNICIOUS.—"Snow in summer and rain in harvest" are in nature mischievous elements. Their tendency is to rob the agriculturist of the rewards of his labour, to disappoint the expectations of all, and to bring on a famine in the land. Far more mischievous is it when the people of a country sink so morally low as to render honour to men who are destitute of moral goodness. The perniciousness is also expressed by another figure in the verses. "As he that bindeth a stone in a sling, so is he that giveth honour to a fool." The word translated " sling " means a heap of stones, and the word "stone" a precious stone. Hence the margin reads " as he that putteth a precious stone into a heap of stones, so is he that giveth honour to a fool." The idea evidently is, as a precious stone amongst rubbish, so is honour given to a fool. To honour a fool is an act as mischievous as the throwing of precious stones into a heap of rubbish. Honour as rendered to fools is as diamonds thrown into the dust hole, or pearls laid before swine. Nothing is more pernicious to the commonwealth, nothing more disastrous to true spiritual and manly progress, than this tendency.

Expect not honour from men, whatever thy lineage, talents, power, or possessions, unless thou art morally wise.

"It is only noble to be good.
Kind hearts are more than coronets,
And simple faith than Norman blood."
TENNYSON

"Our own heart," says Coleridge, "and not other men's opinion, forms our true honour." Nor degrade thy nature to be rendering honour to men who are not *morally* honourable. Do not for the sake of place, power, or fame, render honour to fools. Do not cringe or crawl to flatter and conciliate the worthless. "Wrap yourself," says a foreign author, "in your own virtue, and seek a friend in your daily bread. If you have grown grey with unblenched honour, bless God and die."

"Ye see yon birkie ca'd a lord,
Wha struts and stares and a' that;
Though hundreds worship at his word,
He's but a coof for a' that :
For a' that and a' that,
His riband star and a' that;
The man of independent mind,
He looks and laughs at a' that."—BURNS

Proverbs 26:2

Human Anathemas

"As the bird by wandering, as the swallow by flying, so the curse causeless shall not come."

ANOTHER, and perhaps a better, translation is this:— "Unsteady as the sparrow, as the flight of the swallow, is a causeless curse; it cometh not to pass." "There is a difficulty here," says Dr. Wardlaw, "in settling the precise *point* in the comparison. The ordinary interpretation explains it with reference to curses pronounced by men without cause—imprecations, anathemas, that are unmerited—and the meaning is understood to be—as the bird or sparrow, by wandering, and as the swallow, or wood-pigeon, by flying, *shall not come*—that is, shall not reach us or come upon us in the way of injury, so is it with the *causeless curse*. It will do no more harm than the bird that flies overhead, than Goliath's curses on David. And it might be added that, as these birds return to their own place, to the nests from whence they came, so will such gratuitous maledictions come back upon the persons by whom they are uttered. Thus God turned the curses into a blessing which Balak, the son of Zippor, hired Balaam to pronounce against Israel. Thus the malicious and hard-hearted curses of Shimei against David came not upon him, but fell upon the head of their unprincipled author." The following observations may be made upon these words:

MEN ARE FREQUENTLY THE VICTIMS OF HUMAN IMPRECATIONS.—Few men pass through the world without creating enemies, either intentionally or otherwise. Even the best of men have those who regard them with hostile hearts. There have been those in all ages who "hate without a cause." Men vent their hatred in various ways, —sometimes by slander, sometimes by violence, and not unfrequently by imprecations. They wreak their vengeance by profane appeals to heaven. They invoke the

Eternal to curse those whom they cannot reach. This is by no means an uncommon way of gratifying human wrath. Goliath cursed David, and David in his turn cursed his enemies. There are but few men in any generation who have not been cursed. The Prophets were cursed,—Christ was cursed,—His Apostles were cursed. "Woe unto you when all men speak well of you." Men will always damn you if you run counter to their tastes, gratifications, interests, and predilections. Another observation here is that:

Human imprecations are SOMETIMES UNDESERVED.—The curse is "causeless." Sometimes the imprecations of men are deserved. Those on whose heads David invoked the judgments of God deserved the ill he sought. There are two classes of causeless curses. Those that are hurled at us because we have done the right thing. When you are cursed for reproving evil, for proclaiming an unpopular truth, or pursuing a righteous course which clashes with men's prejudices or interests, the curse is "causeless." The other class is those that are uttered without reason or feeling. There are men who are so in the habit of using profane language, that it almost flows from their lips without malice or meaning. And there are those, also, who are such fools that they regard profane language as an indication of manly courage and even gentlemanly bearing. There is neither reason nor feeling in their oaths. To be cursed by men when the curse is undeserved is more an honour than a disgrace. The greatest men in history have been cursed, and some of them have died under a copious shower of human imprecations. The greatest souls have always lived under the ban of their age. Another observation is that:—

Undeserved imprecations are ALWAYS harmless.—"The curse causeless shall not come." Was David the worse for Shimei's curse? or Jeremiah for the curse of his persecutors? "He that is cursed without a cause," says Matthew Henry, "whether by furious imprecations or solemn anathemas, the curse will do him no more harm than the sparrow that flies over his head. It will fly away like the sparrow or the wild swallow, which go nobody knows where, until they return to their proper place, as the curse will at length return to him that uttered it." "Cursing," says Shakespeare,

> "Ne'er hurts him, nor profits you a jot.
> Forbear it, therefore,—give your cause to heaven."

But if the curse be not "causeless," it will come. Jotham's righteous curse came upon Abimelech, and the men of Shechem. Elisha's curse fearfully came to the young mockers of Bethel. "The curse abides on Jericho from generation to generation." The following considerations have been given as reasons why men should not swear:— "*It is mean.* A man of high moral standing would almost as soon steal a sheep as swear. *It is vulgar;* altogether too low for a decent man. *It is cowardly.* Implying a fear either of not being believed or obeyed. *It is ungentlemanly.* A gentleman, according to Webster, is a gentle man, well-bred, refined; such a man will no more swear than go into the street and throw mud with a clod-hopper. *It is indecent.* Offensive to delicacy, and extremely unfit for human ears. *It is foolish.* Want of decency is the want of sense. *It is abusive.* To the mind that conceives the oath, to the tongue that utters it, and to the person at whom it is aimed. *It is venomous.* Showing a man's heart to be a nest of vipers, and every time he swears one of them sticks on his head. *It is contemptible.* Forfeiting the respect of the wise and good. *It is wicked.* Violating the Divine law and provoking the displeasure of Him Who will not hold him guiltless who takes His name in vain."

> "Take not His name, who made thy mouth, in vain:
> It gets thee nothing, and hath no excuse.
> Lust and wine plead a pleasure; avarice gain;
> But the cheap swearer, through his open sluice,
> Lets his soul run for naught, as little fearing:
> Were I an epicure, I could bate swearing.
> When thou dost tell another's jest, therein
> Omit the oaths, which true wit cannot need;
> Pick out of tales the mirth, but not the sin.
> He pares his apple that will cleanly feed."
>
> GEORGE HERBERT

Proverbs 26:3-11

Aspects of a Fool

"A whip for the horse, a bridle for the ass, and a rod for the fool's back. Answer not a fool according to his folly, lest thou also be like unto him. Answer a fool according to his folly, lest he be wise in his own conceit.* He that sendeth a message by the hand of a fool cutteth off the feet, *and* drinketh damage. The legs of the lame are not equal: so *is* a parable in the mouth of fools. As he that bindeth a stone in a sling, so *is* he that giveth honour to a fool. *As* a thorn goeth up into the hand of a drunkard, so *is* a parable in the mouth of fools. The great *God* that formed all *things* both rewardeth the fool, and rewardeth transgressors. As a dog returneth to his vomit, *so* a fool returneth to his folly."

SIN is folly. It sacrifices the spiritual for the material, the temporal for the eternal, the pure joys of immortality for the gratification of an hour. In the judgment of Solomon the sinner was a fool. The two terms with him were convertible. Sin makes dolts; for if a man is naturally stupid, it makes him more so. In these verses he gives us various side views of a moral fool.

He appears here as a SERVANT. —"A whip for the horse, a bridle for the ass, and a rod for the fool's back." This proverb inverts our ideas. We should have said, "a bridle for the horse," and "a whip for the ass." But the Eastern asses have much of the fire of our blood horses, while the horses are often heavy and dull. Therefore the ass there requires the bridle, and the horse the whip. The one to accelerate, the other to restrain and guide activity. As the horse and the ass, in order to be used as the servants of man, require the application of force, so does the fool. "A rod for the fool's back." If a stubborn sinner is to be made the servant of society, coercion must be employed. Argument, persuasion, example, these moral appliances will affect him but little. He must have a rod, the bridle of law must restrain him—the whip of menace must drive him on. It is thus that the Great Master Himself often uses them. The still small voice of

---

* This verse is noticed in a previous Reading.

love and reason reaches them but seldom. The rod of poverty, affliction, bereavement, and sore trial, is employed. The Bible represents hardened sinners as more inconsiderate than the brutes. " The ox knoweth his owner, and the ass his master's crib; but Israel doth not know, my people doth not consider." The incorrigible fool can only be managed by the application of the rod. By pain he is restrained, guided, and driven.

He appears here as a DEBATER.—" Answer not a fool according to his folly, lest thou also be like unto him. Answer a fool according to his folly, lest he be wise in his own conceit." There is an apparent contradiction here, but it is only apparent. The *negative* means, we are not to debate with him in his style and spirit, and thus become like him. We are not to descend to his level of speech and temper. The *positive* means, that we are to answer him as his folly deserves. It may be by silence as well as speech. If by silence, we should be dignified and significant. If by speech, whilst we must be always truthful, it might be sarcastic, reproaching, and denunciatory. The fool talks—he is often a great debater. He is often fluent and dogmatic on subjects on which the wise look with reverent silence. More than half the talk of the world is the talk of fools, and the talk is sensual, profane, cavilling, and morally pernicious.

He appears here as a MESSENGER.—" He that sendeth a message by the hand of a fool cutteth off the feet and drinketh damage." The meaning of this is, " He who would trust a fool with a message might as well cut off his feet, for he will have vexation and may be damage." " The fool," says Bridges, " is utterly unfit for service. When a message is sent by his hands, he makes so many mistakes, careless or wilful, that it is like bidding him go when we have cut off his legs. Indeed we can only *drink* damage from his commission. The employment of the unbelieving spies spread damage of discontent and rebellion throughout the whole congregation. How careful should we be to intrust important business to trustworthy persons! Fools are either unqualified for their mission, or they have their own interests to serve, at whatever cost to their masters. Solomon himself 'drank damage,' by employing an 'industrious' servant, but a *fool* in wickedness, who 'lifted up his hand against the king,' and spoiled his son of ten parts of his kingdom. (1 Kings xi. 26-40.) Benhadad drank damage by sending a message by the hands of Hazael, who murdered his master when the way was opened for his own selfish purposes. (2 Kings viii. 8-15.)" Much of the business of life is carried on by messengers or agents. How much a mercantile firm suffers by improper representatives! How much damage have political States sustained by the employment of unworthy diplomatists! How much injury comes to England every year, by sending to Parliament a message by the " hand of fools!"

He appears here as a TEACHER.—" The legs of the lame are not equal: so is a parable in the mouth of fools." It is not very uncommon to find fools sustaining the office and performing the functions of teachers. "They have a parable in their mouth." There are men, with their natural stupidity, augmented by a moral perversity, acting as teachers in many of our schools and churches, as well as in our literature. The verses suggest two things concerning them as teachers—That *they appear very ridiculous*. " The legs of the lame are not equal, so is a parable in the hands of fools." The idea seems to be, as the cripple who desires to appear nimble and agile, appears ridiculous in his lame efforts to walk, so the fool appears ridiculous in his efforts to teach. "As the legs of a fool," says an old author, "are not equal, by reason of which he is unseemly, so unseemly is it for a fool to pretend to speak apophthegms, and give advice, and for a man to talk devoutly, whose conversation is a constant contradiction to his talk, and gives him the lie. His good words raise him up, but then his bad life takes him down, and so his legs are not equal." " A wise saying," says Bishop Patrick, "doth as ill become a fool, as dancing doth a cripple: for as his lameness never so much appears as when he would seem nimble, so the other's folly is never so ridiculous as when he would seem wise. As, therefore, it is best for a lame man to keep his seat, so it is best for a silly man to hold his tongue." The other thing suggested by the text concerning fools is that, as *teachers, they are generally very mischievous*. "As a thorn goeth up into the hand of the drunkard, so is a parable in the mouth of fools." The idea is, that a fool handling the doctrines of wisdom is like a drunken man handling thorns. The besotted inebriate, not knowing what he is about, lays hold of the thorn and perforates his own nerves. The wise sayings in the mouth of a stupid man are self-condemnatory; holy sayings in the mouth of a corrupt man are also self-criminating. Such men condemn themselves in their teachings.

He appears here as a COMMISSIONER.—"The great God that formed all things, both rewardeth the fool and rewardeth transgressors." The word "God" is not in the original. The margin is the more faithful translation—"A great man giveth all, and he hireth the fool, he hireth also transgressors." Elzas gives a similar translation—"The great man terrifieth every one, he hireth fools, he hireth also transgressors." The idea seems to be, that when worldly princes employ fools for the public service, it is a source of great anxiety and trouble to all good citizens. Alas! such men are often employed in public services; and their arrogances, intolerances, and blunderings bring grief to the country. "The lesson has application from the throne downwards, through all the descriptions of subsidiary trusts. Extensive proprietors, who employ overseers of their tenants, or of those engaged in their manufactories, or mines, or whatever else be the description of their property, should see to the character of these *overseers*. Their power may be abused, and multitudes of workmen suffer, when the owner—the master—knows nothing of what is going on. But he *ought* to know. Many complainings and *strikes*, well or ill-founded, have their origin here."

He appears here as a REPROBATE.—"As a dog returneth to his vomit, so a fool returneth to his folly." The emblem here is disgusting, but the thing signified is infinitely more so. Peter quotes this proverb. The wicked man often sickens at his wickedness, and then returns to it again. Thus Pharaoh returned from his momentary conviction, Ahab from his pretended repentance, Herod from his partial amendment. How often men, by a long continuance in a course of sin, are abandoned to wickedness, or given up by their own consciences and by God, to a destiny of low, deepening depravity!

Mark well this hideous character and shun it. Consider well that sin is folly. It blunts the sharpest intellect, and makes the dullest more dull. Seek the wisdom "that is from above, first pure, then peaceable, gentle, and easy to be entreated, full of mercy and good fruits without partiality and without hypocrisy."

Proverbs 26:12, 16

Vanity, One of the Greatest Obstructions to Soul-Improvement

"Seest thou a man wise in his own conceit? *there is* more hope of a fool than of him. . . . The sluggard *is* wiser in his own conceit than seven men that can render a reason."

THESE words suggest—

That soul improvement is one of the GRANDEST OBJECTS OF HUMAN HOPE.—It is a glorious fact that the human soul is *capable* of improvement. Its potentialities are unbounded. It has within it the germ of countless harvests. It is a patent and a solemn fact that the soul *requires* improvement: improvement in its intelligence and spiritual attributes. As the soul improves, our power to enjoy and serve God and His universe advances. The words suggest—That soul-improvement is an ATTAINMENT VERY DIFFICULT FOR A FOOL.—"There is more hope of a fool than of him,"—that is, the conceited man. A fool is one, the dullness of whose faculties, and the grovelling character of whose sympathies, and the deteriorating power of whose habits render soul-improvement well nigh an impossibility. In the preceding verse it is said, "As a dog returneth to his vomit, *so* a fool returneth to his folly." Perhaps in this verse Solomon refers to a fool who began to *feel* himself to be a fool. In truth it is only such a fool that has any chance of improvement. The words suggest—that soul-improvement, however difficult for a fool, IS STILL MORE DIFFICULT TO THE SELF-CONCEITED.—" Seest thou a man who is wise in his own conceit? there is more hope of a fool than of him." Many such men there are. Men so full of self-satisfaction—so encased in self-sufficiency, so elevated in their own esteem, that the voice of wisdom cannot reach them. First: They cannot improve in intelligence, because, instead of being conscious of their ignorance, they exult in the affluence of their knowledge. Pope says, "that every man has just as much vanity as he wants understanding." The more vanity the less understanding. Vanity so fills the mental stomach with gas as to destroy the desire for, and the capacity to receive the food of true knowledge. Vanity blinds the eyes to truth. It has been called the "mental mole," the "dense ophthalmia of the vacant mind." They cannot improve in spiritual excellence, because, instead of being conscious of moral defects, they are elated with their own virtues. The vain man's language is—"I am rich, and increased in goods, and I have need of nothing;" "I thank thee that I am not as other men." One of the verses states that this self-conceit is fed by laziness. "The sluggard is wiser in his own conceit than seven men that can render a reason." Indolence feeds intellectual vanity.

How then can a vain man spiritually improve? "If any man among you seemeth to be wise in this world, let him become a fool that he may be wise." "Wouldest thou not be thought a fool in another's conceit," says quaint old Quarles, "be not wise in thy own: he that trusts to his own wisdom proclaims his own folly: he is truly wise, and shall appear so, that hath folly enough to be thought not worldly wise, or wisdom enough to see his own folly."

Proverbs 26:17-22

Mischievous Citizens

"*He* that passeth by, *and* meddleth with strife *belonging* not to him, *is like* one that taketh a dog by the ears. As a mad *man* who casteth firebrands, arrows, and death, so *is* the man *that* deceiveth his neighbour, and saith, Am not I in sport? Where no wood is, *there* the fire goeth out: so where *there is* no talebearer, the strife ceaseth. *As* coals *are* to burning coals, and wood to fire; so *is* a contentious man to kindle strife. The words of a talebearer *are* as wounds, and they go down into the innermost parts of the belly." *

These verses give us a few specimens of mischievous citizens—men who disturb the commonwealth—grieve the good, and distract the heart of society.

Here is the MEDDLER.—"He that passeth by, and meddleth with strife belonging not to him is like one that taketh a dog by the ears." Here is his *conduct* defined: he "meddleth with strife" with which he has no business. He is one of those busy-bodies whose over-officiousness is a social nuisance. There is of course a proper interposition. Where strife rages in families, churches, and nations, interposition is not only justifiable but imperative. No man is justified in standing by, when his fellow-men are contending for their mutual injury, without endeavouring to terminate the evil. All should act as mediators. "Blessed is the peacemaker." This is, however, very different from the intermeddling to which Solomon refers—acting the partisan, siding with one of the angry disputants, and thus mixing one's-self up with the quarrel. There are many such meddlers in society. There are the ecclesiastical meddlers—the social meddlers—the political meddlers —the literary meddlers. Here is his *mischief* indicated— It "is like one that taketh a dog by the ears." He rouses the dog's fury, and exposes himself to its savage bite. If he should let it go, his danger perhaps would be increased; the animal might turn upon him with greater fury. He had better have left the dog alone. The man who becomes

* Verses 13, 14, 15, are repetitions of Chapter xxii. 13, xix. 24, and their meaning has already been expounded.

partisan in a quarrel that does not concern him, renders himself liable to the anger of one, if not both, of the contending parties.

Here is the LIAR.—"As a mad man who casteth firebrands, arrows, and death, so is the man that deceiveth his neighbour, and saith, 'Am not I in sport?'" Mark his conduct. He deceives his neighbour, and says it is "sport." By his false representations he involves his neighbour in some embarrassment, contention, or pain, and then excuses himself by saying it is "in sport." A lie is no less a lie because it is spoken in a spirit of frolic and jest. Mark his mischievousness. He is represented as a "mad man who casteth firebrands, arrows, and death." Many practical jokes have proved most disastrous. They have indeed been as firebrands, arrows, and death. Many a practical jester does the maniac's mischief without the maniac's excuse. "He that sins in jest must repent in earnest, or his sin will be his ruin."

Here is the QUERULOUS.—"As coals are to burning coals, and wood to fire, so is a contentious man to kindle strife." Observe the work he accomplishes. He promotes strife. He kindles and maintains fires of dissension. Where there is peace he creates discord, and where there is discord he heightens its rage. He is not at peace with himself, and he looks with an envious eye at peace wherever it exists. He desires the storms that beat his own heart should rage around the hearts of others. He is a social incendiary.

Here is the TALEBEARER.—"The words of a talebearer are as wounds." Two things are here indicated concerning the talebearer. He maintains strife. Thus he does the work of the contentious man. Indeed, the contentious man does his fiendish work by tales. The whispering inuendo, the malicious hint, the slandering word, often kindle the fire of strife in that circle where peace had long reigned before. As the microscopic sting of a little insect sometimes poisons the blood and inflames the body of a strong man, the mere whisper of a talebearer will kindle the fire of discord in a whole community. He infects with poison. "The words of a talebearer are as wounds, they go down to the innermost parts of the belly." Soft and gentle as the words are, they drop as poison, they sink into the centre of the system, and do their work of destruction. They destroy the mental peace of him *to* whom they are uttered, the reputation of him *of* whom they are uttered and the social happiness of *both*. The meddler, the liar, the querulous, and the talebearer, are the mischievous citizens which Solomon here depicts.

Proverbs 26:23-28

Clandestine Hatred

"Burning lips and a wicked heart *are like* a potsherd covered with silver dross. He that hateth dissembleth with his lips, and layeth up deceit within him; when he speaketh fair, believe him not : for *there are* seven abominations in his heart. *Whose* hatred is covered by deceit, his wickedness shall be shewed before the *whole* congregation. Whoso diggeth a pit shall fall therein : and he that rolleth a stone, it will return upon him. A lying tongue hateth *those that are* afflicted by it ; and a flattering mouth worketh ruin."

THERE are two kinds of enemies in society, those who are open and avowed, and those who are secret and hypocritic. The former, who will let out their hatred in unmeasured terms and undisguised actions, are neither so numerous or dangerous as those who conceal their ill-feeling under the mask of friendship. To these Solomon refers in the verses. The subject is *clandestine hatred*, and four thoughts are suggested concerning it :— It is often greatly DISGUISED. — " Burning lips and a wicked heart are like a potsherd covered with silver dross." The "wicked heart" of enmity is covered over by the " burning lips "—glowing language—of good feeling and friendship. The allusion is here to the ancient art of silvering earthenware, making clay appear to the eye as silver. The tongue of the "just," we are told is as "choice silver." Such, however, is not the tongue of the man who is a clandestine enemy. His tongue is mere "silver dross." It is only silver in appearance. How often do we find lips that burn with warm affection covering hearts instinct with malice! Hatred has an instinct for the dark, working under cover, and putting on disguises. "He that hateth dissembleth with his lips, and layeth up deceit within him." Cain talked to his brother in the field, while murder was in his heart. Saul pretended to honour David whilst he was plotting his ruin. As a rule, the less good feeling a man has for us the more he will flatter us, the more glowing his language of friendship. He is a fawning parasite, lacquering with the "silver dross" of friendly speech the base malignity of his own heart. Another thought suggested concerning clandestine hatred is:

It is EXCESSIVELY CORRUPT.—"When he speaketh fair, believe him not: for there are seven abominations in his heart." The number "seven" in Scripture denotes "fulness" or "completeness." The idea is, that such a man's heart is *full* of abominations. The man who can not only cover over his hatred, hide it in his heart, but give it the language of love for malignant purposes, must truly be a man having "seven"—a fulness of—abominations within him. He has within him the seeds of the traitor, the assassin, and of all villany.

> "Satan was the first
> That practised falsehood under saintly show,
> Deep malice to conceal, couch'd with revenge."
> MILTON

Another thought suggested concerning clandestine hatred is—

It is LIABLE TO EXPOSURE.—"Whose hatred is covered by deceit, his wickedness shall be showed before the whole congregation." Dissembling never answers in the end. The Providence of God brings dark deeds to light. "The voice of Abel's blood cried from the ground." "Some men's sins are open beforehand, going before to judgment; and some men they follow after." The hand of time often strips off the mask, and exposes the flatterer to shame. His "seven abominations" shall be proclaimed, if not privately, at last yonder, on the great day of doom, when all shall appear, men and angels as they really are, and when the hypocrite shall receive his just recompense of "everlasting contempt." There is nothing hidden that shall not be revealed. All sin will on "that day" be stripped of its mask, and laid bare in all its putrescent hideousness to the open eye of the universe. Another thought suggested concerning clandestine hatred is—

It is SELF-RUINOUS.—"Whoso diggeth a pit shall fall therein." Evil is a hard worker. It digs pits and rolls stones. And what is worse, all its hard work is self-ruinous. Into the pit which they have dug they shall tumble. The stone which they have rolled upward shall come back upon them, with terrible momentum, and shall crush them. Those who plot mischief for others will be overwhelmed with it themselves. Moab, in attempting to curse Israel, fell himself under the curse of God. Haman's gallows for Mordecai was his own "promotion of shame." The enemies of Daniel were devoured in the ruin which they plotted against him. Thus does God "take the wise in his craftiness, the wicked in his wickedness." The death of Christ, which was to be the means of warding off national judgment, was the cause of the deprecated scourge. The malice that meditates the evil is often the cause of its own overthrow. The last thought suggested concerning clandestine hatred is—

It is SOCIALLY PERNICIOUS.—"A lying tongue hateth those that are afflicted by it; and a flattering mouth worketh ruin." It injures by its *slanders*. "A lying tongue hateth those that are afflicted by it." Slander is at once the creature and servant of hatred. A man slanders another because he hates him, and his hatred is intensified on account of his slander. The law of ill-feeling seems to be this—the more we injure a man, the more we dislike him. In order to justify our injury, we create reasons to justify our dislike. It injures by its *flatteries*. "The flattering mouth worketh ruin." One of the first acts performed by George III., after his accession to the throne, was to issue an order prohibiting any of the clergy who should be called to preach before him, from paying him any compliment in their discourses. His Majesty was led to this by the fulsome adulation which Dr. Thomas Wilson, Prebendary of Westminster, thought proper to deliver in the Chapel Royal; and for which, instead of thanks, he received from his royal auditor a pointed reprimand, his Majesty observing, "that he came to chapel to hear the praises of God, and not his own." This act, whilst it reflected credit on the king, reflected disgrace on the sycophancy of the clergy. Flattery is a social curse.

> " A man I knew, who liv'd upon a smile,
> And well it fed him: he look'd plump and fair,
> While rankest venom foamed in every vein:
> Living, he fawn'd on every fool alive;
> And dying, cursed the friend on whom he lived."
> YOUNG

Proverbs 27:1

Man and Tomorrow, a Fact and a Failing

"Boast not thyself of to-morrow; for thou knowest not what a day may bring forth."

Here is a FACT.—What is the fact? "Thou knowest not what a day may bring forth." A day does bring forth wonderful things; diseases, disappointments, a world of fresh existences and thousands of open graves. But who knows the particular things in relation to us individually that will come forth on the morrow? Will it bring sorrow or joy, health or disease, hope or disappointment, life or death? No one knows. "Ye know not what shall be on the morrow." This ignorance of to-morrow is *necessary to the prosecution of our duties on earth.* Could we draw aside the veil of the future, and look at the things which are coming to us, our energies would be so paralysed as to incapacitate us for the ordinary avocations of life: mercy has woven the veil of concealment. This ignorance of to-morrow *is our incentive to preparation for the future.* Christ used this argument, "Be ye therefore ready, for in such an hour as ye think not the Son of Man cometh." Prepare for the future by living well to-day.

> " Lo, here hath been dawning another blue day:
> Think, wilt thou let it slip useless away ?
> Out of eternity, this new day is born,
> Into eternity at night will return.
>
> " Behold it aforetime, no eye ever did ;
> So soon it for ever from all eyes is hid.
> Here hath been dawning another blue day:
> Think, wilt thou let it slip useless away ?"
>
> T. CARLYLE

Here is a FAULT.—" Boast not thyself of to-morrow." This admonition implies a presuming on the future. This is a fault, and it is *universal*. We are all, more or less, guilty of it. All our purposes and plans reach into a future which will never be ours. This fault is *inexcusable*. Every day Providence delivers homilies to us on the uncertainty of the future. In presuming on it, we go not only against inspiration, but also against our own judgment. This fault is *hazardous*. "Abner promised a kingdom, but could not insure his life for an hour. Haman plumed himself upon the prospect of the queen's banquet, but was hanged like a dog before night. The fool's soul was required of him on the very night of his worldly projects for many years to come." " Serious affairs of to-morrow" —was the laughing reply of Archias, warned of a conspiracy which hurried him into eternity the next hour. The infidel Gibbon calculated upon fifteen years of life, and died within a few months at a day's warning.

"Now is the accepted time." Do not calculate on the morrow. To-morrow's sun may shine on your corpse : on the corpse of many a man as strong as you its rays will fall. " An artist solicited permission to paint a portrait of the Queen. The favour was granted—and the favour was great, for probably it would make the fortune of the man. A place was fixed, and a time. At the fixed place and time the Queen appeared, but the artist was not there—he was not ready yet. When he did arrive, a message was communicated to him that her Majesty had departed, and would not return. Such is the tale: we have no means of verifying its accuracy; but its moral is not dependent on its truth. If it is not a history, let it serve as a parable; such a disappointment might spring from such a cause. Translate it from the temporal into the eternal: employ the earthly type to print a heaven lesson."—*Arnot.*

Proverbs 27:2

Self-praise

"*Let another man praise thee, and not thine own mouth; a stranger, and not thine own lips.*"

THIS verse implies that all should possess *a praiseworthy character*. Praise from others is here recognised by Solomon as a proper thing, and this implies the commendable in character. The praiseworthy qualities of character are patent. They are honesty, sincerity, disinterestedness, chastity, moral heroism. All should seek the possession of these. All should struggle after whatever things are of good report. The verse implies also that where the praiseworthy exists it is right that *praise should be rendered*. The man who cannot recognise excellence in another is morally blind, whilst he who discovers it without commendation is without the sentiments of honest manhood. Whilst flattery is base, honest commendation is a sign of nobility. The verse declares, moreover, that the praise rendered *should not be rendered to self*. "Let another man praise thee, and not thine own mouth." Occasions may occur in every man's life when he is justified in using the word of self-commendation. His motives may be impugned. Slander and vilification may degrade him before his compeers. All manner of evil things may be said about him falsely. Under such circumstances it becomes him, nay it is incumbent on him, to stand up and vindicate, and even commend himself. The great Apostle of the Gentiles did this—"For I suppose I was not a whit behind the very chiefest apostles. But though I be rude in speech, yet not in knowledge; but we have been thoroughly made manifest among you in all things." But it is against self-praise that Solomon speaks, and why should it be spoken against? For the two following reasons—

It generally implies the LACK OF TRUE, GENUINE EXCELLENCE.—The man who parades his own merits, who sings his own praises, is generally self-ignorant; he has not so measured his own faculties as to feel his weakness; so gauged his own resources as to be impressed with his own deficiencies; so searched into his own motives, as to become conscious of his own spiritual unworthiness. Poor, miserable, blind, and naked, yet he fancies himself rich, increasing in goods, and having need of nothing. He lacks that humility which is a leading attribute of all moral worth, that charity which lies at the foundation of all goodness, and which vaunteth not, and is not puffed up. As a rule, the man who praises himself most is the most unpraiseworthy. The other reason is that,—

It is always SOCIALLY OFFENSIVE. — "Praise," says an old author, " is sweet music, but is never tunable in thine own mouth; it is a comely garment, but its beauty, to be seen, must be put on by another, not by thyself." Nothing is more offensive to the ear of the listener than self-laudatory language. The heart of an honest man burns when sycophancy speaks to him in flattery, and it recoils with disgust when the lip of vanity is speaking its own praises in his ear. It is too prevalent in all circles. You hear it at the domestic hearth, in the social gatherings, from the platform, the hustings, and the senate house. Alas, it speaks too often in our pulpits. The vanity of preachers is becoming almost proverbial. Solomon did right, then, in speaking a strong word against self-praise. Even the great Apostle, who stood up in his own self-defence, so strongly felt the impropriety of speaking of his own merits, that he said, "I speak as a fool."

Do not be impatient for praise. Be praiseworthy, and

the praise that is worth having will come. Sallust said of Cato that he "would rather *be* than *seem* to be a good man." The better a man is, the more he deserves praise, but the less he cares for it. A man honours himself not by self-laudatory language, but by noble works, that will shine as the light of day. He who, like the Pharisee in the temple, sounds his own praise, shall step down from his elevation into contempt and oblivion: but he who, in solitude and obscurity, cultivates general excellency, shall come forth to light and be rewarded openly.

Proverbs 27:3-6

Social Wrath and Social Friendliness

"A stone *is* heavy, and the sand weighty; but a fool's wrath *is* heavier than them both. Wrath *is* cruel, and anger *is* outrageous; but who *is* able to stand before envy? Open rebuke *is* better than secret love. Faithful *are* the words of a friend; but the kisses of an enemy *are* deceitful."

THESE verses contain two opposite elements in social life—wrath and friendship.

Here is WRATH.—Here are two kinds of wrong wrath. Wrath *without reason*. The wrath of a fool. "A stone is heavy, and the sand weighty, but a fool's wrath is heavier than them both." This wrath is *weighty*—weighty as a "stone" or "sand." It is a sullen, stubborn thing. It came into the fool's heart without reason; he broods over it, and it grows heavier with days. No reason will modify it. No argument will bear it away. It is there. He carries it with him, like a bag of sand. Nay, it is heavier, Solomon says, than either stone or sand. You may pulverise the stone, you may scatter the sand, you may give both to the winds to bear away, but a fool's anger continues. This wrath is not only weighty but *outrageous*. "Wrath is cruel, and anger is outrageous." Or, as the margin has it, "overflowing." Being altogether without reason it runs into passion; it fires the blood, and makes the man savage, and furious as a beast of prey. This wrath is seen on all battle-fields. The men who fight, for the most part fight without any intelligible reason, and hence their wrath heaves and dashes like the billows when lashed by the hurricane. Here is another kind of wrong wrath, viz.,— Wrath *with a bad reason*. "Who is able to stand before envy?" Envy implies a reason. We do not envy another without knowing something about him. Its reason is that what another has we should possess. Reason feeds this passion of envy. Intellect becomes its nurse and minister. The thought of its possessor acts rather as oil to make the flames more furious, than as water to put them out. This passion is one of the principalities in the malignant passions of the soul. Like the apocalyptic star called wormwood, it embitters all the waters into which it falls. Socrates has well-defined this envy: "The greatest flood has the soonest ebb; the sorest tempest the most sudden calm; the hottest love the coolest end; and from the deepest desire oftentimes ensues the deadliest hate. A wise man had rather be envied for providence than pitied for prodigality. Revenge barketh out at the stars, and spite spurns at that she cannot reach. An envious man waxeth lean with the fatness of his neighbours. Envy is the daughter of pride, the author of murder and revenge, the beginner of secret sedition, and the perpetual tormentor of virtue. Envy is the filthy slime of the soul, a venom, a poison, a quicksilver which consumeth the flesh, and drieth up the marrow of the bones." "What," says Wardlaw, "can stand before it? It was *envy* that murdered Abel, and dyed the earth with the first blood of innocence. It was *envy* that plotted against Joseph, consulted to put him to death, sold him into bondage, dipped his hated vest in blood, and presented it to the eyes of his distracted parent—thus slaying at once the fraternal and the filial affections in the bosom of its subjects. It was *envy* that delivered up to condemnation and death the Lord of glory, the prince of life, the pattern of benevolence and purity, and every divine and human excellence. O! if we cannot help being its *objects*, let us beware of being its *subjects*." On the other hand,—

Here is FRIENDSHIP.—"Open rebuke is better than secret love. Faithful are the wounds of a friend; but the kisses of an enemy are deceitful." Thank God, there are the virtuous and beneficent in social life, as well as the vile and disastrous! There is friendship as well as wrath. But what passes for friendship is often spurious. In these words we have the feigned and the faithful.

Here is the *feigned*. Here we have what is called secret love—"the kisses of an enemy." It is suggested here that feigned friendship will not utter rebukes even when rebukes are needed. It always seeks to please. The face has always the bland smile, and the tongue the flattering oil. It is fond of caressing. It deals in glowing grasps and "kisses." But it is the mere semblance of the true thing, and nothing more. The tree blossoms richly, and it pleases you. When the time comes that you almost die for fruit, there is nothing but the barren branch. We have here the *faithful*. It speaks in "open rebuke." It inflicts "wounds." The faithful friend wounds, not for the sake of wounding, but wounds as the good surgeon wounds—as a means of health.

Rather let us be the objects of wrath than the subjects of envy, the objects of feigned friendship than the subjects of it. Of the two evils—wrath or feigned friendship—I think I should prefer being the victim of the former rather than the latter. Though the antagonism of the one would be more positive and virulent than the other, yet both tend to injury. The one brandishes its deadly implement over men in the broad sun, with the frown of the demon on its brow; the other conceals the javelin under its cloak, and, with a kiss, stabs me in the dark. The one thunders out my faults, the other exaggerates virtues which I never had. Kind heaven, give me the faithful friend—a friend who shall be truthful even though his words cut me to the quick. "False friendship, like the ivy, decays and ruins the walls it embraces; but true friendship gives new life and animation to the object it supports."

Proverbs 27:7

An Appetite for Good Things Essential for Their Enjoyment

"The full soul loatheth an honeycomb; but to the hungry soul every bitter thing is sweet."

THE principle underlying this proverb is, that to appreciate a thing you must first feel its want—that we must have a craving for it before we can enjoy it. This principle applies—

To CORPOREAL good.—It is the appetite that makes the bodily food sweet and enjoyable. The dainty epicure sits at the banquet table with the choicest viands spread before him, and instead of a relish he has a nausea. The very "honeycomb," symbol of the choicest dainty, his "soul loatheth." His appetite, has, through gastric indulgences, been so vitiated that the best provisions are unpleasant to his palate. Delicious was the manna to the Israelites at first. It was like "wafers mixed with honey;" but overindulgence in it caused them at last to say, "Our soul loatheth this light bread. Who will give us flesh to eat?" Whilst to the pampered epicure the choicest dainties are unenjoyable, to the hungry wayfarer and toiling workman "every bitter thing is sweet." Who of the two is the more blest? The man who has the abundance of the enjoyable without the power of enjoying, or he who has the scarcest of the humblest fare, with the full relish of a "hungry soul"? After all, as far as this material life is concerned, better be a hungry pauper than a pampered epicure. "Hunger is the best sauce." This principle applies—

To INTELLECTUAL good.—There appear before you two men—the one the occupant of a mansion, the possessor of a magnificent library. Every volume on his large and crowded shelves is "an honeycomb" amidst the literary productions of all ages; but he has no hunger for knowledge—not because his soul is full of intelligence, for the more knowledge a man has, the more will he crave for an increase, every accession of knowledge whetting the appetite—but because the soul is full of worldliness, self-conceit, nonsense. He has no appetite for any of these books. Nay, the choicest productions of genius are the most distasteful to him. To him the priceless library is worse than worthless. There is another man, whose books are few, whose time for reading and study is not only exceedingly short, but very unseasonable; in the midnight hour, or in minutes seized after the bodily energies have been well-nigh exhausted by labour, the commonest tract containing truth, is seized with avidity, and perused with relish. He picks up the very crumbs of truth, and devours them with a ravenous appetite. Which of the two men is the better off? I'd rather be the man of one book, nay of no book at all but the book of my own soul,—the book of nature—with an appetite for truth, than the owner of the choicest library in the world, with no desire for knowledge. This principle applies—

To SPIRITUAL good.—There is a man to whom Providence has vouchsafed spiritual privileges, choice in their character and abundant in amount. He lives in a family whose members are intelligent and devoted followers of the illustrious Nazarene, and where the sanctities of religion are cheerfully and reverently regarded. The church is near his dwelling, it throws its shadow on his lawns. It has all the appliances for spiritual quickening and growth. Its minister is a preacher of the highest type, free from all dogmatism and exclusiveness, and permeated with the sublime spirit of Him Who spake as never man spake. In his neighbourhood and amongst his acquaintances are devout men of every sect. But he has a "full soul." He has no hungering or thirsting after righteousness, no desire for the "sincere milk of the word," and loatheth the whole. So distasteful is the whole to him, that he is free in the use of terms to designate his abhorrence. All to him is cant, hypocrisy, superstition, fanaticism. There is another man the opposite of this. His spiritual provisions are of the fewest in number and the scantiest in character. He lives in the tents of wickedness. Depravity runs riot through the whole sphere of his daily activities. Bibles, if not unattainable, are rare, churches are distant and inaccessible, a preacher's voice never falls on his ear; but he hungers after righteousness, and enjoys the dimmest rays of spiritual light. The low, occasional, distant whisperings of truth, as they come to him through nature, history, and conscience, are heard eagerly, and interpreted with devotion. Which of these two men is better off—your Socrates in Athens, or your sceptical nobleman here in England? The former, a thousand times. "He"—the Great God—hath always "filled the hungry with good things, and the rich he hath sent empty away."

Proverbs 27:8

The Evil of a Roaming Disposition

"As a bird that wandereth from her nest, so *is* a man that wandereth from his place."

SELF-INJURY is here implied. The bird that wandereth from her nest and never returns, injures herself thereby. She sacrifices all the labour of building, risks her own safety, and if it be in the period either of incubation, or when her nestlings are unfledged, brings ruin on her progeny. So with the man of a roving and unsettled disposition. He exposeth himself to great disadvantages and perils. The language will apply to a roving man in many aspects of life. It will apply to him *domestically*. A man's home is his "place." It is his earthly rest, the Canaan on whose improvement he should bestow his best energies, and from which he should derive his chief social enjoyments. He who wanders from it and seeks his earthly pleasures elsewhere, in clubs or taverns, brings injury both on himself and others. How many wives sigh out a miserable existence and children grow up in ignorance and recklessness, in consequence of the fathers who wander from their place. The language will apply to man *avocationally*. The "place" of a man in business is the occupation in which he has been trained, and into which he has been brought by the ruling circumstances of his life. Success in any avocation depends upon a settled purpose and a systematic procedure therein. The men who wander from their business, who from a fickle and roving tendency are constantly changing their occupations, generally involve themselves and others in injury. The old adage that "a rolling stone gathers no moss," receives illustrations every day. Men who wander from their callings in life often find their way into bankruptcy and ruin. The language will also apply to man *ecclesiastically*. Every man, as a worshipper, should find his way into some church. He should have a religious house, where on stated occasions, he would appear with his neighbours to worship the Common Father. David desired "to dwell in the house of the Lord all the days of his life." The men who wander from their place of worship most frequently do an injury to their own nature. Such men abound in this age. There are those who have been called religious vagrants. They are, either from an idle curiosity, from hope of gain, or from a desire to avoid contributing to the expenses of public worship, never found in regular attendance at the same church. The man who wanders from his home, his business, or his church, is like the bird who "wandereth from her nest:" he involves himself and others in the inconvenient and pernicious. But the proverb receives a profounder and a more universal application when regarded *spiritually*. Man spiritually has wandered from his place in three respects :

As an ENQUIRER after TRUTH.—Man is an intellectual being, he is made to enquire after truth. As the body hungers after food and has the power of appropriating, and requires it as an indispensability, so the soul craves for truth, has faculties for attaining it, and demands it as the one thing needful, and Heaven has kindly spread the universe around him as a field for his researches. What is his "place" as an enquirer? In other words, in what state of mind should he start forth on his investigations Undoubtedly from a supreme sympathy with God: faith in Him, and love for Him should be the starting point of his enquiring mission. Men have gone out in search of truth. They have interrogated nature, and they have obtained what they consider explanations of the various phenomena which have come under their notice. They have systematised *these* explanations and called them science. But what are these sciences? Are they intellectually satisfactory? are they morally so? Do they answer the profoundest questions of the human soul? No. Why? They have not taken the idea and love of God with them into the arcana of nature. He who does not look at the universe through God can never see it —never interpret philosophically its phenomena. Hence our so-called philosophers have been in relation to their work "as the bird that has wandered from her nest." They have not started from the true theistic sentiment, the resting place of intellect. How precious are the works of those we deeply love! With what interest do we study their productions! How interesting the universe would appear to us if we supremely loved its Maker! In truth, this love is the interpreting faculty. If we would understand nature we must look at it through God, that is, through our belief in Him, and love for Him. As enquirers, then, how sadly men have wandered from their place. Man has also wandered—

As a MEMBER OF THE RACE.—He is a social being, he is not isolated, he is a member of a vast community of kindred existencies, and with them he has to do. He has to live with them, by them, and for them. How should he treat them? What is his "place" in relation to them? It is that of brotherhood. He should look on all mankind as the offspring of a common father, endowed with a common nature, burdened with common responsibilities, possessing common rights, destined to a common eternity. This feeling of brotherhood would not only inspire him to act out the golden rule,

"Whatsoever ye would that men should do to you, do ye even so to them," but would inspire him to lay himself out for men's good. But how has man in his conduct to his race wandered from this point! He has treated his fellow men as victims to gratify his own lust and greed, as beasts of burden, and as fiendish foes. Alas, how He has wandered from the true social idea of life! he has also wandered from his place—

As a CREATURE OF WORSHIP.—Man is a religious being. He is made to worship. Worship is a necessity of his nature; he must have a deity and a shrine. What is his place in relation to his worshipping propensities and engagements? A settled, loving, faith in *one* God, the Maker of all. From this he should start in all his religious activities. But how sadly has he wandered from this true religious place of his soul! And in his wanderings, he has found his way into the chilly midnight of atheism; into the cloud land of pantheistic revelries; and into the loathsome, cruel, and superstitious domain of polytheistic dreams. Ah, spiritually, indeed, men are like the bird that has wandered from her nest! They have left their normal place in relation to truth, society, and God. Like the prodigal, they are in a far country; or like the sheep, lost in the wilderness. The spiritual roamers are in a worse condition than the bird. The wandering bird may find another lodgement, build another nest in a more sheltered and salubrious spot; but man has no power to do this, he must return to his place or be lost for ever. Like Noah's dove, he will find no rest until he returns to his true ark—a settled loving faith in God. "Let every man wherein he is called therein abide with God."

"Return, O wanderer, to thy home,
Thy Father calls for thee;
No longer now an exile roam,
In sin and misery.
Return, return!"

Proverbs 27:9-11
A Genuine Friendship, and a Happy Fathership

"Ointment and perfume rejoice the heart: so *doth* the sweetness of a man's friend by hearty counsel. Thine own friend, and thy father's friend, forsake not; neither go into thy brother's house in the day of thy calamity: *for* better *is* a neighbour *that is* near than a brother far off. My son, be wise, and make my heart glad, that I may answer him that reproacheth me."

Here is a GENUINE FRIENDSHIP. Solomon has already said much about friendship, and we shall find further utterances of his on the subject, before the end of the book is reached. The definition of friendship given by Addison is, perhaps, as good as can be presented. He says, "it is a strong and habitual inclination in two persons to promote the interest of each other." The passage suggests two or three of the features of genuine friendship—*Pleasantness.* —"Ointment and perfume rejoice the heart." A better rendering of the verse, perhaps, would be this, although it alters not the sense—"Oil and perfume gladden the heart: so the sweetness of a man's friend by hearty counsel." "Behold," says one who knew what true friendship was, "how good and how pleasant it is for brethren to dwell together in unity! It is like the precious ointment upon the head, that ran down upon the beard, even Aaron's beard: that went down to the skirts of his garments." As refreshing as the oil, and as fragrant as the most delicious aromas to the senses, is true friendship to the soul. It heals our wounds, it soothes our sorrows. How refreshing was the friendship of Jethro to Moses, and of Jonathan to David, when in the wood "he strengthened his hands in God." "Every friend," says Richter, "is to the other a sun and a sun-flower also; he attracts and follows." And Sir Walter Scott expresses its beatific influence, in words of poetic beauty and tenderness—

"When true friends meet in adverse hour,
'Tis like a sunbeam through a shower;
A watery ray an instant seen,
The darkly closing clouds between."

What makes it so refreshing and beautiful is, its heartiness. "So doth the sweetness of a man's friend by hearty counsel." It is not the words, but the heart that is thrown into the words. Friendship is delicious and refreshing in proportion to its depth and thoroughness. Hearty friendship, to a man in sorrow, is like the angel that appeared to Hagar in the wilderness. It points the soul to the "well" of water for which it thirsts. Another feature of genuine friendship is *constancy*.—"Thine own friend, and thy father's friend, forsake not." Here is the sketch of a friend, the forsaking of whom would be criminal indeed. He is "thine own friend, and thy father's friend:" he has not only served thee, but also thy father, who is infirm in years, or, perhaps, sleeping beneath the clod. Both gratitude and filial loyalty should link thee with adamantine chains to him. Friendship, like certain wines, becomes valuable with years. The old family friend, with whom are associated the touching memories of many loved ones in the dust, his presence is more than sunshine to the soul, his voice richer than any music. Of such a friend, Solomon says, "Forsake him not." Do not neglect or undervalue his counsels; ever appreciate his offices of love. "Forsake him not," though you may rise in the world, and he go down to obscurity and want; be his strength in his declining life. Hold his hand in your warm grasp as it grows cold in death. The other feature of genuine friendship is *considerateness*.—"Neither go into thy brother's house in the day of thy calamity." "This certainly," says an excellent writer, "has the appearance of a very strange advice. Whither in the day of our calamity should we go, if not to the house of a brother? Where are we to expect a kind reception, and the comfort we require, if not there? But the proverb, like all others, must be understood generally, and applied in the circumstances and the sense obviously and mainly designed. The meaning seems to be, do not choose 'the day of thy calamity' for making thy visit, if thou hast not shown the same inclination to court and cultivate intimacy before, in the day of thy success and prosperity. This undoubtedly would look not like the impulse of affection, but of felt necessity or convenience and self interest. 'Aye, aye,' your brother will be naturally apt to say, I saw little of you before: you are fain to come to me *now*, when you feel your need of me, and fancy I may be of some service to you.' Or the meaning may be, let not sympathy be forced and extorted. In the day of thy calamity, if thy brother has the heart of a brother, and really feels for thee, he will come to thee, he will seek and find thee. If he does not, then do not press yourself upon his notice, as if you would constrain and oblige him to be kind. This may, and probably will, have the effect of disgusting and alienating him, rather than gaining his love. Love and sympathy must be unconstrained, as well as unbought. When they are either got by a bribe, or got by dint of urgent solicitation, they are alike heartless, and worthless. The reason is, ' for better is a neighbour that is near than a brother far off. The antithetical phrases 'at hand' and 'far off' have evident reference here not to locality, but to disposition. A friendly and kindly disposed neighbour, who bears no relation to us save that of neighbourhood, is greatly preferable to a brother,—to any near relative whatever that is cold, distant, and alienated."

Here is a HAPPY FATHERSHIP.—" My son, be wise and make my heart glad, that I may answer him that reproacheth me." "The joys of parents," says Lord Bacon, " are secret, and so are their griefs and fears; they cannot utter the one, they will not utter the other. Children sweeten labour, but they make misfortunes more bitter: they increase the cares of life, but they mitigate the remembrance of death." It is stated here that a truly virtuous and noble son gladdens the heart of the parent: and truly he does. Such a son is an ample compensation for all his care and sacrifices; is an inspiring object of his sympathies and love; is the stay and hope of his old age. It is stated also that such a son will prepare the parent to meet his enemies. "That I may answer him that reproacheth me." All men are liable to the reproaches of enemies. Those reproaches which are ever painful become more so as years steal from the spirit its buoyancy and from the body its vigour. What, in such circumstances, is a better solace and support than the presence of a noble son: one who, in the full vigour of manhood and the consciousness of rectitude, can stand up, refute, battle, and silence the parental foe? The best defence of a father's character, when impugned, is the character and conduct of wise and noble children. Happy the parent who is thus blest:

> " Thou art the only comfort of my age:
> Like an old tree, I stand amongst the storms:
> Thou art the only limb that I have left me,
> My dear green branch! and how I prize thee, child,
> Heaven only knows."—LEE

Proverbs 27:12, 14

Imprudence and Flattery

"A prudent man foreseeth the evil, *and* hideth himself; *but* the simple pass on, *and* are punished. . . . . He that blesseth his friend with a loud voice, rising early in the morning, it shall be counted a curse to him." *

HERE we have,—

IMPRUDENCE.—" A prudent man foreseeth the evil and hideth himself, but the simple pass on and are punished." "A prudent man foreseeth the evil and hideth himself." We are so constituted that certain evils grow out of certain conduct. He who does not deal rightly either with his body, intellect, or soul, brings, by an eternal law of nature, evils on himself. The prudent man has the necessary forecast. He sees this, he sees the effects in the cause, he sees the upas in the germ, and he so regulates his life as to avoid the evils. But mark the imprudent man.—" The simple pass on, and are punished." Blinded by lust, and the creatures of impulse, the thoughtless and the im

* The 13th verse is the same as the 16th verse of the 20th chapter.

prudent move on utterly regardless of the law of causation that governs human experience. They ignore the inevitable tendency of certain physical conduct to produce physical suffering, intellectual conduct to produce mental weakness and disease, spiritual conduct to produce soul confusion and misery. Thus, in every step they take, start up swarms of fiendish ills. Alas! how many imprudent men there are: men without foresight and preparation. Here is—

FLATTERY.—"He that blesseth his friend with a loud voice, rising early in the morning, it shall be counted a curse to him." Flattery is a species of conduct generally most pleasing, always most pernicious. The flattery referred to in the verse, is a loud vaunting; it is not something that comes out incidentally in eulogistic phrase, but it intrudes itself on all occasions; it is busy and demonstrative. How sadly prevalent is this ostentatious flattery: not merely in the social circle, but at civic banquets, in journalistic columns, in literary criticisms, in senatorial debates, and even in ecclesiastical gatherings! Solomon says this is a curse. It is a curse to its *author*. "It shall be counted a curse to him." He who practises sycophancy inflicts an incalculable injury on his own spiritual nature: he destroys his self-respect, he dishonours his conscience, he degrades his nature. The spirit of independency, the feeling of honest manhood, gives way to a crawling, creeping instinct. It generally implies the untruthful, the selfish, and the vain; in its nature it is a lie, in its aim it is either pelf, position, or praise—

"'Tis the death of virtue,
Who flatters is of all mankind the lowest,
Save him who courts the flattery."

More, it is a sneaking art used to cajole and soften fools. It is a curse to its *victim*. Perhaps this is what Solomon means when he says, "it shall be counted a curse to him," *i.e.*, the object of it. "Of all wild beasts," says Johnson, "preserve me from a flatterer." The following remarks of Sir Walter Raleigh are to the point. "Take care thou be not made a fool by flatterers, for even the wisest men are abused by these. Know therefore that flatterers are the worst kind of traitors, for they will strengthen thy imperfections, encourage thee in all evils, correct thee in nothing, but so shadow and paint all thy vices and follies, as thou shalt never, by their will, discern evil from good or vice from virtue; and because all men are apt to flatter themselves, to entertain the addition of other men's praises, is most perilous. Do not, therefore, praise thyself, except thou wilt be counted a vain-glorious fool; neither take delight in the praise of other men, except thou deserve it; and receive it from such as are worthy and honest, and withal warn thee of thy faults: for flatterers have never any virtue—they are ever base, creeping, cowardly persons. A flatterer is said to be a beast that biteth smiling. It is said by Isaiah in this manner, "My people, they that praise thee, seduce thee, and disorder the paths of thy feet:" and David desired God to cut out the tongue of a flatterer. But it is hard to know them from friends, they are so obsequious and full of protestations: for a wolf resembleth a dog, so doth a flatterer a friend. A flatterer is compared to an ape, who, because she cannot defend the house like a dog, labour as an ox, or bear burdens as a horse, doth therefore play tricks and provoke laughter."

Proverbs 27:17 *

The Soul, Its Bluntness and Its Whetstone

"Iron sharpeneth iron; so a man sharpeneth the countenance of his friend."

How frequently does Solomon refer to the contentious woman! In the two preceding verses, he points to her again. "A continual dropping in a very rainy day and a contentious woman are alike. Whosoever hideth her hideth wind, and the ointment of his right hand which

* Verses 15 and 16 have been noticed in Readings on chaps. xix. 13, xxi. 9.

bewrayeth itself." Ah, the droppings of her spirit are worse than rain-drops, that only wet the skin and chill perhaps the blood; they fall on the heart, and they inflame the brain. You cannot subdue it. "Whoso hideth her hideth the wind." Who can hide the wind, or who, by pressing the ointment in his hand, can conceal it? Its very fragrance will betray its presence. The following is a new, truthful, and poetic rendering of the verses:

> "A continual dropping in a very rainy day
> And a quarrelsome wife are alike:
> He who would restrain her,
> As well might restrain the wind,
> Or conceal the oil which is upon his right hand."

But as we have noticed this subject before, we must confine our remarks to the proverb before us, which includes two things—

The soul's BLUNTNESS.—"Iron sharpeneth iron: so a man sharpeneth the countenance of his friend." As all our implements of steel, domestic, agricultural, artistic, or military, become blunt by use, so the soul gets sadly blunted in the wear and tear of this life. How often do we find the edge taken from our souls, so that they become almost unfit for service! *Corporeal affliction* sometimes blunts the soul. The nerves are shaken, the brain has lost its vigour, and the intellect becomes obtuse; there comes a film over its eyes. *Worldly disappointment* sometimes blunts the soul. Shattered plans, broken purposes, blasted hopes, often so stun and benumb us that our faculties lose their spring and activity. *Social bereavement* sometimes blunts the soul. Our loved ones leave us either by death, or, what is worse, by unfaithfulness; the heart sinks in sadness, and the atmosphere of the soul grows sunless and depressing. The soul is blunted; it cannot cut its way through the path of duty. The proverb includes—

The soul's WHETSTONE.—"Iron sharpeneth iron, so a man sharpeneth the countenance of his friend." That is, as iron is sharpened, "so a man sharpeneth the countenance of his friend." Learn that—As you can only sharpen iron by iron, you can *only sharpen souls by souls*. Neither dead matter, however majestic in aspect or thunderous in melody, nor irrational life, however graceful in form or mighty in force, can sharpen a blunted soul. Mind alone can quicken mind; it is in all cases the Spirit that quickeneth. Although each mind is a unit, a distinct personality, it can only be quickened and developed by the action of other minds. Iron must sharpen iron, soul must sharpen soul; the action of God's soul sharpens the soul of the universe. *The truly sharpening soul is the soul inspired by love.* "The countenance of his friend." The countenance is the revealer of the soul: the quivering lip, the sparkling eye, the beaming brow; through these the soul speaks volumes of thought and emotion in a moment. Who has not often felt the truth of this? Who, when his own soul has been jaded, blunted, saddened, has not sprung into agility and light at the beamings of a friendly countenance? It is the Divine *love* in the spirit that quickens. Love is the sharpening property of souls. The strongest soul has found the exhilarating influence of a friendly countenance. Paul says, "We were troubled on every side; without were fightings, within were fears, nevertheless God, that comforteth those who are cast down, comforted us by the coming of Titus."

Friendly intercourse is the action of similar natures on each other for mutual advantage. Few men have described true friendship with more truthfulness and poetic beauty than Dryden, in the following words:

> "I had a friend that loved me.
> I was his soul : he lived not but in me :
> We were so closed within each other's breast,
> The rivets were not found that joined us first,
> That do not reach us yet : we were so mix'd,
> As meeting streams ; but to ourselves were lost :
> We were one mass : we could not give or take
> But from the same ; for he was I. Then
> Return, my better half, and give me all myself,
> For thou art all.
> If I have any joy when thou art absent,
> I grudge it to myself: methinks I rob
> Thee of thy part."

Proverbs 27:18

Man Honored in Service

"Whoso keepeth the fig tree shall eat the fruit thereof: so he that waiteth on his master shall be honoured."

SERVICE is the order of the universe. Everything in the *material* creation, both inorganic and organic, is made to serve; no atom, element, blade, insect, is made for itself; it has a work to perform, a service to render. It is so in the *spiritual* domain. No mind is made for itself,—all souls are made for service. Man is made to serve. Wealth, social elevations, political power, instead of raising him above the obligation of service add urgency to the duty. No man is too low for service, no man too high. He who is the greatest shall be the servant of all. The proverb suggests two remarks—

Honour comes to man in FAITHFUL SERVICE.—"He that waiteth on his master shall be honoured." "He that waiteth" faithfully on a *human* master shall be honoured. His master may be a humble householder, and his work that of a menial drudge. Yet if his service is faithfully rendered, honour will come to him in that little circle; it will come in approving smiles, in commendatory words, if not in an augmentation of stipend. Or his master may be a political constituency, and his work may be to represent the interest of a large number of his countrymen in Parliament. Yet if he is faithful to his promises at the hustings, and honest in the discharge of his public duties, honour will come to him, not only in the loud applause, but in the renewal of the trust and confidence of the burgesses. Or his master may be a whole kingdom; for kings are servants, and their duties are numerous, heavy, and continual. Yet if they discharge them faithfully, the whole nation will honour them with loyalty and love. "He that waiteth" faithfully on the *Divine* Master shall be honoured. Indeed such is the connexion between the service we have to render to God and to man, that both must be served properly in order for either to be served effectively. We cannot serve the human master faithfully unless we serve the Divine, and we are sure to serve the Divine if we serve the human. "If any man serve me," says Christ, "him will my Father honour." He will proclaim his honour in the open ear of the universe. "Well done, good and faithful servant."

Honour comes to a man NATURALLY in faithful service. —" Whoso keepeth the fig tree shall eat the fruit thereof." The idea is, that just as by the law of nature, the fig-tree yields fruit to the man who properly cultivates it, so will honour, both human and Divine, come to the man whose life is a faithful service. The conscience of all men is bound by its constitution to render honour to all *faithful* servants. And, with reverence be it spoken, the conscience of God binds Him to do the same. True honour is not something put upon a man, as a crown or a robe, something which he can live and breathe without, distinct from his being. It is something that grows out of a noble life, and cannot be taken from him. As the blossom grows out of the tree, honour grows out of a genuine life : but unlike the blossom of a tree which may wither, die, and leave the tree unhurt, it is something inseparable. All the emperors of the world are unable to dignify a man. Though they confer on him all the titles at their disposal, they will not make him a whit the more honourable. No man can be carried up the hill of greatness ; he must climb the slopes inch by inch himself if he would reach the apex. Moral crowns, the only crowns worth having, cannot be given, they must be won.

Proverbs 27:19

The Uniformity and Reciprocity of Souls

"As in water face *answereth* to face, so the heart of man to man."

THE idea of these words is very obvious: the same face with which you look into a crystal lake will look back upon you by reflection; the exact form, features, and expression will be mirrored to your view. Solomon may mean to convey one of two truths by this proverb; either uniformity, or reciprocity of soul. It may be regarded as expressing both—

UNIFORMITY of soul.—There is as great an agreement between the heart of one man and that of another as there is between the face and the reflection in the water. Whatever may be the superficial mental peculiarities of men, and they are confessedly numerous, arising often from climate and culture, there are broad underlying and unobliterable features in which they all agree. We may specify a few as examples—There is *the sentiment of worship*. In all human minds, the world over and the ages through, there is found, with more or less distinctness and force, the instinct of worship. This instinct has been widely and lamentably perverted, it is true; it has created false gods, and filled the world with superstition. But there it is, demonstrating its existence and its power, as well in the spurious as in the genuine. There is *a sense of obligation*. This is nearly akin to the sentiment of worship: it grows out of it, or perhaps is a modification of it. It is conscience; and what is conscience but the feeling of duty? Has there ever been found a rational man who has not had within him the feeling that he owed certain duties to the Supreme Power that is over him? Conscience does not give us the right standard of duty, that comes to man from an outward revelation, but it does give the feeling. Conscience is like a clock, in perpetual motion, but it always strikes the wrong hour of duty, until the Divine Horolographer puts it right. There is *consciousness of wrong*. In all souls there seems to be a feeling that the character is not what it ought to be, that the Great Master has been offended, and that punishment must come sooner or later. Hence the enormous sacrifices made throughout the world in order to put men right with themselves and with God. Most men have had at times the feeling of St. Paul when he said, "O wretched man that I am! who shall deliver me from the body of this death?" The cry of the world is, " Wherewithal shall I come before the Lord? how shall I bow before the Most High?" There is *forbodement of coming retribution*.—" Traverse," says Hamilton, " the earth, enter the gorgeous cities of idolatry, or accept the hospitality of its wandering tribes; go where you will, where worship is most fantastic, and superstition most gross, and you will find in man a 'fearful looking for of judgment.' The mythology of Nemesis may vary, their Elysium and Tartarus may be differently depicted, the Metempsychosis may be the passage of bliss and woe, still the fact is only confirmed by the diversity of the forms in which it is presented."

This uniformity of moral heart may be looked upon in two aspects, as contributing an argument in favour of the unity of the human race. This psychological argument, we cannot but think, is more conclusive than either the philological or the physiological:* and also as contributing an argument in favour of the universal spread of the Gospel. The Gospel appeals to those broad features of the soul which are common to all. It reveals the true God to the sentiment of worship, the Eternal Law to the sense of obligation, the grand redemption to the consciousness of wrong, the day of judgment to the forebodement of retribution. The soul of humanity answers to the Gospel, and consequently the Gospel must make way. The proverb may be regarded as expressing—

RECIPROCITY of soul.—" As in water face answereth to face, so the heart of man to man." It may mean this, that

* See "Christ and other Masters." By Charles Hardwicke, M.A.

just as the water will give back to you the exact expression which you gave to it, the frown or the smile, the hideous or the pleasing, so human hearts will treat you as you treat them. "With what measure you mete, it shall be meted to you again." This is true, manifestly true,—kindness begets kindness, anger anger, justice justice, fraud fraud, the world through. As a rule, if you look kindly at a man he will look kindly at you, if you are tender he will be tender with you, if you thunder he will thunder at you. As the rocks reverberate thunder, hearts echo hearts; they give back what they receive. This fact exposes the absurdity of attempting to subdue men by violence. "He that taketh the sword shall perish by the sword." You may as well endeavour to shiver the rocks by argument as to create peace by war. This fact reveals the philosophy of Christianity as a means of subduing the world to love. Christianity is a system of tenderest compassion and of mightiest love. "No cord or cable can draw so forcibly or bind so fast as love can do with a single thread." "The power of love," says Longfellow, "in all ages creates angels."

Proverbs 27:20

The Insatiability of Man's Inquiring Faculty

"Hell and destruction are never full; so the eyes of man are never satisfied."

"HELL," or Sheol, here means the place of the dead—the grave; and "destruction" the agent that strikes men down, and conveys them to the grave. This hell, and this destructive force "are never full." They have never done their work, they are never satisfied; the grave, which has received all the generations that have been, is ravenously yawning still; and destruction, whose sword has slain its millions, stands with outstretched arm ready to strike down as many more. Now the proverb says that as insatiable as "hell and destruction" are the eyes of men—that is, their inquisitiveness. Man's desire for knowledge is never satisfied, and never can be; every accession of intelligence whets the appetite into a keener edge, intensifies its cravings. "The eyes of man are never satisfied." "Thou hast made us for Thyself," says Augustine, "and our hearts can have no rest until they rest in Thee." This insatiability of man's inquiring faculty suggests—

THE INFINITUDE OF TRUTH.—Wherever in any creature there is a strong natural desire, we may conclude, from the benevolence of the Creator Who planted the desire, that there is an adequate provision somewhere. As man has this ever craving desire for knowledge, we are bound to infer the infinitude of truth. How much is to be known! The known to the most intelligent creature in the universe is as nothing to the knowable. Our greatest sciences are but a few small blades in a boundless landscape, where grow not only the choicest flowers, but also the most majestic forests. At best we can learn but the alphabet of truth here: the great volumes fill the universe. This insatiability of man's inquiring faculty suggests—

THE GREATNESS OF THE SOUL.—How great is man! Nothing but the infinite can satisfy him: he may comprehend the universe, and yet be empty: he wants God Himself, and never will he be satisfied until he wakes up in His image.

> "Were men to live coeval with the sun,
> The patriarch pupil would be learning still,
> And dying, leave his lesson half unlearnt."
> DR. YOUNG

"It doth not yet appear what we shall be." This insatiability of man's inquiring faculty suggests—

THE OFFICE OF THE TEACHER.—What is the office of the true Teacher? To direct the soul to the satisfying supplies. And where are they? Not on this earth. His work is to stand upon the banks of the eternal river of truth, and cry, "Ho! every one that thirsteth, come ye to the waters, and ye that have no money, come, buy wine and milk without price."

> " Should I this spacious earth possess,
> And all the spreading skies,
> They never could my thirst appease,
> Or yield me full supplies.
>
> " Without my God, with all this store,
> I should be wretched still :
> With thirst insatiate crave for more,
> My empty mind to fill.
>
> " But when my soul's of God possessed,
> What can I wish for more ?
> Here let me ever fix my rest,
> And give all wandering o'er !"

Proverbs 27:21

Popularity, the Most Trying Test of Character

"*As* the fining pot for silver, and the furnace for gold ; so *is* a man to his praise."

MEN, in ancient times as well as in modern, submitted precious metals, such as silver and gold, to the test of the fire. Fire revealed their impurity, and made them appear in their true character. What fire is to these metals, Solomon says, popularity or applause is to man's character; it tests him. " As the fining pot for silver and the furnace for gold, so is a man to his praise."

Popularity reveals the VANITY OF THE PROUD MAN.—He who by some brilliant faculty, or dexterous deed, or propitious circumstance, has won the applause of the multitude, and become for a time one of the popular idols of the day, has his vanity conspicuously revealed. He is puffed up. His soul is of that type which vaunteth itself. He shows his vanity in his fashionable costume, in his strutting gait, in his haughty looks, and in his great swelling words.

How did Absalom appear in the blaze of popularity? How did Herod appear? Amidst the shouts of his flatterers he assumed to be a god. So it is ever: a sadder sight can scarcely be witnessed than empty-minded men standing on a pedestal, feeding on the hozannas of a brainless crowd.

Popularity reveals the HUMILITY OF A TRUE MAN.—A true man shrinks from popular applause and feels humbled amidst its shouts. Dr. Payson, a careful self-observer, mentions among his trials "well-meant but injudicious commendations." "Every one here," he writes to his mother, "whether friends or enemies, are conspiring to ruin me. Satan and my own heart of course will lend a hand, and if you join too, I fear all the cold water which Christ can throw upon my pride will not prevent it from breaking out in a destructive flame. As certainly as anybody flatters and caresses me, my Father has to scourge me for it, and an unspeakable mercy it is that He condescends to do it." Great men have always felt more or less contempt for vulgar popularity. "The people," says Milton, "a miscellaneous rabble, extol things vulgar, not worth praise: they praise and they admire they know not what." And Shakespeare says:

> "I love the people,
> But do not like to stage me to their eyes;
> Though it do well, I do not relish well
> Their loud applause, and *Aves* vehement,
> Nor do I think the man of safe discretion
> That does affect it."

Popularity is indeed to character as the "fining pot for silver and the furnace for gold." Few things in life show us the stuff of which men are made more than this. Little men court this fire, but cannot stand it. Corks float to the surface and dance on the popular wave, where oak rests quietly in the sands out of sight. "Small men," says Garibaldi, "always rush to the surface."

Proverbs 27:22

The Moral Obstincay of Sin

"Though thou shouldest bray a fool in a mortar among wheat with a pestle, *yet* will not his foolishness depart from him."

"In Japan and China," says a modern author, "rice is beaten in a tub, with a pestle having a heavy head-piece in order to increase its weight and force. The grain is pounded with a view of clearing away those extraneous matters which would render the rice unwholesome for food. The workman exerts every sinew to the utmost in wielding the pestle. In some cases it is moved by the foot." Dr. Thomson, when near Sidon, observed many people braying or pounding wheat with a pestle in a mortar, and says:—"Every family has one of these large stone mortars, and you may hear the sound of the braying at all hours as you walk in the streets of the city." Reference is made to this in the verse. The process of driving out the chaff and refuse from the grain is attended with success: but with some men, however severe may be the efforts you employ to drive out the folly that is in them, your labour is in vain. There is no correction that will cure them. Repeated reproofs accomplish nothing. Their folly cleaves to them still. They are so incorrigibly bad that, like Ahaz, they trespass yet more.

There are *incorrigible* sinners; men whose natural obstinacy of disposition has been strengthened by habits of depravity. The antediluvians were of this class; so was Pharaoh, so was Ahaz, so was Ephraim, who was joined to idols and who was given up; so were the Jews in the time of Christ, who went forth with a mulish stubbornness to fill up the measures of their iniquity. "There is something," says Johnson, "in obstinacy which differs from every other passion. Whenever it fails, it never recovers, but either breaks like iron, or crumbles sulkily away like a fractured arch. Most other passions have their periods of fatigue and rest, their sufferings and their cure, but obstinacy has no resource, and the first wound is mortal." "An obstinate man," says Pope, "does not hold opinions, they hold him." "Stiff in opinion," says Dryden, "always in the wrong." The fact that there are such sinners is—

A WARNING TO ALL.—There is a danger of every sinner passing into the incorrigible state. Whilst it is true that some men have natural temperaments more obstinate than others, the tendency of sin, in all cases, is to make men stubborn and foolhardy. The power of sinful habits renders their natures so stiff and rigid that sooner would the Ethiopian change his skin than they would change their beliefs and plans. The figure in the proverb is not too strong to express their incorrigibility. In the mortar they brayed off the chaff from the wheat and got at the true grain; but wickedness, in the heart of the incorrigible, is not the husk, it is the *grain* itself; it cannot be reached without pounding it to pieces. The day of probation, it is to be feared, terminates with many before the day of death. God says to them, "My spirit shall no longer strive with you; you are joined to idols, I shall let you alone." "The things that belong to your peace are hid from your eyes." The fact is—

A GUIDE TO TEACHERS.—On such characters it is useless to waste any time, they are the reprobate. "Speak not in the ears of a fool, for he will despise the wisdom of thy mouth." "Give not that which is holy to the dogs, neither cast you your pearls before swine." The "dogs" represent men of a sour, malignant, and snarlish spirit, who, instead of listening to your counsels, will bark at you with the rage of a virulent depravity. The "swine" represent men of the grossest materialism immersed in sensuality, whose hearts are made fat; they are moral swine. All your arguments will fall on them as flakes of snow on the flinty rock—they will make no impression. "Then Paul and Barnabas waxed bold, and said, It was necessary that the word of God should first have been spoken to you: but, seeing ye put it from you, and judge yourselves unworthy of everlasting life, lo, we turn to the Gentiles." What do such passages as these mean but this, that there are incorrigible sinners, and on them you are not to waste your time and energy? Such characters are to be found, undoubtedly, within the circle of every man's observation. Who does not know of some character whom he feels it would be foolish, if not perilous, to counsel about religion? There is not only a time for the good to speak, but a *class* to speak to. Jesus Himself would not speak to some, not even in answer to their appeals. Do not use the "pestle" of your argument and rhetoric in the "mortar" of your ministry; their wickedness is ingrained, it is not *husk*, it is *heart*. On then—

> " You may as well
> Forbid the sea for to obey the moon,
> As, by oath remove, or counsel shake
> The fabric of his folly."—SHAKESPEARE

Proverbs 27:23-27

A Picture of Life, Rural and General

"Be thou diligent to know the state of thy flocks, *and* look well to thy herds. For riches *are* not for ever: and doth the crown *endure* to every generation? The hay appeareth, and the tender grass sheweth itself, and herbs of the mountains are gathered. The lambs *are* for thy clothing, and the goats *are* the price of the field. And *thou shalt have* goats' milk enough for thy food, for the food of thy household, and *for* the maintenance for thy maidens."

HERE is a picture of RURAL life.—Here we read of flocks and herds, of hay and tender grass, herbs of the mountains, lambs and goats. It is a picture of life in such a land as Palestine in the days of Solomon, where pastures and flocks constituted the wealth of the people, and herding and husbandry their chief occupations. It indicates—the beautiful variety *in the scenery* of rural life. "The hay appeareth, and the tender grass sheweth itself, and herbs of the mountains are gathered." How charming is the green and glittering freshness of a dewy and summer morning; when every blade of grass is decked with diamonds, sparkling in the light of the rising sun: when the mower plies his task, and the fragrance of the new-mown hay scents the air; and the corn-fields wave in promise of the coming autumn, and the hills are clothed with their appropriate trees, and shrubs, and herbage! How preferable such a scene to the dirty smoke and manifold pollutions of the crowded city! Custom and habit, it is true, and diverse association of ideas, both form and change men's tastes. But surely nature is on the side of the country :—" God made the country, and man made the town." It indicates also the beautiful *simplicity of the provisions* of rural life. All that men want here below is food and raiment, and this the country gives in the simplest and, at the same time, most efficient way. "Herbs from the mountains, milk from the goats, and fleece from the lambs." How different from the elaborate and artificial provisions which are found in civic life! Human ingenuity is taxed to the utmost, in order to produce food that shall afford the highest gratification to the gastric faculty, and clothing which shall feed the vanity of the wearer, and attract the admiration of the spectators. Rural life for me! Beautiful in its scenery, simple in its provisions, and innocent, and healthful in the occupation of its inhabitants. Here is, moreover—

A picture of GENERAL life.—The sketch of nature here suggests several things concerning the provisions for life in general. They are manifold. Here are various vegetable productions. "Hay" and "grass," and "herbs of the mountains;" and here are various animal productions, "goats" and "lambs." How manifold are God's provisions for man in this world! They are equal to his need. Man only wants food and raiment, and here are the supplies, the clothing and the food. They are entrusted to his keeping, "Be thou diligent in keeping thy flocks, and look well to thy herds." Man is a steward, he has to use them according to the directions of his Master. They are transient. "For riches are not for ever: and doth the crown endure to every generation?" What we have we can only inherit for a short time.

Whether in rural or civic life, let us appreciate, and rightfully employ, the provisions which our merciful Maker has prepared for our needs: let us be diligent in the exercise of our stewardship, take care of our flocks, and rightly cultivate our fields ; and let us do all this religiously, as in the presence and for the honour of our God. Though many of us have been driven long ago from the scenes of rural life, their memory within us is yet green, and full of delicious aroma. We can say with the poet—

> "Not all the sights your boasted garden yields
> Are half so lovely as my father's fields,
> Where large increase has bless'd the fruitful plain,
> And we, with joy, behold the swelling grain,
> Whose heavy ears, towards the earth inclined,
> Wave, nod, and tremble to the whisking wind."

But, though we have left the sunny fields and silent groves of the country for the smoke and din of civic life, Mercy has followed us with its provisions. Heaven help us to use them with faithful diligence and reverential responsibility!

Proverbs 28:1

Conscience

"The wicked flee when no man pursueth: but the righteous are bold as a lion."

MEN differ in their definitions of *conscience*, but agree in the facts and functions of its existence: it is not an attribute of the mind, but its moral substance: it is not a limb of the soul, but the heart of the man: it is the moral I. It is that without which the human creature would cease to be a man: it is what Coleridge calls "the pulse of reason." "Conscience," says Trench, "is a solemn word, if there be such in the world. Now there is not one of us whose Latin will not bring him so far as to tell him that this word is from *con* and *scire*. But what does that *con* intend? Conscience is not merely that which I know, but that which I know with some one else; for this prefix cannot, as I think, be esteemed superfluous or taken to imply merely that which I know with or to myself. That other knower whom the word implies is God; His law making itself known and felt in the heart; and the work of conscience is the bringing of each of our acts and thoughts as a lesser to be tried and measured by this as a greater; the word growing out of and declaring that awful duplicity of our moral being, which arises from the presence of God in the soul—our thoughts by the standard which that presence supplies, and as the result of a comparison with it, 'accusing or excusing one another.'" Notice—

THE TIMIDITY OF A GUILTY CONSCIENCE.—" The wicked fleeth when no man pursueth." No man pursued Adam in lovely Eden, yet he fled. "I heard thy voice in the garden, and was afraid." No man pursued Cain when the world was in the freshness and beauty of youth; yet he fled. The murderer, whose reason well assures him that no man can ever discover him as the author of the dreadful deed, flees from the scene with the utmost rapidity: the rustling of a leaf, the creaking of a branch, the chirping of a bird, sound in his ear as the tread of the avenger. *From what* does a man under a sense of guilt flee? Not from man: "no man pursueth." From the visionary creation of his own conscience. The pursuer is a mere phantom, still not the less real, not the less near, not the less terrific on this account. He cannot escape it; no rapid bounds over seas or continents would separate him from it; it is not at his heels, it is in his heart. He hears the visionary pursuer in every sound; he feels his warm breath in the atmosphere around him; he expects his avenging clutch every instant.

"Suspicion always haunts the guilty mind."
"The thief doth fear each bush an officer."
SHAKESPEARE

Whither can he flee from its presence? Ah, whither, indeed? *Why* does a man under a sense of guilt flee? This is the profoundest question in the nature of man. Why should sin awaken fear where no man is? Between the conscience and the Judge of the universe there is an electric bond, binding them indissolubly together. Every sin acts upon that mystic wire, and sends the shock of judgment into the guilty soul. *Whither* does a man under a sense of guilt flee? Sometimes to the Lamb of God; then

all is safe and right. But oftener, alas, to carnal revelry and debauch, where all is wrong and peril. Notice—
THE HEROISM OF A RIGHTEOUS CONSCIENCE.—"The righteous are bold as a lion." A man whose conscience is with him can dare the universe. " Though hosts shall encamp against me, yet will I not fear." There are many noble instances of this in sacred history. How heroically Caleb and Joshua stood against the rebellion of their countrymen; how bravely Elijah dared the wrath of Ahab; with what undaunted courage did Nehemiah discharge his perilous work! "Should such a man as I flee?" With what an invincible defiance did the three Hebrew youths oppose Nebuchadnezzar and enter the fiery furnace! The boldness of the Apostles in their evangelic labours struck astonishment into the men of their age: " They are bold as a lion," the boldest of all animals. "This noble animal," says Paxton, " is the most perfect model of boldness and courage. He never flies from the hunters, nor is frightened by their onset. If their numbers force him to yield, he retires slowly, step by step, frequently turning upon his pursuers. He has been known to attack a whole caravan, and when obliged to retire, he always retires fighting, and with his face to the enemy." Rectitude is the heart of true moral courage; where this is not, there may be brutal daring, but no true heroism.

Proverbs 28:2-5

A Threefold Glimpse of Life

"For the transgression of a land, many *are* the princes thereof: but by a man of understanding *and* knowledge the state *thereof* shall be prolonged. A poor man that oppresseth the poor *is like* a sweeping rain that leaveth no food. They that forsake the law praise the wicked: but such as keep the law contend with them. Evil men understand not judgment: but they that seek the LORD understand all *things*."

HERE we have three sides of life.

We have a glimpse of POLITICAL life.—" For the transgression of a land many are the princes thereof." These verses enable us to see—The influence of *wickedness* upon the politics of a country. Transgression makes many princes. Wickedness has ever split up kingdoms into political factions, and created rival interests. It is said by the greatest of all teachers that a "kingdom divided against itself cannot stand," and the tendency of wickedness is disruption. The higher the morality of a nation, the more united the people in their loyalty and obedience to their ruling head. As knowledge and virtue extend through the world, the smaller states and kingdoms will, by moral influence, be absorbed in one kingdom, and thus on until "the kingdoms of this world shall become the kingdom of our God and of His Christ." A wicked man can never be a good citizen. What is bad in morality is injurious in politics. The verses enable us to see—The influence of *moral excellence* upon the politics of a country. "By a man of understanding and knowledge, the state thereof shall be prolonged." The good men in a kingdom counteract the tendency to anarchy and disruption. "Righteousness exalteth a nation." The guarantee of a nation's progress and stability is to be found, not in the invincibility of its armies, not in the vastness of its commerce, not in the genius, the learning, or the wealth of its citizens, but in the sound morality and true religious sentiment of the people. "It seems to me," says Carlyle, "a great truth that human things cannot stand on selfishness, mechanical utilities, economies, and law courts; that if there be not a religious element in the relations of men, such relations are miserable, and doomed to ruin." Here we have—

A glimpse of SOCIAL life.—"A poor man that oppresseth the poor is like a sweeping rain which leaveth no food." Here is *the oppression of the poor by the poor*. The oppression of the poor by any class is a great evil. The existence of an indigent class in society is not an accident; it is a Divine ordination; "the poor shall not cease out of the land;" their existence is intended to awaken the compassion, and afford scope for the practical benevolence of the classes above. Their oppression, therefore, is an outrage on the Divine order of things, involves a cowardice the most contemptible, and a cruelty the most revolting. But when this oppression is enacted by the *poor*, its evil seems to be intensified. It is not what might have been expected. One would naturally suppose that the poor would ever be disposed to enter into the sorrows of the poor, and give them a helping hand. But the poor to whom, perhaps, Solomon refers, are those whom fortune has put into power, and who are destitute of the means of supporting the dignity of their position, and therefore have recourse to most unrighteous exactions. A poor king has often been found in the history of the world to lay heavy burdens upon the shoulders of the poor. Or, perhaps, he means the men who have risen from poverty into political authority. It is a sad fact that such have frequently become the most haughty, heartless, and oppressive towards the class from which they have risen. "It is in a matter of power," says Bishop Sanderson, "as it is in matter of learning. They that have but a smattering of scholarship, you will ever observe to be the forwardest to make ostentation of those few ends they have; because they fear there would be little notice taken of their learning if they should not now show it when they can. It is even so in this case. Men of base spirit and condition, when they have gotten the advantage of a little power, conceive that the world would not know what goodly men they are if they should not do some act or other to show forth their power to the world; and then their minds being too narrow to comprehend any generous way whereby to do it, they cannot frame to do any other way than by trampling upon those that are below them; and that they do beyond all reason and without all mercy." The oppression of such men is here represented as a mighty deluge sweeping all before them; their rapacity is unbounded. *Here is the praising of the wicked by the wicked.* "They that forsake the law praise the wicked." The world loveth its own; the sinner countenances his brother in sin. There are many reasons why the wicked praise the wicked. It gratifies their vanity.

By praising those of the same character they virtually praise themselves, and get the praised ones to flatter them in return. It promotes their self-interest; thus they ingratiate themselves into the favour of men, and get their patronage and support. Tertullus, the orator, whom the Jews hired to criminate Paul, was a type of this miserable class. "Seeing that by thee we enjoy great quietness," said he, " and that very worthy deeds are done to this nation by thy providence; we accept it always and in all places, most noble Felix." What a wretched state of society is this! the wicked praising the wicked—yet it is common. Here in England, and in this late hour of the world's history, we are deluged with this in every department of life. Society has now, as ever, its slimy limpets, its sucking parasites, and its fawning flatterers. Here is *the opposing of the wicked by the good.*—" But such as keep the law contend with them." This is one of the brightest features in society. There have been men in all ages who have had the manly honesty to stand up against the hollowness and the corruptions of their age. Noah, the prophets, Christ and His apostles, and in later ages the martyrs and confessors have done this. Here we have—

A glimpse of RELIGIOUS life.—" Evil men understand not judgment: but they that seek the Lord understand all things." Hence we learn that *depravity blinds the moral judgment.* " Evil men understand not judgment." Men under the influence of sin have their understanding darkened, their judgment is blinded. Their intellect may see secular truths and political expediencies, but great moral principles are hidden from them. The atmosphere of depravity around the heart is so dense that the stars of spiritual truth cannot break through it. "Wickedness," says Bishop Taylor, "corrupts a man's reasonings, gives him false principles, and evil measuring of things." A man may as truly read the letter of right without eyes, as appreciate its spirit without goodness. Another thing taught here is—that *piety is a guarantee of knowledge.* "They that seek the Lord understand all things." This agrees with many utterances of Scripture, such as the following:—" If any man will do his will he shall know of the doctrine, whether it be of God or whether I speak of myself." "The meek will He guide in judgment, and the meek will He teach His way." "Ye have an unction from the Holy One, and ye know all things. The anointing which ye have received of him abideth in you, and you need not that any man teach you: but as the same anointing teacheth you of all things, and is truth and is no lie, and even as it hath taught you, ye shall abide in him."

Proverbs 28:7-9

Life in the Home, the Market and the Sanctuary

"Whoso keepeth the law *is* a wise son: but he that is a companion of riotous *men* shameth his father. He that by usury and unjust gain increaseth his substance, he shall gather it for him that will pity the poor. He that turneth away his ear from hearing the law, even his prayer *shall be* abomination." *

LIFE in the HOME.—"Whoso keepeth the law is a wise son, but he that is a companion of riotous men shameth his father." "*The* law,"—what law? Not, of course, the law of the country, or of custom, but the moral law of God, the law of eternal right. He that keepeth this law "is a wise son." Obedience to Heaven is true wisdom, there is no other wisdom. The family with such a son as this is a blessed family, a happiness to the parents, a sunshine to all. But here is another side of the family picture. "But he that is a companion of riotous men shameth his father." The margin has it—"He that feedeth gluttons." The idea is, that the carousing, self-indulgent, extravagant spendthrift, "shameth" his father. He dishonoureth him.

How many such sons abound in England in this age! The "young men of the period" are fast, intemperate, in-

---

* The subject of verse 6 is noticed in Reading on chap. xix. 1.

tolerable snobs. To a true parent nothing is more grievous to the heart, nothing more crushing to the spirit, than the senseless conduct of such miserable progeny. It is a sad fact that many parents beget offspring that run into swine or grow into devils. Here we have—

Life in the MARKET.—"He that by usury and unjust gain increaseth his substance, he shall gather it for him that will pity the poor."

Observe—wealth obtained by improper means. "By usury," which may be regarded as standing for all overreaching and fraudulent efforts to get gain. Fraud is the chief factor of fortunes. As a rule, the less conscience a man has, other things being equal, the more cash he will accumulate. There are "tricks of trade" which are the ladders to commercial eminence.

Observe also, wealth rightly distributed by Providence. "He shall gather it for him that will pity the poor." The idea is, that the wealth gotten by dishonesty will ultimately fall into the hands of some one who will pity the poor, and distribute it. The selfish man works for himself, and ignores the universe. Providence works for humanity, and will one day distribute fortunes gained by unrighteousness amongst the poor. The greatest fortune ever built up by a mercenary man is only a castle of ice: it may glisten beautifully to his eye, and stand for a while on his own grounds, in a certain temperature of the atmosphere, but Providence in its majestic course, will appear one day as the hot sun on his horizon, melt it with his beams, and make it run into a thousand rivers, to bless those who are living in the vales of indigence and want. "I know that the Lord will maintain the cause of the afflicted, and the right of the poor." Here we have—

Life in the SANCTUARY.—"He that turneth away his ear from hearing the law, even his prayer shall be abomination." Three features are observable in this picture. *Immorality.*—You can scarcely describe an immoral man more strikingly and correctly than as representing him turning away his ear from the law—practically disregarding moral law. One who acts from his own impulses, social influences and customs, but habitually neglects law, is an immoral man. Another point in the character before us is *immorality praying.* " Even his prayer." Many an immoral man is devout after his fashion. There is often found in men, who outrage every principle of morality, a certain sentiment of devotion, so that they pray and sing. Rogues often bend their knees at altars, attend prayer-meetings and join in litanies. And moreover we have immorality praying *insulting the Almighty.* " His prayer shall be abomination."

Israel of old presented a multitude of sacrifices as a price for the neglect of practical morality, but God pronounced them vain oblations, and their incense as abomination. " Ye hypocrites, well did Esaias prophecy of you, saying—This people draweth nigh unto me with their mouth, and honoureth me with their lips, but their heart is far from me."

Let us attend to our families; endeavour to keep the law, that they may be wise. Let us in the market be honest and generous in our transactions, knowing that the products of unrighteousness will be wrested from our grasp. Let us, in our devotions at the altar, see that our lives are in harmony with the law; for if we regard iniquity in our heart, the Lord will not hear us.

Proverbs 28:10

Opposite Characters and Opposite Destinies

"Whoso causeth the righteous to go astray in an evil way, he shall fall himself into his own pit; but the upright shall have good *things* in possession."

HERE are—

Opposite CHARACTERS—The perverse and upright. Notice the *perverse.* Who are the perverse? " Whoso causeth the righteous to go astray in an evil way." Here is a sad possibility. What is the possibility?

That the righteous should "go astray." This possibility is implied in moral responsibility. Were it impossible for the righteous to go astray, they would be mere machines, not moral agents; there would be no virtue in their obedience, no guilt in their transgression. When you say that a being is moral, you say that he is free to stand or fall, free to pursue the course of life in which he is placed, or to step into another. Moral beings are not like planets, bound ever to roll in the orbits in which they were first placed, and move with the same speed and regularity; they can bound into another, and move at what rate they please. This possibility is demonstrated in facts. Righteous *angels* have fallen. "Angels kept not their first estate." Righteous *men* have fallen. Adam, Lot, David, Peter. This possibility is assumed in the appeals of Scripture. All the warnings against apostasy, all the encouragements to perseverance, imply it. "Let him that thinketh he standeth take heed lest he fall." Again here is an infernal attempt. The attempt is to "cause the righteous to go astray." Wicked men are constantly making the attempt in a thousand different ways. By suggesting doubts as to the existence of God, the immortality of the soul and the truth of the Bible, and by insidious but potent appeals to those elements of depravity, which linger to a greater or less degree in the souls of even the best men to the end of life. Society abounds with tempters, who ply their seductive influences even upon the best. The children of the devil are all like their father—tempters. Notice on the other hand the *upright*. "The upright shall have good things in his possession." The "upright" here stand in contrast to those who tempt the righteous to go astray. Who are the upright? The men of incorruptible truth, inflexible rectitude; the men, in one word, who "do justice, love mercy, and walk humbly with their God." The men who stand erect in the consciousness of pure motives, holy principles, and Divine approval. Job was an upright man, one that feared God and eschewed evil. Here are—

Opposite DESTINIES.—The destiny of the one is self-ruin. "Shall fall himself into his own pit." The retribution of the wicked is a "pit"—dark, cold, dismal, bottomless. It is a pit that they dig for themselves. Every sin is a deepening of this pit. What is the wicked man about in this life? Sinking a pit for himself: a pit into which he shall one day fall, never to be recovered. It is not God or the devil that digs this pit, it is the man himself. The destiny of the other is a blessed inheritance. "The upright shall have good things in possession." What good things are in store for the upright? "Eye hath not seen, ear hath not heard, neither hath it entered into the heart of man to conceive the things that God hath prepared for them that love Him." Theodore Parker, heretic though he be, has given a better idea of heaven than many an orthodox divine. "The joys of heaven will begin as soon as we attain the character of heaven, and do its duties. That may begin to-day. It is everlasting life to know God—to have His Spirit dwelling in you—yourself at one with Him. Try that, and prove its worth. Justice, usefulness, wisdom, religion, love, are the best things we hope for in heaven. Try them on—they will fit you here not less beseemingly. They are the best things of earth. Think no outlay of goodness and piety too great. You will find your reward. Begin here. As much goodness and piety, so much heaven. Men will not pay you; God will pay you now: pay you hereafter and for ever."

> "Surely yon Heaven, where angels see God's face,
> Is not so distant as we deem
> From this low earth. 'Tis but a little space,
> The narrow crossing of a slender stream.
> 'Tis but a veil, which winds might blow aside;
> Yes, these are all that us of earth divide
> From the bright dwelling of the glorified—
> The Land of which I dream."—HORATIUS BONAR.

Proverbs 28:11

Vanity in the Rich and Penetration in the Poor

"The rich man *is* wise is in his own conceit: but the poor that hath understanding searcheth him out."

THIS proverb leads to two remarks:

THAT WEALTH IS OFTEN ASSOCIATED WITH INTELLECTUAL VANITY.—"The rich man is wise in his own conceit." There are wealthy men who are not vain, not wise in their own eyes; men who have employed their leisure and their means to gain that amount of knowledge which humbles on account of their own ignorance. Like Sir Isaac Newton, their intelligence leads them to see that they are only like children picking up pebbles on the sea-shore. Still, perhaps, this is the exception, and wealth as a rule is associated with inflated notions of mental superiority. Lord Bacon says, "It was prettily devised of Æsop, that the fly sat upon the axletree of the chariot-wheel, and said, 'What a dust do I raise!' So are there some vain persons, that, whatsoever goeth alone, or moveth upon greater means, if they have never so little hand in it, they think it is they that carry it. They stalk society in peacocks' feathers." Wealth has a tendency to make the weak-minded and self-indulgent, opinionated and oracular. What the Pharisee of old felt in relation to morality they feel in relation to mind; they thank God that they "are not as other men." They imagine their mental tastes more refined, their thoughts more elevated, their intelligence more clear and comprehensive than those of other men. Hence they speak with an air of authority, they feel themselves too big for controversy, too great to enter the arena of debate. All this is nourished by the flattery of their dependents, and the sycophantic spirit of the social grades beneath them.

Because of their wealth parasites accept their inanity as power, their eccentricity as genius, their dictates as laws. Our authors from the sixteenth century downward almost to the present age, have, to the disgrace of our literature, ministered to the vanity of rich men, by dedicating, in a fawning spirit and in fulsome terms, their productions to their acceptance and patronage. Their dedicatees, who in many cases they must have known, were ignoramuses and dolts, they addressed as men of great genius, erudition, and philosophic power. Thank God, English authorship is getting more honest and independent in this respect! The time will come when a millionaire or a monarch if a fool, shall be called a fool.

> " Oh, what a world of vile, ill-favoured faults
> Look handsome in the rich to sordid minds."
> SHAKESPEARE

The proverb leads us further to remark that:
POVERTY IS OFTEN ASSOCIATED WITH SPIRITUAL PENETRATION.—" The poor that hath understanding searcheth him out." Poverty has a strong temptation to flatter the rich. Hunger often overcomes honesty, breaks down manhood, and crushes independency. But there are men amongst the poor and ever have been, who stand manfully against this evil force—men to whom truth is greater than trade, principle than property. Such are the poor referred to in the proverb. "But the poor that hath understanding searcheth him out"—they see ignorance under the decorated brow and the splendid attire. Poverty often whets the mental faculties, makes men keen observers and shrewd critics of their fellow-men. Well would it be for the rich who are inflated with vanity, if they realised the fact that there are men in the grades beneath them, who read them through and through. Sooner give me poverty with this mental penetration than wealth with intellectual shallowness and pretence.

Ye rich men! your wealth, unless it leads to mental power, sound intelligence, and true spiritual culture, is a curse to you. "Charge them that are rich in this world that they be not highminded, nor trust in uncertain riches but

722 / Book of Proverbs

in the living God, who giveth us richly all things to enjoy."

> "They are but beggars that can count their wealth."
> SHAKESPEARE,

Ye poor men! thank God if you have the power to search things out. As you look a little into things you will not be envious of the rich, and you will anticipate the day when the righteous Governor of the world, shall balance all human affairs.

Proverbs 28:12, 28; 29:2

Secular Prosperity

"When righteous *men* do rejoice, *there is* great glory: but when the wicked rise, a man is hidden. . . . When the wicked rise, men hide themselves: but when they perish, the righteous increase."

"When the righteous are in authority, the people rejoice: but when the wicked beareth rule, the people mourn."

WE put these three verses together because they refer to the same subject. Intervening verses either have been or will be noticed as we proceed.

The word "rejoice" here evidently points to secular advancement. It is implied in the verses that worldly prosperity is open alike to the wicked and the righteous. There are certain well-known conditions by which men rise in life. Skill, industry, economy, these are amongst the settled laws. He who attends to them as a rule will rise, be he righteous or wicked. Indeed, the wicked man sometimes works these means with greater success; he adds cunning to skill, devotion to industry, parsimony to economy, and moral recklessness to all: so that as a rule he often rises more frequently, rapidly, and eminently in the world than the righteous. Worldly prosperity is no proof of piety, no test of moral character. The proverbs teach—

THAT THE PROSPERITY OF THE RIGHTEOUS IS A PUBLIC BLESSING.—" When righteous men do rejoice there is great glory." We have many examples of this in the Bible. "There was," says one, "glorying among all the truly good in Israel, when David assembled them to bring up to its place the ark of the covenant. When Solomon dedicated the temple; when Hezekiel restored the passover; when Jehoshaphat dispersed the Levites through all the cities to teach the law and the fear of the Lord; and when young Josiah wept and humbled himself at the contents of the long-neglected and hidden book of God's covenant. So it was in the days of Mordecai, when deliverance came through him to his people, and they had "light and joy, and gladness and honour, and ' a good day.'" The prosperity of a righteous man, whether it involves his elevation to political power or to personal competence and affluence, may be justly regarded as a public blessing. There are good reasons why the people should " rejoice." Why? Because the position has been fairly won. There has been no over-reaching in the effort, no outrage of honesty, no injustice done. Nay, whilst no injury has been inflicted upon any in the process, benefits have been conferred on all who have rendered their assistance, and indirectly on their dependents and neighbours too. Why? Because the position is rightly used. The righteous man uses his power and his property not for his own aggrandisement and indulgence, but for the common weal. He acts as a steward under God, he holds himself as a trustee, not as a proprietor, he employs his talents to promote human rights, ameliorate human woes, educate human minds, redeem human souls. Like the clouds that have drunk in the ocean, he pours forth his possessions in fertilising showers upon the parched districts of society: his influence is as rain upon the new mown grass. In the prosperity of such a man let the people rejoice, and the nations be glad. The verses teach—

THAT THE PROSPERITY OF THE WICKED IS A PUBLIC CALAMITY.—" When the wicked rise a man is hidden." The Vulgate has it, " When the ungodly reign it is the ruin of men." But our version gives, I think, the truest sense. The idea is that men have reason to fear, to shrink into obscurity. This is especially the case when a wicked man rises to sovereign authority in a country. " There was this 'hiding,'" says a modern expositor, "when, in Saul's time, David was hunted to death ; when in Ahab's, Elijah—even the intrepid Elijah—fled for his life, and when good Obadiah, at the risk of his own head, hid fifty of the Lord's prophets in a cave, and fed them with bread and water, and when Micaiah, 'faithful among the faithless,' had to be sought and sent for, and for the fidelity of his words was ordered to prison, while the hundreds of the prophets of Baal were in favour and triumphed. What hiding and fear there were when the wicked Haman ' rose,' and what exultation when he fell and the righteous came in his room." When a wicked man gets to the throne it is an eclipse of the sun, the people are all struck as under a portentous gloom. But whatever is the prosperity, whether public or personal, it is a calamity to see a wicked man prosper. The prosperity of such a man increases the power of oppression ; the more money he has, the more power to be haughty, tyrannic, and exacting. It always promotes monopoly; what he has gathered from the common provisions of the world he holds with a tenacious hand, and distributes not to others. It, moreover, starts in the minds of the thoughtful perplexing questions concerning the righteousness of the Divine Government; they stand heart-stricken and amazed, and ask, "Wherefore do the wicked prosper ?"

Good speed to the righteous in his career! In his march in the path of industry he scatters blessings as he goes, and in the possession of the prize he gives as the Lord hath prospered him. Failure to the wicked! It is a mercy when their commercial purposes are broken, when their tricks are frustrated, when they tumble down to bankruptcy and pauperism. It is not just to the universe —not kind to the wicked man himself—to wish him commercial prosperity—the more wealth he has the more he damns himself and others.

Proverbs 28:13

Man's Treatment of His Own Sins

"He that covereth his sins shall not prosper: but whoso confesseth and forsaketh *them* shall have mercy."

AT the outset this verse starts the following observations:—
First: All men have sins. Sin is a little word, but a tremendous thing, It always implies law, the power of understanding law, the capability of obeying or disobeying law. "All men have sinned, and come short of the glory of God." "There is not a just man on earth that doeth good, and sinneth not." "If we say that we have no sin, we deceive ourselves, and the truth is not in us." Our consciences testify that we have sins numerous, aggravated, and hell-deserving. There is no arguing against the fact. To argue against it is to argue against universal consciousness. Secondly: All men have something to do with their sins. Sins are not amongst the things that we may deal with or not. We *must* deal with them. We can no more avoid it than we can avoid breathing the air if we would live. All men deal with their sins either foolishly or wisely, and the proverb points to this twofold treatment. Notice—

The FOOLISH treatment of our sins.—"He that covereth his sins." There are various ways of endeavouring to cover sins. By *denying* them. A lie is a cover which men put over their sins to conceal them from others. They sin and deny the fact; they wrap up their crimes in falsehoods. Thus Cain, Rachel, Joseph's brethren, Peter, Ananias and Sapphira, endeavoured to hide their sin. By *extenuating* them. Men plead excuses. The influence of others, the power of circumstances, the moral weakness of the constitution. Extenuation is a common cover. By *forgetting* them. They endeavour to sweep them from the memory by revelry and mirth, by sensuality, worldliness, and intemperance. But these and all other attempts to cover sin are not only futile but injurious. "He that covereth his sins shall not prosper." He shall not prosper in his attempt. Sins must reveal themselves sooner or later. They will not only break through the fig-leaf covering, but rive the mountains and flame under the heavens. They have a voice, which though men may not hear, like Abel's blood, penetrates the heavens, and enters the ear of God. "There is no darkness nor shadow of death, where the workers of iniquity may hide themselves." They shall not prosper in their own natures. "To hide a sin with a lie," says Jeremy Taylor, "is like a crust of leprosy over an ulcer." David tried to do it, and he says, "When I kept silent my bones waxed old, through my roarings all the day long." The soul whose sins are covered up, hidden, unconfessed, can no more break forth into life, power, and fruitfulness, than the husbandman's seed can spring to life, and rise to perfection, under the frosty sky of night. The proverb points to—

The WISE treatment of our sins.—"Whoso confesseth and forsaketh them shall have mercy." Here is in the wise treatment of sin *confession*—not a cold, formal confession, but a deep, penitential, humble, acknowledgment. Then here is *abandonment*—"forsaketh." The wicked man "forsakes his ways and the unrighteous man his thoughts." There is an utter renunciation. When this is done, there comes "mercy." Mercy breaks through the cloud, quickening the soul into new life. "I acknowledged my sin unto Thee," said David, "and mine iniquity have I not hid." "I said I will confess my transgressions unto the Lord, and Thou forgavest the iniquity of my sin."

What shall we do with our sins? Deny, extenuate, bury them? All our efforts to cover them in this way will be futile; "murder will out." "To cover," says Dr. Arnot, "the sin which lies on the conscience with a layer of earnest efforts to do right will not take the sin away; the underlying sin will assimilate all the dead works that may be heaped upon it, and the result will be a greater mass of sin." Confess and forsake. One leak may sink a ship, one sin covered may damn the soul.

Proverbs 28:14

Reverence and Recklessness

"Happy *is* the man that feareth alway: but he that hardeneth his heart shall fall into mischief."

THE proverb teaches—

That REVERENCE IS HAPPINESS.—"Happy is the man that feareth alway." This could not be true of *fear* in the slavish sense of the word. Servile fear is an element of misery; it "hath torment;" there is no happiness in terror. The "fear" here is reverence; it is a loving awe. It implies a supreme love for the Great Father blended with a sense of His infinite greatness. It is a state of mind foreign alike to the frivolous and the timid: it is serious and brave. Whatever of fear there may be in this state of mind, it is not the fear of receiving injury, it is the fear of wounding and dishonouring the object of love. There is happiness in this reverence; it implies the highest love, and love is blessedness; it implies a settled trust, and trust is magnanimous and heroic; it implies a well-balanced soul—a soul where all the faculties are rightly poised, and such a balance is harmony. The man with this reverence is like David, "who set the Lord always before him;" and he is no longer afraid of men or devils. He is a happy man who has this reverence; happy, not in the sense of the thoughtless, the gay, the voluptuous, who enjoy occasional titillations, and passing flashes of sensational pleasure; but happy as a true man alone can be happy. "The happiness of life," says Richter, "consists, like the day, not in single flashes of light, but in one continuous mild serenity. The most beautiful period of the heart's existence is in the calm, equable light, even although it be only moonshine or twilight. Now the mind alone can obtain for us this heavenly cheerfulness and peace." The proverb teaches—

That RECKLESSNESS IS RUIN.—"He that hardeneth his

heart shall fall into mischief." There are men who harden their hearts; they turn the heart of flesh into stone by resisting moral impressions, and by living a life of indifference, worldliness, and self-indulgence. So obdurate do their hearts become, that the seeds of truth fall on them as on stony ground—holy influences descend upon them as showers on a flinty rock. Thus Pharoah's heart was hardened, and thus the hearts of the children of Israel became hardened during their journey in the wilderness. Such recklessness is ruin. "He that hardeneth his heart shall fall into mischief." This is inevitable in the nature of things. The reckless man is like the mariner who in the tempest disregards the compass and the chart, neglects the rudder, and is driven into the yawning abyss; or, like the man who sleeps on the bosom of a volcanic hill when the subterranean fires are heaving under him, and are about to break into thunder and flame. "He that being often reproved hardeneth his neck, shall be suddenly cut off, and that without remedy."

> "In the corrupted currents of this world,
> Offence's gilded hand may shove by justice;
> And oft 'tis seen the wicked prize itself
> Buys out the law. But 'tis not so above:
> There is no shuffling: there the action lies
> In its true nature, and we ourselves compelled,
> Even to the teeth and forehead of our faults,
> To give an evidence. What then? What rests?
> Try what repentance can: what can it not?
> Yet what can it, when one cannot repent?"
> SHAKESPEARE

Proverbs 28:15-17

Types of Kings

"*As* a roaring lion, and a ranging bear; *so is* a wicked ruler over the poor people. The prince that wanteth understanding *is* also a great oppressor: *but* he that hateth covetousness shall prolong *his* days. A man that doeth violence to the blood of *any* person shall flee to the pit: let no man stay him."

CIVIL government is evidently a divine institution. Society cannot exist without laws; these laws require to be expressed and enforced, and whoever does this is Ruler. Again, whilst the millions have the instinct of obedience, and lack the faculty to rule, there are always some in whom there is the tendency and the power to govern. Hence men always have had, and will ever have, rulers. In these verses there are four distinct types of rulers.

Here is the HEARTLESS ruler.—"As a roaring lion and a ranging bear, so is a wicked ruler over the poor people." There have in all ages been men on thrones so intoxicated with power, so rapacious in greed, so tyrannic in heart, as to treat the people as savage beasts the harmless lamb, mere victims to gratify their passions. They have regarded the people as made for them—slaves to execute their will —victims to gratify their lusts for pelf and power. The people dreaded them as wild beasts, shrunk with terror from them, as the herd on the mountain from the roar of the lion and the bear. England at one time had rulers of this class, but, thank God! they are gone. We look at them in the cage of history now with defiance and disgust.

Here is the FOOLISH ruler.—"The prince that wanteth understanding is also a great oppressor." A king lacking mental capacity is not a very uncommon character in human history. Feeble-minded men have often sat on thrones; and the country where hereditary kingship is practically recognised is ever more or less liable to this calamity.

Weakness in a king is for some reasons as bad as wickedness. Wickedness in a king puts the country on its guard, but weakness destroys confidence, and inspires contempt. A weak ruler has often been an "oppressor." Haughty and heartless advisers have used him to gratify their own selfish and ambitious ends. A weak policy has often outraged the liberties of men, and destroyed the peace of kingdoms. "A prince that wanteth understanding" is a man out of his place, an anomaly, and a curse. He is like an infant at the rudder of a ship in a tempest.

"Let not the world see fear, and sad mistrust
Govern the motion of a kingly eye."—SHAKESPEARE

Here is the GENEROUS ruler.—" He that hateth covetousness shall prolong his days." Here is a King of the true kingly type, a man who rules not for his own selfish ends but for the people's good. A man free from all sordid motives, devoted to the public service, identifying himself with the interests of his people, making their happiness and honour his own. Such a man "shall prolong his days." He establishes his throne in the affections of his people, the love of his people is his impregnable fortress of defence.

Here is the ABANDONED ruler.—" A man that doeth violence to the blood of any person shall flee to the pit : let no man stay him." This verse may be taken in connection with the preceding, as presenting a further description of the same character there depicted. The cruelty of an oppressive ruler frequently incurs blood-guiltiness. "Thus it was with Ahab in the case of Naboth : thus has it been in thousands of instances. Whatever be the high station of him who acts the murderer's part, how independent and irresponsible soever he may imagine himself to be—vengeance shall pursue him—his sin shall find him out. Even his crown and sceptre shall not protect him from righteous retribution. There is a higher than he—'the righteous Lord who loveth righteousness.' Both on Ahab and Jezebel came the blood of Naboth." Let such a monster "flee to the pit" of ignominy, and "let no man stay him ;" let the nations send him howling to the infamy that befits him. Like glowworms that in the night seem brilliant, but in the day contemptible grubs ; weak, ignorant, and tyrannic kings appear glorious in the sight of popular ignorance, but abhorrent as the day of mental intelligence advances.

Let it be remembered that the character of kings depends upon the people. Rulers for the time are always as good as the nation can afford to have.

"It is the curse of kings to be attended
By slaves, that take their humours for a want."
SHAKESPEARE.

Proverbs 28:20-23

Avarice

"A faithful man shall abound with blessings : but he that maketh haste to be rich shall not be innocent. To have respect of persons *is* not good : for a piece of bread *that* man will transgress. He that hasteth to be rich *hath* an evil eye, and considereth not that poverty shall come upon him. He that rebuketh a man afterwards shall find more favour than he that flattereth with the tongue." *

AVARICE is the ruling subject of these verses. Of all the base passions of human nature, there are none baser than an insatiable eagerness for worldly gain. Nor can any man work out more immoral and miserable results. It has been called the "great sepulchre of all other passions." Unlike other tombs, however, it is enlarged by repletion, and strengthened by age. It is a pestiferous plant that grows even in the most sterile natures. The verses suggest the following facts concerning it.

IT STANDS IN OPPOSITION TO FAITHFULNESS.—" A faithful man shall abound with blessings, but he that maketh haste to be rich shall not be innocent" (*margin*, un-

* The truths contained in the two previous verses have been contemplated preceding Readings.

punished). The avaricious man is the man that "maketh haste to be rich." He is intensely eager in pursuit of wealth, and he is here put in opposition to the "faithful man." It is suggested that a man may be rich and *faithful* at the same time, but that he cannot "make haste" to be rich and faithful together. He in whom a desire for wealth is a ruling, raging passion, must be unfaithful—unfaithful to his own conscience, unfaithful to the claims of society, unfaithful to the principles of everlasting right, unfaithful to the great God. In verse 22 it is stated: "He that hasteth to be rich hath an evil eye." What is an "evil eye"? An earthly, grudging, envious eye, an eye fastened to the earth, never directed to Heaven—an eye that sees no worth, beauty or grandeur, but in worldly wealth. In sooth, this passion is essentially immoral. "Covetousness is idolatry." It is the soul worshipping the dust, not the Deity. The Bible ranks the covetous man with those who are excluded from the Kingdom of Heaven. Another fact taught concerning this avarice is that:

IT RENDERS ITS POSSESSOR PARTIAL IN HIS JUDGMENT OF HIS FELLOW MEN.—"To have respect of persons is not good; for a piece of bread that man will transgress." The avaricious man is so wretchedly sordid, so intensely selfish, that he will allow his judgment of others to be governed by "a piece of bread." The man who is his patron, client, customer, any one who smooths his path to fortune, he will extol in flattering words and kneel before in crouching awe, corrupt and hollow though he be. On the other hand, those around him who contribute not to satisfy his miserable greed, are treated not only with indifference, but often with disrespect and haughty insolence. It is sad to see on every hand how a "piece of bread" regulates the conduct of many men towards their contemporaries. Statesmen flatter their country for a "piece of bread," merchants their customers for a "piece of bread," and often, alas, preachers their congregations for a "piece of bread." Another fact taught concerning this avarice is that—

It generates a base sycophancy of spirit.—"He that rebuketh a man afterwards shall find more favour than he that flattereth with the tongue." Duty sometimes calls upon a man to *rebuke*. Truth has been outraged, wrong has been done, obligations have been omitted by our neighbour, and we are called upon to administer an honest reproof. At the time the rebuke may not find favour, it may be disagreeable, it may wound self-respect and bring shame and remorse. Still it should be given, and ultimately, Solomon assures us, that our ministry of rebuke will find "more favour," than if our ministry had been that of fawning flattery. "He," says Matthew Henry, "that cries out against his surgeon for hurting him when he is searching his wound, will yet pay him well, and thank him too when he has cured it." Who is he that "flattereth with the tongue"? It is the avaricious man. "He that hasteth to be rich." Selfishness is the root of flattery, and the inspiration of flunkeyism. The more free a man is of avarice and selfishness, and the more full of generosity and love, the more faithful, brave, heroic, and independent will he be in his conduct to others. Great souls can never adulate or cringe. It is not until the divinity is taken out of a man, that he becomes the lap-dog to lick and fawn. Another fact taught concerning this avarice is that—

It ends in results contrary to aim.—What is the aim of avarice? Wealth and fame. But it often leads to poverty and disgrace. He "considereth not that poverty shall come upon him." Those who gain most of the world must lose it sooner or later, and be stripped of all earthly good. Lot hasted to be rich, but his wealth became his high road to poverty; step by step he proceeds till he ends his days a forlorn pauper, in the desolate cave of Zoar. The most abject destitution awaits all avaricious souls. The world leaves them at last, and they are robbed of everything but their own wretched existence. "The covetous man," says old Adams, "is like Tantalus, up to the chin in water, yet thirsty." As the dogs, in Æsop's fable, lost the real flesh for the shadow of it, so the covetous man casts away the true riches for the love of the shadowy. What is the aim? Fame. But instead of that there comes contempt. "He that rebuketh a man afterwards shall find more favour than he that flattereth with the tongue." He flattered men, hoping to please them, and to win their approbation, but instead of that there comes at last disgust. The time hastens with all, whose ears have been most charmed with the voices of human flattery, when they will recoil with disgust from the words and memory of their miserable sycophants.

Take care of avarice, my friend! If it is in thee, crush it forthwith, and that without mercy or delay. "A man's life consisteth not in the abundance of the things of this life."

> "Some, o'er enamour'd of their bags, run mad,
> Groan under gold, yet weep for want of bread."
> YOUNG.

Proverbs 28:24

Robbery of Parents

"Whoso robbeth his father or his mother, and saith, *It is* no transgression; the same *is* the companion of a destroyer."

"As Christ," says an old expositor, " shows the absurdity and wickedness of those children who think it is no duty, in some cases, to maintain their parents, so Solomon shows here the absurdity and wickedness of those who think it is no sin to rob their parents, either by force or secretly, by wheedling them or threatening them, or by wasting what they have, and (which is no better than robbing them), running into debt and leaving them to pay it." Here is—

A GREAT sin.—Children robbing their parents. "Thou shalt not steal," is one of the cardinal laws in the Divine code, and to take without their knowledge or consent, the property of parents is not only as truly a theft as the taking the property of any other, but a theft of a more aggravated enormity. Whilst the property of a parent is no more the property of a child than that of any other, it should be regarded by him as far more sacred. "The aggravation of sin," says Mr. Bridges, "is proportioned to the obligation of duty. A murderer is a heinous transgressor; how much more a parricide! To rob a stranger, a friend, is evil, how much more a father and mother! The filial obligation of cherishing care is broken. Ingratitude is added to injustice." Here is—

An UNRECOGNISED sin.—" Whoso robbeth his father and mother and saith it is no transgression." The general impression of young people in relation to the appropriation of their parents' property is that it is "no transgression." They imagine that they have a right to make free use of whatever is in the house, and that what is their parents' is theirs also. Why should such an impression as that prevail? Amongst many reasons that may be suggested, two very opposite ones may be stated. The lavish kindness and over indulgence of parents. Parental love is often so exuberant that it gives the impression to children that they have not only a right to all in the house, but that they gratify their parents by making use of it. The devil has no mightier or more efficient organ than parental love. By it he destroys in children the sense of moral distinctions and claims. Meanness and niggardliness of parents may be regarded as another reason. There are parents so miserly in their dispositions and habits that they deny to their children that which is necessary not only to innocent gratification but to common comforts. They are so rigorously economical that they deny to their children the means and the opportunities for those recreations which are almost essential to health and to an appreciation of life. Hence children are tempted to get, by little acts of deception and fraud, that which their parents in their niggardliness deny; and they rob their parents, and feel it is "no transgression." These two opposites, then— lavish generosity and miserly meanness—go to give children the impression that there is "no transgression" in robbing their father and their mother. Here is—

A RUINOUS sin.—"The same is the companion of a destroyer." When a child once begins to cheat his parents he starts on a downward path; one act of deception and fraud leads to another. The spirit of covetousness and self-gratification is increased; self-indulgence is promoted, conscience is weakened, passions are strengthened, self-control has gone, and the youth becomes the companion of the *destroyer*. The little pilferings that began in the family lead to those swindlings and depredations abroad in society which conduct to the prison and the gallows.

Sons and daughters, let your filial love and reverence be associated with a conscience that will lead you to recognise and honour your parents' rights. Neither waste nor steal a fraction of their property; regard it as sacred. For what they give you be thankful, and for what they hold back respect them; it will be no doubt for your ultimate advantage.

Proverbs 28:25-26

Self-sufficiency and Godly Confidence

"He that is of a proud heart stirreth up strife: but he that putteth his trust in the LORD shall be made fat. He that trusteth in his own heart is a fool: but whoso walketh wisely, he shall be delivered."

HERE is—

SELF-SUFFICIENCY.—There is a twofold description of this in the text, *Pride*—"A proud heart," and self-trust—"he that trusteth in his own heart." Some read for "proud heart" a "covetous soul." The original means large in mind. There is a largeness of soul that is desirable and virtuous, involving great thoughts, vast intelligence, and world-wide sympathies. But the largeness here points to something very different, viz.,—a selfish ambition. There are different kinds of pride; there is the pride of self-esteem, the pride of property, and the pride of ambition; the last is the "proud heart" here. What Shakspeare describes as the "eagle-winged pride, sky-aspiring and ambitious thoughts." The other description of this sufficiency is *self-trust*. "Trusteth in his own heart." There is a self-reliance that is good, that lies at the foundation of all noble character and endeavours; but Solomon does not mean this; he means that self-conceit, which proudly disdains the counsels of others. It is self-sufficiency; it is that by which the man is everything to himself, and esteems all others scarcely worthy of note. Two things are here indicated concerning this self-sufficiency. It is *mischievous*. It "stirreth up strife." Truly, as we have seen in a former reading, by "pride cometh contention." Ambition, this proud-crested fiend, this restless, raging thirst for power, this hellish mother, breeding ever swarms of social devils. Who can tell the strifes and wars which it has created?

"Towns turned to ashes, fanes involved in fire!
These deeds the guilt of rash ambition tell."

It is *foolish* also.—"He that trusteth to his own heart is a fool." Truly so; what is there in the heart to trust? It is "deceitful above all things and desperately wicked." "The heart is the great impostor," says Bishop Hall. In all of us it has been "a liar from the beginning" of our conscious existence. Trust to the heart and you trust that which is as false as the mirage in the desert, as changeful as the vane which veers about with every wind. Peter, to his cost, felt what a fool he had been in trusting to his own heart, and so have thousands in every age." "Wouldest thou," says an old writer, "not be thought a fool in another's conceit, be not wise in thine own. He that trusts to his own wisdom proclaims his own folly; he is truly wise and shall appear so, that hath folly enough to be thought not worldly wise, or wisdom enough to see his own folly." Here is—

GODLY CONFIDENCE.—"He that putteth his trust in the

Lord shall be made fat." Trust in Him, implies a knowledge of Him, an appreciation of His transcendent excellencies, a consciousness of His willingness and ability to sustain our being amidst all the changes and epochs of our interminable future. Trusting in Him instead of inclining to our own opinions stimulates to action. Two things are here indicated concerning this trust. It leads to *prosperity*. "Shall be made fat," which means shall enjoy abundance. He who "trusts in the Lord" is the man who is active in duty, and looks to the Lord for a blessing upon his labours, leaves the result in His hands, and is satisfied with His appointments. This man "shall be made fat." He has comfort and peace and happiness in all situations; an inward satisfaction, a heart feast, a prosperity of soul, to which the other is a stranger. It is indicated also that this trust in God is characterised by wisdom of conduct. "Whoso walketh wisely he shall be delivered." The Eternal guides the man safely who trusts in Him. "Though the mariner," says Archbishop Leighton, "sees not the Pole star, yet the needle of the compass, which points to it tells him which way he sails. Thus the heart that is touched with the loadstone of Divine love, trembling with godly fear, and yet still looking towards God by fixed believing, interprets the fear by the love in the fear, and tells the soul that its course is heavenward towards the haven of eternal rest." "Blessed is the man who trusteth in the Lord, and whose hope the Lord is. For he shall be as a tree planted by the waters, and that spreadeth out her roots by the river, and shall not see when heat cometh, but her leaf shall be green; and shall not be careful in the year of drought, neither shall cease from yielding fruit." *

> " Trust to that which aye remains the bliss of Heaven above,
> Which time, nor fate, nor word, nor storm are able to remove ;
> Trust to that sure Celestial Rock that rests on glorious throne,
> That hath been, is, and must be still, our anchor-hold alone."
> KINWELMERSHE

* Jer. xvii. 7, 8.

Proverbs 29:1

Restorative Discipline

"He, that being often reproved hardeneth *his* neck, shall suddenly be destroyed, and that without remedy."*

WHAT is the great end of human existence in this life? To amass wealth? To acquire knowledge? To rise to social distinctions—to gratify the appetites and indulge the passions? *No!* A thousand times no. It is the attainment of a holy moral character—a character that shall gain the approval and qualify for the fellowship and service of the Great Father of our souls. The great aim of God with the human race here is to make it "mete for the inheritance of the saints in light." Human life is a moral school. The discipline is here presented in three aspects.

As EXPERIENCED.—"He that being often reproved." The case here is of a man who has been subject to discipline; has been often reproved. Reproof implies that in the human school of moral culture there is something to be got rid of in the pupil. The training is something more than education, the bringing out of dormant faculties, the full development of what is in the soil. There is something to be removed—moral weeds, thorns, and thistles to be extracted and thrown away. Hence reproof enters into the discipline, and truly how many and constant are the reproofs which the Great Father administers to His children here. They come through Providence, in secular adversities, personal afflictions and social bereavements. They come through the Bible, in a thousand forms of admonitions and counsels. They come through the ministry of the good, through Christian friends, pious parents, and faithful ministers. They come through the monitions and accusations of conscience. Who is the man that has not

---

* The subject contained in the 27th and 28th verses of the foregoing chapter have engaged meditations in preceding Readings.

been "often reproved?" The discipline is here presented—

As ABUSED.—"Hardeneth his neck." The allusion is to the intractable, stubborn ox. Stephen, the martyr, addressed the Jewish people in these words: "Ye stiffnecked and uncircumcised in heart and ears, ye do always resist the Holy Ghost; as your fathers did so do ye."* In all ages men have grown hard under the disciplinary ministries of Heaven. So great is the moral force that man has in him, and so great the perversity of his heart, that he uses the very means intended to soften and mellow his nature for the purpose of hardening it into stone. By Divine reproofs Pharaoh hardened his heart, and in the same way the Jewish nation became morally stubborn and incorrigible. The hardening process goes on with every reproof resisted, with every impression that runs to waste. God hardens hearts in every age, and especially the hearts here in England, in the same way as He hardened Pharaoh's heart on the banks of the Nile, even by His restorative discipline. Men turn God's blessings into curses—convert the elements of spiritual health, life, and growth into deadly poison. Though we cannot alter the laws of the universe or change the nature of things, we can alter their bearings on us. Herein is our freedom. The discipline is here presented—

As TERMINATING.—"Shall suddenly be destroyed, and that without remedy." There is a limit to discipline—it has so many influences, so many days and no more. When its hour terminates with the man who abuses it, his retributive destruction ensues. The destruction will be *sudden*. "Shall suddenly be destroyed." Sudden—not because there lacked warning, but because the warning was not believed. Death always comes suddenly to a man unprepared. The destruction will be *irremediable*. "Without remedy." When the final blow is struck all will be over; the ministries of discipline give way to the ministry of inexorable destiny. The voice of mercy is lost in the thunders of justice—the star of hope is buried in the midnight of despair;

* Acts vii. 51.

the man feels himself lost, and in all the billows of regrets and foreboding that roll over his wretched spirit there is the echo of the words " without remedy." Let us hail the disciplinary ministrations of Heaven, and rightly use them when they come.

> " In the still air music lies unheard :
> In the rough marble beauty hides unseen.
> To wake the music and the beauty needs
> The master's touch, the sculptor's chisel keen.
> Great Master! touch us with thy skilful Hand :
> Let not the music that is in us die.
> Great Sculptor! hew and polish us, nor let,
> Hidden and lost, Thy form within us lie.
> Spare not the stroke : do with us as Thou wilt :
> Let there be naught unfinished, broken, marred :
> Complete Thy purpose, that we may become
> Thy perfect image, O our God and Lord!"

Proverbs 29:3, 15, 17

Parental Life

" Whoso loveth wisdom rejoiceth his father : but he that keepeth company with harlots spendeth *his* substance. . . . The rod and reproof give wisdom : but a child left *to himself* bringeth his mother to shame. . . . Correct thy son, and he shall give thee rest; yea, he shall give delight unto thy soul." *

PARENTAL life is a life whose sympathies and solicitudes parents alone can understand and appreciate : a man must be a parent in order to interpret a parent. The three verses at the head selected from different parts of this chapter point to three things connected with parental life.

Parental DELIGHT.—" Whoso loveth wisdom rejoiceth his father." " Correct thy son and he shall give thee rest; yea, he shall give delight unto thy soul." Expressions identical in import with these have already come under

* The second verse has been discussed in a previous Reading.

our notice.* Who is the son that "rejoiceth his father," gives him "rest" and "delight"? He is here described as one that "loveth wisdom." He not only listens to the lessons of wisdom and practises externally the principles of wisdom, but he *loves* it. It not only fascinates and charms him but draws him, for we evermore follow the objects of our love. He pursues it as the river pursues the ocean. What we love is the chief thought of our understandings, the chief theme of our talk, the chief centre of our being, the chief fashioner of our character. He who truly loves wisdom does not merely love an abstraction or a theory, but a soul-commanding personality, he loves Him Who is the "Wisdom of God." What a source of delight will the spirit and conduct of such a son be to his parents! They will see in it the highest form of filial obedience, that which springs from the Divinest motives, that has its seat in the heart. They will see in it the guarantee of future prosperity. He who thus "loveth wisdom" will have his "steps ordered of the Lord," and will pass through life, if not in affluence and wealth, with contentment and honour. They will see in it the certainty of a happy destiny; for they know that "godliness is profitable in all things, having the promise of the life which now is, and of that which is to come."

Parental DISTRESS.—Here we have two things that bring distress to parents. Corrupt society. "He that keepeth company with harlots spendeth his substance." The deadly influence of a harlot is well described by Pollock :

> "She weaves the winding-sheets of souls, and lays
> Them in the urn of everlasting death."

This odious character is graphically described in the seventh chapter of this book. He who gives himself up to her influence "spendeth his substance." The licentious profligacy of sons has brought many a father to beggary and want. Harlots play sad havoc with families; they draw sons to ruin and parents to an untimely grave. Un--

* See chap. xxiii. 24, 25; xxviii. 7—19.

restrained conduct. "A child left to himself bringeth his mother to shame." Leave the most beautiful garden to itself, and it will soon be overrun with noxious weeds and thorns, leave the young mind to itself and it will run into all that is morally filthy and foul. "Rousseau," says Mr. Bridges, "inculcated this system to its fullest extent, that no kind of habits ought to be impressed on children, that you should leave them to the natural consequences of their own actions, and that when reason comes to exert itself in a matured state, all will be right. Upon which the following beautiful apostrophe has been given— 'Emilius, how I tremble for thee, while I see thee exposed to the care of thy too ingenious tutor. I see thee wilful to thy parents, domineering in the nursery, surfeiting on meats, inflaming thy body with noxious humours, thy mind with unquiet passions, running headlong into dangers which thou canst not foresee, and habits which thou canst not eradicate, mischievous to others, but fatal to thyself.'" This unrestrainedness in the conduct of children, Solomon says, will bring the "mother to shame." Why the mother? Because perhaps in the folly of her maternal fondness and indulgence this unrestrainedness in the child's conduct has come to pass, the strength of her affections and the weakness of her judgment have mingled for herself this bitter cup.

Parental DISCIPLINE.—"The rod and reproof give wisdom." "Correct thy son and he shall give thee rest." Here is discipline. The "rod" does not necessarily mean corporeal infliction, although in some cases that may not only be warranted but required, but it stands for *pain*. The pain of the soul is greater than the pain of the senses, and pain can reach the soul in many ways without the literal rod. The reproof, the parental frown, the denial of gratifications, the restrictions of liberty, all these are moral chastisements, and moral chastisement must be employed. The words of quaint old Quarles are not only worthy of record here, but seem to claim a place. "Be very vigilant over thy child in the April of his understanding, lest the frosts of May nip his blossoms; while he is a tender twig straighten him, whilst he is a new vessel season him; such as thou makest him such commonly shalt thou find him. Let his first lesson be obedience, and his second shall be what thou wilt. Give him education in good letters to the utmost of thy ability, and his capacity. Season his youth with the love of his Creator, and make the fear of his God the beginning of his knowledge. If he have an active spirit, rather rectify than curb it, but reckon idleness among his chiefest faults. As his judgment ripens observe his inclination, and tender him a calling that shall not cross it. Forced marriages and callings seldom prosper. Show him both the mow and the plough, and prepare him as well for the danger of the skirmish, as possess him with the honour of the prize." Let parents so train their children that they may become their strength, succour, and joy in their old age. All children should have the heart of the poet towards their parents:

> "I'll be thy crutch, my father! lean on me:
> Weakness knits stubborn whilst it's bearing thee;
> And hard shall fall the shock of fortune's frown,
> To eke thy sorrows, ere it breaks me down.
> My mother too: thy kindness shall be met,
> And ere I'm able will I pay the debt:
> For what thou'st done, and what gone through for me,
> My last-earned sixpence will I break with thee;
> And when my dwindled sum won't more divide,
>   Then take it all—to fate I'll leave the rest:
> In helping thee I always feel a pride,
>   Nor think I'm happy till we both are blest."—CLARE

Proverbs 29:4, 12, 14

Human Rulership

"The king by judgment establisheth the land : but he that receiveth gifts overthroweth it. . . . If a ruler hearken to lies, all his servants *are* wicked. . . . The king that faithfully judgeth the poor, his throne shall be established for ever." *

DIVERSITIES in the tendencies and powers of men, the necessities of society, and the word of God, establish the fact that civil government is a Divine institution. But this Divine thing, like many other Divine things, has been used most *un*-divinely, the blessing has often been turned into a curse, the angel transformed into a demon. The king, for which God has built up a throne in human society, and the king that man has put upon that throne, are often as opposite as light and darkness, Heaven and hell. Whilst "the powers that be"—institutions—are always "ordained of God," the kings that be are often ordained of the devil. Here we have human rulership—

RIGHTLY EXERCISED.—It is here implied that in the right exercise of this rulership there is judgment. "The king by judgment," that is, the king that rules by judgment. The word must be taken here not merely in the sense of wisdom but in the sense of equity. Wisdom, the power of selecting the best end and employing the best measures, in a ruler, is important, but rectitude is more so. Indeed, the latter is necessary to the former, aye, and involves it : honesty is evermore the best policy. What is morally wrong can never be politically right. What is right is evermore expedient, and what is *really* expedient is always essentially right. " He that ruleth over men must be just, ruling in the fear of God." " A king," says Lord Bacon, "must make religion the rule of Government, and not to balance the scale; for he that casteth in religion only to make the scales even, his own weight is contained in those characters,

* The subject of the thirteenth verse has been elsewhere discussed.

—*Mene, mene, tekel, upharsin*, he is found too light, his kingdom shall be taken from him. Religion is rectitude. It is here implied, that in the right exercise of this rulership there is mercy. "The king that faithfully judgeth the poor." Whilst the Divine purpose of kings is to help and elevate the poor, they have too frequently not only ignored their existence, but cursed them with unrighteous exactions. The King of kings has said, the "prince shall not take of the people's inheritance by oppression." He says to them, "Take away your exactions from my people." "What mean ye, that ye beat my people to pieces, and grind the faces of the poor?" Kings that are taken up with the grandees of the kingdom and neglect the poor, are not God's kings but the devil's. A true king will always be kind. His justice will always be tempered with mercy. In sooth these two things are one, where there is true justice there will always be mercy. There is a conventional justice, a parchment justice, a letter justice; that is not justice, it is a fiction, a misnomer. Justice is a dictate of the Divine heart, and this is the Fountain of love. Justice, indeed, is but love guarding the universe from all that will disturb its happiness and break its peace. It is love speaking in the imperative mood. It is love weeding God's garden of all that mars its beauty, taints its fragrance, or checks its growth.

Here we have human rulership—

SADLY PERVERTED.—"If a ruler hearken to lies." No men in society have so many lies poured into their ears as kings. The vanity, the greed, the servility, the fawning sycophancy, of society, are always fabricating lies for the ears of kings. Here in England, during the illness of the Prince of Wales, what hosts of falsehoods have reached the Royal ears. Through the leading journals our royal personages have been told that the hearts of "all England were breaking during the period of our Prince's sufferings, and that all the souls of the British nation, forgetful of their own personal concerns, gathered about the Royal bed at Sandringham." In sermons we have had the same outrageous exaggerations over and over again during the last few months. How untrue the whole has been to fact! Ask our merchants, our shopkeepers, our mechanics, our labourers, where in their circle they have seen this distress ? Where have they witnessed one breaking heart, or where, even a single tear ? An honest monarchical loyalty, genuine respect for the Queen of England, good wishes for her children, and sworn allegiance to the spirit and teachings of the Prince of the Kings of the earth, as represented in His Sermon on the Mount, and in all His discourses and deeds, urge us here to record our humble protest against these "lies" that have thus streamed from hollow pulpits and a venal press. It is our relief to know that neither the Queen of England nor the Prince of Wales will "hearken to lies;" otherwise they would mistake their position, and might assume an attitude that would lead to national anarchy and confusion. In all ages the "lies" of a base people have been the chief instruments in ruining kings and kingdoms. All true kings will despise these "lies."

> "Some are born kings,
> Made up of three parts fire ; so full of heaven,
> It sparkles at their eyes : inferior souls
> Know 'em as soon as seen, by sure instinct
> To be their lords, and naturally worship
> The secret God within them."—DRYDEN.

Here we have human rulership—

NATIONALLY DEVELOPED.—The conduct of rulers influences the character and destiny of kingdoms. It is here said of the true ruler, the man that rules by judgment and mercy, that he "establishes the land," and that his "throne shall be established for ever." On the other hand, it is said that the king who "receiveth gifts, (or, as in the margin, a man of oblations) overthroweth it." He who will dispose of justice for some personal consideration, will bring himself and his country to ruin. "We will sell justice to none," says our Magna Charta, implying that prior to the existence of this glorious national standard justice had been sold. Aye, aye, kings have sold justice, and there are strong temptations to do so, but when they do so they endanger their kingdom. "The want of uprightness in Saul shook the kingdom in his grasp, and the covetousness of Jehoakim destroyed its foundations, and buried him in its ruins." It is also said here, that if the ruler hearken to lies, "all his servants are wicked." The credulous ruler becomes not only the victim but the implement and the cause of wickedness. He takes in lies, acts upon them, and thus promotes lies in his servants.

Conclusion: Let us pray that a true Rulership may everywhere prevail over the nations of the earth. "Let it please thee to bless rulers, that they may learn to fear the Lord their God, that their heart be not lifted up above their brethren, and that they turn not aside from the commandment to the right hand or to the left." "Let judgment run down as waters, and righteousness as a mighty stream."—*Biblical Liturgy.*

Proverbs 29:5

Flattery, a Net

"A man that flattereth his neighbour spreadeth a net for his feet."

FLATTERY is the subject of these words, and we have had the subject before.* We have it here under the figure of a net—

VARIOUSLY WROUGHT. — "Some praises," says Lord Bacon, "proceed merely of flattery, and if he be an ordinary flatterer, he will have certain common attributes which may serve every man; if he be a cunning flatterer, he will follow the arch flatterer, which is man's self, and wherein a man thinketh best of himself, therein the flatterer will uphold him most. But if he is an impudent flatterer look wherein a man is conscious to himself that he is most defective, and is most out of countenance in himself, that will the flatterer entitle him to, perforce, conscience being

* See Reading on chap. xxvi. 23, 28.

silenced." These nets of flattery are indeed woven of many threads, and of various hues—some are as coarse as a rope, others as fine as a gossamer web; some have their texture of flax, others of silk; some have their hues glaring and coarse, others subdued and delicate—all suited to the character of the prey to be caught. All souls are not to be caught in the same way. What is a vulnerable point in one heart, is impenetrable granite in another. All, however, are more or less susceptible of flattery of some kind or other.

> "As unicorns may be betray'd with trees,
> And bears with glasses, elephants with holes,
> Lions with toils :—so men with flatterers."
>   SHAKESPEARE

Flattery is a net—

WIDELY SPREAD.—"The net of flattery" is spread in all circles and in every path of life. There is more or less of vanity in all natures, and vanity likes flattery; it flatters in order to be flattered. "Flattery," says La Rochefoucauld, "is a bad sort of money to which our vanity gives currency." "Beware of the flatterer," says Bunyan. Yes, beware of him indeed. Flattery is a dangerous net that lies near to every man's foot. It is a cup whose taste is generally delicious, but whose effects are always pernicious, and often mortal. The feet of the strongest men have been entangled in this net; they have fallen into it and been ruined. When Alexander the Great had received from an arrow a wound that would not heal, he said to his parasites, "You say that I am Jupiter's son, but this wound proves me a feeble man." Undeserved praise is always fatal in its effects on the vain-glorious dupe. More dangers lurk in adulation than in abuse, since it is the saliva that kills, and not the bite. Those who are voracious of vain compliments, drink from a Circean cup, which first exhilarates to madness and then destroys.

> "Oh! it is worse than mockery, to listen to the flatterer's tone :
> To lend a ready ear to thoughts the cheeks must blush to own :
> To hear the red lip whispered of, and the flowing curl and eye
> Made constant theme of eulogy extravagant and high :
> And the charm of person worshipped in an homage offered not
> To the perfect charm of virtue and the majesty of thought."
>   J. C. WHITTIER

Proverbs 29:6

The Snare and the Song

"In the transgression of an evil man *there is* a snare: but the righteous doth sing and rejoice."

THE words remind us—

That there is a SNARE FOR THE WICKED.—"In the transgression of an evil man there is a snare." An evil man is a transgressor; it is in fact his transgression that makes him evil. What is transgression? It is not a mere condition of being, it is a positive act, it is a violation of the right; it is not a mere omission, but a commission. Sin is the transgression of the law. The Divine law is so spiritual, penetrating, comprehensive, that it can be transgressed without any overt act; transgressed by thought, desire, volition. In every transgression there is a "*snare*." A snare often to *others*. Every sin is not only an act but a seed; it has in it a self-propagating instinct. No sooner does a man sin than he gets the spirit of the tempter, and with every sin the seductive animus gets strength. Angels sinned and they became the tempters of men. Eve sinned and she became the tempter of Adam. Thus sinners are always ensnaring men. By their specious talk, their mock pleasures, and their seductive arts, they draw the less wary into a "snare." But he is not only a snare to others, but to *himself*. "His foot is taken in his own net." Not only does the trap which he had set for others often bring him to ruin, as did the conduct of the Jews in relation to Christ, but each sin of his is a new entanglement. It increases the terribleness of his moral predicament, it curtails his liberty, renders his freedom more impossible, and his embarrassments more confounding. He is like a man descending a steep road covered with thick mud, and deepening and stiffening as he descends. He cannot go back. His attempt to extricate himself is by taking another step onwards, and this only increases his difficulty; with every sin his feet get deeper and deeper into the "miry clay." There is no liberty where there is sin. The best acts of Parliament passed by a thousand Solons cannot make one sinner free. Every sin tightens his chains, curtails the precincts, and darkens the windows of his cell. Verily in the "transgression of an evil man there is a snare."

That there is A SONG FOR THE RIGHTEOUS.—"The righteous doth sing and rejoice." There is a song in the soul of the good ever ready to break into music; it is the song of gratitude, of liberty, of celestial hope, of holy adoration. Paul and Silas are cast into prison, and the jailor is charged to keep them safely. How do they feel? "At midnight Paul and Silas prayed and sang praises unto God." The righteous alone can truly rejoice. Joy is a dove that can find rest nowhere, but in the heart of a righteous man. "Light is sown for the righteous, and gladness for the upright in heart." "Light seed is sown in the vale of fogs, though often hidden seedlike for a time under the dark clouds of sorrow, it is only taking root in the chastened heart; soon it will appear and bring forth the fragrant flower and mellow fruit, and bloom and grow sweetly and usefully in the garden of God." Happiness as an object of pursuit, is never, can never be attained. It grows out of goodness. The righteous "sing and rejoice" because they are righteous.

"To aim at thine own happiness is an end idolatrous and evil
 In earth : yea, in heaven, if thou seek'st for thyself, seeking thou shalt not find.
 Happiness is a roadside flower, growing on the highway of usefulness :
 Plucked, it shall wither in thy hand ; passed by, it is a fragrance to thy spirit.
 Love not thine own soul ; regard not thine own weal :
 Trample the thyme beneath thy feet : be useful, and be happy."

M. F. TUPPER.

Proverbs 29:7

The Treatment of the Poor, a Test of Character

"The righteous considereth the cause of the poor: *but* the wicked regardeth not to know *it*."

WHILST this verse has perhaps a special reference to the duty of magistrates and judges in relation to the poor, it has a far wider and profounder application. It teaches the doctrine that our treatment of the poor is one test of character: if we are righteous, we consider "the cause of the poor:" if we are wicked, their cause is disregarded by us.

The test is DIVINE.—Everywhere in the Bible the same truth is taught. In the Old Testament we have such passages as these, "Wash you, make you clean: put away the evil of your doings from before mine eyes: cease to do evil: learn to do well: seek judgment: relieve the oppressed: judge the fatherless: plead for the widow."* "Is not this the fast that I have chosen? to loose the bands of wickedness, to undo the heavy burdens, and to let the oppressed go free, and that ye break every yoke? Is it not to deal thy bread to the hungry, and that thou bring the poor that are cast out to thy house? when thou seest the naked that thou cover him: and that thou hide not thyself from thine own flesh?"† And in the New Testament we have such statements as the following:— "Pure religion, and undefiled before God, and the Father is this, To visit the fatherless and widows in their affliction: and to keep himself unspotted from the world."‡ "Whoso hath this world's good, and seeth his brother have need, and shutteth up his bowels of compassion from him, how dwelleth the love of God in him? My little children, let us not love in word, neither in tongue: but in deed and in

---

* Isaiah i. 16, 17.   † Isaiah lviii. 6, 7.   ‡ James i. 27.

truth. And hereby we know that we are of the truth, and shall assure our hearts before him."*

There is no mistaking, then, the fact, that this is a Divine test. The great Judge does not determine our character by the conformity of our belief to any standard of faith, by the mode of our worship, or by the zeal, regularity, and devotion, with which we work out our religious opinions. No, but by our practical kindness to the poor. Practical philanthropy is the Divine test of religion. This is like the diamond, pure and white. "Other graces," we are told, "shine like the precious stones of nature, each with its own hue of brilliance: the diamond emitting all colours in one beautiful and simple white. Love emits all graces." To bear each other's burdens is to fulfil the law of Christ.

The test is PRACTICAL.—It is a test within the reach of every man. Had the test been a standard of theological knowledge, or an ornate method of religious worship, it would have lain out of the reach of many. But practical kindness is always available; for the poor we have ever with us. On all hands there are the naked to be clothed, the hungry to be fed, the diseased to be cured, the ignorant to be enlightened, the destitute to be relieved. Nor can we say, we have not the means to help. Though we may not have worldly goods to supply their need, we have sympathy, we have kind words, we have influence. John Howard, the illustrious philanthropist, wrote in the midst of his perils and dangers in Riga, "I hope I have sources of enjoyment that depend not on the particular spot I inhabit: a rightly cultivated mind, under the power of religion, and the exercise of beneficent dispositions, affords a ground of satisfaction, little affected by *heres* and *theres."*

The test is BLESSED.—Doing good to the poor not only blesses the recipient, but the giver too. Listen to Job's experience. "When the ear heard me, then it blessed: and when the eye saw me, it gave witness to me: because I delivered the poor that cried, and the fatherless, and him

* 1 John iii. 17, 19.

that had none to help him. The blessing of him that was ready to perish came upon me : and I caused the widow's heart to sing for joy. I put on righteousness, and it clothed me : my judgment was as a robe and a diadem. I was eyes to the blind, and feet was I to the lame. I was a father to the poor : and the cause which I knew not I searched out." " Tiberias II. was so liberal to the poor, that his wife blamed him for it. Speaking to him once of his wasting his treasures by this means, he told her, he should never want money so long as, in obedience to Christ's command, he supplied the necessities of the poor. Shortly after this he found a great treasure, under a marble table which had been taken up, and news was also brought him of the death of a very rich man, who had left his whole estate to him." Wilberforce says, " There is a special blessing on being liberal to the poor, and on the family of those who have been so : and I doubt my children will fare better, even in this world, than if I had been saving £20,000 or £30,000 of what has been given away."

The test is FINAL.—What is that which will separate the righteous from the wicked on the last great day? The separation will not be the result of caprice or arbitrary power, but according to a special law in the Divine government. What is that? *Beneficence.* Why are some placed on the right hand? What is the reason the Great Arbiter assigns? Hear it : " I was an hungered, and ye gave me meat ; I was naked, and ye clothed me." This is the principle that determines our destiny. The man who does not live here a life of godly benevolence can never, in the nature of the case, be admitted into heaven. Without this there is no conformity to God. " God is love." "He that loveth not, knoweth not God." Without this there is not fitness for heaven. All in heaven is love. Without this there is no possibility of happiness. Practical benevolence is heaven, practical selfishness is perdition.

" Come, blessed of my heavenly Father, come !
In the high heaven your kingdom is prepared :
Yours is the sceptre and the rich reward.
Haste, for the Saviour calls you to your home :

For I was hungry, and ye brought me bread ;
I thirsted, and your cooling draughts were mine :
O'er my cold limbs the needed vest ye spread ;
A stranger was I, and ye took me in :
I pined in sickness, and ye brought relief :
In the deep dungeon, and ye soothed my grief :
For there my brethren, there, the lowly poor,
Ye sent not cold and empty from your door ;
But ye relieved their wants, and heard their plea :
'Twas done for my sake, and 'tis done for me !"

Proverbs 29:8-11, 20, 22, 23

The Genius of Evil

"Scornful men bring a city into a snare : but wise *men* turn away wrath. *If* a wise man contendeth with a foolish man, whether he rage or laugh, *there is* no rest. The bloodthirsty hate the upright : but the just seek his soul. A fool uttereth all his mind : but a wise *man* keepeth it in till afterwards. . . . Seest thou a man *that is* hasty in his words ? *there is* more hope of a fool than of him. . . An angry man stirreth up strife, and a furious man aboundeth in transgression. A man's pride shall bring him low ; but honour shall uphold the humble in spirit."

WE have gathered these verses together from the chapter because they represent one subject,—the genius of evil. This subject indeed occupies a large portion of the whole book, comes out in almost every page of the Bible, is revealed in every chapter of the world's history, and flashes from all points of social life the world over. Evil is here and has been for sixty long centuries. There is no denying the fact of its existence. It is an ubiquitous presence. It is an all-permeating force. It is a universal pulse throbbing through the life-blood of the race.

It is ESSENTIALLY MALIGNANT.—It is here represented as an *element of contempt*. "Scornful men." Scorn is not only eternally antagonistic to all that is loving and benign, but is a form and expression of the malific. Scorn is fiendish, it has in it the venom of hell. It is here represented as *bloodthirsty*. "The bloodthirsty hate the upright." There is murder in evil. Its advent to this earth was speedily marked by murder. Cain rose up against Abel, his brother, and slew him. It is not only the parent of all assassinations and wars, but of all religious persecutions too. In truth, the better the men the more intent its thirst for their blood; it "hates the upright." John in his apocalyptic vision saw this evil in a human form, the form of a woman. "I saw a woman drunken with the blood of the saints and the blood of the martyrs of Jesus." It is here represented as *furious*. "A furious man aboundeth in transgression." Evil is not like the placid lake but like the troubled sea, the sea whose waters are often lashed by the tempest into the battlings of mountain billows. It is not like the lamb or the dove, but like the ravenous wolf or the bloodthirsty lion in search of prey. It is represented as *proud*. "A man's pride shall bring him low." Pride is sometimes represented as the very spring and heart of evil. "It is a vice," says the illustrious Hooker, "which cleaveth so fast unto the hearts of men, that if we were to strip ourselves of all faults one by one we should undoubtedly find it the very last and hardest to put off." Tupper has put the same idea into a poetical form :—

> "Deep is the sea, and deep is hell; but pride mineth deeper.
> It is coiled as a poisonous worm about the foundations of the soul.
> If thou expose it in thy motives and track it in thy springs of thought,
> Complacent in its own detection, it will seem indignant virtue.
> Smoothly it will gratulate thy skill. O subtle anatomist of self!
> And spurn its very being, while it nestleth the deeper in thy bosom."

Again—

It is ALWAYS UNREASONABLE.—It will not submit to the force of argument. "If a wise man contendeth with a foolish man, whether he rage or laugh, there is no rest." "It would generally be far better not to meddle with such a fool as is here described. We can only deal with him on very disadvantageous terms, and with little prospect of good.* If a wise man contend with the wise, he can make himself understood, and there is some hope of bringing

---

* Chap. xvii. 12; xxvi, 4; Eccles. x. 13; Matt. vii. 6.

the debate to a good issue. But to contend with a fool there is no rest, no peace, no quiet. It will go on without end. He will neither listen to reason nor yield to argument. So intractable is he, that he will either rage or laugh: either vent upon us the fury of an ungoverned temper, or laugh us to scorn." Its unreasonableness is pointed out here by another fact: its speech is not controlled by judgment. "A fool uttereth all his mind, but a wise man keepeth it in till afterwards." "Seest thou a man that is hasty in his words? there is more hope of a fool than of him."* There is an outspokenness that is not only justifiable but praiseworthy, the full, frank, utterance of the mind, where the communication is vital to the interests of others. But this is not like the reckless speech of the man of ungoverned passion. He "uttereth all his mind." All the filth of his heart, all the bitterness of his temper, all the profanity of his spirit, rush out without discretion or control. An old expositor remarks that the "words of a fool are at the very door of his mind, which being always open they readily fly abroad." "A wise man reflects before he speaks, a fool speaks and then reflects on what he has uttered." Evil is against reason, it is eternally opposed to all true philosophy and wisdom: it can only live and work as reason is kept down. As reason rises, widens, and grows, evil must decay and die.

Further—

It is INFLUENTIALLY PERNICIOUS.—It is injurious to *society*. "Scornful men bring a city into a snare, but wise men turn away wrath." In the margin it is rendered, they "set a city on fire." Evil is socially destructive; it is a deadly enemy not only to social order, peace, and prosperity, but to the existence of society. It is everlastingly gnawing at the ties of sympathy and confidence that bind man to man. It is a mighty anarch, eternally warring against all harmony and light, seeking to reduce all to the darkness and the confusion of chaos. Were it not for the good men here, the world would soon rush into a pande-

* Similar expressions have engaged our attention in Readings on chap. xii. 23; xiv. 23; xv. 2; xxvi. 12.

monium. "Wise men turn away wrath"—"the just seek his soul." Every good man is a link in that golden chain with which mercy belts the human world, and prevents the explosive force of its sins from riving it to pieces. It is injurious to *self*. "A man's pride shall bring him low; but honour shall uphold the humble in spirit." "This proverb," says Bishop Hall, "is like unto Shushan, in the streets whereof honour is proclaimed to the humble Mordecai; in the palace whereof an engine of death is erected for the proud Haman." "A man's pride shall bring him low." On its gaudy flaunting pinions it had borne him high up amongst the aerial castles of affluence and splendour, but the time comes when judgment breaks the wings, and down like a millstone he falls.

> "He that is proud eats up himself. Pride is
> His own glass, his own trumpet, his own chronicle,
> And whatever praises itself but in
> The deed, devours the deed in the praise."
> SHAKESPEARE

Proverbs 29:16

The Fall of Evil

"When the wicked are multiplied, transgression increaseth: but the righteous shall see their fall." *

"THE former part of this verse," it has been said, "seems like a truism. The multiplication of the wicked, and the increase of transgression are next to one and the same thing—the former being the increase of the agents of evil, and the latter, of the evil done. They are different; but they are inseparable: the one necessarily includes the other. The meaning may be, that wicked men encourage and embolden one another in iniquity, and that by this means the corruption spreads. Or as, in the second verse

* Verse 15 has been elsewhere discussed.

of the chapter, the same word here rendered 'are multiplied,' is translated ' are in authority,' the reference is in all probability to the influence of wicked rulers in promoting the increase of wickedness in the community, which requires not either illustration or proof." The text points to the fall of evil. Evil will not stand for ever, it is not a moral rock in God's universe, it is a mere creature edifice built on the shifting sand.

It will fall NOTWITHSTANDING ITS INCREASE.—" When the wicked are multiplied, transgression increaseth." Wicked men have been multiplying in this world since the beginning: perhaps they are more numerous to-day than ever in England, as well as in other and more benighted lands. The more numerous they are, the more transgression there is in the world. The more numerous the coral insects, the faster grows the island: and the more numerous sinners become, the higher rises the hellish mountain of transgression. But to whatever proportion evil may grow in the world, however broad its base, and towering its summit, it shall fall; its " mountains shall depart, and its hills be removed." It will fall because it is opposed to the constitution of things: there is nothing in God's universe in which evil can take a lasting roothold. Its roots are only like those of certain marine plants that spring up from one floating wavelet, to be destroyed by the next: or rather like the roots of those atmospheric plants, of which I have somewhere read, that strike only into a wave of air that rolls swiftly on—Heaven knows where. It is not a river rolling from ocean to ocean, fed evermore by the boundless, but a mere stagnant pool which has to be exhaled by the sun. Evil has a thousand forms, it appears not only in the thoughts, words, and deeds of individual life, but in a thousand systems of thoughts, in innumerable institutions and methods of action. But what are these? They have no solid foothold in God's creation; they are only bubbles that appear in the stream of destiny, just here where it is a little agitated; they must break as it swells in volume and approaches the great sea. Evil must fall, because it has in it the seeds of destruction. Error and wrongs in all their forms, carry with them the seeds of dissolution: their bulk is but an unnatural growth, their beauty, but the hectic flush of consumption. Night can only last till the day comes: sin is night, and eternal day is to break on our planet. It must fall, because the Gospel is undermining its foundations. Christ came to destroy the works of the devil. The little stone is put in motion, it shall smite and shiver the huge colossus. It must fall, because Heaven has decreed it. "The kingdoms of this world shall become the kingdoms of our Lord, and of His Christ, and He shall reign for ever and ever." Before the fires of truth and love which Christ kindled in this world, the heaven and earth of evil shall pass away with a great noise, and there shall appear a new heaven and a new earth wherein dwelleth righteousness.

> " One song employs all nations ; and all cry :
> ' Worthy the Lamb, for He was slain for us !'
> The dwellers in the vales and on the rocks
> Shout to each other, and the mountain tops
> From distant mountains catch the flying joy,
> Till nation after nation, taught the strain,
> Earth rolls the rapturous Hosanna round."
> COWPER

It will fall AND THE RIGHTEOUS WILL WITNESS ITS END.—"But the righteous shall see their fall." Noah saw the destruction of the old world; Abraham, the conflagration of Sodom and Gomorrah; Israel beheld the Egyptians sink like lead into the sea. The righteous will survive the fall of evil; their existence, therefore, will stretch far into the ages of the future: for the end of evil is not yet, nay, it is far distant. In the great moral warfare no weapons will ever be invented, by which to slay the enemies in haste; the march is slow; the strokes, however, rapid and powerful, are tardy in working out their deadly results. The wounds are long before they issue in mortification. Sin dies slowly: yet, however remote the period of its utter destruction, the righteous will live to witness it. With what joy will they listen to its death throes, with what rapture will they witness the extinction of its final spark! "Mine eyes shall see my desire on my enemies, and mine ears shall hear my desire of the wicked which rise up against me." "This is, indeed," says Bridges, "the supporting joy of faith; to realise the glory of this day, when the righteous shall see the fall of the now triumphing wicked, and one universal shout shall swell throughout the earth—"Alleluia! Salvation and glory, and honour, and power, unto the Lord our God, for true and righteous are his judgments. Alleluia! .... for the Lord God omnipotent reigneth."

> "The time shall come when every evil thing
> From being and remembrance both shall die:
> The world one solid temple of pure good."
>
> FESTUS

Proverbs 29:18

Divine Revelation

"Where *there is* no vision, the people perish; but he that keepeth the law, happy *is* he." *

WE take the word "*vision*" here to mean the redemptive revelations of God. Such revelations exist. God has at "sundry times and in divers manners" made redemptive revelations of His mind to human souls. These communications were recorded by "holy men, who spake as they were moved by the Holy Ghost." The records form the book we call the Bible. Concerning this Book of books Dryden has well said:

> "Whence but from Heaven could men, unskilled in arts,
> In several ages born, in several parts,
> Weave such agreeing truths? or how or why
> Should all conspire to cheat us with a lie?
> Unasked their pains, ungrateful their advice:
> Starving their gain, and martyrdom their price."

The text presents two facts concerning this redemptive revelation.

Its ABSENCE IS A GREAT CALAMITY.—"Where there s no vision the people perish." The word "perish" has

* Verse 17 has been noticed in a previous Reading.

been variously rendered: some read "will apostatize," others "are made naked," others "are dispersed," others "are become disorderly." All renderings agree in expressing the idea of calamity, and truly is it not a sad calamity to be deprived of the Bible? What is the intellectual, social, and spiritual condition of the millions of heathendom? Are not the dark places of the earth full of the habitations of cruelty? What was the condition of our forefathers before the Bible reached our shores? Where the Bible is not, where is the Father God? Where are pure friendships, where are immortal hopes, where are progressive sciences, where are beneficent institutions, where are the streams of pure social loves, where are the raptures of liberty and the sunbeams of unearthly joys? Men in this life without this "*vision*"—the Bible—are like voyagers on a boundless waste of waters without a star, a pilot, or a compass to direct them, in a condition as miserable as the two hundred three score and sixteen souls who, after being "driven up and down Adria" for fourteen sunless and tempestuous days, were wrecked with Paul on the shores of Melita.

> "Star of eternity! The only star
> By which the bark of man can navigate
> The sea of life, and gain the coast of bliss
> Securely: only star which rose on time,
> And, on its dark and troubled billows, still,
> As generation, drifting swiftly by,
> Succeeded generation, threw a ray
> Of Heaven's own light, and, to the hills of God,
> The eternal hills, pointed the sinner's eye."
>
> POLLOCK

Another fact here concerning this revelation is—

ITS REGULATIVE EXPERIENCE IS A GREAT BLESSING.—"He that keepeth the law happy is he." This "vision" is not an abstraction or a speculative system, it is a "*law.*" It comes with Divine authority; it demands obedience; it is not the mere subject for a creed, but the code for a life; its aim is to regulate all the movements of the soul. It is only those who are ruled by it that are made happy. Those who have it and are not controlled by it, will as assuredly perish as those into whose possession it has never come. It is not the hearers of the law who are just before God, but the doers of the law. "If ye know these things happy are ye if ye do them." "Whoso looketh into the perfect law of liberty and continueth therein, he being not a forgetful hearer, but a doer of the work, this man shall be blessed in his deed." Who is the happy man? Not the man who has the "vision" and does not study it, nor the man who studies it and never reduces it to practice; it is the man who translates the "vision" into his life. "He that keepeth the law happy is he." There is no heaven for man but in obedience to God. "It is foolish to strike," says Seneca, "with what we cannot avoid: we are born subjects, and to obey God is perfect liberty: he that does this shall be free, safe, and quiet; all his actions shall succeed to his wishes."

Proverbs 29:19, 21

Types of Servants

"A servant will not be corrected by words: for though he understand he will not answer. . . . He that delicately bringeth up his servant from a child shall have him become *his* son at the length." *

WE mistake when we think of servants as a class of persons confined to the lower grades of life. Most men are servants; those who are masters in relation to some, are servants in relation to others, and so on, from the humblest cottager to the waiters in palaces and attendants at courts. It is probable, however, that Solomon here refers to the servants of the more menial order, those who serve not as private secretaries, commercial clerks, or political ministers, but as farm labourers and domestic attendants. Of these there are two types in these verses.

The STUBBORN.—"A servant will not be corrected by

* Verse 20 has been noticed in a previous Reading.

words." The language does not mean that masters are authorised to employ any other correcting instruments than words: it lends no authority to the use of corporeal violence or force. It means that correcting words for some servants are utterly unavailing. "Though he understand he will not answer." There are servants of such stubborn make and sulky mood, that the correcting words of their employers make no more impression than rain-drops on the granite rock. Some render the language thus—"a servant will not be corrected by words; though he understand, yet will he not obey." How are such servants to be dealt with? By an immediate discharge from your employment? This would show a hastiness of temper which, in itself, is bad; it might also be to your own disadvantage, for there might be a possibility of making them useful. And then, too, it would be too harsh and cruel treatment towards a fellow-creature with whom you have been brought into a somewhat close relationship. How then? By the infliction of corporeal punishment? This would be morally wrong: you are not to lay violent hands on any man. If stubbornness is the only fault, there is a way to overcome it; it is by kindness, a strong, manly, dignified, unmistakeable kindness. As ice to the sunbeam, stubbornness yields to kindness. Where this fails the servant is incorrigible, and discharge from your employment is the only alternative. The advice of Quarles to masters is worthy of notice. "If thou wouldest have a good servant, let the servant find thee a good master. Be not angry with him too long, lest he think thee malicious; nor too soon, lest he conceive thee rash; nor too often, lest he count thee humorous."

THE TRACTABLE.—"He that delicately bringeth up his servant from a child, shall have him become his son at the length." Elzas gives this rendering to these words, "He who indulgeth his slave from his youth will find him in the end behaving as his offspring." Some suppose the idea to be this, "He who treats his slave with greater tenderness than is suited to his condition, will find that he will presume upon the kindness of his master, and conduct

himself in a manner utterly unsuited to his station in life."
There is another side, however, to the kindness of the
master to his servant, that is, the making of the servant
feel towards him all the sympathy and interest of a
son. There are those servants so tractable in nature
as to be inspired with the love of children to their
masters when kindness has been shown. As a rule, those
in our employ serve us best who love us most; they
are not eye, but heart servants; they move not by the
letter of command, but by the spirit of duty. The kindest
master and mistress will generally have the best servants.
He who can make his servant feel towards him as a loving,
faithful, dutiful child, will reap the greatest comfort and
advantage from his service. Steele has said that, "it is
not only paying wages, and giving commands that constitutes a master of a family, but prudence, equal behaviour,
with a readiness to protect and cherish them, is what
entitles a man to that character in their very hearts and
sentiments."

Proverbs 29:24

Commercial Partnerships

"Whoso is partner with a thief hateth his own soul: he heareth cursing, and bewrayeth *it* not." *

A PARTNERSHIP life is becoming more and more common
and necessary in our commercial England. Great undertakings can only be carried out by companies. Modern
legislation has greatly encouraged these combinations, by
limiting the monetary liability of its members. Hence,
joint-stock companies are multitudinous and multiplying.
Such companies are often, perhaps, generally projected,
promoted, and managed, by selfish, needy, and unprincipled
speculators; and honest men are often tempted by the

---

* Verses 22 and 23 have been discussed in a previous Reading.

glowing promises of their lying programmes to become their adherents, and they soon find themselves in the unfortunate position referred to in the text—"partners with thieves." The text suggests as to this position:

That it is SOUL-RUINOUS.—"Whoso is partner with a thief hateth his own soul." Whether he be a partner with one thief or one hundred, he is doing an injury to his own spiritual nature. Being a partner, he gives his sanction to the fallacious statements, the dishonest principles, and the dishonourable tricks of the Firm; he participates in the results of legalized frauds and falsehoods. Hence he has contracted a guilt which unless removed will damage his soul for ever. " He may," says a modern expositor, " screen his conscience under the pretext of his not doing the deed; but such a screen is a mere cobweb; it will not stand a breath. He may possibly be even worse. If he flatters himself that he is getting the profit without the sin, when he is coolly and deliberately allowing another to damn his own soul—taking no concern about that, provided he get something by it—he must indeed be under the power of a strong delusion. The receiver and resetter is at least as guilty as the thief. I say at least; for in one obvious respect he is worse. His is a general trade, which gives encouragement to many thieves, by holding out to them the means of disposing of their stolen property, and evading the law. He is, in fact, a partaker in the guilt of all. One thief cannot set up and maintain a resetter, but one resetter may keep at their nefarious trade many thieves. Moreover, when the thief swears falsely, the partner is tempted to allow the perjury to pass undetected, lest he should expose himself as well as the thief; by which means he covers the guilt of another doubly—in the theft and the perjury. Nay, if he were summoned as a witness, he is tempted to similar perjury himself, and so to bring additional guilt more directly upon his own soul." On this subject we could write pages from our own bitter experience. Years ago we embarked in two companies, not for mercenary or commercial ends, but in order to work out our philanthropic aspirations—one, indeed, we not only originated ourselves, but obtained by our advocacy, nearly 10,000 adherents, and a nominal capital of £240,000. We soon found ourselves in partnership with thieves. Numbers joined it who not only had no sympathy with its lofty purpose, but who were influenced by a rapacious greed. As hungry vultures gather about a dead carcase, they hastened to clutch the funds. Our efforts to extricate ourselves from the ungodly partnership gave us years of distracting agony, and led to the frustration of our objects.* The other, which we joined from similar unmercenary and benevolent motives, brought us in association with the same wretched class of men, and terminated in a serious loss to all the honest members, and a rich harvest to the managing swindlers. Thank Heaven, we are free from such associations; we have escaped like a bird from the hand of the fowler. We record our experience here, in order to warn young men who in this and in future times may peruse these pages. My young brother, "have no fellowship with the unfruitful works of darkness, but rather reprove them."

That it is SOCIALLY UNJUST.—" He heareth cursing and bewrayeth it not." Dishonesty is committed by the members of the Firm, he is called to give evidence on his oath concerning his knowledge of the deed. His interests and reputation are so involved in the company, and he is so solemnly bound to secrecy, that he will perjure himself rather than betray his swindling partners. When the solemn adjuration is put to him in the court in the name of God to declare the truth, he "bewrayeth it not." Thus he injures society: he allows the swindling Firm to proceed plundering society, rifling the pockets and ruining the homes of honest men.

Conclusion: Eschew bad company. It is said of Pythagoras that before he admitted any one into his school he inquired who were his intimates, implying his belief that those who chose bad companions would not be profited by his instructions. But whilst bad companions in free, social life, are an evil to be denounced and shunned, they are worse in commercial life; worse when you are linked to them by

* See *Homilist*, vol. xxxix., p. 393.

selfishness sanctioned by law. Young men, believe me that England teems with reckless speculators, hungry sharks who are ever in quest of their prey. Most plausible men for the most part they are: they fawn and guile you into their meshes. "One rotten apple," says Feltham, "will infect the store: the putrid grape corrupts the whole sound cluster. If I have found any good companions I will cherish them as the choicest of men, or as angels which are sent as guardians to me. If I have any bad ones, I will study to lose them, lest by keeping them I lose myself in the end."

> "Some love the glow of outward show:
> Some love mere wealth, and try to win it:
> The house to me may lowly be,
> If I but like the people in it.
> What's all the gold that glitters cold,
> When linked to hard or haughty feeling?
> Whate'er we're told, the nobler gold
> Is truth of heart and manly dealing.
> Then let them seek whose minds are weak
> Mere fashion's smile, and try to win it:
> The house to me may lowly be,
> If I but like the people in it."
> CHARLES SWAIN

> "Avoid a villain as you would a brand;
> Which, lighted, burns; extinguished, smuts the hand."
> *Oriental*

Proverbs 29:25-27

Social Life

"The fear of man bringeth a snare: but whoso putteth his trust in the LORD shall be safe. Many seek the ruler's favour; but *every* man's judgment *cometh* from the LORD. An unjust man *is* an abomination to the just; and *he that is* upright in his way *is* an abomination to the wicked."

THESE verses lead us to consider two subjects belonging to social life:—infirmities, and their moral antidotes; antipathies and their true cause.

SOCIAL INFIRMITIES AND THEIR MORAL ANTIDOTE.—
What are the infirmities referred to in this passage? There
are two. (1) Social *timidity*. "The fear of man bringeth
a snare." Account for it how you like, there is in the
human heart a "fear of man." It shows itself in many
ways, and is manifest in all departments of activity. It
seems to be the fear of servility rather than of alarm;
it implies an exaggerated opinion of man's greatness and power. This fear makes the author tremble
before his critic, the preacher before his congregation,
and the orator before his audience; it "bringeth a
snare." It often prevents men from honestly working
out their convictions. Whatever is unpopular, however
righteous and urgent, is kept in silence if not denied.
"It was the fear of man that tempted Abraham, and
after him his son Isaac, to similar and repeated pre-
varication and falsehood." It was the fear of man in
Aaron that made the molten calf even when the vision of
the burning mount should have impressed the fear of God.
It was the fear of man that stained the page of David's
history with such deplorable instances of duplicity and
dissembling. It was the fear of man that led Peter to
deny Christ, and at a later period to dissemble so unwor-
thily as to draw down upon him the censure of his fellow
apostle. It was the fear of man that made the friends and
fellow servants of Paul, when he was brought to trial
before Nero, act with such dastardly unkindness as to give
him cause to say, "No man stood with me, all forsook
me." Secret disciples are afraid publicly to acknowledge
their faith in Christ, because Christianity is unpopular in
their circle. This is the worst and most prevalent of
cowardices. Men who can stand calm in the battle-field
in the presence of the advancing host are too cowardly to
propound an unpopular doctrine, perform an unpopular
act, or espouse an unpopular cause. There is (2) Social
servility. "Many seek the ruler's favour." This state of
mind is nearly akin to the former; it branches from the same
root:—the desire for that honour which cometh from men.
There are those in society whose eyes are ever upturned

with a suppliant expression; to them a smile from their superiors is a sunbeam. They are found in all social grades, from the lowest to the highest. They are generally tyrants as well as sycophants. Whilst they fawn on those above them, they treat with haughty insolence those beneath. It is a crawling, cringing, miserable spirit this, that takes possession of men; it is a canker in the heart of a nation eating out its independency and manhood.

What is the *antidote* referred to in the passage? Trust in the Lord. "Whoso putteth his trust in the Lord shall be safe." He who centres his trust in the supremely wise and good, will soon rise superior to the smiles and frowns of man. To those who look out upon society from the stand-point of trust in God, the greatest magnates of the world will appear only as grasshoppers. They know that "Every man's judgment cometh from the Lord." There is a Providence over all, without whose permission the greatest men can do nothing. He who can say, "Surely my judgment is with the Lord," will stand before his race with undaunted heroism, and before his God with devotion. Conscious dependence on the Almighty is the spirit of independence towards men. Here are—

SOCIAL ANTIPATHIES AND THEIR TRUE CAUSE.—"An unjust man is an abomination to the just." There is a mutual hatred between the good and the bad, old as the devil, deep as hell, strong and universal as death. The antagonisms between the righteous and the wicked though mutual are not identical in reason. The one springs from conscience, the other from passion; the one refers to the character the other to the existence. The righteous hate the character, not the persons of the wicked, whereas the wicked hate not the character but the persons of the righteous. It is a terrible thing to be an "abomination to the just." It is to be in antagonism with the will of God, and the cause of universal order and happiness. On the contrary, it is a glorious and blessed thing to be an abomination to the wicked, their hatred is but the hatred of passion not conscience, for conscience is bound, in all worlds and for ever, to reverence the right. So long as wickedness exists this mutual antagonism must continue. O come the time when the woman's conquering seed shall bruise the serpent's head!

> " Drums and battle cries
> Go out in music of the morning star;
> And soon we shall have thinkers in the place
> Of fighters; each formidable as a man
> To strike electric influence through a race,
> Unstayed by city-wall and barbican."
> ELIZABETH BARRETT BROWNING

Proverbs 30:1-9
Agur, as a Philosopher, a Bibleist and a Suppliant

"The words of Agur the son of Jakeh, *even* the prophecy: the man spake unto Ithiel, even unto Ithiel and Ucal, surely I *am* more brutish than *any* man, and have not the understanding of a man. I neither learned wisdom, nor have the knowledge of the holy. Who hath ascended up into heaven, or descended? who hath gathered the wind in his fists? who hath bound the waters in a garment? who hath established all the ends of the earth? what *is* his name, and what *is* his son's name, if thou canst tell? Every word of God *is* pure: he *is* a shield to them that put their trust in him. Add thou not unto his words, lest he reprove thee, and thou be found a liar. Two *things* have I required of thee; deny me *them* not before I die: remove far from me vanity and lies: give me neither poverty nor riches; feed me with food convenient for me: lest I be full, and deny *thee*, and say, Who *is* the LORD? or lest I be poor, and steal, and take the name of my God *in vain*."

THESE verses to the end of the book form a kind of supplement to what are properly called the Proverbs of Solomon. His proverbs, those selected by himself and those copied by the men of God in the days of Hezekiah, closed with the close of the 29th chapter. It may be that the men who copied his proverbs were Divinely inspired to publish this appendix. Whoever Agur was, whether he was one of the sons of the prophets or not, he was evidently a 'man of God," and endowed with the gift of prophecy.

It is supposed that the others, Ithiel and Ucal, were two of his scholars. The words lead us to look on him as representing a devout philosopher, an intelligent Bibleist, and an enlightened suppliant.

As a DEVOUT PHILOSOPHER.—As a devout sage he seems to have been deeply conscious of two things :—First : Of his *ignorance*. " Surely I am more brutish than any man, and have not the understanding of a man. I neither learned wisdom, nor have the knowledge of the holy." This is not the language of some one else about him, but the language of himself, and it indicates a profound sense of his own ignorance. Perhaps his two disciples, Ithiel and Ucal, were young men, and, like young students generally, were disposed to pride themselves on their mental ability and attainments ; and hence their teacher thus expressed himself strongly concerning his own intellectual deficiency in order to check their vanity. " I neither learned wisdom nor have the knowledge of the holy." The word " holy " in the original is " holies," by which, perhaps, he means the Divine reasons of things, the eternal principles that underlie the universe. Thus he shows his humility. Humility is at once the characteristic and qualification of all true philosophy. The first lesson for every man who would get knowledge to learn is, that he knows nothing. This was the great Newton's experience. Secondly : He was conscious of *universal mystery*. " Who hath ascended up into heaven or descended ? who hath gathered the wind in his fists ? who hath bound the water in a garment ? who hath established all the ends of the earth ? What is his name, and what is his son's name, if thou canst tell ? " The spirit of these words is the same as that contained in Job vii. 9, 12. Agur means to say, there was no one amongst the sons of men able to penetrate into the reason of things, to reach and reveal the eternal secrets of nature. He challenges his disciples to bring forward the name of any man who has ever done so. " What is his name, and what is his son's name ?" Go amongst the greatest philosophers, select one of the chief of their number, and tell me how much he knows of the universe. He means perhaps farther to intimate, that he who could comprehend the works of God must be God Himself.

So far this Agur reveals the spirit of a *true* philosopher. No man is a genuine sage who has not this profound spirit of humility. The words lead us to look on Agur—

As an INTELLIGENT BIBLEIST.—" Every word of God is pure." " He is a shield unto them that put their trust in Him." " Add thou not unto His words, lest He reprove thee, and thou be found a liar." Here he turns from nature to the Scriptures—the Word of God—that which we call the Bible. He was more than a naturalist; he was a Bibleist. Here we have his views of the Word of God. First: He regarded it as *holy*. " Every word of God is pure." The book that we call the Bible contains other words besides the word of God, but all that it contains of the word of God is pure, pure in its essence and in its influence. It commends itself to the universal conscience. Secondly: He regarded it as *trustworthy*. "A shield unto them that put their trust in Him." God's word is Himself —Himself revealed, and it can be trusted, and he who trusts it is in safe keeping. " Scepticism and infidelity," says a writer on this passage, "unsettle the mind. They leave it without confidence and without security. The mind under their influence is like a vessel that has drifted from its moorings, and has been left to drive out to sea without rudder and without anchor—unmanned, and at the mercy of the winds and waves and currents, or, to keep nearer to the allusion in the verse under comment, it is like a soldier in the thick and peril of the battle without a shield, in danger from every arrow that flies, and every sword that is raised against him. They make their unhappy subject the sport and victim of every delusive theory and every temptation of Satan. Thirdly: He regarded it as *sufficient*. "Add thou not unto his words lest he reprove thee, and thou be found a liar." It requires no addition, nor will it suffer subtraction; it is like a vital germ, you can neither attempt to add anything to it or take anything from it, without injuring it. Christ Himself repeats these words of Agur: "I testify unto every man that heareth the words of the prophecy of this book," &c., &c. (Revelation xxii. 18, 19.)

Such was Agur as a Bibleist. Would that we all practically estimated the Bible as he did! The words lead us to look on Agur—

As an ENLIGHTENED SUPPLIANT.—"Two things have I required of thee; deny me them not before I die; remove far from me vanity and lies; give me neither poverty nor riches; feed me with food convenient for me; lest I be full and deny thee, and say who is the Lord? or lest I be poor and steal, and take the name of my God in vain." Here Agur turns both from nature and the Bible to God Himself, and prays; and what does he pray for? Two things. First: *Deliverance from moral evil*—"Remove far from me vanity and lies." An expression this that covers all wrong; all wrong in theory and practice—in sentiment and life. Sin is a delusion, an unreality, a huge falsehood. David felt this, and said, "Who can understand his error? Cleanse thou me from secret faults." He prays Secondly: *For a moderate amount of worldly goods.*—"Give me neither poverty nor riches." Why not poverty? Because of the sufferings and hardships it entails? No. Why not riches? Because of the anxieties and responsibilities connected with them? No. Here is the reason, "Lest I be full and deny thee, and say—Who is the Lord? or lest I be poor and steal, and take the name of my God in vain." The words imply his conviction that dishonesty was a far more terrible evil than poverty, that piety was infinitely more valuable than gold. The man was fully alive to the power of circumstances upon character, and devoutly desired that his external circumstances should be such as to conduce to spiritual excellence.

Here is a man worthy of our study and imitation. As philosophic enquirers into the secrets of nature, let us endeavour to get the humility which animated Agur; as professed believers in the Bible, let us have the same practical confidence in its purity, trustworthiness, and sufficiency, as Agur had; and as suppliants addressing our petitions to heaven, let us seek to be placed amongst those circumstances which will prove subservient to our spiritual culture and growth in goodness. Thus did Agur.

Proverbs 30:10

The False Accuser

"Accuse not a servant unto his master, lest he curse thee, and thou be found guilty."

THERE is a great tendency in a large number of persons to find fault with others, and to make accusations; their eyes are generally open and keen to detect imperfections in their fellow-men, and their tongues are always ready to proclaim them. This tendency in a man is powerful and operative in proportion to the depravity of his own heart. He who has the "beam" in his own eye is ever more anxious to discover the "mote" that is in his brother's. The greatest sinner is always the greatest censor. All history shows this. How severe was the judgment which David pronounced upon the man whose portrait Nathan drew! How vigorous and hasty was the judgment which the proud Pharisee in the temple passed upon the penitent publican! How ready were the Scribes and Pharisees ever to pronounce the severest judgment upon the conduct of Christ and His disciples! The greatest sinners adjudged to death the holiest Being that ever trod this earth, even the blessed Son of God Himself. There is no difficulty in accounting for this remarkable, but patent fact. (1.) There is the self-blinding influence of evil. The greater the sinner, the more ignorant he is of himself and the more unconscious he becomes of the "beam" that is in his own eye. He fancies himself spiritually rich and increased in goods, and needing nothing. (2.) There is the self-hardening influence of evil. The more a man sins, the less he cares for others. He respects neither the claims of society nor of God. He has no regard for the feelings or the reputation of others; fault finding and slander become his most pleasing work. (3.) There is the self-dissatisfying influence of evil. Sin makes his spirit restless as the "troubled sea." It is ever characteristic of a dissatisfied soul to envy the happiness of others, and to seek its destruction. Let us remember that censoriousness grows with sin, and every desire to pass rash judgments upon others is an indication of some great wrong in ourselves. "Charity hopeth all things." The prince of criminals in the universe is the chief of all accusers.

The verse under notice points to an accusation that must be regarded as unjust, heartless, and self-injurious. It is—

UNJUST.—"Accuse not (or, as it is in the margin, hurt not with thy tongue) a servant unto his master." The writer of course does not mean that accusation is not to be made where there is real and righteous cause for it. He who hears the character of an employer calumniated, sees his property plundered, and his interests injured by his servant, would be unjust not to make the accusation. Not to give information to the master against such a servant would be a dereliction of duty, and an encouragement to immorality. There are two kinds of accusations that come under this interdict. One is the *officious* with very *small* reasons. Some little fault, some duty forgotten or mistake committed, which good sense and charity would allow to pass unnoticed, is from an officious spirit brought under the notice of the master, and thus a fictitious significance of culpability is given to it. There is a meddlesome class in all circles, who are constantly doing work of this kind, and they deserve the condemnation of all honourable, righteous, and peace-loving men. The other kind of accusation that comes under this interdict is, what we might call *vicious*, with *false* reasons. The charge is a fabrication presented from dishonest and malicious motives. The accuser has some selfish end to gain, some base passion to gratify; and he does not hesitate to inflict injury upon "the servant." To both these accusers, the officious and the vicious, these words of Agur are addressed, "Accuse not a servant unto his master." The verse points to an accusation, that is—

HEARTLESS.—It is a *"servant"* that is accused "unto his master." An unjust accusation brought against anyone—brought against a rich man to his dependents, or an employer to his employés, is morally reprehensible; but an additional element of turpitude is added to it when the accusation is brought against a servant to his master. It must be borne in mind that the Jewish servants were ordinarily slaves. They were at the absolute disposal of their masters, and were frequently the victims of cruelty. He who, by a false accusation, sought to damage such, would be guilty of a ruthless inhumanity. Albeit there are men of this miserable type—men who are too cowardly to inflict a righteous chastisement upon the wrongs of the rich, but who gratify their miserable malevolence by adding to the sufferings of the indigent and oppressed. The verse points to an accusation that is

SELF-INJURIOUS.—"Lest he curse thee, and thou be found guilty." The vile slanderer, who unjustly destroys the confidence of a master in his servant, and deprives the latter of his reputation and his livelihood, will have his reward. He will be cursed. Poor as his victim is, he has the heart of a man, and he can hate and curse. He can flash the lightnings of indignation and hurl the fulminations of revenge. It is no small evil to be hated by any man. Could we see things as they are, we should feel that it is a far more terrible thing to live amongst men burning with indignation towards us, than to dwell upon the volcanic mountain, whose fiery jaws are about opening to engulf our habitation. But this is not the only evil. He will not only be "cursed" by the servant, but be "found guilty." Found guilty at the bar of his own conscience, and found guilty at the tribunal of the Great Judge.

Let masters be cautious in listening to accusations

brought against their servants. Remember the words of our great dramatist :

> " To urge an accusation is no proof,
> Without more certain and more overt test
> Than their slight habits and poor likelihoods,
> And seemings passion-framed prefer in judgment."

Proverbs 30:11-14

Many Races in One

" *There is* a generation *that* curseth their father, and doth not bless their mother. *There is* a generation *that are* pure in their own eyes, and *yet* is not washed from their filthiness. *There is* a generation, O how lofty are their eyes! and their eyelids are lifted up. *There is* a generation, whose teeth *are as* swords, and their jaw teeth *as* knives, to devour the poor from off the earth, and the needy from *among* men."

THAT there is but *one* human race is a fact well-established and generally received; all men are of common origin, nature, and responsibility. " God hath made of one blood all nations of men to dwell on the face of the earth." But the verses before us teach, that whilst the human race is one *physically*, it is many in a *moral* respect. They speak of four distinct generations, races or families. Paul says, " All flesh is not the same flesh—there is one kind of flesh of men, another flesh of beasts, another of fishes, and another of birds." And verily, in moral temperament and characteristics there is as great a difference between men of the same generation as there is between the beasts of the forest, the finny tribes of ocean, and the fowls of Heaven. Why Agur calls these various moral classes of men " generations " I know not; unless it be that, like the physical generations, they *succeed* and *propagate* each other. These moral classes are found in every age; they come down in regular succession. Man transmits to posterity his moral character as well as his physical attributes.

Like produces like in the spiritual, as well as in the material domain. The four moral generations here are the unnatural, the self-deluded, the haughty, and the cruel.

The UNNATURAL.—"There is a generation that curseth their father and doth not bless their mother." This is an outrage on the natural instinct that teaches love and obedience. Children who curse their father and bless not their mother are human beings "without natural affection," as Paul would say. This is a moral generation which has been large in every age, and which, from the number of "fast young men" and "girls of the period," is, I trow and fear, rapidly on the increase. The young are always the most numerous and important class in society. They come into the inheritance of all the good of the past, and they have to determine all the destinies of the future. To a genuine philanthropist, therefore, no sight is more saddening than a generation that "curseth their father and doth not bless their mother." It is the most infamous, pernicious, and detestable race. "I am a father," says Dr. Wardlaw, "but I trust I do not speak as a father only, but as a son too, whose memory blesses the departed objects of filial love, when I say that with nothing that concerns me would I trust the youth or the man that "curseth his father and doth not bless his mother." There is nothing that is good there; no principle on which to depend. It is well that men have agreed to execrate conduct so unnatural. Notice another moral generation here, which is—

The SELF-DELUDED.—"There is a generation that are pure in their own eyes, and yet is not washed from their filthiness." These are morally corrupt,—Whatever may be the brilliancy of their genius, the greatness of their talents, the vastness of their information, the orthodoxy of their creed, the regularity of their devotions and the refinement of their manners, their souls are not "washed from their filthiness." And yet, notwithstanding this fact, they are so deluded that "they are pure in their own eyes." The moral filth within them they have covered over, and on the covering they have painted the picture of an angel as the portrait of themselves, and on it they look with the eye of admiration. The men of this generation are like the fabled Narcissus, who, having resisted all the charms of others, one day came to an open fountain of silvery clearness. He stooped down to drink and saw his own image, and thought it some beautiful water spirit living in the fountain. He gazed and admired the eyes, the neck, the hair, the lips. He fell in love with himself. In vain he sought a kiss and an embrace. He talked to the charmer, but received no response. He could not break the fascination, and so he pined away and died. These men judge themselves by conventional standards, not by the principles of everlasting right; they are the Pharisees of every age. They are found in every church; and they are the vaunting leaders of little sects and have their sycophantic bigots to cheer them on. They "thank God they are not as other men." Notice yet another moral generation, which is—

The HAUGHTY.—"There is a generation, O how lofty are their eyes? And their eyelids are lifted up." Why are they proud? What are the objects in which this generation pride themselves? They are very various. Some are proud of their personal beauty. How absurd is this, since for neither form nor feature can they take any credit. Some of their lineage. They think of their aristocratic birth, and look with lofty scorn upon all who are plebeian born; a reason still more absurd is this than the former. Some of their wealth. Purse-pride is perhaps the most common and at the same time the most contemptible of all prides. Some pride themselves on their office. Such men move about with the ludicrous air of those who are clothed with a little brief authority. You find this from the holders of high office down to some little mayor or common councilman, from the Archbishop to the poor half-starved curate. Some pride themselves on their own learning. This is certainly more reasonable than the pride of the others, since man deserves some credit for labouring after knowledge. Some pride themselves on their own goodness. They thank God they are not as other men, and say, "Stand by thyself, come not near me, for I am holier than thou." Indeed this is the common language of this generation; they seem to say, "Stand by thyself, for I am nobler, I am wiser, I am richer, I am higher in office, and more religious than thou." "A kite," says the fable, "having risen to a very great height moved in the air as stately as a prince, and looked down with much contempt on all below." "What a superior being I am now!" said the kite; "who has ever ascended so high as I have? What a poor, grovelling set of beings are those beneath me! I despise them." And then he shook his head in derision, and then he wagged his tail; and again he steered along with so much state as if the air were all his own, and as if everything must make way before him, when suddenly the string broke, and down fell the kite with greater haste than he ascended, and was greatly hurt in the fall." When Severus, Emperor of Rome, found his end approaching, he cried out, "I have been everything and everything is nothing." Then ordering the urn to be brought to him, in which his ashes were to be enclosed on his body being burned, he said, "Little urn, thou shalt contain one for whom the world was too little."

Notice the other generation here which is—

The CRUEL.—"There is a generation whose teeth are as swords, and their jaw teeth as knives, to devour the poor from off the earth and the needy from among men." The class of men here are the heartless, ruthless, insatiable oppressors, men utterly destitute of all tenderness of heart, of all loving sympathy, with their fellow creatures. History abounds with them; they teem in every page of the history of wars, colonizations, slaveries, merchandize, hard as iron, cold as death. Occasions sometimes occur when this generation appears in all its strength and savage heartlessness. It is said that at the time of the destruction of the man-of-war, "Prince George," by fire, off Lisbon, by which 485 persons perished, some of the fishermen and merchantmen, of whom there were many around the burning ship, instead of rescuing their fellow creatures, busied themselves in picking up fowls, and whatever else floated to them from the wreck, except drowning sailors. With this generation moral argument has seldom any power.

> "You may as well use question with the wolf,
> Why he hath made the ewe bleat for the lamb;
> You may as well forbid the mountain pines
> To wag their high tops, and to make no noise
> When they are fretted with the gusts of heaven.
> You may as well do anything most hard,
> As seek to soften that (than which, what's harder?)—
> A cruel heart."
>
> SHAKESPEARE

Proverbs 30:24-28

Practical Lessons from Insect Life

"There be four *things which are* but little upon the earth, but they *are* exceeding wise: the ants *are* a people not strong, yet they prepare their meat in the summer; the conies *are but* a feebie folk, yet they make their houses in the rocks; the locusts have no king, yet go they forth all of them by bands; the spider taketh hold with her hands, and is in kings' palaces." *

THERE are four classes of creatures here presented to our study. The *Ants*. The history of these little creatures is most interesting and remarkable. They show their wisdom in their social habits and economical arrangements, in their unwearied industry and prudent foresight. Cicero believed that the ant was furnished not only with senses, but also with mind, reason, and memory. The *Conies*. Some consider this animal to be a well-known creature of Mount Libanus, of the rabbit size and form. Its usual home and refuge is in the holes and clefts of the rocks. Some render the word here "mountain mice." There is no way, however, of settling what animal is meant, with exactness. All that is taught here is, that because they are feeble and incapable of protecting themselves, they

---

* The subject of verse 17 has been discussed in previous Reading. Verses 15, 16, 18, 19, 20, 21, 22, and 23 are omitted for obvious reasons.

seek their refuge in high rocks. The *Locusts*. These, it is said, "have no king, yet go they forth all of them by bands." Naturalists and travellers furnish astonishing accounts of these creatures. They tell us how their countless myriads travel in such immense and compact legions as to darken the air and desolate the most fertile plains. It is not, however, to their number or their destructiveness that these words refer, but to the order and simultaneousness of their movements. They keep time and rank as if they were under the direction of a consummate general. Here is the *Spider*. This creature, it is here said, "taketh hold with her hands, and is in kings' palaces." The structure of this little creature is full of wonders, and the ingenuity, delicacy, and adaptation of its workmanship is marvellous. Its web is constructed with as much accuracy as if it were acquainted with all the laws of architecture and mathematics. What lessons are taught by these various tribes of inferior life? In the "ant" we discover foresight, industry, discretion; in the "coney," prudence in the selection of safe and suitable dwellings; in the "locust," we learn the benefit of order, union, and co-operation in the object of our efforts; and in the "spider" the advantage of ingenuity and diligence in the arts of life. It has been remarked by some that these four tribes of life symbolize all that is requisite for the well-being of a home, a state, or a kingdom. There is the supply of food which the ants work for, suitable dwellings which the conies select, united action which the locusts perform, and skilfulness and perseverance represented by the spider. There are, however, two great practical lessons that we may learn from these little creatures.

That we SHOULD ACT OUT OUR NATURE.—These little creatures differ widely in their constitution, yet they all agree in this—they all act out their respective powers. They war not against their instincts. A man ought to act according to his whole nature, intellectual and spiritual. When does man act naturally? When he subordinates the body to intellect, the intellect to conscience, and conscience to God. The unnaturalness of man is his condemnation, confusion, and misery. Universal depravity is universal unnaturalness. The mission of Christianity is to restore men to the Divine naturalness of life and action.

That we should act out our nature FOR ITS HIGHEST PERFECTION.—All these little creatures work for their well being. The ant that provides in summer for winter, the conies that find their palaces in the wild rocks, the locusts that go forth in armies for the fruits of the earth, and the spider that climbs its way into kings' palaces, all seek their well-being. They work out their whole natures, not for their ruin but safety, and not for their safety only, but for their strength, development, and enjoyment. So it should be with man. There are nourishment, security, and dignity for man, but they can only be reached in connection with his own persevering and well-directed activity; activity and happiness are everywhere connected in the universe.

> "The chiefest action for a man of spirit
> Is never to be out of action: we should think
> The soul was never put into the body,
> Which has so many rare and curious pieces
> Of mathematical motion, to stand still."
> WEBSTER

Proverbs 31:1-9

The Counsels of a Noble Mother to Her Son

"The words of king Lemuel, the prophecy that his mother taught him. What, my son? and what, the son of my womb? and what, the son of my vows? Give not thy strength unto women, nor thy ways to that which destroyeth kings. It is not for kings, O Lemuel, it is not for kings to drink wine; not for princes strong drink: lest they drink and forget the law, and pervert the judgment of any of the afflicted. Give strong drink unto him that is ready to perish, and wine unto those that be of heavy hearts. Let him drink, and forget his poverty, and remember his misery no more. Open thy mouth for the dumb in the cause of all such as are appointed unto destruction. Open thy mouth, judge righteously, and plead the cause of the poor and needy." *

WHO was King Lemuel? Some say he was the elder brother of Agur; others that it was a name given to

---

* We pass over verses 29 to 33 in the preceding chapter, because they contain nothing of importance that has not been frequently noticed.

Solomon himself; others that he was some neighbouring prince whose mother was a pious Jewess; others that the name was a figurative appellation of an ideal king, as it denotes consecration to God. But the identity of this man is lost in the mist of ages. Our belief is that he had an historic existence, exercised regal authority, and through the training of a noble mother, was inspired by the sentiments of true religion. The words before us and the whole of this chapter contain "the prophecy that his mother taught him." She was probably one of those Hebrew females on whom the spirit of inspiration sometimes descended, and her words here were so evidently the words of an oracle, that they were admitted into the sacred canon.

A motherly ministry is the tenderest, the strongest, and the most influential of all the Divine ministries of the world. But when that ministry is the expression of a genuinely religious nature, and specially inspired by Heaven, its character is still more elevated, and its influence still more beneficent and lasting. Such was the ministry of the mother of Lemuel. Her counsel to her son here involves—

An earnest INTERDICT.—With what earnestness does she break forth! Her motherly heart seems all in a flame. "What, my son? and what, the son of my womb? and what, the son of my vows?" The thrice repeated exclamation implies intensity of passion. What am I to say to thee? How passionately do I love thee, how intensely anxious am I that thou shouldest be a good man and a noble king! My heart is too full to utter all the precepts which I wish to inculcate! "The son of my womb,"—part of my very self, my own flesh and blood. "Son of my vows,"—granted to me as an answer to my prayers, and consecrated by me at thy birth to Jehovah. Now mark her earnest interdict. "Give not thy strength unto women, nor thy ways to that which destroyeth kings. It is not for kings, O Lemuel, it is not for kings to drink wine; nor for princes strong drink: lest they drink and forget the law." Her vehement inhibition is against animal indulgence in its two great forms—debauchery and intemperance; against inordinate gratification of the passions and the appetites. She thought perhaps of the *seraglio* and the ruin it had entailed upon the kings of the past, as well as upon the young men of her age, and she thought of the banquet, remembered the numbers that Bacchus had destroyed, and she uttered her prohibition with her soul on fire. She knew and said that lust "destroyeth kings," and so it does. It has shattered many a crown, and ruined many a kingdom. Perhaps her memory reverted to Elah Benhadad, Belshazzar, and the princes, "that made him sick with bottles of wine." Well might a mother thus lift up an earnest protest to her children against animal indulgences! The reign of animalism is a reign that manacles, enfeebles, and damns the soul. Lust blunts the moral sense, pollutes the memory, defiles the imagination, sends a withering influence through all the faculties of man. Robert Burns knew its power, and exclaimed—

"But oh! it hardens a' within,
And petrifies the feeling."

And thus the sightless bard of England has graphically described its terrible power:

"But when lust,
By unchaste looks, loose gestures, and foul talk,
But most by lewd and lavish acts of sin,
Lets in defilement to the inward parts,
The soul grows clotted by contagion,
Embodies and imbrutes till she quite lose
The divine property of her first being."

Her counsel to her son involves also—

An earnest INJUNCTION.—Having earnestly prohibited animal indulgence, she proceeds to a positive injunction of moral virtues. She enjoins social compassion. "Give strong drink unto him that is ready to perish, and wine unto those that be of heavy hearts. Let him drink and forget his poverty, and remember his misery no more." Why should she who had just spoken so strongly against her son drinking wine here enjoin him to give it to others? Wine as a beverage indulged in is a curse, wine as a medicine is a blessing; and it is as a medicine that she here recommends her son to give it to others. Some imagine that in the phrase "ready to perish" there is an allusion to the practice of administering a potion of strong mixed wine to criminals for the purpose of deadening their sensibility to suffering. If she meant this, there was mercy in it. But there are cases of general suffering and distress when wine may be administered with salutary effect. The Samaritan gave it to the wounded traveller, and Paul prescribed it for the infirmities of his "beloved son in the faith." "Give strong drink unto him that is ready to perish;" not to the strong and robust in order to gratify the palate and drown the reason, but to the men that are "ready to perish,"—men in intense suffering and ready to die. Give it to them in order to soothe, refresh, and restore them. In their case it may deaden the pain, quicken the action of the heart, and lead to restoration. What she inculcates here is compassion to the poor. Give to the suffering what they require; if they need bread, give it; if they want wine, as a restorer and cordial, give it. His compassion was to be shown not only in this but in other ways as required. "Open thy mouth for the dumb, in the cause of all such as are appointed to destruction. . . . . and plead the cause of the poor and needy." Which means, "Stand by the oppressed, those against whom false accusations are made, and who are unable to protect themselves; take their part." It is the duty and honour of kings to espouse the cause of the distressed. Mercy is one of the strongest pillars of a throne. She enjoins not only compassion but justice. "Open thy mouth, judge righteously." Deal justice to all, both rich and poor!

Here is a model mother! Would that mothers the world over would imitate the example of this noble Jewess, warn, with all the vehemence of maternal love, their sons against all the "fleshly lusts that war against the soul," and inculcate those principles of compassion and justice, apart from which kings have no dignity, and peoples neither progress or peace! Napoleon being asked what is the great want of the French nation, replied, "Mothers;" by which I presume he meant maternal parents doing the true work of mothers, not allowing their offspring to run into animals or to grow into fiends, but moulding them into angels, that excel in strength, and become the ministers of God.

> "The mother, in her office, holds the key
> Of the soul: and she it is who stamps the coin
> Of character, and makes the being, who would be a savage
> But for her gentle cares, a Christian man."

Proverbs 31:10-31

A Noble Woman's Picture of True Womanhood

"Who can find a virtuous woman? for her price *is* far above rubies. The heart of her husband doth safely trust in her, so that he shall have no need of spoil. She will do him good and not evil all the days of her life. She seeketh wool, and flax, and worketh willingly with her hands. She is like the merchants' ships; she bringeth her food from afar. She riseth also while it is yet night, and giveth meat to her household, and a portion to her maidens. She considereth a field, and buyeth it: with the fruit of her hand she planteth a vineyard. She girdeth her loins with strength, and strengtheneth her arms. She perceiveth that her merchandise *is* good: her candle goeth not out by night. She layeth her hands to the spindle, and her hands hold the distaff. She stretcheth out her hand to the poor; yea, she reacheth forth her hands to the needy. She is not afraid of the snow for her household: for all her household *are* clothed with scarlet. She maketh herself coverings of tapestry; her clothing *is* silk and purple. Her husband is known in the gates, when he sitteth among the elders of the land. She maketh fine linen, and selleth *it;* and delivereth girdles unto the merchant. Strength and honour *are* her clothing; and she shall rejoice in time to come. She openeth her mouth with wisdom; and in her tongue *is* the law of kindness. She looketh well to the ways of her household, and eateth not the bread of idleness. Her children arise up and call her blessed; her husband *also,* and he praiseth her. Many daughters have done virtuously, but thou excellest them all. Favour *is* deceitful, and beauty *is* vain; *but* a woman *that* feareth the LORD, she shall be praised. Give her of the fruit of her hands; and let her own works praise her in the gates."

THIS is a poetic picture of true womanhood, presented by a noble woman to her son. It is moulded after the principle exemplified in the 119th Psalm, a principle in which each verse begins with one of the successive letters of the Hebrew alphabet. Her son here remembers and repeats the poetic descriptions, though perhaps the lips that uttered them and the heart that beat them out were silent in the grave. With the modesty of a true woman, and especially a woman of genius, she did not recite her poem to a public assembly, but quietly breathed it into the soul of her boy, and there it did its work. Her death, it may be, quickened it in his memory, gave it new significance, and forced him to publish it to the world. The death of a mother is often one of the most life-creating events; it opens in her children the graves of memory, and calls forth her long forgotten words in striking forms and tones.

Looking at the splendid picture of a true woman which is here presented, we are struck with her conduct as a wife, her management as a mistress, her blessedness as a mother, her generosity as a neighbour, and her excellence as an individual.

Mark her CONDUCT AS A WIFE—Here is *inviolable faithfulness*. " The heart of her husband doth safely trust in her, so that he shall have no need of spoil. She will do him good and not evil all the days of her life." The husband trusts her character. She is so chaste, so truthful, so incorruptible, that he reposes in her his utmost confidence, and such feelings as jealousy and suspicion in relation to her never enter his breast. He trusts her management too, for it is said, " so that he shall have no need of spoil." Her management is so skilful, industrious, and economic that he has no temptation to go out of his way to do aught that is dishonest in order to increase his resources. Many a husband has been prompted to deeds of dishonesty through the indolence and extravagance of the partner of his life. Here is *practical affection*. "She will do him good and not evil all the days of her life." She loves—but her love is not an animal sympathy, that goes off in kisses and florid verbosities, but a deep and resistless current running through her nature, bearing her on in her daily duties. It is a love that "will do him good and not evil." Not merely temporal good, but intellectual and moral, stimulating his higher faculties and ennobling his character. And this constantly, "All the days of her life." There is a wifely love that is fitful, capricious, passionate in its endearments to-day, to-morrow cold, sulky, and sometimes splenetic; this is not the love of a true wife, it is the love of a selfish woman that seeks only her own gratification. Genuine wifely love seeks the good of her husband, is constant as nature. It is not a meteoric spark that comes and goes—however brilliant, always worthless—but a sunbeam that continues through all life the same. Here is *elevating influence*. "Her husband is known in the gates, when he sitteth among the elders of the land." She is a crown to her husband. In consequence of what she has been to him, and done for him as a wife, he has risen in worldly wealth and social power. Her words have inspired him with honourable ambitions, and her diligence and frugality have contributed the means by which to reach his lofty aims. Here is *merit acknowledged*. "Her husband also praiseth her." There are men who are incapable of appreciating the character or reciprocating the love of a noble wife. Blessed is the man who has found a wife approaching this ideal! May every reader of this sketch be able to join the writer in his thankful acknowledgments to Him who superintends all human affairs, for blessing his life with one whose faithfulness has been inviolable, whose affection pure and practical; and whose services through "all the days of her life" have contributed to improve his position, elevate his character, and widen his influence for good.

Mark her MANAGEMENT AS A MISTRESS.—The first thing to be noticed is her industry. "She seeketh wool and flax, and worketh willingly with her hands. She layeth her hands to the spindle, and her hands hold the distaff." Her industry was cheerful. She does not merely work, but works "willingly." Her industry was varied. She works as a manufacturer. Her work is of a skilful kind. She learnt the art of spinning, she gets the "wool and the flax," spins and prepares them for personal and household purposes. It was customary among the Jews to bring up all the youth to useful and handicraft occupation. An excellent custom this, but sadly neglected in these modern times. This mother of a king here tells her royal son what a woman should be: handicraft is not unworthy of Queens. The picture here of this woman spinning the clothing for herself and family reminds the writer of the days of his boyhood. He well remembers on a lonely farm in Cambria, his ever beloved and lamented mother preparing the wool, "laying her hands to the spindle," taking "hold of the distaff," and spinning garments for domestic use. Well he recollects the pride with which his noble father put on for the first time the coat, the yarn of which she had spun. The pride was mutual. What coat would be so prized by a true man as that which was woven by the hands of a loving and industrious wife?

This form of female industry is superseded in this country by larger and more complicated machinery, worked by steam; but the duty is not abrogated. Diligence in useful pursuits should be the grand lesson in all female education. The most brilliant accomplishments by the side of useful productions are simply contemptible in the eye of intelligence. True ladyhood consists not in birth, in jewelled fingers, in splendid attire or in brilliant accomplishments, but in the diligent pursuit of those objects which contribute to the weal of mankind. Alexander the Great is said to have shown to the Persian princesses his garments made by his mother. And Augustus, we are told, would wear no clothes but such as were made by members of his family. But this noble woman not only works as a manufacturer, but as a merchant too. She buys and sells. "She is like the merchant ships; she bringeth her food from afar? . . . She considereth a field and buyeth it. . . . She maketh fine linen and selleth it, and delivereth girdles unto the merchant." Why does she "bring her food from afar"? Because, undoubtedly, she could not get it so good and so cheap at home. "She buyeth a field," she understands the value of things and buys them on the best terms. But she toils as a farmer also. "With the fruit of her hands she planteth a vineyard." The field she has purchased she cultivates. Again, her industry was not only cheerful and varied but earnest. "She riseth also while it is yet night. . . . . . Her candle goeth not out by night." She threw her heart into the work. The woman who lies late in her bed sleeps away the spirit of diligence, and hastens to the habits of the indolent sloven or the canting invalid. All honour to the mistress who is first from her bed, and, like a general, summons her domestics to action. Her industry is useful. She works for others. "She giveth meat to her household and a portion to her maidens. . . . . . She is not afraid of the snow for her household, for her household are clothed with scarlet:" or as in the margin, "double garments." "She looketh well to the ways of her household." She sees that all her domestics are well fed and well clad; her aim is to see her husband, her children, and her maidens comfortable and happy. Here then is a woman that "eateth not the bread of idleness;" and all who eat such bread eat bread they have no right to, and are dead weights on the industry of the world.

Mark her BLESSEDNESS AS A MOTHER.—"Her children arise up and call her blessed." In the spirit, the character and the lives of her children she meets with an ample reward for all her self-denying efforts to make them happy and good. They mark her noble life, and in the first stages of thoughtfulness they are impressed with the charms of her disinterestedness and devotion, and as they grow up under the advantages of her noble example and spiritual instruction, they love her not only as the instrumental author of their being, but as to them a ministering angel from God. Noble mother! There she sits, weakened by age, crowned with years, and beautiful to behold. Her children grown up, gather around her with a veneration the most sacred, and a love the most tender and strong. Their lives are a grateful acknowledgment of all her kindness, and in their spirit and conversation she reaps a rich harvest of delight. Her children "call her blessed." Their hearts will not allow them to go into detail, nor can they say less than "blessed mother." "Ye wives—ye mothers!" says an able author, "what a lovely, what an enviable scene is this! How earnestly should each one of you strive to realise it in your own happy experience! Your children—affectionate, grateful, pious—united in love to one another and to you—owning and commending, with tears of sensibility and delight, their loved mother as the guardian, all kind and fond and faithful, of their infant years, blessing her, speaking well of her, praying for her, praising her: growing up into a life of credit to her early care, and requiting that care in every kind of practical attention to the well-being of her declining, perhaps her widowed years!"

Mark her GENEROSITY AS A NEIGHBOUR. — "She stretcheth out her hand to the poor; yea, she reacheth forth her hand to the needy." Although she "looketh well to the ways of her household," she works hard for the comforts of all under her roof; her sympathies are not confined to the domestic sphere. They overflow the boundary of family life, they go forth into the neighbourhood. What she does for the poor she does not in a half-hearted way. "She stretcheth forth her hand to the poor; yea, she reacheth forth her hand to the needy." This woman had a right to give,—a right altogether irrespective of even her husband's sanction. She herself had created property; she had acted on the principle laid down by Paul, "Let him labour, working with his hands that which is good, that he may have to give to him that is needy." What we produce is our own. This noble woman, through manufacturing, farming, and bartering, had created property herself, and now she was giving it to them who were in need, and she seems to have given it with her whole heart. You cannot get some people to move their "hands" at all in efforts to help the poor, while others will only lift them a little way after all your arguments and persuasions. But this woman "stretcheth forth her hand,"—she went as far as her means would allow.

"The presence of the poor," says Dr. Arnot, "is, like the necessity of labour, a blessing to mankind; it provides a field for the exercise of affections which are necessary to the perfection of human character. When material acquisitions are great, and benevolent efforts small, the moral health cannot be maintained; when much flows in, and none is permitted to flow out, wealth becomes a stagnant pool, endangering the life of those who reside on its brim. The sluice which love opens to pour a stream upon the needy sweetens all the store. The matron who really does good to her own house will also show kindness to the poor; and she who shows kindness to the poor, thereby brings back a blessing on her own dwelling."

Mark her EXCELLENCE AS AN INDIVIDUAL. — "Many daughters have done virtuously, but thou excellest them all." This is a confession that no woman in the days of Lemuel's mother realised her idea of womanhood; indeed, she starts the poem with the expression of her belief of the rarity of such a character. "Who can find a virtuous woman?" Had Solomon started such a question, who would have been surprised? His knowledge of women was perhaps confined to his hundreds of princesses in his seraglio, and all virtues had forsaken them. But it certainly does reflect sadly upon the female contemporaries of this godly and inspired Jewess, when she puts the question, "Who can find a virtuous woman?"

But let us look for a moment into the personal characteristics of this model woman. She was *vigorous in body*. "She girdeth her loins with strength, and strengtheneth her arms." Such a state of body as this is not thought genteel or even respectable for ladies in this age. A somewhat attenuated frame, impaired health, and sundry ailments are popularly regarded as constituents of ladyhood. But laziness, which is depravity, is the source of these attributes of gentility. This woman lived on wholesome food, worked her muscles, plied her limbs, breathed the mountain air, and won firm tissue and vigorous health. "She girdeth her loins with strength and strengtheneth her arms." Again, it appears that she was *elegant in her dress*. "She maketh herself coverings of tapestry, her clothing is silk and purple." What an index is to a book, dress is to the wearer; it indicates the contents. The quality of this woman's dress was good; it was of "tapestry," "silk and purple." She had a right to such raiment, it was the product of her own hard earnings, and in all probability she made it with her own hands. Every woman should earn her own attire, and not only know how to make it, but do so, unless she is engaged in some higher occupations. Much has been written in the present day on woman's dress, and certainly it is a subject so startling as to challenge criticism, and often to awaken disgust. A woman's dress should always be modest, never arrest attention, or suggest the unchaste. "Madam," says old John Newton, "so dress and so conduct yourself that persons who have been in your company shall not recollect what you had on." A fashionably dressed lady once asked a clergyman if there was any harm in wearing feathers and ornaments. He answered, "If you have the ridiculous vanity in your heart to wish to be thought pretty and fine, you may as well hang out the sign." Dress should not only be modest, but becoming—becoming to the stature, gait, complexion, and station of the wearer. Neatness also should characterize it; ugliness gains nothing, and beauty loses much by the gaudy and the grand. The dress of our modern lady, with her hanging sacks of hair cut from the heads of paupers, convicts, raging maniacs, and the dead, with bolsters of silk and satin piled up on her back, and moving about limping and crooked with the "Grecian Bend," is not only an outrage on decency, but on all æsthetics. To me, I confess, the plain cotton costume of the honest servant, the product of her own industry, and the work of her own hands, is far more beautiful than the mountains of silk, branches of streaming ribbons, and rows of glittering jewellery that cover the would-be-fashionable lady. Furthermore, she was *dignified and cheerful in bearing*. "Strength and honour are her clothing: And she shall rejoice in time to come." She stood erect in strength, and her habits of diligence and honesty gave a dignity to her bearing. Her neighbours would feel themselves, when they looked at her, in the presence of true nobility. And with all she was cheerful. "She shall rejoice in time to come." The life she had lived and was living, was not only a source of pleasure to her now, but would be so in retrospection in years to come. Every day in a true life plants new flowers in the Paradise of the past. The memory of a noble past is one of the chief sources of present delight. Moreover, she was *prudent and kind in speech*. "She openeth her mouth in wisdom: And in her tongue is the law of kindness." Her conversation consisted not in simpering inanities, idle gossip, or unchaste narrations, nor was it ever tinged with unkindness. As there was no spleen in her nature, there was nothing sardonic in her speech. She was too rich in love for envies, too noble for jealousies, too confiding for suspicions, too truthful for falsehood, too good for scandal. And to crown the whole she was *devout and honoured in religion*. "Favour is deceitful and beauty is vain, but a woman that feareth the Lord she shall be praised." Religion was the spirit of her character, the germ from which grew all the fruits of her noble life. Supreme love to God, which is religion, is that which generates, animates, and adorns all other virtues of character. This woman had it, and hence the beauty of her moral stature and the usefulness of her life.

Conclusion.—Our subject furnishes another reason for prizing the Bible. Where in any other book, ancient or modern, can you find such a splendid ideal of womanhood, an ideal that commends itself to our highest philosophy, our conscience, and our hearts? Let us hold up this ideal of womanhood, and in its presence we shall feel that the modern ladyism of England, with its preposterous costumes, unnatural movements, and empty talk, is a thing for loathing and contempt. Young men, take this ideal of womanhood with you into society, hang it about your neck as a glass through which to search out a companion to share the sorrows and the joys, the triumphs and defeats, of your earthly life. Remember ever what a woman's true mission is :—

> " 'Tis woman's to nourish affection's tree,
> And its fruit domestic bliss shall be :
> 'Tis hers to cultivate with patient toil
> Each heaven-born plant in the heart's deep soil;
> And fruits and flowers her toil shall greet,
> Richest flavours and odours on earth that meet.
>
> " 'Tis woman's to fashion the infant mind,
> To kindle its thoughts, and its hopes unbind :
> To guide its young mind in the earliest flight,
> And lure it to worlds of unsullied light :
> To teach him to sing, in his gladsome hours,
> Of a Saviour's love, with an angel's powers.
>
> " 'Tis woman's to bind up the broken heart,
> And soften the bleeding spirit's smart,
> With the balm that in Gilead's garden grows,
> With the stream that from Calvary's fountain flows;
> And to light, in this world of pain and sin,
> The lamp of love and joy again."

Additional Study Aids on the Book of Proverbs

EXPOSITION OF PROVERBS
George Lawson
The author draws on his knowledge of the Hebrew and Greek Scriptures to reveal the practical instruction provided. His understanding of God's sense-of-right commends this thoroughly sound and useful commentary to anyone who seeks to know God's will for his life.   890 pages

STUDIES IN PROVERBS
William Arnot
With a Scriptural depth of a Spurgeon and a literary polish of a Robert G. Lee, Arnot illuminates each proverb with a commentary breathing forth the fresh aroma of one who has walked with the Rose of Sharon. Spurgeon said of this work "For a happy blending of illustrative faculty, practical sound sense, and spirituality, Dr. Arnot was almost unrivalled."   585 pages

Index

You will find here the headings of each commentary classified according to both subject matter and its alphabetical beginning

ABHORRED of the Lord, the, 552
Abominations, the seven, 84
Accusation, an unjust, morally reprehensible, 777
Accusers, the officious and vicious, 776
Action necessary for man, 514
Action, occasional and incidental, lines of, 314
Activity, necessity for, 80
Adams Thomas, quoted, 134, 504, 733
Addison quoted, 335, 372, 549
Adversity, day of, a trial of moral strength, 596
Adversity, day of, for all, 596
Æsop quoted, 513
Afflictions, beneficial influence of, 45
Afflictions, tokens of parental love, 45
Age, righteousness conducive to old, 329
Age, when to be honoured, 328
Agriculture, moral, the inevitable work of human life, 541
Agur a devout philosopher, 772
Agur a man worthy of our imitation, 774
Agur as a philosopher, a bibleist, and a suppliant, 771
Alcoholic drink, the great false prophet in England, 439
Alexander the Great quoted, 749
Ambition, 625, 737
Ambition, corrupt, liable to humiliation, 627
Ancestry, an, that is the glory of its posterity, 344
Anger, a righteous, 503, 647
Anger controlled and uncontrolled, 416
Anger controlled by a wise man, 416
Anger generously overcome, 503
Anger, reasons for the implacability of a brother's, 403
Anger, uncontrolled, self injurious, 417
Anger, unrighteously provoked, 503
Animals, obligation of kindness towards, 163
Animal world, marvels of the, 163
Answering before hearing, flippant habit of, 394

Antiphilus quoted, 513
Apostasy, two kinds of, 505
Apostate, description of the, 231
Apostate, doom of the, 231
Apostate, hopeless, conduct of the, 506
Apostate, hopeless ruin of the, 506
Appeal of parental piety, an, 580
Appetite, an, for good things essential for their enjoyment, 682
Arguments useless to the incorrigible sinner, 705
Arnold, Dr., anecdote of, 417
Arnot, Dr. quoted, 145, 315, 495, 640, 676, 726, 794
Arrogance resembles spleen, 189
Aspects of a fool, 664
Aspects of depravity 594
Attainment of knowledge, the, and the power of kindness, 398
Augustine quoted, 701, 650
Authority of Divine wisdom, the, 92
Authors and their dedicatees 721
Autobiography of wisdom, the, 95
Avarice, 731
Avarice, designs of, 556
Avarice ends in results contrary to aim, 733
Avaricious man governed by a "piece of bread," 732
Avaricious man unfaithful, 732

BACKBITER, baseness of the, 648
Bacon, Lord, quoted, 11, 16, 45, 60, 102, 108, 116, 222, 299, 356, 365, 381 414, 450, 469, 690, 720, 748
Bad neighbours, 643
Bailey quoted, 526
Bancroft quoted, 144
Banquets made for sordid ends, 571
Battling instinct, perversion of, 53
Baxter quoted, 275
Beauty of a reprovable disposition, the, 633
Bedizened wickedness, 148
Beggary entailed by indolence, 444
Benefactor, the greatest, 196
Beneficence, 51
Beneficence God's test on the last day, 754

Benevolence a duty, 52
Benevolent impulse, reason for obeying, 52
Better man, the, 410
Bible, absence of the, a great calamity, 761
Bible, ancient price of, 194
Bible, a reason for prizing the, 796
Bible, language of, often anthropomorphic, 258
Bible, the, a mirror of human life, 130
Bibles, two, in existence, 38
Blessedness of wisdom, the, 46
Bodily health dependent on mental moods, 369
Boethius quoted, 31
Bonar, Dr., quoted, 536, 719
Bowes quoted, 137
Bowring quoted, 192
Briareus quoted, 151
Bribe, definition of, 371
Bribery, 371
Bribery, aim of, pernicious, 371
Bribery, disgrace of constitutional governments, 371
Bridges quoted, 472, 525, 542, 546, 735, 743, 761, 473, 665
Brodie, Sir Benjamin, quoted, 317
Brougham, Lord, quoted, 48
Browne, Sir T., quoted, 197, 317, 557
Browning, Elizabeth Barrett, quoted, 771
Buffon quoted, 459
Bunyan quoted, 455, 596, 632, 749
Burke quoted, 275, 493
Burnet, Bishop, quoted, 650
Burns quoted, 62, 660, 786
Bushnell, Dr., quoted, 368, 489
Business economics, 464
Business, the perfection of system in, 318
Butler, Allen, quoted, 22
Butler, Archer, quoted, 16, 226
Butler, Bishop, quoted, 117, 216
Byron quoted, 188, 522, 529, 642

CABINET secrecies, 624
Caird, Dr., quoted, 658
Calumny gratifying bad men, 340
Cambyses' regard to justice, 576
Capacity without will, 359
Carlyle, quoted, 51, 229, 261, 347, 358, 454, 712, 676
Cash and character, 109
Cautiously believing, reasons for, 234
Celibacy not the best mode of social life, 405
Chapman quoted, 345
Character, 105
Character and doom of the wicked, the, 438
Character formed on the principle of imitation, 206

Character, foundation and blessedness of a good, 104
Character man's only property, 104
Character, value of a righteous man's, 110
Characters, wrong in all, should be chastised, 434
Charms, external, and moral deformity an incongruous conjunction, 149
Charnock quoted, 228
Chastisement, effects of, varying according to character, 435
Chastisement, the kind of, should be according to character, 434
Chatham, Lord, quoted, 459
Cheat, the, 462
Cheever, Dr., quoted, 325
Chicanery, 460
Chief good, of what composed, 58
Childhood, special trainability of, 536
Children, an appeal of pious parents to their, 580
Children, mistake of rebuking, for trivial irregularities, 288
Children robbing parents a theft of great enormity, 735
Children, tendency of, to go wrong, 210
Child training, 536
Child, wickedness of punishing the, in passion or revenge, 425
Christianity a system of love, 700
Christianity indispensable to health, 247
Christianity, sanitary influence of, 370
Christian truths analogous to physical necessaries, 100
Church institution, the, a beneficent appointment, 207
Chrysostom quoted, 502
Cicero quoted, 51, 483
Civil liberty, when truly appreciated, 179
Claims of Divine wisdom, the, 97
Clandestine hatred, 672
Clarendon, advice of, 311
Clare quoted, 744
Clean, crib the, or indolence, 218
Clothes, remembrancers of our lost innocence, 150
Coleridge quoted, 315, 360, 445, 660, 709
Collier quoted, 188
Colton quoted, 137, 188, 549
Comfort independent of display, 162
Commerce, achievements of modern, the result of system, 319
Commercial partnerships, 765
Companions, importance of the choice of, 206
Compassion, social, 786
Concealment, the right, of offences, 349
Conditions of a happy life, the, 318

Conduct, infamous, 521
Confidence godly, 737
Confucius quoted, 173
Conqueror, the, of self the greatest conqueror, 331
Conquest, the most righteous, 331
Conscience, 480, 709
Conscience a divine light in man, 480
Conscience a self-revealing light, 480
Conscience, heroism of a right, 711
Conscience, the work of, 709
Conscience, timidity of a guilty, 710
Conservative, subjects should be, 609
Conservatism, true, described, 609
Conservatives, stereotyped, and men's rights, 565
Constancy essential to genuine friendship, 361
Constantius and his test, 311
Constitutional governments, 441
Consultation, advantages of, 144
Content is the poor man's riches, 305, 335
Contrasts, 120, 276
Contrasts in conditions and characters, 531
Conventional evangelicalism the devil of selfishness, 228
Conventional society, its estimate of human possessions, 109
Conversational likings of bad men, the 339
Cornwall Barry quoted, 179.
Corrupt ambition, a, 625
Cosmological absurdities, three, 298
Counsels of a noble mother to her son, the, 784
Counsels to young men in relation to bad women, 88
Countenance of man, the, a mirror, 268
Countenance the revealer of the soul, 695
Courage, condition of true, 50
Covetousness, evils of, 282
Cowardice of keeping silent or denying what is unpopular, 769
Cowper quoted, 58, 92, 109, 150, 164, 221, 245, 344 444. 574, 760
Craftiness essential to the wicked, 166
Crafty and the honest, the, 166
Creature power, the highest, 593
Credit, caution in giving, inculcated, 464
Credulity, consequences of yielding to, 233
Credulous and the cautious, the, 232
Crimes may be conscientiously perpetrated, 200
Criminal apostates, two classes of, 506
Cry of the poor, the, 500
Culinary art productions of, injurious to body and soul. 567

Cursed home, a, and a blessed home, 418
Curses, 662

DARKNESS, 188
Darkness, cause of, in sinner's path 65
Darkness of sin, the, 65
Dark thoughts, power of, 369
Davy, Sir Humphrey, quoted, 28
Day of adversity, the, 596
Death, 134
Death depending on character, 250, 251
Degenerative principle, force of, 10
Degrees and duties of true friendship, the, 361
Deliberation, 276
Deliberation, importance of, 465
Departmental system in Heaven's remedial work, 620
Depraved woman, influence of, a ' deep pit,'' 551
Depravity blinds the moral judgment, 714
Depravity mischievous in purpose, 594
Deserving poor, the 422, 500
Devices, the many, in man's heart, 427.
Difficulties, the indolent and righteous in relation to, 275, 550
Difficulties to true souls a challenge to action, 551
Difficulty our helper, 275
Dignity, the true, 317
Diligence, 490, 541
Diligence and dignity, 173
Dinner of herbs and the stalled ox, 270
Diogenes quoted, 192
Disappointing man, the, 637
Discipline, a limit to, 740
Discipline, God's, of his children sometimes severe, 484
Discipline, parental, 425
Discord and strife, differences between, 355
Discord generated by pride, 188
Dishonesty a rapid road to wealth, 491
Display, domestic, without comforts, 162
Disputes, best way of settling, 629
Disputes, bitterness of, often aggravated by blood relationship, 402
Disputes, settlement of social, requires the hearing of both disputants, 401
Distress, social, 500
Diverse families, 262
Divine control interferes not with human responsibility, 486
Divine discipline, 337
Divine revelation, 761
Divine ruler of all, 722
Divine wisdom accessible to early seekers, 93
Divine wisdom the queen of the world, 92

Docile, wisdom of the, 169, 203
Doddridge quoted, 459
Domestic modesty and display, 161
Double picture, a, 373
Dress of our modern lady, 795
Dress the index to the wearer, 795
Dress, the proper characteristics of, 795
Drexelius quoted, 332
Drunkard, appearance of the, 585
Drunkard, easy temptability of the, 586
Drunkard, offensive garrulousness of the, 585
Drunkard, reckless stupidity of the, 587
Drunkard's effigy, the, hung up as a beacon, 584
Drunkard, sensual indulgence of the, 585
Drunkenness, 440, 584
Drunkenness, effects of, 586
Dryden, quoted, 168, 555, 605, 695, 705, 747, 761
Duke of Brunswick, anecdote of the, 511
Duty of man under a sense of injuries, the, 469
Dwight quoted, 199

EARLY rising, 458, 792
Ear, the, as a great inlet to the mind, 399, 456
Earthly good, its insufficiency, 10
Edmeston quoted, 605
Educational temple, the, or Christianity a school, 99
Edwards, Jonathan, quoted, 634
Elizabeth, Queen, quoted, 29
Eloquence, importance of, 322
Emerson quoted, 173
Empire, an, that might be permanent, 540
Enemies, the, of a good man, 303
Enemies, the way to overcome, 641
Enemies, winning the good will of, 303
England, pauperism in, 501
Enlightened piety, 591
Entail, the law of, 109
Envy a compliment to its object, 606
Envy, analysis of, 680
Envy, definition of, 606
Envy, folly of, 607
Envy, three things involved by, 606
Epicure, the, and his soul, 568
Epicure, the; or, gastric temptation, 566
Establishment of thoughts, the, 296
Evangelicalism, the right and the wrong, 228
Evermore, 226
Evil, 300
Evil always unreasonable, 756
Evil and the good. 146
Evil essentially malignant, 755

Evil, its numerous forms, 759
Evil of a roaming disposition, the, 684
Evils of avarice, the, 555
Evils of covetousness and the blessings of generosity, the, 282
Evil men, envy of, 590
Evil, punishment of, 354
Evil, self-blinding influence of, 775
Evil, self-dissatisfying influence of, 776
Evil, self-hardening influence of, 776
Evil socially destructive, 757
Evil, spirit of, 353
Evil will fall notwithstanding its increase, 759
Example of the folly of envy, an, 606
Excelsior, 280
Excellency of fitly spoken words, 630
Excuses of laziness, the, 549
Existence, all, has one author, 298
"Eye, a good," 544
"Eye, an evil," described, 732
Eye, wonderful arrangement of the, 456

FABER, F. W., quoted, 652
Face, man's, the index to the soul, 373
Facts, false statements of, 401
Faithfulness, definition of, 448
Faithful man, the, 448
Faithful man, the, a refreshing object, 636
Faithless man, the, 645
Fall of evil, the, 758
False accuser, the, 775
Falsehood, 414, 491
Falsehood ruinous to reputation, 415
Falsehood ruinous to the soul, 415
Fame, love of, 529
Family life, 154
Family scenes, 335
Farrer, Dr., quoted, 552
Fathership, a happy, 690
Father, the unworthy, 179
Faults of others, how to correct, 102, 288
Fear of man, the, 769
Fear of the Lord, definition of the, 241
Feasts, men's motives for making, 571
Feasts to be avoided, 572
Feltham quoted, 223, 768
Festus quoted, 37, 53, 120, 488, 761
Fichte quoted, 11
Fidelity to principle, 40
Fielding quoted, 141
Filial depravity and parental warning, 436
Filial obedience, 17
Fitly spoken words, what distinguishes them, 631
Flatterers, 339, 611, 692, 748

Flattery a curse to its author, 572
Flattery a curse to its victims, 592
Flattery a net, 748
Fool, a, despises parental instruction, 262, 425
Foolish man, the attempting and talking of the, 199, 321
Foolish, recklessness and ruin of the, 583
Foolish, three reasons for avoiding the society of the, 222
Foolish wisdom, 569
Foolishness, three facts concerning, in the heart of a child, 554
Fools abominate departing from evil, 204
Fool's mockery of sin, 222, 290
Fools, Solomon's definition of, 16, 388
Fool, the, as a debater, 665
Fool, the, negatively and positively, 365
Forethought, imporatance of, 613
Formalistically religious, the, 227
Fortune making, virtue a hindrance to, 304
Foster, John, quoted, 24
Franklin, Dr. quoted, 323, 458
Freedom in religion, man's right, 575
Freedom, perfect, four parts of, 199
Freedom, personal, man's right, 574
Free will necessary to human goodness, 306
French quoted, 308, 579
Friendly intercourse, 695
Friendship, an interdicted, 563
Friendship delights of. 689
Friendship loses in death only its alloy, 364
Friendship one of man's greatest needs, 361, 411
Friendship, the degrees of true, 361
Friendship, the real and the spurious, 681
Frivolity a joy to the foolish, 276
Frugality in speech, 377
Frugality in speech frequently favourable to one's reputation, 378
Fruits of personal religion, the, 431
Fuller quoted, 150, 389, 462

GALEN, the conversion of, 457
Garibaldi quoted, 703
Gastric temptation, 566
Gastric temptation, elements of, 566
Gastric temptation, manner of resistance of, 567
General life, picture of, 708
Generations, four moral, on the earth, 778
Generation, the cruel, 781
Generation, the haughty, 780
Generation, the self-deluded, 779

Generation, the unnatural, 779
Generosity and avarice, respective operations of, 151
Generosity, fruits of, 237, 283
Generosity, the blessedness of, 283
Generous and avaricious, the, 150
Generous and avaricious, social estimate of the, 152
Generous and ungenerous, 145
Generous disposition, blessings of a, 145, 237
Gentleman, the, when a felon, 324
Gentleness, the commanding power of, 368
Genuine friendship, a, and a happy fathership, 788
Genuine philanthropy, 543
Genuine student defined, 14
Genius and punishment of evil, the, 353
Genius of evil, the, 755
George III.'s prohibition of flattery, 674.
Getting of wisdom from the wise, 444
Gibbon quoted, 426
Gifts, two kinds of, 399
Giving, highest, the effects of, 43
Glory of aged piety, the, 328
Glory in godliness, both in youth and age, the, 481
God and the human race, 485
God and the sinner in time and eternity, 25
God's discipline of his children, 483
God's inspection of the world, 258
God's omniscience, 623
God's overruling Providence a difficult problem, 472
God, procedure, of, 281
God, tender sensibilities of, 264, 282
God the judge of human character, 487
God the controller of human hearts, 485
God, the master of the universe, 299
God, searching omniscience of, 295
God the protector of the helpless, 575
God-trusting and self-trusting, 40
God, what is necessary to know, 600
Godliness and humanity, 248
Godliness, safety and life, 241
Godliness, true, a tree of life, 47, 242
Godliness the true object for man's pursuit, 514
Godly fear and genuine humility, 290
Good and evil, their co-existence in same soul, 9
Good and evil, pursuit of, 153
Good, happiness of the, 231
Good man, a, overcomes difficulties, 517
Good man and his worldly circumstances, the, 303
Good man, blessedness of a, 549
Good man, influence of the, 548

Good man, the, 547
Good men and their God, 30
Good men, character of, 30
Good men, overthrow of, 387
Good men overthrown by the employment of the wicked, 387
Good reputation, why more valuable than wealth, 530
Good, security of the, 158
Good, strength of the, 517
Good, the blessed in their existence, 113
Good, the, alone, truly, great, 235
Goodness and happiness, 420
Goodness, pride of, 780
Goodness, spiritual, the grand object of life, 421
Good news from a far country, 651
Goodness the only nobility, 660
Göethe quoted, 203, 632
Gold, power of, 263 348, 372
Gospel minister, true work of a, 241
Gotthold quoted, 239
Government, civil, a divine institution, 729, 745
Government, essentials of a good, 143 478
Government, mercy essential for a good, 479
Government, necessity for, 143
Government of the tongue, the, 518
Government, policy of a good, 478
Grand fellowship and assimilation in life's path, the, 205
Grave, the, never full, 700
Great fortunes, fleeting character of, 570
Great men's contempt for popularity, 703
Great men honouring the generous, instances of, 399
Great mischief-maker, and great peacemaker, the, 118
Great mischief-maker, the, and great peace-maker, 118
Great teacher, a, and a genuine student, 12
Great I and little you, 189
Greatest men, definition of the, 31
Greed, 523
Grey head, three things which give beauty to a, 482
Grief, profound, causes for concealing, 224
Group of social principles, a, 236
Guardians, duty of the, of childhood and youth, 370
Guilty "hits," 190
Gurnell quoted, 189

HABIT, terrible force of, 537
Hall, Bishop, quoted, 24, 84, 340, 439, 567, 737, 758
Hall, Robert, quoted, 364

Hamilton quoted, 699
Happiness dependent on keeping the law, 762
Happiness, how to attain it, 422, 515
Happiness independent of external things, 195, 231, 304
Happiness in the soul, not the body, 568
Happiness the attendant of godliness, 515
Happiness, worldly and spiritual, conrasted, 321
Happy marriage, a, 405
Hare, Archdeacon, quoted, 358
Hatred, a mutual, between the good and the bad, 770
Hatred, open and hidden, 672
Haughtiness, definition of, 521
Havard quoted, 347
Having and being, 272, 305
Health, a man's, dependent on himself, 247, 369
Health, bodily, as affected by the soul, 212, 246, 329, 369
Hearing ear and the seeing eye, 455
Heart, a bountiful, 544
Heart, a merry, influence of, on the health, 213, 247
Heart and health, 246
Heart, a sound, 246
Heart, hardening the, 728, 740
Heart, hidden bitternesses of the, 223, 269
Heart's hidden depths, the, 223
Heart, hidden joys of the, 224, 319
Heart, man's, a property urgently claimed 583
Heart, pureness of, what it implies, 547
Heart, a well-stayed, 319
Heartlessness, social, 501
Hearts of the wise man and fool compared, 374
Heaven, joys of, may begin to-day, 719
Hell, description of, 354
Hell, existence of, 280
Helps quoted, 77
Hemans, Mrs., quoted, 155
Henry, Matthew, quoted, 103, 321, 733, 662
Herbert, George, quoted, 663
Highest giving the condition of the highest getting, 43
Highest knowledge, the, 286
History of strife 119
Hoarding wealth, results of, 151
Hobbs quoted, 426, 607, 751
Holiness, 451
Home, a blessed, 419
Home a place of confidence, 154, 418
Home, a religious, 56, 226, 418
Home, consequences to those who break the peace of, 155 367

Home, cursed, a, 418
Home of the wicked, 225
Home, reasons for potency of its influence, 58, 367
Home training, of, 57
Homer quoted, 253
Honesty in dealing, 465
Honesty, strength of, 167, 454, 465
Honey, 600
Honey, the varieties of, in life, 642, 655
Honour comes to man in faithful service, 696
Honour paid to bad men unseemly and pernicious, 658
Honour, real, 203
Honour, true, described, 697
Hooker quoted, 611, 756
Hope deferred, 191
Hope, definition of, 191
Hope, departure of, 135
Hopeless apostasy, 505
Hope, long delayed, good results from, 191
Hope, man clinging to, 192
Hope realised compensating for its delay 192
Horace quoted, 87, 328
Horne Bishop, quoted, 258
Hostility of the wicked towards the good, 602
"Household Words" quoted, 544, 599
House, in what a real, consists, 225
House of Commons, a vice of the, 447
House of Commons' neglect of pauperism, 501
Housetops, eastern, 494
Housewifery, 214
Housewife, necessary qualifications for a, 215
Howard, John, quoted, 195, 502 753
Howe, John quoted 204, 590, 595
Human anathemas, 661
Human conduct, 215
Human existence, the great end of, 739
Human government, 608
Human hearts, 268
Human missions and their discharge, 200
Human labour, 612
Human life, 541
Human mind, fertility of the, when engaged in the service of God, 620
Human possessions, Heaven's estimate of, 110
Human rulership, 745
Human rulership rightly exercised, 745
Human suffering reformative, 45
Humble, salvation to, 281
Humility an adornment, 633, 635
Humility as the pledge of good, 317
Humility, genuine, 291, 317
Humility negatively described, 533

Humility revealed in a true man by popularity, 703
Hunger, physical and moral, 182
Hunger the spring of human activity, 325
Hurdis quoted, 460
Hustings, unlawful use of patronage at the, 348
Hypocrisy and knowledge, 137
Hypocrite, definition of the, 137
Hypocrisy, destructiveness of, 137

IDEAL eloquence, 322
Ideal society, definition of, 401
Idleness, 617
Idleness and industry, 111
Idleness creates false excuses, 550
Idleness foolish, 617
Idleness, its connection with wickedness, 83, 174
Idleness ruinous, 618
Idle talebearer, and the wicked son, 467
Ignorant man garrulous, 199
Ignorance not good for the soul, 412
Ignorance perilous to the soul, 413
Ill temper easily propagated, 563
Impetuous flippancy, 394
Impetuous flippancy characterized, 395
Imprudence and flattery, 691
Incongruous unions, 495
Incorrigible and the docile, the, 201
Incorrigible sinner, the, 573
Incorrigible, the, described, 573, 704
Indolence, 443
Indolence and righteousness, 274
Indolence causing vexation 129
Indolence, dishonesty of, 274
Indolence leading to constant procrastination, 617
Indolence, negative gain of, 218
Indolence not justified by feebleness, 79
Indolence parasitical, 165
Indolence, positive loss of, 219
Indolent, the tendency of the, is to create difficulties, 274, 443, 550
Industrious and slothful man contrasted, 112, 524
Industry, definition of, 111
Industry, honest, the strength of, 274
Industry, manly, rewarded, 165, 210
Infamous, the, 520
Influence of a depraved woman, 551
Influence of the child's character upon the parent's heart, 107
Influence of the tongue, the, 404
Inhumanity is ungodliness, 236, 248
Injudicious man, the, 646
Insatiability of man's inquiring faculty, the, 700
Insolent man, the, 141
Inspired men, words of, 384

Instruction, eloquence a means of useful, 323
Instruction that leads to wrong, 437
Intellectual matters, laziness in, 432
Intellectual poverty of the self-indulgent, 508
Intelligence and ignorance contrasted, 120
Intelligence, by whom loved and hated, 157
Intelligence, disparity between that of different men, 445
Intemperate use of strong drink, an, 439
Intemperate use of strong drink, evils of the, 440
Interdicted conduct, 563
Interpreters, two, in life's school, 320
Intrusive people, offensiveness of, 644
Investigator, the true, 380
Involuntary influence of a good man's life, 156
Irving, Washington, quoted, 572

JENKIN, Dr. T. W., quoted, 451
Jewel, Bishop, quoted, 87
Jewel in swine's snout, 149
Johnson quoted, 191, 388, 413, 491, 692, 704, 654
Joint-stock companies, their promoters, 765
Jones, Sir William, quoted, 256, 299, 384
Jonson, Ben, quoted, 159, 494, 524
Josephus quoted, 636
Judges, unjust, 357
Judgment, partiality of, 610
Justice, a dictate of the Divine heart, 746
Justice done to all, 129, 207
Justice, importance of doing, 505
Just man, a, near to the heart of God, 603
Juvenal quoted, 166

KANT quoted, 52
Keble quoted, 41
Kindness, 429
Kindness, the power of, 399, 430
Kind words, power of, 639
King, a, of the true type, 730
King, a weak, for some reasons as bad as a wicked king, 730
Kinghood, 622
King, paramount duties of a, 450
Kings, character of, dependent on the character of their ministers, 624
Kingship, who entitled to, 449
Kings, honest enquiry in, always an excellency, 623
Kings, real and ideal, 310, 449
Kings should be Godlike, 608
Kings, the devil's, 746
Kinwelmershe quoted, 738,

Kitto quoted, 23
Knave's, the, treatment of absent friends, 328
Knight, Edward, quoted, 392
Knowledge, advantages of, 445
Knowledge, cheering, 286
Knowledge, exquisite pleasures of spiritual, 601
Knowledge, great, always reticent, 446
Knowledge, how to draw it from the wise man, 446
Knowledge is light, 413
Knowledge, man's desire for, never satisfied, 701
Knowledge most required least cared for, 577
Knowledge of God the aliment for man's spiritual nature, 600
Knowledge, piety a guarantee of, 714
Knowledge, pleasures of, 381
Knowledge, reasons for the attainment of spiritual, 576
Knowledge, restorative power of, 138
Knowledge, spiritual, personal application required to attain it, 577
Knowledge, spiritual, satisfying, 601
Knowledge, strengthening, 287
Knowledge, the highest, 59, 286, 600
Knowledge, two things required for the attainment of, 398

LABOUR, 324
Labour as enhancing the relative value of a man's possessions, 177, 191
Labour brings enjoyment, 524
Labour, man's right to the produce of his, 575
Labour, necessity of forethought in, 613
Labour, profitable, 238
Labour, talk, wealth, 238
Labour without God vain, 297
Lack of self-mastery, 657
Ladyhood, popular constituents of, 794
Ladyhood, true, in what it consists, 791
Landmarks, 575
La Rochefoucauld quoted, 749
Laughter, definition of, 229
Laughter, different kinds of, 229
Laughter, hypocritical, 230
Law of the good, the, 194
Laws of life, 69
Laziness, 432
Laziness in worldly concerns, 432
Lazy man, the, a cheat, 82
Lazy man, the, and the wicked man, 82
Leading journals fabricating lies for the ears of kings, 746
Lee quoted, 691
Legislation of Heaven, comprehensiveness of, 71
Legislatures, power of, to reduce pauperism, 501

Index / 807

Leighton, Archbishop, quoted, 252, 738, 650,
Lemuel, King, his identity, 784
Lessons from insects, 782, 783
Liar, the, 671
Liberality its own reward, 151
Liberality, real and sham, 185
"Lies" of a base people, chief instrument in ruining kings, 747
Lies the language of craftiness, 167
Life a lottery and a plan, 333
Life, a school, 320
Life, highest purpose of a good man's, 156
Life, inevitable retribution of a good man's, 157
Life in the home, the market, and the sanctuary, 715
Life of the good, 156, 334
Life, pernicious interpretation of, 321
Life prosperous and perilous, 533
Life, the beneficent interpretation of, 320
Life, the perils of, incurred, 535
Light of souls, the, 187
Literature, falsehoods in, 527
Literature, inestimable value of a pure, 206
Little preachers and great sermons, 78
Livingstone, Dr., quoted, 452
Locke quoted, 13, 203, 538
London as a city at play, 154
Longevity, the true, 61
Longfellow quoted, 700
Look, the power of a, 649
Loquaciousness, a sin against the hearer, 124
Loquaciousness, the sin of, 123
Loquacity an indication of folly, 253, 258
"Lot," a, useful in settling disputes, 402
Lottery, the human side of life is a, 333
Louis IX. quoted, 347
Love, a brotherly, 362
Love, a super-brotherly, 363
Love, distinction between natural and spiritual, 56
Love, perfect, casting out fear, 290
Love, strength of a brother's, 403
Love, the right, the best security, 319
Lowell quoted, 622
Lucretius quoted, 60
Lying witness, motives of a, 240
Lyte, H. F., quoted, 597

MAJESTY of goodness, the, 234
Malice, 522
Man, a glorious possibility for, 302
Man, a religious being, 687
Man a trader, 453
Man a voluntary agent, 472

Man and to-morrow, a fact and a failing, 675
Man as known of God, 73
Man, as known of God, and punished by sin, 73
Man as punished by sin, 74
Man, chastising the wrong, 433
Man, description of an immoral, 716
Man, devotion of an immoral, 717
Man, each, a world to himself, 223
Man honoured in service, 696
Man in a threefold aspect, 114
Man in mischief, 116, 201, 326
Man in peril, 115
Man in safety, 114
Man is consciously a free agent, 473
Man, life of every, divided into two chapters, 471
Man proposes, God disposes, 292
Man, responsibility of, for his physical health, 369
Man speaking, 181
Man, tendency in, to find fault with others, 775
Man, the good, in poverty, 271, 411
Man, the highest end of, 205
Man, the indolent, 617
Man, the valuable and worthless in connection with, 337
Man trusting, 153
Man when acting unnaturally, 783
Man, why he is great, 621
Management, skilful, 318
Manifestation and mightiness of moral power, 638
Manly industry and parasitical indolence, 164
Man's freedom and God's control, 307
Man's freedom of action, 306
Man's "goings" under the control of the Lord, 472
Man's heart, 582
Man's heart, a property that he has to dispose of, 582
Man's heart, God alone a right to it, 583
Man's propensity to believe, 232
Man's respect to man, what should rule it, 342
Man's treatment of his own sins, 725
Manward feeling, and the infinite intelligence of God, the, 264
Many races in one, 778
March of the good, 63
Market, aspects of the, 453
Market, the, 453
Market the scene of divine inspection, 454
Marriage contrasted with celibacy, 72
Marston quoted, 449
Master, the kindest, will have best servants, 765
Masters, advice to, 764

Material wealth, 208, 462
Material wealth and intelligent speech, 462
Material wealth, true appreciation of, 178, 304, 312
Matrimonial alliances, the caution required in, 496
Matrimonial misery, 494
McCosh, Dr., quoted, 286
Meddler, the, 670
Meddling, 442
Medical science, a paramount defect in, 247
Meeting-place of the rich and poor, 531
Memory, functions and power of the, 208
Men, all, have sins, 725
Men as moral sowers and reapers, 541
Men, good, in all ages poor, 304
Men gregarious, 148
Men, most, are servants, 763
Men, some good things in all, 338
Men, the most valuable, 255, 256
Mental force superior to muscular, 516
Mercy, a necessary element in government, 479
Mercy and truth, 37
Mercy and truth necessary to soul, 39
Messages, God's and man's, 200
Might and misery, 131
Miller, Hugh, quoted, 298
Milton quoted, 15, 44, 135, 138, 144, 259, 274, 397, 459, 518, 528, 658, 673, 703
Mind of man, the, and the mind of God, 426
Ministry, a motherly, 785
Ministry of temptation, the, 105
Mischief done in sport, 128
Mischief-maker, the great, 118
Mischievous citizens, 670
Mischievous men, 326
Miserable twinship, 390
Misers, the, 185
Misery, causes of matrimonial, 496
Misery, ignorance of, no excuse for neglected benevolence, 598
Misery of the apostate and the happiness of the good, the, 230
Mistake, terrible, of human life, 542
Mistress, a true wife's management as a, 790
Model monarchs, 308
Monarchs, mysterious grandeur assumed by, 624
Money, power of, 372
Money-making, an all absorbing game, 154
Monogamy the true marriage, 406
Montgomery, J., quoted, 291, 452
Montgomery, R., quoted, 32, 242, 452
Moral and corporeal chastisement, 351

Moral and corporeal chastisement both legitimate in their spheres, 351
Moral and material wealth, 312
Moral causation, the law of, 207
Moral code of Universe, 30
Moral contrasts, 54, 504
Moral impropriety of sloth and waste, 391
Moral obstinacey of sin, the, 704
Moral paths of men, the, 61
Moral phases of life, 127
Moral purity, 451
Moral purity, lamentable rarity of, 452
Moral qualities and their results, 526
Moral strength, 131
Moral, the, more essential than the ceremonial, 487
Moral traps, 20
Moral truthfulness, 183
Moral virtues, a positive injunction of, 786
Morality, conventional, 227
More, Sir Thomas, quoted, 522
Mother, a blessed, 793
Mother, a model, 787
Mother, an earnest appeal of a, 785
Motion, rule of, 194

NAME, an infamous, 521
Napoleon quoted, 639, 787
Natural desires running too far, 655
Nature, God's goodness in, 601
Nature, man should act out his, for its highest perfection, 784
Neglect of social benevolence punished, 598
Neglect of social benevolence, the, 597
Neighbour, the good and bad, 643, 647
Nemesis, destiny following character, 207
Net of flattery widely spread, 749
Nets of flattery, 749
Newton, John, quoted, 795
Nitre, meaning of the word, as used in scripture, 646
Noble woman's picture of true womanhood, a, 788

OBJECT, an, of pursuit necessary for man, 514
Obstinacy different from every other passion, 704
Obtrusive ambition, 626
Opinionated and the docile, the, 169
Opinionated man described, the, 169
Opposite characters and opposite destinies, 717
Opposite characters and destinies, 113
Oppression of the poor by the poor, 712
Oppression of the poor, the, 561

Oppressors, types of, 53
Orphans, outrages on, 575
Ornaments, 50
Otway quoted, 611

PAIN, moral, harder to bear than physical, 352
Pain of soul greater than pain of the senses, 743
Pain the Divine rod, 555
Parasite, the social, 66, 236
Parental delight, 741
Parental discipline, 210, 578, 743
Parental discipline and filial improvement, 424
Parental discipline, the right end of, 579
Parental life, 741
Parents, duty of, to children, 211, 425
Parents, influence of, on children not absolute, 343
Parents responsible for their children's destiny, 448
Parents, robbery of, 734
Parents, the joys of, 365
Parents, the solemn accountability of, 538
Parents, two things that bring distress to, 365, 742
Parents, young, a lesson for, 368, 425
Parker, Theodore, quoted, 719
Partner with thieves, to be a, is socially unjust, 767
Partners with thieves, 766
Path of wickedness, 62
Pathways, the four, of the soul, 176
Patrick, Bishop, quoted, 666
Patronage and servility, 165
Patronage, lawful use of, 347
Patronage power in the life of the receiver, 348
Patronage, unlawful use of, 347
Paxton quoted, 711
Payson, Dr., quoted, 703
Peace, importance of, in home, 155
Peace-maker, the great, 119
Peace-maker, the true, 356
Perceptions, operation of the, 456
Pericles, quoted, 103
Perils of life described, the, 535
Perjury the worst form of lying, 220
Persecution and treason, 375
Personal decoration, passion for, condemned, 149
Perverse treatment of the characters of men, 357
Philanthropy a "profession," 543
Philanthropy, reward of genuine, 544
Philanthropy, practical, the Divine test of religion, 753
Philip of Macedon quoted, 348
Philosophy of health and happiness, the, 35
Phylactery, 38

Physical health, condition of, 36
Physical health improves as morality advances, 248
Physical succession of the race, the, 344
Picture of a noble king, the, 449
Picture of life, rural and general, 707
Piety, 15
Piety, analysis of, 15, 16
Piety conducive to honour, 329
Piety, enlightened, conducive to power, 592, 593
Piety, enlightened, conducive to safety, 593
Place of refuge, remarks on the, 243
Plan of man and the plan of God in human life, the, 305
Plato quoted, 199, 283
Pleasing God, 302
Pleasure, animal, 655
Pleasure, quality and permanence of, 204
Pliny quoted, 606
Plutarch quoted, 119, 274
Political and social importance of morality, the, 254
Politics of a country, influence of moral excellence on the, 712
Pollock quoted, 433, 742, 762
Poor, compassion to the, 787
Poor, contempt for the, punishable, 342
Poor, contempt for the unfortunate, impious, 341
Poor, doing good to the, blesses the giver, 753
Poor, God's acknowledgment of service rendered to the deserving, 424
Poor, God's interest in the deserving, 423
Poor, happiness of those who have mercy on the, 237, 753
Poor man, desertion of the, 408
Poor, oppression of the, by the poor, 712
Poor, oppression of the, prohibited, 561
Poor, punishment of the oppressors of the, 562
Poor, temptations of the, 540
Poor, the deserving, 500
Poor, the presence of the, a blessing to mankind, 794
Poor, the reasons why they are despised, 236
Poor, the, their advantages, 186, 271, 411
Poor, value of the labour of the, 561
Pope, quoted, 133, 140, 184, 189, 210, 232, 349, 380, 417, 570, 616, 705
Popularity in relation to greatness, 656
Popularity reveals the vanity of the proud man, 702
Popularity, the most trying test of character, 702

Population, increase of a, reflects honour on the government, 243
Population of an empire, the, 243
Porteous quoted, 633
Possession without capacity to enjoy it, 360
Posterity, a good man's interest in, 209
Posterity, a, that is the glory of its ancestry, 343
Posterity and its ancestors, 343
Posthumous fame, the inheritors of, 114
Poverty and wealth, 184, 271
Poverty not always a disgrace, 271, 500
Poverty often associated with spiritual penetration, 721
Poverty, riches, and social selfishness, 408
Power, the three kinds of, 638
Poverty, the trials of, 408
Poverty, when a calamity, 341
Poverty, when a shame, 202
Power of patronage, the, 347
Practical kindness always available, 753
Practical lessons from insect life, 782
Praise, the desire for, 656
Praising of the wicked by the wicked, 713
Prating fool, description of, 116
Prayer, philosophy of the action of, 286
Prejudice, 395
Prevalent vice, a, and a rare virtue, 447
Pride, 188, 316
Pride, advent and fall of, 132, 316
Pride, an offence, 84
Pride and humility, 316
Pride arising from ignorance, 488
Pride, definition of, 132
Pride, different kinds of, 737
Pride, divine correctives of, 301
Pride, essential odiousness of, and necessary punishment, 300
Pride, evil of, 133, 188, 300
Pride is garrulous, 253
Pride the precursor of ruin, 316
Pride, various objects of, 780
Priesthood, reign of, explained by man's credulity, 233
Prince, quoted, 35
Princes, two kinds of, 375
Principle, advantages of fidelity to, 49
Procedure and propensity of God, the, 281
Prosperity of the wicked for this life only, 607
Prosperity of the wicked is sin, the, 488
Prosperity, true, the condition of, 44
Prosperous life, characteristics of a, 534
Prosperous life, elements of a, 533
Proverb defined, 12
Proverbs, sections of the book of, 558
Proverbs, to produce, requires a fertile mind, 620

Providence over man, a, 471
Provision, God's, for the good, 31
Prudence, indications of true, 234
Prudent man, forecast of the, 691
Public conscience in relation to moral character, 139
Punishment, a, that is persecution, 375
Punishment, self-imposed, of the wicked, 26
Purifying process employed by God, the, 338
Purposes, disappointed, 277, 296
Purposes, realized, 277

Quarles quoted, 31, 84, 181, 279, 447, 520, 545, 605, 699, 743, 764
Queen of the household, the, 159
Queens, handicraft not unworthy of, 791
Querulous man, the, 671
Quiet mind better than a crown, 337

Raleigh, Sir Walter, quoted, 115, 239, 584, 692
Randolph quoted, 435
Rash speech, the folly of, 171
Rebuke, how received by the wise, 103, 289
Reciprocity of soul, 699
Regenerate, way of the, 492
Regeneration, moral, the urgency of a, 372
Rectitude exalts a nation, 254
Religion, significations of an enlightened, 592
Religion, vitality of true, 431
Religious apostacy, 653
Religious dissimulation the most heinous, 526
Reproof, 102, 288
Reproof necessary for the scorner, 267
Reproofs from God, how administered, 739
Reproving the wrong, delight of, 612
Reputation and riches, 528
Reputation, value of a good, 530
Respect commended by good men, 161
Respectability, the only true, 329
Respectful man, the, 141
Restorative discipline, 739
Reticence and loquacity, 252
Retributions of the life inevitable, 168, 237, 498, 541
Retributions of the lip and life, 167
Revealment, the wrong, of offences, 350
Revenge, 604
Revenge, definition of, 604
Revenge, gratification of, 605
Revenge is wild justice, 469, 604
Revenge, the avenger of, 605
Revenge, the object of, 604
Reverence and recklessness, 727.

Index / 811

Reverence is happiness, 727
Revolutionism often obstructive, 609
Rice, mode of preparing it in China and Japan, 704
Rich and poor socially distant from each other, 531
Riches not to be laboured for as an end, 568
Riches, possessions which are more valuable than, 411, 530
Riches, unsubstantial character of, 569
Riches, when not enviable, 272, 313
Richter quoted, 256, 380, 630, 688, 727
Right and wrong road to plenty, the, 490
Right concealment and the wrong revealment of offences, the, 349
Right, might of the, 358
Right road, the, 490
Righteous and the wicked, the, 157, 160, 176, 284
Righteous anger, 647
Righteous, God's nearness to the, 268
Righteous men have fallen, 718
Righteous path of life, the, 537
Righteous, possibility of the, going astray, 718
Righteous, prosperity of the, a public blessing, 723
Righteous, the death of the, 251
Righteous, the light of the, 187
Righteous, the, will survive the fall of evil, 760
Righteous: their deliverance out of trouble, 136
Ripeness, the glory of spiritual, 329
Roaming disposition, the, 684
Robbery of parents, 734
Robbery of parents, reason why children deem it no transgression, 735
Robbing parents a ruinous sin, 736
Robertson, Rev. F. W., quoted, 154, 306, 418, 485
Robinson quoted, 616
Rod, corrective, two things must mark it, 554
Rod, material or mental, necessary for children, 211, 425, 578
Ruin, interminable, 507
Ruinous tendency of sloth and waste, 391
Ruler, the abandoned, 730
Ruler, the credulous, the implement of wickedness, 748
Ruler, the foolish, 729
Ruler, the generous, 730
Ruler, the heartless, 729
Ruler, the world's, not to be mistrusted, 510
Rural Life, a picture of, 707
Ruskin quoted, 153, 238, 524
Russell, Earl, quoted, 12

SADDENING and the succouring, the, 174
Saddening in life, the, 174
St. Augustine quoted, 223
St. Chrysostom quoted, 405
Saint, picture of an old, 330
Sallust quoted, 679
Salvation, easiness of the conditions of, 233
Sanderson, Bishop, quoted, 713
Satan adapts his temptations, 19, 20
Satisfaction of the body determined by the condition of the soul, 212
Scepticism and infidelity, their effects on the mind, 773
Scheming, vicious, 86
Scorn, bloodthirsty, 755
Scorner, the, 545
Scorner, the, an abomination to men, 595
Scorner, the, a social disturber, 545
Scorner, the, described, 102, 221, 267, 433, 521, 545
Scorner, necessity for "casting out" the, 546
Scott, Sir Walter, quoted, 626, 688
Secker quoted, 189
Secret disciples, 769
Secrets, 467
Secular prosperity, 722
Seeking and trusting, 152
Seeming right often ruinous, the, 227
Self-complacency of sinners and the Omniscience of God, 294
Self-conceit a hindrance to improvement, 669
Self-conceit, effects of, 42
Self-examination, the duty of, 295
Self-government the noblest rule, 658
Self-improvement, 67
Self-improvement and self-control, 67
Self-indulgence a source of poverty, 507
Self-indulgence involves extravagance, 508
Self-indulgence, prevalency of, 507
Self-praise, 677
Self-reliance right, 41
Self-sufficiency and godly confidence, 736
Self-sufficiency, foolish, 737
Selfish host, spirit of a, 571
Selfish man, portrait of the, 477
Selfishness in religion, 474
Selfishness, reasons of its failure, 185
Seneca quoted, 31, 42, 44, 512, 763
Sentiments in which men all agree, 698
Servant, moral influence of a, 336
Servants, correcting words for some, utterly unavailing, 764
Servants, treatment of stubborn, 764
Service the order of the universe, 696
Servility, offensiveness of, 236, 769

Seven abominations, 84
Shakespeare quoted, 2, 43, 107, 142, 145, 165, 170, 180, 183, 196, 198, 212, 263, 336, 347, 351, 354, 355, 356, 373, 390, 412, 417, 425, 440, 469, 496, 503, 614, 615, 636, 643, 649, 656, 663, 703, 706, 710, 721, 722, 728, 731, 737, 749, 758, 782
Shenstone quoted, 388
Sheridan quoted, 142, 615
Silence, necessity of, 123
Simple man described, the, 433
Sin a great deceiver, 590
Sin, absurdity of, 589
Sin, every, a seed, 750
Sin its own punishment, 74, 98, 204, 207, 213, 251
Sin, pleasure of, ever-cloying, 590
Sin slow in dying, 760
Sinful mirth, 229
Sinful mirth boisterous in expression, 229
Sinful mirth, the end of, 230
Sinner, path of the, a path of self-entrapment, 603
Sinner, self-complacency of, 294
Sinner, the, a snare to himself, 750
Sinners, a description of, 589
Sinners, conduct of the impenitent, towards God in eternity, 26
Sinners, God's conduct towards, in eternity, 26
Sinners, God's conduct towards, in time, 25
Sins, foolish treatment of, 725
Slander compared to poison, 616
Slanderer, the, 86, 273, 616
Slanderer, the, cursed, 777
Slanderous man, the, 644
Sleep as a blessing and the reverse, 458
Sloth, 522
Slothfulness and servility, 173
Slothfulness creates unmanly excuses, 550
Sluggard denounced, 78
Small-brained men obtrusively ambitious, 626
Smith, Alexander, quoted, 47
Smith, Henry, quoted, 300
Smollett quoted, 541
Snare, the, and the song, 750
Social anger, 503
Social antipathies and their true cause, 770
Social conduct, 610
Social contrast, a, 121
Social discord, 273
Social discord, evil of, 273
Social discord, the appeasers of, 273
Social disputes, 401
Social harmony a good all should seek, 350
Social infirmities and their moral antidote, 769

Social injustice, 574
Social life, 768
Social position a matter of relative value, 178
Social retribution, 502
Social rule of wealth, the, 539
Social suretiships, 75
Social wrath and social friendliness, 679
Society to be shunned, the, 221
Society, selfishness of, 409
Socrates quoted, 71, 497, 513, 597, 607, 680
Solitude and silence necessary to the pursuit of knowledge, 380
Solomon's classification of men, 146
Solomon's life, its spiritual significance, 9
Solomon's three thousand proverbs, 619
Son, a depraved, described, 436
Son, a high aim for a, 108
Son, a worthless, 336, 365, 468
Son, the foolish, 366, 418
Son, the, that rejoices his father, 742
Son, the unteachable, 180, 336
Song, a, for the righteous, 751
Soul craving, 182
Soul craving, allayed only by labour, 183
Soul, five gates of the, 455
Soul, greatness of the, 701
Soul pleasure and soul pain, 203
Soul satisfied by God alone, 584
Soul, strength of the, 287
Soul, the, its bluntness and its whetstone, 693
Soul, the, preservation of, dependent on conduct, 315
Soul, uniformity of, 698
Soul without knowledge, the, 412
Soul's bluntness, the, 694
Soul's home, the, 225
Soul's necessity to love, 583
Soul's tower, the, 392
Sound intellect, a, 195
South, Dr., quoted, 334, 350, 383
Southey quoted, 625
Southwell quoted, 82
Speaking truth, definition of, 171
Speculation without capital, 77
Speech, 117, 170, 216, 260, 377
Speech, acceptable, 126, 463
Speech a rod, 216
Speech, controlled and reckless, 181, 377
Speech, false, 346
Speech, frugality in, frequently symptomatic of something good, 377
Speech, good, described, 168, 253
Speech, gracious, 547
Speech, healing, 260
Speech, hypocritical 345
Speech, incongruous and false, 345

Speech, killing, 125, 217, 405
Speech, living, 260
Speech, mischievous, 172, 217
Speech, moral elements of, 127
Speech, natural, 117
Speech, nourishing, 125, 217
Speech of a splenetic fool, the, 388
Speech of the good, influence of, 117, 216, 319, 463
Speech of the righteous and wicked compared, 125, 217, 282
Speech of the wicked, 118, 160, 217
Speech, piercing, 171
Speech, powers and perversion of, 69
Speech, provocational, 389
Speech, querulous, 388
Speech, satisfying, 168, 404
Speech, self-profiting in, 181
Speech, self-ruinous in, 181, 389
Speech, tender, 639
Speech, useful, 277
Speech, useful, the joys of, 277
Speech, wounding, 261, 389
Spinning, 790
Spiritual excellence, 27
Spiritual excellence defined, 27
Spiritual excellence, how attained, 28
Spiritual excellence, influence of, 28
Spiritual happiness, requirements of, 38
Spiritual interests, laziness in, 433
Spiritual knowledge, 2
Spiritual science, 599
Spiritual verities, 557
Spiritual verities, experimental knowledge of, a transcendent blessing, 558
Spiritual verities, experimental knowledge of, attainable, 559
Spurious charity, 423
Spurious hospitality, a, 570
Spurious hospitality abhorrent, 572
Standard, the right, 493
Standards by which the rights of men are to be determined, 565
State, promotion of the best interests of a, 255
Steele quoted, 85, 229, 765
Sterne quoted, 371, 645
Stevens, Sir J., quoted, 105
Stillingfleet quoted, 635
Strange woman, the, and the true wife, 71
Strife, 355
Strife, a lawful, 441
Strife and oppression, 53
Strife hasty, 628
Strife inherent in the soul, 53
Strife makers, 87
Strife, the honour of ceasing from unlawful, 442
Strife, three ideas concerning, 355
Strong drink, intemperate use of, deceitful, 439
Strong government, a, 478

Stuart quoted, 630
Student's spirit, a, 379
Subjects should be conservative, 609
Success, what is necessary for, 360
Suffering, ordinary means which sustain a man under, 396
Suicidal tendencies of slothfulness, 522
Summum bonum, the, 58
Sun, the emblem of the good man, 64
Suretiship, special caution necessary in, 564
Suretiships, 75
Swaggering generosity, 63/
Swain, Charles, quoted, 768
Swearing, objections to, 663
Swift, Dean, quoted, 354, 458, 468, 645
Sycophancy, 556
Sycophancy, offensiveness of, to an honest man, 678
Sympathy, power of, 206
Syrens, fable of the, 19

TALEBEARER, mischievous officiousness of the, 467
Talebearer, the, 671
Talebearer, words of a, 389
Talfourd quoted, 430
Talk, 238
Talk, impoverishing, 238
Talkers, the merely showy, 429
Tattler, the mischievous, 141, 467
Taylor, Bishop, quoted, 714
Taylor, Jeremy, quoted, 72,189, 424, 726
Teachable and the unteachable son, the, 179
Teachable, the destiny of the, 202
Teacher, office of the true, 701
Temper, 244
Temper, a discontented, 335
Temper controlled, 243
Temper uncontrolled, 244, 331, 335
Temple, Sir W., quoted, 389
Tennyson quoted, 12, 203, 660
Terrible evil a, and a severe cure, 553
Terrible in human history, the, 34
Terrific in human governments, the, 440
Testimony, a causeless, 615
Things that are good for some, not good for others, 511
Thompson Dr., quoted, 704
Thomson quoted, 202, 293, 428
Thought, man's dignity consists in, 621
Thought, power of, 397
Thoughtlessness, 276
Thoughtfulness a law of life, 70
Thoughts of the wicked, 160, 282
Thoughts that should be established, 296
Thoughts, two classes of sinful, 595
Threats idle wind, 183
Three bad things, 386

Threefold glimpse of life, a, 711
Threshing, way of in the East, 478
Throne, the, should be established by righteousness, 310
Tiberias II. quoted, 754
Todd, Dr. J., quoted, 259, 458
Tombs, the, of old disputes, 327
To-morrow, the uncertainty of, 675
Tongue, government of the, practicable, 520
Tongue, influence of the, on the speaker, 404
Tongue, influence of the, upon society, 405
Tongue, the froward, 126
Tongue ungoverned, troubles through an, 519
Torture, the, of the continual dropping, 419
Tower, the soul's false, 393
Tower, the soul's true, 392
Trader, man by instincts and necessities is a, 453
Training, definition of, 536
Transgression described, 750
Transgressors, the way of, 197
Treasonable rebellion, 376
Treatment of animals, the, 163
Treatment of the poor, a test of character, 752
Trials, use of, 485
Trophy, the highest, 332
Trouble in its relation to the righteous and wicked, 135
True humanity is godliness, 249
True pathway of souls, the, 176
True patriot, the, 139
True pursuit of mankind, the, 514
True thoughts, superiority to all other productions, 11
True thoughts, their vitality, 11
True witness, the, 240
Trustworthy man, the, 142
Trustfulness, true, the advantages of, 41
Truth alone imperishable, 99, 171
Truth, infinitude of, 701
Truthfulness a safeguard against evil, 184
Truthfulness an instinct to the righteous, 183
Tullock, Dr., quoted, 318
Tupper quoted, 118, 751, 756
Two interpreters, the, 320
Types of character in social life, 140
Types of corrupt testimony, 615
Types of kings, 729
Types of servants, 763
Tyrant, the throne of a, 470

UNBEARABLE wound, the, 396
Understanding, a good, defined, 195
Understanding a well-spring of life, 320

Undeserving poor, the, 500
Uniformity and reciprocity of souls, the, 698
Unfortunate poor, the, 341
Ungenerous disposition a curse, 146
Uninstructible persons, 202
Universal existence, 298
Universe not eternal, 48
Universe organised by one being, 49, 96, 278
Unlawful strife, 441
Unregenerate and the regenerate, the, 492
Unregenerate, the way of the, 492
Unscrupulous accumulating, 466
Upright, the, described, 718
Uprightness and self-control, 528

VALUE of a good messenger to his employers, the, 635
Vanity an obstruction to self-improvement, 447
Vanity an unsuccessful agent, 448
Vanity, description of, 161, 395
Vanity in the rich, and penetration in the poor, 720
Vanity of wealthy men nourished by the flattery of their dependents, 720
Vanity, one of the greatest obstructions to soul-improvement, 668
Veracity and safety, 527
Veracity and wisdom, 219
Verities, spiritual, 558
Villany and absurdity of sin, the, 589
Virtue its own reward, 505
Virtuous woman, definition of a, 159
Virtuous woman, power of a, 159
Visits, how and when, to make, 644
Voice of divine wisdom, 90
Voice of wisdom to the world, 22
Voltaire quoted, 198, 426
Volubility, evils of, 123
Voluntary connection with wicked men, 386
Vows broken by selfishness, 476
Vows, obligation of performing right, 476
Vows, proper and improper, 476
Vows, wrong, 476
Vulgarity likes finery, 150

WALKING uprightly, 215
Wardlaw quoted, 14, 118, 379, 483, 779, 661, 680
Wastefulness, two causes of, 390
Way of transgressors, the, 197
Way of the upright, 314
Way of the wise, the, 279
Way to ruin, the, 132
Way to strength, the, 131, 314
Wealth, 238, 263
Wealth a blessing when rightly used, 529

Wealth and poverty, tendencies of, 121, 185, 313
Wealth desirable for the good, 511
Wealth, dignifying, 239, 312
Wealth, enlightened piety conductive to 592
Wealth gotten by vanity, 190
Wealth in relation to character, 511
Wealth making friends, 409
Wealth making happy, 128, 263, 312
Wealth, rightly distributed by Providence, 716
Wealth, rule of, should be a generous rule, 539
Wealth, secular and spiritual, contrasted, 410
Wealth, tendency of, to promote haughtiness, 409
Wealth undesirable for the wicked, 511
Wealth, worthlessness of a wicked man's, 109, 263, 313
Wealth, wrong kinds of, 679
Wealthy men, vanity of, 720
Webster quoted, 371, 784
Wesley quoted, 459
Whetstone, the soul's, 694
Whisperer, the, a separator of friends, 327
White, H. Kirke, quoted, 252
Whitehead quoted, 203
Whittier, J. C., quoted, 400, 749
Wicked a ransom for the righteous, 509
Wicked, a snare for the, 750
Wicked, an argument for the future punishment of, 157, 498
Wicked, aversion of the, to the truly pious, 602
Wicked, best services of the, an abomination to the Lord, 525
Wicked, destiny of the, 719
Wicked, doom of the, 34, 265, 438
Wicked, flattery of the, execrable, 611
Wicked, influence of the, 33
Wicked, influence of their punishment on others, 498, 509
Wicked, insecurity of the, 161
Wicked, malignity of the, 498
Wicked men, the character of, 438
Wicked, prosperity of the, a public calamity, 723
Wicked, prosperity of the, increases the power of oppression, 724
Wicked, prosperity of the, wrong, 489
Wicked, seeming prosperity of the, 234, 488
Wicked, the, 497
Wicked, the, cannot ruin the good, 602
Wicked, the, have no prosperity in the future, 607
Wicked, the lamp of the, 187
Wicked, the, mere sacrifices for the good and true, 510
Wicked, the, not to be envied, 510
Wicked, troubles of the, 136, 198
Wicked, work of the, 146
Wickedness, 524
Wickedness, a means of exhibiting certain perfections of God's nature, 299
Wickedness and effrontery, 527
Wickedness and wisdom, the bane and the antidote, 32
Wickedness, arguments for the certain punishment of the, 498
Wickedness contemptible and contemptuous, 382
Wickedness contemptuous in spirit, 383, 498.
Wickedness promoted by personal ornament, 149
Wickedness, some of the elements of, 382
Widow, Jehovah's special regard for the, 281
Wife, a contentious, 419, 494, 693
Wife, a good, a divine gift, 407
Wife, a true woman's conduct as a, 789
Wife, blessedness as a mother of a true, 792
Wife, earnest and varied industries of a true, 791
Wife, elevating influence of a true, 790
Wife, excellence as an individual of a true, 794
Wife, generosity as a neighbour of a true. 793
Wife, industry of a true, 790
Wife, management of a true, 789
Wife, practical affection of a, 789
Wife, the good influence and characteristics of, 159, 214, 406, 495
Wife, the true, 72, 214, 789
Wife, torturing power of a brawling, 494
Wilberforce quoted, 754
Wine a mocker, 439
Wine as a beverage and a medicine, 787
Wisdom, attainment of, dependent on the spirit of the seeker, 220
Wisdom, delivering influence of, 35, 205
Wisdom, endowments of, 46
Wisdom, means of getting, 359
Wisdom, right reception of, 34
Wisdom the source and sovereign of worlds, 48
Wisdom, the voice of, 22, 90
Wisdom the want of states, 142

Wisdom, true, always associated with forecast, 533
Wisdom, value and permanence of her gifts, 94, 199
Wise and the foolish, the, 198
Wise man, mind of the, and mind of the fool compared, 373
Wise men, transforming power of the ideas of, 206
Wise spirit, a, 381
Wise treatment of our sins, 726
Witnesses, false, 526, 615
Wolsey, Cardinal, quoted, 627
Woman, dignified and cheerful bearing of a true, 795
Woman, personal character of a model, 794
Woman, the strange, 71
Woman, true, devout and honoured in religion, 796
Womanhood, a poetic picture of true, 788
Word, the, 193
Word of God, penalty of despising, 193
Word of God, the, 193
Words, 160, 193, 256, 278
Words, all, should breathe a kind spirit, 632
Words, examples of, spoken in due season, 279
Words, fertilising, 385
Words, flowing, 385
Words, good, 175, 282
Words, human, 193
Words, lasting effect of, 285
Words of inspired wisdom, the, 383
Words, naturally flowing, 632
Words, pacifying and irritating power of, 256
Words, right and wrong use of, 257

Words that hide truth, 631
Words, value of, dependent on their seasonable utterance, 278, 631
Wordsworth quoted, 54, 214, 295, 317, 493, 538
Work, the important, should be done first in labour, 613
Works, all, bring results to the worker, 147, 541
Works, committal of, to the Lord, 297
Works, good, 315
World's honey, the, 641
Worldly prosperity no proof of piety, 722
Worldly wealth, 190
Worldly wealth a good thing, 190, 208, 312, 569
Worship, instinct of, in all, 698
Worst and best way of treating social dissensions, 628
Worth, real, how to be determined, 410
" Wounds of a wound," the, 484
Wrong may exist in very different characters, 433
Wrong, reproof of the, blessed, 612
Wrong road, the, 491

YOUNG man, the, 18
Young men counselled in relation to women, 88
" Young men of the period," 715
Young, Dr., quoted, 49, 230, 364, 701
Young quoted, 163, 340, 456, 618, 675, 734
Youth, godliness in, makes strength glorious, 482